Lecture Notes in Artificial Intelligence 4603

Edited by J. G. Carbonell and J. Siekmann

Subseries of Lecture Notes in Computer Science

Frank Pfenning (Ed.)

Automated Deduction – CADE-21

21st International Conference on Automated Deduction
Bremen, Germany, July 17-20, 2007
Proceedings

 Springer

Series Editors

Jaime G. Carbonell, Carnegie Mellon University, Pittsburgh, PA, USA
Jörg Siekmann, University of Saarland, Saarbrücken, Germany

Volume Editor

Frank Pfenning
Carnegie Mellon University
Department of Computer Science
Pittsburgh, PA 15213, USA
E-mail: fp@cs.cmu.edu

Library of Congress Control Number: 2007930705

CR Subject Classification (1998): I.2.3, F.4.1, F.3, F.4, D.2.4

LNCS Sublibrary: SL 7 – Artificial Intelligence

ISSN   0302-9743
ISBN-10   3-540-73594-1 Springer Berlin Heidelberg New York
ISBN-13   978-3-540-73594-6 Springer Berlin Heidelberg New York

Springer is a part of Springer Science+Business Media

springer.com

Typesetting: Camera-ready by author, data conversion by Scientific Publishing Services, Chennai, India
Printed on acid-free paper   SPIN: 12089642   06/3180   5 4 3 2 1 0

Preface

This volume contains the proceedings of the 21st International Conference on Automated Deduction, which was held July 17–20, 2007 at the Jacobs University in Bremen, Germany. CADE is the major forum for the presentation of research in all aspects of automated deduction. There were also a number of affiliated workshops on the days preceding CADE, which helped to make the conference a success.

A total of 28 regular papers and 6 system descriptions were selected for presentation from 64 submissions. Each submission was reviewed by at least 4 members of the Program Committee, with the help of 115 external referees. I would like to thank all the members of the Program Committee for their diligent, careful, and timely work and thoughtful deliberations, and Andrei Voronkov for providing the EasyChair system which greatly facilitated the reviewing process, the electronic Program Committee meeting, and the preparation of the proceedings.

In addition to the contributed papers, the program contained four invited talks by Peter Baumgartner, Rustan Leino, Colin Stirling, and Ashish Tiwari. I would like to thank the invited speakers not only for their presentations, but also for contributing abstracts or full papers to the proceedings.

During the conference, the 2007 Herbrand Award for Distinguished Contributions to Automated Reasoning was given to Alan Bundy in recognition of his outstanding contributions to proof planning and inductive theorem proving, as well as to many other areas of automated reasoning and artificial intelligence.

Many people helped to make CADE-21 a success. I am particularly grateful to Michael Kohlhase (Conference Chair), Christoph Benzmüller (Workshop Chair), Amy Felty (CADE Secretary and Publicity Chair), Geoff Sutcliffe (CASC Chair), and all the individual workshop organizers.

May 2007   Frank Pfenning

Conference Organization

Program Chair

Frank Pfenning   Carnegie Mellon University

Program Committee

David Basin	ETH Zürich
Christoph Benzmüller	The University of Cambridge
Maria Paola Bonacina	Università degli Studi di Verona
Simon Colton	Imperial College London
Gilles Dowek	École Polytechnique
Rajeev Goré	Australian National University
Jean Goubault-Larrecq	ENS Cachan
Reiner Hähnle	Chalmers University of Technology
John Harrison	Intel Corporation
Michael Kohlhase	Jacobs University Bremen
Dale Miller	INRIA-Futurs and École Polytechnique
Tobias Nipkow	Technical University Munich
Hans de Nivelle	University of Wroclaw
Albert Oliveras	Technical University of Catalonia
Frank Pfenning	Carnegie Mellon University
Ulrike Sattler	University of Manchester
Manfred Schmidt-Schauß	University of Frankfurt
Cesare Tinelli	University of Iowa
Andrei Voronkov	University of Manchester
Toby Walsh	National ICT Australia and University of New South Wales

Conference Chair

Michael Kohlhase   Jacobs University Bremen

Workshop Chair

Christoph Benzmüller   The University of Cambridge

System Competition

Geoff Sutcliffe   University of Miami

External Reviewers

Wolfgang Ahrendt
Anbulagan
Flemming Andersen
Serge Autexier
David Baelde
Marc Bezem
Jesse Bingham
Magnus Björk
Richard Bonichon
Achim Brucker
Richard Bubel
Linda Buisman
Elie Bursztein
Amine Chaieb
Ching-Tsun Chou
Koen Claessen
Hubert Comon-Lundh
Cas Cremers
Jeremy Dawson
Christian Dax
Anatoli Degtyarev
Louise Dennis
Francesco Donini
Mnacho Echenim
Amy Felty
Christian Fermueller
Maribel Fernandez
Jean-Christophe Filliatre
Alexander Fuchs
Murdoch Gabbay
Didier Galmiche
Silvio Ghilardi
Martin Giese
Juergen Giesl
Birte Glimm
Guillem Godoy
Amit Goel
Jeremy Gow
Bernhard Gramlich

Jim Grundy
Olivier Hermant
Jan Hladik
Ullrich Hustadt
Dieter Hutter
Paul Jackson
Felix Klaedtke
Gerwin Klein
Konstantin Korovin
Laura Kovacs
Alexander Krauss
Sava Krstic
Oliver Kullmann
Hermann Lehner
Christopher Lynch
Michael Maher
Maarten Marx
Fabio Massacci
Laurent Mauborgne
Stefan Maus
William McCune
Jia Meng
Tommie Meyer
Aart Middeldorp
Jean-Francois Monin
Boris Motik
Normen Mueller
Cesar Munoz
Juan Antonio
    Navarro Perez
Linh Nguyen
Joachim Niehren
Robert Nieuwenhuis
Immanuel Normann
Michael Norrish
Jens Otten
Peter Patel-Schneider
Christine Paulin-Mohring
Larry Paulson

Andrew Pitts
Randy Pollack
Florian Rabe
Silvio Ranise
Christophe Ringeissen
Enric
    Rodriguez-Carbonell
Philipp Ruemmer
Michael Rusinowitch
David Sabel
Alexis Saurin
Gerhard Schellhorn
Marvin Schiller
Norbert Schirmer
Lutz Schröder
Stephan Schulz
Jan Schwinghammer
Rob Shearer
Andrew Slater
Viorica
    Sofronie-Stokkermans
Volker Sorge
Christoph Sprenger
Graham Steel
Werner Stephan
Lutz Strassburger
Murali Talupur
Dmitry Tsarkov
Tarmo Uustalu
David Wahlstedt
Angela Wallenburg
Makarius Wenzel
Freek Wiedijk
Claus-Peter Wirth
Burkhard Wolff
Jin Yang
Calogero Zarba
Evgeny Zolin
Roland Zumkeller

Table of Contents

Session 6. Satisfiability Modulo Theories

Session 7. Induction, Rewriting, and Polymorphism

Session 8. First-Order Logic

Session 9. Invited Talk: K. Rustan M. Leino

Session 10. Model Checking and Verification

Session 11. Invited Talk: Peter Baumgartner

Session 12. Termination

Session 13. Tableaux and First-Order Systems

Games, Automata and Matching

Colin Stirling

School of Informatics
University of Edinburgh
cps@inf.ed.ac.uk

Higher-order matching is the problem given $t = u$ where t, u are terms of simply typed λ-calculus and u is closed, is there a substitution θ such that $t\,\theta$ and u have the same normal form with respect to $\beta\eta$-equality: can t be pattern matched to u? The problem was conjectured to be decidable by Huet [4]. Loader showed that it is undecidable when β-equality is the same normal form by encoding λ-definability as matching [6].

In previous work, we confirm Huet's conjecture [12]: a full (and very complicated) proof is in the long version of [12] available from the author's web page. It first appeals to Padovani's and Schubert's reduction of matching to the conceptually simpler (dual) interpolation problem [9,8]. It is then inspired by model-checking games (such as in [10]) where a model, a transition graph, is traversed relative to a property and players make choices at appropriate positions. We define a game where the model is a closed λ-term t and play moves around it relative to a (dual) interpolation problem P. The game captures the dynamics of β-reduction on t without changing it (using substitution). Unlike standard model-checking games, play may arbitrarily jump around a term because of binding. The principal virtue of the game is that small pieces of a solution term can be understood in terms of their subplays and how they, thereby, contribute to solving the problem P. Simple transformations on terms are defined and combinatorial properties shown. Decidability of matching follows from the *small model property*: if there is a solution to a problem then there is a small solution to it. The proof of this property uses "unfolding" a λ-term with respect to game playing, analogous to unravelling a transition system in modal logic, followed by its inverse refolding.

In the talk our interest is with a different, although related, question: can we independently characterize the set of *all* solution terms to an interpolation problem? Part of the hope is that this may lead to a simpler proof of decidability of matching. Again, we start with the term checking game. However, we slightly reformulate it and show that it underpins an automata-theoretic characterization relative to *resource*: given a problem P, a finite set of variables and constants the (possibly infinite) set of terms that are built from those components and that solve P is regular. The characterization uses standard bottom-up tree automata. The states of the automaton are built from abstractions of sequences of moves in the game. The automaton construction works for all orders. Comon and Jurski define tree automata that characterize all solutions to a 4th-order problem [2]. The states of their automata appeal to Padovani's observational equivalence classes of terms [8]. To define the states of their automata at higher-orders, one

F. Pfenning (Ed.): CADE 2007, LNAI 4603, pp. 1–2, 2007.

would need to solve the problem of how to quotient the potentially infinite set of terms into their respective finite observational equivalence classes: however, as Padovani shows this problem is, in fact, equivalent to the matching problem itself. Ong shows decidability of monadic second-order logic of the tree generated by an arbitrary higher-order scheme [7]. The proof uses a game-semantic characterization of a scheme as an infinite λ-term. A property, expressed as an alternating parity tree automaton, of the tree has to be transferred to the infinite term. A key ingredient of the transition from game to automaton is Ong's abstraction "variable profile" that captures a sequence of back-and-forth play jumping in a term which is also central to our analysis.

References

1. Comon, H., Dauchet, M., Gilleron, R., Jacquemard, F., Lugiez, D., Tison, S., Tommasi, M.: Tree Automata Techniques and Applications. Draft Book (2002) http://l3ux02.univ-lille3.fr/tata/
2. Comon, H., Jurski, Y.: Higher-order matching and tree automata. In: Nielsen, M. (ed.) CSL 1997. LNCS, vol. 1414, pp. 157–176. Springer, Heidelberg (1998)
3. Dowek, G.: Higher-order unification and matching. In: Robinson, A., Voronkov, A. (ed.) Handbook of Automated Reasoning, vol. 2, pp. 1009–1062, North-Holland (2001)
4. Huet, G.: Rèsolution d'èquations dans les langages d'ordre 1, 2, ... ω. Thèse de doctorat d'ètat, Universitè Paris VII (1976)
5. Jung, A., Tiuryn, J.: A new characterisation of lambda definability. In: Bezem, M., Groote, J.F. (eds.) TLCA 1993. LNCS, vol. 664, pp. 245–257. Springer, Heidelberg (1993)
6. Loader, R.: Higher-order β-matching is undecidable. Logic Journal of the IGPL 11(1), 51–68 (2003)
7. Ong, C.-H.L.: On model-checking trees generated by higher-order recursion schemes. In: Procs LICS, pp. 81–90 (Longer version available from Ong's web page) (2006)
8. Padovani, V.: Decidability of fourth-order matching. Mathematical Structures in Computer Science 10(3), 361–372 (2001)
9. Schubert, A.: Linear interpolation for the higher-order matching problem. In: Bidoit, M., Dauchet, M. (eds.) CAAP 1997, FASE 1997, and TAPSOFT 1997. LNCS, vol. 1214, pp. 441–452. Springer, Heidelberg (1997)
10. Stirling, C.: Modal and Temporal Properties of Processes. In: Texts in Computer Science, Springer, Heidelberg (2001)
11. Stirling, C.: Higher-order matching and games. In: Ong, L. (ed.) CSL 2005. LNCS, vol. 3634, pp. 119–134. Springer, Heidelberg (2005)
12. Stirling, C.: A game-theoretic approach to deciding higher-order matching. In: Bugliesi, M., Preneel, B., Sassone, V., Wegener, I. (eds.) ICALP 2006. LNCS, vol. 4052, pp. 348–359. Springer, Heidelberg (2006)

Formalization of Continuous Probability Distributions

Osman Hasan and Sofiène Tahar

Dept. of Electrical & Computer Engineering, Concordia University
1455 de Maisonneuve W., Montreal, Quebec, H3G 1M8, Canada
{o_hasan,tahar}@ece.concordia.ca

Abstract. Continuous probability distributions are widely used to mathematically describe random phenomena in engineering and physical sciences. In this paper, we present a methodology that can be used to formalize any continuous random variable for which the inverse of the cumulative distribution function can be expressed in a closed mathematical form. Our methodology is primarily based on the Standard Uniform random variable, the classical cumulative distribution function properties and the Inverse Transform method. The paper includes the higher-order-logic formalization details of these three components in the HOL theorem prover. To illustrate the practical effectiveness of the proposed methodology, we present the formalization of Exponential, Uniform, Rayleigh and Triangular random variables.

1 Introduction

Theorem proving [7] is an interactive verification approach that can be used to prove mathematical theorems in a computer based environment. Due to its inherent soundness, theorem proving is capable of providing precise answers and is thus more powerful than testing or simulation-based system analysis techniques. In this paper, we propose to perform probabilistic analysis within the environment of a higher-order-logic theorem prover in order to overcome the inaccuracy and enormous CPU time requirement limitations of state-of-the-art simulation based probabilistic analysis approaches.

The foremost criteria for constructing a theorem-proving based probabilistic analysis framework is to be able to formalize the commonly used random variables in higher-order logic. This formalized library of random variables can be utilized to express random behavior exhibited by systems and the corresponding probabilistic properties can then be proved within the sound environment of an interactive theorem prover. Random variables are basically functions that map random events to numbers and they can be expressed in a computerized environment as probabilistic algorithms. In his PhD thesis, Hurd [14] presented a methodology for the verification of probabilistic algorithms in the higher-order-logic (HOL) theorem prover [8]. Hurd was also able to formalize a few discrete random variables and verify their corresponding distribution properties. On the

F. Pfenning (Ed.): CADE 2007, LNAI 4603, pp. 3–18, 2007.

other hand, to the best of our knowledge, no higher-order-logic formalization of continuous random variables exists in the open literature so far.

In this paper, we propose a methodology for the formalization of continuous random variables in HOL. Our methodology utilizes Hurd's formalization framework and is based on the concept of the nonuniform random number generation [5], which is the process of obtaining random variates of arbitrary distributions using a Standard Uniform random number generator. The main advantage of this approach is that we only need to formalize one continuous random variable from scratch, i.e., the Standard Uniform random variable, which can be used to model other continuous random variables by formalizing the corresponding nonuniform random number generation method.

Based on the above methodology, we now present a framework, illustrated in Figure 1, for the formalization of continuous probability distributions for which the inverse of the *Cumulative Distribution Function* (CDF) can be represented in a closed mathematical form. Firstly, we formally specify the Standard Uniform random variable and verify its correctness by proving the corresponding CDF and measurability properties. The next step is the formalization of the CDF and the verification of its classical properties. Then we formally specify the mathematical concept of the inverse function of a CDF. This formal specification, along with the formalization of the Standard Uniform random variable and the CDF properties, can be used to formally verify the correctness of the *Inverse Transform Method* (ITM) [5], which is a well known nonuniform random generation technique for generating nonuniform random variates for continuous probability distributions for which the inverse of the CDF can be represented in a closed mathematical form. At this point, the formalized Standard Uniform random variable can be used to formally specify any such continuous random variable and its corresponding CDF can be verified using the ITM.

The rest of the paper is organized as follows: In Section 2, we briefly review Hurd's methodology for the verification of probabilistic algorithms in HOL. The next three sections of this paper present the HOL formalization of the three major steps given in Figure 1, i.e., the Standard Uniform random variable, the CDF and the ITM. In Section 6, we utilize the proposed framework of Figure

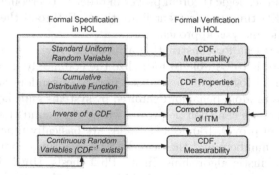

Fig. 1. Proposed Formalization Framework

1 to formalize the Exponential, Uniform, Rayleigh and Triangular random variables. In Section 7, we discuss potential probabilistic analysis applications for the formalized continuous random variables. A review of related work in the literature is given in Section 8 and we finally conclude the paper in Section 9.

2 Verifying Probabilistic Algorithms in HOL

In this section, we provide an overview of Hurd's methodology [14] for the verification of probabilistic algorithms in HOL. The intent is to introduce the main ideas along with some notation that is going to be used in the next sections.

Hurd [14] proposed to formalize the probabilistic algorithms in higher-order logic by thinking of them as deterministic functions with access to an infinite Boolean sequence B^∞; a source of infinite random bits. These deterministic functions make random choices based on the result of popping the top most bit in the infinite Boolean sequence and may pop as many random bits as they need for their computation. When the algorithms terminate, they return the result along with the remaining portion of the infinite Boolean sequence to be used by other programs. Thus, a probabilistic algorithm which takes a parameter of type α and ranges over values of type β can be represented in HOL by the function

$$\mathcal{F} : \alpha \to B^\infty \to \beta \times B^\infty$$

For example, a $Bernoulli(\frac{1}{2})$ random variable that returns 1 or 0 with equal probability $\frac{1}{2}$ can be modeled as follows

  ⊢ bit = λs. (if shd s then 1 else 0, stl s)

where s is the infinite Boolean sequence and shd and stl are the sequence equivalents of the list operation 'head' and 'tail'. The probabilistic programs can also be expressed in the more general state-transforming monad where the states are the infinite Boolean sequences.

  ⊢ ∀ a,s. unit a s = (a,s)
  ⊢ ∀ f,g,s. bind f g s = let (x,s')← f(s) in g x s'

The unit operator is used to lift values to the monad, and the bind is the monadic analogue of function application. All monad laws hold for this definition, and the notation allows us to write functions without explicitly mentioning the sequence that is passed around, e.g., function bit can be defined as

  ⊢ bit_monad = bind sdest (λb. if b then unit 1 else unit 0)

where sdest gives the head and tail of a sequence as a pair $(shd\ s,\ stl\ s)$.

Hurd [14] also formalized some mathematical measure theory in HOL in order to define a probability function $\mathbb{P}$ from sets of infinite Boolean sequences to *real* numbers between 0 and 1. The domain of $\mathbb{P}$ is the set $\mathcal{E}$ of events of the probability. Both $\mathbb{P}$ and $\mathcal{E}$ are defined using the Carathéodory's Extension theorem, which ensures that $\mathcal{E}$ is a σ-algebra: closed under complements and countable unions. The formalized $\mathbb{P}$ and $\mathcal{E}$ can be used to prove probabilistic properties for probabilistic programs such as

$\vdash \mathbb{P}\ \{s\ |\ \text{fst (bit s)} = 1\} = \frac{1}{2}$

where the function fst selects the first component of a pair. In Hurd's formalization of probability theory, a set of infinite Boolean sequences, S, is said to be measurable if and only if it is in $\mathcal{E}$, i.e., $S \in \mathcal{E}$. Since the probability measure $\mathbb{P}$ is only defined on sets in $\mathcal{E}$, it is very important to prove that sets that arise in verification are measurable. Hurd [14] showed that a function is guaranteed to be measurable if it accesses the infinite Boolean sequence using only the unit, bind and sdest primitives and thus leads to only measurable sets.

Hurd formalized a few discrete random variables and proved their correctness by proving the corresponding *Probability Mass Function* (PMF) properties [14]. The algorithms for these discrete random variables are either guaranteed to terminate or satisfy probabilistic termination, meaning that the probability that the algorithm terminates is 1. Thus, they can be expressed using Hurd's methodology by either well formed recursive functions or the *probabilistic while loop* [14]. On the other hand, the implementation of continuous random variables requires non-terminating programs and hence calls for a different approach.

3   Formalization of the Standard Uniform Distribution

In this section, we present the formalization of the Standard Uniform distribution that is the first step in the proposed methodology for the formalization of continuous probability distributions as shown in Figure 1. The Standard Uniform random variable can be characterized by the CDF as follows:

$$Pr(X \leq x) = \begin{cases} 0 \text{ if } x < 0; \\ x \text{ if } 0 \leq x < 1; \\ 1 \text{ if } 1 \leq x. \end{cases} \tag{1}$$

3.1   Formal Specification of Standard Uniform Random Variable

The Standard Uniform random variable can be formally expressed in terms of an infinite sequence of random bits as follows [11]

$$\lim_{n \to \infty} (\lambda n. \sum_{k=0}^{n-1} (\frac{1}{2})^{k+1} X_k) \tag{2}$$

where, X_k denotes the outcome of the kth random bit; *true* or *false* represented as 1 or 0, respectively. The mathematical expression of Equation (2) can be formalized in the HOL theorem prover in two steps. The first step is to define a discrete Standard Uniform random variable that produces any one of the equally spaced 2^n dyadic rationals, of the form $\frac{i}{2^n}$ ($0 \leq i \leq 2^n$), in the interval $[0, 1-(\frac{1}{2})^n]$ with the same probability $(\frac{1}{2})^n$ using Hurd's methodology.

Definition 3.1:

std_unif_disc: $(num \rightarrow (num \rightarrow bool) \rightarrow (real \times (num \rightarrow bool)))$
$\vdash$ (std_unif_disc 0 = unit 0) $\land$
$\forall$ n. (std_unif_disc (suc n) =
      bind (std_unif_disc n) (λm. bind sdest
          (λb. unit (if b then $((\frac{1}{2})^{n+1} + m)$ else m))))

The function std_unif_disc allows us to formalize the *real* sequence of Equation (2) in the HOL theorem prover. Now, the formalization of the mathematical concept of limit of a *real* sequence in HOL [10] can be used to formally specify the Standard Uniform random variable of Equation (2) as follows

Definition 3.2:

std_unif_cont: $((num \rightarrow bool) \rightarrow real)$
$\vdash \forall$ s. std_unif_cont s = lim (λn. fst (std_unif_disc n s))

where, *lim* is the HOL function for the limit of a *real* sequence [10].

3.2 Formal Verification of Standard Uniform Random Variable

The formalized Standard Uniform random variable, std_unif_cont, can be verified to be correct by proving its CDF to be equal to the theoretical value given in Equation (1) and its *Probability Mass Function* (PMF) to be equal to 0, which is an intrinsic characteristic of all continuous random variables. For this purpose, it is very important to prove that the sets $\{s \mid std\_unif\_cont\ s \leq x\}$ and $\{s \mid std\_unif\_cont\ s = x\}$ arising in this verification are measurable. The fact that the function std_unif_disc accesses the infinite Boolean sequence using only the unit, bind and sdest primitives can be used to prove

Lemma 3.1:

$\vdash \forall$ x n. $\{$s $\mid$ fst (std_unif_disc n s) $\leq$ x$\} \in \mathcal{E}\ \land$
      $\{$s $\mid$ fst (std_unif_disc n s) = x$\} \in \mathcal{E}$

On the other hand, the definition of the function std_unif_cont involves the *lim* function and thus the corresponding sets cannot be proved to be measurable in a very straightforward manner. Therefore, in order to prove this, we leveraged the fact that each set in the sequence of sets $(\lambda n.\{s \mid fst(std\_unif\_disc\ n\ s) \leq x\})$ is a subset of the set before it. In other words, this sequence of sets is a monotonically decreasing sequence. Thus, the countable intersection of all sets in this sequence can be proved to be equal to the set $\{s \mid std\_unif\_cont\ s \leq x\}$

Lemma 3.2:

$\vdash \forall$ x. $\{$s $\mid$ std_unif_cont s $\leq$ x$\}$ =
    $\bigcap_n$ (λ n. $\{$s $\mid$ fst (std_unif_disc n s) $\leq$ x$\}$)

Now the set $\{s \mid std\_unif\_cont\ s \leq x\}$ can be proved to be measurable since $\mathcal{E}$ is closed under countable intersections [14] and all sets in the sequence

$(\lambda n. \{s \mid fst(std\_unif\_disc \; n \; s) \; \leq \; x\})$ are measurable according to Lemma 1. Using a similar reasoning, the set $\{s \mid std\_unif\_cont \; s \; = \; x\}$ can also be proved to be measurable.

Theorem 3.1:
$$\vdash \forall \; x. \; \{s \mid std\_unif\_cont \; s \leq x\} \in \mathcal{E} \; \wedge$$
$$\{s \mid std\_unif\_cont \; s \; = x\} \in \mathcal{E}$$

Theorem 3.1 can now be used along with the *real* number theories [10] to verify the correctness of the function *std_unif_cont* in the HOL theorem prover by proving its *Probability Mass Function* (PMF) and CDF properties [11].

Theorem 3.2:
$$\vdash \forall \; x. \; \mathbb{P}\{s \mid std\_unif\_cont \; s = x\} = 0 \; \wedge$$
$$\mathbb{P}\{s \mid std\_unif\_cont \; s \leq x\} =$$
$$\text{if } (x < 0) \text{ then } 0 \text{ else } (\text{if } (x < 1) \text{ then } x \text{ else } 1)$$

4   Formalization of the Cumulative Distribution Function

In this section, we present the verification of classical CDF properties in the HOL theorem prover, which is the second step in the proposed methodology.

4.1   Formal Specification of CDF

The CDF of a random variable, R, is defined by $F_R(x) = Pr(R \leq x)$ for any *real* number x, where Pr represents the probability. It follows from this definition that the CDF can be formally specified in HOL by a higher-order-logic function that accepts a random variable and a *real* argument and returns the probability of the event when the given random variable is less than or equal to the value of the given *real* number.

Definition 4.1:
$$\text{cdf}: \; (((num \rightarrow bool) \rightarrow real) \rightarrow real \rightarrow real)$$
$$\vdash \forall \; R \; x. \; \text{cdf } R \; x = \mathbb{P} \; \{s \mid R \; s \leq x\}$$

4.2   Formal Verification of CDF Properties

Using the formal specification of the CDF, we are able to verify classical CDF properties [16] (details are given below) in HOL. The formal proofs for these properties not only ensure the correctness of our CDF specification but also play a vital role in proving the correctness of the ITM as will be discussed in Section 5. The formal proofs of these properties are established using the HOL set, measure, probability [14] and *real* number [10] theories and under the assumption that the set $\{s \mid R \; s \leq x\}$, where R represents the random variable under consideration, is measurable for all values of x. The details of the HOL verification steps for these properties can be found in [12].

CDF Bounds. $(0 \leq F_R(x) \leq 1)$
This property states that if we plot the CDF against its *real* argument x, then the graph of the CDF is between the two horizontal lines $y = 0$ and $y = 1$.

Theorem 4.1:
⊢ ∀ R x. (0 ≤ cdf R x) ∧ (cdf R x ≤ 1)

CDF is Monotonically Increasing. (*if* $a < b$, *then* $F_R(a) \leq F_R(b)$)
For all *real* numbers a and b, if a is less than b, then the CDF value of a random variable, R, at a can never exceed the CDF value of R at b.

Theorem 4.2:
⊢ ∀ R a b. a < b ⇒ (cdf R a ≤ cdf R b)

Interval Probability. (*if* $a < b$ *then* $Pr(a < R \leq b) = F_R(b) - F_R(a)$)
This property is very useful for evaluating the probability of a random variable, R, lying in any given interval (a,b] in terms of its CDF.

Theorem 4.3:
⊢ ∀ R a b. a < b ⇒ (ℙ {s | (a < R s) ∧ (R s ≤ b)} =
                        cdf R b - cdf R a)

CDF at Positive Infinity. ($\lim_{x \to \infty} F_R(x) = 1$; *that is*, $F_R(\infty) = 1$)
This property states that the value of the CDF for any given random variable, R, always tends to 1 as its *real* argument approaches positive infinity.

Theorem 4.4:
⊢ ∀ R. lim (λ n. cdf R (&n)) = 1

where *lim M* represents the formalization of the limit of a *real* sequence M (i.e., $\lim_{n \to \infty} M(n) = lim\ M$) [10] and "&" represents the conversion function from *natural* to *real* numbers in HOL.

CDF at Negative Infinity. ($\lim_{x \to -\infty} F_R(x) = 0$; *that is*, $F_R(-\infty) = 0$)
This property states that the value of the CDF for any given random variable, R, always tends to 0 as its *real* argument approaches negative infinity.

Theorem 4.5:
⊢ ∀ R. lim (λ n. cdf R (-&n)) = 0

CDF is Continuous from the Right. ($\lim_{x \to a^+} F_R(x) = F_R(a)$)
In this property, $\lim_{x \to a^+} F_R(x)$ is defined as the limit of $F_R(x)$ as x tends to a through values greater than a. Since F_R is monotone and bounded, this limit always exists.

Theorem 4.6:
⊢ ∀ R a. lim (λ n. cdf R (a + $\frac{1}{\&(n+1)}$)) = cdf R a

CDF Limit from the Left. ($\lim_{x \to a^-} F_R(x) = Pr(R < a)$)

In this property, $\lim_{x \to a^-} F_R(x)$ is defined as the limit of $F_R(x)$ as x tends to a through values less than a.

```
Theorem 4.7:
        ⊢ ∀ R a. lim (λ n. cdf R (a - 1/&(n+1))) = ℙ {s | (R s < a})
```

5   Formalization of the Inverse Transform Method

In this section, we present the formal specification of the inverse function for a CDF and the verification of the ITM in HOL. It is the third step in the proposed methodology for the formalization of continuous probability distributions as shown in Figure 1. The ITM is based on the following proposition [21].

Let U be a Standard Uniform random variable. For any continuous CDF F, the random variable X defined by $X = F^{-1}(U)$ has CDF F, where $F^{-1}(U)$ is defined to be the value of x such that $F(x) = U$.

Mathematically,

$$Pr(F^{-1}(U) \leq x) = F(x) \tag{3}$$

5.1   Formal Specification of the Inverse Transform method

We define the inverse function for a CDF in HOL as a predicate *inv_cdf_fn*, which accepts two functions, f and g, of type $(real \to real)$ and returns true if and only if the function f is the inverse of the CDF g according to the above proposition.

```
Definition 5.1:
        inv_cdf_fn: ((real → real) → (real → real) → bool)
        ⊢ ∀ f g. inv_cdf_fn f g =
            (∀x. (0 < g x ∧ g x < 1) ⇒ (f (g x) = x) ∧
            (∀x. 0 < x ∧ x < 1 ⇒ (g (f x) = x))) ∧
            (∀x. (g x = 0) ⇒ (x ≤ f (0))) ∧
            (∀x. (g x = 1) ⇒ (f (1) ≤ x))
```

The predicate *inv_cdf_fn* considers three separate cases, the first one corresponds to the strictly monotonic region of the CDF, i.e., when the value of the CDF is between 0 and 1. The next two correspond to the flat regions of the CDF, i.e., when the value of the CDF is either equal to 0 or 1, respectively. These three cases cover all possible values of a CDF since according to Theorem 4.1 the value of CDF can never be less than 0 or greater than 1.

The inverse of a function f, $f^{-1}(u)$, is defined to be the value of x such that $f(x) = u$. More formally, if f is a one-to-one function with domain X and range Y, its inverse function f^{-1} has domain Y and range X and is defined by

$f^{-1}(y) = x \Leftrightarrow f(x) = y$, for any y in Y. The composition of inverse functions yields the following result.

$$f^{-1}(f(x)) = x \; for \; all \; x \in X, \quad f(f^{-1}(x)) = x \; for \; all \; x \in Y \qquad (4)$$

We use the above characteristic of inverse functions in the predicate inv_cdf_fn for the strictly monotonic region of the CDF as the CDF in this region is a one-to-one function. On the other hand, the CDF is not injective when its value is either equal to 0 or 1. Consider the example of some CDF, F, which returns 0 for a *real* argument a. From Theorems 4.1 and 4.2, we know that the CDF F will also return 0 for all *real* arguments that are less than a as well, i.e., $\forall x. \; x \leq a \Rightarrow F(x) = 0$. Therefore, no inverse function satisfies the conditions of Equation (4) for the CDF in these flat regions. When using the paper-and-pencil proof approach, this issue is usually resolved by defining the inverse function of a CDF in such a way that it returns the infimum (inf) of all possible values of the *real* argument for which the CDF is equal to a given value, i.e., $f^{-1}(u) = inf\{x|f(x) = u\}$ [5], where f represents the CDF. Even though this approach has been shown to analytically verify the correctness of the ITM [5], it was not found to be sufficient enough for a formal definition in our case. This is due to the fact that in order to simplify the formalization task, Hurd [14] used the standard *real* numbers $\mathbb{R}$, formalized in HOL by Harrison [10], rather than the extended real numbers $\overline{\mathbb{R}} = \mathbb{R} \bigcup\{-\infty, +\infty\}$ to formalize the mathematical measure theory. Thus, if the inf function is used to define the inverse function, then the problem arises for the case when the value of the CDF is equal to 0. For this case, the set $\{x|f(x) = 0\}$ becomes unbounded at the lower end because of the CDF property given in Theorem 4.5 and thus the value of the inverse function becomes undefined. In order to overcome this problem, we used two separate cases for the two flat regions in the predicate inv_cdf_fn. According to this definition the inverse function of a CDF is a function that returns the maximum value of all arguments for which the CDF is equal to 0 and the minimum value of all arguments for which the CDF is equal to 1.

5.2   Formal Verification of the Inverse Transform Method

The correctness theorem for the ITM can be expressed in HOL as follows:

Theorem 5.1:
$$\vdash \forall \; f \; g \; x. \; (is\_cont\_cdf\_fn \; g) \land (inv\_cdf\_fn \; f \; g) \Rightarrow$$
$$(\mathbb{P} \; \{s \; | \; f \; (std\_unif\_cont \; s) \leq x\} = g \; x)$$

The antecedent of the above implication checks if f is a valid inverse function of a continuous CDF g. The predicate inv_cdf_fn has been described in the last section and ensures that the function f is a valid inverse of the CDF g. The predicate $is\_cont\_cdf\_fn$ accepts a *real*-valued function, g, of type $(real \rightarrow real)$ and returns true if and only if it represents a continuous CDF. A *real*-valued function can be characterized as a continuous CDF if it is a continuous function and satisfies the CDF properties given in Theorems 4.2, 4.4 and 4.5. Therefore, the predicate $is\_cont\_cdf\_fn$ is defined in HOL as follows:

Definition 5.2:

> is_cont_cdf_fn: $((real \rightarrow real) \rightarrow bool)$
> ⊢ ∀ g. is_cont_cdf_fn g =
>> (∀ x. (λx. g x) contl x) ∧
>> (∀ a b. a < b ⇒ g a ≤ g b) ∧
>> (lim (λ n. g (-&n)) = 0) ∧
>> (lim (λ n. g (&n)) = 1)

where $(\forall \; x.f \; contl \; x)$ represents the HOL definition for a continuous function [10] such that the function f is continuous for all x.

The conclusion of the implication in Theorem 5.1 represents the correctness proof of the ITM given in Equation (3). The function std_unif_cont in this theorem is the formal definition of the Standard Uniform random variable, described in Section 3. Theorem 3.2 can be used to reduce the proof goal of Theorem 5.1 to the following subgoal:

Lemma 5.1:

> ⊢ ∀ f g x. (is_cont_cdf_fn g) ∧ (inv_cdf_fn f g) ⇒
>> ($\mathbb{P}$ {s | f (std_unif_cont s) ≤ x} =
>> $\mathbb{P}$ {s | std_unif_cont s ≤ g x})

Next, we use the theorems of Section 3 and 4 along with the formalized measure and probability theories in HOL [14] to prove the measurability of the sets that arise in this verification, i.e., they are in $\mathcal{E}$.

Lemma 5.2:

> ⊢ ∀ f g x. (is_cont_cdf_fn g) ∧ (inv_cdf_fn f g) ⇒
>> ({s | f (std_unif_cont s) ≤ x} ∈ $\mathcal{E}$) ∧
>> ({s | std_unif_cont s ≤ g x} ∈ $\mathcal{E}$) ∧
>> ({s | f (std_unif_cont s) = x} ∈ $\mathcal{E}$)

Lemma 5.1 can now be proved using Lemma 5.2, the theorems from Section 3 and 4 and Hurd's formalization of probability theory in HOL. The details of the HOL verification steps can be found in [13]. The main advantage of the formally verified ITM (i.e., Theorem 5.1) is the simplification of the verification task of proving the CDF property of a random variable. Originally the verification of the CDF property involves a reasoning based on the measure, probability and *real* number theories and the theorems related to the Standard Uniform random variable. Using the ITM, the CDF verification goal can be broken down to two simpler sub-goals, which only involve a reasoning based on the *real* number theory; i.e., (1) verifying that a function g, of type $(real \rightarrow real)$, represents a valid CDF and (2) verifying that another function f, of type $(real \rightarrow real)$, is a valid inverse of the CDF g.

6   Formalization of Continuous Probability Distributions

In this section, we present the formal specification of four continuous random variables; Uniform, Exponential, Rayleigh and Triangular and verify the correctness of these random variables by proving their corresponding CDF properties in the HOL theorem prover.

6.1   Formal Specification of Continuous Random Variables

All continuous random variables for which the inverse of the CDF exists in a closed mathematical form can be expressed in terms of the Standard Uniform random variable according to the ITM proposition given in Section 5. We selected four such commonly used random variables, i.e., Exponential, Uniform, Rayleigh and Triangular, which are formally expressed in terms of the formalized Standard Uniform random variable (std_unif_cont) in Table 1 as HOL functions exp_rv, $uniform\_rv$, $rayleigh\_rv$ and $triangular\_rv$, respectively. The functions ln, exp and $sqrt$ in Table 1 are the HOL functions for *logarithm*, *exponential* and *square root*, respectively [10].

Table 1. Continuous Random Variables (for which CDF^{-1} exists)

Distribution	CDF	Formalized Random Variable
Exponential(l)	$0 \quad$ if $x \leq 0$; $1 - exp^{-lx}$ if $0 < x$.	$\vdash \forall s\ l.\ exp\_rv\ l\ s =$ $-\frac{1}{l}ln(1 - std\_unif\_cont\ s)$
Uniform(a, b)	$0 \quad$ if $x \leq a$; $\frac{x-a}{b-a}$ if $a < x \leq b$; $1 \quad$ if $b < x$.	$\vdash \forall s\ l.\ uniform\_rv\ a\ b\ s =$ $(b - a)(std\_unif\_cont\ s) + a$
Rayleigh(l)	$0 \quad$ if $x \leq 0$; $1 - exp^{\frac{-x^2}{2l^2}}$ if $0 < x$.	$\vdash \forall s\ l.\ rayleigh\_rv\ l\ s =$ $l * sqrt(-2ln(1 - std\_unif\_cont\ s))$
Triangular($0, a$)	$0 \quad$ if $x \leq 0$; $(\frac{2}{a}(x - \frac{x^2}{2a}))$ if $x < a$; $1 \quad$ if $a \leq x$.	$\vdash \forall s\ a.\ triangular\_rv\ l\ s =$ $a(1 - sqrt(1 - std\_unif\_cont\ s))$

6.2   Formal Verification of Continuous Random Variables

The first step in verifying the CDF property of a continuous random variable, using the correctness theorem of the ITM, is to express the given continuous random variable as $F^{-1}(U\ s)$, where F^{-1} is a function of type $(real \rightarrow real)$ and U represents the formalized Standard Uniform random variable. For example, the Exponential random variable given in Table 1 can be expressed as $(\lambda x. -\frac{1}{l} * ln(1 - x))(std\_unif\_cont\ s)$. Similarly, we can express the CDF of the given random variable as $F(x)$, where F is a function of type $(real \rightarrow real)$ and x is a *real* data type variable. For example, the CDF of the Exponential random variable can be expressed as $(\lambda x.\ if\ x \leq 0\ then\ 0\ else\ 1 - exp^{-\lambda x}))\ x$.

The next step is to prove that the function F defined above represents a valid continuous CDF and the function F^{-1} is a valid inverse function of the CDF F. The predicates $is\_cont\_cdf\_fn$ and inv_cdf_fn, defined in Section 5, can be used for this verification and the corresponding theorems for the Exponential random variable are given below

Lemma 6.1:
>   ⊢ ∀ 1. is_cont_cdf_fn
>   (λx. if x ≤ 0 then 0 else (1 - exp (-1 * x)))

Lemma 6.2:
>   ⊢ ∀ 1. inv_cdf_fn (λ x. $-\frac{1}{l}$ * ln (1 - x))
>   (λx. if x ≤ 0 then 0 else (1 - exp (-1 * x)))

The above lemmas along with Theorem 5.1 and Lemma 5.2 can be used to verify the CDF and the measurability of the sets corresponding to the given continuous random variable, respectively. These theorems for the Exponential random variable are given below

Theorem 6.1:
>   ⊢ ∀ 1 x. (0 < 1) ⇒ cdf (λs. exp_rv 1 s) x =
>   if x ≤ 0 then 0 else (1 - exp (-1 * x))

Theorem 6.2:
>   ⊢ ∀ 1 x. (0 < 1) ⇒ ({s | exp_rv r s ≤ x} ∈ $\mathcal{E}$) ∧
>   ({s | exp_rv r s = x} ∈ $\mathcal{E}$)

The above results allow us to formally reason about interesting probabilistic properties of continuous random variables within a higher-order-logic theorem prover. The measurability of the sets $\{s|\ F^{-1}(U\ s) \le x\}$ and $\{s|\ F^{-1}(U\ s) = x\}$ can be used to prove that any set that involves a relational property with the random variable $F^{-1}(U\ s)$, e.g., $\{s\ |\ F^{-1}(U\ s) < x\}$ and $\{s\ |\ F^{-1}(U\ s) \ge\ x\}$, is measurable because of the closed under complements and countable unions property of $\mathcal{E}$. The CDF properties proved in Section 4 can then be used to determine probabilistic quantities associated with these sets [13].

The CDF and measurability properties of the rest of the continuous random variables given in Table 1 can also be proved in a similar way [13]. For illustration purposes the corresponding CDF theorems are given below

Theorem 6.3:
>   ⊢ ∀ a b x. (a < b) ⇒ cdf (λs. uniform_rv a b s) x =
>   if x ≤ a then 0 else (if x < b then $\frac{x-a}{b-a}$ else 1)

Theorem 6.4:
>   ⊢ ∀ x 1. (0 < 1) ⇒ cdf (λs. rayleigh_rv 1 s) x =
>   if x ≤ 0 then 0 else (1 - $\frac{exp(x^2)}{(2l^2)}$)

Theorem 6.5:
>   ⊢ ∀ a x. (0 < a) ⇒ cdf (λs. triangular_rv a s) x =
>   if (x ≤ 0) then 0 else
>   (if (x < a) then ($\frac{2}{a}$(x - $\frac{x^2}{2a}$)) else 1)

7 Applications

A distinguishing characteristic of the proposed probabilistic analysis approach is the ability to perform precise quantitative analysis of probabilistic systems. In this section, we first illustrate this statement by considering a simple probabilistic analysis example. Then, we present some probabilistic systems which can be formally analyzed using the continuous random variables defined in Section 6.

Consider the problem of determining the probability of the event when there is no incoming request for 10 seconds in a Web server. Assume that the *interarrival* time of incoming requests is known from statistical analysis and is exponentially distributed with an average rate of requests $\lambda = 0.1$ jobs per second. We know from analytical analysis that this probability is precisely equal to $(\frac{1}{exp\ 1})$. This result can be verified in the HOL theorem prover by considering the probability of the event when the value of the Exponential random variable, with parameter 0.1 (i.e., $\lambda = 0.1$), lies in the interval $[10, \infty)$.

$$\vdash \mathbb{P} \ \{s \ | \ 10 < \texttt{exp\_rv} \ 0.1 \ s\} = \frac{1}{exp\ 1}$$

The first step in evaluating a probabilistic quantity is to prove that the event under consideration is measurable. The set in the above proof goal is measurable since it is the complement of a measurable set $\{s|exp\_rv\ 0.1\ s \leq 10\}$ (Theorem 6.2) and $\mathcal{E}$ is closed under complements and countable unions. The next step is to express the unknown probabilistic quantity in terms of the CDF of the given random variable. This can be done for the above proof goal by using the measurability property of the set under consideration and using the *complement law* of probability function, i.e., $(\mathbb{P}(\bar{S}) = 1 - \mathbb{P}(S))$.

$$\vdash \mathbb{P} \ \{s \ | \ 10 < \texttt{exp\_rv} \ 0.1 \ s\} = 1 - (\texttt{cdf} \ (\lambda s. \ \texttt{exp\_rv} \ 0.1 \ s) \ 10)$$

The CDF of the Exponential random variable given in Theorem 6.1 can now be used to simplify the right-hand-side of the above equation to be equal to $(\frac{1}{exp\ 1})$. Thus, we were able to determine the unknown probability with 100% precision; a novelty which is not available in simulation based approaches.

The higher-order-logic theorem proving based probabilistic analysis can be applied to a variety of different domains, for instance, the sources of error in computer arithmetic operations are basically quantization operations and are modeled as uniformly distributed continuous random variables [24]. A number of successful attempts have been made to perform the statistical analysis of computer arithmetic analytically or by simulation (e.g., [15]). These kind of analysis form a very useful case study for our formalized continuous Uniform distribution as the formalization of both floating-point and fixed-point numbers already exist in HOL [1]. Similarly, the continuous probability distributions are extensively used for the analysis of probabilistic algorithms and network protocols [18]. Using our formalized models, these kind of analysis can be performed within the sound environment of the HOL theorem prover. The Exponential distribution in particular, due to its memoryless property and its relationship to the Poisson process [23], can be used to formalize the Birth-Death process which is a Continuous-Time Markov Chain. The higher-order-logic formalization of the Birth-Death process may open the door for the formalized probabilistic analysis of a wide range of queuing systems, e.g., the CSMA/CD protocol [6], the IEEE 802.11 wireless LAN protocol [17], etc.

8   Related Work

Hurd's PhD thesis [14] can be regarded as one of the pioneering works in regards to formalizing probabilistic programs in a higher-order-logic theorem prover. An alternative method has been presented by Audebaud *et. al* [2]. Instead of using the measure theoretic concepts of probability space, as is the case in Hurd's approach, Audebaud *et. al* based their methodology on the monadic interpretation of randomized programs as probabilistic distribution. This approach only uses functional and algebraic properties of the unit interval and has been successfully used to verify a sampling algorithm of the Bernoulli distribution and the termination of various probabilistic programs in the Coq theorem prover. The main contribution of our paper is the extension of Hurd's framework to verify sampling algorithms for continuous probability distributions in HOL, a novelty that has not been available in any higher-order-logic theorem prover so far.

Another promising approach for conducting formal probabilistic analysis is to use probabilistic model checking, e.g., [3], [22]. Like traditional model checking, it involves the construction of a precise mathematical model of the probabilistic system which is then subjected to exhaustive analysis to verify if it satisfies a set of formal properties. This approach is capable of providing precise solutions in an automated way; however, it is limited to systems that can be expressed as a probabilistic finite state machine. It is because of this reason that probabilistic model checking techniques are not capable of providing precise reasoning about quantitative probabilistic properties related to continuous random variables. On the other hand, it has been shown in this paper that higher-order-logic theorem proving provides this capability. Another major limitation of probabilistic model checking is the state space explosion [4], which is not an issue with our approach.

A number of *probabilistic languages*, e.g., Probabilistic cc [9], λ_o [19] and IBAL [20], can be found in the open literature, which are capable of modeling continuous random variables. These probabilistic languages allow programmers to perform probabilistic computations at the level of probability distributions by treating probability distributions as primitive data types. It is interesting to note that the probabilistic language, λ_o, is based on sampling functions, i.e., a mapping from the unit interval [0,1] to a probability domain $\mathfrak{D}$ and thus shares the main ideas formalized in this paper. The main benefit of these probabilistic languages is their high expressiveness but they have their own limitations. For example, either they require a special treatment such as the lazy list evaluation strategy in IBAL and the limiting process in Probabilistic cc or they do not support precise reasoning as in the case of λ_o. The proposed theorem proving approach, on the other hand, is not only capable of formally expressing most continuous probability distributions but also to precisely reason about them.

9 Conclusions

In this paper, we have proposed to use higher-order-logic theorem proving for probabilistic analysis as a complementary approach to state-of-the-art simulation based techniques. Because of the formal nature of the models the analysis is free of approximation errors, which makes the proposed approach very useful for the performance and reliability optimization of safety critical and highly sensitive engineering and scientific applications.

We presented a methodology for the formalization of continuous probability distributions, which is a significant step towards the development of formal probabilistic analysis methods. Based on this methodology, we described the construction details of a framework for the formalization of all continuous probability distributions for which the inverse of the CDF can be expressed in a closed mathematical form. The major HOL definitions and theorems in this framework have been included in the current paper and more details can be found in [13]. We demonstrated the practical effectiveness of our framework by formalizing four continuous probability distributions; Uniform, Exponential, Rayleigh and Triangular. To the best of our knowledge, this is the first time that the formalization of these continuous random variables has been presented in a higher-order-logic theorem prover.

For our verification, we utilized the HOL theories of *Boolean Algebra*, *Sets*, *Natural Numbers*, *Real Numbers*, *Measure* and *Probability*. Our results can therefore be used as an evidence for the soundness of existing HOL libraries and the usefulness of theorem provers in proving pure mathematical concepts. The presented formalization can be utilized for the formalization of a number of other mathematical theories as well. For example, the CDF properties can be used along with the derivative function [10] to formalize the Probability Density Function, which is a very significant characteristic of continuous random variables and can be used to formalize the corresponding statistical quantities. Similarly, the formalization of the Standard Uniform random variable can also be transformed to formalize other continuous probability distributions, for which the inverse CDF is not available in a closed mathematical form. This can be done by exploring the formalization of other nonuniform random number generation techniques such as Box-Muller and acceptance/rejection [5]. Another interesting area that needs to be explored is the support of multiple independent continuous random variables.

References

1. Akbarpour, B., Tahar, S.: Formalization of Fixed-Point Arithmetic in HOL. Formal Methods in Systems Design 27(1-2), 173–200 (2005)
2. Audebaud, P., Paulin-Mohring, C.: Proofs of Randomized Algorithms in Coq. In: Uustalu, T. (ed.) MPC 2006. LNCS, vol. 4014, pp. 49–68. Springer, Heidelberg (2006)
3. Baier, C., Haverkort, B., Hermanns, H., Katoen, J.P: Model Checking Algorithms for Continuous time Markov Chains. IEEE Trans. on Software Engineering 29(4), 524–541 (2003)

4. Clarke, E.M, Grumberg, O., Peled, D.A: Model Checking. MIT Press, Cambridge (2000)
5. Devroye, L.: Non-Uniform Random Variate Generation. Springer, Heidelberg (1986)
6. Gonsalves, T.A, Tobagi, F.A: On the Performance Effects of Station Locations and Access Protocol Parameters in Ethernet Networks. IEEE Trans. on Communications 36(4), 441–449 (1988)
7. Gordon, M.J.C: Mechanizing Programming Logics in Higher-0rder Logic. In: Current Trends in Hardware Verification and Automated Theorem Proving, pp. 387–439. Springer, Heidelberg (1989)
8. Gordon, M.J.C, Melham, T.F: Introduction to HOL: A Theorem Proving Environment for Higher-Order Logic. Cambridge University Press, Cambridge (1993)
9. Gupta, V.T, Jagadeesan, R., Panangaden, P.: Stochastic Processes as Concurrent Constraint Programs. In: Principles of Programming Languages, pp. 189–202. ACM Press, New York (1999)
10. Harrison, J.: Theorem Proving with the Real Numbers. Springer, Heidelberg (1998)
11. Hasan, O., Tahar, S.: Formalization of the Standard Uniform Random Variable. Theoretical Computer Science (to appear)
12. Hasan, O., Tahar, S.: Verification of Probabilistic Properties in HOL using the Cumulative Distribution Function. In: Integrated Formal Methods. LNCS, vol. 4591, pp. 333–352. Springer, Heidelberg (2007)
13. Hasan, O., Tahar, S.: Formalization of Continuous Probability Distributions. Technical Report, Concordia University, Montreal, Canada (February 2007) http://hvg.ece.concordia.ca/Publications/TECH_REP/FCPD_TR07
14. Hurd, J.: Formal Verification of Probabilistic Algorithms. PhD Thesis, University of Cambridge, Cambridge, UK (2002)
15. Kaneko, T., Liu, B.: On Local Roundoff Errors in Floating-Point Arithmetic. ACM 20(3), 391–398 (1973)
16. Khazanie, R.: Basic Probability Theory and Applications. Goodyear (1976)
17. Köpsel, A., Ebert, J., Wolisz, A.: A Performance Comparison of Point and Distributed Coordination Function of an IEEE 802.11 WLAN in the Presence of Real-Time Requirements. In: Proceedings of Seventh International Workshop on Mobile Multimedia Communications, Tokyo, Japan (2000)
18. Mitzenmacher, M., Upfal, E.: Probability and Computing. Cambridge University Press, Cambridge (2005)
19. Park, S., Pfenning, F., Thrun, S.: A Probabilistic Language based upon Sampling Functions. In: Principles of Programming Languages, pp. 171–182. ACM Press, New York (2005)
20. Pfeffer, A.: IBAL: A Probabilistic Rational Programming Language. In: International Joint Conferences on Artificial Intelligence, pp. 733–740. Morgan Kaufmann Publishers, Washington (2001)
21. Ross, S.M: Simulation. Academic Press, San Diego (2002)
22. Rutten, J., Kwaiatkowska, M., Normal, G., Parker, D.: Mathematical Techniques for Analyzing Concurrent and Probabilisitc Systems. CRM Monograph Series. American Mathematical Society, vol. 23 (2004)
23. Tridevi, K.S: Probability and Statistics with Reliability, Queuing and Computer Science Applications. Wiley, Chichester (2002)
24. Widrow, B.: Statistical Analysis of Amplitude-quantized Sampled Data Systems. AIEE Trans. (Applications and Industry) 81, 555–568 (1961)

Compilation as Rewriting in Higher Order Logic

Guodong Li and Konrad Slind

School of Computing, University of Utah
{ligd, slind}@cs.utah.edu

Abstract. We present an approach based on the use of deductive rewriting to construct a trusted compiler for a subset of the native functions of higher order logic. Program transformations are specified by equality theorems that characterize the transformations; and the mechanical application of these rules is directed by programs written in the meta-language of the logical framework. Each application of a rule ensures that the transformed code is equivalent to the original one, thus warranting the correctness of the entire compiler.

1 Introduction

There has recently been a surge of research on verified compilers for imperative languages like C and Java, conducted with the assistance of logical frameworks [2,11,10,9]. In these compilers, the syntax and semantics of all languages, from the source language to various intermediate forms, and finally to the target language, are defined explicitly as data-types and evaluation relations. The verification of the transformations between different languages is often performed by proving semantics preservation for the translation based on these definitions, *e.g.*, simulation arguments based on rule-induction over the evaluation relation modeling the operational semantics. However, such compilers do not make full use of the support provided by the logical framework, e.g. efficient substitution and automatic renaming of variables. What's worse, it is hard to reason about their source and intermediate languages unless laborious work is done to provide reasoning mechanisms for these languages. Furthermore, they do not isolate small-step program transformations clearly and verify them individually, thus a slight modification of the compilation algorithm often leads to a heavy burden on the revision of the proofs done previously.

In this paper, we present an alternative approach, based on the use of verified rewrite rules, to construct a certified compiler for a simple functional programming language inherent in a general-purpose logical framework. Specifically, a subset of the term language dwelling within the higher order logic in HOL [19] is taken as the source language; and most intermediate languages introduced during compilation are specific forms of this language. That is, source programs and intermediate forms are mathematical functions whose properties can be transparently stated and proved correct using the ordinary mathematics provided by the logical framework. As a consequence, we do not need to define the syntax and semantics of these languages in the framework. And, transformations can

F. Pfenning (Ed.): CADE 2007, LNAI 4603, pp. 19–34, 2007.

be isolated clearly and specified as term rewrites, making it easy to construct a "new" certified compiler by applying the rewrites in a different order. The essence of our approach is: for each rewriting step, a theorem that establishes the equality of the original program and result of the transformation is given as by-product (we call this technique *compilation by proof*).

Proof producing compilation has already been investigated in a prototype hardware compiler [5], which synthesizes Verilog netlists, and a software compiler [12], which produces ARM code, from first-order HOL functions. In the software compiler, the core intermediate languages and the target language are imperative languages with syntax and operational semantics explicitly defined. And the verification of the translation from an intermediate language L_1 to another one is performed by comparing execution states. Actually, semantics preservation is proved by inducting on the data types representing the syntax of L_1 programs.

The software compiler [12] also includes simple intermediate languages that are restricted forms of the term language of HOL. Their operational semantics are not explicitly defined; and transformations over them are performed by applying rewrite rules. However, since these rules are designed for generating programs in imperative intermediate languages, they are far from enough for translating a source program to a form that is suitable for code generation, not to mention the lack of optimizations over them. Now in this paper, we extend this method to construct a compiler by purely applying term rewrites, where no imperative intermediate languages are introduced.

Namely, we present a new approach based on deductive rewriting to implement a software compiler with source language similar to that in [12]. The features of this new approach include: (1) The automation provided by the host logic logical framework are fully utilized; (2) All intermediate languages except for the one at the last step can be reasoned directly using ordinary mathematics provided by the logical framework; (3) Program transformations are cleanly isolated and specified as certified rewrite rules. This approach overlaps only a little with the implementations in our previous work [5,12]. In fact, less than 5% of the code is shared between our previous work and the work presented here.

2   Motivation

It is well-known that higher order logic (HOL) has a simple purely functional programming language built into it. Most algorithms can be represented by functional programs in HOL, *i.e.*, as mathematical functions whose properties can be transparently stated and proved correct using ordinary mathematics. This feature is a strength of higher order logic and is routinely exploited in verifications carried out in any HOL implementation (*e.g.* [17,18]).

We take a large subset of the language built into HOL-4 [19] as the source language and built a variety of intermediate languages over it. Programs in these languages represent mathematical functions and can be understood as λ expressions. This has several benefits:

1. Proofs about programs in these languages may be conducted in ordinary mathematics supported by HOL. This supports much flexibility and allows the meaning of a program to be transparent. In particular, we say that two programs are equivalent when the mathematical functions represented by them are equal.
2. Both the syntax and the semantics of these languages are already defined in HOL. Thus many front end tasks are already provided: lexical analysis, parsing, type inference, overloading resolution, function definition, and termination proof.
3. The syntax (see Fig. 1) and semantics of the language resembles the pure core subset of some widely-used functional programming languages such as ML and OCAML. Thus our results can be easily extended to these practical languages.

op_b	$::= + \mid - \mid * \mid \ggg \mid \gg \mid > \mid \ll \mid \& \mid \mid \mid \ldots$	arithmetic / bitwise operator
op_r	$::= = \mid \neq \mid < \mid > \mid \leq \mid \geq$	relational operator
op_l	$::= \wedge \mid \vee$	logic operator
e_c	$::= \top \mid \bot \mid e \; op_r \; e \mid \neg \, e_c \mid \; ; e_c \; op_l \; e_c$	logic expressions
e	$::= i \mid v$	integer and variable
	$\mid (e_1, \ldots, e_n)$	tuple
	$\mid e \; op_b \; e$	binary operation
	$\mid \lambda v.e$	anonymous function
	$\mid$ if e_c then e else e	conditional
	$\mid$ let $(v_1, \ldots, v_n) = e$ in e	let definition
	$\mid e \; e_1 \; \ldots \; e_n$	function application
	$\mid f$	named function
f	$::= f_{id} \, (v_1, \ldots, v_n) =_{def} e$	function definition

Fig. 1. Syntax of the source language

Each intermediate language is derived from the source language of Fig. 1 by restricting its syntax to certain formats and introducing new administrative terms to facilitate compilation and validation. In essence, an intermediate language is a restricted instance of the source language. This leads to an advantage that intermediate forms can also be reasoned about using ordinary mathematics.

Our compiler applies transformations such as normalization, inline expansion, closure conversion, register allocation and structured assembly generation and a couple of optimizations to translate a source program into a form that is suitable for machine code generation. The transformations occurring in these translations are specified rewrite rules whose application is guided by programs written in the meta language of the logical framework (*e.g.* LCF-style tactics). Generally, the process of deciding when and where to apply these rewrites is syntax-directed. Since each rewrite rule has been formally proven in HOL-4, each rewriting step ensures that the transformed code is equivalent to the source one. We use two ways to generate such a proof:

1. *Prove Beforehand.* The correctness of a rewrite rule is proven once and for all: a single object logic theorem establishes that all successful applications of this rule always generates code that is equivalent to original program.
2. *Prove Dynamically.* A per-run correctness check is performed. The result of a rewrite is verified each time it is applied to a program.

The format of a rewrite rule is [name] redex $\longleftrightarrow$ contractum $\Leftarrow$ P. It specifies an expression that matches the redex can be replaced with the contractum provided that the side condition P over the redex holds. The declarative part of the rule, redex $\longleftrightarrow$ contractum, is a theorem that characterizes the transformation to be performed; while the control part, P, specifies in what cases the rewrite should be applied. When no restriction is put on the application of a rule, P is omitted. Notation $e[v]$ stands for an expression that has free occurrences of expression v; and $e[v_1, \ldots, v_n] \longleftrightarrow e[w_1, \ldots, w_n]$ indicates that, for $\forall i.\, 1 \leq i \leq n$, all occurrences of v_i in e are replaced with w_i. In addition, $x \in_{fv} e$ indicates that there is at least one free occurrence of x in e.

3   Compilation by Proof

In this section we state the compilation steps used to bridge the gap between high-level languages and low-level representations. As an illustration we show some intermediate forms of a simple program f_1 in Fig.2 and Fig.3.

```
fact i =def
    if i = 0 then 1
    else i * fact (i − 1)

f1 (k0, k1, k2) =def
    let y = k2 + 100 in
    let g (x, y) = y − (x * k0) in
    let z =
        if fact 3 < 10 ∧ y + 2 * k1 > k0
        then g (k1, k2) else y
    in z * y

              (a)

fact =
    λv1.
    if v1 = 0 then 1
    else
        let v2 = v1 − 1 in
        let v3 = fact v2 in
        let v4 = v1 * v3 in v4

              (b)
```

```
f1 =
    letrec v4 = (
        λv11λ(v12, v13).
        let v14 = v11 * v12 in
        let v15 = v13 − v14
        in v15)
    in
    λ(v1, v2, v3).
    let v5 = v3 + 100 in
    let v6 = 2 * v2 in
    let v7 = v5 + v6 in
    let v8 = (
        if v7 ≤ v1 then v5
        else
            let v10 = v4 v1 (v2, v3)
            in v10)
    in
    let v9 = v5 * v8 in v9

              (c)
```

Fig. 2. (a) Source programs fact and f_1; (b) fact's intermediate form before register allocation; (c) f_1's intermediate form after closure conversion

3.1 Pre-processing

The first step is to pre-process a source program so that subsequent transformations become easier. For a program, we first simplify those expressions that contain boolean constants $\top$ and $\bot$; then apply rewrite rules based on the de Morgan theorems to moving negations in over the connectives (conjunction, disjunction and conditional expressions). Meanwhile the decision procedure for formulas of Presburger arithmetic is called to simplify and normalize arithmetic expressions (this is essentially a proof-based implementation of *constant folding*).

$$[\text{split\_and}] \quad \text{if } c_1 \wedge c_2 \text{ then } e_1 \text{ else } e_2 \longleftrightarrow$$
$$\text{let } x = e_2 \text{ in (if } c_1 \text{ then (if } c_2 \text{ then } e_1 \text{ else } x) \text{ else } x)$$
$$[\text{split\_or}] \quad \text{if } c_1 \vee c_2 \text{ then } e_1 \text{ else } e_2 \longleftrightarrow$$
$$\text{let } x = e_1 \text{ in (if } c_1 \text{ then } x \text{ else (if } c_2 \text{ then } x \text{ else } e_2))$$
$$[\text{if\_true}] \quad \text{if } \top \text{ then } e_1 \text{ else } e_2 \longleftrightarrow e_1$$
$$[\text{if\_false}] \quad \text{if } \bot \text{ then } e_1 \text{ else } e_2 \longleftrightarrow e_2$$
$$[\text{norm\_gt}] \quad \text{if } a > b \text{ then } e_1 \text{ else } e_2 \longleftrightarrow \text{if } a \leq b \text{ then } e_2 \text{ else } e_1$$
$$[\text{norm\_ge}] \quad \text{if } a \geq b \text{ then } e_1 \text{ else } e_2 \longleftrightarrow \text{if } b \leq a \text{ then } e_1 \text{ else } e_2$$
$$[\text{norm\_lt}] \quad \text{if } a < b \text{ then } e_1 \text{ else } e_2 \longleftrightarrow \text{if } b \leq a \text{ then } e_2 \text{ else } e_1$$

3.2 Normalization

In a high level program, the value of a compound expression is computed by a sequence of low level instructions. By defining every intermediate result of computation as a variable, we can convert such compound expressions into sequences of let-expressions corresponding to assembly instructions.

This leads to our first intermediate language that is a combination of K-normal forms [1] and A-normal forms [4], where intermediate computations and their results are made explicit. The core of the transformation is to remove compound expressions so that every target of basic operations such as arithmetic operations and function applications is now a variable. After the transformation, the control flow is pinned down into a sequence of elementary steps.

The first step is to perform a continuation-passing style (CPS) transformation. It repeatedly rewrites with the following theorems in a syntax-directed manner to transform a program into its continuation form. Here $C\ e\ k$ deontes the application of the continuation k to an expression e, and its value is equal to $k\ e$.

$$[\text{C\_intro}] \quad e \longleftrightarrow C\ e\ (\lambda x.x)$$
$$[\text{C\_binop}] \quad C\ (e_1\ \text{op}_b\ e_2)\ k \longleftrightarrow C\ e_1\ (\lambda x. C\ e_2\ (\lambda y. C\ (x\ \text{op}_b\ y)\ k))$$
$$[\text{C\_pair}] \quad C\ (e_1, e_2)\ k \longleftrightarrow C\ e_1\ (\lambda x. C\ e_2\ (\lambda y. C\ (x,y)\ k))$$
$$[\text{C\_let\_ANormal}] \quad C\ (\text{let } v = e \text{ in } f\ v)\ k \longleftrightarrow C\ e\ (\lambda x. C\ (f\ x)\ (\lambda y. k\ y))$$
$$[\text{C\_let\_KNormal}] \quad C\ (\text{let } v = e \text{ in } f\ v)\ k \longleftrightarrow C\ e\ (\lambda x. C\ x\ (\lambda y. C\ (f\ y)\ (\lambda z. k\ z)))$$
$$[\text{C\_abs}] \quad C\ (\lambda v.\ f\ v)\ k \longleftrightarrow C\ (\lambda v.(C\ (f\ v)\ (\lambda x.x)))\ k$$
$$[\text{C\_app}] \quad C\ (f\ e)\ k \longleftrightarrow C\ f\ (\lambda g. C\ e\ (\lambda x. C\ (g\ x)\ (\lambda y. k\ y)))$$
$$[\text{C\_cond}] \quad C\ (\text{if } (c_1\ \text{op}_r\ c_2) \text{ then } e_1 \text{ else } e_2)\ k \longleftrightarrow$$
$$C\ c_1\ (\lambda p. C\ c_2\ (\lambda q. C\ (\text{if } (p\ \text{op}_r\ q) \text{ then}$$
$$C\ e_1\ (\lambda x.x) \text{ else } C\ e_2\ (\lambda y.y))\ (\lambda z.\ k\ z)))$$

As apparent from the C_cond rule, we translate conditional branches into special forms combining comparisons and branches. This translation bridges a gap between high level programs and assembly where branch instructions must follow comparison instructions.

In order to avoid unnecessary let-expression insertion in subsequent phases, during this transformation we rewrite an expression e to atom e, where atom $=$ $\lambda x.\, x$, when e is simply a constant or a variable or a function name. The next step converts the continuation form into a readable, 'let'-based normal form using following theorems. Since the logical framework takes care of program scoping and substitution implicitly, during the rewriting fresh variables are generated and bound to the results of intermediate computations automatically.

$$
\begin{array}{lll}
[\text{atom\_intro}] & v \longleftrightarrow \text{atom } v & \Longleftarrow \quad v \text{ is a constant, a variable or a name} \\
[\text{C\_atom}] & \text{C (atom } v)\; k \longleftrightarrow v & \\
[\text{C\_to\_let}] & \text{C } e\; k \longleftrightarrow \text{let } x = e \text{ in } k\; x &
\end{array}
$$

3.3 Transformations of Normal Forms

SSA (Static Single-Assignment) Form. In the SSA format, each variable has only one definition in the program text. This format supports subsequent transformations such as inlining and closure conversion; and it is necessary for the correctness of our register allocation algorithm. The core of this transformation is to rename all bound variables of a program to fresh names. Initially, all free variables in a function (*i.e.* arguments) are replaced with fresh variables beginning with "v". Then any variable in the lefthand side of a let-expression is substituted by a fresh new variable. As a result, an α-equivalent expression is returned with a proof showing that this expression is indeed α-equivalent to the original expression.

Simplification of Let-expressions. It is often useful both for clarification and for efficiency, to reduce expressions such as let $v_1 = v_2$ in $e[v_1]$ to $e[v_2]$ by expanding the aliasing of variables. Rule atom_let supports such reduction; obviously it is a special case of inline expansion. Rule flatten_let is used to expose the values of nested let-expressions for subsequent transformations (e.g. closure conversion). Rule useless_let is for eliminating unused variable/function definitions. It requires that x does not appear free in e_2 (thus the execution of expression e_1 is unnecessary).

$$
\begin{array}{ll}
[\text{atom\_let}] & \text{let } x = \text{atom } v \text{ in } e[x] \longleftrightarrow e[v] \\
[\text{flatten\_let}] & \text{let } x = (\text{let } y = e_1 \text{ in } e_2[y]) \text{ in } e_3[x, y] \longleftrightarrow \\
& \quad \text{let } y = e_1 \text{ in let } x = e_2[y] \text{ in } e_3[x, y] \\
[\text{useless\_let}] & \text{let } x = e_1 \text{ in } e_2 \longleftrightarrow e_2
\end{array}
$$

Constant Folding. After some optimization, an expression may include only constant values, thus creating new opportunities for constant folding. This is accomplished by invoking a decision procedure for unquantified Presburger arithmetic, plus the application of other relevant rules such as if_true and if_false.

Inline Expansion. This transformation replaces calls to small functions with their bodies. If the size of the body e in a function definition let $f = e$ in ... is less than a specific threshold t, f will be expanded. Although the variables may have the same names in the inlining function and inlined function, no problem will be incurred during substitution since the logical framework will capture program scope and rename variables automatically. For a recursive function, we avoid code explosion by expanding its body for only a certain number of times. The expression obtained from inline expansion is further simplified by applying other transformations such as the let-expression simplifications and constant folding until no more simplications can be made.

[fun_intro]	let $v = \lambda x.e_1[x]$ in $e_2[v]$ $\longleftrightarrow$ let $v =$ fun $(\lambda x.e_1[x])$ in $e_2[v]$
	$\Leftarrow$ size $e_1 < t$
[unroll_rec]	let $f =$ fun $e_1[f]$ in $e_2[f]$ $\longleftrightarrow$ let $f =$ fun $(e_1[e_1[f]])$ in $e_2[f]$
	$\Leftarrow$ size $e_1 < t$
[inline_expand]	let $f =$ fun e_1 in $e_2[f]$ $\longleftrightarrow$ $e_2[e_1]$

3.4 Closure Conversion

Another gap still remaining between the intermediate forms and assembly is nested function definitions. In this phase we flatten them by closure conversion. The core of this conversion is to push the values of all free variables in a function's body into the closure, then extract from the closure the values of free variables and supply them as arguments when a function call is made.

As in inline expansion, we identify all function definitions via the fun_intro rule and pretty print them to be a "letrec" format, where letrec $f = \lambda x.\, e_1$ in e_2 is a short hand of let $f =$ fun $\lambda x.\, e_1$ in e_2.

[abs_one]	letrec $f = e_1[v]$ in e_2 $\longleftrightarrow$ let $v =$ atom v in letrec $f = e_1[v]$ in e_2
[close_one]	let $v =$ atom v in letrec $f = e_1$ in e_2 $\longleftrightarrow$
	letrec $f = \lambda v.\, e_1$ in $e_2[f\ v]$
[close_all]	letrec $f = e_1[v_1, \ldots, v_n]$ in $e_2[f]$ $\longleftrightarrow$
	letrec $f = \lambda(v_1, \ldots, v_n).\, e_1[v_1, \ldots, v_n]$ in $e_2[f\ (v_1, \ldots, v_n)]$
	$\Leftarrow$ $v_i \in_{fv} e_1$ for $1 \le i \le n$
[top_level_let]	let $v = e_1$ in letrec $f = e_2$ in $e_3[f]$ $\longleftrightarrow$
	letrec $f = e_2$ in let $v = e_1$ in $e_3[f]$
[top_level_cond_1]	if e_1 then letrec $f = e_2$ in $e_3[f]$ else e_4 $\longleftrightarrow$
	letrec $f = e_2$ in if e_1 then $e_3[f]$ else e_4
[top_level_cond_2]	if e_1 then e_3 else letrec $f = e_2$ in $e_4[f]$ $\longleftrightarrow$
	letrec $f = e_2$ in if e_1 then e_3 else $e_4[f]$
[top_level_abs]	$\lambda x.$ letrec $f = e_1$ in $e_2[f]$ $\longleftrightarrow$ letrec $f = e_1$ in $\lambda x.\, e_2[f]$

We distinguish functions without free variables from those requiring closure conversion. Upon seeing a general function definition, we first check whether this function has no free variables. If yes, no closure conversion is needed. Otherwise, for each free variable in the function's body, we add it as the argument of the function, and replace the application of this function with a new one where the value of this variable is taken from the closure. As the program is already in SSA format, the value of this variable will not be altered since the point where it is defined. Thus the value taken from the closure equals to its original value. This process is repeated until no free variable remains in the function body. In practice, a free variable is identified and abstracted using the abs_one rule; then a closure containing its value is passed as the argument to the function (close_one). To speed up this conversion, we can adopt the *Prove Dynamically* technique as shown in the close_all: in one step we put the values of all free variables into the closure (which is modeled as a tuple) rather than process only one variable each time (close_one). Finally, we move the definition of a function to the top level; and store its definition (as a theorem) in the logical framework or inline expand it.

3.5 Register Allocation

One of the most sophisticated processes in the compiler is register allocation. Although many register allocation algorithms exist for imperative languages, we find them unnecessarily complicated for our purely functional languages because variables are never destructively updated, obviating the standard notion of def-use chains. Operating on the SSA format, our algorithm is a simple greedy algorithm with backtracking for early spilling.

The basic policy of register allocation is to avoid registers already assigned to live variables. Variables live at the same time should not be allocated to the same register. We adopt a naming convention: variables yet to be allocated begin with v, variables spilled begin with m (memory variable) and those in registers begin with r (register variable). Notation _ matches a variable of any of these kinds. And $\hat{v}$, $\hat{r}$ and $\hat{m}$ stand for a fresh variable, a unused register and a new memory location respectively. Predicate $r \leftarrow v$ specifies that variable v is assigned to register r; by definition $\forall r \in S_{mach}. r \leftarrow r$ and $\forall r \in S_{mach} \forall m. r \nleftarrow m$ (where S_{mach} is the set of machine registers). Notation avail e returns the set of available registers after allocating e, i.e., avail $e = S_{mach} - \{r \mid \forall w. w \in e \wedge r \leftarrow w\}$. Administrative terms app, save and restore are all defined as $\lambda x.x$. app is used to mark function applications. Finally, loc $(v, l) = l$ indicates that variable v is allocated to location l (where $l = r$ or m).

[assgn_reg]	let $v = e_1$ in $e_2[v]$ $\longrightarrow$ let $\hat{r} = e_1$ in $e_2[\text{loc}(v, \hat{r})]$	$\Leftarrow$	avail $e_2 \neq \phi$
[spill]	let $v = e_1$ in $e_2[v, \text{loc}(w, r)]$ $\longrightarrow$		
	let $\hat{m} = $ save r in let $r = e_1$ in $e_2[\text{loc}(v, r), \text{loc}(w, \hat{m})]$	$\Leftarrow$	avail $e_2 = \phi$
[early_spill]	let $v = e_1$ in $e_2[v, \text{loc}(w, r)]$ $\longrightarrow$		
	let $\hat{m} = $ save r in let $v = e_1$ in $e_2[v, \text{loc}(w, \hat{m})]$	$\Leftarrow$	avail $e_2 = \phi$
[restore]	$e[\text{loc}(v, m)]$ $\longrightarrow$ let $\hat{v} = $ restore m in $e[\hat{v}]$		
[caller_save]	let _ = app f in $e[\_, \text{loc}(w, r)]$ $\longrightarrow$		
	let $\hat{m} = $ save r in let _ = app f in $e[\_, \text{loc}(w, \hat{m})]$		
[spill_if]	let _ = if e_1 then $e_2[\text{loc}(w, r_1)]$ else $e_3[\text{loc}(w, r_2)]$ in $e_4[\text{loc}(w, r_0)]$ $\longrightarrow$		
	let $\hat{m} = $ save r_0 in let _ = if e_1 then $e_2[\text{loc}(w, \hat{m})]$ else $e_3[\text{loc}(w, \hat{m})]$ in		
	$\quad e_4[\text{loc}(w, \hat{m})]$ $\quad \Leftarrow \quad \neg(r_0 = r_1 = r_2)$		

When variable v in expression let $v = e_1$ in $e_2[v]$ is to be assigned a register, the live variables to be considered are just the free variables in e_2 excluding v. If live variables do not use up all the machine registers, then we pick an available register and assign v to it by applying rule assgn_reg. Otherwise, we spill to the memory a variable consuming a register, and assign this register to v. In some cases we prefer to spill a variable as early as possible: in the early_spill rule variable w's value is spilled from r for future use; but r may not be allocated to v in the subsequent allocation. When encountering a memory variable in later phases, we need to generate code that will restore its value from the memory to a register (the $\hat{v}$ in rule restore will be assigned a register by the subsequent application of rule assgn_reg).

Saving is necessary not only when registers are spilled, but also when functions are called. Our compiler adopts the *caller-save* convention, so every function call is assumed to destroy the values of all registers. Therefore, we need to, as implemented in the caller_save rule, save the values of all registers that are live at that point. In addition, as we allocate the two branches of a conditional expression separately, a variable may be assigned different registers by the branches. This will contradict the convention that a variable should be assigned only one register. In this case, we will early spill it through the spill_if rule.

At the final step, all save, store and loc in an expression are eliminated. This results in an equivalent expression containing only register variables and memory variables. In practice, in order to improve the performance we do not have to perform equivalence check for every rewrite step. Instead, after all the rewrites are done, by applying the following rules to the produced expression, we will obtain an expression that is α-equivalent to the original expression, thus validating that the register allocation on the entire expression is correct.

$$[\text{elim\_save}] \quad \text{let } m = \text{save } r \text{ in } e[m] \longleftrightarrow e[r]$$
$$[\text{elim\_store}] \quad \text{let } r = \text{store } m \text{ in } e[r] \longleftrightarrow e[m]$$

In order to see the effect of spilling and restoring, we specify the number of available registers to be 3 when running the allocator for f_1. The resulting intermediate form (*i.e.* FIL) is shown at the left of Fig.3.

$f_1 =$
  $\lambda(r_0, r_1, r_2).$
    let $m_1 = r_2$ in let $m_2 = r_0$ in
    let $r_0 = m_1$ in let $r_0 = r_0 + 100$ in
    let $m_3 = r_0$ in let $r_0 = 2 * r_1$ in
    let $r_2 = m_3$ in let $r_0 = r_2 + r_0$ in
    let $r_2 = m_2$ in
    let $r_0 = ($
      if $r_0 \leq r_2$ then let $r_0 = m_3$ in r_0
      else
        let $r_0 = r_2 * r_1$ let $r_1 = m_1$ in
        let $r_0 = r_1 - r_0$ in $r_0)$
    in
    let $r_1 = m_3$ in let $r_0 = r_1 * r_0$
    in r_0

program: f_1
input: (r_0, r_1, r_2)
output: r_0
$(l_1 \ \{m_1 := r_2\} \ \uplus \ \{m_2 := r_0\} \ \uplus$
  $\{r_0 := m_1\} \ \uplus \ \{r_0 := r_0 + 100\} \ \uplus$
  $\{m_3 := r_0\} \ \uplus \ \{r_0 := 2 * r_1\} \ \uplus$
  $\{r_2 := m_3\} \ \uplus \ \{r_0 := r_2 + r_0\} \ \uplus$
  $\{r_2 := m_2\}$
$l_2) \ \uplus$
$(l_2 \ \text{ifgoto } (r_0 \leq r_2) \ l_3 \ l_4) \ \uplus$
$(l_4 \ \{r_0 := r_2 * r_1\} \ \uplus \ \{r_1 := m_1\} \ \uplus$
  $\{r_0 := r_1 - r_0\}$
$l_5) \ \uplus$
$(l_3 \ \{r_0 := m_3\} \ l_5) \ \uplus$
$(l_5 \ \{r_1 := m_3\} \ \uplus \ \{r_0 := r_1 * r_0\} \ l_6)$

Fig. 3. f_1's FIL (left) and f_1's SAL (right)

4   Code Generation

After the transformations in Section 3 are over, a source program has been converted into equivalent form that is much closer to assembly code. This form, with syntax shown in Fig.4, is called Functional Intermediate Language (FIL). The transformation presented in this section admits only tail recursive programs.

$$
\begin{array}{llll}
x & ::= r \mid m \mid i & & \text{register variable, memory variable and integer} \\
y & ::= r \mid i & & \text{register variable and integer} \\
v & ::= r \mid m & & \text{register and memory variable} \\
e & ::= (e_1, \dots, e_n) & & \text{tuple} \\
& \mid x \ \mathsf{op}_b \ x & & \text{binary operation} \\
& \mid \mathsf{if} \ r \ \mathsf{op}_r \ y \ \mathsf{then} \ e \ \mathsf{else} \ e & & \text{conditional} \\
& \mid f_{id} \ x_1 \ \dots \ x_n & & \text{function application} \\
& \mid \mathsf{let} \ (v_1, \dots, v_n) = e \ \mathsf{in} \ e & & \text{let definition} \\
f & ::= f_{id} = \lambda v_1 \dots \lambda v_n . e & & \text{function definition}
\end{array}
$$

Fig. 4. Syntax of the Functional Intermediate Language (FIL)

For those non-tail recursive programs, we rely on third party translator to turn them into equivalent tail recursion. A preliminary tool linRec has been developed to translate linear recursions to tail-recursions [5].

We further convert a tail recursive program into the sequential composition of its body loop (represented by a tr structure) and its basic base through theorem conv_tr. Theorem tr_ind enables us to reason about tr structures through induction. At the next step this tail recursive equation is translated to abstract assembly code.

$$
\begin{array}{lll}
\Vdash_{def} & \mathsf{tr} \ c \ f \doteq \lambda x.\mathsf{if} \ c \ x \ \mathsf{then} \ x \ \mathsf{else} \ \mathsf{tr} \ (f \ x) & \text{[tr\_def]} \\
\Vdash_{thm} & (f \ x = \mathsf{if} \ c \ x \ \mathsf{then} \ f_1 \ x \ \mathsf{else} \ f \ (f_2 \ x)) \Leftrightarrow (f \ x = \mathsf{let} \ v = \mathsf{tr} \ c \ f_2 \ x \ \mathsf{in} \ f_1 \ v) & \text{[conv\_tr]} \\
\Vdash_{thm} & \forall P. (\forall x. (\neg c \ x \Longrightarrow P \ (f \ x)) \Longrightarrow P \ x) \Longrightarrow \forall v. P \ v & \text{[tr\_ind]}
\end{array}
$$

4.1   Structured Assembly Language

Validation of the translation from high-level language programs to low-level codes is believed to be difficult due to inherent non-modularity the of low-level programs. This is attributed to low-level code being flat and to the prominent presence of unrestricted jumps.

Fortunately, although low-level code seems to be just flat finite sets of instructions, it is structured by finite unions naturally: a compilation produces code structurally by combining smaller pieces of code together to generate larger code. Technically, we can formulate a structured version for a piece of low level instructions and develop compositional natural semantics for it. With this spirit, Saabas and Uustalu [20] propose a compositional natural semantics and a Hoare logic for a structured low-level language. Siminarly, Tan and Appel [23] propose a continuation-style compositional logic with a rather sophisticated interpretation of Hoare triples involving explicit fix-point approximations.

We introduce a structured assembly language (SAL) with a compositional (natural) semantics as the next intermediate representation. The translation from FIL to SAL is shown to be correct with respect to this compositional semantics. This language has the following grammar. For optimization purpose, some of the labels in a code may be omitted when the control flow is clear (see section 4.2).

$$sc ::= (\ell \ \{v := e\} \ \ell) \mid l \ \textsf{ifgoto} \ cond \ \ell \ \ell \mid \ell \ \textsf{goto} \ \ell \mid sc \uplus sc$$

The natural semantics of SAL is specified as evaluation rules which relate a piece of code (with entry label and exit label) with the functional expression it implements. Rule $\vdash \langle l_1 \rangle \ S \ \langle l_2 \rangle \Rightarrow (w, v)$ indicates: (1) Structure S computes a FIL expression w and stores the result of computation in v; (2) The control flow starts at label l_1 and ends at label l_2 (by convention $l_i \neq l_j$ if $i \neq j$). In this case we say S is reducible to (w, v). Roughly (w, v) can be understood as $\textsf{C} \ w \ (\lambda v. \dots)$ where $\textsf{C}$ is the CPS combinator defined in section 3.2. A code being reducible to (v, v) means that it computes nothing but moving the control flow. Actually (v, v) is often abbreviated to be (). If a piece of SAL code c is reducible to (e, v), then we claim that c implements FIL expression let $v = e$ in v, and the translation from this expression to c is correct.

The idea behind this natural semantics is an assembly program can be structured as a union of labeled structures such that the control flow is represented by the jumps between labels of these structures. Since the composition of these labeled structures is flat and the only connection between them is labels, the gap between high level programs (which exhibit complicated control flow structures) and low level assembly code (which is flat) is met.

As shown in Fig.5, a SAL program is built by composing labeled structures according to their entry labels and exit labels. Most of these rules are self-explanatory. Rule loop says if a round of computation of the body of a loop returns value $e[v]$, and subsequent rounds takes $e[v]$ as arguments and computes $f[e[v]]$, then the effect of these rounds together is to compute $f[v]$. Clearly this rule characterizes the behavior of tail recursions.

$$\frac{}{\vdash \langle l_1 \rangle \ l_1 \ \{v := w\} \ l_2 \ \langle l_2 \rangle \Rightarrow (w, v)} \ \textsf{inst} \qquad \frac{\vdash \langle l_1 \rangle \ S_1 \ \langle l_2 \rangle \Rightarrow () \quad \vdash \langle l_2 \rangle \ S_2 \ \langle l_3 \rangle \Rightarrow e}{\vdash \langle l_1 \rangle \ S_1 \uplus S_2 \ \langle l_3 \rangle \Rightarrow e} \ \textsf{nop}$$

$$\frac{\vdash \langle l_1 \rangle \ S_1 \ \langle l_2 \rangle \Rightarrow e_1 \quad \vdash \langle l_3 \rangle \ S_2 \ \langle l_4 \rangle \Rightarrow e_2}{\vdash \langle l_1 \rangle \ S_1 \uplus S_2 \ \langle l_2 \rangle \Rightarrow e_1} \ \textsf{skip}$$

$$\frac{\vdash \langle l_1 \rangle \ S_1 \ \langle l_2 \rangle \Rightarrow (e, v) \quad \vdash \langle l_2 \rangle \ S_2 \ \langle l_3 \rangle \Rightarrow (f \ v, w)}{\vdash \langle l_1 \rangle \ S_1 \uplus S_2 \ \langle l_3 \rangle \Rightarrow (\textsf{let} \ v = e \ \textsf{in} \ f \ v, w)} \ \textsf{seq}$$

$$\frac{}{\vdash \langle l_1 \rangle \ \textsf{ifgoto} \ \top \ l_2 \ l_3 \ \langle l_2 \rangle \Rightarrow ()} \ \textsf{ift} \qquad \frac{}{\vdash \langle l_1 \rangle \ \textsf{ifgoto} \ \bot \ l_2 \ l_3 \ \langle l_3 \rangle \Rightarrow ()} \ \textsf{iff}$$

$$\frac{}{\vdash \langle l_1 \rangle \ l_1 \ \textsf{goto} \ l_2 \ \langle l_2 \rangle \Rightarrow ()} \ \textsf{goto}$$

$$\frac{\vdash \langle l_1 \rangle \ S \ \langle l_1 \rangle \Rightarrow (e[v], v) \quad \langle l_1 \rangle \ S \ \langle l_2 \rangle \Rightarrow (f[e[v]], v)}{\vdash \langle l_1 \rangle \ S \ \langle l_2 \rangle \Rightarrow (f[v], v)} \ \textsf{loop}$$

Fig. 5. Compositional semantics of SAL

Based on the basic rules, we derive some advanced rules for more complicated control flow structures such as conditional jumps, tail recursions and function calls:

$$\frac{\vdash \langle l_2\rangle\, S_1\, \langle l_4\rangle \Rightarrow (e_1, v) \qquad \vdash \langle l_3\rangle\, S_2\, \langle l_4\rangle \Rightarrow (e_2, v)}{\vdash \langle l_1\rangle\, (l_1 \text{ ifgoto } c\, l_2\, l_3)\uplus S_2 \uplus S_1\, \langle l_4\rangle \Rightarrow (\text{if } c \text{ then } e_1 \text{ else } e_2, v)} \ \text{conditional}$$

$$\frac{\neg c\, v \Longrightarrow \langle l_3\rangle\, S\, \langle l_4\rangle \Rightarrow (f\, v, v)}{\vdash \langle l_1\rangle\, (l_1 \text{ ifgoto } (c\, v)\, l_2\, l_3)\uplus S \uplus (l_4 \text{ goto } l_1)\, \langle l_2\rangle \Rightarrow (\text{tr } c\, f\, v, v)} \ \text{tr}$$

$$\frac{\vdash \langle l_2\rangle\, S\, \langle l_3\rangle \Rightarrow (f\, w_1, v_1)}{\vdash \langle l_1\rangle\, (l_1\, \{w_1 := w_2\}\, l_2)\uplus S \uplus (l_3\, \{v_2 := v_1\}\, l_4) \Rightarrow (f\, w_2, v_2)} \ \text{fun\_call}$$

The detailed derivation of them is shown below. The proof of rule conditional goes by case analysis on the condition c; so does the proof of rule tr. The proof of rule fun_call is based on the fact that the pre-processing and post-processing for a function call take care of argument passing and result passing respectively.

Derivation of rule conditional

$asm_1 = \vdash \langle l_1\rangle\, l_1 \text{ ifgoto } \top\, l_2\, l_3\, \langle l_2\rangle \Rightarrow () \qquad asm_2 = \vdash \langle l_3\rangle\, S_2\, \langle l_4\rangle \Rightarrow (e_2, v)$

$asm_3 = \vdash \langle l_2\rangle\, S_1\, \langle l_4\rangle \Rightarrow (e_1, v) \qquad asm_4 = \vdash \langle l_1\rangle\, l_1 \text{ ifgoto } \bot\, l_2\, l_3\, \langle l_3\rangle \Rightarrow ()$

$lem_1 = \langle l_1\rangle\, (l_1 \text{ ifgoto } \top\, l_2\, l_3)\uplus S_2\, \langle l_2\rangle \Rightarrow ()$

$thm_1 = \vdash \langle l_1\rangle\, (l_1 \text{ ifgoto } \top\, l_2\, l_3)\uplus S_2 \uplus S_1\, \langle l_4\rangle \Rightarrow (e_1, v)$

$lem_2 = \vdash \langle l_1\rangle\, (l_1 \text{ ifgoto } \bot\, l_2\, l_3)\uplus S_2\, \langle l_4\rangle \Rightarrow (e_2, v)$

$thm_2 = \vdash \langle l_1\rangle\, (l_1 \text{ ifgoto } \bot\, l_2\, l_3)\uplus S_2 \uplus S_1\, \langle l_4\rangle \Rightarrow (e_2, v)$

$$\cfrac{\cfrac{\cfrac{asm_1 \quad asm_2}{lem_1}\text{skip} \quad asm_3}{thm_1}\text{nop} \qquad \cfrac{\cfrac{asm_4 \quad asm_2}{lem_2}\text{nop} \quad asm_3}{thm_2}\text{skip}}{\langle l_1\rangle\, (l_1 \text{ ifgoto } c\, l_2\, l_3)\uplus S_2 \uplus S_1\, \langle l_4\rangle \Rightarrow (\text{if } c \text{ then } e_1 \text{ else } e_2, v)}$$

Derivation of rule tr

$body = \langle l_1\rangle\, (l_1 \text{ ifgoto } (c\, v)\, l_2\, l_3)\uplus S \uplus (l_4 \text{ goto } l_1)\, \langle l_2\rangle$

$asm_1 = \vdash \langle l_1\rangle\, l_1 \text{ ifgoto } \top\, l_2\, l_3\, \langle l_2\rangle \Rightarrow () \qquad asm_2 = \vdash \langle l_3\rangle\, S\, \langle l_4\rangle \Rightarrow (e, v)$

$asm_3 = \vdash \langle l_4\rangle\, l_4 \text{ goto } l_1\langle l_1\rangle \qquad lem_1 = \vdash \langle l_1\rangle\, (l_1 \text{ ifgoto } \top\, l_2\, l_3)\uplus S\, \langle l_2\rangle \Rightarrow ()$

$thm_1 = \vdash c\, v \Longrightarrow body \Rightarrow () \qquad thm_2 = \vdash c\, v \Longrightarrow body \Rightarrow (\text{tr } c\, f\, v, v)$

$asm_4 = \vdash \neg c\, v \Longrightarrow body \Rightarrow (\text{tr } c\, f\, (f\, v), v)$

$asm_5 = \vdash \neg c\, v \Longrightarrow \langle l_1\rangle\, (l_1 \text{ ifgoto } (c\, v)\, l_2\, l_3)\uplus S \uplus (l_4 \text{ goto } l_1)\, \langle l_1\rangle \Rightarrow (f\, v, v)$

$thm_3 = \vdash \neg c\, v \Longrightarrow body \Rightarrow (\text{tr } c\, f\, v, v)$

$$\cfrac{\cfrac{\cfrac{\cfrac{asm_1 \quad asm_2}{lem_1}\text{skip} \quad asm_3}{thm_1}\text{nop}}{thm_2}\text{tr\_def} \qquad \cfrac{\cfrac{asm_4 \quad asm_5}{thm_3}\text{case}}{}\text{loop, tr\_def}}{\vdash body \Rightarrow (\text{tr } c\, f\, v, v)}$$

Derivation of rule fun_call

$$pre = l_1\, \{w_1 := w_2\}\, l_2 \qquad post = l_3\, \{v_2 := v_1\}\, l_4$$

$$\frac{\vdash \langle l_1 \rangle \; pre \; \langle l_2 \rangle \; \Rightarrow \; (w_2, w_1) \qquad \vdash \langle l_2 \rangle \; S \; \langle l_3 \rangle \; \Rightarrow \; (f \; w_1, \; v_1)}{\vdash \langle l_1 \rangle \; pre \uplus S \; \langle l_3 \rangle \; \Rightarrow \; (\text{let } w_1 = w_2 \text{ in } f \; w_1, v_1)} \; \text{seq}$$

$$\frac{\dfrac{\langle l_3 \rangle \; post \; \langle l_4 \rangle \; \Rightarrow \; (v_1, v_2)}{\vdash \langle l_1 \rangle \; pre \uplus S \uplus post \; \langle l_4 \rangle \; \Rightarrow \; (\text{let } v_1 = (\text{let } w_1 = w_2 \text{ in } f \; w_1) \text{ in } v_1, \; v_2)} \; \text{seq}}{\vdash \langle l_1 \rangle \; pre \uplus S \uplus post \; \langle l_4 \rangle \; \Rightarrow \; (f \; w_2, v_2)} \; \text{let\_def}$$

These rules immediately validate the following rewrites whose repeated application will convert a FIL program to an equivalent SAL program. Notation l_{+i} stands for the ith new label introduced during the conversion. As an example, the SAL of f_1 (after the application of rule elim_blk_lab explained in the next section) is shown at the right of Fig.3.

[conv_exp] conv $(l \; (e, v) \; l') \longleftrightarrow (l, \{v := e\}, l')$

[conv_let] conv $(l \; (\text{let } v = e \text{ in } f \; v, \; w) \; l') \longleftrightarrow$
$\qquad$ (conv $(l \; (e, v) \; l_{+1})) \uplus$ conv $(l_{+1} \; (f \; v, w) \; l')$

[conv_cond] conv $(l \; (\text{if } c \text{ then } e_1 \text{ else } e_2, v) \; l') \longleftrightarrow$
$\qquad (l \text{ ifgoto } c \; l_{+1} \; l_{+2}) \uplus$ conv $(l_{+2} \; (e_2, v) \; l') \uplus$ conv $(l_{+1} \; (e_1, v) \; l')$

[conv_tr] conv $(l \; (\text{tr } c \; f \; v, \; v) \; l') \longleftrightarrow$
$\qquad (l \text{ ifgoto } c \; l' \; l) \uplus$ conv $(l \; (f \; v, v) \; l_{+1}) \uplus (l_{+1} \text{ goto } l)$

[conv_app] conv $(l \; (f \; w_2, \; v_2) \; l') \longleftrightarrow$
$\qquad (l \; \{w_1 := w_2\} \; l_{+1}) \uplus$ (conv $(l_{+1} \; bd \; l_{+2})) \uplus (l_{+2} \; \{v_2 := v_1\} \; l')$
$\qquad$ where v_1, bd and w_1 are the input, body and output of f respectively

4.2   Machine Code Generation

This phase pretty-prints SAL programs into assembly code with respect to the instruction set of the target machine. Since we do not specify the semantics of the machine language, this conversion does not go by proof. However, the high similarity between SAL and realistic assembly language makes the correctness of this conversion easy to check (*e.g.* by hand).

One optimization in this phase is to eliminate labels that are not the targets of existing jumps. For instance, internal labels within a block consisting of sequential assignment instructions can be removed safely. And, the exit label of a structure is superfluous when the control flow after its execution goes directly to the next structure. Furthermore, since a ifgoto instruction is always followed immediately by its false block, it is safe to remove its exit label pointing to the false block.

[elim_blk_lab] $(l_1 \; \{v_1 := w_1\} \; l_2) \uplus (l_2 \; \{v_2 := w_2\} \; l_3) \longrightarrow$
$\qquad l_1 \; (\{v_1 := w_1\} \uplus \{v_2 := w_2\}) \; l_3$

[elim_seq_lab] $(l_1 \; S_1 \; l_2) \uplus (l_2 \; S_2 \; l_3) \longrightarrow (l_1 \; S_1) \uplus (l_2 \; S \; l_3)$

[elim_ifgoto_lab] (ifgoto $c \; l_2 \; l_3) \uplus (l_3 \; S \; l_4) \longrightarrow$ (ifgoto $c \; l_2) \uplus (l_3 \; S \; l_4)$

The process of producing assembly from an optimized SAL program is trivial: (1) An assignment instruction with a single variable as target is replaced with a corresponding machine instruction; (2) A goto instruction is inserted for the exit label of a structure; (3) A ifgoto instruction is replaced with a comparison instruction followed by a jump. When both the target and source of an assignment are tuple and the machine model does not support parallel move, this assignment can be implemented by first pushing the value of source into the stack and then loading it back from the stack.

We have modeled an ARM machine in HOL and mechanically verify the translation from an intermediate language similar to the FIG to ARM assembly [12]. By compiling-by-proof FIG into this intermediate language, we can produce certified ARM assembly for FIG programs.

5   Related Work

There are systems that use rewrite rules to specify program transformations. For instance, in the ASF+SDF environment [24] transformations and evaluation can be specified as rewrite rules. There are also some work that uses logical frameworks to simplify the construction of compilers. For instance, Liang [13] implements a compiler for a simple imperative language using a higher-order abstract syntax implementation in λ-Prolog. Boyle, Resler and Winter [8], propose using rewrites that model code transformation to build trusted compilers. They also introduce a transformation grammar to guide the application of rewrites [25]. Similarly, Sampaio [21] uses term rewriting to convert source programs to their normal forms representing object code. However, these works do not not address the issue of validation of the compiler.

Hickey and Nogin [7] base on the MetaPRL logical framework to construct a compiler from a full higher order, untyped, functional language to Intel x86 code, based entirely on higher-order rewrite rules. A set of unverified rewriting rules are used to convert a higher level program to a lower level program. They use higher-order abstract syntax to represent programs and do not define the semantics of these programs. Thus no formal verification of the rewriting rules is done. Although the source language and intermediate languages of their compiler are different from ours, our work can be regarded as an extension of their work by now verifying the rewrite rules for program transformation.

Hannan and Pfenning [6] construct a verified compiler in LF for the untyped λ calculus. The target machine is a variant of the CAM runtime and differs greatly from real machines. In their work, programs are associated with operational semantics; and both compiler transformation and verifications are modeled as deductive systems.

Leroy [2,11] verifies a compiler from a subset of C, $i.e.$ Clight, to PowerPC assembly code in the Coq system. The semantics of Clight is completely deterministic and specified as big-step operational semantics. Several intermediate languages are introduced and translations between them are verified. The proof of semantics preservation for the translation proceeds by induction over the Clight evaluation derivation and case analysis on the last evaluation rule used; in contrast, our proofs proceed by verifying the rewrite rules.

A purely operational semantics based development is that of Klein and Nipkow [9] which gives a thorough formalization of a Java-like language. A compiler from this language to a subset of Java Virtual Machine is verified using Isabelle/HOL. However, that compiler targets fairly high-level code, and assumes an unbounded number of registers. The Isabelle/HOL theorem prover is also used to verify the compilation from a type-safe subset of C to DLX assembly code [10], where a big step semantics and a small step semantics for this language are defined. In addition, Meyer and Wolff [14] derive in Isabelle/HOL a verified compilation of a lazy language (called MiniHaskell) to a strict language (called MiniML) based on the denotational semantics of these languages.

There has recently been a large amount of work on verifying low-level languages (e.g. [15]), originally prompted by the ideas of proof carrying code and typed assembly language [16]. Of course, compiler verification itself is a venerable topic, with far too many publications to survey (see Dave's bibliography [3]).

6 Summary and Future Work

We have shown how term rewriting can be used to construct and verify a compiler for a subset of the computable functions accepted by the TFL package [22], i.e., functions definable by well-founded recursion and ML-style pattern matching. This allows a smooth passage from recursively defined logical functions to assembly code that is guaranteed to implement those functions.

We are considering a systematic way for users to apply the rewrite rules to obtain a trusted compiler of their own. A simple programming language is being introduced for users to write programs to guide the application of the verified rules. By programming such guiding procedures, users will be able to obtain customized trusted compilers.

We also consider to build compilers for widely-used functional languages like ML. They have the similar syntax and semantics as our source language, but have many more advanced features. To start, we need to strengthen the front end translation to support ML-style datatypes, polymorphism and other features.

References

1. Birkedal, L., Tofte, M., Vejlstrup, M.: From region inference to von neumann machines via region representation inference. In: 23rd ACM SIGPLAN-SIGACT Symposium on Principles of Programming Languages (POPL'96) (1996)
2. Blazy, S., Dargaye, Z., Leroy, X.: Formal verification of a C compiler front-end. In: Misra, J., Nipkow, T., Sekerinski, E. (eds.) FM 2006. LNCS, vol. 4085, Springer, Heidelberg (2006)
3. Dave, M.A.: Compiler verification: a bibliography. ACM SIGSOFT Software Engineering Notes 28(6), 2–2 (2003)
4. Flanagan, C., Sabry, A., Duba, B.F., Felleisen, M.: The essence of compiling with continuations. In: ACM SIGPLAN-SIGACT 93 Conference on Programming Language Design and Implementation (PLDI'93) (1993)
5. Gordon, M., Iyoda, J., Owens, S., Slind, K.: Automatic formal synthesis of hardware from higher order logic. In: Proceedings of Fifth International Workshop on Automated Verification of Critical Systems (AVoCS 2005), ENTCS, vol. 145 (2005)
6. Hannan, J., Pfenning, F.: Compiler verification in LF. In: Proceedings of the 7th Symposium on Logic in Computer Science (LICS'92) (1992)

7. Hickey, J., Nogin, A.: Formal compiler construction in a logical framework. Journal of Higher-Order and Symbolic Computation 19(2-3), 197–230 (2006)
8. Resler, R., Boyle, J., Winter, K.: Do you trust your compiler? applying formal methods to constructing high-assurance compilers, High-Assurance Systems Engineering Workshop (1997)
9. Klein, G., Nipkow, T.: A machine-checked model for a Java-like language, virtual machine and compiler. TOPLAS 28(4), 619–695 (2006)
10. Leinenbach, D., Paul, W., Petrova, E.: Towards the formal verification of a C0 compiler: Code generation and implementation correctnes. In: 4th IEEE International Conference on Software Engineering and Formal Methods (2005)
11. Leroy, X.: Formal certification of a compiler backend, or: programming a compiler with a proof assistant. In: Symposium on the Principles of Programming Languages (POPL 2006), ACM Press, New York (2006)
12. Li, G., Owens, S., Slind, K.: Structure of a proof-producing compiler for a subset of higher order logic. In: 16th European Symposium on Programming (ESOP'07) (2007)
13. Liang, C.C.: Compiler construction in higher order logic programming, Practical Aspects of Declarative Languages (2002)
14. Meyer, T., Wolff, B.: Tactic-based optimized compilation of functional programs. In: Filliâtre, J.-C., Paulin-Mohring, C., Werner, B. (eds.) TYPES 2004. LNCS, vol. 3839, Springer, Heidelberg (2006)
15. Moore, J.S.: Piton: A mechanically verified assembly-level language. Automated Reasoning Series. Kluwer Academic Publishers, Dordrecht (1996)
16. Morrisett, G., Walker, D., Crary, K., Glew, N.: From System F to typed assembly language. TOPLAS 21(3), 527–568 (1999)
17. Nipkow, T., Paulson, L.C., Wenzel, M. (eds.): Isabelle/HOL. LNCS, vol. 2283. Springer, Heidelberg (2002)
18. Norrish, M., Slind, K.: A thread of HOL development. The Computer Journal 45(1), 37–45 (2002)
19. Norrish, M., Slind, K.: HOL-4 manuals (1998-2006) , Available at http://hol.sourceforge.net/
20. Saabas, A., Uustalu, T.: A compositional natural semantics and hoare logic for low- level languages, SOS 2005 (2005)
21. Sampaio, A.: An algebraic approach to compiler design. In: amast series in computing, vol. 4, World Scientific, Singapore (1997)
22. Slind, K.: Reasoning about terminating functional programs, Ph.D. thesis, Institut für Informatik, Technische Universität München (1999)
23. Tan, G., Appel, A.W.: A compositional logic for control flow. In: Emerson, E.A., Namjoshi, K.S. (eds.) VMCAI 2006. LNCS, vol. 3855, Springer, Heidelberg (2005)
24. Brand, M.v.d., Heering, J., Klint, P., Olivier, P.A.: Compiling language definitions: The ASF+SDF compiler. ACM Transactions of Programming Language Systems 24(4), 334–368 (2003)
25. Winter, V.L.: Program transformation in hats. In: Proceedings of the Software Transformation Systems Workshop (1999)

Barendregt's Variable Convention in Rule Inductions

Christian Urban[1], Stefan Berghofer[1], and Michael Norrish[2]

[1] TU Munich, Germany
[2] NICTA, Australia

Abstract. Inductive definitions and rule inductions are two fundamental reasoning tools in logic and computer science. When inductive definitions involve binders, then Barendregt's variable convention is nearly always employed (explicitly or implicitly) in order to obtain simple proofs. Using this convention, one does not consider truly arbitrary bound names, as required by the rule induction principle, but rather bound names about which various freshness assumptions are made. Unfortunately, neither Barendregt nor others give a formal justification for the variable convention, which makes it hard to formalise such proofs. In this paper we identify conditions an inductive definition has to satisfy so that a form of the variable convention can be built into the rule induction principle. In practice this means we come quite close to the informal reasoning of "pencil-and-paper" proofs, while remaining completely formal. Our conditions also reveal circumstances in which Barendregt's variable convention is not applicable, and can even lead to faulty reasoning.

1 Introduction

In informal proofs about languages that feature bound variables, one often assumes (explicitly or implicitly) a rather convenient convention about those bound variables. Barendregt's statement of the convention is:

> **Variable Convention:** *If $M_1, \ldots, M_n$ occur in a certain mathematical context (e.g. definition, proof), then in these terms all bound variables are chosen to be different from the free variables.* [2, Page 26]

The reason for this convention is that it leads to very slick informal proofs—one can avoid having to rename bound variables.

One example of such a slick informal proof is given in [2, Page 60], proving the substitutivity property of the $\longrightarrow_1\!\!\twoheadrightarrow$ (or "parallel reduction") relation, which is defined by the rules:

$$
\frac{}{M \longrightarrow_1\!\!\twoheadrightarrow M} \; \text{One}_1 \qquad\qquad \frac{M \longrightarrow_1\!\!\twoheadrightarrow M'}{lam(y.M) \longrightarrow_1\!\!\twoheadrightarrow lam(y.M')} \; \text{One}_2
$$

$$
\frac{M \longrightarrow_1\!\!\twoheadrightarrow M' \quad N \longrightarrow_1\!\!\twoheadrightarrow N'}{app(M,N) \longrightarrow_1\!\!\twoheadrightarrow app(M',N')} \; \text{One}_3 \qquad \frac{M \longrightarrow_1\!\!\twoheadrightarrow M' \quad N \longrightarrow_1\!\!\twoheadrightarrow N'}{app(lam(y.M),N) \longrightarrow_1\!\!\twoheadrightarrow M'[y := N']} \; \text{One}_4
$$
$$\tag{1}$$

The substitutivity property states:

F. Pfenning (Ed.): CADE 2007, LNAI 4603, pp. 35–50, 2007.
© Springer-Verlag Berlin Heidelberg 2007

Lemma. If $M \longrightarrow_{1} M'$ and $N \longrightarrow_{1} N'$, then $M[x := N] \longrightarrow_{1} M'[x := N']$.

In [2], the proof of this lemma proceeds by an induction over the definition of $M \longrightarrow_{1} M'$. Though Barendregt does not acknowledge the fact explicitly, there are two places in his proof where the variable convention is used. In case of rule One$_2$, for example, Barendregt writes (slightly changed to conform with the syntax we shall employ for λ-terms):

Case One$_2$. $M \longrightarrow_{1} M'$ is $lam(y.P) \longrightarrow_{1} lam(y.P')$ and is a direct consequence of $P \longrightarrow_{1} P'$. By induction hypothesis one has $P[x := N] \longrightarrow_{1} P[x := N']$. But then $lam(y.P[x := N]) \longrightarrow_{1} lam(y.P'[x := N'])$, i.e. $M[x := N] \longrightarrow_{1} M'[x := N']$. $\qquad\square$

However, the last step in this case only works if one knows that

$$lam(y.P[x := N]) = lam(y.P)[x := N] \quad \text{and}$$
$$lam(y.P'[x := N']) = lam(y.P')[x := N']$$

which only holds when the bound variable y is not equal to x, and not free in N and N'. These assumptions might be inferred from the variable convention, provided one has a formal justification for this convention. Since one usually assumes that λ-terms are α-equated, one might think a simple justification for the variable convention is along the lines that one can always rename binders with fresh names. This is however *not* sufficient in the context of inductive definitions, because there rules can have the same variable occurring both in binding and non-binding positions. In rule One$_4$, for example, y occurs in binding position in the subterm $lam(y.M)$, and in the subterm $M'[y := N']$ it is in a *non*-binding position. Both occurrences must refer to the same variable as the rule

$$\frac{M \longrightarrow_{1} M' \quad N \longrightarrow_{1} N'}{app(lam(z.M), N) \longrightarrow_{1} M'[y := N']} \; \text{One}'_4$$

leads to a nonsensical reduction relation.

In the absence, however, of a formal justification for the variable convention, Barendregt's argument considering only a well-chosen y seems dubious, because the induction principle that comes with the inductive definition of $\longrightarrow_{1}$ is:

$\forall M. \; P \, M \, M$

$\forall y \, M \, M'. \; P \, M \, M' \Rightarrow P \, (lam(y.M)) \, (lam(y.M'))$

$\forall M \, M' \, N \, N'. \; P \, M \, M' \wedge P \, N \, N' \Rightarrow P \, (app(M, N)) \, (app(M', N'))$

$\forall y \, M \, M' \, N \, N'. \; P \, M \, M' \wedge P \, N \, N' \Rightarrow P \, (app(lam(y.M), N)) \, (M'[y := N'])$

$$\overline{M \longrightarrow_{1} N \Rightarrow P \, M \, N}$$

where both cases One$_2$ and One$_4$ require that the corresponding implication holds for **all** y, not just the ones with $y \neq x$ and $y \notin FV(N, N')$. Nevertheless, we will show that Barendregt's apparently dubious step can be given a faithful, and sound, mechanisation. Being able to restrict the argument in general to a suitably chosen bound variable will, however, depend on the form of the rules in an inductive definition. In this paper we will make precise what this form is and will show how the variable convention can be built into the induction principle.

The interactions between bound and free occurrences of variables, and their consequences for obtaining a formal argument, seem to often be overlooked in the literature when claiming that proofs by rule inductions are straightforward. One example of this comes with a weakening result for contexts in the simply-typed λ-calculus.

We assume types are of the form $T ::= X \mid T \rightarrow T$, and that typing contexts (finite lists of variable-type pairs) are *valid* if no variable occurs twice. The typing relation can then be defined by the rules

$$\frac{valid(\Gamma) \quad (x{:}T) \in \Gamma}{\Gamma \vdash var(x) : T} \; \text{Type}_1 \qquad \frac{\Gamma \vdash M : T_1 \rightarrow T_2 \quad \Gamma \vdash N : T_1}{\Gamma \vdash app(M, N) : T_2} \; \text{Type}_2$$

$$\frac{x \mathbin{\#} \Gamma \quad (x{:}T_1){::}\Gamma \vdash M : T_2}{\Gamma \vdash lam(x.M) : T_1 \rightarrow T_2} \; \text{Type}_3 \tag{2}$$

where $(x : T) \in \Gamma$ stands for list-membership, and $x \mathbin{\#} \Gamma$ for x being fresh for Γ, or equivalently x not occuring in Γ. Define a context Γ' to be weaker than Γ (written $\Gamma \subseteq \Gamma'$), if every name-type pair in Γ also appears in Γ'. Then we have

Lemma (Weakening). *If $\Gamma \vdash M : T$ is derivable, and $\Gamma \subseteq \Gamma'$ with Γ' valid, then $\Gamma' \vdash M : T$ is also derivable.*

The informal proof of this lemma is straightforward, provided(!) one uses the variable convention.

Informal Proof. By rule induction over $\Gamma \vdash M : T$ showing that $\Gamma' \vdash M : T$ holds for all Γ' with $\Gamma \subseteq \Gamma'$ and Γ' being valid.

Case Type_1: $\Gamma \vdash M : T$ *is* $\Gamma \vdash var(x) : T$. *By assumption we know* $valid(\Gamma')$, $(x{:}T) \in \Gamma$ *and* $\Gamma \subseteq \Gamma'$. *Therefore we can use* Type_1 *to derive* $\Gamma' \vdash var(x) : T$.

Case Type_2: $\Gamma \vdash M : T$ *is* $\Gamma \vdash app(M_1, M_2) : T$. *Case follows from the induction hypotheses and rule* Type_2.

Case Type_3: $\Gamma \vdash M : T$ *is* $\Gamma \vdash lam(x.M_1) : T_1 \rightarrow T_2$. *Using the variable convention we assume that* $x \mathbin{\#} \Gamma'$. *Then we know that* $((x{:}T_1){::}\Gamma')$ *is valid and hence that* $((x{:}T_1){::}\Gamma') \vdash M_1 : T_2$ *holds. By appealing to the variable convention again, we have that* $\Gamma' \vdash lam(x.M_1) : T_1 \rightarrow T_2$ *holds using rule* Type_3 □

However, in order to make this informal proof work with the induction principle that comes with the rules in (2), namely

$$\frac{\begin{array}{l} \forall \Gamma\, x\, T. \; valid(\Gamma) \wedge (x{:}T) \in \Gamma \Rightarrow P\, \Gamma\, (var(x))\, T \\ \forall \Gamma\, M\, N\, T_1\, T_2. \; P\, \Gamma\, M\, (T_1 \rightarrow T_2) \wedge P\, \Gamma\, N\, T_1 \Rightarrow P\, \Gamma\, (app(M, N))\, T_2 \\ \forall x\, \Gamma\, M\, T_1\, T_2. \; x \mathbin{\#} \Gamma \wedge P\, ((x{:}T_1){::}\Gamma)\, M\, T_2 \Rightarrow P\, \Gamma\, (lam(x.M))\, (T_1 \rightarrow T_2) \end{array}}{\Gamma \vdash M : T \Rightarrow P\, \Gamma\, M\, T} \tag{3}$$

we need in case of rule Type_3 to be able to rename the bound variable to be suitably fresh for Γ'; by the induction we only know that x is fresh for the smaller context Γ. To be able to do this renaming depends on two conditions: first, there must exist a fresh variable which we can choose. In our example this means that the context Γ' must not contain all possible free variables. Second, the relation $\Gamma \vdash M : T$ must be invariant under suitable renamings. This is because when we change the goal from $\Gamma' \vdash lam(x.M_1) : T_1 \to T_2$ to $\Gamma' \vdash lam(z.M_1[x := z]) : T_1 \to T_2$, we must be able to infer from $((x : T_1) :: \Gamma') \vdash M_1 : T_2$ that $((z : T_1) :: \Gamma') \vdash M_1[x := z] : T_2$ holds. This invariance under renamings does, however, *not* hold in general, not even under renamings with fresh variables. For example if we assume that variables are linearly ordered, then the relation

$$\frac{v = min\{v_0, \ldots, v_n\}}{(\{v_0, \ldots, v_n\}, v)}$$

that associates finite subsets of these variables to the smallest variable occurring in it, is *not* invariant (apply the renaming $[v := v']$ where v' is a variable that is bigger than every variable in $\{v_0, \ldots, v_n\}$). Other examples are rules that involve a substitution for concrete variables or a substitution with concrete terms. In order to avoid such pathological cases, we require that the relation for which one wants to employ the variable convention must be invariant under renamings; from the induction we require that the variable convention can only be applied in contexts where there are only finitely many free names.

However, these two requirements are *not* yet sufficient, and we need to impose a second condition that inductive definitions have to satisfy. Consider the function that takes a list of variables and binds them in λ-abstractions, that is

$$bind\ t\ [] \overset{\text{def}}{=} t \qquad bind\ t\ (x :: xs) \overset{\text{def}}{=} lam(x.(bind\ t\ xs))$$

Further consider the relation $\hookrightarrow$, which "unbinds" the outermost abstractions of a λ-term and is defined by:

$$\frac{}{var(x) \hookrightarrow [], var(x)}\ \text{Unbind}_1 \qquad \frac{}{app(t_1, t_2) \hookrightarrow [], app(t_1, t_2)}\ \text{Unbind}_2 \qquad (4)$$

$$\frac{t \hookrightarrow xs, t'}{lam(x.t) \hookrightarrow x :: xs, t'}\ \text{Unbind}_3$$

Of course, this relation cannot be expressed as a function because the bound variables do not have "particular" names. Nonetheless it is well-defined, and not trivial. For example, we have

$$lam(x.lam(y.app(var(x), app(var(y), var(z)))))$$
$$\hookrightarrow [x, y], app(var(x), app(var(y), var(z)))\ \text{and}$$
$$lam(x.lam(y.app(var(x), app(var(y), var(z)))))$$
$$\hookrightarrow [y, x], app(var(y), app(var(x), var(z)))$$

but we also have $\forall t'.\ lam(x.lam(y.app(x, app(var(y), var(z))))) \not\hookrightarrow [x, z], t'$.

Further, one can also easily establish (by induction on the term t) that for every t there exists a t' and a list xs of distinct variables such that $t \hookrightarrow xs, t'$ holds, demonstrating that the relation is "total" if the last two parameters are viewed as results.

If one wished to do rule inductions over the definition of this relation, one might imagine that the variable convention allowed us to assume that the bound name x was distinct from the free variables of the conclusion of the rule, and in particular that x could not appear in the list xs. However, this use of the variable convention quickly leads to the *faulty* lemma:

Lemma (Faulty). *If* $t \hookrightarrow (x :: xs), t'$ *and* $x \in FV(t')$ *then* $x \in FV(bind\ t'\ xs)$.

The "proof" is by an induction over the rules given in (4) and assumes that the binder x in the third rule is fresh with respect to xs. This lemma is of course false as witnessed by the term $lam(x.lam(x.var(x)))$. Therefore, including the variable convention in the induction principle that comes with the rules in (4), would produce an inconsistency. To prevent this problem we introduce a second condition for rules, which requires that all variables occurring as a binder in a rule must be fresh (a notion which we shall make precise later on) for the conclusion of this rule, and if a rule has several such variables, they must be mutually distinct.

Our Contribution. We introduce two conditions inductive definitions must satisfy in order to make sure they are compatible with the variable convention. We will build a version of this convention into the induction principles that come with the inductive definitions. Moreover, it will be shown how these new ("vc-compatible") induction principles can be automatically derived in the nominal datatype package [11,9]. The presented results have already been extensively used in formalisations: for example in our formalisations of the CR and SN properties in the λ-calculus, in a formalisation by Bengtson and Parrow for several proofs in the pi-calculus [3], in a formalisation of Crary's chapter on logical relation [4], and in various formalised proofs on structural operational semantics.

2   Nominal Logic

Before proceeding, we briefly introduce some important notions from nominal logic [8,11]. In particular, we will build on the three central notions of *permutations*, *support* and *equivariance*. Permutations are finite bijective mappings from atoms to atoms, where atoms are drawn from a countably infinite set denoted by $\mathbb{A}$. We represent permutations as finite lists whose elements are swappings (i.e., pairs of atoms). We write such permutations as $(a_1\ b_1)(a_2\ b_2) \cdots (a_n\ b_n)$; the empty list $[]$ stands for the identity permutation. A permutation π *acting* on an atom a is defined as:

$$[] \cdot a \stackrel{\text{def}}{=} a \qquad ((a_1\ a_2) :: \pi) \cdot a \stackrel{\text{def}}{=} \begin{cases} a_2 & \text{if } \pi \cdot a = a_1 \\ a_1 & \text{if } \pi \cdot a = a_2 \\ \pi \cdot a & \text{otherwise} \end{cases}$$

where $(a\ b) :: \pi$ is the composition of a permutation followed by the swapping $(a\ b)$. The composition of π followed by another permutation π' is given by list-concatenation, written as $\pi' @ \pi$, and the inverse of a permutation is given by list reversal, written as π^{-1}. Our representation of permutations as lists does not give unique representatives: for example, the permutation $(a\ a)$ is "equal" to the identity permutation. We equate permutations with a relation $\sim$:

Definition 1 (Permutation Equality). *Two permutations are equal, written* $\pi_1 \sim \pi_2$, *provided* $\pi_1 \bullet a = \pi_2 \bullet a$, *for all* $a \in \mathbb{A}$.

The permutation action on atoms can be lifted to other types.

Definition 2 (The Action of a Permutation). *A permutation action* $\pi \bullet (-)$ *lifts to a type* T *provided it the following three properties hold on all values* $x \in T$

$$(i) \quad [\,] \bullet x = x$$
$$(ii) \quad (\pi_1 @ \pi_2) \bullet x = \pi_1 \bullet (\pi_2 \bullet x)$$
$$(iii) \quad \text{if } \pi_1 \sim \pi_2 \text{ then } \pi_1 \bullet x = \pi_2 \bullet x$$

For example, lists and tuples can be given the following permutation action:

$$\text{lists:} \qquad \pi \bullet [\,] \stackrel{\text{def}}{=} [\,]$$
$$\pi \bullet (h :: t) \stackrel{\text{def}}{=} (\pi \bullet h) :: (\pi \bullet t) \qquad (5)$$
$$\text{tuples:} \quad \pi \bullet (x_1, \ldots, x_n) \stackrel{\text{def}}{=} (\pi \bullet x_1, \ldots, \pi \bullet x_n)$$

Further, on α-equated λ-terms we can define the permutation action:

$$\pi \bullet var(x) \stackrel{\text{def}}{=} var(\pi \bullet x)$$
$$\pi \bullet app(M_1, M_2) \stackrel{\text{def}}{=} app(\pi \bullet M_1, \pi \bullet M_2) \qquad (6)$$
$$\pi \bullet lam(x.M) \stackrel{\text{def}}{=} lam(\pi \bullet x. \pi \bullet M)$$

The second notion that we use is that of *support* (roughly speaking, the support of an element is its set of free atoms). The set supporting an element is defined in terms of permutation actions on that element, so that as soon as one has defined a permutation action for a type, one automatically derives its accompanying notion of support, which in turn determines the notion of freshness (see [11]):

Definition 3 (Support and Freshness). *The* support *of* x *is defined as:* $\text{supp}(x) \stackrel{\text{def}}{=} \{a \mid \text{infinite}\{b \mid (a\,b) \bullet x \neq x\}\}$. *An atom* a *is said to be* fresh *for an* x, *written* $a \,\#\, x$, *if* $a \notin \text{supp}(x)$.

We will also use the auxiliary notation $a \,\#\, xs$, in which xs stands for a collection of objects $x_1 \ldots x_n$, to mean $a \,\#\, x_1 \ldots a \,\#\, x_n$. We further generalise this notation to a collection of atoms, namely $as \,\#\, xs$, which means $a_1 \,\#\, xs \ldots a_m \,\#\, xs$.

Later on we will often make use of the following two properties of freshness, which can be derived from the definition of support, the permutation action on $\mathbb{A}$ and the requirements of permutation actions on other types (see [11]).

Lemma 1
- (a) $a \,\#\, x$ *implies* $\pi \bullet a \,\#\, \pi \bullet x$; *and*
- (b) *if* $a \,\#\, x$ *and* $b \,\#\, x$, *then* $(a\,b) \bullet x = x$.

Henceforth we will only be interested in those objects which have finite support, because for them there exists always a fresh atom (recall that the set of atoms $\mathbb{A}$ is infinite).

Lemma 2. *If x is finitely supported, then there exists an atom a such that $a \mathrel{\#} x$.*

Unwinding the definitions of permutation actions and support one can often easily calculate the support of an object:

atoms:	$\mathsf{supp}(a) = \{a\}$
tuples:	$\mathsf{supp}(x_1, \ldots, x_n) = \mathsf{supp}(x_1) \cup \ldots \cup \mathsf{supp}(x_n)$
lists:	$\mathsf{supp}([\,]) = \varnothing$, $\mathsf{supp}(h :: t) = \mathsf{supp}(h) \cup \mathsf{supp}(t)$
α-equated λ-terms:	$\mathsf{supp}(var(x)) = \{x\}$
	$\mathsf{supp}(app(M, N)) = \mathsf{supp}(M) \cup \mathsf{supp}(N)$
	$\mathsf{supp}(lam(x.M)) = \mathsf{supp}(M) - \{x\}$

We therefore note the following: all elements in $\mathbb{A}$ and all α-equated λ-terms are finitely supported. Lists (similarly tuples) containing finitely supported elements are finitely supported. The last three equations show that the support of α-equated λ-terms coincides with the usual notion of free variables. Hence, $a \mathrel{\#} M$ with M being an α-equated λ-term coincides with a not being free in M. If b is an atom, then $a \mathrel{\#} b$ coincides with $a \neq b$.

The last notion of nominal logic we use here is that of *equivariance*.

Definition 4 (Equivariance)
- *A relation R is* equivariant *if $R\,(\pi{\cdot}xs)$ is implied by $R\,xs$ for all π.*
- *A function f is* equivariant *provided $\pi{\cdot}(f\,xs) = f\,(\pi{\cdot}xs)$ for all π.*

Remark 1. Note that if we regard the term-constructors *var*, *app* and *lam* as functions, then they are equivariant on account of the definition given in (6). Because of the definition in (5), the cons-constructors of lists are equivariant. By a simple structural induction on the list argument of *valid*, we can establish that the relation *valid* is equivariant. By Lem. $1(a)$ freshness is equivariant. Also list-membership, $(-) \in (-)$, is equivariant, which can be shown by an induction on the length of lists.

3   Schematic Terms and Schematic Rules

Inductive relations are defined as the smallest relation closed under some schematic rules. In this section we will formally specify the form of such rules. Diagrammatically they have the form

$$\frac{premises \quad side\text{-}conditions}{conclusion}\,\varrho \tag{7}$$

where the premises, side-conditions and conclusions are predicates of the form $R\,ts$ where we use the letters R, S, P and Q to stand for predicates; ts stands for a collection of schematic terms (the arguments of R). They are either variables, abstractions or functions, namely $t ::= x \mid a.t \mid f\,ts$ where a is a variable standing for an atom and f stands for a function. We call the variable a in $a.t$ as being in *binding position*. Note that a schematic rule may contain the same variable in binding and non-binding positions (One$_4$ and Type$_3$ are examples).

Assuming an inductive definition of the predicate R, the schematic rule in (7) must be of the form

$$\frac{R\,ts_1\ \ldots\ R\,ts_n\quad S_1\,ss_1\ \ldots\ S_m\,ss_m}{R\,ts}\ \varrho \tag{8}$$

where the predicates $S_i\,ss_i$ (the ones different from R) stand for the side-conditions in the schematic rule.

For proving our main result in the next section it is convenient to introduce several auxiliary notions for schematic terms and rules. The following functions calculate for a schematic term the set of variables in non-binding position and the set of variables in binding position, respectively:

$$\begin{aligned}
vars(x) &= \{x\} & varsbp(x) &= \varnothing \\
vars(a.t) &= vars(t) - \{a\} & varsbp(a.t) &= varsbp(t) \cup \{a\} \\
vars(f\,ts) &= vars(ts) & varsbp(f\,ts) &= varsbp(ts)
\end{aligned} \tag{9}$$

The notation $t[as; xs]$ will be used for schematic terms to indicate that the variables in binding position of t are included in as and the other variables of t are either in as or xs. That means we have for $t[as; xs]$ that $varsbp(t) \subseteq as$ and $vars(t) \subseteq as \cup xs$ hold.

We extend this notation also to schematic rules: by writing $\varrho[as; xs]$ for (8) we mean

$$\frac{R\,ts_1[as; xs]\ \ldots\ R\,ts_n[as; xs]\quad S_1\,ss_1[as; xs]\ \ldots\ S_m\,ss_m[as; xs]}{R\,ts[as; xs]}\ \varrho \tag{10}$$

However, unlike in the notation for schematic terms, we mean in $\varrho[as; xs]$ that the as stand *exactly* for the variables occurring somewhere in ϱ in binding position and the xs stand for the rest of variables. That means we have for $\varrho[as; xs]$ that $varsbp(\varrho) = as$ and $vars(\varrho) = xs$ hold.

assuming suitable generalisations of the functions $vars$ and $varsbp$ to schematic rules. To see how the schematic notation works out in examples, reconsider the definitions for the relations One, given in (1), and Type, given in (2). Using our schematic notation for the rules, we have

$$\begin{aligned}
&\mathrm{One}_1[-; M] & &\mathrm{Type}_1[-; \Gamma, x, T] \\
&\mathrm{One}_2[y; M, M'] & &\mathrm{Type}_2[-; \Gamma, M, N, T_1, T_2] \\
&\mathrm{One}_3[-; M, N, M', N'] & &\mathrm{Type}_3[x; \Gamma, M, T_1, T_2] \\
&\mathrm{One}_4[y; M, N, M', N']
\end{aligned}$$

where '$-$' stands for no variable in binding position.

The main property of an inductive definition, say for the inductive predicate R, is that it comes with an induction principle, which establishes a property $P\,ts$ under the assumption that $R\,ts$ holds. This means we have an induction principle diagrammatically looking as follows

$$\frac{\begin{array}{c} \cdots \\ \forall as\,xs.\ P\,ts_1[as; xs]\ \wedge\ \ldots\ \wedge\ P\,ts_n[as; xs]\ \wedge \\ S\,ss_1[as; xs]\ \wedge\ \ldots\ \wedge\ S\,ss_m[as; xs]\ \Rightarrow\ P\,ts[as; xs] \\ \cdots \end{array}}{R\,ts \Rightarrow P\,ts} \tag{11}$$

where for every schematic rule ϱ in the inductive definition we have to establish an implication. These implications state that we can assume the property for all premises and also can assume that the side-conditions hold; we have to show that the property holds for the conclusion of the schematic rule.

As explained in the introduction, we need to impose some conditions on schematic rules in order to avoid faulty reasoning and to permit an argument employing the variable convention. A rule $\varrho[as; xs]$, as given in (10), is *variable convention compatible*, short *vc-compatible*, provided the following two conditions are satisfied.

Definition 5 (Variable Convention Compatibility). *A rule $\varrho[as; xs]$ with conclusion $R\,ts$ is* vc-compatible *provided that:*

- *all functions and side-conditions occurring in ϱ are equivariant, and*
- *the side-conditions $S_1\,ss_1 \wedge \ldots \wedge S_m\,ss_m$ imply that $as \,\#\, ts$ holds and that the as are distinct.*

If every schematic rule in an inductive definition satisfies these conditions, then the induction principle can be strengthened such that it includes a version of the variable convention.

4   Strengthening of the Induction Principle

In this section we will show how to obtain a stronger induction principle than the one given in (11). By stronger we mean that it has the variable convention already built in (this will then enable us to give slick proofs by rule induction which do not need any renaming). Formally we show that induction principles of the form

$$\frac{\begin{array}{c}\ldots \\ \forall as\ xs\ C.\ (\forall C.P\,C\,ts_1[as; xs]) \wedge \ \ldots \ \wedge (\forall C.P\,C\,ts_n[as; xs]) \wedge \\ S\,ss_1[as; xs]\ \wedge\ \ldots\ \wedge\ S\,ss_n[as; xs]\ \wedge\ \boxed{as\,\#\,C}\ \Rightarrow P\,C\,ts[as; xs] \\ \ldots \end{array}}{R\,ts \Rightarrow P\,C\,ts} \tag{12}$$

can be used, where C stands for an *induction context*. This induction context can be instantiated appropriately (we will explain this in the next section). The only requirement we have about C is that it needs to be finitely supported. The main difference between the stronger induction principle in (12) and the weaker one in (11) is that in a proof using the stronger we can assume that the as, i.e. the variables in binding-position, are fresh with respect to the context C (see highlighted freshness-condition). This additional assumption allows us to reason as in informal "paper-and-pencil" proofs where one assumes the variable convention (we will also show this in the next section).

The first condition of vc-compatibility implies that the inductively defined predicate R is equivariant and that every schematic subterm occurring in a rule is equivariant.

Lemma 3. *(a) If all functions in a schematic term $t[as; xs]$ are equivariant, then (viewed as a function) t is equivariant, that is $\pi \bullet t[as; xs] = t[\pi \bullet as; \pi \bullet xs]$. (b) If all functions and side-conditions in the rules of an inductive definition for the predicate R are equivariant, then R is equivariant, that is if $R\,ts$ holds than also $R\,(\pi \bullet ts)$ holds.*

Proof. The first part is by a routine induction on the structure of the schematic term t. The second part is by a simple rule induction using the weak induction principle given in (11).

We now prove our main theorem: if the rules of an inductive definition are vc-compatible, then the strong induction principle in (12) holds.

Theorem 1. *Given an inductive definition for the predicate R involving vc-compatible schematic rules only, then a strong induction principle is available for this definition establishing the implication $R\,ts \Rightarrow P\,C\,ts$ with the induction context C being finitely supported.*

Proof. We need to establish $R\,ts \Rightarrow P\,C\,ts$ using the implications indicated in (12). To do so we will use the weak induction from (11) and establish that the proposition $R\,ts \Rightarrow \forall \pi\,C.P\,C\,(\pi \bullet ts)$ holds. For each schematic rule $\varrho[as; xs]$

$$\frac{R\,ts_1[as; xs] \ \ldots \ R\,ts_n[as; xs] \quad S_1\,ss_1[as; xs] \ \ldots \ S_m\,ss_m[as; xs]}{R\,ts[as; xs]} \, \varrho$$

in the inductive definition we have to analyse one case. The reasoning proceeds in each of them as follows: By induction hypothesis and side-conditions we have

$$(\forall \pi\,C.P\,C\,(\pi \bullet ts_1[as; xs])) \ \ldots \ (\forall \pi\,C.P\,C\,(\pi \bullet ts_n[as; xs])) \tag{13}$$

$$S_1\,ss_1[as; xs] \ \ldots \ S_m\,ss_m[as; xs] \tag{14}$$

hold. Since ϱ is assumed to be vc-compatible, we have by Lem. 3 that (*) $\pi \bullet ts_i[as; xs]$ is equal to $ts_i[\pi \bullet as; \pi \bullet xs]$ in (13). For (14) we can further infer from the vc-compatibility of ϱ that

$$(a) \ as \,\#\, ts[as; xs] \qquad \text{and} \qquad (b) \ distinct(as) \tag{15}$$

hold. We have to show that $P\,C\,(\pi \bullet ts[as; xs])$ holds, which because of Lem. 3 is equivalent to $P\,C\,ts[\pi \bullet as; \pi \bullet xs]$.

The proof proceeds by using Lem. 2 and choosing for every atom a in as a fresh atom c such that for all the cs the following holds:

$$(a) \ cs \,\#\, ts[\pi \bullet as; \pi \bullet xs] \quad (b) \ cs \,\#\, \pi \bullet as \quad (c) \ cs \,\#\, C \quad (d) \ distinct(cs) \tag{16}$$

Such cs always exists: the first and the second property can be obtained since the schematic terms $ts[\pi \bullet as; \pi \bullet xs]$ and $\pi \bullet as$ stand for finitely supported objects; the third can also be obtained since we assumed that the induction context C is finitely supported; the last can be obtained by choosing the cs one after another avoiding the ones that have already been chosen.

Now we form the permutation $\pi' \stackrel{\text{def}}{=} (\pi \bullet as \ cs)$ where $(\pi \bullet as \ cs)$ stands for the sequence of swappings $(\pi \bullet a_1 \ c_1) \ldots (\pi \bullet a_j \ c_j)$. Since permutations are bijective renamings, we can infer from (15.b) that $distinct(\pi \bullet as)$ holds. This and the fact in (16.d) implies that

$$\pi' @ \pi \bullet as = \pi' \bullet (\pi \bullet as) = cs \tag{17}$$

We then instantiate the π in the induction hypotheses given in (13) with $\pi' @ \pi$ and obtain using (17) and (*) so that

$$(\forall C.P \ C \ ts_1[cs; \pi' @ \pi \bullet xs])) \ \ldots \ (\forall C.P \ C \ ts_n[cs; \pi' @ \pi \bullet xs])) \tag{18}$$

hold. Since the rule ϱ is vc-compatible, we can infer from (14) and the equivariance of the side-conditions that

$$S_1 \ ss_1[cs; \pi' @ \pi \bullet xs] \ \ldots \ S_m \ ss_m[cs; \pi' @ \pi \bullet xs] \tag{19}$$

hold (we use here the fact that $\pi' @ \pi \bullet (ss_i[as; xs])$ is equal to $ss_i[cs; \pi' @ \pi \bullet xs]$). From (16.$c$), (18), (19) and the implication from the strong induction principle we can infer $P \ C \ ts[cs; \pi' @ \pi \bullet xs]$ which by Lem. 3 is equivalent to

$$P \ C \ \pi' \bullet ts[\pi \bullet as; \pi \bullet xs] \tag{20}$$

From (15.a) we can by Lem. 1(a) infer that $\pi \bullet as \ \# \ ts[\pi \bullet as; \pi \bullet xs]$ holds. This however implies by (16.a) and by repeated application of Lem. 1(b) that

$$\pi' \bullet ts[\pi \bullet as; \pi \bullet xs] = ts[\pi \bullet as; \pi \bullet xs] \tag{21}$$

Substituting this equation into (20) establishes the proof obligation for the rule ϱ. Provided we analysed all such cases, we have shown $R \ ts \Rightarrow \forall \pi \ C.P \ C \ (\pi \bullet ts)$. We obtain our original goal by instantiating π with the identity permutation. $\quad\square$

5   Examples

We can now apply our technique to the examples from the Introduction.

5.1   Simple Typing

Given the typing relation defined in (2), we must first check the conditions spelt out in Definition 5. The first condition is that all of the definition's functions (namely var, app, lam and ::) and side-conditions (namely $valid$, $\in$ and $\#$) must be equivariant. This is easily confirmed (see Remark 1). The second condition requires that all variables in binding positions be distinct (there is just one, the x in Type$_3$); and that it be fresh for all the terms appearing in the conclusion of that rule, namely $\Gamma \vdash lam(x.M) : T_1 \to T_2$, under the assumption that the side-condition, $x \# \Gamma$, of this rule holds.

In this case, therefore, we must check that $x \# \Gamma$, $x \# lam(x.M)$ and $x \# T_1 \to T_2$ hold. The first is immediate given our assumption; the second follows from the definition of support for lambda-terms ($x \# lam(x.M)$ for all x and M); and the third follows from the definition of support for types (we define permutation on types T as $\pi \bullet T \stackrel{\text{def}}{=} T$ and thus obtain that $\text{supp}(T) = \varnothing$).

With these conditions established, Theorem 1 tells us that the strong, or vc-compatible principle exists, and that it is

$$\forall \Gamma\, x\, T\, C.\ valid(\Gamma) \wedge (x:T) \in \Gamma \Rightarrow P\, C\, \Gamma\, (var(x))\, T$$
$$\forall \Gamma\, M\, N\, T_1\, T_2\, C.\ (\forall C.\ P\, C\, \Gamma\, M\, (T_1 \to T_2)) \wedge (\forall C.\ P\, C\, \Gamma\, N\, T_1) \Rightarrow$$
$$P\, C\, \Gamma\, (app(M,N))\, T_2$$
$$\forall \Gamma\, x\, M\, T_1\, T_2\, C.\ x \,\#\, \Gamma \wedge (\forall C.\ P\, C\, ((x:T_1)::\Gamma)\, M\, T_2) \wedge x \,\#\, C \Rightarrow$$
$$P\, C\, \Gamma\, (lam(x.M))\, (T_1 \to T_2)$$

$$\overline{\Gamma \vdash M : T \ \Rightarrow\ P\, C\, \Gamma\, M\, T}$$

This principle can now be used to establish the weakening result. The statement is

$$\Gamma \vdash M : T \ \Rightarrow\ \Gamma \subseteq \Gamma' \ \Rightarrow\ valid(\Gamma') \ \Rightarrow\ \Gamma' \vdash M : T \qquad (22)$$

With the strong induction principle, the formal proof of this statement proceeds like the informal one given in the Introduction. There, in the Type$_3$ case, we used the variable convention to assume that the bound x was fresh for Γ'. Given this information, we instantiate the induction context C in the strong induction principle with Γ' (which is finitely supported). The complete instantiation of the vc-compatible induction principle is

$$P = \lambda \Gamma\, M\, T\, \Gamma'.\ \Gamma \subseteq \Gamma' \Rightarrow valid(\Gamma') \Rightarrow \Gamma' \vdash M : T$$
$$C = \Gamma' \qquad\qquad \Gamma = \Gamma \qquad\qquad M = M \qquad\qquad T = T$$

which after some beta-contractions gives us the statement in (22). The induction cases are then as follows (stripping off the outermost quantifiers):

(1) $valid(\Gamma) \wedge (x : T) \in \Gamma \Rightarrow \Gamma \subseteq \Gamma' \Rightarrow valid(\Gamma') \Rightarrow \Gamma' \vdash var(x) : T$

(2) $(\forall \Gamma''.\ \Gamma \subseteq \Gamma'' \Rightarrow valid(\Gamma'') \Rightarrow \Gamma'' \vdash M_1 : T_1 \to T_2) \wedge$
$(\forall \Gamma''.\ \Gamma \subseteq \Gamma'' \Rightarrow valid(\Gamma'') \Rightarrow \Gamma'' \vdash M_2 : T_1) \Rightarrow$
$\Gamma \subseteq \Gamma' \Rightarrow valid(\Gamma') \Rightarrow \Gamma' \vdash app(M_1, M_2) : T_2$

(3) $(\forall \Gamma''.\ (x : T_1) :: \Gamma \subseteq \Gamma'' \Rightarrow valid(\Gamma'') \Rightarrow \Gamma'' \vdash M : T_2) \wedge x \,\#\, \Gamma' \Rightarrow$
$\Gamma \subseteq \Gamma' \Rightarrow valid(\Gamma') \Rightarrow \Gamma' \vdash lam(x.M) : T_1 \to T_2$

The first two cases are trivial. For (3), we instantiate Γ'' in the induction hypothesis to be $(x : T_1) :: \Gamma'$. From the assumption $\Gamma \subseteq \Gamma'$ we have $(x : T_1) :: \Gamma \subseteq (x : T_1) :: \Gamma'$. Moreover from the assumption $valid(\Gamma')$ we also have $valid((x : T_1) :: \Gamma')$ using the variable convention's $x \,\#\, \Gamma'$. Hence we can derive $(x : T_1) :: \Gamma' \vdash M : T_2$ using the induction hypothesis. Now applying rule Type$_3$ we can obtain $\Gamma' \vdash lam(x.M) : T_1 \to T_2$, again using the variable convention's $x \,\#\, \Gamma'$. This completes the proof. Its *readable* version expressed in Isabelle's Isar-language [12] and using the nominal datatype package [9] is shown in Fig. 1.

By way of contrast, recall that a proof without the stronger induction principle would not be able to assume anything about the relationship between x and Γ', forcing the prover to α-convert $lam(x.M)$ to a form with a new and suitably fresh bound variable, $lam(z.((z\,x)\bullet M))$, say. At this point, the simplicity of the proof using the variable convention disappears: the inductive hypothesis is much

lemma *weakening*:
   assumes a_1: $\Gamma \vdash M{:}T$ **and** a_2: $\Gamma \subseteq \Gamma'$ **and** a_3: *valid* Γ'
   shows $\Gamma' \vdash M{:}T$
using a_1 a_2 a_3
proof (*nominal-induct* Γ M T *avoiding*: Γ' *rule*: *strong-typing-induct*)
   case (*Type$_3$* x Γ T_1 T_2 M)
   have *vc*: $x\#\Gamma'$ **by** *fact* — variable convention
   have *ih*: $(x{:}T_1){::}\Gamma{\subseteq}(x{:}T_1){::}\Gamma' {\Longrightarrow} valid\ ((x{:}T_1){::}\Gamma'){\Longrightarrow}(x{:}T_1){::}\Gamma'{\vdash}M{:}T_2$ **by** *fact*
   have $\Gamma \subseteq \Gamma'$ **by** *fact*
   then have $(x{:}T_1){::}\Gamma \subseteq (x{:}T_1){::}\Gamma'$ **by** *simp*
   moreover
   have *valid* Γ' **by** *fact*
   then have *valid* $((x{:}T_1){::}\Gamma')$ **using** *vc* **by** (*simp add*: *valid-cons*)
   ultimately have $(x{:}T_1){::}\Gamma' \vdash M{:}T_2$ **using** *ih* **by** *simp*
   with *vc* **show** $\Gamma' \vdash lam(x.M) : T_1 \rightarrow T_2$ **by** *auto*
qed (*auto*) — cases Type$_1$ and Type$_2$

Fig. 1. A readable Isabelle-Isar proof for the weakening lemma using the strong induction principle of the typing relation. The stronger induction principle allows us to assume a variable convention, in this proof $x \# \Gamma'$, which makes the proof to go through without difficulties.

harder to show applicable because it mentions M, but the desired goal is in terms of $(z\,x){\bullet}M$.

5.2 Parallel Reduction

In [2], the central lemma of the proof for the Church-Rosser property of beta-reduction is the substitutivity property of the $\longrightarrow_1{\twoheadrightarrow}$-reduction. To formalise this proof while preserving the informal version's simplicity, we will need the strong induction principle for $\longrightarrow_1{\twoheadrightarrow}$.

Before proceeding, we need two important properties of the substitution function, which occurs in the redex rule One$_4$. We characterise the action of a permutation over a substitution (showing that substitution is equivariant), and the support of a substitution. Both proofs are by straightforward vc-compatible *structural* induction over M:

$$\pi{\bullet}(M[x := N]) = (\pi{\bullet}M)[(\pi{\bullet}x) := (\pi{\bullet}N)] \tag{23}$$

$$\mathbf{supp}(M[x := N]) \subseteq (\mathbf{supp}(M) - \{x\}) \cup \mathbf{supp}(N) \tag{24}$$

With this we can start to check the vc-compatibility conditions: the condition about equivariance of functions and side-conditions is again easily confirmed. The second condition is that bound variables are free in the relation's rules' conclusions. In rule One$_2$, this is trivial because $y \# lam(y.M)$ and $y \# lam(y.M')$ hold. A problem arises, however, with rule One$_4$. Here we have to show that $y \# app(lam(y.M), N)$ and $y \# M'[y := N']$, and we have no assumptions to hand about y.

It is certainly true that y is fresh for $lam(y.M)$, but it may occur in N. As for the term $M'[y := N']$, we know that any occurrences of y in M' will be masked by the substitution (see (24)), but y may still be free in N'.

We need to reformulate One$_4$ to read

$$\frac{y \# N \quad y \# N' \quad M \xrightarrow{}_{1}\!\!\twoheadrightarrow M' \quad N \xrightarrow{}_{1}\!\!\twoheadrightarrow N'}{app(lam(y.M), N) \xrightarrow{}_{1}\!\!\twoheadrightarrow M'[y := N']} \quad \text{One}_4''$$

so that the vc-compatibility conditions can be discharged. In other words, if we have rule One$_4''$ we can apply Theorem 1, but not if we use One$_4$. This is annoying because both versions can be shown to define the same relation, but we have no general, and automatable, method for determining this. For the moment, we reject rule One$_4$ and require the user of the nominal datatype package to use One$_4''$. If this is done, the substitutivity lemma is almost automatic:

lemma *substitutivity-aux*:
    assumes a: $N \longrightarrow_1 N'$
    shows $M[x{:=}N] \longrightarrow_1 M[x{:=}N']$
using a **by** (*nominal-induct M avoiding*: x N N' *rule*: *strong-lam-induct*) (*auto*)

lemma *subtitutivity*:
    assumes a_1: $M \longrightarrow_1 M'$ **and** a_2: $N \longrightarrow_1 N'$
    shows $M[x{:=}N] \longrightarrow_1 M'[x{:=}N']$
using a_1 a_2 **by** (*nominal-induct M M' avoiding*: N N' x *rule*: *strong-parallel-induct*)
                    (*auto simp add*: *substitutivity-aux substitution-lemma fresh-atm*)

The first lemma is proved by a vc-compatible *structural* induction over M; the second, the actual substitutivity property, is proved by a vc-compatible *rule* induction relying on the substitution lemma, and the lemma *fresh-atm*, which states that $x \# y$ is the same as $x \neq y$ when y is an atom.

6   Related Work

Apart from our own preliminary work in this area [10], we believe the prettiest formal proof of the weakening lemma to be that in Pitts [8]. This proof uses the equivariance property of the typing relation, and includes a renaming step using permutations. Because of the pleasant properties that permutations enjoy (they are bijective renamings, in contrast to substitutions which might identify two names), the renaming can be done with relatively minimal overhead. Our contribution is that we have built this renaming into our vc-compatible induction principles once and for all. Proofs using the vc-compatible principles then do not need to perform any explicit renaming steps.

Somewhat similar to our approach is the work of Pollack and McKinna [6]. Starting from the standard induction principle that is associated with an inductive definition, we derived an induction principle that allows emulation of Barendregt's variable convention. Pollack and McKinna, in contrast, gave a "weak" and "strong" version of the typing relation. These versions differ in the way the rule for abstractions is stated:

$$\frac{x \# M \quad (x : T_1) :: \Gamma \vdash M[y := x] : T_2}{\Gamma \vdash lam(y.M) : T_1 \to T_2} \text{ weak}$$

$$\frac{\forall x.\, x \# \Gamma \Rightarrow (x : T_1) :: \Gamma \vdash M[y := x] : T_2}{\Gamma \vdash lam(y.M) : T_1 \to T_2} \text{ strong}$$

They then showed that both versions derive the same typing judgements. With this they proved the weakening lemma using the "strong" version of the principle, while knowing that the result held for the "weak" relation as well. The main difference between this and our work seems to be of convenience: we can relatively easily derive, in a uniform way, an induction principle for vc-compatible relations (we have illustrated this point with two examples). Achieving the same uniformity in the style of McKinna and Pollack does not seem as straightforward.

7 Future Work

Our future work will concentrate on two aspects: first on generalising our definition of schematic rules so that they may, for example, include quantifiers. Second on being more liberal about which variables can be included in the induction context. To see what we have in mind with this, recall that we allowed in the induction context only variables that are in binding position. However there are examples where this is too restrictive: for example Crary gives in [4, Page 231] the following mutual inductive definition for the judgements $\Gamma \vdash s \Leftrightarrow t : T$ and $\Gamma \vdash p \leftrightarrow q : T$ (they represent a type-driven equivalence algorithm for lambda-terms with constants):

$$\frac{s \Downarrow p \quad t \Downarrow q \quad \Gamma \vdash p \leftrightarrow q : T}{\Gamma \vdash s \Leftrightarrow t : b} \text{Ae}_1 \quad \frac{(x : T_1) :: \Gamma \vdash s\,x \Leftrightarrow t\,x : T_2}{\Gamma \vdash s \Leftrightarrow t : T_1 \to T_2} \text{Ae}_2 \quad \frac{}{\Gamma \vdash s \Leftrightarrow t : unit} \text{Ae}_3$$

$$\frac{(x : T) \in \Gamma}{\Gamma \vdash x \leftrightarrow x : T} \text{Pe}_1 \quad \frac{\Gamma \vdash p \leftrightarrow q : T_1 \to T_2 \quad \Gamma \vdash s \leftrightarrow t : T_1}{\Gamma \vdash p\,s \leftrightarrow q\,t : T_2} \text{Pe}_2 \quad \frac{}{\Gamma \vdash k \leftrightarrow k : b} \text{Pe}_3$$

What is interesting is that these rules do not contain any variable in binding position. Still, in some proofs by induction over those rules one wants to be able to assume that the variable x in the rule Ae_2 satisfies certain freshness conditions. Our implementation already deals with this situation by explicitly giving the information that x should appear in the induction context. However, we have not yet worked out the theory.

8 Conclusion

In the POPLMARK Challenge [1], the proof of the weakening lemma is described as a "straightforward induction". In fact, mechanising this informal proof is *not* straightforward at all (see for example [6,5,8]). We have given a novel rule induction principle for the typing relation that makes proving the weakening lemma mechanically as simple as performing the informal proof.

Importantly, this new principle can be derived from the original inductive definition of the typing relation in a mechanical way. This method extends our earlier work [10,7], where we constructed our new induction principles by hand.

By formally deriving principles that avoid the need to rename bound variables, we advance the state-of-the-art in mechanical theorem-proving over syntax with binders. The results of this paper have already been used many times in the nominal datatype package: for example in the proofs of the CR and SN properties in the λ-calculus, in proofs about the pi-calculus, in proofs about logical relations and in several proofs from structural operational semantics.

The fact that our technique may require users to cast some inductive definitions in alternative forms is unfortunate. In the earlier [10], our hand-proofs correctly derived a vc-compatible principle from the original definition of $\longrightarrow_{\neg}^{\twoheadrightarrow}$; we hope that future work will automatically justify comparable derivations.

Acknowledgements. We are very grateful to Andrew Pitts for the many discussions with him on the subject of this paper.

References

1. Aydemir, B.E., Bohannon, A., Fairbairn, M., Foster, J.N., Pierce, B.C., Sewell, P., Vytiniotis, D., Washburn, G., Weirich, S., Zdancewic, S.: Mechanized Metatheory for the Masses: The PoplMark Challenge. In: Hurd, J., Melham, T. (eds.) TPHOLs 2005. LNCS, vol. 3603, pp. 50–65. Springer, Heidelberg (2005)
2. Barendregt, H.: The Lambda Calculus: its Syntax and Semantics. Studies in Logic and the Foundations of Mathematics, vol. 103, North-Holland (1981)
3. Bengtson, J., Parrow, J.: Formalising the pi-Calculus using Nominal Logic. In: Proc. of the 10th International Conference on Foundations of Software Science and Computation Structures (FOSSACS). LNCS, vol. 4423, pp. 63–77. Springer, Heidelberg (2007)
4. Crary, K.: Advanced Topics in Types and Programming Languages. In: chapter Logical Relations and a Case Study in Equivalence Checking, pp. 223–244. MIT Press, Cambridge (2005)
5. Gallier, J.: Logic for Computer Science: Foundations of Automatic Theorem Proving. Harper & Row (1986)
6. McKinna, J., Pollack, R.: Some type theory and lambda calculus formalised. Journal of Automated Reasoning 23(1-4) (1999)
7. Norrish, M.: Mechanising λ-calculus using a classical first order theory of terms with permutation. Higher-Order and Symbolic Computation 19, 169–195 (2006)
8. Pitts, A.M.: Nominal Logic, A First Order Theory of Names and Binding. Information and Computation 186, 165–193 (2003)
9. Urban, C., Berghofer, S.: A Recursion Combinator for Nominal Datatypes Implemented in Isabelle/HOL. In: Furbach, U., Shankar, N. (eds.) IJCAR 2006. LNCS (LNAI), vol. 4130, pp. 498–512. Springer, Heidelberg (2006)
10. Urban, C., Norrish, M.: A formal treatment of the Barendregt Variable Convention in rule inductions. In: MERLIN '05: Proceedings of the 3rd ACM SIGPLAN workshop on Mechanized reasoning about languages with variable binding, pp. 25–32. ACM Press, New York (2005)
11. Urban, C., Tasson, C.: Nominal techniques in Isabelle/HOL. In: Nieuwenhuis, R. (ed.) Automated Deduction – CADE-20. LNCS (LNAI), vol. 3632, pp. 38–53. Springer, Heidelberg (2005)
12. Wenzel, M.: Isar — A Generic Interpretative Approach to Readable Formal Proof Documents. In: Bertot, Y., Dowek, G., Hirschowitz, A., Paulin, C., Théry, L. (eds.) TPHOLs 1999. LNCS, vol. 1690, pp. 167–184. Springer, Heidelberg (1999)

Automating Elementary Number-Theoretic Proofs Using Gröbner Bases

John Harrison

Intel Corporation, JF1-13
2111 NE 25th Avenue, Hillsboro OR 97124, USA
johnh@ichips.intel.com

Abstract. We present a uniform algorithm for proving automatically a fairly wide class of elementary facts connected with integer divisibility. The assertions that can be handled are those with a limited quantifier structure involving addition, multiplication and certain number-theoretic predicates such as 'divisible by', 'congruent' and 'coprime'; one notable example in this class is the Chinese Remainder Theorem (for a specific number of moduli). The method is based on a reduction to ideal membership assertions that are then solved using Gröbner bases. As well as illustrating the usefulness of the procedure on examples, and considering some extensions, we prove a limited form of completeness for properties that hold in all rings.

1 Introduction

Various classes of mathematical problems, when expressed in formal logic, can be solved automatically by suitable algorithms. This is often valuable, if only for dealing with relatively uninteresting subtasks of larger formal proofs. Some algorithms implement decision procedures for theories or logical fragments known to be decidable, such as Cooper's algorithm [7] for Presburger arithmetic [17]. Others are more heuristic in nature, e.g. automated induction proofs employing conjecture generalization [4], though many of these can be understood in a general framework of proof planning [6].

Here we present a new algorithm for a useful class of elementary number-theoretic properties. We will introduce and motivate the procedure by focusing on the integers $\mathbb{Z}$, though we will see later that the procedure is only complete for properties that hold in the class of *all* rings. (Thus it is perhaps neither a heuristic method nor a decision procedure, but rather a heuristic application *of* a decision procedure outside its domain of completeness.) The formulas that can be handled are expressed in a first-order language. The terms can be built up using integer constants, negation, addition, subtraction and multiplication, as well as exponentiation with constant nonnegative exponents. (For example, $2x^2 - y^3(w - 42z)^9$ is allowed, but not x^y.) The formulas can be built from these terms using the equality symbol as well as three 'divisibility' relationships, all of which we consider as mere shorthands for other formulas using equality as the only predicate:

F. Pfenning (Ed.): CADE 2007, LNAI 4603, pp. 51–66, 2007.
© Springer-Verlag Berlin Heidelberg 2007

- $s \mid t$, read 's divides t' abbreviates $\exists d.\, t = sd$
- $s \equiv t \pmod{u}$, read 's is congruent to t modulo u', abbreviates $\exists d.\, t - s = ud$
- $\mathrm{coprime}(s, t)$, read 's and t are coprime', abbreviates $\exists x\, y.\, sx + ty = 1$.

Over the integers, $\mathrm{coprime}(m, n)$ holds precisely if m and n have no common factors besides ± 1. This equivalence is proved in many elementary number theory texts [2,8].

We attempt to explain any algebraic terminology as it is used, but a reader may find it helpful to refer to an algebra textbook such as [21] for more on rings, polynomials and ideals. It is worth noting that we tend to blur the distinction between three distinct notions of 'polynomial': (i) a first-order formula in the language of rings, (ii) a polynomial itself as an algebraic object, and (iii) a polynomial function or its evaluation for a specific argument. When we want to emphasize the polynomial as a function we tend to write the arguments (so $p(\overline{x})$ rather than just p), and when treating it as an element of the ring of polynomials we tend to omit arguments, and perhaps emphasize that equations are to be understood as polynomial identities. Sometimes, however, we write the arguments just to emphasize which variables are involved in the polynomial. Over an infinite base ring such as $\mathbb{Z}$, two polynomials are equal as algebraic objects ($p = q$) if and only if the associated functions are equal on all arguments ($\forall \overline{x}.\, p(\overline{x}) = q(\overline{x})$). By contrast, over a 2-element ring the polynomials $x^2 + x$ and 0 are considered distinct even though they determine the same function.

2   Example

We will explain the procedure by a typical example first, proving this 'cancellation' property for congruences:

$$\forall a\, n\, x\, y.\, ax \equiv ay \pmod{n} \wedge \mathrm{coprime}(a, n) \Rightarrow x \equiv y \pmod{n}$$

The first step is to expand away the number-theoretic predicates:

$$\forall a\, n\, x\, y.\, (\exists d.\, ay - ax = nd) \wedge$$
$$(\exists u\, v.\, au + nv = 1)$$
$$\Rightarrow (\exists e.\, y - x = ne)$$

and we then pull out the existential quantifiers in the antecedent:

$$\forall a\, n\, x\, y\, d\, u\, v.\, ay - ax = nd \wedge au + nv = 1 \Rightarrow \exists e.\, y - x = ne$$

We prove this by proving something related, but in general stronger, namely that over the ring $\mathbb{Z}[a, n, x, y, d, u, v]$ the polynomial $y - x$ is contained in the ideal generated by the polynomials in the antecedent ($ay - ax - nd$ and $au + nv - 1$) and the multiplier (n) for the existentially quantified variable:

$$(y - x) \in \mathrm{Id}\,\langle ay - ax - nd,\, au + nv - 1,\, n \rangle$$

i.e. that there exist 'cofactor' polynomials $p(a, n, x, y, d, u, v)$, $q(a, n, x, y, d, u, v)$ and $r(a, n, x, y, d, u, v)$ such that the following is a polynomial identity:

$$y - x = (ay - ax - nd)p(a, n, x, y, d, u, v)+$$
$$(au + nv - 1)q(a, n, x, y, d, u, v)+$$
$$nr(a, n, x, y, d, u, v)$$

To see that the identity implies the original claim, note that if $ay - ax = nd$ and $au + nv = 1$, the identity reduces to $y - x = nr(a, n, x, y, d, u, v)$, which certainly implies $\exists e.\ y - x = ne$. In fact, it shows something stronger: there is a polynomial expression for the witness e in terms of the other variables.

To prove the ideal membership goal, the most natural and straightforward technique is to apply Buchberger's algorithm [5] to find a Gröbner basis for the ideal, and then show that $y - x$ reduces to 0 w.r.t. this basis. A suitably instrumented version of the algorithm can actually produce the explicit cofactor polynomials, giving a simple 'certificate' of the result. For our example, one natural possibility for the cofactors is:

$$p(a, n, x, y, d, u, v) = u$$
$$q(a, n, x, y, d, u, v) = x - y$$
$$r(a, n, x, y, d, u, v) = ud + vy - vx$$

We can then verify the polynomial identity simply by normalizing both sides in some reasonable way.

3   Detailed Procedure

We aim to reduce the initial problem to one or more sub-problems of the following standard form, where the $e_i(\overline{x})$, $a_i(\overline{x})$ and $p_{ij}(\overline{x})$ are polynomials in variables $\overline{x} = x_1, \ldots, x_l$:

$$\forall \overline{x}. \bigwedge_{i=1}^{m} e_i(\overline{x}) = 0 \Rightarrow \exists y_1 \cdots y_n.\ p_{11}(\overline{x})y_1 + \cdots + p_{1n}(\overline{x})y_n = a_1(\overline{x}) \wedge$$
$$\cdots \wedge$$
$$p_{k1}(\overline{x})y_1 + \cdots + p_{kn}(\overline{x})y_n = a_k(\overline{x})$$

We need to test whether this formula holds over the integers, and we do it by testing the following ideal membership problem in $\mathbb{Z}[x_1, \ldots, x_l, u_1, \ldots, u_k]$, where the u_i are fresh variables not occurring in the original problem:

$$(a_1 u_1 + \cdots + a_k u_k)$$
$$\in \mathrm{Id}\, \langle e_1, \ldots, e_m, (p_{11}u_1 + \cdots + p_{k1}u_k), \ldots (p_{1n}u_1 + \cdots + p_{kn}u_k) \rangle$$

(Note that we are considering *integer* polynomials only in the ideal membership.) In the common special case $k = 1$, as in the example of the previous section, we do not need to introduce the auxiliary variables, but can use simply:

$$a_1 \in \mathrm{Id}\, \langle e_1, \ldots, e_m, p_{11}, \ldots, p_{1n} \rangle$$

3.1   Incompleteness over the Integers

The standard problem above takes in the degenerate case ($n = 0$ and $k = 0$) of proving that a Diophantine equation has no solutions over the integers: $\forall \overline{x}. \bigwedge_{i=1}^{m} e_i(\overline{x}) = 0 \Rightarrow \bot$. Since this is known to be undecidable [16] while ideal membership over the integers is decidable [1] it follows that our test based on ideal membership cannot be both sound and complete. And indeed, it is not hard to find examples of incompleteness, where the existential assertion holds over $\mathbb{Z}$ but the corresponding ideal membership does not. The following are all variations on a theme that $x^2 + x$ is always even:

- $\forall x. \exists a. x^2 + x = 2a$ holds over the integers, yet $(x^2 + x) \notin \mathrm{Id}\,\langle 2 \rangle$.
- $\forall x\, y.\, y = 1 \Rightarrow \exists a.\, x^2 + x = (y+1)a$ holds over the integers, yet $(x^2 + x) \notin \mathrm{Id}\,\langle y - 1, y + 1 \rangle$
- $\forall x\, y.\, \exists a\, b.\, x^2 + x = (y+1)a + (y-1)b$ yet $(x^2 + x) \notin \mathrm{Id}\,\langle y - 1, y + 1 \rangle$

Nevertheless, we will show (i) that our procedure is sound, and (ii) that it is complete for properties that hold in *all rings*, not just in the integers.

3.2   Soundness

Consider first the special case $k = 1$, when we just test

$$a_1 \in \mathrm{Id}\,\langle e_1, \ldots, e_m, p_{11}, \ldots, p_{1n} \rangle$$

If this ideal membership assertion holds, then concretely there are cofactor polynomials $f_1, \ldots, f_m, g_1, \ldots, g_n$ such that

$$e_1 f_1 + \cdots + e_m f_m + p_{11} g_1 + \cdots + p_{1n} g_n = a_1$$

Evaluating when $\bigwedge_{i=1}^{m} e_i(\overline{x}) = 0$ we get

$$p_{11}(\overline{x}) g_1(\overline{x}) + \cdots + p_{1n}(\overline{x}) g_n(\overline{x}) = a_1(\overline{x})$$

which does indeed show that there exist $y_1, \ldots, y_n$ such that

$$p_{11}(\overline{x}) y_n + \cdots + p_{1n}(\overline{x}) y_n = a_1(\overline{x})$$

and from the cofactors in the ideal membership, we obtain a simple and explicit proof of the original formula, with witnesses for the existentially quantified variables that are polynomials in the other variables. In the general case (not requiring $k = 1$), suppose that the ideal membership holds:

$$(a_1 u_1 + \cdots + a_k u_k)$$
$$\in \mathrm{Id}\,\langle e_1, \ldots, e_m, (p_{11} u_1 + \cdots + p_{k1} u_k), \ldots, (p_{1n} u_1 + \cdots + p_{kn} u_k) \rangle$$

which means explicitly we have a polynomial identity of the form:

$$(a_1 u_1 + \cdots + a_k u_k) =$$
$$e_1(\overline{x}) r_1(\overline{x}, \overline{u}) + \cdots + e_m(\overline{x}) r_m(\overline{x}, \overline{u}) +$$
$$(p_{11} u_1 + \cdots + p_{k1} u_k) q_1(\overline{x}, \overline{u}) + \cdots + (p_{1n} u_1 + \cdots + p_{kn} u_k) q_n(\overline{x}, \overline{u})$$

with the q_i and r_i polynomials in $\mathbb{Z}[x_1, \ldots, x_l, u_1, \ldots, u_k]$. Let us separate each $q_i(\overline{x}, \overline{u})$ into:

$$q_i(\overline{x}, \overline{u}) = c_i(\overline{x}) + d_i(\overline{x}, \overline{u})$$

where $c_i(\overline{x})$ does not involve any of the u_i, and all monomials in $d_i(\overline{x}, \overline{u})$ contain at least one of the u_i. Similarly we decompose $r_i(\overline{x}, \overline{u})$ into:

$$r_i(\overline{x}, \overline{u}) = s_i(\overline{x}, \overline{u}) + t_i(\overline{x}, \overline{u})$$

where each monomial in $s_i(\overline{x}, \overline{u})$ has degree 1 in exactly one of the u_i (e.g. $3u_1$ or $x_5^2 u_2$) and each monomial in $t_i(\overline{x}, \overline{u})$ either does not involve any u_i, involves more than one, or has a degree higher than 1 in one of them (e.g. 42, $7u_1u_2$, xu_3^2). Now:

$$
\begin{aligned}
(a_1 u_1 + \cdots + a_k u_k) = \\
e_1(\overline{x})s_1(\overline{x}, \overline{u}) + \cdots + e_m(\overline{x})s_m(\overline{x}, \overline{u}) + \\
e_1(\overline{x})t_1(\overline{x}, \overline{u}) + \cdots + e_m(\overline{x})t_m(\overline{x}, \overline{u}) + \\
(p_{11}u_1 + \cdots + p_{k1}u_k)c_1(\overline{x}) + \cdots + (p_{1n}u_1 + \cdots + p_{kn}u_k)c_n(\overline{x}) + \\
(p_{11}u_1 + \cdots + p_{k1}u_k)d_1(\overline{x}, \overline{u}) + \cdots + (p_{1n}u_1 + \cdots + p_{kn}u_k)d_n(\overline{x}, \overline{u})
\end{aligned}
$$

Note that all terms on the LHS have degree exactly 1 in just one of the u_i. Thus all terms on the right that are not of that form must cancel, leaving:

$$
\begin{aligned}
(a_1 u_1 + \cdots + a_k u_k) = \\
e_1(\overline{x})s_1(\overline{x}, \overline{u}) + \cdots + e_m(\overline{x})s_m(\overline{x}, \overline{u}) + \\
(p_{11}u_1 + \cdots + p_{k1}u_k)c_1(\overline{x}) + \cdots + (p_{1n}u_1 + \cdots + p_{kn}u_k)c_n(\overline{x})
\end{aligned}
$$

Evaluating when $\bigwedge_{i=1}^{m} e_i(\overline{x}) = 0$ gives:

$$
\begin{aligned}
(a_1 u_1 + \cdots + a_k u_k) = \\
(p_{11}u_1 + \cdots + p_{k1}u_k)c_1(\overline{x}) + \cdots + (p_{1n}u_1 + \cdots + p_{kn}u_k)c_n(\overline{x})
\end{aligned}
$$

Successively setting $u_i = 1$ and $u_j = 0$ for all $j \neq i$, we find that for all $1 \leq i \leq k$ the following holds:

$$a_i = c_1(\overline{x})p_{i1}(\overline{x}) + \cdots + c_n(\overline{x})p_{in}(\overline{x})$$

which does indeed show that there exist $y_1, \ldots, y_n$ such that

$$
\begin{aligned}
p_{11}(\overline{x})y_1 + \cdots + p_{1n}(\overline{x})y_n = a_1(\overline{x}) \wedge \\
\cdots \wedge \\
p_{k1}(\overline{x})y_1 + \cdots + p_{kn}(\overline{x})y_n = a_k(\overline{x})
\end{aligned}
$$

and once again we obtain explicit polynomials $y_i = c_i(\overline{x})$ as witnesses.

3.3 Completeness over All Rings

We will now prove that the ideal membership assertion is equivalent to *the validity of the starting formula in all rings* (as usual, we mean commutative rings with 1). The reasoning in the previous section extends easily from $\mathbb{Z}$ to an arbitrary ring, showing that the ideal membership implies the validity of the starting formula in all rings. To establish the other direction, we first recall that a *Horn clause* is a first-order formula that is either of the form:

$$\forall v_1, \ldots, v_n. \, P_1[v_1, \ldots, v_n] \wedge \cdots \wedge P_n[v_1, \ldots, v_n] \Rightarrow Q[v_1, \ldots, v_n]$$

including the degenerate case

$$\forall v_1, \ldots, v_n. \, Q[v_1, \ldots, v_n]$$

or

$$\forall v_1, \ldots, v_n. \, P_1[v_1, \ldots, v_n] \wedge \cdots \wedge P_n[v_1, \ldots, v_n] \Rightarrow \bot$$

where $Q[v_1, \ldots, v_n]$ and all $P_i[v_1, \ldots, v_n]$ are atomic formulas. In particular, the axioms for commutative rings with 1 are just (implicitly universally quantified) equations, and are therefore Horn clauses. In fact, all truly *algebraic* axioms are just universally quantified equations, and thus Horn clauses. For example, we can add the infinite set of axioms $x^k = 0 \Rightarrow x = 0$ for all $k \geq 1$ to axiomatize the class of *reduced* rings (rings without nilpotent elements). However neither the integral domain axiom $xy = 0 \Rightarrow x = 0 \vee y = 0$ nor the field axiom $\neg(x = 0) \Rightarrow x^{-1}x = 1$ is a Horn clause, and so the special results we will note for Horn clause theories are not directly applicable, though analogous results can be derived for general theories by considering canonical resolution proofs [14].

In order to state these special properties of Horn clause theories, it is more convenient to consider first-order logic without special treatment of equality. By a standard result [13], a formula is valid in first-order logic with equality iff it is a general first-order consequence of the set of equivalence and congruence properties of equality for the language at issue. In particular, a formula holds in all rings iff it is a first-order consequence of the following axioms, all of which are Horn clauses:

$$x + y = y + x$$
$$x + (y + z) = (x + y) + z$$
$$x + 0 = x$$
$$x + (-x) = 0$$
$$xy = yx$$
$$x(yz) = (xy)z$$
$$x1 = x$$
$$x(y + z) = xy + xz$$
$$x = x$$
$$x = y \Rightarrow y = x$$
$$x = y \wedge y = z \Rightarrow x = z$$
$$x = x' \Rightarrow -x = -x'$$
$$x = x' \wedge y = y' \Rightarrow x + y = x' + y'$$
$$x = x' \wedge y = y' \Rightarrow xy = x'y'$$

If Γ is a set of Horn clauses and A an atomic formula or $\bot$, then $\Gamma \vdash A$ if and only if there is a 'Prolog-style' proof of A from Γ, i.e. a tree whose nodes are atomic formulas, with A as the top node, such that for every node B in the tree, there is a clause in the axiom set that can be instantiated so its conclusion is B and its antecedent atoms are the nodes below B in the tree [10]. This special canonical proof format for deductions from Horn clauses allows us to deduce some interesting consequences. We start with a theorem due to Simmons [19,12,21]:

Theorem 1. *Let* $p_1(\overline{x})$, ..., $p_r(\overline{x})$ *and* $p(\overline{x})$ *be polynomials with integer coefficients over the variables* $\overline{x} = x_1, \ldots, x_l$. *Then the following holds in all commutative rings with* 1:

$$\forall x_1, \ldots, x_l. \, p_1(\overline{x}) = 0 \wedge \cdots \wedge p_r(\overline{x}) = 0 \Rightarrow p(\overline{x}) = 0$$

iff the following ideal membership holds over $\mathbb{Z}[\overline{x}]$:

$$p \in Id\langle p_1, \ldots, p_r \rangle$$

in other words, if there are cofactor polynomials $q_1(\overline{x})$, ..., $q_r(\overline{x})$ *with integer coefficients such that the following is a polynomial identity:*

$$p(\overline{x}) = p_1(\overline{x})q_1(\overline{x}) + \cdots + p_r(\overline{x})q_r(\overline{x})$$

Proof. (*Sketch.*) *The bottom-to-top direction is immediate, because given that identity, the right-hand side collapses to zero when all the* $p_i(\overline{x})$ *are zero. Conversely, if the top result holds in all rings, then there is a Prolog-style proof from the Horn clause axioms for rings and equality. By induction on this tree, for every equation* $s(\overline{x}) = t(\overline{x})$ *deduced,* $s(\overline{x}) - t(\overline{x})$ *is in the ideal generated by* $p_1, \ldots, p_r$. $\qquad\square$

The following is essentially Theorem 7.0.6 ("Horn-Herbrand theorem") in [10]. It states that for deduction from Horn clauses we can strengthen the usual classical Herbrand theorem to one with the same 'existence property' as in intuitionistic logic:

Theorem 2. *Let* T *be a set of Horn clauses and* $A_i[y_1, \ldots, y_n]$ *atomic formulas (in a language with at least one individual constant). Then*

$$T \models \exists y_1, \ldots, y_n. \, A_1[y_1, \ldots, y_n] \wedge \cdots \wedge A_k[y_1, \ldots, y_n]$$

(where '$T \models P$' means 'P is a first-order consequence of Γ') if and only if there are ground terms $t_1, \ldots, t_n$ *in the language such that:*

$$T \models A_1[t_1, \ldots, t_n] \wedge \cdots \wedge A_k[t_1, \ldots, t_n]$$

Proof. (*Sketch.*) *The bottom-to-top direction is immediate. For the other direction, note that the top is equivalent to*

$$T \cup \{(\forall y_1, \ldots, y_n. \, A_1[y_1, \ldots, y_n] \wedge \cdots \wedge A_k[y_1, \ldots, y_n] \Rightarrow \bot)\} \models \bot$$

The usual 'Prolog style' backchaining proof for Horn clauses can only apply the extra clause once, and will give rise to the corresponding instantiation. $\qquad\square$

Thus we can deduce a corollary:

Theorem 3. *The following formula:*

$$\forall \overline{x}. \bigwedge_{i=1}^{m} e_i(\overline{x}) = 0 \Rightarrow \exists y_1 \cdots y_n. \; p_{11}(\overline{x})y_1 + \cdots + p_{1n}(\overline{x})y_n = a_1(\overline{x}) \wedge$$
$$\cdots \wedge$$
$$p_{k1}(\overline{x})y_1 + \cdots + p_{kn}(\overline{x})y_n = a_k(\overline{x})$$

holds in all rings iff there are terms $q_1(\overline{x}),\ldots,q_n(\overline{x})$ in the language of rings (i.e. polynomials with integer coefficients) such that the following holds in all rings:

$$\forall \overline{x}. \bigwedge_{i=1}^{m} e_i(\overline{x}) = 0 \Rightarrow p_{11}(\overline{x})q_1(\overline{x}) + \cdots + p_{1n}(\overline{x})q_n(\overline{x}) = a_1(\overline{x}) \wedge$$
$$\cdots \wedge$$
$$p_{k1}(\overline{x})q_1(\overline{x}) + \cdots + p_{kn}(\overline{x})q_n(\overline{x}) = a_k(\overline{x})$$

Proof. We can replace the variables $\overline{x}$ by constants, and regard the $e_i(\overline{x})$ as new (Horn) axioms. The result is then an immediate consequence of Theorem 2 and the Horn nature of the ring and equality axioms.   □

This leads us to the following:

Theorem 4. *The following formula:*

$$\forall \overline{x}. \bigwedge_{i=1}^{m} e_i(\overline{x}) = 0 \Rightarrow \exists y_1 \cdots y_n. \; p_{11}(\overline{x})y_1 + \cdots + p_{1n}(\overline{x})y_n = a_1(\overline{x}) \wedge$$
$$\cdots \wedge$$
$$p_{k1}(\overline{x})y_1 + \cdots + p_{kn}(\overline{x})y_n = a_k(\overline{x})$$

holds in all rings iff there are terms $q_1(\overline{x}),\ldots,q_n(\overline{x})$ and $r_{1j}(\overline{x}),\ldots,r_{mj}(\overline{x})$ in the language of rings (i.e. polynomials with integer coefficients) such that the following is a polynomial identity for each j with $1 \le j \le k$:

$$e_1(\overline{x})r_{1j}(\overline{x}) + \cdots + e_m(\overline{x})r_{mj}(\overline{x}) + p_{j1}(\overline{x})q_1(\overline{x}) + \cdots + p_{jn}(\overline{x})q_n(\overline{x}) = a_j(\overline{x})$$

Proof. Just combine the previous theorem and Theorem 1.   □

The case $k = 1$ takes a particularly simple form, which was used in the motivating example of the previous section:

Theorem 5. *The formula:*

$$\forall \overline{x}. \bigwedge_{i=1}^{m} e_i(\overline{x}) = 0 \Rightarrow \exists y_1 \cdots y_n. \; p_1(\overline{x})y_1 + \cdots + p_n(\overline{x})y_n = a(\overline{x})$$

holds in all rings iff the following ideal membership holds for integer polynomials:

$$a \in Id \langle e_1, \ldots, e_m, p_1, \ldots, p_n \rangle$$

Proof. Just a special case of the previous theorem.   □

The conclusion of Theorem 4 for general k is not just a conjunction of independent ideal membership assertions, because we need to constrain the cofactors $q_i(\overline{x})$ to be the same for each one. However, by introducing auxiliary variables $u_1, \ldots, u_k$ we will show:

Theorem 6. *The following formula:*

$$\forall \overline{x}. \bigwedge_{i=1}^{m} e_i(\overline{x}) = 0 \Rightarrow \exists y_1 \cdots y_n. \begin{array}{l} p_{11}(\overline{x})y_1 + \cdots + p_{1n}(\overline{x})y_n = a_1(\overline{x}) \wedge \\ \cdots \wedge \\ p_{k1}(\overline{x})y_1 + \cdots + p_{kn}(\overline{x})y_n = a_k(\overline{x}) \end{array}$$

holds in all rings iff the following ideal membership assertion, where the u_i are fresh variables not occurring in the original problem, holds in $\mathbb{Z}[x_1, \ldots, x_l, u_1, \ldots, u_k]$:

$$(a_1 u_1 + \cdots + a_k u_k)$$
$$\in Id\langle e_1, \ldots, e_m, (p_{11}u_1 + \cdots + p_{k1}u_k), (p_{1n}u_1 + \cdots + p_{kn}u_k) \rangle$$

Proof. The bottom-to-top direction was dealt with above under 'soundness'. For the other direction, note that by Theorem 4, the initial assertion is equivalent to the existence of $q_1(\overline{x}), \ldots, q_n(\overline{x})$ and $r_{1j}(\overline{x}), \ldots, r_{mj}(\overline{x})$ such that for all $1 \leq j \leq k$:

$$e_1(\overline{x})r_{1j}(\overline{x}) + \cdots + e_m(\overline{x})r_{mj}(\overline{x}) + p_{j1}(\overline{x})q_1(\overline{x}) + \cdots + p_{jn}(\overline{x})q_n(\overline{x}) = a_j(\overline{x})$$

Multiplying this identity by u_j and summing over $1 \leq j \leq k$ we obtain

$$\begin{array}{l} a_1 u_1 + \cdots + a_k u_k = \\ e_1(\overline{x})(u_1 r_{11}(\overline{x}) + \cdots + u_k r_{1k}(\overline{x})) + \cdots + \\ e_m(\overline{x})(u_1 r_{m1}(\overline{x}) + \cdots + u_k r_{mk}(\overline{x})) + \\ (p_{11}u_1 + \cdots + p_{k1}u_k)q_1(\overline{x}) + \cdots + (p_{1n}u_1 + \cdots + p_{kn}u_k)q_n(\overline{x}) \end{array}$$

which verifies the claimed ideal membership. □

4 Reduction to Standard Form

In reducing the initial problem to standard form, we expand the number-theoretic predicates into existentially quantified equations. Note that the equivalence assumed between $\exists x\, y.\, sx + ty = 1$ and coprime(s, t), in the usual sense of having no non-unit common factors, does not hold over an arbitrary ring (though it does in all principal ideal domains). For example, $x + 1$ and 2 are coprime over the polynomial ring $\mathbb{Z}[x]$, but there are no integer polynomials p and q such that $(x + 1)p(x) + 2q(x) = 1$. This means that even though the core reduction is complete w.r.t. the class of all rings, the initial processing into standard form relies on additional axioms. Moreover, we will sometimes want to exploit the integral domain property $st = 0 \Leftrightarrow s = 0 \vee t = 0$ (see below), which also fails in an arbitrary ring (e.g. $2 \cdot 3 = 0$ in $\mathbb{Z}/6$ but $2 \neq 0$ and $3 \neq 0$). This mismatch between a preprocessing step valid only in certain rings and a core procedure sound and complete with respect to *all* rings gives our overall procedure a somewhat heuristic flavour.

But once we accept the mappings of the basic concepts down to algebraic statements, then we can translate a wide variety of assertions into the standard form. In particular, any Horn clause built up from the basic number-theoretic concepts works, e.g. our first example:

$$ax \equiv ay \pmod{n} \wedge \text{coprime}(a, n) \Rightarrow x \equiv y \pmod{n}$$

as well as numerous others such as

$d|a \wedge d|b \Rightarrow d|(a - b)$
$a|b \Rightarrow (ca)|(cb)$
$x|y \wedge y|z \Rightarrow x|z$
$(xd)|a \Rightarrow d|a$
$a|b \wedge c|d \Rightarrow (ac)|(bd)$
$\text{coprime}(d, a) \wedge \text{coprime}(d, b) \Rightarrow \text{coprime}(d, ab)$
$\text{coprime}(d, ab) \Rightarrow \text{coprime}(d, a)$
$m|r \wedge n|r \wedge \text{coprime}(m, n) \Rightarrow (mn)|r$
$x \equiv x' \pmod{n} \wedge y \equiv y' \pmod{n} \Rightarrow xy \equiv x'y' \pmod{n}$
$x \equiv y \pmod{m} \wedge n|m \Rightarrow x \equiv y \pmod{n}$
$\text{coprime}(a, b) \wedge x \equiv y \pmod{a} \wedge x \equiv y \pmod{b} \Rightarrow x \equiv y \pmod{(ab)}$
$x^2 \equiv y^2 \pmod{(x + y)}$
$x^2 \equiv a \pmod{n} \wedge y^2 \equiv a \pmod{n} \Rightarrow n|((x + y)(x - y))$

It is also clear we can solve problems of the form $P \Leftrightarrow Q$ by separating them into $P \Rightarrow Q$ and $Q \Rightarrow P$; more generally we can place a problem in conjunctive normal form and split up the conjuncts. For example, this deals with:

$$x \equiv y \pmod{n} \Rightarrow (\text{coprime}(n, x) \Leftrightarrow \text{coprime}(n, y))$$
$$x \equiv 0 \pmod{n} \Leftrightarrow n|x$$
$$x + a \equiv y + a \pmod{n} \Leftrightarrow x \equiv y \pmod{n}$$
$$\text{coprime}(xy, x^2 + y^2) \Leftrightarrow \text{coprime}(x, y)$$

Additional negated equations can easily be absorbed into the conclusion using the integral domain property, passing from $\neg(t = 0) \wedge P \Rightarrow \exists \overline{y}.\ s(\overline{y}) = 0$ to $P \Rightarrow \exists \overline{y}.\ s(\overline{y})t = 0$, which allows us to handle things like:

$$\neg(c = 0) \Rightarrow ((ca)|(cb) \Leftrightarrow a|b)$$

Perhaps more interesting is that we can even handle existential quantifiers present in the original problem before the algebraic reduction, e.g.

$$\text{coprime}(a, n) \Rightarrow \exists x.\ ax \equiv b \pmod{n}$$

We will treat a somewhat more general version of that problem in detail below ('extension with GCDs'). Here we will run through the basic binary Chinese Remainder Theorem, which also has an existential quantifier in the conclusion:

$$\forall a\ b\ u\ v.\ \text{coprime}(a, b) \Rightarrow \exists x.\ x \equiv u \pmod{a} \wedge x \equiv v \pmod{b}$$

If we proceed as usual we obtain the goal:

$$\forall a\ b\ u\ v\ w\ z.\ aw + bz = 1 \Rightarrow \exists x\ d\ e.\ u - x = da \wedge v - x = eb$$

Since we have multiple equations under the existential quantifier, the reduction to ideal membership introduces two new variables r and s:

$$(ur + vs) \in \mathrm{Id}\ \langle aw + bz - 1, r + s, ar, bs \rangle$$

and this is true since we have

$$ur + vs = (aw + bz - 1)(rv - ru) + (r + s)(v + buz - bvz) + (ar)(uw - vw) + (bs)(vz - uz)$$

5   Extensions

Although the basic procedure above is already quite powerful, we can extend its scope by a number of perhaps ad hoc but quite natural refinements.

5.1   Introduction of GCDs

It is often convenient to express properties using greatest common divisors (GCDs). One simple approach for handling $\gcd(a, b)$ is to replace it with a variable g while adding as an additional hypothesis a characterizing theorem:

$$g \mid a \wedge g \mid b \wedge (\exists u\ v.\ au + bv = g)$$

This does not characterize g uniquely because of the ambiguity over sign (or multiplication by a unit in a general ring), but any divisibility relationships are also invariant under such a change, so this is not a severe obstacle. For example, consider proving a basic condition for the solvability of a congruence:

$$\gcd(a, n) \mid b \Rightarrow \exists x.\ ax \equiv b\ (\mathrm{mod}\ n)$$

After the initial augmentation we get:

$$g \mid a \wedge g \mid n \wedge (\exists u\ v.\ au + nv = g) \wedge g \mid b \Rightarrow \exists x.\ ax \equiv b\ (\mathrm{mod}\ n)$$

and the usual expansion, normalization and prenexing yields:

$$gq = a \wedge gr = n \wedge au + nv = g \wedge gs = b \Rightarrow \exists x\ y.\ ax + yn = b$$

giving the ideal membership question

$$b \in \mathrm{Id}\ \langle gq - a, gr - n, au + nv - g, gs - b, a, n \rangle$$

which is true since

$$b = (gq - a)0 + (gr - n)0 + (au + nv - g)(-s) + (gs - b)(-1) + a(su) + n(sv)$$

The converse implication $\exists x.\ ax \equiv b\ (\mathrm{mod}\ n) \Rightarrow \gcd(a, n) \mid b$ can be proved in a similar way.

5.2 Elimination Using Linear Equations

For a motivating example here, consider again the binary Chinese Remainder Theorem:

$$\forall a\ b\ u\ v.\ \mathrm{coprime}(a, b) \Rightarrow \exists x.\ x \equiv u\ (\mathrm{mod}\ a) \wedge x \equiv v\ (\mathrm{mod}\ b)$$

If we proceed as before we obtain the goal:

$$\forall a\ b\ u\ v\ w\ z.\ aw + bz = 1 \Rightarrow \exists x\ d\ e.\ u - x = da \wedge v - x = eb$$

Earlier, we introduced auxiliary variables to handle the double equation. However, in this case it is fairly obvious that we can get an equivalent that just eliminates x between the two equations:

$$\forall a\ b\ u\ v\ w\ z.\ aw + bz = 1 \Rightarrow \exists d\ e.\ v - u = eb - da$$

This gives a reduction to the ideal membership goal:

$$(v - u) \in \mathrm{Id}\ \langle aw + bz - 1, b, -a \rangle$$

which is true since

$$v - u = (aw + bz - 1)(u - v) + b(zv - zu) + -a(wu - wv)$$

This elimination does not help with the ternary Chinese Remainder Theorem, whereas the method using auxiliary variables still works perfectly. However, on a heuristic level it seems prudent always to eliminate existentially quantified variables when there is a simple linear equation that allows us to do so.

5.3 Sequential Treatment of Equations

Our standard form requires each equation to be linear in the existentially quantified variables. However, note that linearity is irrelevant to Theorem 2, and only appears as a restriction in order to reduce witness-finding to ideal membership. So we can consider more general means of finding witnesses by building in techniques for nonlinearity. Elimination using linear equations, as in the previous example, may enable us to get round this restriction in some cases. Otherwise, we can at least find witnesses for those equations we can, and hope that they will then in turn allow us to solve the overall problem. For example, consider:

$$\gcd(a, b) \neq 0 \Rightarrow \exists a'\ b'.\ a = a' \gcd(a, b) \wedge b = b' \gcd(a, b) \wedge \mathrm{coprime}(a', b')$$

Proceeding in the usual way, eliminating number-theoretic concepts, we obtain:

$$a = gx \wedge b = gy \wedge g = ua + vb \wedge \neg(g = 0) \Rightarrow \exists a'\ b'\ w\ z.\ a = a'g \wedge b = b'g \wedge a'w + b'z = 1$$

and as usual we eliminate the negated equational hypothesis using the integral domain property:

$$a = gx \wedge b = gy \wedge g = ua + vb \Rightarrow \exists a' \ b' \ w \ z. ag = a'g^2 \wedge bg = b'g^2 \wedge a'wg + b'zg = g$$

This does not fall into our subset because of the nonlinearity: in $a'wg$ we have two existentially quantified variables a' and w multiplied together. On the other hand, we might heuristically try to find witnesses by considering the equations one at a time. First

$$a = gx \wedge b = gy \wedge g = ua + vb \Rightarrow \exists a'. ag = a'g^2$$

gives the ideal membership assertion

$$(ag) \in \mathrm{Id}\, \langle gx - a, gy - b, ua + vb - g, g^2 \rangle$$

from whose solution

$$ag = (gx - a)(-g) + g^2 x$$

we extract the witness $a' = x$. Similarly solving the next equation gives us $b' = y$. After inserting those, two equations in the problem are trivial and everything reduces to:

$$a = gx \wedge b = gy \wedge g = ua + vb \Rightarrow \exists w \ z. xwg + yzg = g$$

giving the ideal membership

$$g \in \mathrm{Id}\, \langle gx - a, gy - b, ua + vb - g, xg, yg \rangle$$

which is true since

$$g = (gx - a)(-u) + (gy - b)(-v) + (ua + vb - g)(-1) + (xg)u + (yg)v$$

and in particular we obtain the witnesses $w = u$, $z = v$.

6   Implementation

We have implementéd a simple prototype of the routine, containing fewer than 100 lines of code, in the HOL Light theorem prover [9]; in version 2.20, it is included in the standard release. The implemented version does not yet use the extension to multiple equations using auxiliary variables, and some of the initial normalization is a little ad hoc. But it does include all the extensions in the previous section, and all the examples we have mentioned in this paper can be proved automatically by it. Here is a typical interaction, proving a slight generalization of the binary Chinese remainder theorem, not assuming that the moduli are coprime: if $a_1 \equiv a_2 \pmod{\gcd(n_1, n_2)}$ then there is an x such that $x \equiv a_1 \pmod{n_1}$ and $x \equiv a_2 \pmod{n_2}$. The user passes the desired result as a parameter to `INTEGER_RULE` on the first line, and after some informative messages, the required theorem is proved automatically:

```
# INTEGER_RULE
  '!a1 a2 n1 n2:int.
        (a1 == a2) (mod (gcd(n1,n2)))
        ==> ?x. (x == a1) (mod n1) /\ (x == a2) (mod n2)';;
4 basis elements and 1 critical pairs
5 basis elements and 0 critical pairs
1 basis elements and 0 critical pairs
Translating certificate to HOL inferences
val it : thm =
  |- !a1 a2 n1 n2.
        (a1 == a2) (mod gcd (n1,n2))
        ==> (?x. (x == a1) (mod n1) /\ (x == a2) (mod n2))
```

We just use the normal Buchberger algorithm for polynomial ideals over $\mathbb{Q}$, implemented in HOL via `int_ideal_cofactors`. Properly speaking, we should use a version of Buchberger's algorithm tailored to the ring $\mathbb{Z}$ [11]. For example, consider proving just $x+y = 0 \land x-y = 0 \Rightarrow x = 0$. This does not hold in all rings (e.g. set $x = y = 1$ in the integers modulo 2). The Gröbner basis algorithm over the rationals, however, would appear to prove it giving coefficients of $1/2$ in the cofactors. However, testing ideal membership over $\mathbb{Z}$ is in general somewhat more difficult [1], and we have found almost no cases where the distinction mattered (most problems involve no explicit constants $|c| > 1$, which helps). Because the actual HOL Light proof proceeds rigorously by logical inference, no false result could be generated, but the proof construction step will fail if the ideal cofactors contain rationals.

7   Conclusions and Related Work

We are not aware of any related work on automating problems involving both multiplication and 'divisibility' concepts. Indeed, as we have noted, the problem is in general unsolvable and our procedure, though remarkably effective, is a combination of a preprocessing step tailored to the integers followed by a decision procedure complete only over the class of rings in general.

There are established results for decidability of universal linear formulas in the language of Presburger arithmetic including divisibility by non-constants [3,15], though we are not aware of any actual implementation. Allowing a richer quantifier structure soon leads to undecidability, even in the linear case; for example multiplication can be defined in terms of divisibility, successor and 1 only [18], so even that theory is undecidable. In contrast, we allow more or less unrestricted use of multiplication, which in principle leads to undecidability. But the approach of seeking properties true in all rings seems to work very well.

We have found the procedure very useful in practice. Just as it is convenient to have automated provers for routine facts of linear arithmetic and propositional tautologies, being able to generate routine lemmas about divisibility with so little effort is a considerable help in proofs. In fact, we were inspired to create this procedure during the formal verification of an arithmetic algorithm, when we found ourselves repeatedly proving trivialities about divisibility by hand. The procedure has also been useful in some HOL proofs in pure mathematics, e.g. quadratic reciprocity.

In all the examples we have tried, the ideal membership goals are easy: our straightforward Gröbner basis algorithm works in a fraction of a second. It might be interesting to try some large (even if artificial) problems, such as n-ary Chinese remainder theorems for large n. Perhaps in such cases more care would be needed, e.g. over the monomial order in the Gröbner basis algorithm. At present we order the monomials by total degree then reverse lexicographic order of variables [21], ordering the variables themselves alphabetically. Other optimizations might be worthwhile, e.g. using reduced Gröbner bases or constructing the basis more incrementally when dealing with equations sequentially.

Also, it would be more satisfactory to use a Gröbner basis algorithm tailored to the integers. This would open up the possibility of dealing with a wider range of problems involving specific numbers. It is even conceivable that the approach could then be used to reason about machine arithmetic modulo 2^n in a useful way. Perhaps the results here could also be used in other situations where restricted quantifier instantiation is needed, e.g. checking that universally quantified polynomial equations are invariant over a program block.

Acknowledgements

I am grateful to the anonymous referees for their valuable work; they offered everything from thought-provoking general observations to lists of subtle typos in doubly indexed variables.

References

1. Aschenbrenner, M.: Ideal membership in polynomial rings over the integers. Journal of the American Mathematical Society 17, 407–441 (2004)
2. Baker, A.: A Concise Introduction to the Theory of Numbers. Cambridge University Press, Cambridge (1985)
3. Beltyokov, A.P.: Decidability of the universal theory of natural numbers with addition and divisibility (Russian). Sem. Leningrad Otd. Mat. Inst. Akad. Nauk SSSR 40, 127–130 (1974) English translation in Journal Of Mathematical Sciences 14, 1436–1444 (1980)
4. Boyer, R.S., Moore, J.S.: A Computational Logic. In: ACM Monograph Series, Academic Press, San Diego (1979)
5. Buchberger, B.: Ein Algorithmus zum Auffinden der Basiselemente des Restklassenringes nach einem nulldimensionalen Polynomideal. PhD thesis, Mathematisches Institut der Universität Innsbruck (1965) English translation to appear in Journal of Symbolic Computation (2006)
6. Bundy, A.: A science of reasoning. In: Lassez, J.-L., Plotkin, G. (eds.) Computational Logic: Essays in Honor of Alan Robinson, pp. 178–198. MIT Press, Cambridge (1991)
7. Cooper, D.C.: Theorem proving in arithmetic without multiplication. In: Melzer, B., Michie, D. (eds.) Machine Intelligence 7, pp. 91–99. Elsevier, Amsterdam (1972)
8. Hardy, G.H., Wright, E.M.: An Introduction to the Theory of Numbers, 5th edn. Clarendon Press, Oxford (1979)

9. Harrison, J.: HOL Light: A tutorial introduction. In: Srivas, M., Camilleri, A. (eds.) FMCAD 1996. LNCS, vol. 1166, pp. 265–269. Springer, Heidelberg (1996)
10. Hodges, W.: Logical features of Horn clauses. In: Gabbay, D.M., Hogger, C.J., Robinson, J.A. (eds.) Handbook of Logic in Artificial Intelligence and Logic Programming (logical foundations), vol. 1, pp. 449–503. Oxford University Press, Oxford (1993)
11. Kandri-Rody, A., Kapur, D.: Algorithms for computing Gröbner bases of polynomial ideals over various Euclidean rings. In: Fitch, J. (ed.) EUROSAM 84. LNCS, vol. 174, pp. 195–206. Springer, Heidelberg (1984)
12. Kandri-Rody, A., Kapur, D., Narendran, P.: An ideal-theoretic approach to word problems and unification problems over finitely presented commutative algebras. In: Jouannaud, J.-P. (ed.) Rewriting Techniques and Applications. LNCS, vol. 202, pp. 345–364. Springer, Heidelberg (1985)
13. Kreisel, G., Krivine, J.-L.: Elements of mathematical logic: model theory. Studies in Logic and the Foundations of Mathematics. North-Holland, revised second edition, 1971. First edition 1967. Translation of the French 'Eléments de logique mathématique, théorie des modeles' published by Dunod, Paris (1964)
14. Lifschitz, V.: Semantical completeness theorems in logic and algebra. Proceedings of the American Mathematical Society 79, 89–96 (1980)
15. Lipshitz, L.: The Diophantine problem for addition and divisibility. Transactions of the American Mathematical Society 235, 271–283 (1978)
16. Matiyasevich, Y.V.: Enumerable sets are Diophantine. Soviet Mathematics Doklady 11, 354–358 (1970)
17. Presburger, M.: Über die Vollständigkeit eines gewissen Systems der Arithmetik ganzer Zahlen, in welchem die Addition als einzige Operation hervortritt. In: Sprawozdanie z I Kongresu metematyków slowiańskich, Warszawa 1929, pp. 92–101, 395. Warsaw, 1930. Annotated English version by [20]
18. Robinson, J.: Definability and decision problems in arithmetic. Journal of Symbolic Logic. Author's PhD thesis 14, 98–114 (1949)
19. Simmons, H.: The solution of a decision problem for several classes of rings. Pacific Journal of Mathematics 34, 547–557 (1970)
20. Stansifer, R.: Presburger's article on integer arithmetic: Remarks and translation. Technical Report CORNELLCS:TR84-639, Cornell University Computer Science Department (1984)
21. Weispfenning, V., Becker, T.: Groebner bases: a computational approach to commutative algebra. In: Graduate Texts in Mathematics, Springer, Heidelberg (1993)

Optimized Reasoning in Description Logics Using Hypertableaux

Boris Motik, Rob Shearer, and Ian Horrocks

University of Manchester, UK

Abstract. We present a novel reasoning calculus for Description Logics (DLs)—knowledge representation formalisms with applications in areas such as the Semantic Web. In order to reduce the nondeterminism due to general inclusion axioms, we base our calculus on hypertableau and hyperresolution calculi, which we extend with a blocking condition to ensure termination. To prevent the calculus from generating large models, we introduce *"anywhere" pairwise blocking*. Our preliminary implementation shows significant performance improvements on several well-known ontologies. To the best of our knowledge, our reasoner is currently the only one that can classify the original version of the GALEN terminology.

1 Introduction

Description Logics (DLs) [2]—knowledge representation formalisms with well-understood formal properties—have been applied to numerous problems in computer science. A central component of most DL applications is an efficient and scalable reasoner. Modern reasoners, such as Pellet [15], FaCT++ [21], and RACER [8], are typically based on tableau calculi [2, Chapter 2]. These calculi demonstrate (un)satisfiability of a knowledge base $\mathcal{K}$ via a constructive search for an abstraction of a model of $\mathcal{K}$. Numerous optimizations have been developed in an effort to reduce the size of the search space [2, Chapter 9].

Despite major advances in recent years, ontologies are still encountered in practice that cannot be handled by existing reasoners. This is mainly because many different models might need to be examined, and each model might be very large [2, Chapter 3]. The former problem is due to *or-branching*: given a disjunctive assertion $C \sqcup D(s)$, a tableau algorithm nondeterministically guesses that either $C(s)$ or $D(s)$ holds. To show unsatisfiability of $\mathcal{K}$, *every* possible guess must lead to a contradiction: if assuming $C(s)$ leads to a contradiction, the algorithm must backtrack and assume $D(s)$. This can clearly result in exponential behavior. General concept inclusions (GCIs)—axioms of the form $C \sqsubseteq D$—are the main source of disjunctions: to ensure that $C \sqsubseteq D$ holds, a tableau algorithm adds a disjunction $\neg C \sqcup D(s)$ to each individual s in the model. Various *absorption* optimizations [2, Chapter 9][11,20] reduce the high degree of nondeterminism in such a procedure; however, they often fail to eliminate all sources of nondeterminism. This may be the case even for ontologies that can be translated into Horn clauses (such as GALEN, NCI, and SNOMED), for which reasoning without any nondeterminism should be possible in principle.

F. Pfenning (Ed.): CADE 2007, LNAI 4603, pp. 67–83, 2007.
© Springer-Verlag Berlin Heidelberg 2007

The size of the model being constructed is determined by *and-branching*—the expansion of a model due to existential quantifiers. Apart from memory consumption problems, and-branching can increase or-branching by increasing the number of individuals to which GCIs are applied.

In this paper, we present a reasoning calculus that addresses both sources of complexity. We focus on the DL $\mathcal{SHIQ}$; however, our calculus should be applicable to most DLs with known tableau algorithms. A $\mathcal{SHIQ}$ knowledge base is first preprocessed into *DL-clauses*—universally quantified implications containing DL concepts and roles as predicates. The main inference rule for DL-clauses is hyperresolution: an atom from the head of a DL clause is derived *only if* all atoms from the clause body have been derived. On Horn clauses, this calculus is deterministic, which eliminates all or-branching. This is in contrast with existing DL tableau calculi, which often behave nondeterministically on Horn problems. Our algorithm can thus be viewed as a hybrid of resolution and tableau, and is related to the hypertableau [3] and hyperresolution [17] calculi.

Hyperresolution decides many first-order fragments (see, e.g., [6,5] for an overview). Unlike most of these fragments, $\mathcal{SHIQ}$ allows for cyclic GCIs of the form $C \sqsubseteq \exists R.C$, on which hyperresolution can generate infinite paths of successors. Therefore, to ensure termination, we use the pairwise blocking technique from [10] to detect cyclic computations. Due to hyper-inferences, the soundness and correctness proofs from [10] do not carry over to our calculus. In fact, certain simpler blocking conditions for weaker DLs cannot be applied in a straightforward manner in our setting. To limit and-branching, we extend the blocking condition from [10] to *anywhere pairwise blocking*: an individual can be blocked by an individual that is not necessarily an ancestor. This significantly reduces the sizes of the constructed models. Anywhere blocking has already been used with *subset* blocking [1]; however, to the best of our knowledge, it has neither been used with the more sophisticated pairwise blocking nor tested in practice.

We have implemented our calculus in a new reasoner. Even with a relatively naïve implementation, our reasoner outperforms existing reasoners on several real-world ontologies. For example, the deterministic treatment of GCIs significantly reduces the classification time for the NCI ontology. Furthermore, the pairwise anywhere blocking strategy seems to be very effective in limiting model sizes. To the best of our knowledge, our reasoner is currently the only one that can classify the original version of the GALEN terminology.

2 Preliminaries

The DL $\mathcal{SHIQ}$ is defined as follows. For N_R a set of *atomic roles*, the set of *roles* is $N_R \cup \{R^- \mid R \in N_R\}$. For $R \in N_R$, let $\mathsf{Inv}(R) = R^-$ and $\mathsf{Inv}(R^-) = R$. An *RBox* $\mathcal{R}$ is a finite set of role inclusion axioms $R \sqsubseteq S$ and transitivity axioms $\mathsf{Trans}(R)$, where R and S are roles. Let $\sqsubseteq^*$ be the reflexive transitive closure of $\{R \sqsubseteq S, \mathsf{Inv}(R) \sqsubseteq \mathsf{Inv}(S) \mid R \sqsubseteq S \in \mathcal{R}\}$. A role R is *transitive* in $\mathcal{R}$ if a role S exists such that $S \sqsubseteq^* R$, $R \sqsubseteq^* S$, and either $\mathsf{Trans}(S) \in \mathcal{R}$ or $\mathsf{Trans}(\mathsf{Inv}(S)) \in \mathcal{R}$; R is *simple* if no transitive role S exists with $S \sqsubseteq^* R$.

Table 1. Model-Theoretic Semantics of $\mathcal{SHIQ}$

Semantics of Roles and Concepts		Semantics of Axioms
$\top^I = \triangle^I$	$\bot^I = \emptyset$	$C \sqsubseteq D \;\; \Rightarrow C^I \subseteq D^I$
$(\neg C)^I = \triangle^I \setminus C^I$	$(R^-)^I = \{\langle y, x\rangle \mid \langle x, y\rangle \in R^I\}$	$R \sqsubseteq S \;\; \Rightarrow R^I \subseteq S^I$
$(C \sqcap D)^I = C^I \cap D^I$	$(C \sqcup D)^I = C^I \cup D^I$	$\mathsf{Trans}(R) \Rightarrow (R^I)^+ \subseteq R^I$
$(\forall R.C)^I = \{x \mid \forall y : \langle x, y\rangle \in R^I \to y \in C^I\}$		$C(a) \qquad \Rightarrow a^I \in C^I$
$(\exists R.C)^I = \{x \mid \exists y : \langle x, y\rangle \in R^I \land y \in C^I\}$		$R(a, b) \;\; \Rightarrow \langle a^I, b^I\rangle \in R^I$
$(\leq n\, S.C)^I = \{x \mid \sharp\{y \mid \langle x, y\rangle \in S^I \land y \in C^I\} \leq n\}$		$a \approx b \;\; \Rightarrow a^I = b^I$
$(\geq n\, S.C)^I = \{x \mid \sharp\{y \mid \langle x, y\rangle \in S^I \land y \in C^I\} \geq n\}$		$a \not\approx b \;\; \Rightarrow a^I \neq b^I$

Note: $\sharp N$ is the number of elements in N, and R^+ is the transitive closure of R.

For a set of *atomic concepts* N_C, the set of *concepts* is the smallest set containing $\top$, $\bot$, A, $\neg C$, $C \sqcap D$, $C \sqcup D$, $\exists R.C$, $\forall R.C$, $\geq n\, S.C$, and $\leq n\, S.C$, for $A \in N_C$, C and D concepts, R a role, S a simple role, and n a nonnegative integer. A TBox $\mathcal{T}$ is a finite set of *general concept inclusions* (GCIs) $C \sqsubseteq D$.

For a set of *individuals* N_I, an ABox $\mathcal{A}$ is a finite set of assertions $C(a)$, $R(a, b)$, and (in)equalities $a \approx b$ and $a \not\approx b$, where C is a concept, R is a role, and a and b are individuals. A $\mathcal{SHIQ}$ knowledge base $\mathcal{K}$ is a triple $(\mathcal{R}, \mathcal{T}, \mathcal{A})$.

An *interpretation* for $\mathcal{K}$ is a tuple $I = (\triangle^I, \cdot^I)$, where $\triangle^I$ is a nonempty set, and $\cdot^I$ assigns an element $a^I \in \triangle^I$ to each individual a, a set $A^I \subseteq \triangle^I$ to each atomic concept A, and a relation $R^I \subseteq \triangle^I \times \triangle^I$ to each atomic role R. The function $\cdot^I$ is extended to concepts and roles as shown in the left-hand side of Table 1. I is a *model* of $\mathcal{K}$, written $I \models \mathcal{K}$, if it satisfies all axioms of $\mathcal{K}$ as shown in the right-hand side of Table 1. The basic inference problem for $\mathcal{SHIQ}$ is checking satisfiability of $\mathcal{K}$—that is, checking whether a model of $\mathcal{K}$ exists.

The *negation-normal form* of a concept C, written $\mathsf{nnf}(C)$, is the concept equivalent to C containing negations only in front of atomic concepts; $\dot{\neg} C$ is an abbreviation for $\mathsf{nnf}(\neg C)$. $|\mathcal{K}|$ is the size of $\mathcal{K}$ with numbers coded in unary. The DL $\mathcal{ALCHIQ}$ is obtained from $\mathcal{SHIQ}$ by disallowing transitive roles.

3 Algorithm Overview

To see how GCIs can increase or-branching and thus cause performance problems, consider the following knowledge base $\mathcal{K}_1$:

$$\mathcal{T}_1 = \{\exists R.A \sqsubseteq A\}$$
$$\mathcal{A}_1 = \{\neg A(a_0),\ R(a_0, b_1),\ R(b_1, a_1), \ldots, R(a_{n-1}, b_n),\ R(b_n, a_n),\ A(a_n)\} \tag{1}$$

To satisfy the GCI, a tableau algorithm derives $(\forall R.\neg A \sqcup A)(a_i)$, $0 \leq i \leq n$ and $(\forall R.\neg A \sqcup A)(b_j)$, $1 \leq j \leq n$. Assuming that a_i are processed before b_j, the algorithm derives $\forall R.\neg A(a_i)$, $0 \leq i \leq n$ and $\neg A(b_i)$, $1 \leq i \leq n$, after which it derives $\forall R.\neg A(b_i)$, $1 \leq i \leq n-1$ and $\neg A(a_i)$, $1 \leq i \leq n$. The ABox now contains a contradiction on a_n, so the algorithm flips its guess on b_{n-1} to $A(b_{n-1})$. This generates a contradiction on b_{n-1}, so the algorithm backtracks from all guesses for b_i. Next, the guess on a_n is changed to $A(a_n)$ and the work for all b_i is repeated. This also leads to a contradiction, so the algorithm must revise its guess for a_{n-1}; but then, two guesses are again possible for a_n. In general, after revising a guess for a_i, all possibilities for a_j, $i < j \leq n$, must be reexamined, which results in exponential behavior. Note that none of the standard backtracking optimizations [2, Chapter 9] help us avoid this problem. Namely, the problem arises because the order in which the individuals are processed makes the guesses on a_i independent from the guesses on a_j, $i \neq j$. It is difficult to estimate in advance which order is optimal; in fact, the processing order is typically determined by implementation side-effects (such as the data structures used to store $\mathcal{K}$).

The GCI $\exists R.A \sqsubseteq A$ is not inherently nondeterministic: it is equivalent to the Horn clause $\forall x, y : [R(x,y) \wedge A(y) \rightarrow A(x)]$. By hyperresolution, we derive the facts $A(b_n), A(a_{n-1}), \ldots, A(a_0)$, and eventually we derive a contradiction on a_0. These inferences are deterministic, so we can conclude that $\mathcal{K}_1$ is unsatisfiable without any backtracking. This example suggests that the way tableau algorithms handle GCIs can be "unnecessarily" nondeterministic.

Absorption [2, Chapter 9] reduces the nondeterminism introduced by GCIs. If possible, it rewrites GCIs as $B \sqsubseteq C$ with B an atomic concept; then, during reasoning, it derives $C(s)$ only if the ABox contains $B(s)$. This localizes the applicability of the rewritten GCIs. Absorption has been extended to *binary absorption* [11], which rewrites a GCI to $B_1 \sqcap B_2 \sqsubseteq C$, and to *role absorption* [20], which rewrites a GCI to $\exists R.\top \sqsubseteq C$. Note, however, that the axiom $\exists R.A \sqsubseteq A$ cannot be absorbed directly. It can be absorbed if it is rewritten as $A \sqsubseteq \forall R^-.A$. In practice, it is often unclear in advance which combination of transformation and absorption techniques will yield the best results. Therefore, implemented absorption algorithms are guided primarily by heuristics.

Our algorithm can be seen as a generalization of absorption. It first translates GCIs into *DL-clauses*—universally quantified implications of the form $\bigwedge U_i \rightarrow \bigvee V_j$, where U_i are of the form $R(x,y)$ or $A(x)$, and V_j are of the form $R(x,y)$, $A(x)$, $\exists R.C(x)$, $\geq n R.C(x)$, or $x \approx y$. DL-clauses are used in *hyperresolution* inferences, which derive some V_j, but only if all U_i are matched to assertions in the ABox. This calculus is quite different from the standard DL tableau calculi. For example, it has no *choose*-rule for qualified number restrictions [19], and it can handle implications such as $R(x,y) \rightarrow B(x) \vee A(y)$ (obtained from $\exists R.\neg A \sqsubseteq B$) that contain several universally quantified variables.

It is easy to see that and-branching can cause the introduction of infinitely many new individuals. Consider the following (satisfiable) knowledge base:

$$\mathcal{T}_2 = \left\{ \begin{array}{l} A_1 \sqsubseteq \; \geq 2\,S.A_2, \; \ldots, \; A_{n-1} \sqsubseteq \; \geq 2\,S.A_n, \; A_n \sqsubseteq A_1, \\ A_i \sqsubseteq (B_1 \sqcup C_1) \sqcap \ldots \sqcap (B_m \sqcup C_m) \text{ for } 1 \leq i \leq n \end{array} \right\} \quad \mathcal{A}_2 = \{A_1(a)\} \quad (2)$$

To check satisfiability of $\mathcal{K}_2$, a tableau algorithm builds a binary tree with each node labeled with some A_i and an element of $\Pi = \{B_1, C_1\} \times \ldots \times \{B_m, C_m\}$. A naïve algorithm would try to construct an infinite tree, so tableau algorithms employ *blocking* [10]: if a node a is labeled with the same concepts as some ancestor a' of a, then the existential quantifiers for a are not expanded. This ensures termination; however, the number of elements in Π is exponential, so, with "unlucky" guesses, the tree can be exponential in depth and doubly exponential in total. In the best case, the algorithm can, for example, choose B_j rather than

C_j for each $1 \leq j \leq m$. It then constructs a polynomially deep binary tree and thus runs in exponential time.

To curb and-branching, we extend pairwise blocking [10] to *anywhere pairwise blocking*, in which an individual can be blocked not only by an ancestor, but by any individual satisfying certain ordering requirements. This reduces the worst-case complexity of the tableau algorithm by an exponential factor; for example, on $\mathcal{K}_2$, after we exhaust all members of Π, all subsequently created individuals will be blocked. Such blocking can sometimes also improve the best-case complexity; for example, on $\mathcal{K}_2$, our algorithm can create a polynomial path and then use the individuals from that path to block their siblings.

We explain the remaining two aspects of our algorithm. First, the $\forall_+$-rule traditionally used to deal with transitive roles does not work in our setting, since we represent concepts of the form $\forall R.C$ as DL-clauses. Therefore, we encode transitivity axioms using GCIs in a preprocessing step. Second, to avoid an exponential blowup in the transformation of GCIs to DL-clauses, we apply the well-known *structural transformation* [16]. We take special care, however, to maximize the likelihood that the result can be translated into Horn DL-clauses. For example, given $\top \sqsubseteq \forall R.(C \sqcup \forall S.\neg D)$, if we replace $\forall S.\neg D$ with an atomic concept Q, we obtain the axioms (3), of which the first one does not give us a Horn DL-clause. If, however, we replace $\forall S.\neg D$ with $\neg Q'$, we obtain the axioms (4), which can both be translated into Horn DL-clauses.

$$
\begin{aligned}
\top \sqsubseteq \forall R.(C \sqcup Q) &\quad \rightsquigarrow \quad R(x,y) \rightarrow C(y) \lor Q(y) \\
Q \sqsubseteq \forall S.\neg D &\quad \rightsquigarrow \quad Q(x) \land S(x,y) \land D(y) \rightarrow \bot
\end{aligned}
\tag{3}
$$

$$
\begin{aligned}
\top \sqsubseteq \forall R.(C \sqcup \neg Q') &\quad \rightsquigarrow \quad R(x,y) \land Q'(y) \rightarrow C(y) \\
\neg Q' \sqsubseteq \forall S.\neg D &\quad \rightsquigarrow \quad S(x,y) \land D(y) \rightarrow Q'(x)
\end{aligned}
\tag{4}
$$

In Section 4.1, we present a version of the structural transformation that replaces a complex concept with either a positive or negative atomic concept, depending on the polarity of the concept being replaced. We thus bring GCIs into a *normalized* form in which no complex concept occurs under implicit negations; then, we translate such GCIs into DL-clauses.

4   The Satisfiability Checking Algorithm

4.1   Preprocessing

Elimination of Transitivity Axioms. We first encode a $\mathcal{SHIQ}$ knowledge base $\mathcal{K}$ into an equisatisfiable $\mathcal{ALCHIQ}$ knowledge base $\Omega(\mathcal{K})$. Roughly speaking, an axiom $\mathsf{Trans}(S)$ is replaced with axioms $\forall R.C \sqsubseteq \forall S.(\forall S.C)$, for each R with $S \sqsubseteq^* R$ and C a "relevant" concept from $\mathcal{K}$. This encoding is polynomial and has been presented several times for various description [19] and modal [18] logics. Therefore, we omit the details of the transformation and refer the reader to [14, Section 5.2]. After this transformation, there is no distinction between simple and complex roles, so, without loss of generality, in the rest of this paper we treat $\exists R.C$ as a syntactic shortcut for $\geq 1\, R.C$.

Table 2. The Functions Used in the Structural Transformation

$$\Delta(\mathcal{K}) = \{\top(\iota)\} \cup \bigcup_{\alpha \in \mathcal{R} \cup \mathcal{A}} \Delta(\alpha) \cup \bigcup_{C_1 \sqsubseteq C_2 \in \mathcal{T}} \Delta(\top \sqsubseteq \text{nnf}(\neg C_1 \sqcup C_2))$$

$$\Delta(\top \sqsubseteq \mathbf{C} \sqcup C') = \Delta(\top \sqsubseteq \mathbf{C} \sqcup \alpha_{C'}) \cup \bigcup_{i=1}^{n} \Delta(\alpha_{C'} \sqsubseteq C_i) \text{ for } C' = \bigsqcap_{i=1}^{n} C_i$$

$$\Delta(\top \sqsubseteq \mathbf{C} \sqcup \forall R.D) = \Delta(\top \sqsubseteq \mathbf{C} \sqcup \forall R.\alpha_D) \cup \Delta(\alpha_D \sqsubseteq D)$$

$$\Delta(\top \sqsubseteq \mathbf{C} \sqcup \geq n\,R.D) = \Delta(\top \sqsubseteq \mathbf{C} \sqcup \geq n\,R.\alpha_D) \cup \Delta(\alpha_D \sqsubseteq D)$$

$$\Delta(\top \sqsubseteq \mathbf{C} \sqcup \leq n\,R.D) = \Delta(\top \sqsubseteq \mathbf{C} \sqcup \leq n\,R.\dot{\neg}\alpha_{D'}) \cup \Delta(\alpha_{D'} \sqsubseteq D') \text{ for } D' = \dot{\neg}D$$

$$\Delta(D(a)) = \{\alpha_D(a)\} \cup \Delta(\alpha_D \sqsubseteq D)$$

$$\Delta(R^-(a,b)) = \{R(b,a)\}$$

$$\Delta(\beta) = \{\beta\} \text{ for any other axiom } \beta$$

$$\alpha_C = \begin{cases} Q_C & \text{if } \text{pos}(C) = \text{true} \\ \neg Q_C & \text{if } \text{pos}(C) = \text{false} \end{cases} \text{ where } Q_C \text{ is a fresh atomic concept unique for } C$$

$\text{pos}(\top) = \text{false}$	$\text{pos}(\bot) = \text{false}$
$\text{pos}(A) = \text{true}$	$\text{pos}(\neg A) = \text{false}$
$\text{pos}(C_1 \sqcap C_2) = \text{pos}(C_1) \vee \text{pos}(C_2)$	$\text{pos}(C_1 \sqcup C_2) = \text{pos}(C_1) \vee \text{pos}(C_2)$
$\text{pos}(\forall R.C_1) = \text{pos}(C_1)$	$\text{pos}(\leq n\,R.C_1) = \begin{cases} \text{pos}(\dot{\neg}C_1) & \text{if } n = 0 \\ \text{true} & \text{otherwise} \end{cases}$
$\text{pos}(\geq n\,R.C_1) = \text{true}$	

Note: A is an atomic concept, C_i are arbitrary concepts, $\mathbf{C}$ is a possibly empty disjunction of arbitrary concepts, D is not a literal concept, and ι is a fresh individual.

Structural Transformation. GCIs are next brought into a certain normalized form, defined as follows:

Definition 1. *For A an atomic concept, the concepts A, $\neg A$, $\top$, and $\bot$ are called* literal concepts. *A GCI is* normalized *if it is of the form $\top \sqsubseteq \bigsqcup_{i=1}^{n} C_i$, where each C_i is of the form B, $\forall R.B$, $\geq n\,R.B$, or $\leq n\,R.B$, and B is a literal concept. A TBox $\mathcal{T}$ is* normalized *if all GCIs in it are normalized. An ABox $\mathcal{A}$ is* normalized *if (i) each concept assertion in $\mathcal{A}$ is of the form $B(s)$ or $\geq n\,R.B(s)$, for B a literal concept, (ii) each role assertion in $\mathcal{A}$ contains only atomic roles, and (iii) $\mathcal{A}$ contains at least one assertion. A knowledge base $\mathcal{K}$ is* normalized *if $\mathcal{T}$ and $\mathcal{A}$ are normalized.*

A knowledge base $\mathcal{K}$ can be brought into normalized form $\Delta(\mathcal{K})$ as follows:

Definition 2. *For $\mathcal{K}$ an $\mathcal{ALCHIQ}$ knowledge base, $\Delta(\mathcal{K})$ is the knowledge base computed as shown in Table 2.*

The difference between the well-known structural transformation [16] and Definition 2 is as follows. Assume that we need to rename a nonatomic subconcept D of C. If $\text{pos}(D) = \text{false}$, then D can be converted into clauses with only negative literals, so we rename D by a negative literal concept $\neg Q_D$; otherwise, the clausification of D requires at least one positive literal, so we rename D by a positive literal concept Q_D. In this way, the renaming of D in C does not change the number of positive literals in the clausal representation of C, so renaming preserves Horn-ness. Furthermore, for a Horn-$\mathcal{SHIQ}$ knowledge base $\mathcal{K}$ [12], the knowledge base $\Delta(\mathcal{K})$ is guaranteed also to be a Horn-$\mathcal{SHIQ}$ knowledge base that can be translated into Horn DL-clauses.

Lemma 1. *An $\mathcal{ALCHIQ}$ knowledge base $\mathcal{K}$ is satisfiable if and only if $\Delta(\mathcal{K})$ is satisfiable; $\Delta(\mathcal{K})$ can be computed in polynomial time; and $\Delta(\mathcal{K})$ is normalized.*

Proof. It is easy to see that our transformation is a syntactic variant of the structural transformation from [16], from which the first two claims follow. Observe that Δ essentially rewrites each GCI into a form $\top \sqsubseteq \bigsqcup_{i=1}^{n} C_i$ and then keeps replacing nested subconcepts of C_i as long as the GCI is not normalized. Furthermore, it adds $\top(\iota)$ to the ABox so that it is not empty, and it replaces all inverse role assertions with equivalent assertions on the atomic roles.   □

Translation into DL-Clauses. We next define the notion of DL-clauses:

Definition 3. *Let N_V be a set of variables disjoint from N_I. An* atom *is an expression of the form $C(s)$, $R(s,t)$, or $s \approx t$, for s and t individuals or variables, C a concept, and R a role. A* DL-clause *is an expression of the form*

$$U_1 \wedge ... \wedge U_m \rightarrow V_1 \vee ... \vee V_n \tag{5}$$

where U_i and V_j are atoms, $m \geq 0$, and $n \geq 0$. The conjunction $U_1 \wedge ... \wedge U_m$ is called the antecedent, *and the disjunction $V_1 \vee ... \vee V_n$ is called the* consequent.

Let $I = (\triangle^I, \cdot^I)$ be an interpretation and $\mu : N_V \rightarrow \triangle^I$ a variable mapping. Let $a^{I,\mu} = a^I$ for an individual a and $x^{I,\mu} = \mu(x)$ for a variable x. Satisfaction of an atom, DL-clause, and a set of DL-clauses N in I and μ is defined as follows:

$$
\begin{aligned}
I, \mu &\models C(s) &&\text{if } s^{I,\mu} \in C^I \\
I, \mu &\models R(s,t) &&\text{if } \langle s^{I,\mu}, t^{I,\mu} \rangle \in R^I \\
I, \mu &\models s \approx t &&\text{if } s^{I,\mu} = t^{I,\mu} \\
I, \mu &\models \textstyle\bigwedge_{i=1}^{m} U_i \rightarrow \bigvee_{j=1}^{n} V_n &&\text{if } I, \mu \models V_j \text{ for some } 1 \leq j \leq n \text{ whenever} \\
& &&\quad I, \mu \models U_i \text{ for each } 1 \leq i \leq m \\
I &\models \textstyle\bigwedge_{i=1}^{m} U_i \rightarrow \bigvee_{j=1}^{n} V_n &&\text{if } I, \mu \models \bigwedge_{i=1}^{m} U_i \rightarrow \bigvee_{j=1}^{n} V_n \text{ for all mappings } \mu \\
I &\models N &&\text{if } \quad I \models r \text{ for each DL-clause } r \in N
\end{aligned}
$$

In the rest of this paper, we assume that each atom $s \approx t$ ($s \not\approx t$) also stands for the symmetric atom $t \approx s$ ($t \not\approx s$). Furthermore, we allow ABoxes to contain the assertion $\bot$, which is false in all interpretations. Finally, we denote the empty consequents of DL-clauses with $\bot$. We now show how to transform a normalized $\mathcal{ALCHIQ}$ knowledge base into a set of DL-clauses.

Definition 4. *For a normalized $\mathcal{ALCHIQ}$ knowledge base $\mathcal{K} = (\mathcal{R}, \mathcal{T}, \mathcal{A})$, the set of DL-clauses $\Xi(\mathcal{K})$ is obtained as shown in Table 3.*

To simplify the *Hyp*-rule in Section 4.2, the role atoms in $\mathcal{A}$ and $\Xi(\mathcal{K})$ involve only atomic roles. Thus, the function ar from Table 3 is used to convert inverse role atoms $R^-(s,t)$ in $\Xi(\mathcal{K})$ into atomic role atoms $R(t,s)$. An inverse role can occur only in concepts of the form $\geq n R^-.C$, so the $\geq$-rule (defined in Section 4.2) also uses ar to generate atoms with atomic roles.

Lemma 2. *Let $\mathcal{K}$ be a normalized $\mathcal{ALCHIQ}$ knowledge base. Then, $I \models \mathcal{K}$ if and only if $I \models \Xi(\mathcal{K})$ and $I \models \mathcal{A}$.*

Table 3. Translation of Normalized GCIs to DL-Clauses

$\Xi(\mathcal{K}) = \{[\bigwedge_{i=1}^{n} \mathrm{lhs}(C_i)] \rightarrow [\bigvee_{i=1}^{n} \mathrm{rhs}(C_i)] \mid$ for each $\top \sqsubseteq \bigsqcup_{i=1}^{n} C_i$ in $\mathcal{T}\} \cup$		
$\{\mathrm{ar}(R,x,y) \rightarrow \mathrm{ar}(S,x,y) \mid$ for each $R \sqsubseteq S$ in $\mathcal{R}\}$		

$$\mathrm{ar}(R,s,t) = \begin{cases} R(s,t) & \text{if } R \text{ is an atomic role} \\ S(t,s) & \text{if } R \text{ is an inverse role and } R = S^- \end{cases}$$

Note: Whenever $\mathrm{lhs}(C_i)$ or $\mathrm{rhs}(C_i)$ is undefined, it is omitted in the DL-clause.

C	$\mathrm{lhs}(C)$	$\mathrm{rhs}(C)$
A		$A(x)$
$\neg A$	$A(x)$	
$\geq n\,R.A$		$\geq n\,R.A(x)$
$\geq n\,R.\neg A$		$\geq n\,R.\neg A(x)$
$\forall R.A$	$\mathrm{ar}(R,x,y_C)$	$A(y_C)$
$\forall R.\neg A$	$\mathrm{ar}(R,x,y_C) \wedge A(y_C)$	
$\leq n\,R.A$	$\bigwedge_{i=1}^{n+1}[\mathrm{ar}(R,x,y_C^i) \wedge A(y_C^i)]$	$\bigvee_{i=1}^{n+1}\bigvee_{j=i+1}^{n+1} y_C^i \approx y_C^j$
$\leq n\,R.\neg A$	$\bigwedge_{i=1}^{n+1}\mathrm{ar}(R,x,y_C^i)$	$\bigvee_{i=1}^{n+1} A(y_C^i) \vee \bigvee_{i=1}^{n+1}\bigvee_{j=i+1}^{n+1} y_C^i \approx y_C^j$

Note: Each variable $y_C^{(i)}$ is unique for C (and i), and it is different from x.

Proof. The following equivalences between DLs and first-order logic are known:

$$\forall R.C(x) \equiv \forall y : \neg R(x,y) \vee C(y)$$
$$\leq n\,R.C(x) \equiv \forall y_1, \ldots, y_{n+1} : \bigvee_{i=1}^{n+1}[\neg R(x,y_i) \vee \neg C(y_i)] \vee \bigvee_{i=1}^{n+1}\bigvee_{j=i+1}^{n+1} y_i \approx y_j$$

Clearly, $\Xi(\mathcal{K})$ is obtained from normalized GCIs by expanding the concepts $\forall R.C$ and $\leq n\,R.C$ according to these equivalences, and then moving all negative atoms into the antecedent and all positive atoms into the consequent. $\square$

4.2   The Hypertableau Calculus for DL-Clauses

We now present our hypertableau calculus for deciding satisfiability of $\mathcal{A} \cup \Xi(\mathcal{K})$.

Definition 5. *Unnamed Individuals.* *For a set of* named *individuals* N_I*, the set of all individuals* N_X *is inductively defined as* $N_I \subseteq N_X$ *and, if* $x \in N_X$*, then* $x.i \in N_X$ *for each integer* i*. The individuals in* $N_X \setminus N_I$ *are* unnamed*. An individual* $x.i$ *is a* successor *of* x*, and* x *is a* predecessor *of* $x.i$*;* descendant *and* ancestor *are the transitive closures of* successor *and* predecessor*, respectively.*

Pairwise Anywhere Blocking. *A concept is* blocking-relevant *if it is of the form* A*,* $\geq n\,R.A$*, or* $\geq n\,R.\neg A$*, for* A *an atomic concept. The label of an individual* s *and of an individual pair* $\langle s,t \rangle$ *in an ABox* $\mathcal{A}$ *are defined as follows:*

$$\mathcal{L}_{\mathcal{A}}(s) = \{C \mid C(s) \in \mathcal{A} \text{ and } C \text{ is a blocking-relevant concept}\}$$
$$\mathcal{L}_{\mathcal{A}}(s,t) = \{R \mid R(s,t) \in \mathcal{A}\}$$

Let $\prec$ *be a strict ordering (i.e., a transitive and irreflexive relation) on* N_X *containing the ancestor relation—that is, if* s' *is an ancestor of* s*, then* $s' \prec s$*. By induction on* $\prec$*, we assign to each individual* s *in* $\mathcal{A}$ *a status as follows:*

Table 4. Derivation Rules of the Tableau Calculus

Hyp-rule	If 1. $U_1 \wedge \ldots \wedge U_m \to V_1 \vee \ldots \vee V_n \in \Xi(\mathcal{K})$, 2. a mapping $\sigma : N_V \to N_\mathcal{A}$ exists, for $N_\mathcal{A}$ the set of individuals in $\mathcal{A}$, 3. $\sigma(U_i) \in \mathcal{A}$ for each $1 \le i \le m$, 4. $\sigma(V_j) \notin \mathcal{A}$ for each $1 \le j \le n$, then if $n = 0$, then $\mathcal{A}_1 = \mathcal{A} \cup \{\bot\}$, otherwise $\mathcal{A}_j := \mathcal{A} \cup \{\sigma(V_j)\}$ for $1 \le j \le n$.
$\ge$-rule	If 1. $\ge n\, R.C(s) \in \mathcal{A}$, 2. s is not blocked in $\mathcal{A}$, and 3. there are no individuals $u_1, \ldots, u_n$ such that $\{\mathsf{ar}(R,s,u_i), C(u_i) \mid 1 \le i \le n\} \cup \{u_i \not\approx u_j \mid 1 \le i < j \le n\} \subseteq \mathcal{A}$, then $\mathcal{A}_1 := \mathcal{A} \cup \{\mathsf{ar}(R,s,t_i),\, C(t_i) \mid 1 \le i \le n\} \cup \{t_i \not\approx t_j \mid 1 \le i < j \le n\}$ where $t_1, \ldots, t_n$ are fresh pairwise distinct successors of s.
$\approx$-rule	If 1. $s \approx t \in \mathcal{A}$ and 2. $s \ne t$ then $\mathcal{A}_1 := \mathsf{merge}_\mathcal{A}(s \to t)$ if t is named or if s is a descendant of t, $\mathcal{A}_1 := \mathsf{merge}_\mathcal{A}(t \to s)$ otherwise.
$\bot$-rule	If 1. $s \not\approx s \in \mathcal{A}$ or $\{A(s), \neg A(s)\} \subseteq \mathcal{A}$ and 2. $\bot \notin \mathcal{A}$ then $\mathcal{A}_1 := \mathcal{A} \cup \{\bot\}$.

- s is directly blocked by *an individual* s' *iff both* s *and* s' *are unnamed,* s' *is not blocked,* $s' \prec s$, $\mathcal{L}_\mathcal{A}(s) = \mathcal{L}_\mathcal{A}(s')$, $\mathcal{L}_\mathcal{A}(t) = \mathcal{L}_\mathcal{A}(t')$, $\mathcal{L}_\mathcal{A}(s,t) = \mathcal{L}_\mathcal{A}(s',t')$, *and* $\mathcal{L}_\mathcal{A}(t,s) = \mathcal{L}_\mathcal{A}(t',s')$, *for* t *and* t' *the predecessors of* s *and* s', *resp.*
- s is indirectly blocked *iff its predecessor is blocked.*
- s is blocked *iff it is either directly or indirectly blocked.*

Pruning. *The ABox* $\mathsf{prune}_\mathcal{A}(s)$ *is obtained from* $\mathcal{A}$ *by removing all assertions of the form* $R(t, t.i)$, $R(t.i, t)$, $C(t.i)$, $u \approx t.i$, *and* $u \not\approx t.i$, *where* t *is either* s *or some descendant of* s, i *is an integer, and* u *is an arbitrary individual.*

Merging. *The ABox* $\mathsf{merge}_\mathcal{A}(s \to t)$ *is obtained from* $\mathsf{prune}_\mathcal{A}(s)$ *by replacing the individual* s *with the individual* t *in all assertions.*

Derivation Rules. *Table 4 specifies derivation rules that, given an ABox* $\mathcal{A}$ *and a set of DL-clauses* $\Xi(\mathcal{K})$, *derive the ABoxes* $\mathcal{A}_1, \ldots, \mathcal{A}_n$. *In the Hyp-rule,* σ *is a mapping from* N_V *to the individuals occurring in* $\mathcal{A}$, *and* $\sigma(U)$ *is the atom obtained from* U *by replacing each variable* x *with* $\sigma(x)$.

Derivation. *For a normalized* $\mathcal{ALCHIQ}$ *knowledge base* $\mathcal{K} = (\mathcal{R}, \mathcal{T}, \mathcal{A})$, *a derivation is a pair* (T, λ) *where* T *is a finitely branching tree and* λ *is a function that labels the nodes of* T *with ABoxes such that (i)* $\lambda(\epsilon) = \mathcal{A}$ *for* ϵ *the root of the tree, and (ii) for each node* t, *if one or more derivation rules are applicable to* $\lambda(t)$ *and* $\Xi(\mathcal{K})$, *then* t *has children* $t_1, \ldots, t_n$ *such that* $\lambda(t_1), \ldots, \lambda(t_n)$ *are the result of applying one (arbitrarily chosen) applicable rule to* $\lambda(t)$ *and* $\Xi(\mathcal{K})$.

Clash. *An ABox* $\mathcal{A}$ *contains a clash iff* $\bot \in \mathcal{A}$; *otherwise,* $\mathcal{A}$ *is clash-free.*

In [10], the successor relation is encoded using role arcs, which point only from predecessors to successors. Since our ABoxes contain only atomic roles, role arcs can point in both directions, so we encode the successor relation in the individuals. The ordering $\prec$ ensures that there are no cyclic blocks, so all successors of nonblocked individuals have been constructed. *Ancestor pairwise blocking* from [10] is obtained if $\prec$ is exactly the descendant relation.

Pruning prevents infinite loops of merge-create rule applications—the so-called "yo-yo" effect. Consider the following example:

$$
\begin{aligned}
\mathcal{A}_3 &= \{A(a),\ \exists R.\top(a),\ R(a,b),\ R(a,a)\} \\
\Xi(\mathcal{K}_3) &= \{R(x,y_1) \land R(x,y_2) \to y_1 \approx y_2,\ A(x) \land R(x,y) \to \exists R.\top(y)\}
\end{aligned}
\tag{6}
$$

By the second DL-clause, we derive $\exists R.\top(b)$, which we expand to $R(b,b.1)$. But then, by the first DL-clause, we derive $b \approx a$. Hence, we merge b into a, and obtain $\mathcal{A}'_3 = \{A(a), \exists R.\top(a), R(a,b.1), R(a,a)\}$. The ABox $\mathcal{A}'_3$ is isomorphic to $\mathcal{A}_3$, so we can repeat the whole process, which clearly leads to nontermination. To remedy this, we remove all assertions that involve successors of b before merging b into a; we thus obtain $\mathcal{A}''_3 = \{A(a), R(a,a), \exists R.\top(a)\}$, after which the algorithm terminates. Intuitively, merging ensures that no individual "inherits" successors through merging. In [10], the successors are not physically removed, but are marked as "not present" by setting their edge labels to $\emptyset$. This has exactly the same effect as pruning.

We next prove that our calculus is sound, complete, and terminating.

Lemma 3 (Soundness). *Let $\mathcal{A}$ be an ABox and $\Xi(\mathcal{K})$ a set of DL-clauses such that $\mathcal{A} \cup \Xi(\mathcal{K})$ is satisfiable, and let $\mathcal{A}_1, \ldots, \mathcal{A}_n$ be obtained by applying a derivation rule to $\mathcal{A}$ and $\Xi(\mathcal{K})$. Then, $\mathcal{A}_i \cup \Xi(\mathcal{K})$ is satisfiable for some $1 \le i \le m$.*

Proof. Let I be a model of $\mathcal{A} \cup \Xi(\mathcal{K})$, and let us consider all derivation rules.

(*Hyp*-rule) Since $\sigma(U_i) \in \mathcal{A}$, we have $I \models \sigma(U_i)$ for all $1 \le i \le m$. But then, $I \models \sigma(V_j)$ for some $1 \le j \le n$. Since $\mathcal{A}_j = \mathcal{A} \cup \{\sigma(V_j)\}$, we have $I \models \mathcal{A}_j \cup \Xi(\mathcal{K})$.

($\ge$-rule) Since $\ge n\, R.C(s) \in \mathcal{A}$, we have $I \models\ \ge n\, R.C(s)$, which means that $\alpha_1, \ldots, \alpha_n \in \Delta^I$ exist such that $\langle s^I, \alpha_i \rangle \in R^I$ and $\alpha_i \in C^I$ for $1 \le i \le n$, and $\alpha_i \ne \alpha_j$ for $1 \le i < j \le n$. Let I' be obtained from I by setting $t_i^{I'} = \alpha_i$. Clearly, $I' \models \mathsf{ar}(R, s, t_i)$, $I' \models C(t_i)$, and $I' \models t_i \not\approx t_j$ for $i \ne j$, so $I' \models \mathcal{A}_1 \cup \Xi(\mathcal{K})$.

($\approx$-rule) Since $s \approx t \in \mathcal{A}$, we have $I \models s \approx t$, so $s^I = t^I$. Pruning removes assertions, so I is a model of the pruned ABox by monotonicity. Merging simply replaces an individual with a synonym, so, clearly, $I \models \mathcal{A}_1 \cup \Xi(\mathcal{K})$.

($\bot$-rule) This rule is never applicable if $\mathcal{A} \cup \Xi(\mathcal{K})$ is satisfiable. $\square$

The following corollary follows immediately from Lemma 3:

Corollary 1. *Each derivation for a satisfiable normalized $\mathcal{ALCHIQ}$ knowledge base $\mathcal{K}$ contains a path such that $\lambda(t)$ is clash-free for each node t on the path.*

Lemma 4 (Completeness). *If a derivation for a normalized $\mathcal{ALCHIQ}$ knowledge base $\mathcal{K} = (\mathcal{R}, \mathcal{T}, \mathcal{A})$ contains a leaf node labeled with a clash-free ABox $\mathcal{A}'$, then $\mathcal{A} \cup \Xi(\mathcal{K})$ is satisfiable.*

Proof. We first prove the claim (*): for each ABox $\mathcal{A}'$ occurring in a derivation for $\mathcal{K}$, (*i*) for each $R(s, t) \in \mathcal{A}'$, t is a predecessor or a successor of s, or both s and t are named individuals, and (*ii*) for each $s \approx t \in \mathcal{A}'$, $s = t$, or s and t are both named, or t is a successor of a named individual and s is a named individual, or t and s have a common predecessor, or t is a successor of a successor of s. The proof is by a simple induction on the application of the derivation rules. Initially, $\mathcal{A}$ contains only named individuals. An application of the $\geq$-rule clearly preserves (*). For the $\approx$-rule, (*) holds because $\mathcal{A}'$ satisfies (*ii*) and merging never replaces an individual with a descendant. Finally, let us consider the *Hyp*-rule. By Definition 4, each DL-clause from $\Xi(\mathcal{K})$ is of the form (7), for A_i and B_i atomic concepts, R_i atomic roles, and C_i and D_i blocking-relevant concepts:

$$\bigwedge A_i(x) \wedge \bigwedge \mathsf{ar}(R_i, x, y_i) \wedge \bigwedge B_i(y_i) \rightarrow \bigvee C_i(x) \vee \bigvee D_i(y_i) \vee \bigvee y_i \approx y_j \qquad (7)$$

For each $y_i \approx y_j$, the antecedent contains $\mathsf{ar}(R, x, y_i) \wedge \mathsf{ar}(R, x, y_j)$. Since $\mathcal{A}'$ satisfies (*i*), each $\sigma(y_i)$ is either a successor or a predecessor of $\sigma(x)$ and, if $\sigma(y_i)$ is a named individual, then all $\sigma(y_j)$ are either named individuals or successors of named individuals. Thus, each $\mathcal{A}'_i$ obtained by the *Hyp*-rule satisfies (*).

We now construct a model of $\Xi(\mathcal{K}) \cup \mathcal{A}$. A *path* is a finite sequences of pairs of individuals $p = [\frac{x_0}{x_0'}, \ldots, \frac{x_n}{x_n'}]$. Let $\mathsf{tail}(p) = x_n$, $\mathsf{tail}'(p) = x_n'$, and $q = [p \mid \frac{x_{n+1}}{x_{n+1}'}]$ be the path $[\frac{x_0}{x_0'}, \ldots, \frac{x_n}{x_n'}, \frac{x_{n+1}}{x_{n+1}'}]$; we say that q is a *successor* of p, and p is a *predecessor* of q. The set of all paths $\mathcal{P}(\mathcal{A}')$ is defined inductively as follows: (*i*) $[\frac{a}{a}] \in \mathcal{P}(\mathcal{A}')$ for each named individual a in $\mathcal{A}'$; (*ii*) $[p \mid \frac{s'}{s'}] \in \mathcal{P}(\mathcal{A}')$ if $p \in \mathcal{P}(\mathcal{A}')$, s' is a successor of $\mathsf{tail}(p)$ in $\mathcal{A}'$, and s' is not blocked; and (*iii*) $[p \mid \frac{s}{s'}] \in \mathcal{P}(\mathcal{A}')$ if $p \in \mathcal{P}(\mathcal{A}')$, s' is a successor of $\mathsf{tail}(p)$ in $\mathcal{A}'$, and s' is directly blocked by s. For each blocking-relevant concept C and each path $p \in \mathcal{P}(\mathcal{A}')$, by the definition of blocking, $C(\mathsf{tail}(p)) \in \mathcal{A}'$ iff $C(\mathsf{tail}'(p)) \in \mathcal{A}'$; furthermore, $\mathsf{tail}(p)$ is not blocked. We denote these two properties by (**). Let I be the following interpretation:

$\triangle^I = \mathcal{P}(\mathcal{A}')$

$a^I = [\frac{a}{a}]$ for each named individual a in $\mathcal{A}'$

$a^I = b^I$ if individuals $a = c_0, c_1, \ldots, c_n = b$ exist such that c_{i-1} was merged into c_i in the derivation leading to $\mathcal{A}'$

$A^I = \{p \mid A(\mathsf{tail}(p)) \in \mathcal{A}'\}$

$R^I = \{\langle [\frac{a}{a}], [\frac{b}{b}] \rangle \mid a \text{ and } b \text{ are named individuals and } R(a, b) \in \mathcal{A}'\} \cup$
    $\{\langle p, [p \mid \frac{s}{s'}] \rangle \mid s' \text{ is a successor of } \mathsf{tail}(p) \text{ and } R(\mathsf{tail}(p), s') \in \mathcal{A}'\} \cup$
    $\{\langle [p \mid \frac{s}{s'}], p \rangle \mid s' \text{ is a successor of } \mathsf{tail}(p) \text{ and } R(s', \mathsf{tail}(p)) \in \mathcal{A}'\}$

The ABox $\mathcal{A}'$ is normalized, so $\triangle^I$ is not empty. We now show that, for each $p_s = [q_s \mid \frac{s}{s'}]$ and $p_t = [q_t \mid \frac{t}{t'}]$ from $\triangle^I$, the following claims hold (***):

- *If $s' \approx t' \in \mathcal{A}'$, then $s' = t'$:* Obvious, as the $\approx$-rule is not applicable to $\mathcal{A}'$.
- *If $s' \not\approx t' \in \mathcal{A}'$, then $p_s \neq p_t$:* Since $\perp \notin \mathcal{A}'$ and the $\perp$-rule is not applicable to $s' \not\approx t'$, we have $s' \neq t'$, which implies the claim.
- *If $A(s') \in \mathcal{A}'$, then $p_s \in A^I$:* By (**), we have $A(s) \in \mathcal{A}'$, so $p_s \in A^I$.
- *If $\neg A(s') \in \mathcal{A}'$, then $p_s \notin A^I$.* Since $\perp \notin \mathcal{A}'$ and the $\perp$-rule is not applicable to $\neg A(s')$, we have $A(s') \notin \mathcal{A}'$. By (**), this implies $A(s) \notin \mathcal{A}'$, so $p_s \notin A^I$.

– If $\geq n\,R.C(s') \in \mathcal{A}'$, then $p_s \in (\geq n\,R.C)^I$: By (**), $\geq n\,R.C(s) \in \mathcal{A}'$ and s is not blocked. The $\geq$-rule is not applicable to $\geq n\,R.C(s)$, so individuals $u_1, \ldots, u_n$ exist such that $\mathsf{ar}(R, s, u_i) \in \mathcal{A}'$ and $C(u_i) \in \mathcal{A}'$ for $1 \leq i \leq n$, and $u_i \not\approx u_j \in \mathcal{A}'$ for $1 \leq i < j \leq n$. By (*), these possibilities exist for each u_i:

- u_i is a successor of s. If u_i is directly blocked by u_i', let $p_{u_i} = [p_s \mid \frac{u_i'}{u_i}]$; otherwise, let $p_{u_i} = [p_s \mid \frac{u_i}{u_i}]$.
- u_i is a predecessor of s. Let $p_{u_i} = q_s$. If $\mathsf{tail}'(p_{u_i}) \neq u_i$, this is because s' is blocked, but then, by the conditions of blocking, $C(\mathsf{tail}'(p_{u_i})) \in \mathcal{A}'$ and $\mathsf{ar}(R, s', \mathsf{tail}'(p_{u_i})) \in \mathcal{A}'$.
- u_i is neither a predecessor nor a successor of s. Then, both s and u_i are named individuals, so let $p_{u_i} = [\frac{u_i}{u_i}]$.

In all cases, we have $\mathsf{ar}(R, s', \mathsf{tail}'(p_{u_i})) \in \mathcal{A}'$, which implies $\langle p_s, p_{u_i} \rangle \in R^I$, and $C(\mathsf{tail}'(p_{u_i})) \in \mathcal{A}'$, which implies $p_{u_i} \in C^I$. Consider now each pair of paths p_{u_i} and p_{u_j} with $i \neq j$. If $\mathsf{tail}'(p_{u_i}) \not\approx \mathsf{tail}'(p_{u_j}) \in \mathcal{A}'$, then clearly $p_{u_i} \neq p_{u_j}$. If $\mathsf{tail}'(p_{u_i}) \not\approx \mathsf{tail}'(p_{u_j}) \notin \mathcal{A}'$, this is because $\mathsf{tail}'(p_{u_i}) \neq u_i$, which is possible only if s' is directly blocked by s and u_i is a predecessor of s. Since s can have at most one predecessor, no u_j with $j \neq i$ is a predecessor of s, so $p_{u_i} \neq p_{u_j}$. Thus, we conclude that $p_s \in (\geq n\,R.C)^I$.

Clearly, (***) implies that $I \models \alpha'$ for each assertion $\alpha' \in \mathcal{A}'$ that contains only named individuals. Consider now each $\alpha \in \mathcal{A}$. If $\alpha \notin \mathcal{A}'$, then some named individuals in α were merged into other individuals; but then, $\mathcal{A}'$ contains the assertion α' obtained by this merging, so $I \models \alpha$ by the definition of I.

It remains to be shown that $I \models \Xi(\mathcal{K})$. Consider each DL-clause $r \in \Xi(\mathcal{K})$ of the form (7) and each variable mapping μ. Let $p_x = \mu(x)$, $p_{y_i} = \mu(y_i)$, and $s' = \mathsf{tail}'(p_x)$. Assume now that each atom from the antecedent of r is true in I and μ—that is, $p_x \in A_i^I$, $p_{y_i} \in B_i^I$, and $\langle p_x, p_{y_i} \rangle \in R^I$.

If s' is not blocked, let $s = s'$ and $t_i = \mathsf{tail}'(p_{y_i})$. By the definition of I, we have $A_i(s) \in \mathcal{A}'$, $B_i(t_i) \in \mathcal{A}'$, and $\mathsf{ar}(R_i, s, t_i) \in \mathcal{A}'$.

If s' is blocked, let $s = \mathsf{tail}'(p_x)$; that is, s is the individual that blocks s'. By the definition of I, since $p_x \in A_i^I$, we have $A_i(s) \in \mathcal{A}'$. If $\mathsf{tail}'(p_{y_i})$ is a successor of s, let $t_i = \mathsf{tail}'(p_{y_i})$; now $p_{y_i} \in B_i^I$ and $\langle p_x, p_{y_i} \rangle \in R_i^I$ imply $B_i(t_i) \in \mathcal{A}'$ and $\mathsf{ar}(R_i, s, t_i) \in \mathcal{A}'$. If $\mathsf{tail}'(p_{y_i})$ is not a successor of s, let t_i be the predecessor of s; this predecessor exists by the definition of blocking. Furthermore, $p_{y_i} \in B_i^I$ and $\langle p_x, p_{y_i} \rangle \in R_i^I$ imply $B_i(\mathsf{tail}'(p_{y_i})) \in \mathcal{A}'$ and $\mathsf{ar}(R_i, s', \mathsf{tail}'(p_{y_i})) \in \mathcal{A}'$; by the definition of blocking, we have $B_i(t_i) \in \mathcal{A}'$ and $\mathsf{ar}(R_i, s, t_i) \in \mathcal{A}'$ as well.

Let σ be a mapping such that $\sigma(x) = s$ and $\sigma(y_i) = t_i$. The Hyp-rule is not applicable to $\mathcal{A}'$, so some of the atoms from the consequent of $\sigma(r)$ must be present in $\mathcal{A}'$. Assume first that $C_i(s) \in \mathcal{A}'$ or $D_i(t_i) \in \mathcal{A}'$. By the definition of blocking, $C_i(\mathsf{tail}'(p_x)) \in \mathcal{A}'$ or $D_i(\mathsf{tail}'(p_{y_i})) \in \mathcal{A}'$, respectively; by (***), this implies $p_x \in C_i^I$ or $p_{y_i} \in D_i^I$, respectively. Assume now that $t_i \approx t_j \in \mathcal{A}'$. By (***), we have $t_i = t_j$. If p_{y_i} and p_{y_j} are both successors of p_x, then $t_i = \mathsf{tail}'(p_{y_i})$ and $t_j = \mathsf{tail}'(p_{y_j})$, so $t_i = t_j$ implies $p_{y_i} = p_{y_j}$. If p_{y_i} and p_{y_j} are both predecessors of p_x, we have $p_{y_i} = p_{y_j}$ since p_x can have at most one predecessor. Finally, let us assume that p_{y_i} is a predecessor of p_x, which is a predecessor of p_{y_j}. Then,

$\mathsf{tail}'(p_{y_j}) = t_j$; furthermore, since t_i is not blocked, we have $\mathsf{tail}'(p_{y_j}) \neq t_i$, which contradicts the assumption that $t_i = t_j$. □

If $\prec$ coincides with the descendant relationship, the termination proof is analogous to [10, Lemma 3], so we present here only the intuition. Consider any ABox $\mathcal{A}$ in the derivation. There are at most exponentially many different tuples $\langle \mathcal{L}_\mathcal{A}(s), \mathcal{L}_\mathcal{A}(s,t), \mathcal{L}_\mathcal{A}(t,s), \mathcal{L}_\mathcal{A}(t) \rangle$, so an individual can have at most exponentially many nonblocked ancestors. Thus, $\mathcal{A}$ can be viewed as a tree with exponential depth and a linear branching factor, so the number of nonblocked individuals is at most doubly exponential. When an individual s becomes blocked, at most double exponentially many nonblocked descendants of s can become indirectly blocked, so $|\mathcal{A}|$ is at most doubly exponential in $|\mathcal{K}|$. Due to pruning, the $\geq$-rule can be applied to an individual at most $|\mathcal{K}|$ times. We construct the derivation nondeterministically, so our algorithm runs in 2NExpTime.

If $\prec$ is total, the number of nonblocked individuals in $\mathcal{A}$ is exponential. Analogously to the previous case, we can conclude that the number of individuals is at most exponential, so our algorithm runs in NExpTime. The DL $\mathcal{SHIQ}$ is ExpTime-complete [2], so our algorithm is not worst-case optimal. Worst-case optimal tableau algorithms for fragments of $\mathcal{SHIQ}$ have been presented in [7,4]. These algorithms use caching, which is related to anywhere blocking; however, to obtain the desired complexity result, they use cuts and are thus unlikely to be practical. Furthermore, we are not aware of any practical implementation of these calculi. On Horn-$\mathcal{SHIQ}$ [12] knowledge bases, however, our algorithm is deterministic, so it runs in ExpTime. It is known that Horn-$\mathcal{SHIQ}$ is ExpTime-hard [13], so our algorithm gives a worst-case optimal decision procedure.

Lemma 5 (Termination, [10]). *For a normalized $\mathcal{ALCHIQ}$ knowledge base $\mathcal{K}$, every derivation from $\mathcal{K}$ is finite.*

Lemmas 1, 4, 5, and Corollary 1 immediately imply our main theorem:

Theorem 1. *A $\mathcal{SHIQ}$ knowledge base $\mathcal{K}$ is satisfiable if and only if each derivation from $\mathcal{K}' = \Delta(\Omega(\mathcal{K}))$ contains a leaf node t such that $\lambda(t)$ is clash-free; furthermore, the construction of each such derivation terminates.*

4.3 Applying the Algorithm to Other DLs

For DLs with inverse roles but without number restrictions, traditional tableau algorithms can use simpler *equality blocking* [9]: an unnamed individual s is blocked by an individual s' in $\mathcal{A}$ iff $s' \prec s$ and $\mathcal{L}_\mathcal{A}(s) = \mathcal{L}_\mathcal{A}(s')$. Such blocking must be applied with care in our setting. Consider the knowledge base (8), on which our algorithm produces the ABox (10).

$$\mathcal{K}_4 = \{C \sqsubseteq \exists R.D, \quad D \sqsubseteq \exists S^-.C, \quad \top \sqsubseteq \forall R.\bot \sqcup \forall S.\bot, \quad C(a)\} \tag{8}$$

$$\Xi(\mathcal{K}_4) = \{C(x) \to \exists R.D(x), \ D(x) \to \exists S^-.C(x), \ R(x,y_1) \wedge S(x,y_2) \to \bot\} \tag{9}$$

$$\mathcal{A}_4 = \left\{ \begin{matrix} C(a), \\ \exists R.D(a), \end{matrix} R(a,a.1), \begin{matrix} D(a.1), \\ \exists S^-.C(a.1), \end{matrix} S(a.1.1, a.1), \begin{matrix} C(a.1.1), \\ \exists R.D(a.1.1) \end{matrix} \right\} \tag{10}$$

The individual $a.1.1$ is directly blocked by a, so the algorithm terminates; an expansion of $\exists R.D(a.1.1)$, however, would reveal that $\mathcal{K}$ is unsatisfiable. The problem arises because the DL-clause $R(x, y_1) \wedge S(x, y_2) \to \bot$ contains two role atoms, which allows it to examine both the successors and the predecessor of x. Equality blocking, however, does not ensure that both predecessors and successors of x have been fully built. We can correct this problem by requiring the normalized GCIs to contain at most one $\forall R.C$ concept. For example, if we replace our DL-clause with $R(x, y_1) \to Q(x)$ and $Q(x) \wedge S(x, y_2) \to \bot$, then the first DL-clause additionally derives $Q(a)$, so $a.1.1$ is not blocked.

For DLs without inverse roles, tableau algorithms typically use *subset blocking* [1]: an unnamed individual s is blocked by s' in $\mathcal{A}$ iff $s' \prec s$ and $\mathcal{L}_{\mathcal{A}}(s) \subseteq \mathcal{L}_{\mathcal{A}}(s')$. Subset blocking is not applicable in our setting. Consider the knowledge base (11), on which our algorithm produces the ABox (13):

$$\mathcal{K}_5 = \{C \sqsubseteq \exists R.C, \ C \sqsubseteq \exists S.D, \ \exists S.D \sqsubseteq E, \ \exists R.E \sqsubseteq \bot, \ C(a)\} \tag{11}$$

$$\Xi(\mathcal{K}_5) = \left\{ \begin{array}{ll} C(x) \to \exists R.C(x), & C(x) \to \exists S.D(x), \\ S(x, y) \wedge D(y) \to E(x), & R(x, y) \wedge E(y) \to \bot \end{array} \right\} \tag{12}$$

$$\mathcal{A}_5 = \left\{ \begin{array}{l} C(a), \ \exists S.D(a), \ S(a, a.1), \ \ D(a.1), \ \ E(a), \\ \exists R.C(a), \ R(a, a.2), \ \ C(a.2), \ \exists R.C(a.2), \ \exists S.D(a.2) \end{array} \right\} \tag{13}$$

Now $a.2$ is directly blocked by a. If, however, we expanded $\exists S.D(a.2)$ into $S(a.2, a.2.1)$ and $D(a.2.1)$, we can derive $E(a.2)$; together with $R(a, a.2)$ and the last DL-clause from $\Xi(\mathcal{K}_5)$, we get a contradiction. Even without inverse roles, DL-clauses can propagate information from successors to predecessors.

5   Implementation

Based on the calculus from Section 4, we have implemented a prototype DL reasoner.[1] Currently, it can only handle Horn DL-clauses—our main goal was to show that significant performance improvements can be gained by exploiting the deterministic nature of many ontologies.

To classify a knowledge base $\mathcal{K}$, we run our algorithm on $\mathcal{K}_i = \mathcal{K} \cup \{C_i(a_i)\}$ for each concept C_i, obtaining an ABox $\mathcal{A}_i$. If $D(a_i) \in \mathcal{A}_i$ and $D(a_i)$ was derived without making any nondeterministic choices, then $\mathcal{K} \models C_i \sqsubseteq D$. Since our test ontologies are translated to Horn DL-clauses on which our algorithm is deterministic, $D(a_i) \in \mathcal{A}_i$ iff $\mathcal{K} \models C_i \sqsubseteq D$. Thus, we can classify $\mathcal{K}$ with a linear number of calls to our algorithm. This optimization is also applicable in standard tableau calculi; the nondeterministic handling of GCIs, however, diminishes its value.

We also employ the following optimization: when applying the calculus to $\mathcal{K}_i$, we use the nonblocked individuals from Γ_i as potential blockers, where Γ_i is the union of all satisfiable ABoxes $\mathcal{A}_j$ for $j < i$. Namely, assume that we run our algorithm on $\mathcal{K}'_i = \mathcal{K} \cup \{C_i(a_i)\} \cup \Gamma_i$, where a_i is fresh. In $\mathcal{SHIQ}$, a_i cannot interact with Γ_i; furthermore Γ_i is satisfiable, so $\mathcal{K} \models C_i \sqsubseteq D$ iff our

---

[1] http://www.cs.man.ac.uk/∼ bmotik/HermiT/

Table 5. Results of Performance Evaluation

Ontology	HT	HT-anc	Pellet	FaCT++	Racer
NCI	8 s	9 s	44 min	32 s	36 s
GALEN original	44 s	—	—	—	—
GALEN simplified	7 s	104 s	—	859 s	—

algorithm derives $D(a_i)$ from $\mathcal{K}'_i$. Thus, due to anywhere blocking, we can use the nonblocked individuals from Γ_i as blockers without affecting the correctness of our algorithm. This optimization is applicable even if nondeterministic choices were made in deriving $\mathcal{A}_j$, it is easy to implement, and, like *caching* [2, Chapter 9], it greatly reduces the time needed to classify an ontology since it prevents the computation of the same subtrees in different runs.

Table 5 shows the times that our reasoner, Pellet 1.3, FaCT++ 1.1.4, and Racer 1.9.0 take to classify our test ontologies. To isolate the improvements due to each of the two innovations of our algorithm, we evaluated our system with anywhere blocking (denoted as HT), as well as with ancestor blocking [10] (denoted as HT-anc). All ontologies are available from our reasoner's Web page.

NCI is a relatively large (about 23000 atomic concepts) but simple ontology. FaCT++ and RACER can classify NCI in a short time mainly due to an optimization which eliminates many unnecessary tests, and the fact that all axioms in NCI are definitional so they are handled efficiently by absorption. We conjecture that Pellet is slower by two orders of magnitude because it does not use these optimizations, so it must deal with disjunctions.

GALEN has often been used as a benchmark for DL reasoning. The original version of GALEN contains about 2700 atomic concepts and many GCIs similar to (2). Most GCIs cannot be absorbed without any residual nondeterminism. Thus, the ontology is hard because it requires the generation of large models with many nondeterministic choices. Hence, GALEN has been simplified by removing 273 axioms, and this simplified version of GALEN has commonly been used for performance testing. As Table 5 shows, only HT can classify the original version of GALEN. In particular, anywhere blocking prevents our reasoner from generating the same fragments of a model in different branches.

6   Conclusion

In this paper, we presented a novel reasoning algorithm for DLs that combines hyper-inferences to reduce the nondeterminism due to GCIs with anywhere blocking to reduce the sizes of generated models. In future, we shall extend our reasoner to handle disjunction and conduct a more comprehensive performance evaluation. Furthermore, we shall investigate the possibilities of optimizing the blocking condition and heuristically guiding the model construction to further reduce the sizes of the models created. Finally, we shall try to extend our approach to the DLs $\mathcal{SHOIQ}$ and $\mathcal{SROIQ}$, which provide the logical underpinning of the Semantic Web ontology languages.

References

1. Baader, F., Buchheit, M., Hollunder, B.: Cardinality Restrictions on Concepts. Artificial Intelligence 88(1–2), 195–213 (1996)
2. Baader, F., Calvanese, D., McGuinness, D., Nardi, D., Patel-Schneider, P.F.: The Description Logic Handbook. Cambridge University Press, Cambridge (2003)
3. Baumgartner, P., Furbach, U., Niemelä, I.: Hyper Tableaux. In: Orłowska, E., Alferes, J.J., Moniz Pereira, L. (eds.) JELIA 1996. LNCS, vol. 1126, pp. 1–17. Springer, Heidelberg (1996)
4. Donini, F.M., Massacci, F.: EXPTIME tableaux for ALC. Artificial Intelligence 124(1), 87–138 (2000)
5. Fermüller, C., Tammet, T., Zamov, N., Leitsch, A.: Resolution Methods for the Decision Problem. LNCS, vol. 679. Springer, Heidelberg (1993)
6. Fermüller, C.G., Leitsch, A., Hustadt, U., Tammet, T.: Resolution Decision Procedures. In: Robinson, A., Voronkov, A. (eds.) Handbook of Automated Reasoning (chapter 25), vol. II, pp. 1791–1849. Elsevier, Amsterdam (2001)
7. Goré, R.P., Nguyen, L.: EXPTIME Tableaux with Global Caching for Description Logics with Transitive Roles, Inverse Roles and Role Hierarchies. In: Olivetti, N. (ed.) TABLEAUX 2007. LNCS, vol. 4548, Springer, Heidelberg (2007)
8. Haarslev, V., Möller, R.: RACER System Description. In: Goré, R.P., Leitsch, A., Nipkow, T. (eds.) IJCAR 2001. LNCS (LNAI), vol. 2083, pp. 701–706. Springer, Heidelberg (2001)
9. Horrocks, I., Sattler, U.: A Description Logic with Transitive and Inverse Roles and Role Hierarchies. Journal of Logic and Computation 9(3), 385–410 (1999)
10. Horrocks, I., Sattler, U., Tobies, S.: Reasoning with Individuals for the Description Logic SHIQ. In: McAllester, D. (ed.) Automated Deduction - CADE-17. LNCS, vol. 1831, pp. 482–496. Springer, Heidelberg (2000)
11. Hudek, A.K., Weddell, G.: Binary Absorption in Tableaux-Based Reasoning for Description Logics. In: Proc. DL, Windermere, UK (May 30-June 1, 2006)
12. Hustadt, U., Motik, B., Sattler, U.: Data Complexity of Reasoning in Very Expressive Description Logics. In: Proc. IJCAI 2005, pp. 466–471, Edinburgh, UK (July 30-August 5, 2005)
13. Krötzsch, M., Rudolph, S., Hitzler, P.: Complexity Boundaries for Horn Description Logics. In: Proc. AAAI 2007, Vancouver, BC, Canada, July 22-26, 2007, AAAI Press (to appear)
14. Motik, B.: Reasoning in Description Logics using Resolution and Deductive Databases. PhD thesis, Universität Karlsruhe, Germany (2006)
15. Parsia, B., Sirin, E.: Pellet: An OWL-DL Reasoner. In: McIlraith, S.A., Plexousakis, D., van Harmelen, F. (eds.) ISWC 2004. LNCS, vol. 3298, Springer, Heidelberg (2004)
16. Plaisted, D.A., Greenbaum, S.: A Structure-Preserving Clause Form Translation. Journal of Symbolic Logic and Computation 2(3), 293–304 (1986)
17. Robinson, A.: Automatic Deduction with Hyper-Resolution. Int. Journal of Computer Mathematics 1, 227–234 (1965)
18. Schmidt, R.A., Hustadt, U.: A Principle for Incorporating Axioms into the First-Order Translation of Modal Formulae. In: Baader, F. (ed.) Automated Deduction – CADE-19. LNCS (LNAI), vol. 2741, pp. 412–426. Springer, Heidelberg (2003)

19. Tobies, S.: Complexity Results and Practical Algorithms for Logics in Knowledge Representation. PhD thesis, RWTH Aachen, Germany (2001)
20. Tsarkov, D., Horrocks, I.: Efficient Reasoning with Range and Domain Constraints. In: Proc. DL 2004, Whistler, BC, Canada (June 6-8, 2004)
21. Tsarkov, D., Horrocks, I.: FaCT++ Description Logic Reasoner: System Description. In: Furbach, U., Shankar, N. (eds.) IJCAR 2006. LNCS (LNAI), vol. 4130, pp. 292–297. Springer, Heidelberg (2006)

Conservative Extensions in the Lightweight Description Logic $\mathcal{EL}$

Carsten Lutz[1] and Frank Wolter[2]

[1] Institute for Theoretical Computer Science, TU Dresden, Germany
[2] Department of Computer Science, University of Liverpool, UK
lutz@tcs.inf.tu-dresden.de,frank@csc.liv.ac.uk

Abstract. We bring together two recent trends in description logic (DL): *lightweight DLs* in which the subsumption problem is tractable and *conservative extensions* as a central tool for formalizing notions of ontology design such as refinement and modularity. Our aim is to investigate conservative extensions as an automated reasoning problem for the basic tractable DL $\mathcal{EL}$. The main result is that deciding (deductive) conservative extensions is EXPTIME-complete, thus more difficult than subsumption in $\mathcal{EL}$, but not more difficult than subsumption in expressive DLs. We also show that if conservative extensions are defined model-theoretically, the associated decision problem for $\mathcal{EL}$ is undecidable.

1 Introduction

In recent years, lightweight description logics (DLs) have gained increased popularity. In particular, a number of useful lightweight DLs have been identified for which reasoning is tractable even w.r.t. general TBoxes (i.e., sets of subsumptions between concepts). Such DLs are used in the formulation of large-scale ontologies, which usually require a high level of abstraction and consequently use only limited expressive power from a DL. There are currently two main lines of research on lightweight DLs: the $\mathcal{EL}$ family of tractable DLs investigated in [5,2] aims at providing a logical underpinning of lightweight ontology languages, with a special emphasis on life science ontologies. In contrast, the main purpose of the DL-Lite family of tractable DLs investigated in [7,8] is to allow efficient reasoning about conceptual database schemas, and to exploit existing DBMSs for DL reasoning. In this paper, we will be interested in applications of DLs for ontology design, and thus consider $\mathcal{EL}$ as our basic tractable DL. The main reasoning problem in $\mathcal{EL}$ is *subsumption*, i.e., deciding whether one concept subsumes another one w.r.t. a general TBox. Intuitively, such a TBox can be thought of as a logical theory providing a description of the application domain. In the following, we use the terms "general TBox" and "ontology" interchangeably.

There are a number of important life science ontologies that are formulated in $\mathcal{EL}$ or mild extensions thereof. Examples include the Systematized Nomenclature of Medicine, Clinical Terms (SNOMED CT), which comprises ~0.5 million concepts and underlies the systematized medical terminology used in the health

F. Pfenning (Ed.): CADE 2007, LNAI 4603, pp. 84–99, 2007.

systems of the US, the UK, and other countries [16]; and the thesaurus of the US national cancer institute (NCI), which comprises ~45.000 concepts and is intended to become the reference terminology for cancer research [15]. With ontologies of this size, a principled approach to their design and maintenance is indispensible, and automated reasoning support is highly welcome.

Recently, conservative extensions have been identified as a fundamental notion when formalizing central issues of ontology design such as refinement and modularity [1,10,13,11,12]. Unless otherwise noted, we refer to the deductive version of conservative extensions: the extension $\mathcal{T}_1 \cup \mathcal{T}_2$ of an ontology $\mathcal{T}_1$ is conservative if $\mathcal{T}_1 \cup \mathcal{T}_2$ implies no new subsumptions in the signature of $\mathcal{T}_1$, i.e., every subsumption $C \sqsubseteq D$ that is implied by $\mathcal{T}_1 \cup \mathcal{T}_2$ and where the concepts C and D use only symbols (concept and role names) from $\mathcal{T}_1$ is already implied by $\mathcal{T}_1$.

We briefly sketch how conservative extensions can help to formalize ontology refinement and modularity. *Refinement* means to add more details to a part of the ontology that has not yet been sufficiently described. Intuitively, such a refinement should provide more detailed information about the meaning of concepts of the original ontology, but it should not affect the relationship between such concepts. This requirement can be formalized by demanding that the refined ontology is a conservative extension of the original ontology. The main benefits of *modularity* of ontologies are that changes to the ontology have only local impact, and that modules from an ontology can be re-used in other ontologies. Intuitively, a module inside an ontology should be self-contained in the sense that it contains all the relevant information about the concepts it uses. Formally, this can be captured by requiring that a module inside an ontology $\mathcal{T}$ is a subset $\mathcal{T}'$ of $\mathcal{T}$ such that $\mathcal{T}$ is a conservative extension of $\mathcal{T}'$. See e.g.[11] for more details.

In [10,13], it was proposed to provide automated reasoning support for conservative extensions. For example, if an ontology designer intends to refine his ontology, he may use an automated reasoning tool capable of deciding conservative extensions to check whether his modifications really had no impact on relationships between concepts in the original ontology. The complexity of deciding conservative extensions is usually rather high. For example, it is 2-ExpTime complete in expressive DLs such as $\mathcal{ALC}$ and $\mathcal{ALCQI}$ and even undecidable in $\mathcal{ALCQIO}$ [10,13]; recall that subsumption is decidable in ExpTime and, respectively, NExpTime for those logics.

In this paper, we study conservative extensions in the basic tractable description logic $\mathcal{EL}$. This is motivated by the observation that large-scale ontologies are often formulated in such lightweight DLs, and large-scale ontologies is also where issues of refinement and modularity play the most important role. We provide an alternative characterization of conservative extension in $\mathcal{EL}$, and use this characterization to provide a decision procedure. It is interesting to note that decision procedures for deciding conservative extensions in more expressive DLs such as $\mathcal{ALC}$ can *not* be used for $\mathcal{EL}$, see Section 2 for an example illustrating this effect. We show that our algorithm runs in deterministic exponential time, and prove a matching lower bound. Thus, deciding conservative extension in $\mathcal{EL}$ is

EXPTIME-complete and not tractable like subsumption in $\mathcal{EL}$. However, it is also not more difficult than subsumption in expressive DLs such as $\mathcal{ALC}$ and $\mathcal{ALCQI}$, problems that are considered manageable in practice. We also consider a stronger, model theoretic notion of conservative extensions that is useful for query answering and prove that the associated decision problem for $\mathcal{EL}$ is undecidable.

In this version of the paper, many proof details are omitted for brevity. They can be found in the full version [14].

2 $\mathcal{EL}$ and Conservative Extensions

Let $\mathsf{N_C}$ and $\mathsf{N_R}$ be countably infinite and disjoint sets of *concept names* and *role names*, respectively. $\mathcal{EL}$-*concepts* C are built according to the syntax rule $C ::= \top \mid A \mid C \sqcap D \mid \exists r.C$, where A ranges over $\mathsf{N_C}$, r ranges over $\mathsf{N_R}$, and C, D range over $\mathcal{EL}$-concepts. The semantics is defined by means of an *interpretation* $\mathcal{I} = (\Delta^{\mathcal{I}}, \cdot^{\mathcal{I}})$, where the interpretation *domain* $\Delta^{\mathcal{I}}$ is a non-empty set, and $\cdot^{\mathcal{I}}$ is a function mapping each concept name A to a subset $A^{\mathcal{I}}$ of $\Delta^{\mathcal{I}}$ and each role name $r^{\mathcal{I}}$ to a binary relation $r^{\mathcal{I}} \subseteq \Delta^{\mathcal{I}} \times \Delta^{\mathcal{I}}$. The function $\cdot^{\mathcal{I}}$ is inductively extended to arbitrary concepts by setting $\top^{\mathcal{I}} := \Delta^{\mathcal{I}}$, $(C \sqcap D)^{\mathcal{I}} := C^{\mathcal{I}} \cap D^{\mathcal{I}}$, and $(\exists r.C)^{\mathcal{I}} := \{d \in \Delta^{\mathcal{I}} \mid \exists e \in C^{\mathcal{I}} : (d, e) \in r^{\mathcal{I}}\}$.

A *TBox* is a finite set of *concept inclusions (CIs)* $C \sqsubseteq D$, where C and D are concepts. An interpretation $\mathcal{I}$ *satisfies* a CI $C \sqsubseteq D$ (written $\mathcal{I} \models C \sqsubseteq D$) if $C^{\mathcal{I}} \subseteq D^{\mathcal{I}}$. $\mathcal{I}$ is a *model* of a TBox $\mathcal{T}$ if it satisfies all CIs in $\mathcal{T}$. We write $\mathcal{T} \models C \sqsubseteq D$ if every model of $\mathcal{T}$ satisfies $C \sqsubseteq D$. Here is an example TBox $\mathcal{T}_1$:

$$\mathsf{Human} \sqsubseteq \exists \mathsf{eats}.\top$$
$$\mathsf{Plant} \sqsubseteq \exists \mathsf{grows\text{-}in}.\mathsf{Area}$$
$$\mathsf{Vegetarian} \sqsubseteq \mathsf{Healthy}$$

A *signature* Σ is a finite subset of $\mathsf{N_C} \cup \mathsf{N_R}$. The signature $\mathsf{sig}(C)$ ($\mathsf{sig}(\mathcal{T})$) of a concept C (TBox $\mathcal{T}$) is the set of concept and role names which occur in C (in $\mathcal{T}$). If $\mathsf{sig}(C) = \Sigma$, we also call C a Σ-*concept*. Let $\mathcal{T}_1$ and $\mathcal{T}_2$ be TBoxes. We call $\mathcal{T}_1 \cup \mathcal{T}_2$ a *conservative extension* of $\mathcal{T}_1$ if $\mathcal{T}_1 \cup \mathcal{T}_2 \models C \sqsubseteq D$ implies $\mathcal{T}_1 \models C \sqsubseteq D$ for all $\mathsf{sig}(\mathcal{T}_1)$-concepts C, D. If C, D violate this condition (and thus, $\mathcal{T}_1 \cup \mathcal{T}_2$ is not a conservative extension of $\mathcal{T}_1$), then $C \sqsubseteq D$ is called a *counter-subsumption*. As an example, consider the following TBox $\mathcal{T}_2$:

$$\mathsf{Human} \sqsubseteq \exists \mathsf{eats}.\mathsf{Food}$$
$$\mathsf{Food} \sqcap \mathsf{Plant} \sqsubseteq \mathsf{Vegetarian}$$

It is not too difficult to verify that $\mathcal{T}_1 \cup \mathcal{T}_2$ is a conservative extension of $\mathcal{T}_1$, where $\mathcal{T}_1$ is the TBox defined above. Unsurprisingly, the notion of a conservative extension strongly depends on the description logic used. For example, $\mathcal{ALC}$ is the extension of $\mathcal{EL}$ with a negation constructor $\neg C$, which has the obvious semantics $(\neg C)^{\mathcal{I}} = \Delta^{\mathcal{I}} \setminus C^{\mathcal{I}}$. In $\mathcal{ALC}$, $\forall r.C$ is an abbreviation for $\neg \exists r.\neg C$. If we view the TBoxes $\mathcal{T}_1$ and $\mathcal{T}_2$ from above as $\mathcal{ALC}$ TBoxes, then $\mathcal{T}_1 \cup \mathcal{T}_2$ is not a conservative extension of $\mathcal{T}_1$, with counter-subsumption

$$\mathsf{Human} \sqcap \forall \mathsf{eats}.\mathsf{Plant} \sqsubseteq \exists \mathsf{eats}.\mathsf{Vegetarian}.$$

This shows that we cannot use the existing algorithms for conservative extensions in $\mathcal{ALC}$ [10] to decide conservative extensions in $\mathcal{EL}$.

Another initial observation about conservative extensions in $\mathcal{EL}$ is that minimal counter-subsumptions may be quite large. Define a TBox $\mathcal{T}$ such that it contains only tautologies and $\mathrm{sig}(\mathcal{T}) = \{A, B, r, s\}$. For each $n \geq 0$, we define a TBox $\mathcal{T}'_n$. It has additional concept names $X_0, \ldots, X_{n-1}$ and $\overline{X}_0, \ldots, \overline{X}_{n-1}$ that are used to represent a binary counter X: if X_i is true, then the i-th bit is positive and if $\overline{X}_i$ is true, then it is negative. Define $\mathcal{T}'_n$ as

$$A \sqsubseteq \overline{X}_0 \sqcap \cdots \sqcap \overline{X}_{n-1}$$

$$\textstyle\bigsqcap_{\sigma \in \{r,s\}} \exists \sigma.(\overline{X}_i \sqcap X_0 \sqcap \cdots \sqcap X_{i-1}) \sqsubseteq X_i \qquad \text{for all } i < n$$

$$\textstyle\bigsqcap_{\sigma \in \{r,s\}} \exists \sigma.(X_i \sqcap X_0 \sqcap \cdots \sqcap X_{i-1}) \sqsubseteq \overline{X}_i \qquad \text{for all } i < n$$

$$\textstyle\bigsqcap_{\sigma \in \{r,s\}} \exists \sigma.(\overline{X}_i \sqcap \overline{X}_j) \sqsubseteq \overline{X}_i \qquad \text{for all } j < i < n$$

$$\textstyle\bigsqcap_{\sigma \in \{r,s\}} \exists \sigma.(X_i \sqcap \overline{X}_j) \sqsubseteq X_i \qquad \text{for all } j < i < n$$

$$X_0 \sqcap \cdots \sqcap X_{n-1} \sqsubseteq B$$

Observe that Lines 2-5 implement incrementation of the counter X. Then the smallest new consequence of $\mathcal{T} \cup \mathcal{T}'_n$ is $C_{2^n-1} \sqsubseteq B$, where:

$$C_0 = A$$
$$C_i = \exists r.C_{i-1} \sqcap \exists s.C_{i-1}$$

Clearly, C_{2^n-1} is doubly exponentially large in the size of $\mathcal{T}$ and $\mathcal{T}'_n$. If we use structure sharing (i.e., define the size of C_{2^n-1} as the number of its distinct subconcepts), it is still exponentially large.

3 Characterizing Conservative Extensions

We provide a characterization of when a TBox $\mathcal{T}_1 \cup \mathcal{T}_2$ is not a conservative extension of $\mathcal{T}_1$. This characterization is used in the subsequent section to devise a decision procedure for (non-)conservative extensions in $\mathcal{EL}$.

Let $\mathcal{I}_1$ and $\mathcal{I}_2$ be interpretations and Σ a signature. A relation $S \subseteq \Delta^{\mathcal{I}_1} \times \Delta^{\mathcal{I}_2}$ is a Σ-simulation from $\mathcal{I}_1$ to $\mathcal{I}_2$ if the following holds:

- for all concept names $A \in \Sigma$ and all $(d_1, d_2) \in S$ with $d_1 \in A^{\mathcal{I}_1}$, $d_2 \in A^{\mathcal{I}_2}$;
- for all role names $r \in \Sigma$, all $(d_1, d_2) \in S$, and all $e_1 \in \Delta^{\mathcal{I}_1}$ with $(d_1, e_1) \in r^{\mathcal{I}_1}$, there exists $e_2 \in \Delta^{\mathcal{I}_2}$ such that $(d_2, e_2) \in r^{\mathcal{I}_2}$ and $(e_1, e_2) \in S$.

If $d_1 \in \Delta^{\mathcal{I}_1}$, $d_2 \in \Delta^{\mathcal{I}_2}$, and there is a Σ-simulation S from $\mathcal{I}_1$ to $\mathcal{I}_2$ with $(d_1, d_2) \in S$, then $(\mathcal{I}_2, d_2)$ Σ-simulates $(\mathcal{I}_1, d_1)$, written $(\mathcal{I}_1, d_1) \leq_\Sigma (\mathcal{I}_2, d_2)$. If $\Sigma = \mathsf{N_C} \cup \mathsf{N_R}$, we simply speak of a simulation and write $\leq$ instead of $\leq_\Sigma$. Let $\mathcal{I}$ be an interpretation, Σ a signature, and $d \in \Delta^{\mathcal{I}}$. Then we define the abbreviation $d^{\Sigma,\mathcal{I}} := \{C \mid d \in C^{\mathcal{I}} \wedge \mathrm{sig}(C) \subseteq \Sigma\}$. The out-degree of an interpretation $\mathcal{I}$ is the supremum of the cardinalities of the sets $\{d' \mid (d, d') \in r^{\mathcal{I}}\}$, for $d \in \Delta^{\mathcal{I}}$ and $r \in \mathsf{N_R}$. The following theorem establishes a connection between simulations and $\mathcal{EL}$ formulas. The proof is standard, and therefore omitted, see e.g. [9].

Theorem 1. *If $(\mathcal{I}_1, d_1) \leq_\Sigma (\mathcal{I}_2, d_2)$, then $d_1^{\Sigma, \mathcal{I}_1} \subseteq d_2^{\Sigma, \mathcal{I}_2}$. Conversely, if $\mathcal{I}_1$ and $\mathcal{I}_2$ have finite out-degree and $d_1^{\Sigma, \mathcal{I}_1} \subseteq d_2^{\Sigma, \mathcal{I}_2}$, then $(\mathcal{I}_1, d_1) \leq_\Sigma (\mathcal{I}_2, d_2)$.*

We use $\mathsf{sub}(C)$ to denote the set of subconcepts of a concept C. As usual, this set contains C itself. For a TBox $\mathcal{T}$, we denote by $\mathsf{sub}(\mathcal{T})$ the set of all subconcepts of concepts which occur in $\mathcal{T}$. With each concept C and TBox $\mathcal{T}$, we associate two sets of consequences that will play a central role in what follows.

- $K_\mathcal{T}(C) = \{D \in \mathsf{sub}(\mathcal{T}) \mid \mathcal{T} \models C \sqsubseteq D\};$
- $L_\mathcal{T}(C) = \{D \in \mathsf{sub}(C) \mid \mathcal{T} \models C \sqsubseteq D\} \cup K_\mathcal{T}(C).$

By the results in [5], both sets can be computed in time polynomial in the size of C and $\mathcal{T}$. The *canonical model* $\mathcal{I}_{C,\mathcal{T}} = (\Delta^{C,\mathcal{T}}, \cdot^{C,\mathcal{T}})$ of C and $\mathcal{T}$ is defined as follows, where A ranges over all elements of $\mathsf{N_C}$ and r over all elements of $\mathsf{N_R}$:

- $\Delta^{C,\mathcal{T}} = \{C\} \cup \{C' \mid \exists r.C' \in \mathsf{sub}(C) \cup \mathsf{sub}(\mathcal{T})\};$
- $D \in A^{\mathcal{I}_{C,\mathcal{T}}}$ iff $A \in L_\mathcal{T}(D);$
- $(D, D') \in r^{\mathcal{I}_{C,\mathcal{T}}}$ iff $\exists r.D' \in K_\mathcal{T}(D)$ or $D = E \sqcap \exists r.D'$, for some concept E.

The model $\mathcal{I}_{C,\mathcal{T}}$ is a subtle refinement of the data structure generated by the algorithms in [5,2] to prove correctness of the algorithm in [2].[1] Since the sets $L_\mathcal{T}(C)$ and $K_\mathcal{T}(C)$ can be computed in polytime, the model $\mathcal{I}_{C,\mathcal{T}}$ can also be computed in time polynomial in the size of C and $\mathcal{T}$.

Lemma 1. *Let $\mathcal{T}$ be a TBox and C a concept. For all $D \in \Delta^{C,\mathcal{T}}$ and all $E \in \mathsf{sub}(C) \cup \mathsf{sub}(\mathcal{T})$, we have $D \in E^{\mathcal{I}_{C,\mathcal{T}}}$ iff $\mathcal{T} \models D \sqsubseteq E$.*

Lemma 1 implies that $\mathcal{I}_{C,\mathcal{T}}$ is a model of $\mathcal{T}$, and that $C \in C^{\mathcal{I}_{C,\mathcal{T}}}$. The following lemma summarizes the most important properties of canonical models. Regarding Points 1 and 2, similar (but simpler) lemmas for the case of $\mathcal{EL}$ without TBoxes have been established in [3].

Lemma 2. *Let C, C_1, C_2, D be $\mathcal{EL}$-concepts and $\mathcal{T}$ a TBox. Then the following holds:*

1. *For all models $\mathcal{I}$ of $\mathcal{T}$ and all $d \in \Delta^\mathcal{I}$, the following conditions are equivalent:*
   (a) $d \in C^\mathcal{I};$
   (b) $(\mathcal{I}_{C,\mathcal{T}}, C) \leq (\mathcal{I}, d).$
2. *The following conditions are equivalent:*
   (a) $\mathcal{T} \models C \sqsubseteq D;$
   (b) $C \in D^{\mathcal{I}_{C,\mathcal{T}}};$
   (c) $(\mathcal{I}_{D,\mathcal{T}}, D) \leq (\mathcal{I}_{C,\mathcal{T}}, C).$
3. *If $\exists r.D \in (\mathsf{sub}(C_i) \cup \mathsf{sub}(\mathcal{T}))$ for all $i \in \{1, 2\}$, then $(\mathcal{I}_{C_1,\mathcal{T}}, D) \leq (\mathcal{I}_{C_2,\mathcal{T}}, D)$.*

Let $\mathcal{T}_1, \mathcal{T}_2$ be TBoxes, C a $\mathsf{sig}(\mathcal{T}_1)$-concept, and D a $\mathsf{sig}(\mathcal{T}_1) \cup \mathsf{sig}(\mathcal{T}_2)$-concept. We write $C \Rightarrow_1 D$ if, for all $\mathsf{sig}(\mathcal{T}_1)$-concepts E, $\mathcal{T}_1 \cup \mathcal{T}_2 \models D \sqsubseteq E$ implies $\mathcal{T}_1 \models C \sqsubseteq E$. Our characterization of non-conservative extensions, as stated by the following lemma, is based on this relation. The main benefit of this characterization is that when checking for new subsumptions $\mathcal{T}_1 \cup \mathcal{T}_2 \models C \sqsubseteq D$, it allows

---

[1] Essentially, in those papers we have $(D, D') \in r^{\mathcal{I}_{C,\mathcal{T}}}$ iff $\exists r.D' \in L_\mathcal{T}(D)$.

us to concentrate on concepts D of a very simple form, namely subconcepts of T_1 and T_2. This is achieved by considering $\mathsf{sig}(T_1) \cup \mathsf{sig}(T_2)$-concepts instead of $\mathsf{sig}(T_1)$-concepts as in the definition of conservative extensions. In addition, the characterization provides a bound on the *outdegree* of C, i.e., the maximum cardinality of any set P of pairs of the form (r, C'), with r a role name and C' a concept, such that $\prod_{(r,C') \in P} \exists r.C' \in \mathsf{sub}(C)$. We use $|C|$ and $|T|$ to denote the *length* of a concept C and a TBox T, i.e., the number of symbols needed to write it.

Lemma 3. $T_1 \cup T_2$ *is not a conservative extension of* T_1 *iff there exists a* $\mathsf{sig}(T_1)$-*concept* C *and a concept* $D \in \mathsf{sub}(T_1 \cup T_2)$ *such that*

(a) $T_1 \cup T_2 \models C \sqsubseteq D$;
(b) $C \not\Rightarrow_1 D$;
(c) *the outdegree of* C *is bounded by* $|T_1 \cup T_2|$.

Proof. "$\Leftarrow$". Assume that (a) to (c) are satisfied. By (b), there is a concept E with $T_1 \cup T_2 \models D \sqsubseteq E$ and $T_1 \not\models C \sqsubseteq E$. From the former and (a), we get $T_1 \cup T_2 \models C \sqsubseteq E$, which implies that $T_1 \cup T_2$ is not a conservative extension of T_1.

"$\Rightarrow$". We give only a sketch and refer to the full version [14] for details. Assume that $T_1 \cup T_2$ is not a conservative extension of T_1. In this sketch, we show only (a) and (b). If there is a counter-subsumption $C \sqsubseteq D$ with $D \in \mathsf{sub}(T_1)$, then conditions (a) and (b) hold for C and D and we are done. Assume that no such counter-subsumption exists. Let $C \sqsubseteq D$ be a counter-subsumption such that D is of minimal length. Then D can be shown to be of the form $\exists r.D'$. Using Lemma 2, it is possible to prove that $T_1 \cup T_2 \models C \sqsubseteq \exists r.D'$ implies that one of the following holds:

1. there is a conjunct $\exists r.C'$ of C such that $T_1 \cup T_2 \models C' \sqsubseteq D'$;
2. there is $\exists r.C' \in \mathsf{sub}(T_1 \cup T_2)$ s.t. $T_1 \cup T_2 \models C \sqsubseteq \exists r.C'$ and $T_1 \cup T_2 \models C' \sqsubseteq D'$.

It is possible to show that Case 1 actually yields a contradiction to the minimal length of D. Thus, Case 2 applies. We show that the concepts C and $\exists r.C'$ (substituted for D) satisfy Conditions (a) and (b). First, $T_1 \cup T_2 \models C \sqsubseteq \exists r.C'$ establishes Condition (a). For Condition (b), observe that $T_1 \not\models C \sqsubseteq \exists r.D'$ and $T_1 \cup T_2 \models \exists r.C' \sqsubseteq \exists r.D'$. This means $C \not\Rightarrow_1 \exists r.C'$. $\qquad\square$

The following lemma characterizes the relation $C \Rightarrow_1 D$ semantically and shows that it can be decided in polytime.

Lemma 4. *Let* T_1, T_2 *be TBoxes and* C, D *concepts. Then we have* $C \Rightarrow_1 D$ *iff* $(\mathcal{I}_{D,T_1 \cup T_2}, D) \leq_{\mathsf{sig}(T_1)} (\mathcal{I}_{C,T_1}, C)$. *Hence, the problem* $C \Rightarrow_1 D$ *is decidable in polynomial time in the size of* C, D, *and* $T_1 \cup T_2$.

Proof. "$\Rightarrow$". Let $C \not\Rightarrow_1 D$. Then there is a $\mathsf{sig}(T_1)$-concept E such that $T_1 \cup T_2 \models D \sqsubseteq E$ and $T_1 \not\models C \sqsubseteq E$. By Point 2 of Lemma 2, this yields $D \in E^{\mathcal{I}_{D,T_1 \cup T_2}}$ and $C \notin E^{\mathcal{I}_{C,T_1}}$. Hence, by Theorem 1, $(\mathcal{I}_{D,T_1 \cup T_2}, D) \not\leq_{\mathsf{sig}(T_1)} (\mathcal{I}_{C,T_1}, C)$.

"$\Leftarrow$". Let $(\mathcal{I}_{D,\mathcal{T}_1 \cup \mathcal{T}_2}, D) \not\lesssim_{\text{sig}(\mathcal{T}_1)} (\mathcal{I}_{C,\mathcal{T}_1}, C)$. By Theorem 1, there exists E over $\text{sig}(\mathcal{T}_1)$ with $D \in E^{\mathcal{I}_{D,\mathcal{T}_1 \cup \mathcal{T}_2}}$ but $C \notin E^{\mathcal{I}_{C,\mathcal{T}_1}}$. By Point 2 of Lemma 2, $\mathcal{T}_1 \cup \mathcal{T}_2 \models D \sqsubseteq E$ and $\mathcal{T}_1 \not\models C \sqsubseteq E$. Hence, $C \not\Rightarrow_1 D$.

It is well-known that computing the largest Σ-simulation between two finite graphs can be done in polynomial time [9].   ❑

4   The Algorithm

We devise an algorithm for deciding (non)-conservative extensions in $\mathcal{EL}$, which is based on our characterization of not being a conservative extensions in terms of "$\Rightarrow_1$" (Lemma 3) and of "$\Rightarrow_1$" in terms of simulations (Lemma 4). To check whether $\mathcal{T}_1 \cup \mathcal{T}_2$ is not a conservative extension of $\mathcal{T}_1$, the algorithm searches for a $\text{sig}(\mathcal{T}_1)$-concept C such that for some $D \in \text{sub}(\mathcal{T}_1 \cup \mathcal{T}_2)$, the Points (a)–(c) of Lemma 3 are satisfied. Intuitively, it proceeds in rounds. In the first round, the algorithm considers the case where C is a conjunction of concept names. For every such C and all $D \in \text{sub}(\mathcal{T}_1 \cup \mathcal{T}_2)$, it checks whether Points (a) and (b) are satisfied. By Lemma 4, this can be done in polytime. If all tests fail, the second round is started in which the algorithm considers concepts C of the form $F_0 \sqcap \bigsqcap_{(r,E) \in P} \exists r.E$, where F_0 is a conjunction of concept names and P is a set of pairs (r, E) with r a role name and E a candidate for C from the first round (i.e., E is also a conjunction of concept names). Because of Point (c), it will be sufficient to consider sets P of cardinality bounded by $|\mathcal{T}_1 \cup \mathcal{T}_2|$. To check if such a concept C satisfies Points (a) and (b), we exploit the information that we have gained about the concepts E in the previous round. If again no suitable C is found, then in the third round we use the Cs from the second round as the Es in $F_0 \sqcap \bigsqcap_{(r,E) \in P} \exists r.E$, and so on.

For the algorithm to terminate and run in exponential time, we have to introduce a condition that indicates when enough candidates C have been inspected in order to know that there is no counter-subsumption $C \sqsubseteq D$. To obtain such a termination condition and to avoid having to deal with double exponentially large concepts, our algorithm will not construct the candidate concepts C directly, but rather use a certain data structure to represent relevant information about C. The relevant information about C is suggested by Lemma 3: for each C, we take the quadruple

$$C^\sharp = (F, K_{\mathcal{T}_1}(C), K_{\mathcal{T}_1 \cup \mathcal{T}_2}(C), K_{\mathcal{T}_1, \mathcal{T}_1 \cup \mathcal{T}_2}(C)),$$

where F is the conjunction of all concept names occurring in the top-level conjunction of C (if there are none, then $F = \top$), $K_{\mathcal{T}_1(C)}$ and $K_{\mathcal{T}_1 \cup \mathcal{T}_2}(C)$ are defined in the previous section, and $K_{\mathcal{T}_1, \mathcal{T}_1 \cup \mathcal{T}_2}(C) = \{D \in \text{sub}(\mathcal{T}_1 \cup \mathcal{T}_2) \mid C \Rightarrow_1 D\}$. We call this the *quadruple determined by* C.

By Lemma 3, the quadruple $C^\sharp$ determined by a concept C gives us enough information to decide whether C is the left hand side of a counter-subsumption. In addition, it contains enough information to enable the recursive search described above. This is exploited by our algorithm for deciding (non)-conservative extensions, which is shown in Figure 1. Observe that the Condition $\mathcal{Q}_2 \setminus \mathcal{Q}_3 \neq \emptyset$

Imput: TBoxes $\mathcal{T}_1$ and $\mathcal{T}_2$.

1. Compute the set $\mathcal{N}_0$ of quadruples determined by conjunctions of concept names from $\mathsf{sig}(\mathcal{T}_1)$.
2. if $\mathcal{N}_0$ contains a quadruple $(F, \mathcal{Q}_1, \mathcal{Q}_2, \mathcal{Q}_3)$ such that $\mathcal{Q}_2 \setminus \mathcal{Q}_3 \neq \emptyset$, then output "not conservative extension".
3. Generate the sequence $\mathcal{N}_1, \mathcal{N}_2, \ldots$ of quadruples such that $\mathcal{N}_{i+1} = \mathcal{N}_i \cup \mathcal{N}_i'$, where $\mathcal{N}_i'$ is the set of quadruples $(F_0, \mathcal{F}_1, \mathcal{F}_2, \mathcal{F}_3)$ which can be obtained from a conjunction F_0 of concept names from $\mathsf{sig}(\mathcal{T}_1)$ and a set $Q \subseteq (\mathsf{N_R} \cap \mathsf{sig}(\mathcal{T}_1)) \times \mathcal{N}_i$ of cardinality not exceeding $|\mathcal{T}_1 \cup \mathcal{T}_2|$ in the following way:

  – $\mathcal{F}_1 = K_{\mathcal{T}_1}(F_0 \sqcap \displaystyle\prod_{(r,(F,\mathcal{Q}_1,\mathcal{Q}_2,\mathcal{Q}_3)) \in Q} \exists r.(\prod_{D \in \mathcal{Q}_1} D));$

  – $\mathcal{F}_2 = K_{\mathcal{T}_1 \cup \mathcal{T}_2}(F_0 \sqcap \displaystyle\prod_{(r,(F,\mathcal{Q}_1,\mathcal{Q}_2,\mathcal{Q}_3)) \in Q} \exists r.(\prod_{D \in \mathcal{Q}_2} D));$

  – $\mathcal{F}_3 = \{D \mid D \in \mathsf{sub}(\mathcal{T}_1 \cup \mathcal{T}_2)$ and

      (a) for all $A \in \mathsf{sig}(\mathcal{T}_1)$, $A \in K_{\mathcal{T}_1 \cup \mathcal{T}_2}(D)$ implies $A \in \mathcal{F}_1$;

      (b) if $(D, D') \in r^{\mathcal{I}_{D,\mathcal{T}_1 \cup \mathcal{T}_2}}$ with $r \in \mathsf{sig}(\mathcal{T}_1)$, then
          (i) there is a tuple $(r, (F, \mathcal{Q}_1, \mathcal{Q}_2, \mathcal{Q}_3)) \in Q$ such that $D' \in \mathcal{Q}_3$
          or (ii) there is $\exists r.C' \in \mathcal{F}_1$ with $(\mathcal{I}_{D',\mathcal{T}_1 \cup \mathcal{T}_2}, D') \leq_{\mathsf{sig}(\mathcal{T}_1)} (\mathcal{I}_{C',\mathcal{T}_1}, C')$
  $\}$

This is done until $\mathcal{N}_i$ contains a quadruple $(F, \mathcal{Q}_1, \mathcal{Q}_2, \mathcal{Q}_3)$ such that $\mathcal{Q}_2 \setminus \mathcal{Q}_3 \neq \emptyset$, or $\mathcal{N}_{i+1} = \mathcal{N}_i$. Output "not conservative extension" if the first condition applies. Otherwise, output "conservative extension".

Fig. 1. Algorithm for deciding (non)-conservative extensions in $\mathcal{EL}$

corresponds to satisfaction of Points (a) and (b) in Lemma 3. Also observe that, in Point (b) of the definition of $\mathcal{F}_3$, we refer to the canonical model $\mathcal{I}_{D,\mathcal{T}_1 \cup \mathcal{T}_2}$ for the relevant concepts D. These models are constructed in polytime when needed. To show that this algorithm really implements the initial description given at the beginning of this section, we make explicit the concepts that we describe by means of the quadruples constructed in Step 3 of Figure 1. This is done by the following lemma, which will also be a central ingredient to our correctness proof.

Lemma 5. *Let $(F_0, \mathcal{F}_1, \mathcal{F}_2, \mathcal{F}_3)$ be the quadruple obtained from F_0 and Q in Figure 1. Let, for each $(r, q) \in Q$, $C_{r,q}$ be a concept which determines q. Then $C = F_0 \sqcap \prod_{(r,q) \in Q} \exists r.C_{r,q}$ determines $(F_0, \mathcal{F}_1, \mathcal{F}_2, \mathcal{F}_3)$.*

Proof. Let $(F_0, \mathcal{F}_1, \mathcal{F}_2, \mathcal{F}_3)$ and C be as in the lemma. It is trivial to see that F_0 is as required. To treat $\mathcal{F}_1$ and $\mathcal{F}_2$, we prove the following in [14]: for all TBoxes $\mathcal{T}$ and concepts $C' = F_0' \sqcap \prod_{(r,E) \in P} \exists r.E$ with F_0' a conjunction of concept names,

$$K_{\mathcal{T}}(C') = K_{\mathcal{T}}(F_0' \sqcap \prod_{(r,E) \in P} \exists r.(\prod_{D \in K_{\mathcal{T}}(E)} D)).$$

This implies that $\mathcal{F}_1$ and $\mathcal{F}_2$ are as required. It remains to consider $\mathcal{F}_3$. Fix $D \in \mathsf{sub}(\mathcal{T}_1 \cup \mathcal{T}_2)$. By Lemma 4, $C \Rightarrow_1 D$ iff $(\mathcal{I}_{D,\mathcal{T}_1 \cup \mathcal{T}_2}, D) \leq_{\mathsf{sig}(\mathcal{T}_1)} (\mathcal{I}_{C,\mathcal{T}_1}, C)$. By

definition of simulations and once more by Lemma 4, to check whether $C \Rightarrow_1 D$
it is sufficient to check both of the following:

1. for all concept names $A \in \mathsf{sig}(\mathcal{T}_1)$, $A \in K_{\mathcal{T}_1 \cup \mathcal{T}_2}(D)$ implies $A \in K_{\mathcal{T}_1}(C)$;
2. for all $r \in \mathsf{sig}(\mathcal{T}_1)$ and D' with $(D, D') \in r^{\mathcal{I}_{D, \mathcal{T}_1 \cup \mathcal{T}_2}}$ there exists C' with
   $(C, C') \in r^{\mathcal{I}_{C, \mathcal{T}_1}}$ and $(\mathcal{I}_{D, \mathcal{T}_1 \cup \mathcal{T}_2}, C') \leq_{\mathsf{sig}(\mathcal{T}_1)} (\mathcal{I}_{C, \mathcal{T}_1}, D')$.

Point 1 is checked under (a) since, as we have seen already, $K_{\mathcal{T}_1}(C) = \mathcal{F}_1$.
For Point 2, $(C, C') \in r^{\mathcal{I}_{C, \mathcal{T}_1}}$ and the definition of canonical models implies
that we have (i) $\exists r.C'$ is a conjunct of C or (ii) $\exists r.C' \in K_{\mathcal{T}_1}(C)$. In Case
(i), $C' = C_{r,q}$ for some $(r, q) \in Q$ and $C' \Rightarrow_1 D'$ iff D' is an element of the
fourth component of q. This is what is checked in (b.i) of the algorithm. In
Case (ii), $\exists r.C' \in \mathsf{sub}(\mathcal{T}_1)$ and thus we can use Point 3 of Lemma 1 to show that
$(\mathcal{I}_{D, \mathcal{T}_1 \cup \mathcal{T}_2}, C') \leq_{\mathsf{sig}(\mathcal{T}_1)} (\mathcal{I}_{C, \mathcal{T}_1}, D')$ iff $(\mathcal{I}_{D', \mathcal{T}_1 \cup \mathcal{T}_2}, D') \leq_{\mathsf{sig}(\mathcal{T}_1)} (\mathcal{I}_{C', \mathcal{T}_1}, C')$. This is
exactly what is checked in (b.ii) of the algorithm.   ❏

Theorem 2. *The algorithm for deciding non-conservative extensions is sound,
complete, and runs in exponential time.*

Proof. Soundness follows from Lemmas 3 and 5. For completeness, assume that
$\mathcal{T}_1 \cup \mathcal{T}_2$ is not a conservative extension of $\mathcal{T}_1$. By Lemma 3, there exists C of
outdegree not exceeding $|\mathcal{T}_1 \cup \mathcal{T}_2|$ and $D \in \mathsf{sub}(\mathcal{T}_1 \cup \mathcal{T}_2)$ such that $\mathcal{T}_1 \cup \mathcal{T}_2 \models C \sqsubseteq D$
and $C \not\Rightarrow_1 D$. If C is a conjunction of concept names, then the algorithm outputs
"not conservative extension" in Step 2. Now suppose C has quantifier depth
$n \geq 1$. Using Lemma 5, one can easily show by induction on i that for all
$i \geq 0$, the set $\mathcal{N}_i$ contains all quadruples determined by subconcepts C' of C of
quantifier depth smaller than i. Hence, the algorithm outputs "not conservative
extension" after computing some $\mathcal{N}_i$ with $i \leq n$.

For termination and complexity, observe that, by Lemma 4, the quadruple
determined by a conjunction of concept names from $\mathsf{sig}(\mathcal{T}_1)$ can be computed in
polytime. Hence Steps 1 and 2 run in exponential time. For Step 3 observe that
the number of tuples $(F, \mathcal{Q}_1, \mathcal{Q}_2, \mathcal{Q}_3)$ with F a conjunction of concept names from
$\mathsf{sig}(\mathcal{T}_1)$ and $\mathcal{Q}_i \subseteq \mathsf{sub}(\mathcal{T}_1 \cup \mathcal{T}_2)$ is bounded by $2^{4|\mathcal{T}_1 \cup \mathcal{T}_2|}$. It follows that $\mathcal{N}_i = \mathcal{N}_{i+1}$
for some $i \leq 2^{4|\mathcal{T}_1 \cup \mathcal{T}_2|}$. Hence, the algorithm terminates and to show that it runs
in exponential time it remains to check that $\mathcal{N}_{i+1}$ can be computed in exponential
time from $\mathcal{N}_i$. This follows from the following: first, the number of pairs (F_0, Q),
with F_0 a conjunction of concept names from $\mathsf{sig}(\mathcal{T}_1)$ and $Q \subseteq (\mathsf{N_R} \cap \mathsf{sig}(\mathcal{T}_1)) \times \mathcal{N}_i$
of cardinality not exceeding $|\mathcal{T}_1 \cup \mathcal{T}_2|$, is still only exponential in $|\mathcal{T}_1 \cup \mathcal{T}_2|$; and
second, the computation of $(F_0, \mathcal{F}_1, \mathcal{F}_2, \mathcal{F}_3)$ from F_0 and Q in Figure 1 can be
done in time polynomial in $|\mathcal{T}_1 \cup \mathcal{T}_2|$.   ❏

5   ExpTime-Hardness

We prove ExpTime-hardness of deciding conservative extensions in $\mathcal{EL}$ by reduction of the problem of determining whether a given player has a winning
strategy in the two-player game Peek introduced in [17] (the version G_4). An
instance of Peek is a tuple $(\Gamma_1, \Gamma_2, \Gamma_I, \varphi)$ where:

- Γ_1 and Γ_2 are disjoint, finite sets of Boolean variables, with the intended interpretation that the variables in Γ_1 are under the control of Player 1, and Γ_2 is under the control of Player 2;
- $\Gamma_I \subseteq (\Gamma_1 \cup \Gamma_2)$ are the variables true in the initial state of the game;
- φ is a propositional logic formula over the variables $\Gamma_1 \cup \Gamma_2$, representing the winning condition.

The game is played in a series of rounds, with the Players $i \in \{1, 2\}$ alternating (Player 1 moves first) to select a variable from Γ_i whose truth value is then flipped to reach the next game configuration. The game starts from the initial assignment defined by Γ_I. Variables that were not changed retain the same truth value in the subsequent configuration. A player may also make a skip move, i.e., not change any of its variables. Any player wins in a given round if he makes a move such that the resulting truth assignment defined by that round makes the winning formula φ true. The decision problem associated with Peek is to determine whether Player 1 has a winning strategy in a given game instance $(\Gamma_1, \Gamma_2, \Gamma_I, \varphi)$. A formal definition of winning strategies for this game can be found in [14].

Let us make precise the notion of a winning strategy. A *configuration* of G is a pair (t, p) where t is a truth assignment for the variables in $\Gamma_1 \cup \Gamma_2$ and $p \in \{1, 2\}$ indicates the player that has moved to reach the current configuration. A *winning strategy for Player 1* is a finite tree (V, E, ℓ) where ℓ is a node labelling function that assigns to each node a configuration of G. The labelling is such that

1. the root is labelled with $(\Gamma_I, 2)$;
2. if a node is labelled with $(t, 2)$ (i.e., Player 1 is to move), then it has a single successor labelled $(t', 1)$, where t' is obtained from t by switching the truth value of at most one variable from Γ_1;
3. if a node is labelled with $(t, 1)$ (i.e., Player 2 is to move), then its successors are labelled $(t_0, 1), \ldots, (t_\ell, 2)$, where $t_0, \ldots, t_\ell$ are the configurations of G that can be obtained from t by switching the truth value of at most one variable from Γ_2;
4. if a leaf is labelled (t, i), then $i = 1$ and t satisfies φ.

Note that if $\ell(v) = (t, i)$, then i is the player that has moved in order to reach configuration $\ell(v)$.

Given a game instance $G = (\Gamma_1, \Gamma_2, \Gamma_I, \varphi)$, we define TBoxes $\mathcal{T}_G$ and $\mathcal{T}'_G$ such that $\mathcal{T}_G \cup \mathcal{T}'_G$ is not a conservative extension of $\mathcal{T}_G$ iff Player 1 has a winning strategy in G. More precisely, $\mathcal{T}_G$ and $\mathcal{T}'_G$ are crafted such that witness subsumptions $C \sqsubseteq D$ against conservativity are such that (D is a concept name and) C describes a winning stategy for Player 1. Conversely, every winning strategy can be converted into a witness subsumption against conservativity. For convenience, we assume that the set of variables $\Gamma_1 \cup \Gamma_2$ is of the form $\{0, \ldots, n-1\}$ for some $n \geq 2$. In $\mathcal{T}_G$, we use the following concept and role names to describe a winning strategy (V, E, ℓ):

- the concept names $V_0, \ldots, V_{n-1}$ and $\overline{V}_0, \ldots, \overline{V}_{n-1}$ describe the t component of the configuration $\ell(v) = (t, p)$ associated with a node v, where V_i indicates that variable i is true, and $\overline{V}_i$ indicates that it is false;

- the concept names P_1, P_2 describe the p component of the configuration $\ell(v) = (t, p)$ associated with a node v;
- the concept names $F_0, \ldots, F_n$ denote the variable that is flipped to reach the configuration $\ell(v)$ associated with a node v, with F_n indicating a skip move;
- the role name r represents E.

We also use some auxiliary concept names that are introduced below. Among them the concept name B plays a special role: we will construct $\mathcal{T}_G$ and $\mathcal{T}'_G$ such that if $\mathcal{T}_G \cup \mathcal{T}'_G$ is not a conservative extension of $\mathcal{T}_G$, then there is a witness subsumption $C \sqsubseteq D$ with $D = B$.

We now assemble $\mathcal{T}_G$. We first say that the players alternate:

$$\exists r.P_1 \sqsubseteq P_2$$
$$\exists r.P_2 \sqsubseteq P_1$$

Then, we say that P_1 and P_2 should be disjoint. The idea is as follows: every concept C which enforces to make both P_1 and P_2 true somewhere in the model subsumes the special concept name B already w.r.t. $\mathcal{T}_G$, and thus cannot occur on the left-hand side of a witness subsumtion $C \sqsubseteq B$. The concept name M is used as a marker:

$$P_1 \sqcap P_2 \sqsubseteq M \qquad \exists r.M \sqsubseteq M \qquad M \sqsubseteq B$$

We also need disjointness conditions for truth values and flipping markers:

$$V_i \sqcap \overline{V}_i \sqsubseteq M \;\; \text{for all } i < n$$
$$F_i \sqcap F_j \sqsubseteq M \;\; \text{for all } i, j \leq n \text{ with } i \neq j$$

Next, we say that if the marker F_i is set, the variable V_i flips:

$$\exists r.(F_i \sqcap V_i) \sqsubseteq \overline{V}_i \;\; \text{for all } i < n$$
$$\exists r.(F_i \sqcap \overline{V}_i) \sqsubseteq V_i \;\; \text{for all } i < n$$

If a marker F_j for a different variable V_j is set, then V_i does not flip:

$$\exists r.(F_i \sqcap V_j) \sqsubseteq V_j \;\; \text{for all } i \leq n \text{ and } j < n \text{ with } i \neq j$$
$$\exists r.(F_i \sqcap \overline{V}_j) \sqsubseteq \overline{V}_j \;\; \text{for all } i < n \text{ and } j < n \text{ with } i \neq j$$

Additionally, we would like to ensure that at least one of the F_i markers is true. This cannot be done in a straightforward way in $\mathcal{T}_G$. We will use the TBox $\mathcal{T}'_G$, which we define next. W.l.o.g., we assume that φ is in NNF. We first translate the formula φ into a set of GCIs as follows. For each $\psi \in \mathsf{sub}(\varphi)$, we introduce a concept name X_ψ. For each $\psi \in \mathsf{sub}(\varphi)$, we use $\sigma(\psi)$ to denote

- the concept name X_ψ if ψ is a non-literal and
- the concept name from $V_0, \ldots, V_{n-1}, \overline{V}_0, \ldots, \overline{V}_{n-1}$ corresponding to ψ if ψ is a literal.

Now we can translate each non-literal $\psi \in \mathsf{sub}(\varphi)$ into GCIs:

- if $\psi = \vartheta \wedge \chi$, then the GCI is $\sigma(\vartheta) \sqcap \sigma(\chi) \sqsubseteq X_\psi$;
- if $\psi = \vartheta \vee \chi$, then the GCIs are $\sigma(\vartheta) \sqsubseteq X_\psi$ and $\sigma(\chi) \sqsubseteq X_\psi$.

We introduce concept names $N, N', N'', N_0, \ldots, N_{n-1}$ that will be used as markers. Let k be the cardinality of Γ_1. First we add markers that will help to ensure that (i) each variable has a truth value in every configuration, (ii) a least one of the flipping markers is set in every configuration, and (iii) the flipping marker denotes a variable controlled by the player whose turn it currently is:

$$V_i \sqsubseteq N_i \text{ for all } i < n \qquad \overline{V}_i \sqsubseteq N_i \text{ for all } i < n$$
$$F_i \sqsubseteq N' \text{ for all } i \in \{0, \ldots, k-1, n\} \qquad F_i \sqsubseteq N'' \text{ for all } i \in \{k, \ldots, n\}$$

Next, we set a marker if Player 1 has moved to reach a state in which φ is satisfied:

$$X_\varphi \sqcap P_1 \sqcap N' \sqcap N_0 \sqcap \cdots \sqcap N_{n-1} \sqsubseteq N$$

Then, the marker N is pulled up inductively ensuring that if Player 1 is to move, there is a single successor indicating the move of Player 1 recommended by the strategy; and if Player 2 is to move, there are $n - k + 1$ successors, one for each possible move of Player 2 (including the skip move):

$$P_1 \sqcap N' \sqcap N_0 \sqcap \cdots \sqcap N_{n-1} \sqcap \exists r.N \sqsubseteq N$$
$$P_2 \sqcap N'' \sqcap N_0 \sqcap \cdots \sqcap N_{n-1} \sqcap \bigsqcap_{i \in \{k, \ldots, n\}} \exists r.(N \sqcap F_i) \sqsubseteq N$$

Finally, we require that Player 1 moves first and that the initial configuration is labelled as described by Γ_I. Only if this is satisfied, the concept name B from $\mathcal{T}_G$ is implied:

$$P_2 \sqcap N \sqcap \bigsqcap_{i \in \Gamma_I} V_i \sqcap \bigsqcap_{i \notin \Gamma_I} \overline{V}_i \sqsubseteq B$$

Lemma 6. *Player 1 has a winning strategy in G iff $\mathcal{T}_G \cup \mathcal{T}_G'$ is not a conservative extension of $\mathcal{T}_G$.*

We have thus established the following result.

Theorem 3. *Deciding conservative extensions in $\mathcal{EL}$ is* ExpTime-*hard, thus* ExpTime-*complete.*

6   Model Conservativity

In mathematical logic and software specification, there are (at least) two different kinds of conservative extensions. Until now, we have worked with the deductive version based on the consequence relation "$\models$". The second version is model-theoretic and defined as follows. Let $\mathcal{T}_1$ and $\mathcal{T}_2$ be TBoxes. We say that $\mathcal{T}_1 \cup \mathcal{T}_2$ is a *model conservative extension* of $\mathcal{T}_1$ iff every model $\mathcal{I}$ of $\mathcal{T}_1$ can be extended to a model of $\mathcal{T}_1 \cup \mathcal{T}_2$ by modifying the interpretation of the predicates in $\mathsf{sig}(\mathcal{T}_2) \setminus \mathsf{sig}(\mathcal{T}_1)$ while leaving the predicates in $\mathsf{sig}(\mathcal{T}_1)$ fixed.

Model conservative extensions of DL TBoxes have first been analyzed in [13], where it was argued that model conservative extensions are of interest for query answering modulo ontologies. For example, assume that we are interested in computing the certain answers to a first-order query over an ABox $\mathcal{A}$ as described e.g. in [6]. Then $T_1 \cup T_2$ being a model conservative extension of T_1 means that the answers given w.r.t. the TBoxes T_1 and $T_1 \cup T_2$ are identical. The notion of a model conservative extension is more strict than the deductive one. If $T_1 \cup T_2$ is a model conservative extension of T_1, then it is clearly also a deductive conservative extension of T_1, but the converse does not hold. To show the latter, let $T_1 = \{A \sqsubseteq A\}$ and $T_2 = \{\top \sqsubseteq \exists r.A\}$. It is not hard to see that $T_1 \cup T_2$ is a deductive conservative extension of T_1 if $\mathcal{EL}$ (or even $\mathcal{ALC}$) is the assumed descripion logic, but it is not a model conservative extension.

Also in [13], it was shown that deciding model conservative extensions is undecidable and Π_1^1-complete in $\mathcal{ALC}$. In this section, we show the surprising result that model conservative extensions are undecidable even in $\mathcal{EL}$ (though we are not able to establish Π_1^1-hardness). The proof is by reduction of the halting problem for deterministic Turing machines on the empty tape. We assume w.l.o.g. that our Turing machines are such that the initial state is not reachable (directly or indirectly) from itself and that the halting state does not allow any further transitions. Let $M = (Q, \Sigma, \Gamma, \Delta, q_0, q_h)$ be a Turing machine. We construct TBoxes T_M and T_M' such that $T_M \cup T_M'$ is not a model conservative extension of T_M iff M halts on the empty tape. We use the following concept and role names for describing computations of M:

- the elements of Q and Γ as concept names;
- concept names head, before, and after to represent the relation of a tape cell to the head position;
- role names n (for *next tape cell*) and s (for *successor configuration*).

Our construction is such that models of T_M that cannot be extended to models of T_M' describe halting computations of M on the empty tape. Essentially, such models have the form of a grid, with the vertical edges labelled s and the horizontal ones labelled n. Thus, each row represents a configuration. We will enforce the roles n and s to be functional, except at row 0 and column 0 (because this does not seem possible). Therefore, the actual grid representing the computation of M starts at row 1 and column 1.

We start with the definition of T_M. For now, it is easiest to simply assume n and s to be functional and confluent (which will be enforced later by T_M'). We first set before and after correctly, exploiting the assumed functionality of n:

$$\exists n.\text{before} \sqsubseteq \text{before} \qquad \exists n.\text{head} \sqsubseteq \text{before}$$
$$\text{head} \sqsubseteq \exists n.\text{after} \qquad \text{after} \sqsubseteq \exists n.\text{after}.$$

Then we say that states are uniform over the tape: for all $q \in Q$,

$$q \sqsubseteq \exists n.q \qquad \exists n.q \sqsubseteq q.$$

Exploiting that q_0 cannot reach itself and the above uniformity, we say that the tape is initially blank (where $b \in \Gamma$ is the blank symbol):

$$q_0 \sqsubseteq b.$$

For each transition $\delta(q, a) = (q', a', L)$, exploiting confluence of n and s, we set

$$\exists n.(q \sqcap \mathsf{head} \sqcap a) \sqsubseteq \exists s.(q' \sqcap \mathsf{head} \sqcap \exists n.a'),$$

and for each transition $\delta(q, a) = (q', a', R)$,

$$(q \sqcap \mathsf{head} \sqcap a) \sqsubseteq \exists s.(a' \sqcap q' \sqcap \exists n.\mathsf{head}).$$

We also say that symbols not under the head do not change: for all $a \in \Gamma$, put

$$a \sqcap \mathsf{before} \sqsubseteq \exists s.a, \quad a \sqcap \mathsf{after} \sqsubseteq \exists s.a.$$

We would like to say that certain concept names such as before and head are disjoint. Since disjointness cannot be expressed in $\mathcal{EL}$, we revert to a trick that will become clear when $\mathcal{T}'_M$ is defined. For now, we introduce a concept name D that serves as a marker for problems with disjointness: for all $q, q' \in Q$ with $q \neq q'$ and all $a, a' \in \Gamma$ with $a \neq a'$, put

$$q \sqcap q' \sqsubseteq D \quad a \sqcap a' \sqsubseteq D \quad \mathsf{before} \sqcap \mathsf{head} \sqsubseteq D \quad \mathsf{head} \sqcap \mathsf{after} \sqsubseteq D \quad \mathsf{before} \sqcap \mathsf{after} \sqsubseteq D.$$

Up to now, we simply have assumed the described grid structure, but we did not enforce it. In $\mathcal{T}_M$, we cannot do much more than saying that every point has the required successors:

$$\top \sqsubseteq \exists n.\top \sqcap \exists s.\top.$$

We now define $\mathcal{T}'_M$, introducing new atomic concepts N, A, B and a new role u. The concept name N serves as a marker. It is enforced to be true at the origin of the relevant part of the grid (point $(1,1)$) if the described computation reaches the halting state:

$$q_h \sqsubseteq N \quad \exists n.N \sqsubseteq N \quad \exists s.N \sqsubseteq N$$

It remains to ensure that a model $\mathcal{I}$ of $\mathcal{T}_M$ cannot be extended to a model of $\mathcal{T}'_M$ iff (i) r and s are functional (except in row and column 0), (ii) r and s are confluent, (iii) $D^{\mathcal{I}} = \emptyset$ (thus no problems with disjointness), (iv) the origin $(1, 1)$ satisfies N (thus a halting state is reached), and (v) the described computation starts in the initial state with the head on the left-most cell and reaches the halting state. Suprisingly, all this can be achieved with two simple CIs:

$$\exists n.\exists s.(N \sqcap q_0 \sqcap \mathsf{head}) \sqsubseteq \exists u.(\exists n.\exists s.A \sqcap \exists s.\exists n.B)$$
$$A \sqcap B \sqsubseteq \exists u.D$$

Observe that any model $\mathcal{I}$ of $\mathcal{T}_M$ can indeed be extended to satisfy these additional CIs when any of the conditions (i) to (v) is violated, e.g., when D is non-empty or the roles n and s are functional anywhere except in row 0 and column 0. Conversely (and as shown in the proof of the following lemma), any model $\mathcal{I}$ of $\mathcal{T}_M$ that can be extended to these CIs violates one of (i) to (v).

Lemma 7. $\mathcal{T}_M \cup \mathcal{T}'_M$ *is not a model conservative extension of* $\mathcal{T}_M$ *iff* M *halts on the empty tape*

We have thus shown the following.

Theorem 4. *Deciding model conservative extensions in* $\mathcal{EL}$ *is undecidable.*

7 Conclusion

We have shown that deciding conservative extensions in $\mathcal{EL}$ is ExpTime-complete. As a next step, it is desirable to build on this foundation and design 'practical' algorithms. This is a serious challenge since conservative extensions are rather new as a reasoning problem and no experiences with implementing the associated algorithms have yet been made. (An exception is, of course, classical propositional logic, for which deciding conservative extensions corresponds to deciding the validity of quantified Boolean formulas of the form $\forall p \exists q \varphi(p, q)$). The algorithm and results presented in this paper provide useful insights regarding crucial problems that have to be solve to develop a 'practical' procedure. For example, they indicate that such a procedure will rely on efficient algorithms for checking the existence of simulations between models.

References

1. Antoniou, G., Kehagias, K.: A note on the refinement of ontologies. Int. J. of Intelligent Systems 15, 623–632 (2000)
2. Baader, F., Brandt, S., Lutz, C.: Pushing the EL envelope. In: Proc. of the 19th Int. Joint Conf. on Artificial Intelligence (IJCAI'05), pp. 364–369. Professional Book Center (2005)
3. Baader, F., Küsters, R., Molitor, R.: Computing least common subsumers in description logics with existential restrictions. In: Proc. of the 16th Int. Joint Conf. on Artificial Intelligence (IJCAI'99), pp. 96–101. Morgan Kaufmann, San Francisco (1999)
4. Bloom, B., Paige, R.: Transformational design and implementation of a new efficient solution to the ready simulation problem. Sci. Comput. Program. 24(3), 189–220 (1995)
5. Brandt, S.: Polynomial time reasoning in a description logic with existential restrictions, GCI axioms, and—what else? In: Proc. of the 16th European Conf. on Artificial Intelligence (ECAI-2004), pp. 298–302. IOS Press, Amsterdam (2004)
6. Calvanese, D., De Giacomo, G., Lenzerini, M.: On the decidability of query containment under constraints. In: Proc. of the 17th Symposium on Principles of Database Systems (PODS'98), pp. 149–158 (1998)
7. Calvanese, D., De Giacomo, G., Lembo, D., Lenzerini, M., Rosati, R.: DL-Lite: Tractable description logics for ontologies. In: Proc. of the 20th Nat. Conf. on Artificial Intelligence (AAAI 2005), pp. 602–607 (2005)
8. Calvanese, D., De Giacomo, G., Lembo, D., Lenzerini, M., Rosati, R.: Data complexity of query answering in description logics. In: Proc. of the 10th Int. Conf. on Principles of Knowledge Representation and Reasoning (KR 2006), pp. 260–270 (2006)

9. Clarke, E., Schlinghoff, H.: Model checking. In: Handbook of Automated Reasoning (chapter 24), vol. II, pp. 1635–1790. Elsevier, Amsterdam (2001)
10. Ghilardi, S., Lutz, C., Wolter, F.: Did I damage my ontology? A case for conservative extensions in description logics. In: Proc. of the 10th Int. Conf. on Principles of Knowledge Repr. and Reasoning (KR'06), pp. 187–197. AAAI Press, Stanford (2006)
11. Grau, B.C., Horrocks, I., Kazakov, Y., Sattler, U.: A logical framework for modularity of ontologies. In: Proc. of the 20th Int. Joint Conf. on Artificial Intelligence (IJCAI'07), AAAI Press, Stanford (2007)
12. Grau, B.C., Parsia, B., Sirin, E., Kalyanpur, A.: Modularity and web ontologies. In: Proc. of the 10th Int. Conf. on Principles of Knowledge Repr. and Reasoning (KR'06), pp. 198–209. AAAI Press, Stanford (2006)
13. Lutz, C., Walther, D., Wolter, F.: Conservative extensions in expressive description logics. In: Proc. of the 20th Int. Joint Conf. on Artificial Intelligence IJCAI-07, AAAI Press, Stanford (2007)
14. Lutz, C., Wolter, F.: Conservative extensions in the lightweight description logic EL (2007) http://www.liv.csc.ac.uk/~frank
15. Sioutos, N., de Coronado, S., Haber, M., Hartel, F., Shaiu, W., Wright, L.: NCI thesaurus: a semantic model integrating cancer-related clinical and molecular information. Journal of Biomedical Informatics 40(1), 30–43 (2006)
16. Spackman, K.: Managing clinical terminology hierarchies using algorithmic calculation of subsumption: Experience with SNOMED-RT, Fall Symposium Special Issue (2000)
17. Stockmeyer, L.J., Chandra, A.K.: Provably difficult combinatorial games. SIAM Journal on Computing 8(2), 151–174 (1979)

An Incremental Technique for Automata-Based Decision Procedures

Gulay Unel and David Toman

D.R.Cheriton School of Computer Science
University of Waterloo
{gunel,david}@cs.uwaterloo.ca

Abstract. Automata-based decision procedures commonly achieve optimal complexity bounds. However, in practice, they are often outperformed by sub-optimal (but more local-search based) techniques, such as tableaux, on many practical reasoning problems. This discrepancy is often the result of automata-style techniques global approach to the problem and the consequent need for constructing an extremely large automaton. This is in particular the case when reasoning in theories consisting of large number of relatively simple formulas, such as descriptions of database schemes, is required. In this paper, we propose techniques that allow us to approach a μ-calculus satisfiability problem in an incremental fashion and without the need for re-computation. In addition, we also propose heuristics that guide the problem partitioning in a way that is likely to reduce the size of the problems that need to be solved.

1 Introduction

Propositional μ-calculus, thanks to its high expressive power, is often considered one of the *lingua franca* logical formalism among logics with EXPTIME decision procedures. Indeed, many other modal, dynamic, temporal, and description logics have been shown to be relatively easily encodable in μ-calculus [8,16,24].

The key technique to showing decidability and complexity bounds for μ-calculus is based on capturing *the language of models* of a given formula using an automaton constructed from the formula—usually an *alternating parity automaton*—that accepts infinite tree models of the formula [25,26,27]. Hence, testing for satisfiability reduces to testing for non-emptiness of an appropriate automaton.

In practice, however, automata-based decision procedures do not enjoy the success predicted by the accompanying theory. Indeed, in many cases, theoretically sub-optimal approaches, such as the use of tableaux equipped with appropriate *blocking conditions* that prevent infinite expansions, are more successful [1,12]. This rather surprising observation can be traced to severe difficulties in implementing automata-based decision procedures, in particular when inherently infinite models are considered. For example, the emptiness test for alternating parity automaton, in particular when based on Safra's determinization approach [22,23], is rather difficult to implement. This issue, for μ-calculus

F. Pfenning (Ed.): CADE 2007, LNAI 4603, pp. 100–115, 2007.

formulas, was addressed by using simpler *Safraless* decision procedures based on transforming an alternating parity automaton to a non-deterministic Büchi automaton while preserving emptiness [19].

However, even this improvement does not yield a practical reasoning procedure. The difficulties *inherent in the automata-based approaches* are especially apparent when determining *logical consequences* of moderately large *theories* of the form $\{\varphi_1, \ldots \varphi_n\} \models \varphi$, are considered. Commonly, more local search techniques applied to this problem try to discover an inconsistency in the set $\{\varphi_1, \ldots \varphi_n, \neg\varphi\}$, which in practice rarely involves all the formulas φ_i in the input. Hence, the inconsistency can often be detected much more efficiently than using the automata-theoretic method which is constructing the automaton for the formula $\varphi_1 \wedge \varphi_2 \wedge \ldots \wedge \varphi_n \wedge \neg\varphi$ and then checking for its emptiness. This problem manifests itself in many important settings, in which theories that describe system behavior use a large number of relatively simple constraints, such as database schemes or UML diagrams specified using, e.g., an appropriate description logic [2,7].

In this paper, we explore techniques that attempt to remedy the above difficulties by proposing an incremental and interleaved approach to constructing the automaton corresponding to the logical implication problem while simultaneously testing for satisfiability of the so far constructed fragments. The main contributions of this paper are as follows:

- we show how the decision problem can be split into a sequence of simpler problems,
- we show that in this incremental process, the larger problems can be constructed from the simpler ones, hence avoiding unnecessary recomputation, and
- we show how top-down query evaluation techniques enhanced with memoing can be used to drive the incremental computation.

The rest of the paper is organized as follows: Section 2 provides the necessary definitions and background, Section 3 introduces the incremental approach and outlines the main results, Section 4 discusses heuristics and optimizations of the proposed algorithm, and Section 6 concludes outlining directions of further research.

2 Preliminaries

In this section, we provide definitions needed for the technical development in the rest of the paper.

2.1 μ-Calculus

The propositional μ-calculus is a propositional modal logic augmented with least and greatest fixpoint operators [16]. The syntax of μ-calculus [4] is given below:

Definition 1. *Let* Var *be an (infinite) set of variable names, typically named* $X, Y, Z, \ldots$; Prop *a set of atomic propositions, typically named* $P, Q, \ldots$; *and* $\mathcal{L}$ *a set of labels,* $a, b, \ldots$. *The set of* L_μ *formulas (with respect to* Var, Prop, $\mathcal{L}$) *is defined as follows:*

- $P \in$ Prop *and* $Z \in$ Var *are formulas.*
- *If* ϕ_1 *and* ϕ_2 *are formulas, so is* $\phi_1 \wedge \phi_2$.
- *If* ϕ *is a formula, so are* $[a]\phi$, $\neg\phi$, *and* $\nu Z.\phi$ *provided that every free occurrence of* Z *in* ϕ *occurs positively.*

In the rest of the paper we use derived operators, e.g., $\phi_1 \vee \phi_2$ for $\neg(\neg\phi_1 \wedge \neg\phi_2)$, $\langle a \rangle \phi$ for $\neg[a]\neg\phi$, $\mu Z.\phi(Z)$ for $\neg\nu Z.\neg\phi(\neg Z)$, $[K]\phi$ for $\bigwedge_{a \in K}[a]\phi$, $[-]\phi$ for $[\mathcal{L}]\phi$, etc.

Formulas of L_μ are interpreted with respect to labeled transition systems over Prop in which nodes are labeled by propositional assignments and edges by elements of $\mathcal{L}$; for full definition see [4].

2.2 Alternating Automata

Satisfiable L_μ formulas enjoy the *tree model* property. This property provides a link to automata theory: satisfiability of a L_μ formula is equivalent to checking whether a corresponding tree automaton that accepts tree models of the formula is non-empty.

Definition 2. *Given a set D of directions, a D-tree is a set $T \subseteq D^*$ such that if $x \cdot c \in T$ (an extension of x with c), where $x \in D^*$ and $c \in D$, then also $x \in T$. If $T = D^*$, we say that T is a full D-tree. The empty word ϵ is the root of T and the elements of T are called nodes. A path π of a tree T is a set $\pi \subseteq T$ such that $\epsilon \in \pi$ and for every $x \in \pi$ either x is a leaf or there exists a unique c such that $x \cdot c \in \pi$. Given an alphabet Σ, a Σ-labeled D-tree is a pair $\langle T, \tau \rangle$ where T is a tree and $\tau : T \to \Sigma$ maps each node of T to a letter in Σ.*

For a set X, $\mathcal{B}^+(X)$ is the set of positive Boolean formulas over X; for a set $Y \subseteq X$ and a formula $\phi \in \mathcal{B}^+(X)$, we say that Y satisfies ϕ iff assigning **true** *to elements in Y and assigning* **false** *to elements in $X \setminus Y$ makes ϕ true. An alternating tree automaton is $A = \langle \Sigma, D, Q, q_i, \delta, \alpha \rangle$, where Σ is the input alphabet, D is a set of directions, Q is a finite set of states, $\delta : Q \times \Sigma \to \mathcal{B}^+(D \times Q)$ is a transition function, $q_i \in Q$ is an initial state, and α specifies the acceptance condition.*

An alternating automaton A runs on Σ-labeled full D-trees. A run of A over a Σ-labeled D-tree $\langle T, \tau \rangle$ is a $(T \times Q)$-labeled tree $\langle T_r, r \rangle$ such that:

1. *$\epsilon \in T_r$ and $r(\epsilon) = \langle \epsilon, q_i \rangle$.*
2. *For every $y \in T_r$ such that $r(y) = \langle x, q \rangle$ there is a set*

$$\{(c_0, q_0), (c_1, q_1), \ldots (c_{n-1}, q_{n-1})\} \subseteq D \times Q$$

that satisfies $\delta(q, \tau(x))$, and for all $0 \leq j < n$, $y \cdot j \in T_r$, $r(y \cdot j) = \langle x \cdot c_j, q_j \rangle$.

A run $\langle T_r, r \rangle$ is accepting if all its infinite paths satisfy an acceptance condition. The set of states on a path $\pi \subseteq T_r$ that appear infinitely often is denoted with $\inf(\pi)$ where $\inf(\pi) \subseteq Q$ and $q \in \inf(\pi)$ if and only if there are infinitely many $y \in \pi$ for which $r(y) \in T \times \{q\}$. The types of acceptance conditions are defined as follows:

- *A path π satisfies Büchi acceptance condition $\alpha \subseteq Q$ if $\inf(\pi) \cap \alpha \neq \emptyset$.*
- *A path π satisfies co-Büchi acceptance condition $\alpha \subseteq Q$ if $\inf(\pi) \cap \alpha = \emptyset$.*
- *A path π satisfies parity acceptance condition $\alpha = \{F_1, F_2, \ldots, F_h\}$ with $F_1 \subseteq F_2 \subseteq \ldots \subseteq F_h = Q$ if the minimal index i for which $\inf(\pi) \cap F_i \neq \emptyset$ is even. The number h of sets in α is called the index of the automaton.*

An automaton accepts a tree if there exists a run that accepts it. The set of all Σ-trees that are accepted by A is denoted by $\mathcal{L}(A)$. An alternating automaton is:

- *nondeterministic: if the formulas (c_1, q_1) and (c_2, q_2) appear in δ and are conjunctively related, then $c_1 \neq c_2$,*
- *universal: if all the formulas that appear in δ are conjunctions of atoms in $D \times Q$,*
- *deterministic: if it satisfies the conditions for being nondeterministic and universal at the same time.*

The connection between L_μ formulas and alternating automata is captured by the following theorem [9,13,27].

Theorem 1. *Let $\varphi \in L_\mu$. Then there is an alternating parity tree automaton A_φ that can be constructed effectively from φ, such that the language of trees accepted by A_φ is the set of tree models of φ.*

Hence, it remains to solve the emptiness problem for alternating automata to decide the satisfiability of μ-calculus formulas. Logical implication problems can be solved by using the associated satisfiability problems (possibly with the help of the greatest fixpoint operator when *global axioms* are needed).

2.3 From APT to NBT Via UCT

The standard approach for checking the emptiness of an alternating parity tree automaton (APT) involves Safra's construction [22] which is complicated and not very suitable for efficient implementation. An alternative approach to this problem has been proposed by Vardi and Kupferman [19] and involves the following steps:

1. Translate the APT A representing a μ-calculus formula φ to a Universal Co-Büchi Tree Automaton (UCT) A',
2. Translate the UCT A' to a Non-deterministic Büchi Tree Automaton (NBT) A'', and
3. Check for emptiness of A''.

The above transformations only preserve emptiness for the automata, not the actual languages of trees accepted. This is, however, sufficient for deciding satisfiability. We modify this procedure to operate in an incremental fashion when the original alternating automaton represents a conjunction of L_μ formulas. First, we outline the two main steps in the original construction [19]:

From APT to UCT. Consider an APT $A = \langle \Sigma, D, Q, q_i, \delta, \alpha \rangle$, where $\delta :$ $Q \times \Sigma \to \mathcal{B}^+(D \times Q)$. A *restriction* of δ is a partial function $\eta : Q \to 2^{D \times Q}$. A restriction η is relevant to $\sigma \in \Sigma$ if for all $q \in Q$ for which $\delta(q, \sigma)$ is satisfiable, the set $\eta(q)$ satisfies $\delta(q, \sigma)$. Let R be the set of restrictions of δ.

For $A = \langle \Sigma, D, Q, q_i, \delta, \alpha \rangle$ with $\alpha = \{F_1, F_2, \ldots, F_{2h}\}$, and $F_0 = \emptyset$, the UCT is defined as $A' = \langle \Sigma', D, Q \times \{0, \ldots, h-1\}, \langle q_i, 0 \rangle, \delta', \alpha' \rangle$ where:

- $\Sigma' \subseteq \Sigma \times R$ such that η is relevant to σ for all $\langle \sigma, \eta \rangle \in \Sigma'$.
- For every $q \in Q$, $\sigma \in \Sigma$, and $\eta \in R$:
  - $\delta'(\langle q, 0 \rangle, \langle \sigma, \eta \rangle) = \bigwedge_{0 \le i < h} \bigwedge_{(c,s) \in (\eta(q) \setminus (D \times F_{2i}))} (c, \langle s, i \rangle)$.
  - For every $1 \le i < h$, $\delta'(\langle q, i \rangle, \langle \sigma, \eta \rangle) = \bigwedge_{(c,s) \in (\eta(q) \setminus (D \times F_{2i}))} (c, \langle s, i \rangle)$.
- $\alpha' = \bigcup_{0 \le i < h} (F_{2i+1} \times \{i\})$

Intuitively, the nondeterminism in A is removed in A' since Σ' contains all the pairs $\langle \sigma, \eta \rangle$ for which η is relevant to σ (η chooses from all the possible sets of atoms that satisfy δ). The automaton A' consists of h copies of A such that the ith copy checks if a path in a run of A' visits F_{2i} only finitely often then it also visits F_{2i+1} only finitely often by making sure that the run stays in the ith copy unless it has to move to a state from F_{2i}.

From UCT to NBT. Let $A' = \langle \Sigma', D', Q', q_i', \delta', \alpha' \rangle$, and let $k = (2n!)n^{2n}3^n$ $(n+1)/n!$. Let $\mathcal{R}$ be the set of functions $f : Q' \to \{0, \ldots k\}$ in which $f(q)$ is even for all $q \in \alpha'$. For $g \in \mathcal{R}$, let $odd(g) = \{q : g(q) \text{ is odd}\}$. The definition of $A'' = \langle \Sigma', D', Q'', q_i'', \delta'', \alpha'' \rangle$ is given as follows:

- $Q'' = 2^{Q'} \times 2^{Q'} \times \mathcal{R}$
- $q_i'' = \langle \{q_i'\}, \emptyset, g_0 \rangle$, where g_0 maps all states to k.
- For $q \in Q'$, $\sigma \in \Sigma'$, and $c \in D'$, let $\gamma'(q, \sigma, c) = \delta'(q, \sigma) \cap (\{c\} \times Q)$. For two functions g and g' in $\mathcal{R}$, a letter σ, and direction $c \in D'$, we say that g' *covers* $\langle g, \sigma, c \rangle$ if for all q and q' in Q', if $q' \in \gamma'(q, \sigma, c)$. then $g'(q') \le g(q)$. Then for all $\langle S, O, g \rangle \in Q''$ and $\sigma \in \Sigma'$, δ'' is defined as follows:
  - If $O \ne \emptyset$ then $\delta''(\langle S, O, g \rangle, \sigma)$
    $$= \bigwedge_{c \in D} \bigvee_{g_c \text{ covers } \langle g, \sigma, c \rangle} \langle \gamma'(S, \sigma, c), \gamma'(O, \sigma, c) \setminus odd(g_c), g_c \rangle$$
  - If $O = \emptyset$ then $\delta''(\langle S, O, g \rangle, \sigma)$
    $$= \bigwedge_{c \in D} \bigvee_{g_c \text{ covers } \langle g, \sigma, c \rangle} \langle \gamma'(S, \sigma, c), \gamma'(S, \sigma, c) \setminus odd(g_c), g_c \rangle$$
- $\alpha'' = 2^{Q'} \times \{\emptyset\} \times \mathcal{R}$.

Intuitively, the automaton A'' is the result of a subset construction applied to A' such that for a run of A' that satisfies a particular co-Büchi condition it guesses the possible runs that satisfy its dual Büchi condition. The emptiness problem for NBT is much simpler than the emptiness problem for APT which is shown to be solved symbolically in quadratic time [17].

3   Incremental Approach to Satisfiability of Conjunctions

In this section, we provide the main contribution of this paper: a decomposition technique for the APT to NBT construction based on conjunctive formulas and, in turn, an incremental algorithm for checking the emptiness of an APT A for a formula φ. We also outline a top-down approach for checking the emptiness of the associated NBT.

Assume that we have a conjunctive formula $\varphi = \varphi_1 \wedge \varphi_2 \wedge \ldots \wedge \varphi_n$ and φ is represented by an APT $A = \langle \Sigma, D, Q, q_i, \delta, \alpha \rangle$. We decompose the APT to NBT translation in such a way that we do not need to construct the complete automaton for φ and we can stop checking for emptiness if $\varphi' = \varphi_1 \wedge \varphi_2 \wedge \ldots \wedge \varphi_k$ for $k \leq n$ is unsatisfiable. Otherwise we are able to reuse the facts we computed for φ' in the emptiness check of φ.

The incremental technique first constructs an automaton A_1 for φ_1 and checks for its emptiness, if A_1 is empty then the procedure stops. Otherwise it continues with automata for formulas $\varphi_1 \wedge \varphi_2$, ..., $\varphi_1 \wedge \varphi_2 \wedge \ldots \wedge \varphi_n$ applying the same technique and reusing the automaton computed in step i for computing the automaton in step $i + 1$ as it is shown in Figure 1.

3.1   Decomposition of the APT to NBT Translation

In this section, we describe the proposed decomposition technique for a conjunction of formulas of the form $\varphi = \varphi_1 \wedge \varphi_2 \wedge \ldots \wedge \varphi_n$. We know that there is an APT $A = \langle \Sigma, D, Q, q_i, \delta, \alpha \rangle$ that accepts tree models of φ. To define this automaton, we need the following auxiliary definition:

Definition 3. *The closure of a formula ϕ, $\mathsf{cl}(\phi)$ is the smallest set of formulas that satisfies the following:*

- $\phi \in \mathsf{cl}(\phi)$.
- *If $\phi_1 \wedge \phi_2 \in \mathsf{cl}(\phi)$, then $\phi_1 \in \mathsf{cl}(\phi)$ and $\phi_2 \in \mathsf{cl}(\phi)$.*
- *If $[a]\psi$ or $\neg\psi \in \mathsf{cl}(\phi)$ then $\psi \in \mathsf{cl}(\phi)$.*
- *If $\nu Z.\psi \in \mathsf{cl}(\phi)$, then $\psi(\nu Z.\psi) \in \mathsf{cl}(\phi)$ and $\psi \in \mathsf{cl}(\phi)$.*

Now we define an alternating automaton $A_k = \langle \Sigma_k, D, Q_k, q_{i_k}, \delta_k, \alpha_k \rangle$ for a subformula $\varphi' = \varphi_1 \wedge \varphi_2 \wedge \ldots \wedge \varphi_k$ of φ as follows:

- $\Sigma_k = 2^{AP_k}$ where AP_k is the set of atomic propositions in φ',
- $q_{i_k} = \varphi'$,
- $Q_k = \mathsf{cl}(\varphi')$,
- for all $\sigma \in \Sigma_k$, $\delta(q, \sigma) \in \delta_k$ iff $q \in Q_k$, and
- $\alpha_k = \{F_1 \cap Q_k, F_2 \cap Q_k, \ldots, F_{2h} \cap Q_k\}$.

Emptiness of A_k implies emptiness of A and, in turn, the unsatisfiability of the original formula φ, as A_k represents a subformula $\varphi_1 \wedge \varphi_2 \wedge \ldots \wedge \varphi_k$ of φ. Hence, we can stop checking for the emptiness of the automaton A early: whenever we reach an automaton A_k that is empty. Otherwise we use the following theorem to *extend* A_k to A_{k+1} without the need to recompute all the transitions from scratch:

Theorem 2. *Let* $A'_k = \langle \Sigma'_k, D, Q_k \times \{0, \ldots h-1\}, \langle q_{i_k}, 0 \rangle, \delta'_k, \alpha'_k \rangle$ *be the UCT translation of* A_k, *and* $A' = \langle \Sigma', D, Q \times \{0, \ldots h-1\}, \langle q_i, 0 \rangle, \delta', \alpha' \rangle$ *be the UCT translation of* A.

Then for every $q_k \in Q_k$, $\sigma_k \in \Sigma_k$, $\eta_k \in R_k$, $\eta_l \in R_l$:
$\delta'(\langle q_k, i \rangle, \langle \sigma_k, \eta_k \cup \eta_l \rangle) = \delta'_k(\langle q_k, i \rangle, \langle \sigma_k, \eta_k \rangle)$ *for all* $0 \leq i < h$ *where* R_k *is the set of restrictions* $\eta_k : Q_k \to 2^{D \times Q_k}$ *such that for all* $\langle \sigma_k, \eta_k \rangle \in \Sigma'_k$, η_k *is relevant to* σ_k, *and* R_l *is the set of restrictions* $\eta_l : Q \setminus Q_k \to 2^{D \times Q}$.

Proof. For every $q_k \in Q_k$, $\sigma_k \in \Sigma_k$, $\eta_k \in R_k$, $\eta_l \in R_l$:

$$
\begin{aligned}
- \quad \delta'(\langle q_k, 0 \rangle, \langle \sigma_k, \eta_k \cup \eta_l \rangle) &= \bigwedge\nolimits_{0 \leq i < h} \bigwedge\nolimits_{(c,s) \in (\eta_k(q_k) \cup \eta_l(q_k)) \setminus (D \times F_{2i})} (c, \langle s, i \rangle) \\
&= \bigwedge\nolimits_{0 \leq i < h} \bigwedge\nolimits_{(c,s) \in (\eta_k(q_k)) \setminus (D \times F_{2i})} (c, \langle s, i \rangle) \wedge \\
& \qquad \bigwedge\nolimits_{0 \leq i < h} \bigwedge\nolimits_{(c,s) \in (\eta_l(q_k)) \setminus (D \times F_{2i})} (c, \langle s, i \rangle) \\
&= \bigwedge\nolimits_{0 \leq i < h} \bigwedge\nolimits_{(c,s) \in (\eta_k(q_k)) \setminus (D \times F_{2i})} (c, \langle s, i \rangle) \\
&= \bigwedge\nolimits_{0 \leq i < h} \bigwedge\nolimits_{(c,s) \in (\eta_k(q_k)) \setminus (D \times (F_{2i} \cap Q_k))} (c, \langle s, i \rangle) \\
&= \delta'_k(\langle q_k, 0 \rangle, \langle \sigma_k, \eta_k \rangle), \text{ and}
\end{aligned}
$$

- for all $1 \leq i < h$ we have
$$
\begin{aligned}
\delta'(\langle q_k, i \rangle, \langle \sigma_k, \eta_k \cup \eta_l \rangle) &= \bigwedge\nolimits_{(c,s) \in (\eta_k(q_k) \cup \eta_l(q_k)) \setminus (D \times F_{2i})} (c, \langle s, i \rangle) \\
&= \bigwedge\nolimits_{(c,s) \in (\eta_k(q_k)) \setminus (D \times F_{2i})} (c, \langle s, i \rangle) \wedge \\
& \qquad \bigwedge\nolimits_{(c,s) \in (\eta_l(q_k)) \setminus (D \times F_{2i})} (c, \langle s, i \rangle) \\
&= \bigwedge\nolimits_{(c,s) \in (\eta_k(q_k)) \setminus (D \times F_{2i})} (c, \langle s, i \rangle) \\
&= \bigwedge\nolimits_{(c,s) \in (\eta_k(q_k)) \setminus (D \times (F_{2i} \cap Q_k))} (c, \langle s, i \rangle) \\
&= \delta'_k(\langle q_k, i \rangle, \langle \sigma_k, \eta_k \rangle).
\end{aligned}
$$

Thus we can reuse the transitions computed for a UCT A'_k (i.e., for $\varphi_1 \wedge \varphi_2 \wedge \ldots \wedge \varphi_k$) when computing the transitions of A'_{k+1} for $\varphi_1 \wedge \varphi_2 \wedge \ldots \wedge \varphi_{k+1}$. Similar theorem holds for the UCT to NBT step:

Theorem 3. *Let* $A''_k = \langle \Sigma'_k, D, Q''_k, q''_{i_k}, \delta''_k, \alpha''_k \rangle$ *be NBT translation of* A'_k, *and* $A'' = \langle \Sigma', D, Q'', q''_i, \delta'', \alpha'' \rangle$ *be the NBT translation of* A'.

Then for all $\langle S, O, g \rangle \in Q''_k$, $\sigma' = \langle \sigma_k, \eta_k \rangle \in \Sigma'_k$, $\sigma = \langle \sigma_k, \eta_k \cup \eta_l \rangle \in \Sigma'$, $\delta''(\langle S, O, g \cup f \rangle, \sigma) = \delta''_k(\langle S, O, [g \cup f/g] \rangle, \sigma')$ *where* $g : Q'_k \to \{0, \ldots, k'\}$ $(k' = (2n_k!)n_k^{2n_k} 3^{n_k} (n_k + 1)/n_k!$ *where* n_k *is the number of states in* $A'_k)$, *and* $f : Q' \setminus Q'_k \to \{0, \ldots, k\}$.

Proof. If $O \neq \emptyset$ then

$$\delta''(\langle S, O, g \cup f \rangle, \sigma)$$

$$= \bigwedge_{c \in D} \bigvee_{\substack{g_c \, covers \, \langle g, \sigma, c \rangle \\ f_c \, covers \, \langle f, \sigma, c \rangle}} \langle \gamma'(S, \sigma, c), \gamma'(O, \sigma, c) \setminus odd(g_c \cup f_c), g_c \cup f_c \rangle$$

$$= \bigwedge_{c \in D} \bigvee_{\substack{g_c \, covers \, \langle g, \sigma, c \rangle \\ f_c \, covers \, \langle f, \sigma, c \rangle}} \langle \gamma'_k(S, \sigma', c), \gamma'_k(O, \sigma', c) \setminus odd(g_c), g_c \cup f_c \rangle$$

$$= \delta''_k(\langle S, O, [g \cup f/g] \rangle, \sigma')$$

The proof works analogously for the $O = \emptyset$ case.

This result shows that we can reuse the transitions we compute for an NBT A''_k used for checking the satisfiability of $\varphi_1 \wedge \varphi_2 \wedge \ldots \wedge \varphi_k$ when we are computing the transitions of A''_{k+1} for $\varphi_1 \wedge \varphi_2 \wedge \ldots \wedge \varphi_{k+1}$.

Example 1. Consider a formula $\varphi = \varphi_1 \wedge \varphi_2$ such that $\varphi_1 = \nu X.(\psi \wedge \langle - \rangle X)$ $\varphi_2 = \neg \nu X.(\psi \wedge \langle - \rangle X)$ where $\psi = \mu Y.(b \vee \langle - \rangle Y)$. Let $\Sigma = \{a, b\}$, and $D = \{1, 2\}$, an APT accepting models (which are tree models that have at least one path with infinitely many b's) of φ_1 is $A_1 = \{\Sigma, D, Q_1, q_1, \delta_1, \alpha_1\}$ where:

$Q_1 = \{q_0, q_1\}$
$\delta_1(q_0, a) = (1, q_0) \vee (2, q_0)$
$\delta_1(q_0, b) = (1, q_1) \vee (2, q_1)$
$\delta_1(q_1, a) = (1, q_0) \vee (2, q_0)$
$\delta_1(q_1, b) = (1, q_1) \vee (2, q_1)$
$\alpha_1 = \{\{q_0\}, \{q_0, q_1\}, \{q_0, q_1\}, \{q_0, q_1\}\}$

APT for φ_2, $A_2 = \{\Sigma, D, Q_2, q_2, \delta_2, \alpha_2\}$:

$Q_2 = \{q_2, q_3\}$
$\delta_2(q_2, a) = (1, q_2) \wedge (2, q_2)$
$\delta_2(q_2, b) = (1, q_3) \wedge (2, q_3)$
$\delta_2(q_3, a) = (1, q_2) \wedge (2, q_2)$
$\delta_2(q_3, b) = (1, q_3) \wedge (2, q_3)$
$\alpha_2 = \{\{\}, \{q_2\}, \{q_2, q_3\}, \{q_2, q_3\}\}$

and the APT for φ is $A_3 = \{\Sigma, D, Q_3, q_4, \delta_3, \alpha_3\}$:

$Q_3 = Q_1 \cup Q_2 \cup \{q_4\}$
$\delta_3 = \delta_1 \cup \delta_2$ plus the following transitions:
$\delta_3(q_4, a) = (1, q_0) \wedge (1, q_2)$
$\delta_3(q_4, b) = (1, q_0) \wedge (1, q_2)$
$\alpha_3 = \{\{q_0\}, \{q_0, q_1, q_2\}, \{q_0, q_1, q_2, q_3\}, \{q_0, q_1, q_2, q_3\}\}$

Note that the index of A_3 is 4 and A_1 and A_2 have the same index as A_3 according to the definition of α_k (for k=1 and k=2 in this case). As a result some sets in α_1 and α_2 are repeated at the end.

The incremental strategy used for this formula first checks for the emptiness of A_1 (which is not empty), then checks for the emptiness of A_3 (while re-using the transitions computed for the UCT A_1' and the NBT A_1''), e.g.: $\delta_3'(\langle q_0, 0 \rangle, \langle a, \eta_1 \cup \eta_2 \rangle) = \delta_1'(\langle q_0, 0 \rangle, \langle a, \eta_1 \rangle)$ for all $\eta_1 \in R_1$ and $\eta_2 \in R_2$. Here R_1 is the set of restrictions $\eta_1 : Q_1 \to 2^{D \times Q_1}$ such that for all $\langle \sigma_1, \eta_1 \rangle \in \Sigma_1'$, η_1 is relevant to σ_1, and R_2 is the set of restrictions $\eta_2 : Q_3 \setminus Q_1 \to 2^{D \times Q_3}$.

3.2   The Algorithm

Let A_i be the APT for $\varphi_1 \wedge \varphi_2 \wedge \ldots \wedge \varphi_i$, and let A_i' be the UCT translation of A_i, $A_i''[j]$ be the NBT translation of A_i' where $\mathcal{R}$ is the set of functions $f : Q_i' \to \{0, \ldots, j\}$ for $1 \leq i \leq n$. The algorithm outlined in Figure 1 incrementally

```
1: initial = 1
2: for i = 1 to n do
3:     construct A_i
4:     if i > 1 then
5:         construct A'_i using A'_{i-1}
6:     end if
7:     k = (2n!)n^{2n}3^n(n + 1)/n! for A'_i with n states
8:     for j = initial to k - 1 do
9:         construct A''_i[j]
10:        if A''_i[j] is not empty then
11:            if i = n then
12:                return not empty
13:            else
14:                initial = j
15:                go to 2
16:            end if
17:        end if
18:    end for
19:    if A''_i[k] is empty then
20:        return empty
21:    end if
22: end for
```

Fig. 1. Pseudo-code for Incremental Satisfaction Algorithm

constructs automata $A_i''[j]$ representing φ_i for $1 \leq i \leq n$ and looks for the smallest j, $j_m \leq k$ such that $A_i''[j]$ is not empty reusing the automaton $A_i''[j]$ in the computation of $A_i''[j + 1]$. If $A_i''[k]$ is empty it stops, if not it constructs $A_{i+1}''[j_m]$ reusing the automaton $A_i''[j_m]$. Hence we have two directions first we are checking for the emptiness of a particular automaton $A_i''[j]$ for $1 \leq j \leq k$, second we are checking for the emptiness of automata $A_i''[j]$ for $1 \leq i \leq n$. We are using the proposed incremental technique on computing automata reusing the previous automata in both directions.

Theorem 4. *If $A_i''[k']$ is not empty then $A_{i-1}''[k']$ is also not empty where $1 \leq k' \leq (2n!)n^{2n}3^n(n+1)/n!$ and n is the number of states in A_i'.*

Proof. Let $A_i' = \langle \Sigma, D, Q, q_i, \delta, \alpha \rangle$, and $A_{i-1}' = \langle \Sigma_1, D, Q_1, q_{i_1}, \delta_1, \alpha_1 \rangle$ Starting state of A_i'' is $q_i'' = \langle \{\langle q_i, 0 \rangle\}, \emptyset, g_0 \rangle$, and starting state of A_{i-1}'' is $q_{i_1}'' = \langle \{\langle q_{i_1}, 0 \rangle\}, \emptyset, g_0^1 \rangle$ where R is the set of functions $f : Q \to \{0, \dots k'\}$ and $g_0 \in R$ and $g_0^1 \in R$ map all the states in Q and Q_1 to k' respectively. For each $c \in D$, q_i'' goes to $\langle S, O, g_0 \rangle$. If we remove all the states $Q_2 = Q \setminus Q_1$ from a path π that start with $\langle S, O, g_0 \rangle$ then we get a path π_2 that start with $\langle S_2, O_2, g_0^1 \rangle$ where $\langle q_{i_1}, 0 \rangle \in S_2$ and $\langle q_{i_1}, 0 \rangle \in O_2$. For each $c \in D$, q_{i_1}'' goes to $\langle S_1, O_1, g_0^1 \rangle$ where $S_1 = \{\langle q_{i_1}, 0 \rangle\}$ and $O_1 = \{\langle q_{i_1}, 0 \rangle\}$. Let a path that start with $\langle S_1, O_1, g_0^1 \rangle$ be π_1. If π_2 is accepting then π_1 is also accepting since $O_1 \subseteq O_2$ and we get to $\emptyset$ from O_1 if we get to $\emptyset$ from O_2.

This theorem shows that the smallest j such that $A_{i-1}''[j]$ is not empty is also the smallest possible j such that $A_i''[j]$ is not empty. As a consequence, when we are constructing $A_i''[j]$ we can start from the *last* j. Also, this means we can directly reuse the information computed at stage $i-1$.

3.3 A Top-Down Approach to the APT to NBT Translation and to the NBT Emptiness Algorithm

We represent the general construction algorithm as a logic program and check the emptiness using a goal with respect to the program. The outline of the program for the construction of an NBT A_n'' for a formula $\varphi_1 \wedge \varphi_2 \wedge \dots \wedge \varphi_n$ is as follows:

- $\mathsf{sat}(A_1''[1]) \leftarrow \mathsf{check}(A_1''[1], \_)$
- For all $1 < i \leq k$ and $1 < j \leq n$:
  $\mathsf{sat}(A_j''[i]) \leftarrow \mathsf{sat}(A_j''[i-1])$
  $\mathsf{sat}(A_j''[i]) \leftarrow \mathsf{exists}(A_j''[i-1]), \mathsf{check}(A_j''[i], A_j''[i-1])$
  $\mathsf{sat}(A_j''[i]) \leftarrow \mathsf{exists}(A_{j-1}''[i]), \mathsf{check}(A_j''[i], A_{j-1}''[i])$
  $\mathsf{exists}(A_j''[i]) \leftarrow \mathsf{check}(A_j''[i], \_)$

We ask the following query with respect to this program:

$$\mathsf{sat}(A_1''[k]), \mathsf{sat}(A_2''[k]), \dots, \mathsf{sat}(A_n''[k])$$

Here, $\mathsf{sat}(A_j''[i])$ is true if $A_j''[i]$ is not empty. The predicate $\mathsf{check}(A_j''[i], A_l''[m])$ checks the emptiness of $A_j''[i]$ using $A_l''[m]$ and returns true if $A_j''[i]$ not empty. If an automaton $A_j''[i]$ is constructed $\mathsf{exists}(A_j''[i])$ is marked as true. As a result we check the emptiness of A_1'', A_2'', ... A_n'' and stop if we hit an empty one using a top-down approach with memoing where the automata we compute are kept in the memo tables to be used whenever needed where the construction rules ensure that we reuse the automaton we compute at a particular stage in the next stage.

The proposed NBT emptiness algorithm for a particular automaton (implementation of the check predicate) checks if subtrees which have only final nodes in their leaves are repeated infinitely often. The emptiness query works top-down starting from the transitive closure of the initial state on these types of subtrees and stops checking when it makes certain that they are repeated infinitely often. This means that there is a tree accepted by the automaton. We compute only the transitions that we need to answer the emptiness query. For instance, to answer the emptiness query on an NBT automaton we only need to compute the transitions that are reachable from the starting state of the automaton.

Example 2. Consider an NBT automaton A where $\Sigma = \{a\}$, $D = \{1, 2\}$ $Q = \{q_0, q_1, q_2, q_3, q_4, q_5\}$, $q_i = q_0$, $\delta(q_0, a) = (1, q_1) \wedge (2, q_2)$, $\delta(q_1, a) = (1, q_2) \wedge (2, q_3)$, $\delta(q_2, a) = (1, q_1) \wedge (2, q_1)$, $\delta(q_3, a) = (1, q_1) \wedge (2, q_3)$, $\delta(q_4, a) = (1, q_5) \wedge (2, q_5)$, $\delta(q_5, a) = (1, q_1) \wedge (2, q_1)$, and $\alpha = \{q_2, q_3\}$

When we are running the emptiness algorithm on this automaton we only compute the first four transitions.

4 Heuristics

In this section, we provide several heuristics and optimizations that can be applied to the proposed technique. First, we explain the optimizations in translation of an APT A to a UCT A' which is an incremental technique on the alphabet we use for A'. Then we explain the optimizations in translation of a UCT A' to an NBT A'' which is an incremental technique on the size of the functions in $\mathcal{R}$ we use for A'' which is proposed in [19]. Finally, we describe the heuristics we can use for rewriting conjunctive formulas (i.e. reordering the subformulas in a conjunctive formula) so that we have a better chance for detecting possible contradictions faster.

Optimizations in APT to UCT Translation. First we introduce an optimization used in the translation of APT to UCT.

Since $\Sigma' \subseteq \Sigma \times R$ we can start the construction using a subset Σ'_1 of Σ'. We proceed with a larger subset, Σ'_2, if the satisfiability query is empty, and repeat enlarging the alphabet until either the query becomes non-empty or we reach to the set Σ'. We are also able to reuse the results in the next computation since $\Sigma'_1 \subseteq \Sigma'_2$.

Theorem 5. *Let $A'_1 = \langle \Sigma'_1, D, Q, q_i, \delta'_1, \alpha \rangle$ and $A'_2 = \langle \Sigma'_2, D, Q, q_i, \delta'_2, \alpha \rangle$ are UCT translations of an APT A using Σ'_1 as alphabet of A'_1 and using Σ'_2 as alphabet of A'_2. If $\Sigma'_1 \subseteq \Sigma'_2$, then $\delta'_1 \subseteq \delta'_2$.*

Proof. Since we define $\delta'_2(\langle q, i \rangle, \langle \sigma_2, \eta_2 \rangle)$ for every $q \in Q$, $\sigma_2 \in \Sigma_2$, $\eta_2 \in R_2$, and for all $0 \leq i < h$ where R_2 is the set of restrictions such that for all $\langle \sigma_2, \eta_2 \rangle \in \Sigma'_2$, η_2 is relevant to σ_2 the same way as $\delta'_1(\langle q, i \rangle, \langle \sigma_1, \eta_1 \rangle)$ for every $q \in Q$, $\sigma_1 \in \Sigma_1$, $\eta_1 \in R_1$, and for all $0 \leq i < h$ where R_1 is the set of restrictions such that for all $\langle \sigma_1, \eta_1 \rangle \in \Sigma'_1$, η_1 is relevant to σ_1 then if $\Sigma'_1 \subseteq \Sigma'_2$, $\delta'_1 \subseteq \delta'_2$.

Optimizations in UCT to NBT Translation. In the proposed translation of UCT to NBT we start from an initial value k_1 for k and increase this value up to k_2, as long as the satisfiability query is empty. We continue this process until either the automaton becomes non-empty or we reach the upper bound of $(2n!)n^{2n}3^n(n+1)/n!$ for n the number of states in the UCT automaton. This approach has been proposed in [19]. Our decomposition, however, allows an incremental implementation that reuses *the transitions* computed for k_1 in the subsequent construction for k_2.

Theorem 6. *Let $A_1''[k_1]$ and $A_2''[k_2]$ are NBT translations of an APT A, using k_1 as the maximum range of functions in $\mathcal{R}_1$ for A_1'' and k_2 as the maximum range of functions in $\mathcal{R}_2$ for A_2''. If $k_1 \leq k_2$, then $\delta_1'' \subseteq \delta_2''$.*

Proof. Since $\mathcal{R}_1$ is the set of functions $f_1 : Q' \to \{0, \ldots, k_1\}$ and $\mathcal{R}_2$ is the set of functions $f_2 : Q' \to \{0, \ldots, k_2\}$ and $k_1 \leq k_2$ then $\mathcal{R}_1 \subseteq \mathcal{R}_2$ which means $Q_1'' \subseteq Q_2''$. Thus $\delta_1'' \subseteq \delta_2''$.

Example 3. Consider an alternating automaton A such that: $\Sigma = \{a\}$, $D = \{1, 2\}$, $Q = \{q_0, q_1, q_2, q_3\}$, $q_i = q_0$, $\delta(q_0, a) = (1, q_1) \wedge (2, q_2)$, $\delta(q_1, a) = (1, q_3) \wedge (2, q_3)$, $\delta(q_2, a) = (1, q_3) \wedge (2, q_3)$, $\delta(q_3, a) = (1, q_3)$, and $\alpha = \{\{\}, \{q_0, q_1, q_2, q_3\}\}$ We have calculated the actual number of transitions in the UCT translation of A, A' and the NBT translation of A, A'', and the number of transitions we need to answer the satisfiability query after we apply the above optimizations. The set of restrictions is R and the set of restrictions we used for answering the satisfiability query is R_1. The number of transitions computed for A' with R is 4×2^{32} and the number of transitions computed for A' with R_1 is 4. The results for the NBT translation are given in Figure 2 where $k = 2^{20} \cdot 42525$, and $k_1 = 1$.

# of transitions computed for $A''[k]$	$256 \cdot k^4$
# of transitions computed for $A''[k_1]$	256
# of transitions computed for $A''[k_1]$ with top-down evaluation	70

Fig. 2. Number of transitions in the NBT automata $A''[k]$ and $A''[k_1]$

Heuristics for Ordering of Conjunctive Formulas. Consider a logical consequence question $\{\varphi_1, \varphi_2, \ldots, \varphi_n\} \models \psi$, such that the formula ψ is already inconsistent with a subset of formulas in $\{\varphi_1, \varphi_2, \ldots, \varphi_n\}$. As we use an incremental technique we can use rewriting heuristics to generate a formula $\neg\psi \wedge \varphi_{i_1} \wedge \varphi_{i_2} \wedge \ldots \wedge \varphi_{i_n}$ such that $[i_1, i_2, \ldots i_n]$ is a permutation of $[1, 2, \ldots n]$. For instance, the formulas $\varphi_1, \varphi_2, \ldots, \varphi_n$ can be ordered according to the number of free variables they share with ψ. Hence we improve our chances of finding a possible contradiction faster if we use this formula instead of the original one in the proposed algorithm. The following examples demonstrate the effect of ordering of the subformulas of a conjunctive formula.

Example 4. Consider a formula $\psi = \varphi \wedge \varphi_4$ where φ is the formula given in Example 1, $\varphi_4 = \nu X.(\psi \wedge \langle - \rangle X)$ such that $\psi = \mu Y.(a \vee \langle - \rangle Y)$, $\Sigma = \{a, b\}$, and $D = \{1, 2\}$, an APT for φ_4 is $A_4 = \{\Sigma, D, Q_4, q_5, \delta_4, \alpha_4\}$ where:

$Q_4 = \{q_5, q_6\}$
$\delta_4(q_5, a) = (1, q_5) \vee (2, q_5)$
$\delta_4(q_5, b) = (1, q_6) \vee (2, q_6)$
$\delta_4(q_6, a) = (1, q_5) \vee (2, q_5)$
$\delta_4(q_6, b) = (1, q_6) \vee (2, q_6)$
$\alpha_4 = \{\{q_6\}, \{q_5, q_6\}, \{q_5, q_6\}, \{q_5, q_6\}\}$

APT for ψ, $A_5 = \{D, \Sigma, Q_5, q_7, \delta_5, \alpha_5\}$:

$Q_5 = Q_3 \cup Q_4 \cup \{q_7\}$
$\delta_5 = \delta_3 \cup \delta_4$ plus the following transitions:
$\delta_5(q_7, a) = (1, q_4) \wedge (1, q_5)$
$\delta_5(q_7, b) = (1, q_4) \wedge (1, q_5)$
$\alpha_5 = \{\{q_0, q_6\}, \{q_0, q_1, q_2, q_5, q_6\}, \{q_0, q_1, q_2, q_3, q_5, q_6\}, \{q_0, q_1, q_2, q_3, q_5, q_6\}\}$

Using the proposed strategy we first check whether A_1 defined in Example 1 is empty (it is not empty), then we check the emptiness of A_3 which is empty and thus we do not need to construct A_5' and A_5''. The estimated number of transitions is 10×2^{50} for A_3', and 16×2^{128} for A_5'. The estimated number of transitions for A_3'' and A_5'' are given in Figure 3 where $k_3 = 20! \cdot 10^{20} \cdot 3^{10} \cdot 11/10!$, $k_5 = 32! \cdot 2^{128} \cdot 3^{16} \cdot 17/16!$.

estimated # of transitions for A_3''	$2 \times 2^{10} \times 2^{10} \times k_3^{10}$
estimated # of transitions for A_5''	$2 \times 2^{16} \times 2^{16} \times k_5^{16}$

Fig. 3. Number of transitions in the NBT automata A_3'' and A_5''

Example 5. Consider a logical consequence problem $\{\varphi_2, \varphi_3, \varphi_4, \varphi_5\} \models \varphi_1$ where φ_1 and φ_2 are given in Example 1, $\varphi_3 = \nu X.(\psi_1 \wedge \langle - \rangle X)$ such that $\psi_1 = \mu Y.(a \vee \langle - \rangle Y)$, $\Sigma_3 = \{a, b\}$, $\varphi_4 = \nu X.(\psi_2 \wedge \langle - \rangle X)$ such that $\psi_2 = \mu Y.(c \vee \langle - \rangle Y)$, $\Sigma_4 = \{c, b\}$, $\varphi_5 = \nu X.(\psi_3 \wedge \langle - \rangle X)$ such that $\psi_3 = \mu Y.(d \vee \langle - \rangle Y)$, $\Sigma_5 = \{d, b\}$, and $D = \{1, 2\}$, an APT for φ_3 is $A_3 = \{\Sigma, D, Q_3, q_5, \delta_3, \alpha_3\}$ where:

$Q_3 = \{q_5, q_6\}$
$\delta_3(q_5, a) = (1, q_5) \vee (2, q_5)$
$\delta_3(q_5, b) = (1, q_6) \vee (2, q_6)$
$\delta_3(q_6, a) = (1, q_5) \vee (2, q_5)$
$\delta_3(q_6, b) = (1, q_6) \vee (2, q_6)$
$\alpha_3 = \{\{q_6\}, \{q_5, q_6\}, \{q_5, q_6\}, \{q_5, q_6\}\}$

The APT A_4 for φ_4 and the APT A_5 for φ_5 are the same as A_3 except that the state names are changed and the letter a is replaced with c in A_4 and d in A_5, respectively.

Using the proposed strategy we first check if A_1 defined in Example 1 is empty (it is not empty), then we check the emptiness of the intersection automaton $A_{1,2}$ of A_1 and A_2 which is empty. Hence, we do not need to construct the complete intersection automaton A for A_1, A_2, A_3, A_4, and A_5. The estimated number of transitions for $A''_{1,2}$ and A'' are given in Figure 4 where $k_1 = 20! \cdot 10^{20} \cdot 3^{10} \cdot 11/10!$, $k_2 = 56! \cdot 28^{56} \cdot 3^{28} \cdot 29/28!$.

estimated # of transitions for $A''_{1,2}$	$2 \times 2^{10} \times 2^{10} \times k_1^{10}$
estimated # of transitions for A''	$5 \times 2^{28} \times 2^{28} \times k_2^{28}$

Fig. 4. Number of transitions in the NBT automata $A''_{1,2}$ and A''

5 Related Work

The connection between logic and automata was first considered by Büchi [5] and Elgot [10]. They have shown that monadic second-order logic over finite words and finite automata have the same expressive power, and we can transform formulas of this logic to finite automata and vice versa. Later, Büchi [6], McNaughton [18], and Rabin [21] proved that monadic second-order logic over infinite words (and trees) and finite automata also have the same expressive power. The practical use of this connection was investigated for temporal logics and fixed-point logics which led to the theory of model checking [3,28]. In addition, μ-calculus formulas can be translated to alternating automata [9,13,27]. Unfortunately, the standard way of checking for emptiness of an alternating automaton involves Safra's construction [22]. An alternative approach to this problem is proposed by Vardi and Kupferman [19] that does not use Safra's theorem. An extensive survey on automata and logic can be found in [25].

The connection between logics and automata theory has been used for implementing decision procedures for numerous logics, for example the MONA system [11,14] for deciding monadic second order logics on finite words and trees. It is argued that the success of these procedures relies on efficient operations on a compact representation of automata based on BDDs [14,15]. Recently, an extension of Safraless decision algorithm that is amenable to implementation was proposed for LTL formulas [20] which also improved the complexity of the algorithm.

6 Conclusions and Future Work

In this paper, we have developed an incremental approach to an automata-based decision procedure for μ-calculus. The proposed technique and optimizations are sufficiently general to be applicable to other automata-based techniques. Future research will follow several directions:

1. we attempt to reduce the part of the automaton needed to show satisfia-
   bility/unsatisfiability by introducing additional heuristics in the incremental
   construction,
2. for particular classes of problems, for which other techniques exhibit better
   performance due to reduced search space, we attempt to modify the proposed
   incremental approach to mimic those approaches, and
3. we study how the proposed incremental technique can take advantage of
   the structure of problems formulated in more restricted formalisms such as
   description logics.

References

1. Baader, F., Sattler, U.: An Overview of Tableau Algorithms for Description Logics.
   Studia Logica 69, 5–40 (2001)
2. Berardi, D., Calvanese, D., De Giacomo, G.: Reasoning on UML Class Diagrams
   using Description Logic Based Systems. In: Baader, F., Brewka, G., Eiter, T. (eds.)
   KI 2001. LNCS (LNAI), vol. 2174, Springer, Heidelberg (2001)
3. Bernholtz, O., Vardi, M.Y., Wolper, P.: An automata-theoretic approach to
   branching-time model checking. In: Dill, D.L. (ed.) CAV 1994. LNCS, vol. 818,
   pp. 142–155. Springer, Heidelberg (1994)
4. Bradfield, J., Stirling, C.: Modal Mu-Calculi (chapter 12) (2006)
5. Büchi, J.R.: Weak second-order arithmetic and finite automata. Z. Math. Logik
   Grundl. Math. 6, 66–92 (1960)
6. Büchi, J.R.: On a decision method in restricted second-order arithmetic. In: Proc.
   Int. Congr. for Logic, Methodology and Philosophy of Science 1–11 (1962)
7. Calvanese, D., Lenzerini, M., Nardi, D.: Description logics for conceptual data
   modeling. In: Chomicki, J., Saake, G. (eds.) Logics for Databases and Information
   Systems, pp. 229–264. Kluwer, Dordrecht (1998)
8. Demri, S., Sattler, U.: Automata-theoretic decision procedures for information logics. Fundam. Inform. 53(1), 1–22 (2002)
9. Jutla, C.S., Emerson, E.A.: Tree automata, mu-calculus and determinacy. In: Proceedings of the 32nd annual symposium on Foundations of computer science, pp.
   368–377. IEEE Computer Society Press, Los Alamitos (1991)
10. Elgot, C.C.: Decision problems of finite automata design and related arithmetics.
    Trans. Amer. Math. Soc. 98, 21–52 (1961)
11. Henriksen, J.G., Jensen, J.L., Jörgensen, M.E., Klarlund, N., Paige, R., Rauhe,
    T., Sandholm, A.: MONA: Monadic second-order logic in practice. In: Brinksma,
    E., Steffen, B., Cleaveland, W.R., Larsen, K.G., Margaria, T. (eds.) TACAS 1995.
    LNCS, vol. 1019, pp. 89–110. Springer, Heidelberg (1995)
12. Hladik, J., Sattler, U.: A Translation of Looping Alternating Automata into De-
    scription Logics. In: Baader, F. (ed.) Automated Deduction – CADE-19. LNCS
    (LNAI), vol. 2741, pp. 90–105. Springer, Heidelberg (2003)
13. Janin, D., Walukiewicz, I.: Automata for the modal μ-calculus and related results.
    In: Hájek, P., Wiedermann, J. (eds.) MFCS 1995. LNCS, vol. 969, pp. 552–562.
    Springer, Heidelberg (1995)
14. Klarlund, N.: MONA & FIDO: The logic-automaton connection in practice. Com-
    puter Science Logic 311–326 (1997)
15. Klarlund, N., Møller, A., Schwartzbach, M.I.: MONA implementation secrets. Int.
    J. Found. Comput. Sci. 13(4), 571–586 (2002)

16. Kozen, D.: Results on the propositional *mu*-calculus. Theoretical Computer Science 27, 333–354 (1983)
17. Wolper, P., Vardi, M.Y.: Automata theoretic techniques for modal logics of programs (extended abstract). In: STOC '84: Proceedings of the sixteenth annual ACM symposium on Theory of computing, pp. 446–456. ACM Press, New York (1984)
18. McNaughton, R.: Testing and generating infinite sequences by a finite automaton. Information and Control 9, 521–530 (1966)
19. Vardi, M.Y., Kupferman, O.: Safraless decision procedures. In: Proc. 46th IEEE Symp. on Foundations of Computer Science, pp. 531–540, Pittsburgh (October 2005)
20. Vardi, M.Y., Kupferman, O., Piterman, N.: Safraless compositional synthesis. In: Ball, T., Jones, R.B. (eds.) CAV 2006. LNCS, vol. 4144, pp. 31–44. Springer, Heidelberg (2006)
21. Rabin, M.O.: Decidability of second-order theories and automata on infinite trees. Trans. Amer. Math. Soc. 141, 1–35 (1969)
22. Safra, S.: On the Complexity of ω-Automata. In: FOCS, pp. 319–327 (1988)
23. Safra, S.: Exponential Determinization for omega-Automata with Strong-Fairness Acceptance Condition (Extended Abstract). In: STOC, pp. 275–282 (1992)
24. Sattler, U., Vardi, M.Y.: The Hybrid μ-Calculus. In: Goré, R.P., Leitsch, A., Nipkow, T. (eds.) IJCAR 2001. LNCS (LNAI), vol. 2083, pp. 76–91. Springer, Heidelberg (2001)
25. Thomas, W.: Languages, automata, and logic. In: Handbook of Formal Languages, vol. 3, Springer, Heidelberg (1997)
26. Vardi, M.Y.: What makes Modal Logic so Robustly Decidable. Descriptive Complexity and Finite Models. American Mathematical Society (1997)
27. Vardi, M.Y.: Reasoning about the past with two-way automata. In: Larsen, K.G., Skyum, S., Winskel, G. (eds.) ICALP 1998. LNCS, vol. 1443, pp. 628–641. Springer, Heidelberg (1998)
28. Vardi, M.Y., Wolper, P.: An automata-theoretic approach to automatic program verification. In: Proc. LICS, pp. 322–331 (1986)

Bidirectional Decision Procedures for the Intuitionistic Propositional Modal Logic IS4

Samuli Heilala and Brigitte Pientka

School of Computer Science, McGill University, Montreal, Canada
{sheila1,bpientka}@cs.mcgill.ca

Abstract. We present a multi-context focused sequent calculus whose derivations are in bijective correspondence with normal natural deductions in the propositional fragment of the intuitionistic modal logic **IS4**. This calculus, suitable for the enumeration of normal proofs, is the starting point for the development of a sequent calculus-based bidirectional decision procedure for propositional **IS4**. In this system, relevant derived inference rules are constructed in a forward direction prior to proof search, while derivations constructed using these derived rules are searched over in a backward direction. We also present a variant which searches directly over normal natural deductions. Experimental results show that on most problems, the bidirectional prover is competitive with both conventional backward provers using loop-detection and inverse method provers, significantly outperforming them in a number of cases.

1 Introduction

Intuitionistic modal logics are constructive logics incorporating operators of necessity ($\Box$) and possibility ($\Diamond$). Fitch [7], Prawitz [16], Satre [18], and more recently Simpson [19], Bierman and de Paiva [1], and Pfenning and Davies [15] have investigated a broad range of proof-theoretical properties of various logics of this kind. Recently, such logics have also found applications in hardware verification [6] and proposed type systems for staged computation [3] and distributed computing [13]. A logic frequently used in these settings is either the intuitionistic variant of the classical modal logic **S4**, which we will call **IS4**, or a logic that can be expressed through **IS4**, such as Fairtlough and Mendler's lax logic [6] (see for instance [15] for the relationship between **IS4** and lax logic).

In this light, it is surprising that proof search in **IS4** has not received more attention. Howe has investigated proof enumeration and theorem proving in lax logic [12] and, coming closer to our work, has presented a backward decision procedure for the fragment of propositional **IS4** without the possibility modality [11]. His system performs loop-detection using a history mechanism, but is encumbered by a large number of rules and related provisos (21 axioms and inference rules). It would only grow with the addition of the possibility modality, which would also require a different loop-detection mechanism.

F. Pfenning (Ed.): CADE 2007, LNAI 4603, pp. 116–131, 2007.

Our contributions begin with a sequent calculus for propositional **IS4** suitable for the enumeration of normal proofs. This forms the basis for the development of a sequent calculus-based *bidirectional* **IS4** decision procedure, in which derived inference rules relevant to the query are constructed in a forward direction prior to proof search, while derivations constructed using these derived rules are searched over in a backward direction. We also demonstrate that this approach corresponds very closely to an elegant bidirectional decision procedure that searches directly over normal natural deductions. The key to our theoretical justification of both of these decision procedures is a refinement of the well-known subformula property, which we use to restrict nondeterminism in focused proof search in the presence of multiple contexts. To evaluate our approach empirically, we have put together a set of 50 benchmark formulas for **IS4**. Experimental results show that on most problems, the bidirectional prover is competitive with both conventional backward provers using loop-detection and inverse method provers, significantly outperforming them in a number of cases. Although we concentrate on propositional **IS4** in this paper, we believe that the techniques presented are general enough to find applications in other constructive logics, such as the contextual modal logic of Nanevski, Pfenning, and Pientka [14]. Finally, while this paper contains only proof sketches of many of our results, we provide the full proofs in the accompanying technical report [10].

In Sect. 2 we summarize the relevant background and introduce our core natural deduction formalism, while Sect. 3 presents corresponding sequent calculi for proof search in both backward and forward directions, followed by a more detailed discussion of some of the intricacies of focused forward proof search. In Sects. 4 and 5 we describe our bidirectional decision procedure in both a sequent calculus and a natural deduction setting. Experimental results are given in Sect. 6, while Sect. 7 concludes with related and future work.

2   Natural Deduction

Formulas in the propositional fragment of **IS4** are given by the grammar

$$A \quad ::= \quad P \mid \bot \mid A \supset A \mid A \wedge A \mid A \vee A \mid \Box A \mid \Diamond A$$

where P is taken from a countable set of atomic propositional constants and negation and truth are defined notationally in the usual way. Our starting point is a multi-context natural deduction formulation for **IS4** similar to ones proposed by Pfenning and Davies [15] and Bierman and de Paiva [1], except that we impose a restriction that only natural deductions in normal form can be constructed. This is achieved by annotating judgements with their intended direction of reasoning:

$\Delta; \Gamma \vdash A \uparrow$ A has a normal proof under hypotheses Δ and Γ,

$\Delta; \Gamma \vdash A \downarrow$ A can be extracted from hypotheses in Δ and Γ using only elimination rules,

$$\dfrac{}{\Delta; \Gamma_1, A, \Gamma_2 \vdash A \downarrow} \ \text{hyp}_1 \qquad \dfrac{}{\Delta_1, A, \Delta_2; \Gamma \vdash A \downarrow} \ \text{hyp}_2 \qquad \dfrac{\Delta; \Gamma \vdash \perp \downarrow}{\Delta; \Gamma \vdash C \uparrow} \ \perp\text{E}$$

$$\dfrac{\Delta; \Gamma, A_1 \vdash A_2 \uparrow}{\Delta; \Gamma \vdash A_1 \supset A_2 \uparrow} \ \supset\text{I} \qquad \dfrac{\Delta; \Gamma \vdash A_1 \supset A_2 \downarrow \quad \Delta; \Gamma \vdash A_1 \uparrow}{\Delta; \Gamma \vdash A_2 \downarrow} \ \supset\text{E}$$

$$\dfrac{\Delta; \Gamma \vdash A_1 \uparrow \quad \Delta; \Gamma \vdash A_2 \uparrow}{\Delta; \Gamma \vdash A_1 \wedge A_2 \uparrow} \ \wedge\text{I} \qquad \dfrac{\Delta; \Gamma \vdash A_1 \wedge A_2 \downarrow}{\Delta; \Gamma \vdash A_j \downarrow} \ \wedge\text{E}_j$$

$$\dfrac{\Delta; \Gamma \vdash A_j \uparrow}{\Delta; \Gamma \vdash A_1 \vee A_2 \uparrow} \ \vee\text{I}_j \qquad \dfrac{\Delta; \Gamma \vdash A_1 \vee A_2 \downarrow \quad \Delta; \Gamma, A_1 \vdash C \uparrow \quad \Delta; \Gamma, A_2 \vdash C \uparrow}{\Delta; \Gamma \vdash C \uparrow} \ \vee\text{E}$$

$$\dfrac{\Delta; \cdot \vdash A \uparrow}{\Delta; \Gamma \vdash \Box A \uparrow} \ \Box\text{I} \qquad \dfrac{\Delta; \Gamma \vdash \Box A \downarrow \quad \Delta, A; \Gamma \vdash C \uparrow}{\Delta; \Gamma \vdash C \uparrow} \ \Box\text{E}$$

$$\dfrac{\Delta; \Gamma \vdash A \uparrow}{\Delta; \Gamma \vdash \Diamond A \uparrow} \ \Diamond\text{I} \qquad \dfrac{\Delta; \Gamma \vdash \Diamond A \downarrow \quad \Delta; A \vdash \Diamond C \uparrow}{\Delta; \Gamma \vdash \Diamond C \uparrow} \ \Diamond\text{E} \qquad \dfrac{\Delta; \Gamma \vdash A \downarrow \quad A \text{ is atomic}}{\Delta; \Gamma \vdash A \uparrow} \ \uparrow\downarrow$$

$$j \in \{1, 2\}$$

Fig. 1. $\text{NJ}^{\text{N}}_{\text{IS4}}$

where $\Gamma = A_1, \ldots, A_n$ is a context of true hypotheses and $\Delta = B_1, \ldots, B_m$ is a modal context of *valid* hypotheses. Valid hypotheses are hypotheses whose truth does not depend on the truth of other formulas, that is, hypotheses that are in some sense "always" or necessarily true. The resulting system, which we will call $\text{NJ}^{\text{N}}_{\text{IS4}}$, is shown in Fig. 1. Although the contexts of this system are formally ordered lists, we can afford to be flexible with them, as $\text{NJ}^{\text{N}}_{\text{IS4}}$ has the usual structural properties of weakening, contraction, and exchange for both contexts. For convenience, we will generally think of contexts in $\text{NJ}^{\text{N}}_{\text{IS4}}$ as multisets.

The inference rules of $\text{NJ}^{\text{N}}_{\text{IS4}}$ are largely standard, but to glean some intuition about the modal rules and the two contexts, it is useful to think of the modalities as quantifying truth over worlds in some universe, with some reachability relation defined on the worlds. To say that $\Box A$ is true is to say that A is true in *all* worlds reachable from the current one, while to say that $\Diamond A$ is true is to say that A is true in *some* world reachable from the current one. The current world represents the environment in which the provability of the succedent is to be established. Under this interpretation, the hypotheses in the modal context can be used in all reachable worlds, while those in the regular context can only be used in the current world.

Note that while $\text{NJ}^{\text{N}}_{\text{IS4}}$ defines the normal forms that we are interested in during proof search, an unrestricted variant NJ_{IS4} can be obtained by dropping the arrow annotations and the rule $\uparrow\downarrow$. In the accompanying technical report [10], we show that the two systems NJ_{IS4} and its "normalized" cousin $\text{NJ}^{\text{N}}_{\text{IS4}}$ are equivalent in terms of provability. For the interested reader, we also provide a common Hilbert-style axiomatization of IS4 in [10], along with a proof that the unrestricted system NJ_{IS4} and the axiomatization are equivalent. This lends support to the claim that we are indeed dealing with the intuitionistic variant of **S4**. Finally, we would like to point out that the separation between modal and ordinary hypotheses is not strictly necessary. Building on work by Bierman and de Paiva [1], we obtain a faithful embedding into a single-context system simply by providing every valid hypothesis with a □ operator and merging the two contexts. The details of this embedding are beyond the scope of this paper, but are presented in [10].

While Girard, Lafont, and Taylor suggest that we should think of natural deductions as the "true 'proof' objects" [9], natural deduction systems have traditionally not seen much use as formalisms for proof search, mainly as a result of their lack of syntax-directedness. Although we will ultimately return to natural deduction in our search for bidirectional decision procedures, the relationship between backward and forward proof search is perhaps most vividly demonstrated in a sequent calculus setting, which we turn to next.

3   Sequent Calculi

Following the approach of Dyckhoff and Pinto [5], we can construct a *focused* sequent calculus for propositional **IS4** whose derivations are in bijective correspondence with normal natural deductions. This system, which we will call $\mathbf{MJ_{IS4}}$, is shown in Fig. 2 and involves two forms of sequents:

$$\Delta; \Gamma \to C \qquad C \text{ can be proved from assumptions } \Delta, \Gamma,$$

$$\Delta; \Gamma \triangleright A \to C \qquad \begin{array}{l} C \text{ can be proved from assumptions } \Delta, \Gamma, A, \text{ focusing on} \\ \text{the assumption } A. \end{array}$$

If a sequent is focused on a formula A, then the only applicable rules are those with A as a principal formula. Following Girard [8], we will call the position of the focused formula the *stoup*. As in the natural deduction formulations, contexts in $\mathbf{MJ_{IS4}}$ are technically ordered lists, but the usual structural properties of weakening, exchange, and contraction hold here as well, so an interpretation of contexts as multisets is reasonable. The following key result establishes the close correspondence between $\mathbf{MJ_{IS4}}$ and $\mathbf{NJ_{IS4}^N}$. The soundness and completeness of $\mathbf{MJ_{IS4}}$ with respect to $\mathbf{NJ_{IS4}^N}$ follow from it.

Theorem 1 (Bijection between $\mathbf{MJ_{IS4}}$ and $\mathbf{NJ_{IS4}^N}$ derivations). *Derivations of unfocused sequents in $\mathbf{MJ_{IS4}}$ correspond bijectively to derivations of $\uparrow$ judgements in $\mathbf{NJ_{IS4}^N}$.*

Proof. We define functions mapping derivations from $\mathbf{NJ_{IS4}^N}$ to $\mathbf{MJ_{IS4}}$ and vice versa. Inductive arguments on the structures of the argument derivations show that the functions are bijections.   □

Although $\mathbf{MJ_{IS4}}$ is suitable for proof search in a backward direction, a naive approach still requires loop-detection to achieve a decision procedure. We will not pursue this direction further here, but instead concentrate on forward proof search, and on how we can combine ideas from backward and forward search to perform bidirectional proof search.

$$\frac{A \text{ is atomic}}{\Delta; \Gamma \triangleright A \to A} \text{ init} \qquad \frac{}{\Delta; \Gamma \triangleright \bot \to C} \perp\mathsf{L}$$

$$\frac{\Delta; \Gamma_1, A, \Gamma_2 \triangleright A \to C}{\Delta; \Gamma_1, A, \Gamma_2 \to C} \text{ ch}_1 \qquad \frac{\Delta_1, A, \Delta_2; \Gamma \triangleright A \to C}{\Delta_1, A, \Delta_2; \Gamma \to C} \text{ ch}_2$$

$$\frac{\Delta; \Gamma, A_1 \to A_2}{\Delta; \Gamma \to A_1 \supset A_2} \supset\mathsf{R} \qquad \frac{\Delta; \Gamma \to A_1 \quad \Delta; \Gamma \triangleright A_2 \to C}{\Delta; \Gamma \triangleright A_1 \supset A_2 \to C} \supset\mathsf{L}$$

$$\frac{\Delta; \Gamma \to A_1 \quad \Delta; \Gamma \to A_2}{\Delta; \Gamma \to A_1 \wedge A_2} \wedge\mathsf{R} \qquad \frac{\Delta; \Gamma \triangleright A_j \to C}{\Delta; \Gamma \triangleright A_1 \wedge A_2 \to C} \wedge\mathsf{L}_j$$

$$\frac{\Delta; \Gamma \to A_j}{\Delta; \Gamma \to A_1 \vee A_2} \vee\mathsf{R}_j \qquad \frac{\Delta; \Gamma, A_1 \to C \quad \Delta; \Gamma, A_2 \to C}{\Delta; \Gamma \triangleright A_1 \vee A_2 \to C} \vee\mathsf{L}$$

$$\frac{\Delta; \cdot \to A}{\Delta; \Gamma \to \Box A} \Box\mathsf{R} \qquad \frac{\Delta, A; \Gamma \to C}{\Delta; \Gamma \triangleright \Box A \to C} \Box\mathsf{L}$$

$$\frac{\Delta; \Gamma \to A}{\Delta; \Gamma \to \Diamond A} \Diamond\mathsf{R} \qquad \frac{\Delta; A \to \Diamond C}{\Delta; \Gamma \triangleright \Diamond A \to \Diamond C} \Diamond\mathsf{L}$$

$$j \in \{1, 2\}$$

Fig. 2. $\mathbf{MJ_{IS4}}$

Constructing $\mathbf{MJ_{IS4}}$ proofs in a forward direction — from the top down — is complicated by the presence of multiple contexts, making $\mathbf{MJ_{IS4}}$ less than ideal for forward proof search. All $\mathbf{MJ_{IS4}}$ derivations begin, at the leaves, with focused sequents of the form $\Delta; \Gamma \triangleright A \to A$, with A atomic. After a sequence of (possibly zero) left-rule applications, the stoup formula is dropped from the stoup into one of the contexts by an application of ch_1 or ch_2. In a focused forward calculus used as the basis for the inverse method [4], we would proceed in a similar way, but it is not clear which context a stoup formula should be dropped into.

To address this uncertainty, we refine the idea of focusing and develop the system $\mathbf{MJ^F_{IS4}}$, which is suitable for forward proof search and features sequents of three kinds, involving both modal and nonmodal stoups:

$\Delta; \Gamma \mapsto C$ C can be proved using all assumptions in Δ, Γ,

$\Delta; \Gamma \triangleright A \mapsto C$ C can be proved using all assumptions in Δ, Γ, A, with A assumed true,

$\Delta; \Gamma \triangleright\triangleright A \mapsto C$ C can be proved using all assumptions in Δ, Γ, A, with A assumed valid.

Note that the forms of the focused sequents reveal which context the stoup formula will drop into. For brevity, we write $\Delta; \Gamma \triangleright^i A \mapsto C$, $i \in \{1, 2\}$ for either form of focused sequent.

The inference rules of $\mathbf{MJ^F_{IS4}}$, shown in Fig. 3, are obtained by reinterpreting the rules of $\mathbf{MJ_{IS4}}$ in a forward fashion and by defining the ch_i rules to behave as sketched above. The contexts of $\mathbf{MJ^F_{IS4}}$, however, are interpreted differently,

$$\frac{A \text{ is atomic}}{\cdot; \cdot \rhd^i A \mapsto A} \text{ init}_i \quad \frac{}{\cdot; \cdot \rhd^i \bot \mapsto C} \bot \mathsf{L}_i \quad \frac{\Delta; \Gamma \rhd A \mapsto C}{\Delta; \Gamma, A \mapsto C} \text{ ch}_1 \quad \frac{\Delta; \Gamma \rhd \rhd A \mapsto C}{\Delta, A; \Gamma \mapsto C} \text{ ch}_2$$

$$\frac{\Delta; \Gamma, A_1 \mapsto A_2}{\Delta; \Gamma \mapsto A_1 \supset A_2} \supset \mathsf{R}_1 \quad \frac{\Delta; \Gamma \mapsto A_2}{\Delta; \Gamma \mapsto A_1 \supset A_2} \supset \mathsf{R}_2$$

$$\frac{\Delta_1; \Gamma_1 \mapsto A_1 \quad \Delta_2; \Gamma_2 \rhd^i A_2 \mapsto C}{\Delta_1, \Delta_2; \Gamma_1, \Gamma_2 \rhd^i A_1 \supset A_2 \mapsto C} \supset \mathsf{L}_i$$

$$\frac{\Delta_1; \Gamma_1 \mapsto A_1 \quad \Delta_2; \Gamma_2 \mapsto A_2}{\Delta_1, \Delta_2; \Gamma_1, \Gamma_2 \mapsto A_1 \wedge A_2} \wedge \mathsf{R} \quad \frac{\Delta; \Gamma \rhd^i A_j \mapsto C}{\Delta; \Gamma \rhd^i A_1 \wedge A_2 \mapsto C} \wedge \mathsf{L}_{i,j}$$

$$\frac{\Delta; \Gamma \mapsto A_j}{\Delta; \Gamma \mapsto A_1 \vee A_2} \vee \mathsf{R}_j \quad \frac{\Delta_1; \Gamma_1, A_1 \mapsto C \quad \Delta_2; \Gamma_2, A_2 \mapsto C}{\Delta_1, \Delta_2; \Gamma_1, \Gamma_2 \rhd^i A_1 \vee A_2 \mapsto C} \vee \mathsf{L}_i$$

$$\frac{\Delta; \cdot \mapsto A}{\Delta; \cdot \mapsto \Box A} \Box \mathsf{R} \quad \frac{\Delta, A; \Gamma \mapsto C}{\Delta; \Gamma \rhd^i \Box A \mapsto C} \Box \mathsf{L}_i \quad \frac{\Delta; \Gamma \mapsto A}{\Delta; \Gamma \mapsto \Diamond A} \Diamond \mathsf{R} \quad \frac{\Delta; A \mapsto \Diamond C}{\Delta; \cdot \rhd^i \Diamond A \mapsto \Diamond C} \Diamond \mathsf{L}_i$$

$$i, j \in \{1, 2\}$$

Fig. 3. MJ$^{\mathrm{F}}_{\mathbf{IS4}}$

in that sequents $\Delta; \Gamma \mapsto C$ and $\Delta; \Gamma \rhd^i A \mapsto C$, $i \in \{1, 2\}$ assert that *all* assumptions in Δ and Γ, as well as A if the sequent is focused, are needed to prove C. General weakening, which holds in **MJ$_{\mathbf{IS4}}$**, is thus disallowed, but local weakening is incorporated in the rule $\supset \mathsf{R}_2$. Contexts in **MJ$^{\mathrm{F}}_{\mathbf{IS4}}$** are treated as sets rather than multisets, and we write Γ_1, Γ_2 and Γ, A for $\Gamma_1 \cup \Gamma_2$ and $\Gamma \cup \{A\}$, respectively.

Theorem 2 (Soundness and completeness of MJ$^{\mathrm{F}}_{\mathbf{IS4}}$ with respect to MJ$_{\mathbf{IS4}}$)

1. *(Soundness)*
   (a) If $\Delta; \Gamma \mapsto C$, then $\Delta; \Gamma \to C$.
   (b) If $\Delta; \Gamma \rhd^i A \mapsto C, i \in \{1, 2\}$, then $\Delta; \Gamma \rhd A \to C$.
2. *(Completeness)*
   (a) If $\Delta; \Gamma \to C$, then $\Delta'; \Gamma' \mapsto C$ for some $\Delta' \subseteq \Delta$, $\Gamma' \subseteq \Gamma$.
   (b) If $\Delta; \Gamma \rhd A \to C$ and A is a subformula of a formula in Γ, then either $\Delta'; \Gamma' \mapsto C$ or $\Delta'; \Gamma' \rhd A \mapsto C$ for some $\Delta' \subseteq \Delta$, $\Gamma' \subseteq \Gamma$.
   (c) If $\Delta; \Gamma \rhd A \to C$ and A is a subformula of a formula in Δ, then either $\Delta'; \Gamma' \mapsto C$ or $\Delta'; \Gamma' \rhd \rhd A \mapsto C$ for some $\Delta' \subseteq \Delta$, $\Gamma' \subseteq \Gamma$.

Proof. In both cases by simultaneous induction on the structure of the given derivation, using weakening in **MJ$_{\mathbf{IS4}}$** where necessary. $\Box$

Note that the more fine-grained focusing mechanism of **MJ$^{\mathrm{F}}_{\mathbf{IS4}}$** could just as well have been introduced in a sequent calculus suitable for backward reasoning, such as **MJ$_{\mathbf{IS4}}$**. Indeed, the single type of focused sequent in **MJ$_{\mathbf{IS4}}$** has the role of both types of focused sequents in $\mathbf{MJ^F_{IS4}}$, making the focusing mechanism of $\mathbf{MJ_{IS4}}$ in some sense "overloaded".

The forward calculus $\mathbf{MJ^F_{IS4}}$ suggests itself immediately as a basis for an implementation of the inverse method [4], fundamental to which is the classification of the subformulas of a query formula into positive and negative classes. The sign of a subformula determines where in a sequent it may occur (for instance as a goal formula or in the context) and restricts nondeterminism during proof search. We will refine this notion by classifying subformulas as either

1. positive $(+)$ subformulas, which may occur as goal formulas,
2. negative $(-)$ subformulas, which may occur in the nonmodal context,
3. negative focused $(\sim)$ subformulas, which may occur in the nonmodal stoup,
4. valid $(=)$ subformulas, which may occur in the modal context, or
5. valid focused $(\approx)$ subformulas, which may occur in the modal stoup.

With this intended interpretation, it is straightforward to read the formal definition of refined signed subformulas directly from the inference rules of $\mathbf{MJ^F_{IS4}}$.

Definition 1 (Signed subformulas). *A signed subformula A^* is a formula A with a sign $* \in \{+, -, \sim, =, \approx\}$. The subformula relation $\leq$ is the smallest reflexive and transitive relation between signed subformulas satisfying the following.*

$$A_1^-, A_2^+ \leq (A_1 \supset A_2)^+ \quad A_i^+ \leq (A_1 \wedge A_2)^+ \quad A_i^+ \leq (A_1 \vee A_2)^+$$

$$A^+ \leq (\square A)^+ \quad A^+ \leq (\lozenge A)^+ \quad A^\sim \leq A^-$$

$$A_1^+, A_2^\sim \leq (A_1 \supset A_2)^\sim \quad A_i^\sim \leq (A_1 \wedge A_2)^\sim \quad A_i^- \leq (A_1 \vee A_2)^\sim$$

$$A^= \leq (\square A)^\sim \quad A^- \leq (\lozenge A)^\sim \quad A^\approx \leq A^=$$

$$A_1^+, A_2^\approx \leq (A_1 \supset A_2)^\approx \quad A_i^\approx \leq (A_1 \wedge A_2)^\approx \quad A_i^- \leq (A_1 \vee A_2)^\approx$$

$$A^= \leq (\square A)^\approx \quad A^- \leq (\lozenge A)^\approx$$

$$i \in \{1, 2\}$$

Note that for every negative subformula A^- of a signed formula C^*, C^* also has, as a subformula, the corresponding negative focused subformula $A^\sim$. The converse, however, is not true in general. A similar relation holds for valid and valid focused subformulas. Also, the usual signed subformula property extends to encompass our refined signing scheme, where we write Γ^- and $\Delta^=$ for contexts of signed subformulas of the forms $A_1^-, \ldots, A_n^-$ and $B_1^=, \ldots, B_m^=$, respectively.

Theorem 3 (Signed subformula property). *Every sequent in an $\mathbf{MJ^F_{IS4}}$ derivation of*

$$\Delta^=; \Gamma^- \mapsto C^+ \qquad or \qquad \Delta^=; \Gamma^- \rhd^i A^* \mapsto C^+, \; i \in \{1, 2\}$$

where $*$ is $\sim$ or $\approx$ if $i = 1$ or $i = 2$, respectively, is of the form

1. $D_1^=, \ldots, D_n^=; E_1^-, \ldots, E_m^- \mapsto F^+,$

2. $D_{\bar{1}}^{=}, \ldots, D_{\bar{n}}^{=}; E_{\bar{1}}^{-}, \ldots, E_{m}^{-} \triangleright E^{\sim} \mapsto F^{+}$, *or*

3. $D_{\bar{1}}^{=}, \ldots, D_{\bar{n}}^{=}; E_{\bar{1}}^{-}, \ldots, E_{m}^{-} \triangleright \triangleright D^{\approx} \mapsto F^{+}$,

where all $D_{\bar{j}}^{=}$, E_{k}^{-}, and $E^{\sim}$, $D^{\approx}$, and F^{+} are signed subformulas of $\Delta^{=}$, Γ^{-}, C^{+}, and A^{*}.

Proof. By simultaneous induction on the structure of the given derivation.   □

Theorem 3 guarantees, for instance, that in any $\mathbf{MJ}_{\mathbf{IS4}}^{\mathbf{F}}$ derivation of the sequent $\Delta^{=}; \Gamma^{-} \mapsto C^{+}$, all leaves are of the forms

$$\frac{A \text{ is atomic}}{\cdot; \cdot \triangleright^{i} A^{*} \mapsto A^{+}} \text{ init}_{i} \quad \text{or} \quad \frac{}{\cdot; \cdot \triangleright^{i} \perp^{*} \mapsto B^{+}} \perp L_{i} \quad i \in \{1, 2\}$$

where $*$ is $\sim$ or $\approx$ if $i = 1$ or $i = 2$, respectively, and A^{*}, A^{+}, $\perp^{*}$ and B^{+} must be signed subformulas of $\Delta^{=}$, Γ^{-}, and C^{+}. In general, every rule application considered by an implementation of the inverse method must abide by the conditions set forth by the extended signed subformula property. This provides a foundation for a focused inverse method prover for **IS4** with nondeterminism restricted more strongly than by the usual subformula property.

However, pure forward proof search techniques such as the inverse method also have shortcomings. For instance, the existence of two $\supset$R rules is a concession to the need for localized weakening, something usually handled more elegantly in backward decision procedures by general weakening. Also, the refined focusing we have introduced strongly restricts what rules are applicable, something that a decision procedure should be able to exploit in order to generate fewer intermediate sequents. These issues are addressed in the next section by combining ideas from forward and backward proof search.

4   Bidirectional Proof Search in Sequent Calculus

The idea behind the bidirectional sequent calculus method is that given a query formula A, we can, by exploiting forward proof search techniques, but before performing proof search itself, construct a set of derived inference rules for $\mathbf{MJ}_{\mathbf{IS4}}$ which conceal all left-rule applications that could be needed in a proof of A. We then carry out backward proof search over these relevant derived rules and the usual right-rules of $\mathbf{MJ}_{\mathbf{IS4}}$. By design, our derived inference rules will correspond exactly to the notion of *focused threads* in $\mathbf{MJ}_{\mathbf{IS4}}^{\mathbf{F}}$ derivations, defined as follows.

Definition 2 (Focused threads). *A focused thread of an $\mathbf{MJ}_{\mathbf{IS4}}^{\mathbf{F}}$ derivation is a segment of the derivation that begins, at the top, with an application of init_{i}, $\perp L_{i}$, $\vee L_{i}$, $\square L_{i}$, or $\Diamond L_{i}$, $i \in \{1, 2\}$ (raising a formula into a stoup), includes only focused sequents, and ends with an application of ch_{i} (dropping a formula from the stoup).*

In any $\mathbf{MJ}_{\mathbf{IS4}}^{\mathbf{F}}$ derivation of an unfocused sequent, left-rule applications must occur in focused threads, so we can think of derivations as consisting of focused threads strung together using right-rule applications. The key insight is that all focused threads possibly needed in an $\mathbf{MJ^F_{IS4}}$ proof of a formula A can be deterministically constructed prior to proof search by inspecting the structure of A. To justify this claim, we will use our refined subformula property.

First note that it is straightforward to uniquely label subformula occurrences of a formula to be proved, and that the definition of signed subformulas, the signed subformula property, and the inference rules of $\mathbf{MJ^F_{IS4}}$ can be adjusted to operate on labels rather than formulas, thus differentiating between subformula occurrences.

To give some intuition as to how to construct all the focused threads possibly needed for a proof of a formula, we will illustrate the approach on the following small example:

$$\overbrace{\underbrace{L_1^-,L_1^\sim}_{\underbrace{L_2^=,L_2^\approx}_{\overbrace{L_3^+}\ \overbrace{L_4^\approx}}}\ \underbrace{L_5^+}_{\underbrace{L_6^+}_{\overbrace{L_7^-,L_7^\sim}\ \overbrace{L_8^+}}}}^{L_0^+}$$
$$\Box(\ A\ \supset\ B\ )\supset\Diamond(\ A\ \supset\ B\ )$$

with subformulas

$$L_0^+,L_3^+,L_5^+,L_6^+,L_8^+,\qquad L_1^-,L_7^-,\qquad L_1^\sim,L_7^\sim,\qquad L_2^=,\qquad \text{and}\qquad L_2^\approx,L_4^\approx.$$

The signed subformula property guarantees that in a proof of the sequent $\cdot;\cdot \mapsto L_0^+$, the only axioms we require are

$$\frac{}{\cdot;\cdot\triangleright L_7^\sim\mapsto L_3^+}\ \mathrm{init_1}\qquad\text{and}\qquad\frac{}{\cdot;\cdot\triangleright\triangleright L_4^\approx\mapsto L_8^+}\ \mathrm{init_2}$$

Consider the first of these axioms. Every left-rule either drops the stoup formula into a context or expands it. The immediate parent of $L_7^\sim$ in the subformula hierarchy is L_7^-, indicating that dropping L_7 into the context is a permissible operation. In fact, it is the *only* operation permitted by the signed subformula property operating on labels. We can collapse this short focused thread into a single derived inference rule:

$$\frac{\dfrac{}{\cdot;\cdot\triangleright L_7^\sim\mapsto L_3^+}\ \mathrm{init_1}}{\cdot;L_7^-\mapsto L_3^+}\ \mathrm{ch_1}\qquad\rightsquigarrow\qquad\frac{}{\cdot;L_7^-\mapsto L_3^+}\quad(1)$$

Considering the second axiom, we notice that the parent subformula of $L_4^\approx$ is $L_2^\approx$, also a focused subformula. The next rule application should then be $\supset\mathsf{L}_2$, with $L_2^\approx$ as the principal formula. In fact, it is not difficult to see that since every subformula occurrence has a unique parent subformula, the signed subformula property operating on labels always uniquely dictates which rule may be applied. This game continues until the end of the focused thread. In the case of the second axiom, the immediate parent of $L_2^{\approx}$ is $L_2^{\equiv}$, signalling an application of ch_2 and the end of the thread:

$$\dfrac{\dfrac{\Delta; \Gamma \mapsto L_3^+ \quad \overline{\cdot; \cdot \triangleright \triangleright L_4^{\approx} \mapsto L_8^+}\ \mathsf{init}_2}{\dfrac{\Delta; \Gamma \triangleright \triangleright L_2^{\approx} \mapsto L_8^+}{\Delta, L_2^{\equiv}; \Gamma \mapsto L_8^+}\ \mathsf{ch}_2}\ {\supset}\mathsf{L}_2} \qquad \leadsto \qquad \dfrac{\Delta; \Gamma \mapsto L_3^+}{\Delta, L_2^{\equiv}; \Gamma \mapsto L_8^+}\ (2)$$

Note that this thread, unlike the one concealed by (1), has open premises and is parametric in the contexts Δ and Γ. Finally, the signed subformula property allows one more focused thread, starting with

$$\dfrac{\Delta, L_2^{\equiv}; \Gamma \mapsto M^+}{\Delta; \Gamma \triangleright L_1^{\sim} \mapsto M^+}\ {\square}\mathsf{L}_1$$

The immediate parent subformula of $L_1^{\sim}$ is L_1^-, so this thread ends here, yielding the derived rule

$$\dfrac{\dfrac{\Delta, L_2^{\equiv}; \Gamma \mapsto M^+}{\Delta; \Gamma \triangleright L_1^{\sim} \mapsto M^+}\ {\square}\mathsf{L}_1}{\Delta; \Gamma, L_1^- \mapsto M^+}\ \mathsf{ch}_1 \qquad \leadsto \qquad \dfrac{\Delta, L_2^{\equiv}; \Gamma \mapsto M^+}{\Delta; \Gamma, L_1^- \mapsto M^+}\ (3)$$

Notice that this big step rule is schematic not only in the contexts Δ and Γ, but also in the goal formula M^+. Since the signed subformula property allows no other focused threads, the remainder of the proof, if one exists, may only chain the derived rules (1), (2), and (3) together with right-rule applications. In this case, completing the proof is straightforward:

$$\dfrac{\dfrac{\dfrac{\dfrac{\dfrac{\dfrac{\overline{\cdot; L_7^- \mapsto L_3^+}\ (1)}{L_2^{\equiv}; L_7^- \mapsto L_8^+}\ (2)}{L_2^{\equiv}; \cdot \mapsto L_6^+}\ {\supset}\mathsf{R}}{L_2^{\equiv}; \cdot \mapsto L_5^+}\ {\Diamond}\mathsf{R}}{\cdot; L_1^- \mapsto L_5^+}\ (3)}{\cdot; \cdot \mapsto L_0^+}\ {\supset}\mathsf{R}}$$

In general, to cover all focused threads, the construction of derived rules must begin with focused sequents of the following kinds, where $*$ is $\sim$ or $\approx$, depending on whether $i = 1$ or $i = 2$:

1. $\cdot; \cdot \triangleright^i L_j^* \mapsto L_k^+$, where L_j and L_k denote the same atomic formula,
2. $\cdot; \cdot \triangleright^i L_j^* \mapsto M^+$, where L_j denotes $\bot$ and M is schematic,
3. $\Delta; \Gamma \triangleright^i L_j^* \mapsto M^+$, where L_j denotes some $A_1 \vee A_2$ and M is schematic,
4. $\Delta; \Gamma \triangleright^i L_j^* \mapsto M^+$, where L_j denotes some $\square A$ and M is schematic, and
5. $\Delta; \Gamma \triangleright^i L_j^* \mapsto M^+$, where L_j denotes some $\Diamond A$ and M denotes some $\Diamond C$, C being schematic.

Moreover, the constructed derived rules must end with a stoup formula being dropped into one of the contexts.

The question now is how these forward-constructed derived rules can complement backward proof search. The key observation is that every focused thread of an $\mathbf{MJ^F_{IS4}}$ derivation can be converted into a focused thread of an $\mathbf{MJ_{IS4}}$ derivation by applying weakening, reducing valid focused sequents to focused sequents, and omitting the now unnecessary signs of subformula labels. For instance,

$$
\cfrac{\cfrac{\Delta; \Gamma \mapsto L_3^+ \quad \overline{\cdot; \cdot \rhd \rhd L_4^\approx \mapsto L_8^+}\ \mathsf{init}_2}{\Delta; \Gamma \rhd \rhd L_2^\approx \mapsto L_8^+}\ \supset\!\mathsf{L}_2}{\Delta, L_2^=; \Gamma \mapsto L_8^+}\ \mathsf{ch}_2
$$

can be converted into the $\mathbf{MJ_{IS4}}$ derivation segment

$$
\cfrac{\cfrac{\Delta_1, L_2, \Delta_2; \Gamma \to L_3 \quad \overline{\Delta_1, L_2, \Delta_2; \Gamma \rhd L_4 \to L_8}\ \mathsf{init}}{\Delta_1, L_2, \Delta_2; \Gamma \rhd L_2 \to L_8}\ \supset\!\mathsf{L}}{\Delta_1, L_2, \Delta_2; \Gamma \to L_8}\ \mathsf{ch}_2
$$

This makes it possible to construct derived rules for $\mathbf{MJ_{IS4}}$. The benefit of performing backward proof search over these derived rules and the remaining right rules is that it requires no conventional loop-detection. However, some bookkeeping is still required, since our bidirectional decision procedure has one important termination requirement: that every derived rule that every derived rule instance — characterized by the identity of the schematic derived rule and the concrete goal formula, if applicable — is used is used at most once along every branch of the proof, from root to leaf. The following result of $\mathbf{MJ_{IS4}}$ guarantees that this requirement does not cost us completeness.

Theorem 4 (Uniqueness of stoup and goal formula occurrences on branches). *If a sequent $\Delta; \Gamma \to L$ is derivable, then it has a derivation with the property that no branch (from root to leaf) contains more than one application of ch_i, $i \in \{1, 2\}$ with the same stoup and goal formula occurrences, and the same formula occurrence raised into the stoup at the top of the thread terminated by this application of ch_i.*

Proof. A derivation with loops of this kind can be shortened by collapsing segments between repeated applications of ch_i, $i \in \{1, 2\}$. $\qquad\square$

Since the identity of a focused thread depends on the identities of the focused formula occurrences it contains, and on its goal formula occurrence, we obtain the following important corollary.

Corollary 1. *If a sequent $\Delta; \Gamma \to L$ is derivable, then it has a derivation with the property that no focused thread instance occurs more than once along a branch.*

The consequence of this result is that if a sequent is provable in $\mathbf{MJ_{IS4}}$, then it is provable without using any derived rule instances more than once along a branch. With the observation that every right rule of $\mathbf{MJ_{IS4}}$ reduces the complexity of the goal formula, this means that every rule application during backward proof search in $\mathbf{MJ_{IS4}}$ with derived rule instances either reduces the number of available derived rule instances along the current branch, or leaves the number of available derived rules unchanged but reduces the complexity of the goal formula. This measure gives an immediate termination guarantee without the need for conventional loop-detection. All that is needed is a way of keeping track of which derived rules have been applied along a branch. While this bookkeeping apparatus is reminiscent of a history mechanism, we expect it to be far more lightweight than maintaining histories of previously encountered sequents or goal formulas, as is common in standard loop-detection schemes. Our expectations will, for the most part, be vindicated by our experimental results. Note that the idea of constructing relevant derived rules prior to proof search can also be exploited in forward proof search, where the derived rules described above can take the place of left rules in the inverse method. The main advantages here are that the derived rules are more relevant to proof search for the given query formula, and that the number of intermediate sequents added to the knowledge base during proof search is reduced, since no focused sequents need to be maintained.

5   Bidirectional Proof Search in Natural Deduction

In the backward bidirectional sequent calculus method, we construct derived rules to conceal all required focused threads. Notice that the focused threads of $\mathbf{MJ_{IS4}^F}$ correspond naturally to segments of $\mathbf{NJ_{IS4}^N}$ proofs consisting of elimination rule applications, that is, $\downarrow$ judgements. The beginnings of focused threads, where formulas are placed into the stoup, correspond to *reversing rules* in $\mathbf{NJ_{IS4}^N}$. These are the $\uparrow\downarrow$ rule, as well as all elimination rules with $\uparrow$ judgements as their conclusions. The ends of focused threads, on the other hand, where the stoup formula is dropped into a context, correspond to using a hypothesis with applications of $\mathsf{hyp_1}$ or $\mathsf{hyp_2}$.

This means that the process of building a derived $\mathbf{MJ_{IS4}^F}$ rule in a top-down way corresponds to building a natural deduction derived rule by beginning with an application of a reversing rule, and growing it upwards until we reach a leaf. Just as the construction of derived rules in the sequent calculus is determined uniquely by the form of the query formula, so these natural deduction derived rules can be deterministically constructed before proof search even begins.

This approach is best demonstrated by an example such as the one given in Sect. 4. For instance, given the pair $L_4^{\approx}$ and L_8^+ from that example, we begin with the coercion

$$\frac{\Delta; \Gamma \vdash L_4^{\approx} \downarrow}{\Delta; \Gamma \vdash L_8^+ \uparrow} \uparrow\downarrow$$

Since the immediate parent of $L_4^{\approx}$ in the signed subformula hierarchy is $L_2^{\approx}$, denoting $A \supset B$, the rule application above this coercion must be an application of $\supset$E:

$$\frac{\dfrac{\Delta; \Gamma \vdash L_2^{\approx} \downarrow \quad \Delta; \Gamma \vdash L_3^+ \uparrow}{\Delta; \Gamma \vdash L_4^{\approx} \downarrow}\supset E}{\Delta; \Gamma \vdash L_8^+ \uparrow} \uparrow\downarrow$$

The focused thread continues along the first premise, but the parent of $L_2^{\approx}$ is $L_2^{\overline{=}}$, indicating the end of this focused thread by an application of hyp_2:

$$\frac{\dfrac{\dfrac{L_2^{\overline{=}} \in \Delta}{\Delta; \Gamma \vdash L_2^{\approx} \downarrow}\mathsf{hyp}_2 \quad \Delta; \Gamma \vdash L_3^+ \uparrow}{\Delta; \Gamma \vdash L_4^{\approx} \downarrow}\supset E}{\Delta; \Gamma \vdash L_8^+ \uparrow} \uparrow\downarrow \quad \rightsquigarrow \quad \frac{\Delta_1, L_2^{\overline{=}}, \Delta_2; \Gamma \vdash L_3^+ \uparrow}{\Delta_1, L_2^{\overline{=}}, \Delta_2; \Gamma \vdash L_8^+ \uparrow} \; (2)$$

In similar constructions, the pair $L_7^{\sim}$, L_3^+ and $L_1^{\sim}$, the latter denoting $\square(A \supset B)$, produce, respectively, the natural deduction derived rules

$$\frac{\dfrac{L_7^- \in \Gamma}{\Delta; \Gamma \vdash L_7^{\sim} \downarrow}\mathsf{hyp}_1}{\Delta; \Gamma \vdash L_3^+ \uparrow} \uparrow\downarrow \quad \rightsquigarrow \quad \frac{}{\Delta; \Gamma_1, L_7^-, \Gamma_2 \vdash L_3^+ \uparrow} \; (1)$$

and

$$\frac{\dfrac{L_1^- \in \Gamma}{\Delta; \Gamma \vdash L_1^{\sim} \downarrow}\mathsf{hyp}_1 \quad \Delta, L_2^{\overline{=}}; \Gamma \vdash M^+ \uparrow}{\Delta; \Gamma \vdash M^+ \uparrow}\square E \quad \rightsquigarrow \quad \frac{\Delta, L_2^{\overline{=}}; \Gamma_1, L_1^-, \Gamma_2 \vdash M^+ \uparrow}{\Delta; \Gamma_1, L_1^-, \Gamma_2 \vdash M^+ \uparrow} \; (3)$$

The rest of the proof then uses only these derived rules and introduction rules:

$$\frac{\dfrac{\dfrac{\dfrac{\dfrac{\dfrac{}{L_2^{\overline{=}}; L_1^-, L_7^- \vdash L_3^+ \uparrow}\;(1)}{L_2^{\overline{=}}; L_1^-, L_7^- \vdash L_8^+ \uparrow}\;(2)}{L_2^{\overline{=}}; L_1^- \vdash L_6^+ \uparrow}\supset I}{L_2^{\overline{=}}; L_1^- \vdash L_5^+ \uparrow}\Diamond I}{\cdot; L_1^- \vdash L_5^+ \uparrow}\;(3)}{\cdot; \cdot \vdash L_0^+ \uparrow}\supset I$$

In general, the approach for constructing natural deduction derived rules is analogous to the method for the backward bidirectional sequent calculus, only turned upside-down, in the sense that the rule at the beginning of an $\mathbf{MJ}_{\mathsf{IS4}}^{\mathsf{F}}$ focused thread determines the reversing rule at the bottom of the natural deduction focused thread, while the final application of hyp_i dictates the "principal formula" of the ensuing derived natural deduction rule.

Proof search over natural deductions can then be performed in a backward direction. The only nondeterminism is in whether to apply a derived rule or an introduction rule, the premises of which are uniquely determined by their conclusions. Note that to guarantee termination, we again disallow using a derived rule instance more than once along any branch of a proof.

Table 1. Selection of experimental results

Formula	Size	Modalities	Provable	Histories Time	Inverse Time	Rules	Bidirectional Time	Rules
32	49	0	N	> 1000	1.36	33	0.01	33
36	175	0	Y	0.08	> 1000	159	> 1000	592
37	68	9	Y	84.79	1.18	60	< 0.01	28
39	42	3	N	8.46	1.83	31	< 0.01	15
44	49	14	Y	75.13	> 1000	51	37.11	21
50	44	7	Y	7.38	> 1000	49	48.76	25

6   Experimental Results

While benchmark formulas are available for intuitionistic propositional logic and classical modal logics, we are not aware of any benchmark libraries specific to propositional **IS4**. In order to evaluate the performance of our bidirectional approach, we put together a benchmark set of 50 formulas for **IS4**, mostly problems from Raths et al.'s Intuitionistic Logic Theorem Proving (ILTP) library [17] to which we introduced modalities. Our full benchmark set is provided as an appendix to the accompanying technical report [10].

We implemented three **IS4** decision procedures in SML: (1) an MJ_{IS4}-based backward prover with a history mechanism for loop-detection, (2) an MJ_{IS4}^{F}-based inverse method prover without derived rules, and (3) our bidirectional natural deduction prover. The loop-detection prover maintains two histories to detect repeated modal and nonmodal rule applications, respectively. This approach is a generalization of Howe's decision procedure [11] extended to full **IS4**. Note that the behaviour of our backward bidirectional sequent calculus prover corresponds exactly to that of the bidirectional natural deduction prover, so we have only implemented the more elegant natural deduction prover.

On many of the smaller problems, there was little measurable difference in the performance of the provers, but some of the problems that did elicit noticeably different performances are highlighted in Table 1. The size column shows the complexity of each formula, computed inductively in the usual way, while the modalities column shows the number of modal operators. Times are in seconds.[1] For the inverse method and bidirectional provers, we show the number of inference rules generated (derived rules in the case of the bidirectional prover).

As the results demonstrate, the bidirectional natural deduction prover is a competitive alternative to the more conventional provers, equalling or outperforming them on most problems. Comparing the average proving time for problems that were solved, it is noticeably superior, although we found two formulas on which it was significantly outperformed (formulas 36 and 50 in Table 1).

---

[1] All timing results were obtained on a Pentium III 850 MHz with 256 MB of RAM, running SML/NJ version 110.60.

Interestingly, there is not always a clear connection between the number of derived rules generated and the time required to solve a problem. Presumably, the problematic cases were those whose derived rules were the shortest and least useful. Note also that as derived rules are associated with subformula occurrences, those formulas with many repeated subformulas (e.g. formula 36) caused a very large number of duplicate derived rules to be generated.

7   Related and Future Work

Although **IS4** has undergone thorough proof-theoretical studies, there has been little work in developing proof search strategies specific to it. We have presented a comprehensive study of proof search formalisms for **IS4**, highlighting the duality between backward and forward search. Moreover, we have demonstrated how to combine the benefits of both to yield bidirectional decision procedures based on sequent calculi and natural deduction. Our experimental results reveal that combining the two traditionally disparate paradigms can be fruitful. Although our implementations are naive and unoptimized, we hope that our results might encourage further study of bidirectional proof search, particularly in other logics.

For instance, in the contextual modal logic of Nanevski, Pfenning, and Pientka [14], structural modality is generalized by relativizing the validity judgement and the modal operators. The techniques discussed in this paper extend very naturally to contextual modal logic, yielding sequent calculi suitable for backward and forward proof search, but the exact nature of how such a generalization affects proof search is yet to be explored. The reconciliation of forward and backward proof search has recently also been investigated by Chaudhuri and Pfenning [2], who, in the context of linear logic, propose a focusing inverse method prover incorporating derived rules constructed in a backward way and searched over in a forward direction, precisely opposite to our approach.

In the future, we plan to explore extensions to the first-order case. Although the idea of derived rules extends, in principle, to first-order quantifiers, the constructed derived rules become parametric in terms. The useful property of **MJ**$_{IS4}$ that eliminated the need for conventional loop-detection in our bidirectional method now only holds for particular instantiations of the terms of the parametric derived rules. Unfortunately, requiring the storage of rule instantiations introduces another layer of bookkeeping. How to efficiently overcome this problem and what the proof-theoretical relationship between first-order bidirectional decision procedures and natural deduction provers is remains to be investigated.

Acknowledgements. We would like to thank Daniel Pomerantz for discussions on forward proof search and for the implementation of the inverse method prover, and the reviewers for their insightful comments and suggestions.

References

1. Bierman, G.M., de Paiva, V.C.V.: On an intuitionistic modal logic. Studia Logica 65(3), 383–416 (2000)
2. Chaudhuri, K., Pfenning, F.: Focusing the inverse method for linear logic. In: Ong, L. (ed.) CSL 2005. LNCS, vol. 3634, pp. 200–215. Springer, Heidelberg (2005)
3. Davies, R., Pfenning, F.: A modal analysis of staged computation. Journal of the ACM 48(3), 555–604 (2001)
4. Degtyarev, A., Voronkov, A.: The inverse method. In: Robinson, J.A., Voronkov, A. (eds.) Handbook of Automated Reasoning, pp. 179–272. Elsevier and MIT Press (2001)
5. Dyckhoff, R., Pinto, L.: A permutation-free sequent calculus for intuitionistic logic. Research Report CS/96/9, University of St. Andrews (1996)
6. Fairtlough, M., Mendler, M.: Propositional lax logic. Information and Computation 137(1), 1–33 (1997)
7. Fitch, F.B.: Intuitionistic modal logic with quantifiers. Portugaliae Mathematica 7(2), 113–118 (1948)
8. Girard, J.-Y.: A new constructive logic: Classical logic. Mathematical Structures in Computer Science 1(3), 255–296 (1991)
9. Girard, J.-Y., Lafont, Y., Taylor, P.: Proofs and types. Cambridge University Press, Cambridge (1989)
10. Heilala, S., Pientka, B.: Bidirectional decision procedures for the intuitionistic propositional modal logic IS4. Technical Report SOCS-TR-2007.2, McGill University (May 2007)
11. Howe, J.M.: Proof search issues in some non-classical logics. PhD thesis, University of St. Andrews (1998)
12. Howe, J.M.: Proof search in lax logic. Mathematical Structures in Computer Science 11(4), 573–588 (2001)
13. Moody, J.: Modal logic as a basis for distributed computation. Technical Report CMU-CS-03-194, Carnegie Mellon University (2003)
14. Nanevski, A., Pfenning, F., Pientka, B.: Contextual modal type theory. ACM Transactions on Computational Logic (to appear)
15. Pfenning, F., Davies, R.: A judgmental reconstruction of modal logic. Mathematical Structures in Computer Science 11(4), 511–540 (2001)
16. Prawitz, D.: Natural deduction: A proof-theoretical study. Almqvist & Wiksell (1965)
17. Raths, T., Otten, J., Kreitz, C.: The ILTP problem library for intuitionistic logic, release v1.1. Journal of Automated Reasoning (to appear)
18. Satre, T.W.: Natural deduction rules for modal logics. Notre Dame Journal of Formal Logic 13(4), 461–475 (1972)
19. Simpson, A.K.: The proof theory and semantics of intuitionistic modal logic. PhD thesis, University of Edinburgh (1994)

A Labelled System for IPL with Variable Splitting

Roger Antonsen and Arild Waaler

Department of Informatics, University of Oslo, Norway

Abstract. The paper introduces a free variable, labelled proof system for intuitionistic propositional logic with variable splitting. In this system proofs can be found without backtracking over rules by generating a single, uniform derivation. We prove soundness, introduce a construction that extracts finite countermodels from unprovable sequents, and formulate a branchwise termination condition. This is the first proof system for intuitionistic propositional logic that admits goal-directed search procedures without compromising proof lengths, compared to corresponding tableau calculi.

1 Introduction

Connection-based search methods for intuitionistic logic were enabled by Wallen's introduction of a matrix characterization for intuitionistic logic [16]. Roughly, Wallen's idea was to encode the rule dependencies in Gentzen-style calculi for intuitionistic logic as term dependencies and to satisfy these dependency constraints by unification. On this basis one can design calculi with only nondestructive rules, in the sense that the rules generate single proof objects, without backtracking over the inference rules. At the time of writing the fastest theorem prover for first-order intuitionistic logic, ileanCoP [9, 10], is connection-based and designed over a matrix-based calculus.

However, for intuitionistic propositional logic (IPL) the connection-based methods do not have easily definable termination conditions, and none of the connection-based provers implement efficient termination conditions. Such conditions can easily be formulated for traditional destructive, multi-succedent calculus (in [13] called m-**G3i**) [11], and for the contraction-free calculi for IPL [4, 7]. In both these types of calculi one can decide termination by a branchwise condition. Currently the best decision procedures for IPL implement a contraction-free calculus [10].

The source of this lies in the variable dependencies imposed by the matrix characterization, a point which is discussed in [14] in relation to a labelled sequent calculus for intuitionistic logic. More precisely, two ways of introducing free variables are discussed: *variable-pure* and *variable-sharing*. In the former case fresh variables are introduced in each inference that generates a free variable, a constraint which enables an exact simulation of m-**G3i**-proofs in the variable-pure calculus [14, Lemma 4.16]. However, the variable-pure calculus is

F. Pfenning (Ed.): CADE 2007, LNAI 4603, pp. 132–146, 2007.

sensitive to the order of rule applications in a way that effectively blocks the possibility of connection-based search procedures.

Variable-sharing derivations are produced if the free variables are generated from *formulas*, that is, a given formula generates the same free variable in every branch in which it is expanded. Used in this way the labelled sequent calculus can be viewed as a rendition of the matrix characterization. Variable-sharing derivations are freely permuting and hence admits connection-based search methods. However, the variable dependencies give rise to redundancies in proof objects which, in the general case, make the proofs longer than in traditional Gentzenstyle calculi.

In this paper we propose a proof system[1] for IPL that remedies the situation for the matrix-based camp. In particular, the proof system that we introduce admits both a local termination condition and goal-directed proof procedures. The proof system utilizes *variable splitting*, a technique which we recently proposed for firstorder logic [1, 2]. The idea behind variable splitting is to identify conditions under which different occurrences of the same variable can be taken as independent, and hence treated as distinct variables. Technically, variables that occur in the leaf of a branch are labelled with the name of the branch; the branch is said to *color* the variables that occur in its leaf. The admissibility condition for proofs is formulated in terms of a relation on the nodes of the formula trees, called a *reduction ordering*. (A solution is *admissible* if the associated reduction ordering is irreflexive.) A property that is not explored in this paper, but worthwhile to mention, is that the admissibility condition entails that a variable splitting proof can be transformed, or even permuted, into a variable-pure proof.

After presenting the proof system, we first prove its soundness, and then introduce a construction that is used to generate finite countermodels for unprovable sequents. This construction incorporates a local termination condition which can be stated independently of the rule application order and which is just as tight as for the variable-pure calculi. Since we are addressing a limit case of termination for unprovable sequents, we are content with using ground substitutions. However, the results pave the way for unification-based proof procedures based on the proposed proof system.

2   Language, Indexing and Derivations

The proof system is formulated in the style of block tableaux [12], and we adopt an indexing system for formulas similar to that used by Wallen [16] and Otten and Kreitz [8].

The language of IPL is defined in the standard way from a nonempty set of proposition letters by means of the logical symbols $\neg$, $\wedge$, $\vee$, and $\rightarrow$. A *signed formula* is a formula with a *polarity*, $\top$ or $\bot$. Typically, assumptions have positive polarity and conclusions have negative polarity. A signed formula has a *principal type*, α or β, determined by its main connective and its polarity according to

---

[1] Even though what we introduce is really a matrix characterization of logical validity for IPL, we will follow usual terminology and refer to it as a proof system.

α	α_1	α_2
$(A \wedge B)^\top$	$A^\top$	$B^\top$
$(A \vee B)^\perp$	$A^\perp$	$B^\perp$
$(A \rightarrow B)^\perp$	$A^\top$	$B^\perp$
$(\neg A)^\top$	$A^\perp$	$A^\perp$
$(\neg A)^\perp$	$A^\top$	$A^\top$

β	β_1	β_2
$(A \wedge B)^\perp$	$A^\perp$	$B^\perp$
$(A \vee B)^\top$	$A^\top$	$B^\top$
$(A \rightarrow B)^\top$	$A^\perp$	$B^\top$

ϕ	ψ
$(A \rightarrow B)^\top$	$(A \rightarrow B)^\perp$
$(\neg A)^\top$	$(\neg A)^\perp$

Fig. 1. Types and polarities

the tables in Fig. 1. For a given signed formula, the polarities of its immediate subformulas are as specified in the tables, from which the polarities of its subformulas are defined by recursion. The subformulas β_1 and β_2 of a β-formula have an additional *secondary type*, β_0, and signed formulas with the main connective $\rightarrow$ or $\neg$ have an additional *intuitionistic type*, ϕ or ψ, as given in the tables. The intuitionistic types are commonly used for *special* formulas of IPL, formulas that yield properties of non-permutability when expanded [14, 16].

In derivations ϕ-formulas are generative; when they are expanded, a copy is retained for further expansion. We need a fine-grained system to distinguish different formula occurrences within derivations. This is achieved by means of an indexing system for all potential formula occurrences. Specifically, different copies of formulas will be indexed differently. Think of an *indexed formula tree* as a representation of a signed formula as a tree, where all copies of ϕ-formulas are made explicit and all nodes are marked with an *index*. For every index there is a unique indexed formula and vice versa. When a rule is applied to a ϕ-formula, one of the premisses is always a copy of the formula itself. This *copy* of a ϕ-formula is denoted ϕ', and has an index different from ϕ. The indices of ϕ- and ψ-formulas are called *variables* and *parameters*, respectively. The letters u, v, w etc., are used for variables, and the letters a, b, c etc., are used for parameters. If a formula F has polarity P and index i, we write F_i^P for the corresponding *indexed formula*. From now on, unless otherwise specified, we assume all formulas to be signed and indexed.

A set of formulas is called a *sequent*. A *derivation* of a sequent Γ is a finite tree, with root node Γ, obtained by iteratively applying the derivation rules in Fig. 2.

The rules should be read bottom-up; for example, if Γ, α is the leaf sequent of a derivation, then $\Gamma^*, \alpha_1, \alpha_2$ is a new sequent added above Γ, α. The sequent below the horizontal line is called the *conclusion* of the *inference*, and the sequents above are called the *premisses*. The formulas α and β below the horizontal line

$$\frac{\Gamma^*, \alpha_1, \alpha_2}{\Gamma, \alpha} \qquad \frac{\Gamma^*, \beta_1 \quad \Gamma, \beta_2}{\Gamma, \beta}$$

Fig. 2. Derivation rules. If the expanded formula is of type ϕ, then $\Gamma^* = \Gamma \cup \{\phi'\}$, otherwise $\Gamma^* = \Gamma$

are said to be *expanded* in a derivation. Sequents are for readability displayed in the form $\Gamma^\top \vdash \Gamma^\perp$, where Γ^P is the set of formulas with polarity P, and selected indices are sometimes displayed below the root sequent.

For a derivation to be a *proof* of its root sequent in classical logic, there must be a pair of complementary formulas in each of the leaves in the derivation. This is equivalent to the matrix characterization of logical validity [3, 16]. In order to extend this characterization to intuitionistic logic, one usually associates *prefixes* with formulas and requires the prefixes of complementary formulas to be unifiable. The following ordering is important and used throughout the paper.

The ordering $\ll$ is a partial ordering on indices that captures the subformula ordering, or the order in which formulas must be expanded in a derivation. It is defined as the transitive closure of $\ll_1$, where $i \ll_1 j$ holds if G_j is an immediate subformula, or the copy of, F_i. Intuitively, the formulas occurring in the root sequent of a derivation always have the least indices with respect to the ordering. For example, in Fig. 3, the $\ll_1$-ordering is displayed for the formula $\neg(\neg P \to Q)_a^\perp$.

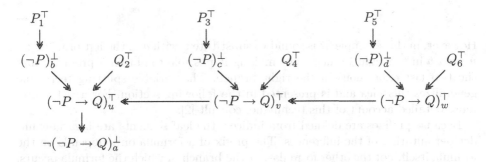

Fig. 3. The $\ll_1$-ordering for $\neg(\neg P \to Q)_a^\perp$. If $F_a \longleftarrow F_b$, then $a \ll_1 b$ holds.

For the purpose of defining prefixes, we do not want to relate copies of indices to each other, so let $i \lessdot_1 j$ if G_j is an immediate subformula of F_i, or the copy of an immediate subformula of F_i. For example, in Fig. 3 we have that $a \lessdot_1 v$ and $v \lessdot_1 c$, but neither that $u \lessdot_1 v$ nor that $u \lessdot_1 c$. Let $\lessdot$ be the transitive closure of $\lessdot_1$. The *prefix* of a formula F_i, or more generally the prefix of i, is the string $a_1 \ldots a_n$, where $a_1 \lessdot \ldots \lessdot a_n$ are all the indices of type ϕ or ψ that are $\lessdot$-less than i. The empty string is denoted ϵ. For example, in Fig. 3, the prefix of $P_3^\top$ is avc. The prefix of a formula is displayed in square brackets, like in $P[avc]$. We require that all formulas in a root sequent of a derivation have the empty prefix. In general, a string over variables and parameters is called a *label*, and a label is called *ground* if it contains only parameters. If p is an initial substring of q, we write $p \preceq q$; if p is an initial proper substring of q, we write $p \prec q$.

For a derivation to be a *proof* of its root sequent in intuitionistic logic, there must be a pair of complementary formulas for each of the leaves in the derivation, as for classical logic. Additionally, there must exist a single substitution that makes p an initial substring of q for each such pair $F[p]^\top$ and $F[q]^\perp$ of complementary formulas [16]. Intuitively, this enforces an order constraint on the expansion of ϕ- and ψ-formulas in calculi *without* free variables [13, 15] due to the fact that the ϕ- and ψ-rules in such calculi do not permute. A proof of a formula F is simply a proof of the sequent $\vdash F$.

Example 1. The following derivation, together with the substitution $\{u/a, v/b\}$, is an intuitionistic proof.

$$\frac{\dfrac{\dfrac{\neg(P \vee Q)[\epsilon], \overline{Q[b]} \vdash P[u], Q[u], P[v], \overline{Q[v]}}{\neg(P \vee Q)[\epsilon], Q[b] \vdash P[u], Q[u], (P \vee Q)[v]}}{\neg(P \vee Q)[\epsilon], Q[b] \vdash P[u], Q[u]}}{} $$

$$\frac{\dfrac{\neg(P \vee Q)[\epsilon], \overline{P[a]} \vdash \overline{P[u]}, Q[u]}{\neg(P \vee Q)[\epsilon] \vdash \neg P[\epsilon], P[u], Q[u]} \qquad \dfrac{\neg(P \vee Q)[\epsilon], Q[b] \vdash P[u], Q[u]}{\neg(P \vee Q)[\epsilon] \vdash \neg Q[\epsilon], P[u], Q[u]}}{\dfrac{\neg(P \vee Q)[\epsilon] \vdash \neg P \wedge \neg Q[\epsilon], P[u], Q[u]}{\dfrac{\neg(P \vee Q)[\epsilon] \vdash \neg P \wedge \neg Q[\epsilon], (P \vee Q)[u]}{\underset{u/v}{\neg} (P \vee Q)[\epsilon] \vdash \underset{a}{\neg} P \wedge \underset{b}{\neg} Q[\epsilon]}}}$$

$\dashv$

However, in this example, it is sound to substitute u with a in the left branch and u with b in the right branch, thus making it possible to obtain a proof *without* the two last expansions in the right branch. The variable splitting technique generalizes this idea and is presented in the following section. For a richer and more detailed account of this technique, consult [2].

Because prefixes are defined from indices, the leaf sequents are invariant under permutation of the inferences. The prefix of a formula only depends on the formula itself, not the other formulas, or the branch in which the formula occurs. Thus, for any two expanded formulas that occur in the same branch, and that are not subformula-related, it is possible to permute the derivation into a form where one formula is expanded below the other, or the other way around. More generally, for any relation $<$ such that the transitive closure of $\ll \cup <$ is irreflexive, a derivation can be permuted such that it *conforms to* $<$, that is, if $a < b$, then a is expanded below b in every branch where both a and b are expanded. For a more thorough explanation of permutability properties, see [14].

There is in fact a proviso for this permutability claim, which is caused by the asymmetry of the β-rule, namely, that an expanded ϕ-formula $(F \rightarrow G)^{\top}$ is copied into the left premiss and not into the right. If we copy the formula into the right premiss as well, we gain full permutability. This can, however, also be achieved without the copy in the right premiss; we shall, however, spare the reader for these details.

3   Variable Splitting and Admissibility

Variable splitting allows us to assign a value to a variable relative to the branch in which it occurs, so that a variable receives a particular value in one branch and a different value in another. A simple way to do this is to annotate a variable with a name of the branch in which it occurs. For each branch of a derivation there is a set B of all the formulas contained in it, and we use the set of indices of the β_0-formulas in B as the name of the branch. For example, if $(P \lor Q)^\top$ is expanded in a derivation, one set contains the index of P and the other set contains the index of Q. In examples, these sets are written as strings. A *colored variable* is a variable u together with the name A of a branch, written u^A. If p is the prefix of a formula in the leaf sequent of a branch B, then $\widehat{p}$ denotes the *colored prefix* where all variables u have been replaced by u^B (the branch will always be always be clear from the context when the notation $\widehat{p}$ is used.)

A *substitution* is a function σ from colored variables to ground labels, which is extended to arbitrary labels in the standard way. The application of σ to an argument p is written in the postfix notation $p\sigma$. For the sake of simplicity, we are here assuming that all substitutions are *total* and *ground*. It is sometimes convenient to define substitutions relative to a branch B, and in this case we simply ignore the colors and view the substitutions as functions from uncolored variables.

Definition 2. Let D be a derivation of Γ. A substitution σ *closes* a leaf sequent Γ' of D if there are formulas $F[p]^\top$ and $F[q]^\perp$ in Γ' such that $\widehat{p}\sigma \preceq \widehat{q}\sigma$. It *closes* D if it closes every leaf sequent of D.   ⊣

In order to characterize intuitionistic validity, it is clearly not sufficient to have a closing substitution, as can be seen from the following example. From now on we omit the copies of ϕ-formula for readability.

Example 3. The following is a derivation of a non-valid root sequent. The variable u occurs in both branch 1 and branch 2, so we obtain the colored variables u^1 and u^2. The derivation is closed by the substitution $\{u^1/a, u^2/b\}$. We shall soon see that this substitution is not admissible.

$$
\cfrac{
\cfrac{
\cfrac{
\cfrac{
\cfrac{
\overline{P[a], Q[b] \vdash \overline{P[u]}} \qquad \overline{P[a], \overline{Q[b]} \vdash \overline{Q[u]}}
}{P[a], Q[b] \vdash (P \land Q)[u]}
}{P[a], Q[b] \vdash}
}{P[a] \vdash \neg Q[\epsilon]}
}{\vdash \neg P[\epsilon], \neg Q[\epsilon]}
}{\underset{u}{\neg} (\underset{1}{P} \land \underset{2}{Q})[\epsilon] \vdash \underset{a}{\neg} P \lor \underset{b}{\neg} Q[\epsilon]}
$$

$$(1 \triangle 2)$$

$$\downarrow\!\!\!\!\!) \; u$$

⊣

Definition 4. If b_1 and b_2 are the indices of the immediate subformulas β_1 and β_2 of a β-formula, then b_1 and b_2 are called *dual*, and $(b_1 \triangle b_2)$ denotes the index of the β-formula. A relation $\sqsubset$ from β-indices to variables is called a *splitting relation* if the following condition holds: if $u^A \sigma \neq u^B \sigma$, then there are dual elements $a \in A$ and $b \in B$ such that $(a \triangle b) \sqsubset u$. The natural way to read $(a \triangle b) \sqsubset u$ is "u depends on $(a \triangle b)$" or "u is split by $(a \triangle b)$". If $\sqsubset$ is a splitting relation, then the transitive closure of $(\ll \cup \sqsubset)$, denoted $\lhd$, is called a *reduction ordering*. We say that a substitution is *admissible* if there exists an irreflexive reduction ordering for it. If D is a derivation of Γ and σ is a substitution, then the tuple $\langle D, \sigma \rangle$ is called a *proof* of Γ if σ closes D and is admissible. $\dashv$

For a given substitution, there can be more than one splitting relation and therefore also more than one reduction ordering. In Example 3, there is only one possible splitting relation and the corresponding reduction ordering is cyclic, as illustrated in the figure on the right-hand side.

A splitting relation can be interpreted as an order constraint on the expansion of β- and ϕ-formulas in calculi where every ϕ-formula introduces a fresh free variable. For instance, if $(a \triangle b) \sqsubset u$, then the formula with index $(a \triangle b)$ should be expanded before the formula with index u, resulting in two occurrences of the u-formula which can introduce different variables.

Example 5. The following is a derivation of a valid root sequent.

$$
\cfrac{
\cfrac{
\cfrac{
\cfrac{
\cfrac{\overline{P[ua], Q[ua] \vdash \overline{P[bv]}}}{(P \wedge Q)[ua] \vdash P[bv]}
}{(P \wedge Q)[ua], \neg P[b] \vdash}
}{(P \wedge Q)[ua] \vdash \neg\neg P[\epsilon]}
\qquad
\cfrac{
\cfrac{
\cfrac{\overline{P[ua], \overline{Q[ua]} \vdash \overline{Q[cw]}}}{(P \wedge Q)[ua] \vdash Q[cw]}
}{(P \wedge Q)[ua], \neg Q[c] \vdash}
}{(P \wedge Q)[ua] \vdash \neg\neg Q[\epsilon]}
}{(P \wedge Q)[ua] \vdash \neg\neg P \wedge \neg\neg Q[\epsilon]}
}{\cfrac{\vdash \neg\neg P \wedge \neg\neg Q[\epsilon], \neg(P \wedge Q)[u]}{\underset{u\,a}{\neg\neg}(P \wedge Q)[\epsilon] \vdash \underset{b\,v}{\neg\neg} P \wedge \underset{c\,w}{\neg\neg} Q[\epsilon]}}
$$

$$
\begin{array}{ccc}
v & w & \\
\downarrow & \downarrow & \\
b & c & a \\
\searrow & \swarrow & \downarrow \\
\triangle & \leftarrow & u
\end{array}
$$

Since $(b \triangle c)$ is the index of the right conjunction, the two branches are named b and c. The leaf sequent of branch b contains $P[ua]^\top$ and $P[bv]^\perp$. The colored prefixes are $\widehat{ua} = u^b a$ and $\widehat{bv} = bv^b$, and this leaf sequent is closed by $\{u^b/b, v^b/a\}$. The substitution $\sigma = \{u^b/b, v^b/a, u^c/c, w^c/a\}$ closes the whole derivation. Let $\sqsubset = \langle (b \triangle c), u \rangle$. It is a splitting relation, since $u^b \sigma = b \neq c = u^c \sigma$ trivially implies that $(b \triangle c) \sqsubset u$. The irreflexivity of the reduction ordering can be seen from the right-hand illustration, where $\triangle \leftarrow u$ stands for $(b \triangle c) \sqsubset u$. We have thus established the admissibility of σ. $\dashv$

4   Labelled Formulas and Semantics

A *labelled formula* is a formula F together with a label p, written $F[p]$. Until now we have only used square brackets to display prefixes of formulas, but from this point we consider all formulas to be labelled. This enables us to apply substitutions to formulas, sequents, and branches.

An *intuitionistic model* is a triple $\langle W, R, V \rangle$, where W is non-empty, R is a partial ordering on W, and V is a function from proposition letters to subsets of W, such that R satisfies the *monotonicity condition*: if $x \in V(P)$ and xRy, then

$y \in V(P)$. The *forcing relation* $\Vdash$ is inductively defined for unsigned formulas in the following way.

$x \Vdash P$	iff	$x \in V(P)$, where P is a proposition letter,
$x \Vdash F \wedge G$	iff	$x \Vdash F$ and $x \Vdash G$,
$x \Vdash F \vee G$	iff	$x \Vdash F$ or $x \Vdash G$,
$x \Vdash F \rightarrow G$	iff	for all y such that xRy, either $y \nVdash F$ or $y \Vdash G$, and
$x \Vdash \neg F$	iff	for all y such that xRy, $y \nVdash F$.

The monotonicity condition transfers from proposition letters to arbitrary formulas: if $x \Vdash F$ and xRy, then $y \Vdash F$. A formula is intuitionistically *valid* if $x \Vdash F$ for every x in every model.

For signed formulas, let $x \Vdash F^{\top}$ iff $x \Vdash F$, and $x \Vdash F^{\perp}$ iff $x \nVdash F$. A *label interpretation function* is a function ι from the set of ground labels to W such that if $p \preceq q$, then $(\iota p)R(\iota q)$. A ground sequent is *falsifiable* if there is a model and a label interpretation function ι such that $\iota(p) \Vdash F$ for all formulas $F[p]$ in Γ (all formulas in Γ have a polarity, by we do not display polarities unless it is needed). In this case we say that Γ is *falsified* under ι and that the model is a *countermodel* for Γ. Note that a formula F is valid exactly when $\vdash F$ is not falsifiable, that is, there is no model such that $x \nVdash F$ for some x.

5   Soundness

In this section we establish the soundness of the variable splitting proof system, that is, we prove that if a formula is provable, it is intuitionistically valid. In brief, we show that if the root sequent of a derivation is falsifiable, then at least one of its leaf sequents is also falsifiable, and therefore not closable by an admissible substitution. In [2] we prove soundness for a similar proof system for first-order logic by an induction over the reduction ordering. While it is perfectly possible to do this also for the current intuitionistic system, we will instead use an alternative, and simpler, approach. Instead of an induction on the reduction ordering, we first permute the derivation into a certain form and then argue by induction on construction of the derivation, that is, we show that each inference preserves falsifiability. As pointed out in Section 2, if the reduction ordering $\lhd$ is irreflexive, a derivation can be permuted such that it conforms to $\lhd$.

To facilitate the argument, we say that a label interpretation function ι is *canonical* if the following two conditions hold.

– if $\iota(p) \nVdash \neg F_a$, then $\iota(pa) \Vdash F$
– if $\iota(p) \nVdash (F \rightarrow G)_a$, then $\iota(pa) \Vdash F$ and $\iota(pa) \nVdash G$

Lemma 6. If a root sequent Γ is falsifiable, then there is a canonical label interpretation function ι such that Γ is falsified under ι.   ⊣

Proof. The proof is by induction on ground labels. Since Γ is falsifiable, and all formulas in Γ have the empty prefix, there must be an x such that $x \Vdash F$ for all formulas F in Γ. Let $\iota(\epsilon) = x$. For all formulas $\neg F^{\perp}$ with index a, if $\iota(p) \not\Vdash \neg F$, then there is a y such that $\iota(p)Ry$ and $y \Vdash F$, so let $\iota(pa) = y$; otherwise, let $\iota(pa) = \iota(p)$. Similarly for all formulas $(F \to G)^{\perp}$.

Lemma 7 (Falsifiability). If the root sequent of a derivation is falsifiable and σ is an admissible substitution, then there is a leaf sequent Γ such that $\widehat{\Gamma}\sigma$ is falsifiable.   ⊣

Proof. Since σ is admissible, there is a splitting relation $\sqsubseteq$ and a reduction ordering $\lhd$ such that $\lhd$ is irreflexive. Permute the derivation such that it conforms to $\lhd$. We shall show that every inference preserves a falsifiability property. In order to state this property, and finally to establish that $\widehat{\Gamma}\sigma$ is falsifiable for some leaf sequent Γ, we shall use σ to assign ground labels to all variables occurring in the derivation. Since σ is defined only for colored variables, we need to propagate the values to uncolored variables. If a variable u occurs in a sequent Γ in a branch B, map this occurrence to $u^B\sigma$. This mapping is well-defined, for suppose for a contradiction that there is a sequent Γ that occurs in both branch B_1 and B_2 and that Γ contains an occurrence of u that is mapped to two different values for the two branches. Then, $u^{B_1}\sigma \neq u^{B_2}\sigma$, so there are dual elements b_1 from B_1 and b_2 from B_2 such that $(b_1 \triangle b_2) \sqsubseteq u$. The formula with index $(b_1 \triangle b_2)$ must have been expanded, otherwise the indices b_1 and b_2 would not be in B_1 and B_2, and this expansion must be somewhere above Γ, since both branches contain Γ. But then, the derivation does not conform to $\lhd$, contrary to the assumption.

By this mapping we can assume that there are only ground labels in the derivation, and by Lemma 6, there is a canonical label interpretation function ι. We proceed to show that if the conclusion of an inference is falsified under ι, then at least one of the premisses is falsified under ι.

- Suppose that the expanded formula is of type ϕ, say $(F \to G)[p]^{\top}$. Then, there is a label pq such that one branch contains $F[pq]^{\perp}$ and one branch contains $G[pq]^{\top}$. By assumption, $\iota(p) \Vdash (F \to G)$. Since $\iota(p)R\iota(pq)$, either $\iota(pq) \Vdash F$ or $\iota(pq) \not\Vdash G$, so one of the premisses is also falsified under ι.
- Suppose that the expanded formula is of type ψ and that its index is a, say $(F \to G)[p]_a^{\perp}$. Then, the premiss contains $F[pa]^{\top}$ and $G[pa]^{\perp}$. By assumption $\iota(p) \not\Vdash (F \to G)_a$. Since ι is canonical, $\iota(pa) \Vdash F$ and $\iota(pa) \not\Vdash G$, so the premiss is also falsifiable under ι.
- The remaining cases are simpler, and left to the reader.

Finally, this yields a branch B with a falsified leaf sequent. If Γ denotes the sequent prior the mapping, and Γ_{σ} denotes the result of the mapping, then Γ_{σ} equals $\widehat{\Gamma}\sigma$, and we are finished.

6   Completeness and Termination

In this section we show how one can construct models from derivations over unprovable sequents. In order to extract information for the model construction in a smooth way we shall restrict the set of substitutions to a set that reflects (parts of) the structure of Kripke models. We also state a property which ensures that the derivation is sufficiently large for the model construction. Since this property always can be satisfied by a finite derivation (we do not prove this in this paper), we shall refer to the property as a *termination condition*. The termination condition stated in this section is defined branchwise and independent of the order of rule application. That the condition is correct follows directly from the completeness theorem.

The condition is defined by constraining the substitutions in a structured way. To this end, let us say that the *weight* of a parameter is 1, that the weight of a variable that is not a copy is 0, and that the weight of the nth copy of a variable is n. Let the weight of a prefix be the sum of the weights of its indices, in particular let the weight of ϵ be 0. For the remainder of the paper, we will only consider substitutions that preserve weights, that is, that map variables of weight n to ground labels of length n. We shall be particularly interested in ground labels that arise on a given branch from substitutions that preserve weights.

Definition 8. The set of *points* for a branch B is inductively defined as follows.

– The empty label, ϵ, is a point for B.
– If p is a point for B, qa is the prefix of a formula in B, and $q\sigma = p$ for a weight-preserving substitution σ, then pa is also a point for B.

For each point p for B, the associated *linear substitution* σ_p is defined by

$$\sigma_p = \bigcup \{\sigma \mid q\sigma \preceq p, q \text{ a prefix in } B, \text{ and } \sigma \text{ weight-preserving}\}. \qquad \dashv$$

Note that the linear substitution maps uncolored variables. Since it is defined branchwise this is just a matter of taste (as a variable u in the domain of σ_p can readily be colored to u^B). Observe that if $p \preceq q$, then $\sigma_p \subseteq \sigma_q$.

Example 9. Let the sequent $\underset{u_0}{\neg\neg P}, \underset{v_0}{\neg\neg Q} \vdash$ be indexed in the following way.

$$
\begin{array}{cccccc}
a & c & e & b & d & f \\
\downarrow & \downarrow & \downarrow & \downarrow & \downarrow & \downarrow \\
u_0 \longleftarrow u_1 \longleftarrow u_2 & & v_0 \longleftarrow v_1 \longleftarrow v_2
\end{array}
$$

After maximally expanding the formulas with indices u_0, u_1, v_0 and v_1, we obtain the following leaf sequent Γ.

$$\underset{u_2}{\neg\neg P}, \underset{v_2}{\neg\neg Q}, P[u_0 a], Q[v_0 b], P[u_1 c], Q[v_1 d] \vdash$$

– The points for the branch are: ϵ, a, b, ac, ad, bc, bd.
– The linear substitution σ_a is $\{u_0/\epsilon, v_0/\epsilon\}$.
– The linear substitution σ_{ac} is $\{u_0/\epsilon, v_0/\epsilon, u_1/a, v_1/a\}$.

We will frequently use the result of mapping linear substitutions to sequents. For example:

- $\Gamma\sigma_a$ equals $\neg\neg P, \neg\neg Q, P[a], Q[b], P[u_1c], Q[v_1d] \vdash$.
- $\Gamma\sigma_{ac}$ equals $\neg\neg P, \neg\neg Q, P[a], Q[b], P[ac], Q[ad] \vdash$.

In particular, we will be interested in the formulas labelled with p in $\Gamma\sigma_p$; for example, the formula $P[a]^\top$ in $\Gamma\sigma_a$ and the formula $P[ac]^\top$ in $\Gamma\sigma_{ac}$.   ⊣

Definition 10. Let B be a branch with leaf sequent Γ. We define, by induction on points, the set of *active points for B*. The empty label, ϵ, is always active. Furthermore, if $F[p]^\top$ is in $\Gamma\sigma_p$, then p is active if

- all points $p' \prec p$ are active, and
- there is no formula $F[p']^\top$ in $\Gamma\sigma_p$ such that $p' \prec p$.

If p is active, we say that p is *active for the ϕ-formula* $F[q]_u^\top$ in Γ if $(qu)\sigma = p$ for some weight-preserving substitution σ.   ⊣

Returning to Example 9, we have the following facts.

- a is active, since $\Gamma\sigma_a$ contains $P[a]^\top$, but not $P[\epsilon]^\top$, and since ϵ is active.
- a is not active for any of the ϕ-formulas in Γ, since there is no weight-preserving σ such that $u_2\sigma = a$ or $v_2\sigma = a$.
- ac is *not* active, since $\Gamma\sigma_{ac}$ contains both $P[a]^\top$ and $P[ac]^\top$.
- ad is active, since $\Gamma\sigma_{ad}$ contains $Q[ad]^\top$, but neither $Q[\epsilon]^\top$ nor $Q[a]^\top$, and since both ϵ and a are active.

Definition 11 (Termination Condition). A derivation is *finished* if each leaf sequent contains only proposition letters and ϕ-formulas for which there are no active points.   ⊣

The derivation from Example 9 is not finished, since the points ad and bc still are active for both ϕ-formulas. After another expansion of the ϕ-formulas, however, the derivation is finished, since there are no active points of length 3.

Recall that an index has a unique prefix. Let the *degree* of an index i, denoted $d(i)$, be the weight of its prefix, plus the weight of i itself, if i is a variable or a parameter. Let the degree of an inference be the degree of the index of the expanded formula. Observe that the degree of an inference equals the weight of the prefix of the formulas introduced in the premisses.

In order to construct the model, we shall assume that a finished derivation is permuted into a form where the inferences are ordered by their degree, that is, if r is above r', then $d(r) \geq d(r')$, or equivalently, no inference decreases the maximum weight of prefixes. Although the size of the derivation may blow up in the permutation process, this is harmless for the sake of the argument since fulfillment of the termination condition is invariant under permutation.

Furthermore, we will restrict the set of admissible substitutions and exploit the fact that if a derivation is not closable with an admissible substitution, then it is not closable with a restricted substitution either. To this end, let $B_1, \ldots, B_m$ be all the branches of a derivation. For each i let p_i be a maximal point for B_i such that if the uppermost common β-inference of B_i and B_j is of degree n, then p_i and p_j agree on their first n symbols. The linear substitutions σ_i can now be combined into a single substitution in the following way. Let σ^B denote the substitution obtained from σ by coloring all variables in the domain with B. Then, the union of $\sigma^{B_i}_{p_i}$, for $1 \leq i \leq n$, is called a *combined substitution*.

When working with combined substitutions we can ignore the admissibility condition for the following reason.

Lemma 12. A combined substitution $\sigma = \bigcup \sigma^{B_i}_{p_i}$ is admissible.   ⊣

Proof. Let $b \sqsubset u$ iff $d(b) < d(u)$. Since the resulting reduction ordering must be irreflexive, it suffices to show that this is a splitting relation. Suppose that $u^{B_1}\sigma \neq u^{B_2}\sigma$. Let $(b_1 \triangle b_2)$ be the index, say of degree n, of the uppermost expanded β-formula such that $b_1 \in B_1$ and $b_2 \in B_2$. By assumption, p_1 and p_2 agree on their first n symbols. If q is the prefix of u, then $(qu)\sigma_{p_1} \neq (qu)\sigma_{p_2}$, so $d(u)$ must be of degree greater than n. Consequently, $(b_1 \triangle b_2) \sqsubset u$.

Definition 13. Let Γ be a sequent, and let p be a point for some branch containing Γ. We say that the linear substitution σ_p is *compatible* with a combined substitution σ if $\sigma^B_p \subset \sigma$ for all branches B containing Γ. The sequent Γ is called *open-ended* for p if every combined substitution compatible with σ_p fails to close at least one leaf sequent above Γ.   ⊣

Example 14. In Example 3, if we require that the variable u has weight 0, all the sequents are trivially open-ended for the points ϵ, a and b. The derivation is not finished, since the leaf sequents contain ϕ-formulas with active points. Let us expand the ϕ-formula, and its β-subformula, in both branches. The derivation becomes finished, and the leftmost part of the derivation is the following.

$$\frac{\dfrac{\overline{P[a], Q[b] \vdash \overline{P[u_1]}} \qquad P[a], \overline{Q[b]} \vdash \overline{Q[u_1]}}{P[a], Q[b] \vdash (P \wedge Q)[u_1]}}{\underset{u_1}{\neg}(\underset{3}{P} \wedge Q)[\epsilon], P[a], Q[b] \vdash \underset{4}{P[u]}}$$

The left leaf sequent is open-ended for b and the right leaf sequent is open-ended for a. The sequent below is open-ended for both a and b.   ⊣

Lemma 15. Let Γ be open-ended for a point p of length n.

- If q is a point such that $p \prec q$, then Γ is open-ended for q.
- If Γ is the conclusion of an inference of degree n, then at least one premiss of the inference is open-ended for p.   ⊣

Proof. For the first claim, note that if Γ can be closed with a combined substitution compatible with σ_q, then it can also be closed with a combined substitution compatible with σ_p, since $\sigma_p \subseteq \sigma_q$. For the second claim, it suffices to prove that if all premisses can be closed with combined substitutions compatible with σ_p, then so can the conclusion. This is trivial for an α-inference; to see that it also holds for a β-inference, suppose that there is a combined substitution σ_1 that closes all leaf sequents above the left premiss and a combined substitution σ_2

that closes all leaf sequents above the right premiss. Let σ_1' be the restriction of σ_1 to the branches above the left premiss and let σ_2' be the restriction of σ_2 to the branches above the right premiss. Since both σ_1 and σ_2 are compatible with σ_p, we have that $\sigma_1' \cup \sigma_2'$ is a combined substitution compatible with σ_p. By construction, it closes the derivation.

Theorem 16. If a derivation is finished and not closed by any combined substitution, then the root sequent has a countermodel.   ⊣

Proof. By repeated applications of Lemma 15 we inductively construct a set O of pairs $\langle \Gamma, p \rangle$ such that Γ is open-ended for p and the following conditions hold.

- $\langle \Gamma, \epsilon \rangle \in O$, where Γ is the root sequent of D.
- If $\langle \Gamma, p \rangle \in O$, the point p is of length n, and Γ is the conclusion of an inference of degree n, then $\langle \Gamma', p \rangle \in O$ for exactly one premiss Γ' of the inference.
- If $\langle \Gamma, p \rangle \in O$, the maximal weight of a prefix in Γ equals the length of p, and pa is a point for a branch containing Γ, then $\langle \Gamma, pa \rangle \in O$.

There is an interdependency between the last two conditions with the effect that one eventually reaches a leaf sequent Γ and a maximal point p. The last condition ensures that the lengths of the points are incremented by one, which makes the second condition apply in cases where the inference increases the maximum weight of prefixes. By induction on the construction of O, one can show that if $\langle \Gamma, p \rangle$ and $\langle \Gamma', p' \rangle$ are in O, and $p' \preceq p$, then Γ and Γ' occur in the same branch.

In fact, the set O now contains enough information to construct a countermodel for the root sequent. We will here only give the outline of a proof. For a full proof in a similar situation, see [14].

From O we define a set S of ground labelled formulas and show that S is falsifiable. Let $F[p] \in S$ iff there is a pair $\langle \Gamma, p \rangle$ in O such that $F[q] \in \Gamma$ and $q\sigma_p = p$. Let $\langle W, \preceq, V \rangle$ be the model defined in the following way.

- Let W be the set of *active* points occurring as labels in S.
- Let $p \in V(F)$ iff $F[p']^\top \in S$ for some $p' \preceq p$.

The label interpretation function ι is defined as follows. If p is an active point, let $\iota(p) = p$. Otherwise, let $\iota(p)$ be the largest active point such that $p' \prec p$. By induction on the length of formulas, we show the following two statements.

- If $F[p]^\top \in S$, then $\iota(p) \Vdash F$, and
- if $F[p]^\perp \in S$, then $\iota(p) \nVdash F$.

The base case for $P[p]^\perp$, where P is a proposition letter, is trivial. Suppose that $P[p]^\perp \in S$. Then, there is a pair $\langle \Gamma, p \rangle \in O$ such that $P[q]^\perp \in \Gamma$ and $q\sigma_p = p$. It suffices to show that there is no $p' \preceq p$ such that $P[p']^\top \in S$, for then $p \nVdash P$. So, suppose for a contradiction that such a p' exists. Then, there is a pair $\langle \Gamma', p' \rangle \in O$ with $P[q']^\top \in \Gamma'$ and $q'\sigma_{p'} = p'$. Since Γ and Γ' must occur in the same branch and P is a proposition letter, either Γ is below Γ', and then $P[q']^\top \in \Gamma$, or Γ' is below Γ, and then $P[q]^\perp \in \Gamma'$. Both cases lead to a contradiction from the assumptions that Γ and Γ' are open-ended for p and p', respectively.

Suppose that $(F \to G)[p]^\top \in S$ and that $p \preceq q$ for some $q \in W$. If there is a $q' \preceq q$ such that $G[q']^\top \in S$, then $\iota(q') \Vdash G$ by the induction hypothesis, and hence $\iota(q) \Vdash G$. Otherwise, since the derivation is finished, there must by construction exist a pair $\langle \Gamma, q \rangle \in O$ with $F[q]^\perp \in \Gamma \sigma_q$. By induction hypothesis, $q \not\Vdash F$.

Suppose that $(F \to G)[p]_a^\perp \in S$. By construction, there is a pair $\langle \Gamma, pa \rangle \in O$ such that both $F[pa]^\top$ and $G[pa]^\perp$ are in $\Gamma \sigma_{pa}$. We can conclude that $\iota(pa) \Vdash F$ and $\iota(pa) \not\Vdash G$ (also in the case that pa is not active).

7   Conclusion and Future Work

We have successfully introduced a free variable proof system for IPL with variable splitting, and proved soundness, completeness, and correctness of a local termination condition. This forms the basis for the design of unification-based goal-directed search procedures.

The variable splitting technique enables us to completely avoid dependence on the order of rule applications. Variable splitting for first-order logic also permits significantly shorter proofs than free variable calculi without variable splitting [2]. An interesting problem is whether there exists a variable splitting system for IPL which also reduces proof lengths and, if so, whether this can be exploited in an even tighter termination condition.

The characterization that we propose is easy to motivate with respect to variable-sharing calculi, but there are also connection-based calculi, like the one used in the ileanCoP implementation [9], that use *renaming of variables* to achieve some of the same effects as variable splitting, as variables introduced in new branches always are renamed. Some of the problems that variable splitting solves for variable-sharing calculi simply do not arise when variables are renamed. The exact relationship between variable splitting and variable renaming is unknown at the time of writing.

We have made some technical simplifications in this paper in order to simplify proofs and increase readability. In particular, we are only considering *ground* and *total* substitutions, and the reduction ordering is formulated with respect to the "full" $\ll$-relation. These restrictions can however be lifted; see [2] for some of the details.

Future work includes the study and implementation of connection-based proof procedures with variable splitting. In particular, we hope to be able to extend the incremental closure technique for first-order logic [5, 6] to the system in this paper. We also plan to exploit the idea of using the classical kernel of the proof objects to first check for classical provability and only upon success invoke the intuitionistic prefix machinery, as already done in [9].

It seems straightforward to adapt this proof system, with its soundness, completeness and termination condition, to propositional modal logics. We also plan to address an extension of it, with minor modifications, to intuitionistic first-order logic in a follow-up work.

Acknowledgements

We thank the anonymous referees, whose detailed comments enabled a significant improvement of the paper. We also thank Jens Otten for very helpful comments.

References

[1] Antonsen, R., Waaler, A.: Consistency of variable splitting in free variable systems of first-order logic. In: Beckert, B. (ed.) TABLEAUX 2005. LNCS (LNAI), vol. 3702, pp. 33–47. Springer, Heidelberg (2005)

[2] Antonsen, R., Waaler, A.: Liberalized variable splitting. Journal of Automated Reasoning 38, 3–30 (2007)

[3] Bibel, W.: Automated Theorem Proving. 2. edn. Vieweg Verlag (1987)

[4] Dyckhoff, R.: Contraction-free sequent calculi for intuitionistic logic. Journal of Symbolic Logic 57, 795–807 (1992)

[5] Giese, M.: Proof Search without Backtracking for Free Variable Tableaux. PhD thesis, Fakultät für Informatik, Universität Karlsruhe (July 2002)

[6] Hansen, C.M., Antonsen, R., Waaler, A.: Incremental closure of variable splitting tableaux, position paper. In: Olivetti, N. (ed.) TABLEAUX 2007, July 3-6, 2007. LNCS, vol. 4548, pp. 3–6. Springer, Heidelberg (2007)

[7] Hudelmaier, J.: Bounds on cut-elimination in intuitionistic propositional logic. Archive for Mathematical Logic 31, 331–353 (1992)

[8] Kreitz, C., Otten, J.: Connection-based theorem proving in classical and non-classical logics. Journal of Universal Computer Science 5(3), 88–112 (1999)

[9] Otten, J.: Clausal connection-based theorem proving in intuitionistic first-order logic. In: Beckert, B. (ed.) TABLEAUX 2005. LNCS (LNAI), vol. 3702, pp. 245–261. Springer, Heidelberg (2005)

[10] Raths, T., Otten, J., Kreitz, C.: The ILTP library: Benchmarking automated theorem provers for intuitionistic logic. In: Beckert, B. (ed.) TABLEAUX 2005. LNCS (LNAI), vol. 3702, pp. 333–337. Springer, Heidelberg (2005)

[11] Sahlin, D., Franzén, T., Haridi, S.: An intuitionistic predicate logic theorem prover. Journal of Logic and Computation 2(5), 619–656 (1992)

[12] Smullyan, R.M.: First-Order Logic. In: Ergebnisse der Mathematik und ihrer Grenzgebiete, vol. 43, Springer, New York (1968)

[13] Troelstra, A.S., Schwichtenberg, H.: Basic Proof Theory, 2nd edn. Cambridge University Press, Cambridge (2000)

[14] Waaler, A.: Connections in nonclassical logics. In: Robinson, A., Voronkov, A. (eds.) Handbook of Automated Reasoning (chapter 22), vol. II, pp. 1487–1578. Elsevier, Amsterdam (2001)

[15] Waaler, A., Wallen, L.: Tableaux for intuitionistic logics. In: D'Agostino, M., Gabbay, D.M., Hähnle, R., Posegga, J. (eds.) Handbook of Tableaux Methods, pp. 255–296. Kluwer Academic Publishers, Dordrecht (1999)

[16] Wallen, L.A.: Automated deduction in nonclassical logics. MIT Press, Cambridge (1990)

Logical Interpretation: Static Program Analysis Using Theorem Proving*

Ashish Tiwari[1] and Sumit Gulwani[2]

[1] SRI International, Menlo Park, CA 94025
tiwari@csl.sri.com
[2] Microsoft Research, Redmond, WA 98052
sumitg@microsoft.com

Abstract. This paper presents the foundations for using automated deduction technology in static program analysis. The central principle is the use of *logical lattices* – a class of lattices defined on logical formulas in a logical theory – in an abstract interpretation framework. Abstract interpretation over logical lattices, called *logical interpretation*, raises new challenges for theorem proving. We present an overview of some of the existing results in the field of logical interpretation and outline some requirements for building expressive and scalable logical interpreters.

1 Introduction

Theorem proving has been one of the core enabling technologies in the field of program verification. The traditional use of theorem proving in program analysis is based on the concept of deductive verification, where the program is *sufficiently* annotated with assertions and verification conditions are generated that, if proved, will establish that the annotated assertions are indeed invariants of the program. The generated verification conditions are discharged using a theorem prover [6]. This traditional approach of integrating theorem proving with program analysis requires theorem provers in the form of satisfiability checkers for various theories and combination of theories.

While deductive verification attempts to *verify* given annotated invariants, abstract interpretation seeks to *generate* invariants for programs. Static analysis and abstract interpretation techniques have seen recent success in the field of software verification. For example, the Slam project and the Astree tool demonstrated effectiveness of static analysis techniques in verifying large pieces of device driver and aerospace code. However, static analysis techniques can verify only simple properties. Most of the current tools based on these techniques target a specific class of programs and prove only specific kinds of properties of these programs. The working hypothesis of this paper is that theorem proving technology can push static analysis techniques to handle larger classes of properties for larger classes of systems.

---

* The first author was supported in part by the National Science Foundation under grant ITR-CCR-0326540.

F. Pfenning (Ed.): CADE 2007, LNAI 4603, pp. 147–166, 2007.

The process of going from checking annotated invariants (deductive verification) to generating the invariants (abstract interpretation) is akin to going from type checking to type inference. While traditional theorem provers, which are essentially satisfiability solvers, can naturally help in invariant checking, how can they be extended to help in this new task of invariant generation?

Shankar [24] proposed the general paradigm of using theorem proving technology in the form of "little engines of proof". The idea was to use components of monolithic theorem provers, such as decision procedures, unification and matching algorithms, and rewriting, as embedded components in an application. This idea gained remarkable traction and lead to the development of several little engines, mostly in the form of *satisfiability modulo theory*, or SMT, solvers. Continued research and development has resulted in dramatic improvements in the performance of these little engines of proof.

Satisfiability checking procedures, while useful in the context of deductive verification, are insufficient for building abstract interpreters. This paper considers the approach of embedding theorem proving technology, in the form of little engines, as an embedded component in modern software verification tools based on abstract interpretation. This integration uses theorem proving technology in a new role and raises several interesting new questions.

How do we formally understand this new approach of integrating theorem proving and program analysis? What little engines are required for this purpose and how can they be built? What is the interface that is required to smoothly embed a little engine inside a static analysis tool based on abstract interpretation?

This paper answers these questions by laying the foundations of *logical interpretation* – the process of performing abstract interpretation on *logical lattices*. A logical lattice is a lattice whose domain consists of formulas and whose ordering relation is (a refinement of) the logical implication relation $\Rightarrow_\mathbb{T}$ in some logical theory $\mathbb{T}$. We present an overview of the existing results in the area of logical interpretation and outline directions for future work.

We start by defining the assertion checking problem in Section 2. We introduce logical lattices in Section 3. In Section 4 we use logical interpretation to solve the assertion checking problem in an intraprocedural setting for various program models. Results for interprocedural analysis are presented in Section 5. In Section 6, we consider the problem of assertion generation using a (forward) logical abstract interpreter. Finally, we briefly discuss richer program models that include heaps in Section 6.2, and the interface of a logical lattice that enables modular construction of quantified logical abstract domains for reasoning about these richer program models in Section 6.3.

2   Problem Definition

We first present the program model and its semantics in Section 2.1, followed by a quick introduction to abstract interpretation in Section 2.2. Section 2.3 will formally define the assertion checking problem.

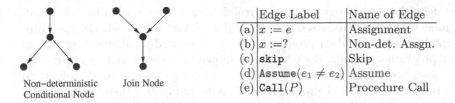

	Edge Label	Name of Edge
(a)	$x := e$	Assignment
(b)	$x :=?$	Non-det. Assgn.
(c)	skip	Skip
(d)	Assume($e_1 \neq e_2$)	Assume
(e)	Call(P)	Procedure Call

Non-deterministic   Join Node
Conditional Node

Fig. 1. Conditional and join nodes in flowcharts and various types of edge labels

2.1 Program Model

A *program* is a directed graph whose edges are labeled by one of the five labels in Figure 1. Each connected component of such a graph, called a *procedure*, is assumed to have a marked entry node with no incoming edges and a marked exit node with no outgoing edges. Each procedure is labeled with a name (of the procedure). Without loss of generality, we assume that, for each node, either its indegree or its outdegree is at most one.

The program model is parameterized by a theory $\mathbb{T}$. We assume, henceforth, that $\mathbb{T}$ is some theory over a signature Σ. Let $Terms(\Sigma \cup X)$ denote the set of terms constructed using signature Σ and variables X. Examples of $\mathbb{T}$ that will be used particularly in this paper are the theory of linear arithmetic, the theory of uninterpreted symbols, the combination of these theories, and the theory of commutative functions.

Let X be a finite set of program variables. The edges of a program are labeled by either (a) an assignment ($x := e$), or (b) a non-deterministic assignment ($x :=?$), or (c) a skip, or (d) an assume (Assume($e_1 \neq e_2$)), or (e) a procedure call (Call(P)). Here $x \in X$, $e, e_1, e_2 \in Terms(\Sigma \cup X)$, and P is a name for a procedure in the program.

A non-deterministic assignment $x :=?$ denotes that the variable x can be assigned any value. Such non-deterministic assignments are used as a safe abstraction of statements (in the original source program) that can not be precisely expressed in the simplified program model.

A *join node* is a node with two (or more) incoming edges. A *non-deterministic conditional node* is a node with two (or more) outgoing edges. This denotes that the control can flow to either branch irrespective of the program state before the conditional. Such nodes can be used as a safe abstraction of guarded conditionals that cannot be expressed precisely in the simplified program model. We assume, without loss of generality, that all (incoming or outgoing) edges incident on a join or non-deterministic conditional node are labeled with skip.

Assume edges, Assume($e_1 \neq e_2$), can be used to partially capture conditionals. Note that a program conditional of the form $e_1 = e_2$ can be reduced to a non-deterministic conditional and assume statements Assume($e_1 = e_2$) (on the true side of the conditional) and Assume($e_1 \neq e_2$) on the false side of the conditional. The presence of disequality assume edges allows us to capture the false branch precisely in this case. Assume labels of the form Assume($e_1 = e_2$) are disallowed in the simplified model.

Our definition of a program is quite restrictive. The extension to richer program models is briefly discussed in Section 6.2. Nevertheless, this simplied program model is also useful for program analysis. It is used by abstracting a given original program using only the edge labels shown in Figure 1 and then using the results described in this paper on the abstracted program. A second motivation for studying the simplified program model is to study the theoretical aspects of static program analysis and characterize the "precision" of static program analysis that is achievable using abstract interpretation techniques.

Semantics of Programs. The semantics of programs in the above program model is given in the standard way. Let *States* denote the set of all possible mappings from X to *Terms*(Σ). In other words, *States* is the set of ground substitutions. Let $(Pow(States), \subseteq)$ be the complete lattice[1] defined over the domain *Pow(States)*, which is the collection of all subsets of *States*, by the usual set operators. Let $Pow(States) \mapsto Pow(States)$ denote the collection of all functions from *Pow(States)* to *Pow(States)*. The preorder in the lattice $(Pow(States), \subseteq)$ induces a (lattice) preorder on the domain $Pow(States) \mapsto Pow(States)$.

The semantics of each node in the program, say π, is given as a function $[\![\pi]\!]$ in $Pow(States) \mapsto Pow(States)$. Intuitively, $[\![\pi]\!](\psi)$ is the set of program states reached at program point π starting from some program state in ψ at the entry point of the procedure containing π. Formally, if $\boldsymbol{\pi}$ is the set of all program points in a program, then the vector of functions $([\![\pi]\!])_{\pi \in \boldsymbol{\pi}}$ is obtained as the least fixpoint of a set of fixpoint equations obtained from the program (using the semantics of the edge labels); that is, $([\![\pi]\!])_{\pi \in \boldsymbol{\pi}} = F(([\![\pi]\!])_{\pi \in \boldsymbol{\pi}})$, where F is the monotone function representing the strongest post-condition transformer. Note that for a join node π with parents π_1 and π_2, $[\![\pi]\!]$ is the join (union) of $[\![\pi_1]\!]$ and $[\![\pi_2]\!]$. See [4] for further details.

2.2   Abstract Interpretation

Abstract interpretation [4] is a generic framework for describing several static program analyses. The idea is to evaluate the program semantics over more *abstract* or *simpler* lattices, rather than the lattices over which the semantics is defined. Thus, abstract interpretation is parameterized by the choice of the abstract lattice. Its effectiveness is dependent on the expressiveness of the abstract lattice and the computational complexity of computing fixpoints in that lattice.

Let $(A, \sqsubseteq)$ be a complete lattice. Such a lattice will be called an *abstract* lattice if there is a Galois connection between $(A, \sqsubseteq)$ and $(Pow(States), \subseteq)$ defined by the monotone abstraction function $\alpha : Pow(States) \mapsto A$ and the monotone concretization function $\gamma : A \mapsto Pow(States)$. Abstract interpretation involves solving the fixpoint equations defining the semantics of the program, but over such an *abstract lattice* $(A, \sqsubseteq)$ (and the induced extension on $A \mapsto A$), rather than on the concrete lattice *Pow(States)*. Formally, $([\![\pi]\!]_A)_{\pi \in \boldsymbol{\pi}} = F_A(([\![\pi]\!]_A)_{\pi \in \boldsymbol{\pi}})$, where

---

[1] A lattice $(A, \sqsubseteq)$ is identified by its domain A and its preorder $\sqsubseteq$. The meet $(\sqcap_A)$ and join $(\sqcup_A)$ are defined as the greatest lower bound and least upper bound respectively. The top and bottom elements are denoted by $\top_A$ and $\bot_A$.

F_A is the strongest (post-condition) transformer on the abstract domain such that $F \subseteq \gamma \circ F_A \circ \alpha$. Note that, since the lattice $(A, \sqsubseteq)$ is assumed to be complete, fixpoints exist (without requiring any widening to achieve convergence), and $[\![\pi]\!]_A$ are well-defined.

Given an abstract domain $(A, \sqsubseteq)$, the *interprocedural* abstract interpretation problem seeks to compute $[\![\pi]\!]_A$ for each program point π. If we consider a program model where there are no edges labeled by $\mathtt{Call}(P)$, then we obtain the simpler problem of *intraprocedural* analysis. In the case of intraprocedural analysis, we can work on the lattice $(A, \sqsubseteq)$ directly by just focusing on computing $[\![\pi]\!]_A(\top_A)$.

We remark here that the requirement that $(A, \sqsubseteq)$ be a complete lattice can be relaxed. Abstract interpretation based analysis can be performed on semi-lattices A that are not closed under (arbitrary) join. In such a case, the join is over-approximated by some element of the lattice A. However, if we insist that there is a unique least fixpoint solution of the semantic equations in A, then we need to assume that A is a complete lattice.

2.3 The Assertion Checking Problem

We now define the assertion checking problem for programs.

Definition 1 (Assertion Checking Problem). *Let $\mathbb{T}$ be a theory and P be a program using the expression language of $\mathbb{T}$. Given an assertion $e_1 = e_2$ at a program point π in P, the assertion checking problem seeks to determine if $e_1\sigma =_\mathbb{T} e_2\sigma$ for every substitution σ in $[\![\pi]\!](\top)$.*

In general, an assertion ϕ can be any set of states, $\phi \in Pow(States)$, and then the assertion checking problem seeks to determine if $[\![\pi]\!](\top) \subseteq \phi$. If the assertion checking problem has a positive solution, we say the assertion *holds* at the given program point.

The term $e_1\sigma$ is just the evaluation of e_1 along some path in the program. Thus, assertion checking problem essentially seeks to determine if e_1 and e_2 are equal at the end of every path to program point π.

Example 1. Consider the program P containing two sequential assignments: $\{\pi_0; x := f(z); \pi_1; y := f(z); \pi_2\}$, where $X = \{x, y, z\}$ are program variables and the signature $\Sigma = \{f, a\}$ contains an uninterpreted function symbol f and constant a. We are interested in checking the assertion $x = y$ at program point π_2. Now, $[\![\pi_2]\!](\top)$ is the set containing all ground instances of the substitution $\sigma := \{x \mapsto fz, y \mapsto fz\}$. Clearly, $x\sigma = y\sigma$ in the theory of uninterpreted symbols, and hence, $x = y$ holds at π_2.

Since computing $[\![\_]\!]$ is often intractable, the assertion checking problem is often solved using abstract interpretation over some abstract domain. However, this can lead to incompleteness.

Example 2. Following up on Example 1, let Φ denote the set of all finite conjunctions of all variable equalities. The relation $\Rightarrow_{\mathtt{EQ}}$, where $\mathtt{EQ}$ is the pure theory of equality, induces a natural ordering on Φ. This ordering defines a lattice structure $(\Phi, \Rightarrow_{EQ})$. Note that $[\![\pi_2]\!]_\Phi = [\![\pi_1]\!]_\Phi = true$. This is because no variable equality holds at point π_1. Even though $x = y$ holds at π_2, the lattice Φ is not expressive enough to prove it. However, if Φ contains all (conjunctions of) equalities on $\Sigma \cup X$, then $[\![\pi_2]\!]_\Phi$ will be $x = y \wedge y = f(z)$.

An abstract lattice $(A, \sqsubseteq)$, with corresponding concretization function γ, is *sufficiently expressive* for assertion checking if for every element $\phi \in A$ such that the assertion $\gamma(\phi)$ holds at point π in a program P, it is the case that $[\![\pi]\!]_A \sqsubseteq \phi$.

The following result, which is central to many results in this paper, relates unification [2] and program analysis for the simplified program model. The notation $\mathtt{Unif}(E)$, where E is some conjunction of equalities, denotes the formula that is a disjunction of all unifiers in some complete set of unifiers for E.

Lemma 1 ([10]). *Let $\mathbb{T}$ be a convex finitary theory and P be a program built using edge labels (a)–(e) from Figure 1 and using the expression language of $\mathbb{T}$. Let π be a program point in P and let ϕ_i be some conjunction of equalities. Then, $\bigvee_i \phi_i$ holds at π iff $\bigvee_i \mathtt{Unif}_{\mathbb{T}}(\phi_i)$ holds at π.*

We will study the assertion checking problem for different choices of the program model. Our approach will be based on using an appropriate choice of the abstract lattice A and using abstract interpretation over A.

3   Logical Interpretation

We now introduce a class of abstract lattices called logical lattices. Abstract interpretation over logical lattices will be used as an approach to solve the assertion checking problem (Sections 4 and 5) and the invariant generation problem (Section 6). The definition below is a generalization of the definition in [9].

Let $\mathbb{T}$ be a theory over signature Σ and Φ be a class of formulas over $\Sigma \cup X$. We shall assume that $\bot$ and $\top$, representing *false* and *true* respectively, are present in Φ. For example, Φ could be the set of conjunctions of atomic formulas over $\Sigma \cup X$.

Definition 2 (Logical Lattice). *A (semi-, complete) lattice $(A, \sqsubseteq)$ is a logical (semi-, complete) lattice over some theory $\mathbb{T}$ if the domain A is Φ and the partial order $\sqsubseteq$ is contained in the implication relationship $\Rightarrow_{\mathbb{T}}$ in theory $\mathbb{T}$, i.e., if $E \sqsubseteq_A E'$ then $E \Rightarrow_{\mathbb{T}} E'$.*

We first note that a complete logical lattice is an *abstract* lattice. This fact is demonstrated by the concretization function, $\gamma(E) := \{s \in States \mid s \models E\}$, and the abstraction mapping, $\alpha(\sigma) := \sqcap\{E \mid \forall s \in \sigma.s \models E\}$ (since A is assumed to be a complete lattice, this is well-defined). Note that the concretization function, γ, is monotone, since $E \sqsubseteq E'$ implies $E \Rightarrow_{\mathbb{T}} E'$ (by definition), which in turn implies $\gamma(E) \subseteq \gamma(E')$.

In this paper, we will mainly use logical lattices in which $\sqsubseteq$ is equal to $\Rightarrow_{\mathbb{T}}$. The first part of this paper will focus on intraprocedural analysis, whereas the second part will consider interprocedural analysis.

4 Intraprocedural Logical Interpretation

In this section we use logical interpretation to solve intraprocedural assertion checking problem. We shall consider different assertion checking problems parameterized by (a) the theory $\mathbb{T}$ which interprets the expressions e that occur in the assignment and assume statements in the program model and (b) the language of the assertions.

4.1 The Theory of Uninterpreted Symbols

Let Σ be a finite set of uninterpreted function symbols and constants. Let $\mathbb{T}_{\mathsf{UFS}}$ be the theory of uninterpreted function symbols. Let X be a set of program variables. We are given a program with edge labels (a)–(c) from Figure 1, where the expression e is any term in $Terms(\Sigma \cup X)$. We are interested in checking assertions of the form $x = e$ at some program point π. Informally, the problem is to determine if the assertion $x = e$ evaluates to true on each program path.

We use a logical lattice defined by the theory $\mathbb{T}_{\mathsf{UFS}}$ to solve this assertion checking problem. The class Φ of formulas we consider is the set of finite *substitutions*, that is, Φ contains formulas of the form, $\bigwedge_i x_i = t_i$, such that $t_i \in Terms(\Sigma \cup X \mid_{\prec x_i})$ where $\prec$ is some total order on the program variables x_i's. We first observe that we can define a lattice over this choice of Φ.

Proposition 1 ([13]). *The set Φ under the $\Rightarrow_{\mathsf{UFS}}$ forms a lattice. If X is finite, then this is a complete lattice.*

The following theorem states that the assertion checking problem is decidable in polynomial time.

Theorem 1 ([7,10]). *Let $\mathcal{P}$ denote the class of programs built using edge labels (a)–(c) and using the expression language $Terms(\Sigma \cup X)$, where X is a finite set of program variables. Let Φ be as defined above. The assertion checking problem for programs in class $\mathcal{P}$ and assertions in Φ is solvable in PTIME .*

Gulwani and Necula [7] presented a polynomial-time *forward* abstract interpreter over the lattice $(\Phi, \Rightarrow_{\mathsf{UFS}})$ to prove Theorem 1. A naive forward interpreter was shown to blow-up the size of generated facts, and hence, Gulwani and Necula had to prune large facts that were not *relevant* to the assertion. This process of making the forward interpreter *goal-directed* was crucial in proving the above PTIME result. Prior to that, there were other either incomplete, or exponential, procedures to solve the above assertion checking problem [1,23]. All these procedures were based on forward abstract interpretation. It should be noted that to prove completeness of forward interpreter for the assertion checking problem, one needs to show that the above abstract domain is *sufficiently expressive*.

Gulwani and Tiwari [10] provided a new proof of a result that is more general than Theorem 1. In contrast to earlier procedures, the result in [10] is based on *backward* propagation. Backward propagation is naturally goal-directed. Unfortunately, backward propagation through assignment edges may create equations that are *not* of the form $x = e$ anymore. This is illustrated below.

Example 3. Let P be $\{\pi_0; x := a; y := f(a); \pi_1; while(*)\{\pi_2; x := f(x); y := f(y); \}; \pi\}$. Suppose we wish to check the assertion $y = f(x)$ at point π. We perform a backward propagation in the logical lattice $(\Phi, \Rightarrow_{UFS})$ defined above. To prove $y = f(x)$ at π, we need to prove $fy = ffx \wedge ffy = fffx \wedge \cdots$ at π_1. This conjunction is not finite and is not in Φ.

Both these problems are solved by Lemma 1, which notes that $e_1 = e_2$ can be replaced by $\mathtt{Unif}(e_1 = e_2)$ during the backward propagation without any loss of soundness (or completeness) [8,10]. This converts arbitrary $e_1 = e_2$ into the form of equalities in Φ. Moreover, it also helps to show that the conjunction will be finite and fixpoint is reached in n steps. The soundness of Lemma 1 provides an alternate proof of the fact that the lattice $(\Phi, \mathtt{UFS})$ is sufficiently expressive for the assertion checking problem described above.

Example 4. By applying $\mathtt{Unif}$ to the assertion $fy = ffx$, we get $y = fx$ as the assertion at π_1. Thus, in Example 3, backward propagation enhanced with unification gives the assertion $y = fx$ at π_1 and π_2, and *true* at π_0 - thus proving that $y = fx$ holds at π.

The backward procedure is now seen to terminate in PTIME since the most-general unifier of a set of equations contains atmost n equations and a substitution can be strengthened at most n times.

If we enrich the programming model to include assume edges, $\mathtt{Assume}(e_1 = e_2)$, then the problem of assertion checking can be easily shown to be undecidable [16]. This is partly the reason why we do not consider guarded conditionals in our program model. Coincidentally, Lemma 1 fails to hold in the presence of such assume edges.

Example 5. Consider the program $\{\mathtt{Assume}(fx = fy); \pi\}$ with just one assume edge. It is evident that $fx = fy$ holds at π, but it is clear that $x = y$, which is $\mathtt{Unif}(fx = fy)$, does not hold at π.

4.2   The Theory of Linear Arithmetic

Let Σ be the signature of linear arithmetic (without inequality predicates). Let X be the program variables. Let $\mathbb{T}_{\mathsf{LAE}}$ denote the theory of linear arithmetic equalities. Let Φ be the class of formulas containing all finite conjunction of linear equations of the form, $\sum_{x \in X} c_x x = c$, where c_x, c are integer constants.

We are given a program with edge labels (a)–(c) from Figure 1, where the expression e is any term in $Terms(\Sigma \cup X)$. We are also given an assertion from the set Φ at some program point π. The following theorem states that this assertion checking problem is decidable in polynomial time.

Theorem 2 ([10]). *Let $\mathcal{P}$ denote the class of programs built using edge labels (a)–(c) and using the expression language $Terms(\Sigma \cup X)$, where X is a finite set of program variables. Let Φ be as defined above. The assertion checking problem for programs in class $\mathcal{P}$ and assertions in Φ is solvable in PTIME .*

The approach to solving this problem is based on using logical interpretation on the lattice $(\varPhi, \Rightarrow_{\mathtt{LAE}})$. Karr [14] presented a forward abstract interpreter over this logical lattice. To prove Theorem 2 using a forward interpreter requires that we also show that this abstract domain is sufficiently expressive.

A simple backward propagation algorithm gives a simple proof of Theorem 2. It is easy to see that $\varPhi$ is closed under backward propagation through assignment edges. This shows that the above logical lattice is sufficiently expressive. Termination of backward propagation follows from the observation that there can be at most n linearly independent (linear) equations. We note here that we do not need to explicitly use unification since it is inbuilt in the theory $\mathtt{LAE}$.

We remark here that the assertion checking problem becomes undecidable if we include assume edges, $\mathtt{Assume}(e_1 = e_2)$, in the program model [17].

Theorem 1 and Theorem 2 give the complexity of the decision version of the problem of abstract interpretation over logical lattices defined by the theories $\mathtt{UFS}$ and $\mathtt{LAE}$.

4.3 Unitary Theory

Theorem 1 and Theorem 2 are special cases of a more-general theorem for unitary theories. Let $\mathbb{T}$ be a unitary theory defined over a signature $\varSigma$. Let X be the program variables. The class $\varPhi$ of formulas consists of conjunctions representing substitutions.

Theorem 3 ([10]). *Let $\mathbb{T}$ be a unitary theory. Assume that for any sequence of equations $e_1 = e'_1, e_2 = e'_2, \ldots$, the sequence of most-general unifiers $\mathtt{Unif}(e_1 = e'_1), \mathtt{Unif}(e_1 = e'_1 \wedge e_2 = e'_2), \ldots$ contains at most n distinct unifiers where n is the number of variables in the given equations. Suppose that $T_{\mathtt{Unif}}(n)$ is the time complexity for computing the most-general $\mathbb{T}$-unifier of equations given in a shared representation.* [2] *Then the assertion checking problem for programs of size n that are specified using edge labels (a)-(c) and whose expressions are from theory $\mathbb{T}$, can be solved in time $O(n^4 T_{\mathtt{Unif}}(n^2))$.*

The proof of this theorem can be obtained by generalizing the proofs of Theorem 1 and Theorem 2. Specifically, we perform backward propagation on the logical lattice $(\varPhi, \Rightarrow_{\mathbb{T}})$. Using unification (Lemma 1), the generated intermediate assertions are always strengthened to elements of $\varPhi$. This shows that we are essentially doing an (backward) abstract interpretation over the logical lattice $(\varPhi, \Rightarrow_{\mathbb{T}})$. The assumption in the statement of Theorem 3 guarantees that fixpoint is reached in n iterations. Thus, Theorem 3 characterizes the complexity of (the decision version of) the abstract interpretation problem over certain logical lattices induced by unitary theories.

4.4 Checking Disequality Assertions Is Intractable

It is natural to wonder about the complexity of checking a disequality assertion in a program containing restricted kinds of edges. Unfortunately, it is easy to

---

[2] We assume that the $\mathbb{T}$-unification procedure returns *true* when presented with an equation that is valid (true) in $\mathbb{T}$.

see that this problem is undecidable even for the simple case of programs using only uninterpreted symbols.

Theorem 4. *Checking disequality assertions is undecidable for programs with edge labels (a)-(c) and whose expression language is restricted to unary uninterpreted function symbols and one constant.*

Proof. Given an instance $\{(u_i, v_i) : i = 1, \ldots, n\}$ of PCP, consider the program:

```
1  u := ε; v := ε;
2  switch (*)
3          case 1:  u := u₁(u); v := v₁(v);
4          case 2:  u := u₂(u); v := v₂(v);

5              ⋮
6          case n:  u := uₙ(u); v := vₙ(v);
7  if (*) then { goto line number 2 } else { }
```

This program can be implemented using only edge labels (a)-(c). It non-deterministically generates (encodings of) all possible pairs (u, v) of strings such that $u = u_{i_1} \ldots u_{i_k}$ and $v = v_{i_1} \ldots v_{i_k}$. The disequality $u \neq v$ holds at the end of the program iff the original PCP does not have a solution.

4.5   Checking Disjunctive Assertions

We briefly consider the problem of checking if disjunctive assertions of the form $e_1 = e_2 \vee e_3 = e_4 \vee \cdots$ hold at program points. The following simple program shows that this problem is coNP-hard even for programs over a very simple expression language containing just two distinct (uninterpreted) constants.

```
IsUnSatisfiable(ψ)
% Suppose ψ has n variables x₁,…,xₙ and m clauses # 1,…,m
% Suppose xᵢ occurs in positive form in clauses # Aᵢ[0],…,Aᵢ[cᵢ]
%                and in negative form in clauses # Bᵢ[0],…,Bᵢ[dᵢ].
for i = 1 to m do
    eᵢ := 0; % eᵢ represents whether clause i has been satisfied.
for i = 1 to n do
    if (*) then % set xᵢ to true
        for j = 0 to cᵢ do e_{Aᵢ[j]} := 1;
    else % set xᵢ to false
        for j = 0 to dᵢ do e_{Bᵢ[j]} := 1;
Assertion(e₁ = 0 ∨ e₂ = 0 ∨ ⋯ ∨ eₘ = 0);
```

We note that the above program can be easily written as a program using edge labels (a)-(c) by simply unrolling the loop and converting it into a loop-free program. It is easy to see that in the above program, the disjunctive assertion at the end of the program holds iff the given 3-CNF formula is unsatisfiable.

Theorem 5. *The problem of checking disjunctive equality assertions in programs with edge labels (a)-(c) and over an expression language containing (at least) two constants is coNP-hard.*

4.6   The Combined Theory of UFS+LAE

We now consider the problem of assertion checking (equality assertions) in programs whose expression language comes from the union of UFS and LAE theories. This problem can be shown to be coNP-hard [8] by creating a program – very similar to the program in Section 4.5 – whose expression language is that of UFS+LAE and in which an equality assertion is valid iff a given 3-CNF formulas is unsatisfiable. A crucial component of the coNP-hardness proof is the fact that an *equality* assertion in UFS+LAE can encode a *disjunctive* assertion. Specifically, note that $x = a \lor x = b$ can be encoded as the (non-disjunctive) assertion $F(a) + F(b) = F(x) + F(a + b - x)$. This idea can be generalized to encode $x = a_1 \lor x = a_2 \lor x = a_3 \lor \cdots$. Note that, by Lemma 1, $Fa + Fb = Fx + F(a + b - x)$ holds at a program point π iff $\text{Unif}(Fa + Fb = Fx + F(a + b - x))$ holds at π. In the theory $\text{UFS} + \text{LAE}$, $\text{Unif}(Fa + Fb = Fx + F(a + b - x))$ is just $x = a \lor x = b$. By recursively using this same idea, we can find an equation whose complete set of unifiers is a disjunction of the form $x = a_1 \lor x = a_2 \lor \cdots \lor x = a_n$. This observation, combined with Theorem 5, proves the following result.

Theorem 6 ([8]). *Let $\mathcal{P}$ denote the class of programs built using edge labels (a)– (c) and using the expression language $Terms(\Sigma \cup X)$, where Σ is the signature of $\text{UFS} + \text{LAE}$ and X is a finite set of program variables. The problem of checking equality assertions for programs in class $\mathcal{P}$ is coNP-hard.*

4.7   Bitary Theories

The proof of coNP-hardness of assertion checking on programs whose expression language comes from UFS+LAE can be generalized to a class of non-unitary theories that can encode the disjunction $x = a \lor x = b$ as (the complete set of) unifiers of some equality.

Specifically, we define a theory $\mathbb{T}$ to be *bitary* if there exists an equality $e = e'$ in theory $\mathbb{T}$ such that $y \mapsto z_1$ and $y \mapsto z_2$ form a complete set of unifiers for $e = e'$, where y, z_1 and z_2 are some variables. In other words, $\text{Unif}(e = e')$ is $y = z_1 \lor y = z_2$. In addition, we also require that for new variables y' and z_1', it is the case that $\text{Unif}(e = e[y'/y, z_1'/z_1])$ and $\text{Unif}(e' = e'[y'/y, z_1'/z_1])$ are both $y = y' \land z_1 = z_1'$. It is easy to see that UFS+LAE is a bitary theory. The proof of Theorem 6 can be generalized for any bitary theory.

Theorem 7 ([10]). *Let $\mathbb{T}$ be a bitary theory over signature Σ. Let $\mathcal{P}$ denote the class of programs built using edge labels (a)-(c) and using the expression language $Terms(\Sigma \cup X)$, where X is a finite set of program variables. The problem of checking an equality assertion for programs in class $\mathcal{P}$ is coNP-hard.*

Some examples of bitary theories are the theories of a commutative function, combination of linear arithmetic and a unary uninterpreted function, and combination of two associative-commutative functions [10].

4.8   Revisiting the Combined Theory of UFS+LAE

We revisit the problem of checking equality assertions for programs built using expressions from UFS + LAE. The fact that there is no single most-general unifier of an equation in UFS+LAE suggests that the logical lattice defined over the domain of substitutions by $\Rightarrow_{\text{UFS}+\text{LAE}}$ is not sufficiently expressible for assertion checking (of $x = e$ assertions) in programs over UFS + LAE. One option would be to consider a more general lattice whose domain elements are conjunctions of arbitrary equations ($e_1 = e_2$). Unfortunately, the ordering relation $\Rightarrow_{\text{UFS}+\text{LAE}}$ does not induce a lattice structure over this domain. This fact is already true for UFS [13] and is illustrated in two examples below.

Example 6. If Φ is the set of finite conjunctions of ground equations, then there is no *least upper bound* element $\phi \in \Phi$ such that

$$x = y \Rightarrow_{\text{UFS}} \phi$$
$$fx = x \wedge fy = y \wedge gx = gy \Rightarrow_{\text{UFS}} \phi$$

The proof of this claim can be found in [13].

Example 7. If Φ is the set of finite conjunctions of ground equations on the signature of UFS + LAE, then there is no *least upper bound* element $\phi \in \Phi$ such that

$$x = a \wedge y = b \Rightarrow_{\text{UFS}+\text{LAE}} \phi$$
$$x = b \wedge y = a \Rightarrow_{\text{UFS}+\text{LAE}} \phi$$

The reason for the nonexistence of a least upper bound $\phi \in \Phi$ is that any such ϕ would have to imply the infinite set of facts $C[x] + C[y] = C[a] + C[b]$, where $C[\_]$ is an *arbitrary* context.

As observed before, this is not a serious obstacle for assertion checking in programs defined using only uninterpreted symbols – as the logical lattice defined over the domain of substitutions, rather than conjunctions of arbitrary equations, is still sufficiently expressive with respect to assertion checking. However, in the case of programs containing symbols from UFS and LAE, this forces us to search for a logical lattice defined over a domain that is more general than just substitutions, and less general than conjunctions of arbitrary equations. A natural choice is the disjunction of substitutions.

Let Φ be the set of formulas that are disjunctions of substitutions. Let $\Rightarrow_{\text{UFS}+\text{LAE}}$ be an ordering relation on Φ. It is easy to see that $\Rightarrow_{\text{UFS}+\text{LAE}}$ induces a lattice structure on Φ. We can show that the assertion checking problem is decidable on this logical lattice, even for program models that include edge label (d) from Figure 1.

Theorem 8 ([8]). *Let $\mathcal{P}$ denote the class of programs built using edge labels (a)–(d) and using the expression language $Terms(\Sigma \cup X)$, where Σ is a signature containing uninterpreted symbols and linear arithmetic symbols, and X is a finite set of program variables. Let Φ be the set of disjunctions of substitutions. The assertion checking problem for programs in class $\mathcal{P}$ and assertions in Φ is decidable.*

Proof. (Sketch) The procedure works by backward propagating formulas in Φ through the flowchart nodes. Due to Lemma 1, we can use unification to strengthen the formulas at each point. Since the UFS+LAE theory is finitary (every equation has a finite complete set of unifiers), it follows that each intermediate assertion obtained in the backward propagation can be converted to a formula in Φ. The remaining part is showing termination (of fixpoint across loops). Note that when a formula $\phi_1 \vee \cdots \phi_k$ in Φ is strengthened by conjuncting with another formula in Φ, then, in the result ϕ', for each $i \in \{1, \ldots, k\}$, it is either the case that (1) ϕ_i appears as a disjunct in ϕ', or (2) ϕ_i gets strengthened in multiple different ways and these strictly stronger forms appear as disjunct in ϕ'. Note that the strictly stronger forms necessarily instantiate some more of the *finitely many* program variables. If it is case (1) for all i, then this indicates that we have reached a fixpoint. If not, then we can see that we are smaller in some appropriately defined multiset extension of the well-founded ordering $>$ on natural numbers.

4.9 Convex and Finitary Theories

The proof of Theorem 8 depends on two critical ingredients: (1) Unification can be used to replace an arbitrary equation by a formula in Φ without compromising soundness; and (2) Unification always returns a finite complete set of unifiers. Property (1) and (2) can be shown to hold for any convex finitary theory. The combined theory of UFS and LAE is just one example of a convex and finitary theory.

Theorem 9 ([10]). *Let $\mathbb{T}$ be a convex finitary theory over signature Σ. Let $\mathcal{P}$ denote the class of programs built using edge labels (a)–(d) and using the expression language $Terms(\Sigma \cup X)$, where X is a finite set of program variables. Let Φ be the set of disjunctions of substitutions. The assertion checking problem for programs in class $\mathcal{P}$ and assertions in Φ is decidable.*

The (rich) theory obtained by combining (some or all) of the theories of linear arithmetic, uninterpreted functions, commutative functions, associative-commutative functions is finitary and convex. Hence, Theorem 9 shows that the assertion checking problem is decidable for programs that contain symbols from this large class of theories.

5 Interprocedural Logical Interpretation

In this section, we study the assertion checking problem for program models that additionally contain procedure call edges. Interprocedural analysis is considerably more difficult than intraprocedural analysis [21]. A modular way to do interprocedural analysis is by means of computing *procedure summaries* [25]. A summary of procedure P is an abstraction $[\![P]\!]_A$ of its meaning $[\![P]\!]$ (which is a mapping from the subsets of input states to subsets of output subsets) in some abstract domain A.

5.1 The Theory of Linear Arithmetic

We first consider the logical lattice defined by the theory of linear arithmetic (LAE). The abstract domain Φ is the set of conjunctions of linear arithmetic equalities of the form $\sum_{i=1}^{n} c_i x_i = c$, where c_i, c are integer constants and x_i's are program variables. The ordering relation is $\Rightarrow_{\text{LAE}}$. A summary of a procedure in this abstract lattice would be a mapping from Φ to Φ.

Since the set Φ has an infinite number of elements, we can not hope to enumerate Φ and compute this abstract mapping. Consider the *generic* equation $\sum_{i=1}^{n} \alpha_i x_i = \alpha_0$, where α_i's are *variables*. The important property of the equation $\sum_{i=1}^{n} \alpha_i x_i = \alpha_0$ is that every element in Φ can be obtained by appropriately instantiating the α_i's by integer constants. Thus, a symbolic representation of the abstract summary can be obtained by backward propagating such a generic equation.

Backward propagation of a generic assertion, $\sum_{i=1}^{n} \alpha_i x_i = \alpha_0$, will result in (a conjunction of) equation of the general form,

$$\sum_{i=1}^{n}\sum_{j=1}^{n} c_{ij}\alpha_i x_j + \sum_{i=1}^{n} d_i \alpha_i = \alpha_0.$$

This can be seen as a *linear* equation *over* $n^2 + n + 1$ variables: n^2 variables representing the unknown product terms $\alpha_i x_j$ and $n + 1$ variables representing the unknown terms α_i. Since there can be at most $n^2 + n + 1$ linearly independent equations of the above form, the backward propagation computation would reach fixpoints in polynomial number of steps. This observation is the main ingredient in the proof of the following result.

Theorem 10 ([18,11]). *Let* LAE *be the theory of linear arithmetic and* Σ *be its signature. Let* $\mathcal{P}$ *denote the class of programs built using edge labels (a)–(c),(e) and using the expression language* $Terms(\Sigma \cup X)$, *where* X *is a finite set of program variables. Let* Φ *be the set of conjunctions of linear equations over* X. *The assertion checking problem for programs in class* $\mathcal{P}$ *and assertions in* Φ *is solvable in polynomial time, assuming that the arithmetic operations can be done in* $O(1)$ *time.*

5.2 The Theory of Unary Uninterpreted Symbols

Consider the logical lattice defined by the theory of *unary* uninterpreted symbols (UUFS). The abstract domain Φ we used before is the set of substitutions, that is, conjunctions of equations of the form $x_i = t_i$, where t_i is a term (not containing

x_i). The ordering relation is $\Rightarrow_{\mathsf{UUFS}}$. A summary of a procedure in this abstract lattice would be a mapping from Φ to Φ.

Again, the set Φ has an infinite number of elements, and hence we can not hope to enumerate Φ and compute this abstract mapping. Since we assume only unary symbols in the signature, the term t_i above can be seen as a string α (of unary symbols) applied to a program variable x_j or a designated constant ϵ. In other words, t_i can be seen as αx_j or $\alpha \epsilon$.

Consider the $n(n-1)$ *generic* equations $x_i = \alpha_{ij} x_j$, for $i \neq j \in \{1, \ldots, n\}$, along with the n *generic* equations $x_i = \beta_i \epsilon$, for $i \in \{1, \ldots, n\}$, where α_{ij}'s and β_i's are *string variables*. The important property of these total n^2 equations is that every equation in Φ can be obtained by appropriately instantiating one of the α_{ij}'s or β_i's by an appropriate string. Thus, a symbolic representation of the abstract summary can be obtained by backward propagating each of these n^2 generic equations.

Backward propagation of a single generic assertion, $x_i = \alpha_{ij} x_j$, will result in (a conjunction of) equations of the general form,

$$Cx_k = \alpha_{ij} Dx_l,$$

where C, D are concrete strings over Σ and x_k, x_l are either some program variables or ϵ. A technical lemma is now required to show that any conjunction of such equations can be simplified to contain at most a quadratic (in n) number of equations. The simplification procedure is only required to preserve the unifiers (and not preserve logical equivalence). A side-effect of the proof of the technical lemma shows that fixpoints are reached in quadratic number of iterations. Putting all these observations together, we get a proof of the following result.

Theorem 11 ([11]). *Let* UUFS *be the theory of unary uninterpreted symbols and* Σ *be its signature. Let* $\mathcal{P}$ *denote the class of programs built using edge labels (a)–(c),(e) and using the expression language* $Terms(\Sigma \cup X)$, *where* X *is a finite set of program variables. Let* Φ *be the set of substitutions over* X. *The assertion checking problem for programs in class* $\mathcal{P}$ *and assertions in* Φ *is solvable in polynomial time, assuming that string operations can be done in* $O(1)$ *time.*

All string operations that arise in the proof of Theorem 11 can indeed be shown to be computable in polynomial using Plandowski's result on singleton context-free grammars [20,11].

5.3 Unitary Theories

Given the identical approach employed in the proofs of Theorem 10 and Theorem 11, it is naturally evident that these results can be generalized to a class of unitary theories that satisfy certain specific conditions. The theory of unary uninterpreted symbols and that of linear arithmetic can then be seen as members of this class. This generalization has been developed in [11]. This generalization is based on defining the concept of a *generic* equation using *context variables*. In the general case, the backward propagation approach requires solving (performing unification on) equations containing context variables.

Unification type of theory of program expressions	Edge Labels	Complexity of assertion checking	Examples	Refs.
Strict Unitary	(a)–(c)	PTIME	LAE, UFS	[7,16,17]
Bitary	(a)–(c)	coNP-hard	LAE+UFS, C	[8]
Finitary,Convex	(a)–(d)	Decidable	LAE+UFS+C+AC	[16,8]
Unitary	(a)-(c),(e)	Decidable	LAE,UUFS	[11]

Fig. 2. Summary of results. If the program model consists of edges with labels given in Col 2 and the theory underlying the program expressions belongs to the class given in Col 1, then its assertion checking problem has time complexity given in Col 3. Row 1,4 require some additional technical assumptions. Col 4 contains examples of theories for which the corresponding result holds, where C denotes commutative functions, and AC denotes associative-commutative functions.

6 Forward Abstract Interpretation over Logical Lattices

In the previous sections, we have discussed approaches based on backward propagation on abstract logical lattices. In the case of intraprocedural analysis (Section 4), we were able to perform complete backward propagation on rich logical lattices, but we always required the specification of a goal assertion. In the case of interprocedural analysis (Section 5), we did not need a goal assertion explicitly (since the backward propagation could be done on generic assertions), but we were able to obtain complete procedures for only very simple logical lattices. While these theoretical results are useful in understanding the limits and issues in abstract interpretation over logical lattices, they are of limited help in practice. This is because, in practice, often there is no specification of goal assertions and often the programs use expressions over richer theories. Hence, it is important to consider the problem of *generating* invariants by performing forward abstract interpretation over logical lattices.

We restrict our discussion to an intraprocedural setting in this section. It is evident that building an efficient forward logical abstract interpretation on programs with edge labels (a)-(c) over a logical lattice $(A, \sqsubseteq)$ requires:

R1. Given two elements E_1 and E_2 in A, the join $E_1 \sqcup E_2$ should be efficiently computable,

R2. Given $E \in A$, and a program variable x, the best over-approximation not containing x, that is, $\sqcap\{E' \mid E \sqsubseteq E', E'$ does not contain $x\}$, is efficiently computable,

R3. Given $E \in A$, and a ground equation $x = e$ where x does not occur in E, $E \sqcap \{x = e\}$ is efficiently computable,

R4. Given $E, E' \in A$, the relation $E \sqsubseteq E'$ is efficiently decidable.

Requirements R1 and R2 ensure that assertions can be propagated forward, respectively, at join points and across non-deterministic assignments. Requirements R2 and R3 together guarantee that assertions can be propagated forward across assignments. Requirement R4 helps in detecting when a fixpoint is reached.

Finding expressive logical lattices for which the Requirements R1–R4 can be satisfied is one of the challenges in building expressive and scalable abstract interpreters. Since, by Definition 2, $\sqsubseteq$ is generally (some refinement of) the implication relation $\Rightarrow_{\mathbb{T}}$ in a logical theory $\mathbb{T}$, Requirement R4 is often easily fulfilled using existing *decision procedures* for various theories. Requirement R3 is also easy to satisfy for many logical lattices since the domain of a logical lattice is frequently closed under conjunction. Requirement R2 asks for a quantifier elimination procedures, but the result is expected to lie in a restricted subclass A of logical formulas. The problems mentioned in Requirements R1 and R2 are not so well-studied in the theorem proving community. We mention some of the known results here. Karr [14] presented a join algorithm for the linear arithmetic logical lattice. Mine [15] discussed the logical lattice on the octagon abstract domain. Join algorithms for nonlinear polynomial abstract domain were studied by [22], and those for initial term algebra by [7,23,13]. We note here that computing join is often more difficult than deciding $\sqsubseteq$ (satisfiability decision procedure) since $E \sqsubseteq E'$ reduces to checking equivalence of $E \sqcap E'$ and E.

The intuitive choice for the domain of a logical lattice is the conjunction of atomic formulas in the theory. The natural choice for the ordering relation $\sqsubseteq$ is the logical implication relation $\Rightarrow_{\mathbb{T}}$ in the theory. Unfortunately, as we saw in Example 6 and Example 7, these common choices, when put together, need not yield a lattice. This problem can often be solved by restricting the domain or the ordering relation.

6.1   Combining Logical Interpreters

One attractive feature of logical lattices is that there is a natural notion of combination of logical lattices that corresponds directly to the notion of combination of logical theories. This notion is called the *logical product* of logical lattices [9]. The logical product is more expressive than the direct product or reduced product [5,3] of lattices.

A natural question related to logical product of logical lattices is the following: Given abstract interpreters for the individual logical lattices (in the form of, say, witnesses for the satisfiability of the four Requirements R1–R4, can we obtain an abstract interpreter for the logical product?

A positive answer for this question, under certain assumptions on the logical theories underlying the logical lattices, was provided in [9]. This combination result (and the assumptions on the logical theories) are inspired by the Nelson-Oppen combination method for decision procedures [19]. Specifically, we require the individual logical theories to be disjoint, convex, and stably-infinite.

6.2   Richer Logical Lattices

We briefly discuss extensions to the program model to make it more realistic. In the program model discussed above, conditionals were abstracted as non-deterministic choices. In reality, conditionals are important when reasoning about programs. This is, however, easily fixed as forward propagation based logical interpreters can use the meet operation to handle conditionals. As pointed out above, adding conditionals makes the assertion checking problem undecidable in many cases. Hence, abstract interpretation approaches necessarily lose either completeness or termination on this rich program model.

A second crucial feature absent in the program model of Section 2.1 is the *heap* and assignments that manipulate the heap. Modeling the heap and analyzing the properties of data-structures in the heap is important for verifying real programs. In programs that manipulate the heap, the lvalue *lval* of an assignment, *lval* := *e*, need not always be a variable. In such a case, one of the first hurdles to overcome is the issue of aliasing. For example, using C notation, an assignment to $x \rightarrow p$ can change the value of $y \rightarrow p$, if x and y contain the same value. As a result, propagating assertions through assignment edges becomes highly nontrivial in presence of aliasing. A second hurdle when analyzing heap manipulating programs is that all interesting invariants of such programs are about unbounded data-structures in heaps. For example, an invariant could state that all elements of an array or list are initialized. Simpler abstract domains like the ones discussed in previous sections are not expressive to represent such invariants.

These two issues can both be resolved using a very carefully designed logical lattice that can express quantified formulas. Quantified formulas can be used to represent aliasing information. Furthermore, it can also be used to represent invariants of unbounded data-structures. Logical interpretation, but over these richer abstract domains, is a promising approach for designing analysis tools for verification of real and complex code.

While designing useful logical abstract domains, one has to make sure that, in an effort to improve expressiveness, the computational aspects outlined as Requirements R1– R4 are not compromised. The reader is referred to [12] for an abstract domain that includes *quantified formulas*, but that is parameterized by a base abstract domain. A logical interpreter over the rich domain is built using a logical interpreter over the simpler base domain. A good choice of base domain gives an expressive and efficient quantified abstract domain [12].

6.3   Interface for a Logical Lattice: The Boolean Interface

In the effort to built new logical interpreters by using existing logical interpreters, we realized that we need a richer interface from an existing logical interpreter. Apart from the ability to (a) compute meet (which is an over-approximation of conjunction) and join (which is an over-approximation of disjunction) on the logical lattice and (b) check for the ordering relation (which is often just a satisfiability checking procedure), we also need functions that (c) compute good over-approximations of join and meet (especially in lattices that are not complete), and (d) good under-approximations of meet (conjunction) and join (disjunction). Additionally, we require the ability to (e) compute good over- and under-approximations of the operation of projecting out a variable (quantifier elimination on a class of formulas that form the domain of the logical lattice). These operations are often required to be done under some context, that is, under the assumption that certain formulas are known to be true. The exact utility of these interface functions in designing new logical interpreters is beyond the scope of this paper.

7 Conclusion

This paper presents *logical interpretation* - a static analysis approach to checking and generating rich invariants based on using logical lattices. Logical interpretations provide a new paradigm for embedding theorem proving techniques in program analysis tools. The various *satisfiability modulo theory* solvers provide just one of the essential interface functions, and many others are required to build logical interpreters. These other little engines of proof are procedures that perform unification, context unification, matching, and compute over- and under-approximations of conjunction, disjunction, and quantifier elimination on a class of formulas in some theory. The design of effective logical interpreters tries to achieve a balance between *expressiveness* and *computational efficiency*. Well-designed logical abstract domains have the potential of making significant impact on automatically verifying the partial correctness of significant parts of domain-specific software components.

Acknowledgments. The authors thank N. Shankar for helpful feedback.

References

1. Alpern, B., Wegman, M.N., Zadeck, F.K.: Detecting equality of variables in programs. In: 15th Annual ACM Symposium on POPL, pp. 1–11 (1988)
2. Baader, F., Snyder, W.: Unification theory. In: Robinson, A., Voronkov, A. (eds.) Handbook of Automated Reasoning (chapter 8), vol. I, pp. 445–532. Elsevier, Amsterdam (2001)
3. Cousot, P.: Forward relational infinitary static analysis, Lecture Notes (2005) Available at http://web.mit.edu/afs/athena.mit.edu/course/16/16.399/www
4. Cousot, P., Cousot, R.: Abstract interpretation: A unified lattice model for static analysis of programs by construction or approximation of fixpoints. In: 4th Annual ACM Symposium on POPL, pp. 234–252 (1977)
5. Cousot, P., Cousot, R.: Systematic design of program analysis frameworks. In: 6th ACM Symp. on POPL, pp. 269–282 (1979)
6. Flanagan, C., Rustan, K., Leino, M., Lillibridge, M., Nelson, G., Saxe, J.B., Stata, R.: Extended static checking for Java. In: PLDI, pp. 234–245 (2002)
7. Gulwani, S., Necula, G.C.: A polynomial-time algorithm for global value numbering. In: Giacobazzi, R. (ed.) SAS 2004. LNCS, vol. 3148, pp. 212–227. Springer, Heidelberg (2004)
8. Gulwani, S., Tiwari, A.: Assertion checking over combined abstraction of linear arithmetic and uninterpreted functions. In: Sestoft, P. (ed.) ESOP 2006 and ETAPS 2006. LNCS, vol. 3924, Springer, Heidelberg (2006)
9. Gulwani, S., Tiwari, A.: Combining abstract interpreters. In: PLDI (June 2006)
10. Gulwani, S., Tiwari, A.: Assertion checking unified. In: Cook, B., Podelski, A. (eds.) VMCAI 2007. LNCS, vol. 4349, Springer, Heidelberg (2007) (to appear)

11. Gulwani, S., Tiwari, A.: Computing procedure summaries for interprocedural analysis . In: Proc. European Symp. on Programming, ESOP 2007. LNCS, Springer, Heidelberg (2007) (to appear)
12. Gulwani, S., Tiwari, A.: Static analysis of heap manipulating low-level software. In: CAV. LNCS, vol. 4590, Springer, Heidelberg (2007)
13. Gulwani, S., Tiwari, A., Necula, G.C.: Join algorithms for the theory of uninterpreted symbols. In: Lodaya, K., Mahajan, M. (eds.) FSTTCS 2004. LNCS, vol. 3328, pp. 311–323. Springer, Heidelberg (2004)
14. Karr, M.: Affine relationships among variables of a program. Acta Informatica 6, 133–151 (1976)
15. Mine, A.: The octagon abstract domain. Higher Order Symbol. Comput. 19(1), 31–100 (2006)
16. Müller-Olm, M., Rüthing, O., Seidl, H.: Checking Herbrand equalities and beyond. In: Cousot, R. (ed.) VMCAI 2005. LNCS, vol. 3385, pp. 79–96. Springer, Heidelberg (2005)
17. Müller-Olm, M., Seidl, H.: A note on Karr's algorithm. In: 31st International Colloquium on Automata, Languages and Programming, pp. 1016–1028 (2004)
18. Müller-Olm, M., Seidl, H.: Precise interprocedural analysis through linear algebra. In: 31st ACM Symposium on POPL, pp. 330–341 (January 2004)
19. Nelson, G., Oppen, D.: Simplification by cooperating decision procedures. ACM Transactions on Programming Languages and Systems 1(2), 245–257 (1979)
20. Plandowski, W.: Testing equivalence of morphisms on context-free languages. In: van Leeuwen, J. (ed.) ESA 1994. LNCS, vol. 855, pp. 460–470. Springer, Heidelberg (1994)
21. Reps, T.: On the sequential nature of interprocedural program-analysis problems. Acta Informatica 33(8), 739–757 (1996)
22. Rodriguez-Carbonell, E., Kapur, D.: An abstract interpretation approach for automatic generation of polynomial invariants. In: Giacobazzi, R. (ed.) SAS 2004. LNCS, vol. 3148, Springer, Heidelberg (2004)
23. Rüthing, O., Knoop, J., Steffen, B.: Detecting equalities of variables: Combining efficiency with precision. In: Cortesi, A., Filé, G. (eds.) SAS 1999. LNCS, vol. 1694, pp. 232–247. Springer, Heidelberg (1999)
24. Shankar, N.: Little engines of proof. In: Eriksson, L.-H., Lindsay, P.A. (eds.) FME 2002. LNCS, vol. 2391, pp. 1–20. Springer, Heidelberg (2002)
25. Sharir, M., Pnueli, A.: Two approaches to interprocedural data flow analysis. In: Program Flow Analysis: Theory and Applications, pp. 189–233. Prentice-Hall, Englewood Cliffs (1981)

Solving Quantified Verification Conditions Using Satisfiability Modulo Theories*

Yeting Ge[1], Clark Barrett[1], and Cesare Tinelli[2]

[1] New York University
{yeting, barrett}@cs.nyu.edu
[2] The University of Iowa
tinelli@cs.uiowa.edu

Abstract. First order logic provides a convenient formalism for describing a wide variety of verification conditions. Two main approaches to checking such conditions are pure first order automated theorem proving (ATP) and automated theorem proving based on satisfiability modulo theories (SMT). Traditional ATP systems are designed to handle quantifiers easily, but often have difficulty reasoning with respect to theories. SMT systems, on the other hand, have built-in support for many useful theories, but have a much more difficult time with quantifiers. One clue on how to get the best of both worlds can be found in the legacy system Simplify which combines built-in theory reasoning with quantifier instantiation heuristics. Inspired by Simplify and motivated by a desire to provide a competitive alternative to ATP systems, this paper describes a methodology for reasoning about quantifiers in SMT systems. We present the methodology in the context of the Abstract DPLL Modulo Theories framework. Besides adapting many of Simplify's techniques, we also introduce a number of new heuristics. Most important is the notion of *instantiation level* which provides an effective mechanism for prioritizing and managing the large search space inherent in quantifier instantiation techniques. These techniques have been implemented in the SMT system CVC3. Experimental results show that our methodology enables CVC3 to solve a significant number of benchmarks that were not solvable with any previous approach.

1 Introduction

Many verification problems can be solved by checking formulas in first order logic. Automated theorem proving (ATP) systems are much more powerful than those of just a few years ago. However, practical verification conditions often require reasoning with respect to well-established first order theories such as arithmetic. Despite their power, ATP systems have been less successful in this domain. A new breed of provers, dubbed SMT solvers (for Satisfiability Modulo Theories) is attempting to fill this gap.

---

* This work was partially supported by a donation from Intel Corp. and by the National Science Foundation grant number 0551645.

F. Pfenning (Ed.): CADE 2007, LNAI 4603, pp. 167–182, 2007.

Solvers for SMT are typically based on decision procedures for the satisfiability of quantifier-free formulas in certain logical theories of interest. As a result, they have been traditionally rather limited in their ability to reason about quantifiers, especially when compared to ATP systems. A notable exception is the prover Simplify [7] which combines a Nelson-Oppen style prover with heuristics for instantiation of quantifiers. Simplify has been successfully applied in a variety of software verification projects including ESC/JAVA [9], and, despite its age, it is still considered state-of-the-art for SMT reasoning with quantifiers.

However, Simplify has a number of drawbacks. Chief among them is the fact that it is old and no longer supported. Additionally, there are several weaknesses in Simplify's heuristics, so that often users must spend considerable manual effort rewriting or annotating their input formulas before Simplify can successfully prove them. Finally, modern SMT solvers have a host of performance and feature enhancements that make them more appealing for use in applications. Unfortunately, users of SMT solvers have had to choose between these improvements and effective quantifier support.

In this paper we discuss efforts to update and improve quantifier reasoning in SMT solvers based on the DPLL(T) architecture [10]. We begin by extending the Abstract DPLL Modulo Theories framework [11], a convenient abstract framework for describing such systems, with rules for quantifiers. We then explain the main heuristics employed by Simplify as strategies within this framework, and introduce several improvements to Simplify's strategies. Most novel is the notion of *instantiation level* which is an effective means of prioritizing and managing the many terms that are candidates for quantifier instantiation.

The techniques discussed in the paper have been implemented in CVC3, a modern DPLL(T)-style solver based on a variant of the Nelson-Oppen combination method [3,4]. We conclude with experimental results demonstrating the effectiveness of our heuristics in improving the performance of CVC3 and in solving verification conditions (in particular, several from the NASA suite introduced in [6]) that no previous ATP or SMT system has been able to solve.

2   Background

We will assume the usual notions and adopt the usual terminology in first order logic with equality. We also assume familiarity with the fundamentals of unification theory (see, e.g., [1]). For brevity, when it is clear from context, we will refer to an atomic formula also as a term. If φ is a first-order formula or a term, t is a term, and x is a variable, we denote by $\varphi[x/t]$ the result of substituting t for all free occurrences of x in φ. That notation is extended in the obvious way to tuples $\overline{x}$ of variables and $\overline{t}$ of terms. The notation $\exists \overline{x}.\varphi$ stands as usual for a formula of the form $\exists x_1.\exists x_2.\cdots \exists x_n.\varphi$ (similarly for $\forall \overline{x}.\varphi$).

The *Satisfiability Modulo Theories* problem consists of determining the satisfiability of some closed first order formula φ, a *query*, with respect to some fixed *background theory* T with signature Σ. Often it is also desirable to allow the formula to contain additional *free symbols*, i.e. constant, function, and predicate symbols not in Σ. We say that φ is T-satisfiable if there is an expansion of a model of T to the free symbols in φ that satisfies φ. Typical background theories in SMT are (combined) theories T such that the T-satisfiability of ground formulas (i.e. closed quantifier-free formulas possibly with free symbols) can be decided by a special-purpose and efficient procedure we call a *ground SMT solver*.

Most modern ground SMT solvers integrate a propositional SAT solver based on the DPLL procedure with a *theory solver* which can check satisfiability of sets of literals with respect to some fragment of T. The Abstract DPLL Modulo Theories framework [2,11] provides a formalism for this integration that is abstract enough to be simple, yet precise enough to model many salient features of these solvers. The framework describes SMT solvers as transition systems, i.e., sets of *states* with a binary relation $\Longrightarrow$ over them, called the *transition relation*, defined declaratively by means of *transition rules*. A state is either the distinguished state *Fail* (denoting T-unsatisfiability) or a pair of the form $M \parallel F$, where M is a sequence of literals currently assumed to hold and F is a formula in conjunctive normal form (CNF) which is being checked for satisfiability.

Assuming an initial state of the form $\emptyset \parallel F_0$, the goal of the transition rules is to make progress towards a *final* state while maintaining equisatisfiability of the formula F_0. A final state is either *Fail* or a state $M \parallel F$ such that (i) the set of literals in M is T-satisfiable, and (ii) every clause in F is satisfied by the assignment induced by M (i.e., assuming that the literals in M are all true). In the latter case, the original formula F_0 is T-satisfiable. We refer the reader to [2,11] for a complete description of the framework. As a sample of its rules we describe here the propositional and the theory propagation rule:

$$\text{UnitPropagate}: \quad M \parallel F, C \vee l \implies M\,l \parallel F, C \vee l \ \text{ if } \begin{cases} M \models \neg C \\ l \text{ is undefined in } M \end{cases}$$

$$T\text{-Propagate}: \quad M \parallel F \quad \implies M\,l \parallel F \quad \text{ if } \begin{cases} M \models_T l \\ l \text{ or } \neg l \text{ occurs in } F \\ l \text{ is undefined in } M \end{cases}$$

In the above rules, a comma is used to separate clauses of the CNF formula, C and l respectively denote a clause and a literal, $\models$ is propositional entailment, and $\models_T$ is first-order entailment modulo the background theory T.

3   Reasoning with Quantifiers in SMT

While many successful ground SMT solvers have been built for a variety of theories and combinations of theories, extending SMT techniques to quantified queries has proven so far quite difficult. This mirrors the difficulties encountered in first order theorem proving, where quantified queries are the norm, in embedding background theories *efficiently* into existing refutation-based calculi.

Following Stickel's original idea of *theory resolution* [15], several first order calculi have been given sound and complete theory extensions that rely on the computation of complete sets of theory unifiers. These nice theoretical results have, however, failed to generate efficient implementations thus far, mostly due to the practical difficulty, or the theoretical impossibility, of computing theory unifiers for concrete background theories of interest.

Recently, attempts have been made to embed ground SMT procedures into successful first-order provers, most notably Vampire [14] and SPASS [18], while aiming at practical usefulness as opposed to theoretical completeness (see, e.g., [12]). The work described here follows the alternative, also incomplete, approach of extending SMT solvers with effective heuristics for quantifier instantiation.

3.1   Modeling Quantifier Instantiation

The Abstract DPLL Modulo Theories framework can be easily extended to include rules for quantifier instantiation. The key idea is to also allow closed quantified formulas wherever atomic formulas are allowed. We define an *abstract atomic formula* as either an atomic formula or a closed quantified formula. An *abstract literal* is either an abstract atomic formula or its negation; an abstract clause is a disjunction of abstract literals. Then, we simply replace ground literals and clauses with their abstract counterparts. For instance, non-fail states become pairs $M \parallel F$ where M is a sequence of abstract literals and F is a conjunction of abstract clauses.

With this slight modification, we can add the two rules below to Abstract DPLL to model quantifier instantiation. For simplicity and without loss of generality, we assume here that abstract literals in M appear only positively (if they are negated, the negation can be pushed inside the quantifier) and that the bodies of abstract atoms are themselves in abstract CNF.

$$\exists\text{-Inst}: \quad M \parallel F \implies M \parallel F, \neg\exists\overline{x}.\varphi \vee \varphi[\overline{x}/\overline{c}] \quad \textbf{if} \quad \begin{cases} \exists\overline{x}.\varphi \text{ is in } M \\ \overline{c} \text{ are fresh constants} \end{cases}$$

$$\forall\text{-Inst}: \quad M \parallel F \implies M \parallel F, \neg\forall\overline{x}.\varphi \vee \varphi[\overline{x}/\overline{s}] \quad \textbf{if} \quad \begin{cases} \forall\overline{x}.\varphi \text{ is in } M \\ \overline{s} \text{ are ground terms} \end{cases}$$

The $\exists$-Inst rule identifies a quantified abstract literal $\exists\overline{x}.\varphi$ currently in M. This formula is then *instantiated* with fresh constants $\overline{c}$ to get $\varphi[\overline{x}/\overline{c}]$. A clause is then added that is equivalent to the implication $\exists\overline{x}.\varphi \rightarrow \varphi[\overline{x}/\overline{c}]$. Note that we cannot just add $\varphi[\overline{x}/\overline{c}]$ because the Abstract DPLL Modulo Theories framework requires that the satisfiability of F be preserved by every rule. The $\forall$-Inst rule works analogously except that the formula is instantiated with ground terms rather than fresh constants.

Example 1. Suppose a and b are free constant symbols and f is a unary free function symbol. We show how to prove the validity of the formula $(0 \leq b \wedge (\forall x. x \geq 0 \rightarrow f(x) = a)) \rightarrow f(b) = a$ in the union T of rational arithmetic, say, and the empty theory over $\{a, b, f\}$. We first negate the formula and put it into abstract CNF. Three abstract unit clauses are the result: $0 \leq b \ \wedge \ \forall x. (x \not\geq 0 \vee f(x) = a) \ \wedge \ f(b) \neq a$. Let l_1, l_2, l_3 denote the three abstract literals in the above clauses. Then the following is a derivation in the extended framework:

$$\begin{array}{lll}
& \emptyset \parallel l_1, l_2, l_3 & \text{(initial state)} \\
\Longrightarrow^* & l_1\, l_2\, l_3 \parallel l_1, l_2, l_3 & \text{(by UnitPropagate)} \\
\Longrightarrow & l_1\, l_2\, l_3 \parallel l_1, l_2, l_3, \neg l_2 \vee b \not\geq 0 \vee f(b) = a & \text{(by } \forall\text{-Inst)} \\
\Longrightarrow & l_1\, l_2\, l_3\, b \geq 0 \parallel l_1, l_2, l_3, \neg l_2 \vee b \not\geq 0 \vee f(b) = a & \text{(by } T\text{-Propagate)} \\
\Longrightarrow & \mathit{Fail} & \text{(by Fail)}
\end{array}$$

The last transition is possible because M falsifies the last clause in F and contains no decisions (case-splits). As a result, we may conclude that the original clause set is T-unsatisfiable, which implies that the original formula is valid in T.

It is not hard to see, using an analysis similar to that in [2], that the $\exists$-Inst and $\forall$-Inst rules preserve the satisfiability of F and therefore the soundness of the transition system. It is also clear that termination can only be guaranteed by limiting the number of times the rules are applied. Of course, for a given existentially quantified formula, there is no benefit to applying $\exists$-Inst more than once. On the other hand, a universally quantified formula may need to be instantiated with several different ground terms to discover that a query is unsatisfiable. For some background theories (e.g., universal theories), completeness can be shown for exhaustive and fair instantiation strategies that consider all possible quantifier instantiations by ground terms. This result, however, is of little practical relevance because of the great inefficiency of such a process. In this paper we focus on strategies for applying $\forall$-Inst that forgo completeness in the interest of efficiency, and simply aim at good *accuracy*, understood ideally here as the ratio of proved over unproved unsatisfiable queries in a given set.

4   Strategies for Instantiation

4.1   Instantiation Via Matching

A naive strategy for applying rule $\forall$-Inst is the following: once $\forall$-Inst has been selected for application to an abstract literal $\forall \overline{x}.\varphi$, the rule is repeatedly applied until $\overline{x}$ has been instantiated with every possible tuple of elements from some finite set G of ground terms. A reasonable choice for G is the set of ground terms that occur in assumed formulas (i.e., in M). We call this approach *naive instantiation*. A refinement of this strategy for sorted logics is to instantiate $\overline{x}$ with all and only the ground tuples of G that have the same sort as $\overline{x}$. Somewhat surprisingly, naive instantiation is sufficient for solving a large number of quantified verification conditions (see Section 6). Still, there are many verification conditions for which naive instantiation is hopelessly inefficient because of the large number of candidates for instantiation.

The Simplify prover uses a better heuristic, that still applies $\forall$-Inst exhaustively to an abstract atom, but selects for instantiation only ground terms that are *relevant* to the quantified formula in question, according to some heuristic relevance criteria. The idea is as follows: given a state $M \parallel F$ and an abstract literal $\forall x.\varphi$ in M,[1] try to find a subterm t of $\forall x.\varphi$ properly containing x, a

---

[1] The general case of an abstract literal of the form $\forall \overline{x}.\varphi$ is analogous.

ground term g in M, and a subterm s of g, such that $t[x/s]$ is equivalent to g modulo the background theory T (written $t[x/s] =_T g$). In this case, we expect that instantiating x with s is more likely to be helpful than instantiating with other candidate terms. Following Simplify's terminology, we call the term t a *trigger* (for $\forall x.\varphi$). In terms of unification theory, the case in which $t[x/s] =_T g$ is a special case of *T-matching* between t and g.

In general, in the context of SMT, given the complexity of the background theory T, it may be very difficult if not impossible to determine whether a trigger and a ground term T-match. The simplest solution is to check only for syntactic matching, by attempting to unify each trigger with each ground term. Simplify implements a simple extension of syntactic matching based on the congruence closure of the ground equations in M (see [7] for details).

Example 2. Consider again the formula in Example 1. At the point where $\forall$-Inst is applied, M consists of the following sequence of literals: $0 \leq b, \forall x. (x \not\geq 0 \vee f(x) = a), f(b) \neq a$. There are four ground terms appearing in M: 0, a, b, and $f(b)$. Thus, naive instantiation would apply $\forall$-Inst four times, once for each ground term. On the other hand, Simplify's matching heuristic would first identify a trigger in $\forall x. (x \not\geq 0 \vee f(x) = a)$. Since a trigger must be a term properly containing the quantified variable, the only candidate is $f(x)$. Now the trigger is compared with the set of ground terms. There is a single match, with $f(b)$, obtained when x is bound to b. Thus, the matching heuristic selects the ground term b for instantiation.

4.2   Eager Instantiation Versus Lazy Instantiation

So far, we have been concerned with the question of *how* to apply the rule $\forall$-Inst to a given abstract atom. An orthogonal question is *when* to apply it. One strategy, which we call *lazy instantiation*, is to apply $\forall$-Inst only when it is the only applicable rule. At the opposite end of the spectrum, another strategy, which we call *eager instantiation*, is to apply $\forall$-Inst to a universally quantified formula as soon as possible (i.e., as soon as it is added to the current M).

In Simplify, propositional search and quantifier instantiation are interleaved. When Simplify has a choice between instantiation and case splitting, it will generally favor instantiation. Thus, Simplify can be seen as employing a form of eager instantiation. Others [8] have advocated the lazy approach. One advantage of lazy instantiation is that an off-the-shelf SAT solver can be used. Eager instantiation typically requires a more sophisticated SAT solver that can accept new variables and clauses on the fly. We compare eager and lazy instantiation in Section 6 below.

5   Improving Instantiation Strategies

In this section we describe several improvements to the basic strategies discussed above. These strategies are implemented in CVC3 and evaluated in Section 6.

5.1   Triggers

Consider a generic quantified formula $\forall \overline{x}.\varphi$. The first step in the matching strategy described above is to find triggers within φ. CVC3 improves on Simplify's automated trigger generation methods in several ways. In CVC3, every subterm or non-equational atom t of φ that contains all the variables in $\overline{x}$ and at least one function or predicate symbol is considered a viable trigger. For example, if $\overline{x} = \{x_1, x_2\}$, then $x_1 \leq x_2$ and $g(f(x_1 + y), x_2)$ are legal triggers, but $0 \leq x_1$ and $f(x_1) + 1 = x_2$ are not. Simplify is slightly more restrictive: it requires that a trigger contain no additional variables besides those in $\overline{x}$. For example, in the formula $\forall x.(f(x) \rightarrow \forall y.g(x, y) < 0)$, the term $g(x, y)$ is not a viable trigger for Simplify because it contains y which is not bound by the outermost quantifier. Our experiments show that this restriction is unnecessary and does cause a loss of accuracy in some cases (in particular, CVC3's better performance on the *nasa* benchmarks described in Section 6.3 is partly due to relaxing this restriction).

Avoiding instantiation loops. Simplify uses a simple syntactic check to prevent its instantiation mechanism from diverging; specifically, it discards a potential trigger t if certain (syntactical) instances of t occur elsewhere in the formula. For example, in $\forall x.P(f(x), f(g(x)))$, the term $f(x)$ will not be selected as a trigger because an instance of $f(x)$, namely $f(g(x))$ occurs in the formula. While simple and inexpensive, this static filtering criterion is unable to detect more subtle forms of loops. For example, consider a state $M \parallel F$ with M containing the abstract literal $\psi = \forall x.(x > 0 \rightarrow \exists y. f(x) = f(y) + 1)$ where f is free. The only trigger for ψ is $f(x)$ and Simplify has no reason to reject this trigger. Now, if the set of ground terms contains $f(3)$, say, then with an application of $\forall$-Inst, it is possible to add the abstract clause $\neg \psi \vee \exists y. f(3) = f(y) + 1$ to F. Then, with an application of UnitPropagate and of $\exists$-Inst the literal $f(3) = f(c_1) + 1$, with c_1 fresh, can be added to M. The introduction of $f(c_1)$ in the set of ground terms can now give rise to a similar round of rule applications generating a new term $f(c_2)$, and so on. In order to prevent such loops, in addition to Simplify's static loop detection method, CVC3 also implements a general method for dynamically recognizing loops (including loops caused by groups of formulas together) and disabling the offending triggers. We do not describe that method here, partly due to space constraints but mainly because the *instantiation level* heuristic described in Section 5.4 below is much more effective.

Multi-trigger generation. Sometimes, there are no triggers that contain all the variables in $\overline{x}$. In this case, Simplify generates *multi-triggers*: small sets of terms in φ which together contain all (and exactly) the free variables in $\overline{x}$. CVC3 has essentially the same mechanism but it limits the number of multi-triggers composed of atomic formulas of φ. It does this by putting together in a multi-trigger only atoms having the same polarity in the overall abstract CNF formula F—where polarity is defined as usual for negation normal form formulas like F.

5.2   Matching Algorithm

Like all DPLL(T) systems, CVC3 checks the satisfiability of a query modulo some background theory T by maintaining at all times a current set M of assumed abstract literals. Ideally, when looking for matches for triggers, one would want to apply theory matching modulo the union of T and M. As mentioned earlier, however, because of the richness of T alone, in general this is highly impractical, if possible at all. CVC3 instead uses a (rather) incomplete theory matching procedure which is easier to implement efficiently, and, as we show in the next section, provides good results experimentally.

As M is modified, CVC3 also computes and stores in its data structures the congruence closure E of the positive ground literals of M over the set G of all ground terms in M. For any theory T, any two terms equal modulo E are also equal modulo $T \cup M$. Then, to apply the rule ∀-Inst to an abstract literal $\forall \overline{x}.\varphi$, CVC3 generates ground instantiations for $\overline{x}$ by matching modulo E the triggers of $\forall \overline{x}.\varphi$ against the terms in G. CVC3 implements a sound and terminating E-matching procedure by extending the standard rule-based syntactic unification algorithm as explained below.

Given a trigger t of the form $f(t_1, \ldots, t_n)$ where f is a free symbol, we select from G all terms of the form $f(s_1, \ldots, s_n)$; for each of these terms we then try to solve the (simultaneous) unification problem $\{t_1 =^? s_1, \ldots, t_n =^? s_n\}$. Standard unification fails when it encounters the case $g(\overline{t}) =^? g'(\overline{s})$ (where g and g' are distinct symbols). In contrast, we do not immediately fail in this case.

In general, when we select an equation of the form $g(\overline{t}) =^? s$, we do not fail in the following two subcases: (i) $g(\overline{t})$ is ground and $g(\overline{t}) =_E s$,[2] and (ii) g is a free symbol and there is a term of the form $g(\overline{u})$ in G such that $s =_E g(\overline{u})$. In the first case, we just remove the equation $g(\overline{t}) =^? s$; in the second case, we replace it by the set of equations $\overline{t} =^? \overline{u}$.

For a simple example, consider matching a trigger like $f(h(x))$ with a ground term $f(a)$ where f, h, a are free symbols and x is a variable. Suppose that $a = h(s) \in E$ for some s. Then the procedure above can generate the non-syntactic unifier $\{x \mapsto s\}$.

It is not difficult to see using standard soundness and termination arguments that this unification procedure converges, and when it does not fail it produces a grounding E-unifier (in fact, an E-matcher) for the problem $f(t_1, \ldots, t_n) =^? f(s_1, \ldots, s_n)$. This unifier is applied to the body of the abstract atom $\forall x.\varphi$ to obtain the clause for ∀-Inst. The procedure is clearly incomplete because E-matching is usually non-unitary[3], but the procedure returns only one solution, chosen arbitrarily, just for simplicity and speed. This source of incompleteness, however, has not shown to be a major limitation in practice so far.

The instantiation mechanism above applies to triggers whose top symbol is a free function symbol. Triggers whose top symbol is a theory symbol are currently

---

[2] Due to the way the congruence closure E is maintained in CVC3, checking that $g(\overline{t}) =_E s$ takes nearly always constant time.

[3] In other words, E-matching problems can have multiple, incomparable solutions. Consider the previous example with also $a = h(s') \in E$ for some $s' \neq_E s$.

treated the same way unless the symbol is an arithmetic symbol. Triggers starting with $+$ or $*$ are just discarded because treating those symbols syntactically is ineffectual and treating them semantically, as AC symbols say, is too onerous. A trigger t of the form $t_1 < t_2$ or $t_1 \leq t_2$, is processed as follows.[4] For every ground atom p of the form $s_1 < s_2$ or $s_1 \leq s_2$ in M, CVC3 generates the E-matching problem $\{t_1 =^? s_2, t_2 =^? s_1\}$ if t has positive polarity and p occurs in M, or t has negative polarity and $\neg p$ occurs in M; otherwise it generates the problem $\{t_1 =^? s_1, t_2 =^? s_2\}$.

5.3 Special Instantiation Heuristics

In addition to E-matching, CVC3 also employs some specialized instantiation heuristics that have proven useful on the kinds of formulas that appear in practical verification conditions. For simplicity, we will refer to these heuristics too as "trigger matching" even if they are not based on matching in the technical sense of unification theory. Some of these heuristics depend on recognizing that a certain free predicate symbol is defined in the query as an antisymmetric or a transitive symbol. Special multi-triggers are set up for these symbols that take those properties into account to improve the usefulness of the instances generated.

Another heuristic applies to formulas involving CVC3's built-in theory of arrays, which defines a read and a write operator. All triggers of the form $read(write(a, x, v), i)$ where x is one of the quantified variables, in addition to acting as normal triggers, also cause x to be instantiated to the index term j of any ground term of the form $read(a, j)$ or $write(a, j, u)$. The rationale is that when instantiating a variable that is used as an index to an array, we want to consider all known ground array index terms. Usually there are not too many of these terms and the standard matching techniques do not discover all of them.

5.4 Trigger Matching by Instantiation Levels

In SMT problems coming from verification applications, one of the main targets of CVC3, the query is a formula of the form $\Gamma \wedge \neg \varphi$ where φ is a verification condition and Γ is a large and more or less fixed T-satisfiable collection of (quantified) axioms about a number of relations and functions that are relevant to the verification application but for which there is no built-in solver. A large number of these axioms typically have no bearing on whether the negation of a particular verification condition is T-satisfiable with Γ. With heuristic instantiation, this entails that too many resources might be easily spent in producing and processing instances of axioms unrelated to the formula φ.

Simplify uses a *matching depth* heuristic to try to address this problem. Each time a new clause is generated by quantifier instantiation, it is assigned a numerical value which is one greater than the largest value assigned so far. This

---

[4] In CVC3, atoms using $>$ and $\geq$ are normalized internally to $<$ and $\leq$ atoms, respectively.

value is the matching depth of the clause. Later, when a literal must be chosen for a case-split, literals from clauses with a lower matching depth are preferred to those with a higher matching depth.

CVC3 uses a different approach, better suited to systems with a DPLL(T) architecture—where case splitting is not necessarily clause-based. Instead of giving a score to clauses, CVC3 assigns an *instantiation level* to every ground term it creates. Intuitively, an instantiation level n for a term t indicates that t is the result of n rounds of instantiations. More precisely, all terms in the original query are given an instantiation level of 0. If a formula $\forall \overline{x}.\varphi$ is instantiated with the ground terms $\overline{s}$, and n is the maximum instantiation level of the terms in $\overline{s}$, then all the new terms in $\varphi[\overline{x}/\overline{t}]$ (as well as any new terms derived from them via theory reasoning) are given the instantiation level $n+1$.

CVC3 provides as an option a trigger matching strategy that visits ground terms by instantiation levels. With this strategy, CVC3 matches triggers only against ground terms whose instantiation level is within a current upper bound b. This bound, whose initial value can be set by the user, is increased, by one, only when CVC3 reaches a (non-fail) state $M \parallel F$ where $\forall$-Inst is the only applicable rule and all terms with instantiation level less than or equal to b have already been considered.

Trigger matching by instantiation levels has proved very effective in our experiments, discussed in the next session. Here we point out that its inherent fairness has also the derived benefit of neutralizing the possible harmful effects of instantiation loops in the eager instantiation strategy. The reason is simply that each of the new ground terms generated within an instantiation level belongs by construction to the next level, and so will not be considered for matching until all other terms in the current level have been considered. As a consequence, checking for instantiation loops, either statically or dynamically, is completely unnecessary. Moreover, using instantiation levels allows us to enable by default those triggers that static or dynamic loop detection would have disabled. Significantly, we discovered that such triggers are actually necessary to prove many examples.

6   Experimental Results

All tests were run on AMD Opteron-based (64 bit) systems, running Linux, with a timeout of 5 minutes (unless otherwise stated) and a memory limit of 1 GB. For our comparisons, we used the latest versions of each prover available to us at the time: CVC3 version 1.1; Vampire 8.1; SPASS 2.2, yices 1.0, and the version of Fx7 available online at http://nemerle.org/~malekith/smt/en.html as of February 2007. A more detailed version of all the results discussed here can be found at http://www.cs.nyu.edu/~barrett/cade07.

6.1   Benchmarks

The benchmarks for our evaluation are from the SMT-LIB library [13] of benchmarks for SMT solvers. It consists of 29004 benchmarks from three different SMT divisions: AUFLIA (arrays, uninterpreted functions, and linear integer arithmetic); AUFLIRA (arrays, uninterpreted functions, and mixed linear integer and real arithmetic); and AUFNIRA (arrays, uninterpreted functions, and mixed non-linear integer and real arithmetic). They are further subdivided according to families. In AUFLIA, there are five families: *Burns, misc* (we lumped the single benchmark in the *check* family in with *misc*), *piVC, RicartAgrawala*, and *simplify*. In AUFLIRA, there are two families: *misc* and *nasa*. And in AUFNIRA, there is a single family: *nasa*. We will comment more specifically on two of these families, *nasa* and *simplify*, below. For more information on the other benchmarks and on the SMT-LIB library, we refer the reader to the SMT-LIB website: http://www.smtlib.org.

The *nasa* families make up the vast majority of the benchmarks with a total of 28065 benchmarks in two families. These cases are *safety obligations* automatically generated from annotated programs at NASA. Following their introduction in [6], these benchmarks were made publicly available in TPTP format [17], a format for pure first-order logic. We then undertook the task of translating them into the SMT-LIB format and contributing them to the SMT-LIB library. In order to adapt these benchmarks for SMT, several steps were required. First, we removed quantified assumptions that were determined to be valid with respect to the background theories ,[5] in this case arrays and arithmetic, and made sure to use the built-in symbols defined in the SMT-LIB standard. Second, since SMT-LIB uses a many-sorted logic, we had to infer sorts for every symbol. We used the following rules to infer types: (i) The index of an array is of type of integer; (ii) The return type of functions *cos, sin, log, sqrt* is real; (iii) The terms on both sides of infix predicates $=$, $<=$, $>=$, $<$ and $>$, must have the same type; (iv) If the type of a term cannot be deduced by the above rules, it is assumed to be real. According to [6], of the 28065 cases, only 14 are supposed to be satisfiable (the rest are unsatisfiable). However, after running our experiments and carefully examining the benchmarks in their present form in the TPTP library, our best guess is that somewhere around 150 of the cases are actually satisfiable (both in the SMT-LIB format and in the original TPTP format). It is difficult to know for sure since for these cases, no tool we are aware of can reliably distinguish between a truly satisfiable formula and one that is simply too difficult to prove unsatisfiable, and determining this by hand is extremely tedious and error-prone. We suspect that some assumptions present in the benchmarks from [6] were lost somehow before their submission to the TPTP library, but we do not know how this happened. In any case, most of the benchmarks are definitely unsatisfiable and while many are easy, a few of them are very challenging.

The other major family is the *simplify* family, which was translated (by others) from a set of over 2200 benchmarks introduced in [7] and distributed with the Simplify theorem prover. Only a selection of the original benchmarks were

---

[5] These are assumptions that were added by hand to enable better performance by ATP systems. They were removed by using CVC3 to automatically check for validity. Note that this returns the benchmarks to a state more faithfully representing the original application.

translated. According to the translator, he excluded benchmarks that were too easy or involved non-linear arithmetic [5]. There are 833 benchmarks in this family, all of which are unsatisfiable.

6.2   Evaluating the Heuristics

We began by running CVC3 using only naive instantiation (trying both the lazy and eager strategies) on all SMT-LIB benchmarks. Of 29004 benchmarks, 23389 can be solved in negligible time by both the eager and the lazy naive strategies. As a result, these benchmarks are not helpful for evaluating our more sophisticated heuristics and so we have chosen to exclude them from the tables below. Also, there are 16 benchmarks that are known to be satisfiable, including all of the benchmarks in the AUFLIRA/misc family, so we have excluded them as well (we did not exclude any of the nasa benchmarks since we do not know for sure which of them are actually satisfiable).

For the remaining 5599 benchmarks that could not be solved using the naive strategy, we tried the following instantiation strategies: (i) basic trigger/matching algorithm (BTBM) with none of the heuristics described in Section 5; (ii) basic triggers with the smarter matching (BTSM) described in Section 5.2; (iii) same as (ii) except with smart triggers (STSM) as described in Section 5.1; and finally (iv) same as (iii) but with the instantiation level (IL) heuristic activated. The results are shown in Table 1. Each table lists the number of cases by family. Then, for each

Table 1. Lazy vs. eager instantiation strategy in CVC3

Lazy strategy		(i) BTBM		(ii) BTSM		(iii) STSM		(iv) IL	
Category	#cases	#unsat	time	#unsat	time	#unsat	time	#unsat	time
AUFLIA/Burns	12	**12**	0.013	12	0.013	12	0.014	12	0.020
AUFLIA/misc	14	10	0.010	14	0.022	**14**	0.021	14	0.023
AUFLIA/piVC	29	25	0.109	25	0.109	29	0.119	**29**	0.117
AUFLIA/RicAgla	14	14	0.052	**14**	0.050	14	0.050	14	0.050
AUFLIA/simplify	769	471	1.751	749	3.846	**762**	0.664	759	0.941
AUFLIRA/nasa	4619	**4113**	1.533	4113	1.533	4113	1.551	4113	1.533
AUFNIRA/nasa	142	46	0.044	**46**	0.043	46	0.043	46	0.044
Total	5599	4691	1.521	4973	1.849	**4990**	1.402	4987	1.409
Eager strategy		(i) BTBM		(ii) BTSM		(iii) STSM		(iv) IL	
Category	#cases	#unsat	time	#unsat	time	#unsat	time	#unsat	time
AUFLIA/Burns	12	**12**	0.012	12	0.020	12	0.019	12	0.019
AUFLIA/misc	14	10	0.008	12	0.013	12	0.013	**14**	0.047
AUFLIA/piVC	29	25	0.107	25	0.108	29	0.127	**29**	0.106
AUFLIA/RicAgla	14	14	0.056	14	0.058	14	0.056	**14**	0.041
AUFLIA/simplify	769	25	18.24	24	39.52	497	30.98	**768**	0.739
AUFLIRA/nasa	4619	4527	0.072	**4527**	0.071	4527	0.074	4526	0.014
AUFNIRA/nasa	142	**72**	0.010	72	0.010	72	0.011	72	0.012
Total	5599	4685	0.168	4686	0.273	5163	3.047	**5435**	0.117

of the four strategies, and for each family, we list the number of cases successfully proved unsatisfiable and the *average* time spent on these successful cases.

As can be seen, the basic matching strategy is quite effective on about 4/5 of the benchmarks, but there are still nearly 1000 that cannot be solved without more sophisticated techniques. Another observation is that the eager strategy generally outperforms the lazy strategy, both on average time taken and on number of cases proved. The notable exception is the *simplify* family. On this family, the lazy strategy performs much better for all except the very last column. This can be explained by the fact that the simplify benchmarks are especially susceptible to getting lost due to looping. However, the lazy strategy is not subject to looping, so it does much better (this also explains why the last column is no better than the third column for the lazy strategy–in fact it's a bit worse, which we suspect is simply due to random differences in the order of instantiations). For the other benchmarks, however, eager instantiation is usually helpful and sometimes critical for finding the proof (this is especially true of the *nasa* families). Thus, the instantiation level heuristic can be seen as a way of combining the advantages of both the eager and lazy strategies. There is one nasa case which is particularly difficult and falls just inside the time limit for the first three columns and just outside the time limit in the last column. This is why one fewer nasa case is proved in the last column.

6.3 Comparison with ATP Systems

One of our primary goals in this paper was to evaluate whether SMT solvers might be able to do better than ATP systems on real verification applications that require both quantifier and theory reasoning. The *nasa* benchmarks provide a means of testing this hypothesis as they are available in both TPTP and SMT-LIB formats (this was, in fact, one of the primary motivations for translating the benchmarks). We also translated the benchmarks into Simplify's format so as to be able to compare Simplify as well. Table 2 compares CVC3 with Vampire, SPASS, and Simplify on these *nasa* benchmarks. For these tests, the timeout was 1 minute. We chose Vampire and SPASS because Vampire and SPASS are among the best ATP systems: Vampire is a regular winner of the CASC competitions [16], and SPASS was the best prover of those tried in [6]. For easier comparison to [6], the benchmarks are divided as in that paper into seven categories: $T_\emptyset$, $T_{\forall,\rightarrow}$, T_{prop}, T_{eval}, T_{array}, T_{policy}, T_{array*}. The first category $T_\emptyset$ contains the most difficult verification conditions. The other categories were obtained by applying various simplifications to $T_\emptyset$. For a detailed description of the categories and how they were generated, we refer the reader to [6]. We also exclude in this breakdown (as was also done in [6]) the 14 known satisfiable cases, so there are 28051 benchmarks in total.

The first observation is that all solvers can prove most of the benchmarks, as most of them are easy. The ATP systems do quite well compared to Simplify: while Simplify is generally much faster, both Vampire and SPASS prove more cases than Simplify. Since at the time these benchmarks were produced, Simplify

Table 2. ATP vs SMT

Category	#cases	Vampire #unsat	Vampire time	SPASS #unsat	SPASS time	Simplify #unsat	Simplify time	CVC3 #unsat	CVC3 time
$T_\emptyset$	365	266	9.2768	302	1.7645	207	0.0679	**343**	0.0174
$T_{\forall,\rightarrow}$	6198	6080	2.1535	6063	0.6732	5957	0.0172	**6174**	0.0042
T_{prop}	1468	1349	4.3218	1343	1.0656	1370	0.0339	**1444**	0.0058
T_{eval}	1076	959	5.6028	948	0.7601	979	0.0423	**1052**	0.0077
T_{array}	2026	2005	1.4438	2000	0.2702	1943	0.0105	**2005**	0.0048
T_{array*}	14931	14903	0.6946	14892	0.2323	14699	0.0101	**14905**	0.0035
T_{policy}	1987	1979	1.4943	1974	0.2716	1917	0.0101	**1979**	0.0050
Total	28051	27541	1.5601	27522	0.4107	27072	0.0145	**27902**	0.0043

was the only SMT solver that could support quantifiers, this can be seen as a validation of the choice of ATP systems over SMT solvers at the time.

However, CVC3 dominates the other systems in both time and number of cases solved. There are only 149 cases that CVC3 cannot solve (as mentioned above we suspect most of these are actually satisfiable) and the average time is less than a hundredth of a second. For the most challenging cases, those in $T_\emptyset$, CVC3 was able to solve 343 out of 365 cases, significantly more than the provers evaluated in [6] (the best system solved 280). As far as we know, this is the best result ever achieved on these benchmarks. This supports our hypothesis that with the additional quantifier techniques introduced in this paper, modern SMT solvers may be a better fit for verification tasks that mix theory reasoning and quantifier reasoning.[6]

6.4   Comparison with Other SMT Systems

As we prepared this paper, we knew of only two other SMT systems that include support for both quantifiers and the SMT-LIB format: yices and Fx7. Yices was the winner of SMT-COMP 2006, dominating every category. Fx7 is a new system recently developed by Michal Moskal. Unfortunately, the quantifier reasoning techniques used in these systems are not published, but our understanding is that they also use extensions of the matching algorithms found in Simplify.

Table 3 compares Fx7, yices, and CVC3 on the same subset of benchmarks used in the first set of experiments. While yices is sometimes faster than CVC3, CVC3 can prove as many or more cases in every category. In total, CVC3 can prove 34 more cases than yices (yices does not support the AUFNIRA division, so we don't count the additional 72 cases CVC3 can prove in this division). Also, CVC3 is significantly faster on the *simplify* and *nasa* benchmarks.

We were also naturally very curious to know how CVC3 compares to Simplify. Results on the *nasa* benchmarks were given above. The other obvious set of

---

[6] It is worth mentioning that the majority of TPTP benchmarks do *not* contain significant theory reasoning and on these, ATP systems are still much stronger than SMT systems.

Table 3. Comparison of SMT systems

Category	#cases	Fx7 #unsat	time	yices #unsat	time	CVC3 #unsat	time
AUFLIA/Burns	12	12	0.4292	12	0.0108	12	0.0192
AUFLIA/misc	14	12	0.6817	14	0.0500	14	0.0479
AUFLIA/piVC	29	15	0.5167	29	0.0300	29	0.1055
AUFLIA/RicAgla	14	14	0.6400	14	0.0257	14	0.0407
AUFLIA/simplify	769	760	3.2184	740	1.4244	**768**	0.7386
AUFLIRA/nasa	4619	4187	0.4524	4520	0.0824	**4526**	0.0138
AUFNIRA/nasa	142	48	0.4102	N/A	N/A	**72**	0.0118
Total	5599	5048	0.8696	5329	0.2681	**5435**	0.1168

benchmarks to compare on is the *simplify* benchmarks. Not surprisingly, Simplify can solve all of these benchmarks very fast: it can solve all 2251 benchmarks in its suite in 469.05 seconds, faster than both yices and CVC3 which take much longer to solve just the 833 benchmarks that were translated into SMT-LIB format. However, Simplify only achieves these impressive results by relying on special formula annotations that tell it which triggers to use. If these annotations are removed, Simplify can only prove 444 of the original 2251 benchmarks. Since the SMT-LIB benchmarks do not have any such annotations, the ability to prove most of the *simplify* benchmarks *automatically* represents a significant step forward for SMT solvers.

Ideally, we would have run Simplify on all of the SMT-LIB benchmarks. Unfortunately, Simplify does not read the SMT-LIB format and we did not have the chance to translate the other benchmarks into Simplify's language. Such translation is non-trivial as it involves moving from a sorted to an unsorted language (translating the *nasa* cases into Simplify's format was easier because both TPTP and Simplify formats are unsorted).

7 Conclusion

In this paper, we presented new formalisms and techniques for quantifier reasoning in the context satisfiability modulo theories. Significantly, our results indicate that these techniques make SMT solvers a better choice than ATP systems on some classes of verification conditions that make use of both theory reasoning and quantifiers. Our techniques are also competitive with other state-of-the art SMT solvers. Indeed, there are several benchmarks from the SMT-LIB library that have been solved for the first time using these techniques.

In future work, we plan to explore extensions of these techniques that allow for more substantial completeness claims. In particular, we plan to explore more sophisticated kinds of theory matching and integration of complete techniques such as quantifier elimination for those theories for which it is applicable.

References

1. Baader, F., Snyder, W.: Unification theory. In: Robinson, A., Voronkov, A. (eds.) Handbook of Automated Reasoning (chapter 8), vol. I, pp. 445–532. Elsevier, Amsterdam (2001)
2. Barrett, C., Nieuwenhuis, R., Oliveras, A., Tinelli, C.: Splitting on demand in SAT Modulo Theories. Technical Report 06-05, Department of Computer Science, The University of Iowa (August 2006)
3. Barrett, C.W.: Checking Validity of Quantifier-Free Formulas in Combinations of First-Order Theories. PhD thesis, Stanford University (January 2003)
4. Barrett, C.W., Dill, D.L., Stump, A.: A generalization of Shostak's method for combining decision procedures. In: Armando, A. (ed.) Frontiers of Combining Systems. LNCS (LNAI), vol. 2309, pp. 132–146. Springer, Heidelberg (2002)
5. de Moura, L.: Private communication (2006)
6. Denney, E., Fischer, B., Schumann, J.: Using automated theorem provers to certify auto-generated aerospace software. In: Basin, D.A., Rusinowitch, M. (eds.) IJCAR 2004. LNCS (LNAI), vol. 3097, pp. 198–212. Springer, Heidelberg (2004)
7. Detlefs, D., Nelson, G., Saxe, J.B.: Simplify: a theorem prover for program checking. J. ACM 52(3), 365–473 (2005)
8. Flanagan, C., Joshi, R., Saxe, J.B.: An explicating theorem prover for quantified formulas. Technical Report HPL-2004-199, HP Intelligent Enterprise Technologies Laboratory (2004)
9. Flanagan, C., Leino, K.R.M., Lillibridge, M., Nelson, G., Saxe, J.B.: Extended static checking for Java. In: Proc. ACM Conference on Programming Language Design and Implementation, pp. 234–245 (June 2002)
10. Ganzinger, H., Hagen, G., Nieuwenhuis, R., Oliveras, A., Tinelli, C.: DPLL(T): Fast decision procedures. In: Alur, R., Peled, D.A. (eds.) CAV 2004. LNCS, vol. 3114, pp. 175–188. Springer, Heidelberg (2004)
11. Nieuwenhuis, R., Oliveras, A., Tinelli, C.: Solving SAT and SAT Modulo Theories: from an Abstract Davis-Putnam-Logemann-Loveland Procedure to DPLL(T). Journal of the ACM 53(6), 937–977 (2006)
12. Prevosto, V., Waldmann, U.: SPASS+T. In: Sutcliffe, G., Schmidt, R., Schulz, S. (eds.) Proceedings of ESCoR: Empirically Successful Computerized Reasoning, CEUR Workshop Proceedings, Seattle, WA, vol. 192, pp. 18–33 (2006)
13. Ranise, S., Tinelli, C.: The satisfiability modulo theories library (SMT-LIB) (2006) www.SMT-LIB.org
14. Riazanov, A., Voronkov, A.: The design and implementation of VAMPIRE. AI Commun. 15(2-3), 91–110 (2002)
15. Stickel, M.E.: Automated deduction by theory resolution. Journal of Automated Reasoning 1(4), 333–355 (1985)
16. Sutcliffe, G.: The IJCAR-2004 Automated Theorem Proving Competition. AI Communications 18(1), 33–40 (2005)
17. Sutcliffe, G., Suttner, C.: The TPTP Problem Library: CNF Release v1.2.1. Journal of Automated Reasoning 21(2), 177–203 (1998)
18. Weidenbach, C., Brahm, U., Hillenbrand, T., Keen, E., Theobald, C., Topic, D.: SPASS Version 2.0. In: Voronkov, A. (ed.) Automated Deduction - CADE-18. LNCS (LNAI), vol. 2392, pp. 275–279. Springer, Heidelberg (2002)

Efficient E-Matching for SMT Solvers

Leonardo de Moura and Nikolaj Bjørner

Microsoft Research, One Microsoft Way, Redmond, WA, 98074, USA
{leonardo,nbjorner}@microsoft.com

Abstract. Satisfiability Modulo Theories (SMT) solvers have proven highly scalable, efficient and suitable for integrating theory reasoning. However, for numerous applications from program analysis and verification, the ground fragment is insufficient, as proof obligations often include quantifiers. A well known approach for quantifier reasoning uses a matching algorithm that works against an E-graph to instantiate quantified variables. This paper introduces algorithms that identify matches on E-graphs incrementally and efficiently. In particular, we introduce an index that works on E-graphs, called *E-matching code trees* that combine features of substitution and code trees, used in saturation based theorem provers. E-matching code trees allow performing matching against several patterns simultaneously. The code trees are combined with an additional index, called the *inverted path index*, which filters E-graph terms that may potentially match patterns when the E-graph is updated. Experimental results show substantial performance improvements over existing state-of-the-art SMT solvers.

1 Introduction

SMT solvers based on a DPLL(T) [1] framework have proven highly scalable, efficient and suitable for integrating theory reasoning. However, for numerous applications from program analysis and verification, an integration of decision procedures for the ground fragment is insufficient, as proof obligations often include quantifiers for capturing frame conditions over loops, summarizing auxiliary invariants over heaps, and for supplying axioms of theories that are not already equipped with ground decision procedures. A well known approach for incorporating quantifier reasoning with ground decision procedures is used in the Simplify theorem prover [2]. Simplify uses an E-matching algorithm that works against an E-graph to instantiate quantified variables, where the E-matching problem is defined as:

input: A set of ground equations E, a ground term t and a term p possibly containing variables.
output: The set of substitutions θ, modulo E, over the variables in p, such that $E \models t \simeq \theta(p)$. Two substitutions are equivalent if their right hand sides are pairwise congruent modulo E.

The E-graph, which maintains congruence relations, is modified during a backtracking search. Each modification to the E-graph may enable new instantiations. E-matching is also used in the several other state-of-the-art SMT solvers:

F. Pfenning (Ed.): CADE 2007, LNAI 4603, pp. 183–198, 2007.

CVC3 [3], Fx7 [4], Verifun [5], Yices [6], Zap [7]. The Stanford Pascal Verifier [8] already included patterns for generating ground instances of axioms. These approaches are also tightly coupled with software verification applications, as found in for instance ESC/Java [9] and Boogie [10,11].

This paper introduces algorithms that identify matches on E-graphs efficiently and incrementally. In particular, we introduce an index that works on E-graphs, called *E-matching code trees* that combines features of substitution and code trees, used in saturation based theorem provers. E-matching code trees allow performing matching against several patterns simultaneously. The code trees are combined with an additional index, called the *inverted path index*, which filters E-graph terms that may potentially match patterns after modifications in the E-graph. The choice and design of these indices reflect upon measured runtime overheads. While E-matching is in theory NP-hard [12], and the number of matches can be exponential in the size of the E-graph, the practical overhead of using E-matching for quantifier instantiation turns out to be searching and maintaining sets of patterns that can efficiently retrieve new matches as soon as E-graph operations introduce them.

Quantifier reasoning is native to saturation based theorem provers where resolution and superposition are the main mechanisms for producing inferences. However, few implementations and experiments have been reported in these systems for reasoning in the context of theories, despite long running attention [13]. Theory resolution [14] provides a framework for adding theory reasoning (as for instance, unification modulo associativity and commutativity) to such systems. In practice, some decision procedures are included in SNARK, including Allen's Interval Temporal Logic and theories used in the Amphion system [15]. Recently [16] investigated an integration of CVC-lite and SPASS, and combinations with super-position calculi and DPLL and BDDs are investigated in haRVey [17].

2   Background

Let Σ be a *signature* consisting of a set of function symbols, and $\mathcal{V}$ be a set of variables. Each function symbol f is associated with a nonnegative integer, called the *arity* of f, denoted $arity(f)$. If $arity(g) = 0$, then g is a constant symbol. The set of terms $T(\Sigma, \mathcal{V})$ is the smallest set containing all constant and variable symbols such that $f(t_1, \ldots, t_n) \in T(\Sigma, \mathcal{V})$ whenever $f \in \Sigma$, $arity(f) = n$, and $t_1 \ldots t_n \in T(\Sigma, \mathcal{V})$. A *f-application* is a term of the form $f(t_1, \ldots, t_n)$. The set of ground terms is defined as $T(\Sigma, \emptyset)$. In our context, the set of non ground terms is called *patterns*. We use p, $f(p_1, \ldots, p_n)$, and x, y, z to range over patterns, and t, $f(t_1, \ldots, t_n)$, and a, b, c to range over ground terms.

In our context, a *substitution* is a mapping from variables to ground terms. Given a substitution β, we denote by $\beta(p)$ the ground term obtained by replacing every variable x in the pattern p by $\beta(x)$.

A binary relation R over T is an *equivalence relation* if it is reflexive, symmetric, and transitive. An equivalence relation induces a partition of T into *equivalence classes*. Given a binary relation R, its *equivalence closure* is the smallest equivalence relation that contains R. A binary relation R on $T(\Sigma, \emptyset)$ is *mono-tonic* if $\langle f(t_1, \ldots, t_n), f(t'_1, \ldots, t'_n) \rangle \in R$ whenever $f \in \Sigma$ and $\langle t_i, t'_i \rangle \in R$ for all i in $1 \ldots n$. A *congruence relation* is a monotonic equivalence relation. Given a binary relation R on $T(\Sigma, \emptyset)$, its *congruence closure* is the smallest congruence relation that contains R.

An *E-graph* data-structure maintains the *congruence closure* of a binary relation $E = \{(t_1, t'_1), \ldots, (t_k, t'_k)\}$ given incrementally (on-line) as a sequence of operations $union(t_1, t'_1), \ldots, union(t_k, t'_k)$. Each equivalence class is represented by its *representative*. For each term t in the E-graph, $find(t)$ denotes the representative of the equivalence class that contains t, $class(t)$ denotes the equivalence class that contains t, $apps_f(t)$ denotes the set of terms $f(t_1, \ldots, t_n)$ such that $f(t_1, \ldots, t_n) \in class(t)$, $apps(f)$ denotes the set of all f-applications in the E-graph, $parents(t)$ denotes the set of terms $f(\ldots, t', \ldots)$ in the E-graph such that $t' \in class(t)$, $parents_f(t)$ is a subset of $parents(t)$ which contains only f-applications, and $parents_{f,i}(t)$ is a subset of $parents_f(t)$ which contains only f-applications where the *i-th* argument t_i is in $class(t)$. The set $ancestors(t)$ is the smallest set such that $parents(t) \subseteq ancestors(t)$, and $ancestors(t_p) \subseteq ancestors(t)$ whenever $t_p \in ancestors(t)$. We suppress references to E-graphs from the above functions, as there is always only one E-graph during proof search.

2.1   SMT Solvers

Modern SMT solvers combine boolean satisfiability solvers based on the Davis-Putnam-Logemann-Loveland (DPLL) procedure, and T-solvers capable of deciding the satisfiability of conjunctions of T-atoms. In this paper, T-atoms are equalities between ground terms, and quantified formulas. A T-solver maintains a state that is an internal representation of the atoms asserted so far. This solver must provide operations for updating the state by asserting new atoms, checking whether the state is consistent, and backtracking. The solver maintains a stack of *checkpoints* that mark consistent states to which the solver can backtrack.

Most SMT solvers incorporate quantifier reasoning using *E-matching*. Semantically, the formula $\forall x_1, \ldots, x_n.F$ is equivalent to the infinite conjunction $\bigwedge_\beta \beta(F)$ where β ranges over all substitutions over the x's. In practice, solvers use heuristics to select from this infinite conjunction those instances that are "relevant" to the conjecture. The key idea is to treat an instance $\beta(F)$ as relevant whenever it contains enough terms that are represented in the current E-graph. That is, non ground terms p from F are selected as *patterns*, and $\beta(F)$ is considered relevant whenever $\beta(p)$ is in the E-graph. An abstract version of the *E-matching* algorithm is shown in Fig. 1. The set of relevant substitutions for a pattern p can be obtained by taking $\bigcup_{t \in E} match(p, t, \emptyset)$. The abstract matching procedure returns all substitutions that E-match a pattern p with term t. That is, if $\beta \in match(p, t, \emptyset)$ then $E \models \beta(p) = t$, and conversely, if $E \models \beta(p) = t$, then there is a β' congruent (when interpreted as a set of equalities) to β such that $\beta' \in match(p, t, \emptyset)$. In [18], this claim is justified in more detail by observing that the abstract matcher may be viewed as a congruence proof search procedure.

$$match(x, t, S) = \{\beta \cup \{x \mapsto t\} \mid \beta \in S, x \notin dom(\beta)\} \cup$$
$$\{\beta \mid \beta \in S, find(\beta(x)) = find(t)\}$$
$$match(c, t, S) = S \ if \ c \in class(t)$$
$$match(c, t, S) = \emptyset \ if \ c \notin class(t)$$
$$match(f(p_1, \ldots, p_n), t, S) = \bigcup_{f(t_1, \ldots, t_n) \in class(t)} match(p_n, t_n, \ldots, match(p_1, t_1, S))$$

Fig. 1. E-matching (abstract) algorithm

3   E-Matching Abstract Machine

It is usual in automated deduction to compile terms into code that can be efficiently executed at retrieval time. The compiler produces code for a real machine, or for a virtual machine as in the case of Prolog's WAM [19]. In this section, we propose an abstract machine for E-matching, its instructions, compilation process, and interpretation. Memory of the abstract machine is divided in the following way:

- register pc for storing the current instruction.
- an array of registers $reg[]$ for storing ground terms.
- a stack $bstack$ for backtracking.

The basic instruction set of our abstract machine consists of: init, bind, check, compare, choose, yield, and backtrack. The semantics of these instructions, shown in Fig. 2, corresponds closely to the steps used by the abstract matching procedure; so if a pattern p is compiled into a code sequence starting with the instruction $instr$, then the set $match(p, t, \emptyset)$ is retrieved by storing t in $reg[0]$, setting pc to $instr$, and executing the instruction stored in pc. This claim is justified in more detail in [18], by observing, for instance, that the compare instruction handles repeated variable occurrences in a pattern. At the moment choose is not relevant, it will be used when we discuss the case of matching against many patterns simultaneously. The instruction bind creates a backtracking point, the idea is to try all f-applications in the equivalence class of the term stored in $reg[i]$. The effect of the backtrack instruction is to pop the top of the backtracking stack, $bstack$, and perform the instruction stored in top. The abstract machine terminates when the backtracking stack $bstack$ is empty. For convenience, we define the function $cont$ on instructions. On all above instructions but yield, $cont$ returns $next$; for example, $cont(\text{check}(i, t, next)) = next$. The pattern $f(x_1, g(x_1, a), h(x_2), b)$ can be compiled in the following code sequence:

$$\text{init}(f, \text{check}(4, b, \text{bind}(2, g, 5, \text{compare}(1, 5, \text{check}(6, a, \text{bind}(3, h, 7, \text{yield}(1, 7)))))))$$

In the rest of the paper, we represent code sequences using *labeled instructions*. A labeled instruction will be written as a pair of the form $n : instr$, where n is

init(f, $next$)	assuming $reg[0] = f(t_1, \ldots, t_n)$ $reg[1] := t_1;\ \ldots;\ reg[n] := t_n$ $pc := next$
bind($i, f, o, next$)	$push(bstack, \text{choose-app}(o, next, apps_f(reg[i]), 1))$ $pc := \text{backtrack}$
check($i, t, next$)	**if** $find(reg[i]) = find(t)$ **then** $pc := next$ **else** $pc := \text{backtrack}$
compare($i, j, next$)	**if** $find(reg[i]) = find(reg[j])$ **then** $pc := next$ **else** $pc := \text{backtrack}$
choose($alt, next$)	**if** $alt \neq nil$ **then** $push(bstack, alt)$ $pc := next$
yield($i_1, \ldots, i_k$)	yield substitution $\{x_1 \mapsto reg[i_1], \ldots, x_k \mapsto reg[i_k]\}$ $pc := \text{backtrack}$
backtrack	**if** $bstack$ is not empty **then** $\quad pc := pop(bstack)$ **else stop**
choose-app($o, next, s, j$)	**if** $|s| \geq j$ **then** $\quad$ **let** $f(t_1, \ldots, t_n)$ be the jth term in s. $\quad reg[o] := t_1;\ \ldots;\ reg[o + n - 1] := t_n$ $\quad push(bstack, \text{choose-app}(o, next, s, j + 1))$ $\quad pc := next$ **else** $pc := \text{backtrack}$

Fig. 2. Semantics of abstract machine instructions

the label/address, and *instr* is the instruction itself. Using labeled instructions, the code sequence above is represented as:

init(f, n_1), n_1 : check($4, b, n_2$), n_2 : bind($2, g, 5, n_3$), n_3 : compare($1, 5, n_4$),

n_4 : check($6, a, n_5$), n_5 : bind($3, h, 7, n_6$), n_6 : yield($1, 7$)

In the function $compile(W, V, o)$, W (*working set*) is a mapping from register indices to patterns, V (*variables*) is mapping from variables to register indices, and o (*offset*) contains the value of the next available register index. The elements of the working set W can be processed in any order, but in our implementation an entry $i \mapsto f(p_1, \ldots, p_n)$ is only processed when W does not contain an entry $i \mapsto t$ or $i \mapsto x_k$. The idea is to give preference to instructions that do not produce backtracking points.

4   E-Matching Code Trees

The time spent on matching patterns with shared structures can be minimized by combining different code sequences in a *code tree*. Code trees were introduced in [20] in the context of saturation based theorem provers. They are used for forward subsumption and forward demodulation in the Vampire theorem prover [21]. The code trees presented in this section are similar to *substitution*

$$compile(f(p_1, \ldots, p_n)) = \mathsf{init}(f, compile(\{1 \mapsto p_1, \ldots, n \mapsto p_n\}, \emptyset, n + 1))$$
$$compile(\{i \mapsto t\} \cup W, V, o) = \mathsf{check}(i, t, compile(W, V, o)), \text{ when } t \text{ is a ground term.}$$
$$compile(\{i \mapsto x_k\} \cup W, V, o) = compile(W, V \cup \{x_k \mapsto i\}, o), \text{ if } x_k \notin dom(V)$$
$$= \mathsf{compare}(i, V(x_k), compile(W, V, o)), \text{ otherwise.}$$
$$compile(\{i \mapsto f(p_1, \ldots, p_n)\} \cup W, V, o) = \mathsf{bind}(i, f, o, compile(W', V, o + n)),$$
$$\text{where } W' = W \cup \{o \mapsto p_1, \ldots, (o + n - 1) \mapsto p_n\}$$
$$compile(\emptyset, \{x_1 \mapsto i_1, \ldots, x_k \mapsto i_k\}, o) = \mathsf{yield}(i_1, \ldots, i_k)$$

Fig. 3. Algorithm for compiling patterns into code sequences

$\mathsf{init}(f, n_1)$

$\quad n_1 : \mathsf{choose}(n_9, n_2), \; n_2 : \mathsf{bind}(2, g, 3, n_3)$

$\quad\quad n_3 : \mathsf{choose}(n_6, n_4), \; n_4 : \mathsf{check}(3, a, n_5), \; n_5 : \mathsf{yield}(1, 4)$

$\quad\quad n_6 : \mathsf{choose}(nil, n_7), \; n_7 : \mathsf{compare}(1, 3, n_8), \; n_8 : \mathsf{yield}(1, 4)$

$\quad n_9 : \mathsf{choose}(nil, n_{10}), \; n_{10} : \mathsf{check}(2, b, n_{11}), \; n_{11} : \mathsf{bind}(1, h, 5, n_{12})$

$\quad\quad n_{12} : \mathsf{choose}(n_{14}, n_{13}), \; n_{13} : \mathsf{yield}(5, 6)$

$\quad\quad n_{14} : \mathsf{choose}(nil, n_{15}), \; n_{15} : \mathsf{bind}(6, g, 7, n_{16}), \; n_{16} : \mathsf{compare}(5, 7, n_{17}), \; n_{17} : \mathsf{yield}(5, 8)$

Fig. 4. Code tree for $\{f(x, g(a, y)), \; f(x, g(x, y)), \; f(h(x, y), b), \; f(h(x, g(x, y)), b)\}$

trees[22], also used in saturation based theorem provers. The key advantage of using code and substitution trees is that matching work common to multiple patterns is "factored out." This advantage results in substantial speedups over a naive approach that would repeatedly match a term against each pattern. A code tree for a small set of patterns is shown in Fig. 4. Each line can be viewed as node (or *code block*) in the tree, indentation is used to suggest a parent-child relationship between nodes, the instruction choose is used to create branches/choices in the tree. The node starting at label n_1 (n_9) contains the instruction(s) common for matching the first and second (third and fourth) patterns. In E-matching code trees, the yield instruction must also store the quantifier that should be instantiated with the yielded substitution, this information is suppressed to simplify the exposition. Our code trees are also very similar to context trees [23]. The main differences with other code, substitution, and context trees, include the use of a stack to handle both backtracking and the branching that arize from matching in the context of an E-graph.

In general, to maintain a code tree C for a dynamically changing set of patterns P, one has to implement operations for integrating and removing code from the tree. In our context, patterns are added to the code tree when the DPLL(T) engine asserts an atom that represents a quantified formula, and are removed when the DPLL(T) engine backtracks. This usage pattern simplifies the insertion and removal operations. In our implementation, each function symbol is mapped to a unique code tree headed by an init instruction. The algorithm for insertion of new patterns into a code tree is shown in Fig. 5.

$$insert(\mathsf{init}(f, n), f(p_1, \ldots, p_m)) = try(n, \{1 \mapsto p_1, \ldots, m \mapsto p_m\}, nreg(\mathsf{init}(f, n)), [\mathsf{init}(f, n)], [\,])$$

$$try(\mathsf{choose}(a, n), W, o, C, I) = \bot, \text{ if } C = [\,]$$
$$= seq(C, firstfit(\mathsf{choose}(a, n), W, o)), \text{ if } I = [\,],$$
$$= branch(C, seq(I, \mathsf{choose}(a, n)), W, o), \text{ otherwise.}$$

$$try(\mathsf{yield}(i_1, \ldots, i_k), W, o, C, I) = \bot, \text{ if } C = [\,],$$
$$= branch(C, seq(I, \mathsf{yield}(i_1, \ldots, i_n)), W, o), \text{ otherwise.}$$

$$try(instr, W, o, C, I) = try(cont(instr), W, o, C, I \hat{\ } [instr]), \text{ if } compatible(instr, W) = \bot,$$
$$= try(cont(instr), compatible(instr, W), C \hat{\ } [instr], I), \text{ otherwise.}$$

$$firstfit(\mathsf{choose}(a, n), W, o) = \mathsf{choose}(a, try(n, W, o, [\,], [\,])), \text{ if } try(n, W, o, [\,], [\,]) \neq \bot,$$
$$= \mathsf{choose}(firstfit(a, W, o), n), \text{ otherwise.}$$

$$firstfit(nil, W, o) = \mathsf{choose}(nil, compile(W, \emptyset, o))$$

$$seq([\,], fchild) = fchild$$
$$seq(\mathsf{check}(i, t, n) : I, fchild) = \mathsf{check}(i, t, seq(I, fchild))$$
$$seq(\mathsf{compare}(i, j, n) : I, fchild) = \mathsf{compare}(i, j, seq(I, fchild))$$
$$seq(\mathsf{bind}(i, f, o, n) : I, fchild) = \mathsf{bind}(i, f, o, seq(I, fchild))$$
$$branch(C, fchild, W, o) = seq(C, \mathsf{choose}(\mathsf{choose}(nil, compile(W, \emptyset, o)), fchild))$$

$$compatible(\mathsf{check}(i, t, n), \{i \mapsto t'\} \cup W) = W, \text{ if } find(t) = find(t')$$
$$compatible(\mathsf{compare}(i, j, n), \{i \mapsto x, j \mapsto x\} \cup W) = \{i \mapsto x\} \cup W$$
$$compatible(\mathsf{bind}(i, f, o, n), \{i \mapsto f(p_1, \ldots, p_m)\} \cup W) = W \cup \{o \mapsto p_1, \ldots, (o + m - 1) \mapsto p_m\}$$
$$compatible(instr, W) = \bot, \text{ otherwise.}$$

Fig. 5. Algorithm for insertion into an E-matching code tree

Function $try(instr, W, o, C, I)$ traverses a code block accumulating instructions compatible (incompatible) with the working set W in the list C (I), it returns $\bot$ if the code block does not contain any instruction compatible with W. A code block always terminates with a choose or yield instruction. When the code block is fully compatible (i.e., I is empty), the insertion should continue in one of its children. Like substitution trees, there may be several different ways to insert a pattern. The algorithm presented uses a *first fit* (function *firstfit*) strategy when selecting a child block. In our concrete implementation, all children are inspected and the one with the highest number of compatible instructions is used. Function $seq(C, fchild)$ returns a code block composed of the instructions in C, whose first child is *fchild*, $branch(C, fchild, W, o)$ returns a code block composed of the instruction in C, and two children: *fchild*, and the code block produced by the compilation of the working set W. Function $compatible(instr, W)$ returns $\bot$ if the instruction *instr* is not compatible with the working set W, otherwise it returns an updated W by factoring in the effect of *instr*. Function $nreg(c)$ returns the maximum register index used in the code tree c plus one. The yield instruction is always considered incompatible because, as mentioned before, each one is associated with a different quantifier. The init instruction is always compatible because we use a different code tree for each root function symbol. In the context of DPLL(T), removal of code trees follow a chronological backtracking discipline, so it suffices to store old instructions from modified *next* fields in a *trail stack*.

5   Incrementality

The operation $union(t_1, t_2)$ has a potential side-effect of producing new matches. For example, a term $f(a, b)$ matches the pattern $f(g(x), y)$ with a potentially new substitution whenever the operation $union(a, g(c))$ is executed.

The Simplify theorem prover [2, page 409] uses two techniques to identify new terms and patterns that become relevant for matching: *mod-time optimization* and *pattern-element optimization*. *Mod-time optimization* is used to identify relevant terms, and is based on the fact that the operation $union(t_1, t_2)$ may change the set of terms congruent to $t_p \in ancestors(t_1) \cup ancestors(t_2)$. The time needed to traverse the ancestors of a term t can be minimized by marking already visited terms. Marks are removed after every round of matching. When experimenting with this approach we found that most of the ancestors do not produce new matches, and the overhead of traversing them is significant. *Pattern-element optimization* is used to identify relevant patterns. The main idea is to identify when the operation *union* is not relevant for a pattern. A pair of function symbols (f, g) is a *parent-child* pair (*pc-pair*) of a pattern p, if p contains a term of the form:

$$f(\ldots, g(\ldots), \ldots)$$

A pair (not necessarily distinct) of function symbols (f, g) is a *parent-parent* pair (*pp-pair*) of a pattern p, if p contains two distinct occurrences of the variable x of the form:

$$f(\ldots, x, \ldots), \quad g(\ldots, x, \ldots)$$

A $union(t_1, t_2)$ is *pc-relevant* for some *pc-pair* (f, g) of a pattern p whenever

$$(parents_f(t_1) \neq \emptyset \wedge apps_g(t_2) \neq \emptyset) \vee (parents_f(t_2) \neq \emptyset \wedge apps_g(t_1) \neq \emptyset)$$

A $union(t_1, t_2)$ is *pp-relevant* for some *pp-pair* (f, g) of a pattern p whenever

$$(parents_f(t_1) \neq \emptyset \wedge parents_g(t_2) \neq \emptyset) \vee (parents_f(t_2) \neq \emptyset \wedge parents_g(t_1) \neq \emptyset)$$

Assuming that any ground term occurring in a pattern is viewed as a constant symbol, then a $union(t_1, t_2)$ cannot produce new instances for a pattern p if it is not relevant for any *pc-pair* or *pp-pair* of p. The cost of this optimization is minimized using *approximated sets*, as they are called in [2], these are also known as Bloom filters [24], which are like real sets except that membership and overlap tests may return false positives. Each equivalence class representative t is associated with two approximated sets of function symbols: *funs*(t) and *pfuns*(t), where *funs*(t) is the approximated set of function symbols in *class*(t), and *pfuns*(t) is the approximated set of functions symbols in *parents*(t).

5.1 Inverted Path Index

Even with mod-time and pattern-element optimizations, many of the matches found are redundant. In this section, we propose a new technique to identify new terms and patterns that become relevant for matching.

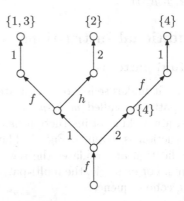

Fig. 6. Inverted path index for *pc-pair* (f, g) and patterns $f(f(g(x), a), x)$, $h(c, f(g(y), x))$, $f(f(g(x), b), y)$, $f(f(a, g(x)), g(y))$

An *inverted path string* over a signature Σ is either the empty string Λ, or $f.i.\pi$, where π is an inverted path string, $f \in \Sigma$, and i is an integer. Intuitively, we can view inverted path strings as a child-to-root path. For example, the inverted path string $g.1.f.2$ is a path to term $f(a, g(h(x), c))$ from subterm $h(x)$.

Given a set of terms T and an inverted path string π, $collect(\pi, T)$ is the set of ancestor terms reached from T following the path π. This set comprises a super-set of terms that participate in new E-matches after a *union* operation. We furthermore seek a sufficiently tight set to avoid redundant E-matching calls. The function *collect* can be formalized as:

$$collect(\Lambda, T) = T$$
$$collect(f.i.\pi, T) = collect(\pi, \{f(t_1, \ldots, t_n) \mid f(t_1, \ldots, t_n) \in parents_{f.i}(t), t \in T\})$$

For example, suppose $pfuns(t_1) = \{f\}$, $funs(t_2) = \{g\}$, and $h(x, f(g(y), a))$ is a pattern. Then, $collect(h.2.f.1, \{t_1\})$ contains all terms that may produce new instances for $h(x, f(g(y), a))$ after executing $union(t_1, t_2)$. Collecting the set of potentially useful candidates for matching per pattern is wasteful when a set of patterns share the same *pc/pp-pairs* and furthermore share portions of the inverted paths. We therefore share repeated prefixes from inverted path strings in an *inverted path index*, which has the form of a trie τ. The nodes of τ consist of a list of branches pointing to children together with a set of patterns (corresponding to a code tree) that share the path down to the node. Thus, a node is of the form $\langle [f_1.i_1.\tau_1, \ldots, f_k.i_k.\tau_k], P \rangle$, where τ_j are nodes, $f_j.i_j$ are different function, integer pairs, and P is a set of patterns. An example of an inverted path index is given in Fig. 6. Adapting a definition of *collect* to inverted path indices is immediate:

$$collect(\langle [f_1.i_1.\tau_1, \ldots f_k.i_k.\tau_k], P \rangle, T) = \{(P, T) \mid P \neq \emptyset\} \cup$$
$$\bigcup_{j=1}^{k} collect(\tau_j, \{f_j(t_1, \ldots, t_n) \mid f_j(t_1, \ldots, t_n) \in parents_{f_j.i_j}(t), t \in T\})$$

Inverted path indices are particularly useful in situations where one has, for example, different instances of frame axioms using similar patterns: $f(t_1, y, g(z))$, $\ldots, f(t_n, y, g(z))$.

6   Additional Instructions

6.1   Multi-patterns

Sometimes it makes sense to instantiate a set of quantified variables only when a set of patterns, called *multi-pattern* is matched. In order to support multi-patterns, a new kind of instruction has been added: continue. The semantics of this instruction is given in Fig. 7. The instruction continue($f, o, next$) *chooses* an f-application and updates the registers from o to $o + arity(f) - 1$ with its arguments. For example, the multi-pattern $\langle f(x, a, y), g(z, x) \rangle$ is compiled in the following code sequence:

init(f, n_1), n_1 : check$(2, a, n_2)$, n_2 : continue$(g, 4, n_3)$, n_3 : compare$(1, 5, n_4)$,

n_4 : yield$(1, 3, 4)$

In our experiments, we observed that a considerable amount of time was spent matching multi-patterns. The problem is that the instruction continue($f, o, next$) is re-executed too many times when the number of f-applications in the E-graph is significant. Considering the code sequence above, a g-application chosen by the continue instruction is only useful to yield an instance if the compare instruction succeeds, that is, the second argument of the chosen g-application is in the same equivalence class of the term stored in register 1. Based on this observation, we added another instruction for compiling multi-patterns: join. The semantics of this instruction is given in Fig. 7. The instruction join($i, \pi, o, next$) chooses a candidate from a set of terms reachable from the term stored in register i following the inverted path string π. When a multi-pattern $\langle p_1, \ldots, p_n \rangle$ is compiled, if p_i contains a variable x that also occurs in p_j for $j < i$, then a join can be used instead of a continue instruction, and π is the path from x to p_i. If there is more than one variable, then we select the one with the shallowest path. Using the join instruction the multi-pattern $\langle f(x, a, y), g(z, x) \rangle$ is compiled in the following code sequence:

init(f, n_1), n_1 : check$(2, a, n_2)$, n_2 : join$(1, g.2, 4, n_3)$, n_3 : yield$(1, 3, 4)$

The instruction compare$(1, 5, n_4)$ is unnecessary, since the join will only select g-applications which the second argument is in the same equivalence class of the term stored in register 1.

6.2   Filters

Consider the pattern $f(g(x), h(y))$; it is compiled in the following sequence of instructions:

init$(f, 2, n_1)$, n_1 : bind$(1, g, 3, n_2)$, n_2 : bind$(2, h, 4, n_3)$, n_3 : yield$(3, 4)$

continue($f, o, next$)	push($bstack$, choose-app($o, next, apps(f), 1$)) $pc :=$ backtrack
join($i, \pi, o, next$)	push($bstack$, choose-app($o, next, collect(\pi, \{reg[i]\}), 1$)) $pc :=$ backtrack
filter($i, fs, next$)	if $fs \cap funs(reg[i]) \neq \emptyset$ then $pc := next$ else $pc :=$ backtrack

Fig. 7. Semantics of additional instructions

Suppose we are trying to match term $f(a, b)$, and $class(a)$ contains n g-applications, but $class(b)$ does not contain any h-application. In this scenario, a lot of wasteful work is performed when interpreting the instructions above, the second bind will fail n times. We address this problem by introducing a new instruction that performs forward pruning: filter. The semantics of this new instruction is shown in Fig. 7. The idea of the new instruction is to use the approximated set $funs(t)$ to quickly test whether the equivalence class of a term t contains an f-application or not. Using the new instruction, the pattern $f(g(x), h(y))$ is compiled as:

$$\mathsf{init}(f, n_1), \ n_1 : \mathsf{filter}(1, \{g\}, n_2), \ n_2 : \mathsf{filter}(2, \{h\}, n_3), \ n_3 : \mathsf{bind}(1, g, 3, n_4),$$
$$n_4 : \mathsf{bind}(2, h, 4, n_5), \ n_5 : \mathsf{yield}(3, 4)$$

The filter instruction is also used for saving unnecessary backtracking prior to a sequence of choose instructions each followed by a bind to a function in fs.

7 Implementation Issues

Relevancy. Simplify retains some of the structure of the input formula as an and-or tree. It then implements a tableau style search: to refute a disjunction, each disjunct is refuted independently. Refuting a conjunction only requires retaining each conjunct. In tableau form, the proof rules used by Simplify are:

$$\frac{\bigvee\{\ell_1, \ldots \ell_k\}}{\ell_1 \mid \ldots \mid \ell_k} \qquad \frac{\neg \bigvee\{\ell_1, \ldots, \ell_k\}}{\neg \ell_1, \ldots, \neg \ell_k} \qquad \frac{\neg\neg\ell}{\ell}$$

The tableau search has the side-effect of eliminating irrelevant literals from the scope of a branch. DPLL(T) based solvers do not have this property, as the search assigns a boolean value to potentially all atoms appearing in a goal. For example, when clausifying $\ell_1 \vee (\ell_2 \wedge \ell_3)$ using a Tseitin [25] style algorithm we obtain the set of clauses:

$$\{\ell_1, \ell_{aux}\}, \ \{\ell_{aux}, \neg\ell_2, \neg\ell_3\}, \ \{\ell_2, \neg\ell_{aux}\}, \ \{\ell_3, \neg\ell_{aux}\}$$

Now, suppose that ℓ_1 is assigned true. In this case, ℓ_2 and ℓ_3 are clearly irrelevant and truth assignments to ℓ_2 and ℓ_3 need not be used, but the Tseitin encoding, which creates a set of clauses, makes the act of discovering this difficult.

The advantage of using relevancy is profound if literals that are pruned from the scope of a branch may produce new quantifier instantiations. We have therefore retained some of the traits of relevancy in our DPLL(T) solver. Our solution does not change how the SAT solver works with respect to case-split heuristics, unit propagation, conflict resolution, etc. Instead, we convert to CNF using a variation of Tseitin algorithm, keep the input formula, and map every (Tseitin) auxiliary variable to a node in the original formula.

Initially, only the auxiliary variable corresponding to the root in the original formula is marked as *relevant*. Relevancy is then propagated to subformulas using the following rules, which effectively simulate the tableau rules. Assume ℓ is marked as relevant. First let ℓ be shorthand for $\bigvee\{\ell_1, \dots, \ell_k\}$, if ℓ is assigned *true*, then the first child ℓ_i that gets assigned *true* is marked relevant. If ℓ is assigned *false*, then all children are marked relevant. If ℓ is shorthand for $\neg\ell'$, then ℓ' is marked as relevant as well.

Congruent terms. If two terms $f(t_1, \dots, t_n)$ and $f(t'_1, \dots, t'_n)$ are congruent, then it is wasteful to try to match both of them, since the set of substitutions produced for each of them will be equivalent. Therefore, it suffices to consider only one term from each set of congruent applications for the bind, continue and join instructions, and when considering new candidates for matching.

Eager vs. Lazy instantiation. Finding the right instantiations prior to case splits can have the effect of pruning the search space dramatically. On the other hand, eager instantiation of quantifiers that are not helpful in closing branches may amplify the search space. A bi-polar approach to instantiation tactics does not seem to work in general; we found that benchmarks where patterns were supplied by the tools generating the quantified formulas worked best with eager instantiation, whereas benchmarks that do not include patterns cannot be solved by eagerly instantiating all quantifiers whenever some subterm can be matched. We therefore collect run-time statistics for when quantifiers are useful for closing branches. Useful quantifiers are promoted to eager instantiations, while quantifiers that were not useful are demoted to a lazy instantiation round when other options have been exhausted. The detailed description of the priority queues used for this scheme is elaborated upon in [18].

Deleting clauses. Quantifier instantiation has a side-effect of producing new clauses containing new atoms into the search space. Retaining these clauses over backtracking is useless if the new clauses were not helpful in closing the branch. A two-tiered [26] combination of SAT solvers address this problem by using different solvers after (a lazy) quantifier instantiation. Work that was potentially useful for other branches has to be reproduced using other means. In our implementation, we use a single SAT solver, but delete clauses generated from quantifier instantiation when backtracking. Conflict clauses and their literals are on the other hand not deleted.

8   Experiments

The experiments were conducted using a 32bit Pentium 4 processor running at 3.6Ghz, 2Gb of memory, and 2Mb of cache. The timeout was set to 10 minutes. We compared our prover, Z3, against CVC3 1.0, Simplify, Yices 1.0, and Zap 2.0. The comparison used more than 3000 publically available benchmarks. It includes the SMT-LIB [27] AUFLIA/simplify, ESC/Java, and Boogie benchmarks.[1] The first set is in SMT-LIB format, and the other two in Simplify format. The most   challenging benchmarks from the SMT-LIB AUFLIA bench-

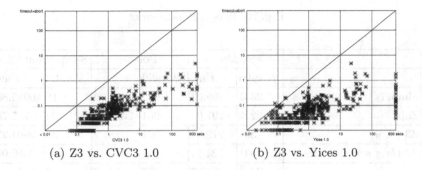

(a) Z3 vs. CVC3 1.0   (b) Z3 vs. Yices 1.0

Fig. 8. SMT-LIB Benchmarks

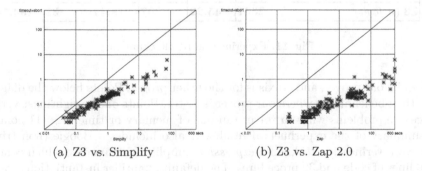

(a) Z3 vs. Simplify   (b) Z3 vs. Zap 2.0

Fig. 9. ESC/Java Benchmarks

marks were derived from the ESC/Java benchmarks. At the time of writing, the SMT-LIB format did not have a standard for specifying patterns for quantified formulas. Most of the benchmarks use linear arithmetic. Fig. 8, 9 and 10 compare Z3 with the other provers, the choice of prover/benchmark set is based on the limitations of the input format accepted by each prover. Each point on the plots represents a benchmark. On each plot the y-axis is the CPU time, in seconds,

---

[1] The benchmarks are also available at http://research.microsoft.com/~leonardo/CADE07

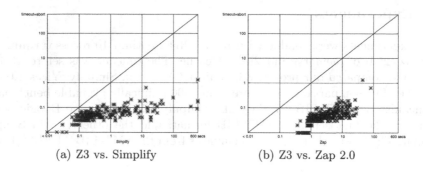

(a) Z3 vs. Simplify   (b) Z3 vs. Zap 2.0

Fig. 10. Boogie Benchmarks

	ESC/Java		Boogie		S-expr Simplifier	
	# valid	time	# valid	time	# valid	time
Simplify	2331	499.03	903	1851.29	18	10985.80
Zap	2222	6297.04	901	2612.64	22	777.78
Z3 (*lazy*)	2331	212.81	907	157.2	32	2904.27
Z3 (*lazy wo. code trees*)	2331	224.14	907	240.44	28	2369.00
Z3 (*eager wo. inc.*)	2331	1495.07	907	229.2	10	2410.52
Z3 (*eager mod-time*)	2331	85.1	907	39.79	32	1341.38
Z3 (*eager wo. code trees*)	2331	48.28	907	26.85	32	654.62
Z3 (*default*)	**2331**	**45.22**	**907**	**18.47**	**32**	**194.54**

Fig. 11. Experimental results: summary

taken by our prover, and x-axis is for the other prover. Points below the diagonal are then benchmarks where our prover is faster. Points on the rightmost vertical edge are problems where a solver ran out of memory or time. Fig. 11 contains a summary of the experimental results. It also includes a Boogie (non trivial) program verification task: an *s-expression* simplification module which contains 500 lines of code and 32 procedures. The default quantifier instantiation strategy in Z3 uses: code trees, inverted path index, and eager instantiation. The table includes other five different settings for Z3: lazy quantifier instantiation (*lazy*), lazy quantifier instantiation without code trees (*lazy wo. code trees*), eager instantiation without any support for incremental E-matching (*eager wo. inc.*), eager instantiation using the mod-time optimization (*eager mod-time*), eager instantiation using inverted path index but without code tress (*eager wo. code trees*). For each set of benchmarks, the table contains the number of successfully proved instances, and the total time in seconds spent on instances where the solver did not timeout. As can be seen, the Z3 default strategy is very effective. E-matching code trees and the inverted path index are particularly useful in non trivial instances such as the s-expression simplifier.

9 Conclusion

We have introduced an abstract machine for E-matching. It combines two indices: the *E-matching code trees* which could efficiently handle matching a term against a large set of patterns simultaneously, and *inverted path indexing*, which narrowly and efficiently finds a superset of terms that will match a set of patterns. Other results of the paper are a new approach for handling multi-patterns, and the use of filters inside of an E-matching procedure. Simple and useful heuristics for handling quantifiers in SMT solvers were also presented. Experimental results show that our new solver outperforms the most competitive SMT solvers that support quantifiers. Possible extensions to the approach include using *context trees* [23] for additional sharing, adding instructions to optimize for large alphabets, and extending *inverted path indexing* to a perfect filter for linear patterns.

References

1. Ganzinger, H., Hagen, G., Nieuwenhuis, R., Oliveras, A., Tinelli, C.: DPLL(T): Fast decision procedures. In: Alur, R., Peled, D.A. (eds.) CAV 2004. LNCS, vol. 3114, pp. 175–188. Springer, Heidelberg (2004)
2. Detlefs, D., Nelson, G., Saxe, J.B.: Simplify: a theorem prover for program checking. J. ACM 52(3), 365–473 (2005)
3. Barrett, C., Berezin, S.: CVC Lite: A New Implementation of the Cooperating Validity Checker. In: Alur, R., Peled, D.A. (eds.) CAV 2004. LNCS, vol. 3114, Springer, Heidelberg (2004)
4. Moskal, M., Lopuszański, J.: Fast quantifier reasoning with lazy proof explication (2006) http://nemerle.org/~malekith/smt/smt-tr-1.pdf
5. Flanagan, C., Joshi, R., Saxe, J.B.: An explicating theorem prover for quantified formulas. Technical Report HPL-2004-199, HP Laboratories, Palo Alto (2004)
6. Dutertre, B., de Moura, L.: A Fast Linear-Arithmetic Solver for DPLL(T). In: Ball, T., Jones, R.B. (eds.) CAV 2006. LNCS, vol. 4144, pp. 81–94. Springer, Heidelberg (2006)
7. Ball, T., Lahiri, S.K., Musuvathi, M.: Zap: Automated theorem proving for software analysis. In: Sutcliffe, G., Voronkov, A. (eds.) LPAR 2005. LNCS (LNAI), vol. 3835, pp. 2–22. Springer, Heidelberg (2005)
8. Nelson, G.: Techniques for program verification. Technical Report CSL81-10, Xerox Palo Alto Research Center (1981)
9. Flanagan, C., Leino, K.R.M., Lillibridge, M., Nelson, G., Saxe, J.B., Stata, R.: Extended static checking for java. In: PLDI, pp. 234–245 (2002)
10. DeLine, R., Leino, K.R.M.: BoogiePL: A typed procedural language for checking object-oriented programs. Technical Report 2005-70, Microsoft Research (2005)
11. Barnett, M., Leino, K.R.M., Schulte, W.: The Spec# programming system: An overview. In: Barthe, G., Burdy, L., Huisman, M., Lanet, J.-L., Muntean, T. (eds.) CASSIS 2004. LNCS, vol. 3362, pp. 49–69. Springer, Heidelberg (2005)
12. Kozen, D.: Complexity of finitely presented algebras. In: STOC, pp. 164–177 (1977)
13. Slagle, J.R.: Automatic theorem proving with built-in theories including equality, partial ordering, and sets. J. of the ACM 19(1), 120–135 (1972)

14. Stickel, M.E.: Automated deduction by theory resolution. J. Autom. Reasoning 1(4), 333–355 (1985)
15. Baalen, J.V., Roach, S.: Using decision procedures to accelerate domain-specific deductive synthesis systems. In: Flener, P. (ed.) LOPSTR 1998. LNCS, vol. 1559, pp. 61–82. Springer, Heidelberg (1999)
16. Waldmann, U., Prevosto, V.: SPASS+T. In: ESCoR, pp. 18–33 (2006)
17. Armando, A., Bonacina, M.P., Ranise, S., Schulz, S.: On a rewriting approach to satisfiability procedures: Extension, combination of theories and an experimental appraisal. In: Gramlich, B. (ed.) Frontiers of Combining Systems. LNCS (LNAI), vol. 3717, pp. 65–80. Springer, Heidelberg (2005)
18. de Moura, L., Bjørner, N.: Efficient E-matching for SMT solvers. Technical report, Microsoft Research (to appear)
19. Aït-Kaci, H.: Warren's abstract machine: a tutorial reconstruction. MIT Press, Cambridge (1991)
20. Voronkov, A.: The anatomy of vampire implementing bottom-up procedures with code trees. J. Autom. Reasoning 15(2), 237–265 (1995)
21. Riazanov, A., Voronkov, A.: Vampire 1.1 (system description). In: Goré, R.P., Leitsch, A., Nipkow, T. (eds.) IJCAR 2001. LNCS (LNAI), vol. 2083, pp. 376–380. Springer, Heidelberg (2001)
22. Graf, P., Meyer, C.: Advanced indexing operations on substitution trees. In: McRobbie, M.A., Slaney, J.K. (eds.) Automated Deduction - Cade-13. LNCS, vol. 1104, pp. 553–567. Springer, Heidelberg (1996)
23. Ganzinger, H., Nieuwenhuis, R., Nivela, P.: Context trees. In: Goré, R.P., Leitsch, A., Nipkow, T. (eds.) IJCAR 2001. LNCS (LNAI), vol. 2083, pp. 242–256. Springer, Heidelberg (2001)
24. Bloom, B.H.: Space/time trade-offs in hash coding with allowable errors. Commun. ACM 13(7), 422–426 (1970)
25. Tseitin, G.S.: On the complexity of derivation in propositional calculus. In: Automation of Reasoning 2: Classical Papers on Computational Logic, pp. 466–483. Springer, Heidelberg (1983)
26. Leino, K.R.M., Musuvathi, M., Ou, X.: A two-tier technique for supporting quantifiers in a lazily proof-explicating theorem prover. In: Halbwachs, N., Zuck, L.D. (eds.) TACAS 2005. LNCS, vol. 3440, Springer, Heidelberg (2005)
27. Ranise, S., Tinelli, C.: The Satisfiability Modulo Theories Library (SMT-LIB) (2006) http://www.SMT-LIB.org

T-Decision by Decomposition

Maria Paola Bonacina and Mnacho Echenim

Dipartimento di Informatica
Università degli Studi di Verona
Strada Le Grazie 15, I-39134 Verona, Italy
mariapaola.bonacina@univr.it, echenim@sci.univr.it

Abstract. Much research concerning Satisfiability Modulo Theories is devoted to the design of efficient SMT-solvers that integrate a SAT-solver with T-satisfiability procedures. The rewrite-based approach to T-satisfiability procedures is appealing, because it is general, uniform and it makes combination of theories simple. However, SAT-solvers are unparalleled in handling the large Boolean part of T-decision problems of practical interest. In this paper we present a decomposition framework that combines a rewrite-based theorem prover and an SMT solver in an off-line mode, in such a way that the prover "compiles the theory away," so to speak. Thus, we generalize the rewrite-based approach from T-satisfiability to T-decision procedures, making it possible to use the rewrite-based prover for theory reasoning and the SAT-solver in the SMT-solver for Boolean reasoning. We prove the practicality of this framework by giving decision procedures for the theories of records, integer offsets and arrays.

1 Introduction

Decision procedures are at the heart of formal verification tools, which invoke them to decide the validity of logical formulæ. In software or hardware verification problems, the validity of a formula is to be tested *modulo* a background theory T; such problems are called *T-decision problems*. Relevant theories include linear arithmetic, or fragments thereof, theories of data structures, and *combinations* of simpler theories. Decision procedures for these problems are commonly called *SMT-solvers*, where SMT stands for Satisfiability Modulo Theories.

Due to the typically large Boolean part of the formulæ to be tested, most SMT-solvers combine sophisticated extensions of the so-called *DPLL procedure* (see, e.g., [18]) for propositional satisfiability, with *T-satisfiability procedures*, that decide the T-satisfiability of sets of unit clauses (see, e.g., [13]). A main issue with this approach is the *combination of theories*, that is, the case where T consists of several simpler theories. Most systems resort to the *Nelson-Oppen combination scheme* [12], so that the theory solver is a Nelson-Oppen reasoner for the combination T of the smaller theories. However, the Nelson-Oppen scheme works without backtracking only if all involved theories are *convex*, otherwise, also the theory solver requires case analysis by backtracking. This makes the design of an SMT-solver that efficiently overlaps the case analysis required by

F. Pfenning (Ed.): CADE 2007, LNAI 4603, pp. 199–214, 2007.

the theory solver with that required by the DPLL procedure a complex engineering problem. Much work is being invested on this issue, for various theories, combinations of theories and classes of clauses. For instance, several of the systems that take part in the SMT competition[1] showcase clever techniques for this integration.

There are several reasons that make a generic theorem prover attractive to solve SMT problems. From a practical point of view, theorem provers offer a well-balanced trade-off of *robustness, reliability* and *efficiency*, as a result of years of research on data structures and algorithms (e.g., those for indexing techniques). Thus, one can take a theorem prover "off the shelf" to solve SMT problems, without worrying about "false negatives" (lack of soundness) or "false positives" (lack of completeness). From a theoretical point of view, theorem provers are *theory-independent* and *expressive*, since the presentation of the considered theory is part of the input. Combination of theories becomes conceptually simple for the same reason: it suffices to provide the theorem prover with the union of the presentations of the theories to be combined.

The rewrite-based inference system $\mathcal{SP}$ was applied to $\mathcal{T}$-satisfiability in [3,1,2,6], by showing that it is guaranteed to terminate on $\mathcal{T}$-satisfiability problems in several theories. Experimental results and a theorem of *modularity of termination* were also obtained [1,2]. The modularity theorem shows that if $\mathcal{SP}$ terminates on $\mathcal{T}$-satisfiability problems in each theory, then it terminates also on $\mathcal{T}$-satisfiability problems in their union, provided the theories are *variable-inactive* and do not share function symbols. Under the same assumption of *variable-inactivity*, an approach to generalize the termination results for $\mathcal{SP}$ from $\mathcal{T}$-satisfiability problems to the more general $\mathcal{T}$-decision problems, that involve ground formulæ, was presented in [5]. However, generic theorem provers are not designed to deal with the Boolean part of a formula as efficiently as possible. Hence, they do not seem to be suited to solve $\mathcal{T}$-decision problems that feature a heavy Boolean part, although this is the case for most problems of practical interest. This issue can be addressed by integrating the theorem prover with a SAT solver, as it is done for instance in the haRVey system[2]. However, state-of-the-art SMT-solvers rely on a *tight* integration of the SAT-solver and the $\mathcal{T}$-satisfiability procedures, which is very problematic if the $\mathcal{T}$-satisfiability procedure is a theorem prover with a proof-confluent inference system that does not require search by backtracking. Furthermore, if the integration were tight, the advantage of using the prover "off the shelf" would be lost.

In this paper, we propose a new framework where a $\mathcal{T}$-decision problem is *decomposed* in such a way that it can be solved *by stages*, by pipe-lining a first-order reasoner and an SMT-solver. Intuitively, a ground formula is decomposed into two parts: one that interacts with the theory, and another that contains the Boolean structure of the formula. In some sense, such a decomposition corresponds to the separation of the *definitional* part of a program (i.e., the part that consists of statements such as "let $x = f(y)$ in ..."), from its *operational* part.

---

[1] http://www.csl.sri.com/users/demoura/smt-comp
[2] http://www.loria.fr/equipes/cassis/softwares/haRVey/

The first-order reasoner is applied to the first part and it "compiles" the theory away, by performing as much theory reasoning as possible. All that remains to do is to test the satisfiability of the union of the boolean part of the formula and the result of this process. In this approach, the call to the theorem prover can be viewed as a *reduction*. However, since this reduction is achieved by generic inferences, it is proof-theoretic in nature and, unlike model-theoretic reductions, it is *independent* of the specific theory or combination of theories under consideration. This new framework may lead to the design of a new generation of SMT-solvers, that will only need to incorporate theory reasoners for the theories left after the reduction, and will thus be easier to implement.

The decomposition framework is general, in that it does not depend on a specific first-order inference system or theorem prover or SMT-solver. In the second part of the paper, we instantiate it to construct $\mathcal{T}$-decision procedures based on $\mathcal{SP}$, and we give specific procedures for the theories of *records*, *integer offsets* and *arrays*. We also show how this scheme enables the system to *postpone* the treatment of a theory: when $\mathcal{T}$ is of the form $\mathcal{T}_1 \cup \mathcal{T}_2$, it is possible to process $\mathcal{T}_1$ first and then deal with $\mathcal{T}_2$. This is especially important when $\mathcal{T}_2$ is a theory that cannot be handled by a theorem prover, such as linear arithmetic: its treatment is passed on to the SMT-solver.

This paper is organized as follows: Section 2 recalls some basic definitions. Section 3 presents the abstract decomposition framework. Section 4 contains its concrete instantiation with the inference system $\mathcal{SP}$. Section 5 shows how the above-mentioned theories of data structures fit into the framework and yield decision procedures. Due to the space limits, all proofs are omitted and can be found in the full version [7].

2   Preliminaries

Given a signature Σ, we assume the standard definitions of Σ-terms, Σ-predicates, Σ-literals and Σ-clauses. As usual, clauses are variable-disjoint. For notation, $\simeq$ is unordered equality, $\bowtie$ is either $\simeq$ or $\not\simeq$, the letters l, r, s, u, v and t denote terms, a, b and c denote constants, w, x, y, z variables, and all other lower-case letters denote constants or function symbols. A theory is presented by a set of sentences, called its *presentation* or *axiomatization*. Given a presentation $\mathcal{T}$, $\mathcal{T}$-*satisfiability* is the problem of deciding whether a set of ground unit clauses is satisfiable in $\mathcal{T}$. The more general $\mathcal{T}$-*decision problem* is the problem of deciding the satisfiability of any ground formula in $\mathcal{T}$. Without loss of generality, we can assume that the considered ground formulæ are sets of clauses.

For sets of clauses S and S', we write $S \equiv_s S'$ to say that S and S' are *equisatisfiable*, that is, S has a model if and only if S' has a model. For a term t, the *depth* of t, denoted by depth(t), is 0 if t is a constant or variable, and depth$(f(t_1, \ldots, t_n)) = 1 + \max\{\text{depth}(t_i) \mid i = 1, \ldots, n\}$ otherwise. For literals, we define depth$(l \bowtie r) = $ depth$(l) + $depth$(r)$. A positive literal is *flat* if its depth is 0 or 1, a negative literal is *flat* if its depth is 0. A literal is *strictly flat* if its depth is 0, and a clause is *flat* (resp. *strictly flat*) if all its literals are.

The operation of *flattening* consists of transforming a finite set of ground clauses S over a signature Σ, into a finite set of ground clauses S' over a signature Σ', in such a way that:

- Σ' is obtained by adding a finite number of constants to Σ;
- every non-unit clause in S' is strictly flat;
- every unit clause in S' is flat and
- for all presentations $\mathcal{T}$, $\mathcal{T} \cup S$ and $\mathcal{T} \cup S'$ are equisatisfiable.

For example, if we flatten the set $\{f(a) \not\simeq f(b) \vee f(a) \not\simeq f(c)\}$, we obtain the equisatisfiable set $\{f(a) \simeq a', \ f(b) \simeq b', \ f(c) \simeq c', \ a' \not\simeq b' \vee a' \not\simeq c'\}$ by introducing fresh constants a', b' and c'.

A *simplification ordering* $\succ$ is an ordering that is *stable, monotonic* and contains the *subterm ordering*: if $s \succ t$, then $c[s]\sigma \succ c[t]\sigma$ for any context c and substitution σ, and if t is a subterm of s then $s \succ t$. A *complete simplification ordering*, or CSO, is a simplification ordering that is total on ground terms. We write $t \prec s$ if $s \succ t$. More details on orderings can be found in surveys such as [10]. An *inference system* Inf consists of a set of *inference rules*, separated into *expansion rules*, that generate clauses, and *contraction rules*, that delete or simplify clauses. If the inference system is based on a CSO $\succ$, we write $\text{Inf}_\succ$ for Inf equipped with $\succ$. An $\text{Inf}_\succ$-*derivation* is a sequence

$$S_0 \vdash_{\text{Inf}_\succ} S_1 \vdash_{\text{Inf}_\succ} \ldots S_i \vdash_{\text{Inf}_\succ} \ldots,$$

where each S_i is a set of clauses, obtained by applying an expansion or a contraction rule to clauses in S_{i-1}. The *limit* of such a derivation is the set of *persistent clauses*: $S_\infty = \bigcup_{j \geq 0} \bigcap_{i \geq j} S_i$. If a derivation is finite and of length n, we may write $S_0 \vdash_{\text{Inf}_\succ}^n S_n$.

The *superposition calculus*, or $\mathcal{SP}$, is a refutationally complete *rewrite-based inference system* for first-order logic with equality (see, e.g., [14]). It consists of expansion and contraction inference rules. Since it is based on a CSO on terms, extended to literals and clauses in a standard way, we write $\mathcal{SP}_\succ$ to specify the ordering. A *strategy*, denoted by $\mathfrak{S}$, is given by an inference system and a search plan that controls the application of the inference rules. A strategy with inference system $\mathcal{SP}_\succ$ is called an $\mathcal{SP}_\succ$-strategy.

3   The Decomposition Framework

When approaching SMT problems in the context of generic first-order reasoning, a problem has the form $\mathcal{T} \cup P$, where $\mathcal{T}$ is the presentation of the theory and P is a set of ground clauses, since the theory is not necessarily built into the inference system. We propose an approach that consists in "compiling" the theory away, so that a problem $\mathcal{T} \cup P$ is transformed into the satisfiability problem of another set of clauses, which does not mention $\mathcal{T}$. Such a problem transformation can be viewed as a *reduction*, with the distinction that the problem is approached from a proof-theoretic point of view and *does not depend on the considered theory*.

In order to investigate under what conditions this problem transformation is correct, we solve a more general problem:

Question: For a presentation $\mathcal{T}$ and sets of clauses S, S', A and A' such that $\mathcal{T} \cup S \equiv_{\mathrm{s}} A$ and $\mathcal{T} \cup S' \equiv_{\mathrm{s}} A'$, what conditions guarantee that $\mathcal{T} \cup S \cup S' \equiv_{\mathrm{s}} A \cup A'$?

3.1 Supported Strategies and $\mathcal{T}$-Compatibility

In order to separate the clauses in $\mathcal{T}$ from the other clauses, we adopt a *supported strategy* (cf. Section 2.6 in [4]), with an inference system $\mathrm{Inf}_{\succ}$, that works on *pairs* $(\mathcal{T}, SOS)$ of sets of clauses, where SOS stands for set-of-support. We assume that all inference rules in $\mathrm{Inf}_{\succ}$ are either unary or binary, all expansion inferences have at least one premise from SOS, all clauses generated by expansion are added to SOS, and $\mathrm{Inf}_{\succ}$ is *refutationally complete for $\mathcal{T}$*. In what follows, when a clause D is generated by a *binary expansion rule* applied to C and C', we will need to distinguish between the first and the second premise of the applied inference rule, hence the following definition:

Definition 1. *A clause D is* generated from parents C and C' *if it is generated by a binary expansion rule applied to C and C', with C as first premise and C' as second premise.*

$A \equiv_{\mathrm{s}} \mathcal{T} \cup S$ and $A' \equiv_{\mathrm{s}} \mathcal{T} \cup S'$ do not imply that $A \cup A' \equiv_{\mathrm{s}} \mathcal{T} \cup S \cup S'$, since equisatisfiability is not preserved by the union operation. A naïve solution would be to impose that A and $\mathcal{T} \cup S$ (resp. A' and $\mathcal{T} \cup S'$) are logically equivalent, but this would be too strong a requirement, satisfied by choosing $A = \mathcal{T} \cup S$ and $A' = \mathcal{T} \cup S'$, which would defeat the purpose. Thus, we relax the model-theoretic condition of logical equivalence by still requiring $\mathcal{T} \cup S \models A$ and $\mathcal{T} \cup S' \models A'$, while replacing $A \models \mathcal{T} \cup S$ and $A' \models \mathcal{T} \cup S'$ with weaker requirements. Then, we define proof-theoretic conditions that suffice to retain equisatisfiability.

Definition 2. *Let C be a clause and S and $\mathcal{T}$ be sets of clauses. The set of $\mathcal{T}$-children of C is defined by:*

$$\mathcal{G}(C, \mathcal{T}) = \{F \mid \exists Q \in \mathcal{T} : F \text{ is generated from parents } C \text{ and } Q\}.$$

The set $\mathcal{D}_i(C, \mathcal{T})$ of i-steps $\mathcal{T}$-descendants of C is defined inductively as follows:

$$\mathcal{D}_0(C, \mathcal{T}) = \{C\} \quad and \quad \mathcal{D}_{i+1}(C, \mathcal{T}) = \bigcup_{F \in \mathcal{D}_i(C, \mathcal{T})} \mathcal{G}(F, \mathcal{T}), \text{ for } i \geq 0.$$

The sets of $\mathcal{T}$-descendants of C and $\mathcal{T}$-descendants of S are defined by:

$$\mathcal{D}(C, \mathcal{T}) = \bigcup_{i \geq 0} \mathcal{D}_i(C, \mathcal{T}) \quad and \quad \mathcal{D}(S, \mathcal{T}) = \bigcup_{C \in S} \mathcal{D}(C, \mathcal{T}).$$

Instead of imposing that A and A' logically entail $\mathcal{T} \cup S$ and $\mathcal{T} \cup S'$ respectively, we only require that they entail the $\mathcal{T}$-descendants of S and S'. This property is termed $\mathcal{T}$*-compatibility*:

Definition 3. *Given a set of clauses A, a clause C (resp. a set of clauses S) is $\mathcal{T}$-compatible with A if $A \models \mathcal{D}(C, \mathcal{T})$ (resp. $A \models \mathcal{D}(S, \mathcal{T})$).*

The name $\mathcal{T}$-compatibility is meant to convey the intuition that this relation between sets is weaker than logical equivalence but stronger than equisatisfiability. Strictly speaking, the notions of $\mathcal{T}$-descendant, $\mathcal{T}$-compatibility, and all those that depend on them, should be parametric with respect to the inference system: for example, a set of clauses may be $\mathcal{T}$-compatible with a given set for one inference system but not for another one. Nevertheless, for the sake of readability, we let the dependence on the inference system remain implicit. We also use the notion of $\mathcal{T}$-compatibility to specify formally what it means for a set of clauses not to "interact" with $\mathcal{T}$. This property is captured by the notion of $\mathcal{T}$-*disconnection*:

Definition 4. *A set of clauses S is $\mathcal{T}$-disconnected if $\mathcal{D}(S, \mathcal{T}) = S$. If $S = \{C\}$, we may also write that C is $\mathcal{T}$-disconnected.*

Intuitively, if a set of clauses S is $\mathcal{T}$-compatible with itself, it means that it does not need to interact with $\mathcal{T}$. The notion of $\mathcal{T}$-disconnection entails this property:

Proposition 1. *If S is $\mathcal{T}$-disconnected, then S is $\mathcal{T}$-compatible with itself.*

3.2   Preserving $\mathcal{T}$-Compatibility

We define a few restrictions guaranteeing that if a set of clauses S is $\mathcal{T}$-compatible with A and $(\mathcal{T}, S) \vdash_{\mathrm{Inf}_\succ} (\mathcal{T}, S')$, then S' is also $\mathcal{T}$-compatible with A. As we introduce them by considering the possible $\mathrm{Inf}_\succ$-inferences, we start with contraction inferences.

Definition 5. *A set of clauses S is $\mathcal{T}$-contraction-compatible if for all sets A, for all contraction inferences $(\mathcal{T}, S) \vdash_{\mathrm{Inf}_\succ} (\mathcal{T}, S')$, if S is $\mathcal{T}$-compatible with A then S' is also $\mathcal{T}$-compatible with A.*

$\mathcal{T}$-compatibility is clearly preserved by contraction rules that delete a clause in S, such as *subsumption* and *tautology deletion*. On the other hand, the behavior of rules such as *simplification* depends on $\mathcal{T}$ and the given set of clauses:

Example 1. Let $\mathcal{T} = \{f(a) \simeq b\}$, $S = \{f(c) \simeq d,\ c \simeq a\}$, and assume that $\mathcal{D}(S, \mathcal{T}) = S$, that is, S is $\mathcal{T}$-compatible with itself. Suppose that $(\mathcal{T}, S) \vdash_{\mathrm{Inf}_\succ} (\mathcal{T}, S')$, where S' is obtained from S by the simplification of $f(c) \simeq d$ by $c \simeq a$, i.e., $S' = \{f(a) \simeq d,\ c \simeq a\}$. If $\mathrm{Inf}_\succ$ features a rule generating $d \simeq b$ from parents $f(a) \simeq d$ and $f(a) \simeq b$, then $b \simeq d \in \mathcal{D}(S', \mathcal{T})$. In this case, S' is not $\mathcal{T}$-compatible with S, since $S \not\models \{b \simeq d\}$.

We proceed with expansion inferences, distinguishing between unary and binary ones.

Unary Expansion Inferences. The property of $\mathcal{T}$-*neutrality* is sufficient to control unary inferences. Intuitively, this notion prevents clauses generated by unary inferences from interacting with clauses in $\mathcal{T}$.

Definition 6. *A clause C is $\mathcal{T}$-neutral if, for every clause D generated from C by a unary inference, D is $\mathcal{T}$-disconnected. A set of clauses is $\mathcal{T}$-neutral if all its clauses are.*

Proposition 2. *Let A be a set of clauses such that S is $\mathcal{T}$-compatible with A, and suppose that S is $\mathcal{T}$-neutral. If $(\mathcal{T}, S) \vdash_{\text{Inf}_\succ} (\mathcal{T}, S \cup \{D\})$, where D is generated from a clause in S by a unary inference, then $S \cup \{D\}$ is $\mathcal{T}$-compatible with A.*

Binary Expansion Inferences Between a Clause in $\mathcal{T}$ and One in S. With Definitions 1, 2 and 3, we defined $\mathcal{T}$-compatibility for binary expansion inferences involving a clause in S as first premise and a clause in $\mathcal{T}$ as second premise. We require these to be the only binary expansion inferences that can take place between clauses in S and clauses in $\mathcal{T}$. This leads to the notion of $\mathcal{T}$-orientation:

Definition 7. *A clause C is $\mathcal{T}$-oriented if no binary expansion inference applies with a clause in $\mathcal{T}$ as first premise and C as second premise. A set of clauses is $\mathcal{T}$-oriented if all its clauses are.*

Proposition 3. *Let A be a set of clauses such that S is $\mathcal{T}$-compatible with A and suppose S is $\mathcal{T}$-oriented. If $(\mathcal{T}, S) \vdash_{\text{Inf}_\succ} (\mathcal{T}, S \cup \{D\})$, where D is generated by a binary inference applied to a clause in S and one in $\mathcal{T}$, then $S \cup \{D\}$ is $\mathcal{T}$-compatible with A.*

Example 2. Let $\mathcal{T} = \{a \simeq b\}$, $S = \{f(b) \simeq c\}$, and let $\text{Inf}_\succ$ be an inference system featuring a rule that generates $f(a) \simeq c$ from parents $a \simeq b$ and $f(b) \simeq c$. Then S is not $\mathcal{T}$-oriented, since this rule involves a clause in $\mathcal{T}$ as first premise and a clause in S as second premise. Suppose further that S is $\mathcal{T}$-compatible with itself. Since $(\mathcal{T}, S) \vdash_{\text{Inf}_\succ} (\mathcal{T}, S')$, with $S' = \{f(b) \simeq c, f(a) \simeq c\}$, and $S \not\models S'$, the set S' is not $\mathcal{T}$-compatible with S.

This example shows how, for inference systems such as $\mathcal{SP}$ where the binary expansion rules are *superposition* and *paramodulation*, the notion of first and second premise instantiates to the traditional notion of clauses paramodulated *from* and *into*, respectively. In such a context, C is $\mathcal{T}$-oriented if no clause of $\mathcal{T}$ paramodulates into C. This property is satisfied by all persistent clauses generated by $\mathcal{SP}$ from $\mathcal{T}$-satisfiability problems in the theories of in [3,2,6].

Binary Expansion Inferences Within S. These are the inferences that require the most control. For this purpose, we define a notion of *associativity*, that lends itself to an easy symbolic representation: informally, let $C \to C'$ denote a clause generated from parents C and C', then C is $[C', D']$-*associative* if either $(C \to C') \to D' = C \to (C' \to D')$, or $(C \to C') \to D'$ is subsumed by $C' \to D'$. This property is relevant when D' is an axiom in $\mathcal{T}$. Intuitively, it means that if an inference between two clauses yields another inference with an axiom as second premise, then an inference with an axiom as second premise could have been done before hand. This disentangles inferences into axioms from the others, allowing us to do them first.

Definition 8. *Given the clauses C, C' and D', the clause C is $[C', D']$-associative if for every clause D generated from parents C and C', and for every clause E generated from parents D and D', there exists a clause E' generated from parents C' and D' such that either E can be generated from parents C and E', or E' subsumes E. The clause C is weakly $\mathcal{T}$-associative for C' if for every $Q \in \mathcal{T}$, C is $[C', Q]$-associative. C is $\mathcal{T}$-associative for C' if it is weakly $\mathcal{T}$-associative for every $E' \in \mathcal{D}(C', \mathcal{T})$. A set of clauses S is weakly $\mathcal{T}$-associative (resp. $\mathcal{T}$-associative) if for all $C, C' \in S$, C is weakly $\mathcal{T}$-associative for C' (resp. $\mathcal{T}$-associative for C').*

One can prove that if S is $\mathcal{T}$-associative, it is also $\mathcal{T}$-contraction-compatible[3]. This requires to instantiate $\mathrm{Inf}_{\succ}$ to a concrete inference system (cf. Lemma 29 in [7] for this result for the system $\mathcal{U}_{\succ}$ of Sec. 5). Since $\mathcal{T}$-associativity is defined using subsumption, to ensure that $\mathcal{T}$-compatibility is preserved by binary inferences between clauses in S, we need subsumption to preserve $\mathcal{T}$-compatibility:

Definition 9. *A clause C is $\mathcal{T}$-subsumption-preserving if for all sets A that C is $\mathcal{T}$-compatible with and for all clauses C' subsumed by C, clause C' is also $\mathcal{T}$-compatible with A. A set of clauses S is $\mathcal{T}$-subsumption-preserving if all its clauses are $\mathcal{T}$-subsumption-preserving.*

$\mathcal{T}$-subsumption-preservation, together with $\mathcal{T}$-associativity, guarantees that if D is generated by a binary expansion inference applied to two clauses in S, then $S \cup \{D\}$ is $\mathcal{T}$-compatible with A. The statement of the following lemma is actually stronger and is also used to prove that $\mathcal{T}$-compatible sets can be combined, provided they are $\mathcal{T}$-associative:

Lemma 1. *Let C, C' and D be clauses such that D is generated from parents C and C', and let A (resp. A') be a set of clauses such that C is $\mathcal{T}$-compatible with A (resp. C' with A'). If $\mathcal{D}(C', \mathcal{T})$ is $\mathcal{T}$-subsumption-preserving and C is $\mathcal{T}$-associative for C', then D is $\mathcal{T}$-compatible with $A \cup A'$.*

3.3 $\mathcal{T}$-Stability

In order to ensure that all relevant properties are preserved by all rules in $\mathrm{Inf}_{\succ}$, we introduce $\mathcal{T}$-*closure* and $\mathcal{T}$-*stability*:

Definition 10. *Given a presentation $\mathcal{T}$, a set of clauses S is $\mathcal{T}$-closed under $\mathrm{Inf}_{\succ}$ if all clauses generated by an inference applied to $(\mathcal{T}, S)$ are in S.*

Definition 11. *Given a presentation $\mathcal{T}$, a set of clauses $\mathcal{B}$ is $\mathcal{T}$-stable for $\mathrm{Inf}_{\succ}$ if every subset of $\mathcal{B}$ is $\mathcal{T}$-contraction-compatible and the set $\mathcal{B}$ is (i) $\mathcal{T}$-oriented, (ii) $\mathcal{T}$-neutral, (iii) weakly $\mathcal{T}$-associative, (iv) $\mathcal{T}$-subsumption-preserving and (v) $\mathcal{T}$-closed under $\mathrm{Inf}_{\succ}$.*

We are now in a position to state the main theorem:

Theorem 1. *Given a presentation $\mathcal{T}$, let $\mathcal{B}$ be a set of clauses that is $\mathcal{T}$-stable for $\mathrm{Inf}_{\succ}$ and consider sets of clauses $S, S' \subseteq \mathcal{B}$. If A and A' are sets of clauses such that (i) $\mathcal{T} \cup S \models A$, (ii) $\mathcal{T} \cup S' \models A'$, (iii) S is $\mathcal{T}$-compatible with A and (iv) S' is $\mathcal{T}$-compatible with A', then $\mathcal{T} \cup S \cup S'$ and $A \cup A'$ are equisatisfiable.*

---

[3] The set of clauses S of Example 1 satisfies neither property.

4   𝒯-Decision Procedures Based on 𝒮𝒫

Let $\mathcal{T}$ be a presentation such that a fair $\mathcal{SP}_\succ$-strategy is a $\mathcal{T}$-satisfiability procedure. We outline how an $\mathcal{SP}$-based $\mathcal{T}$-decision procedure can be designed by applying the decomposition framework. The binary expansion rules of $\mathcal{SP}$ are superposition and paramodulation. We use paramodulation for both for simplicity. In a typical theory presentation (e.g., those considered in [3,2,6]), no paramodulation applies from a non-ground axiom into a strictly flat clause. This, together with the fact that every set of ground clauses can be flattened into an equisatisfiable set containing flat unit clauses and strictly flat clauses, is used to test the satisfiability of $\mathcal{T} \cup P$ as shown in Fig. 1. The set P is decomposed into $S \uplus S'$, where S only contains *flat unit clauses*. A fair $\mathcal{SP}_\succ$-strategy is applied to $\mathcal{T} \cup S$, to generate a finite limit set $\mathcal{T} \cup \bar{S}$. Then the satisfiability of $\bar{S} \cup S'$ is tested. To guarantee that this process is correct, we must prove that $\mathcal{T} \cup P$ and $\bar{S} \cup S'$ are equisatisfiable. Therefore we check whether the hypotheses of Theorem 1 are satisfied. For this purpose, we define first an inference system $\mathrm{Inf}_\succ$, such that S is $\mathcal{T}$-compatible with $\bar{S}$ and S' is $\mathcal{T}$-disconnected. Then, we verify that there exists a set $\mathcal{B}_\mathcal{T}$ that includes S and S' and is $\mathcal{T}$-stable for $\mathrm{Inf}_\succ$. If these conditions are met, Theorem 1 applies with A instantiated to $\bar{S}$ and A' instantiated to S'. Indeed, we have $\mathcal{T} \cup S \models \bar{S}$, $S' \models S'$, S is $\mathcal{T}$-compatible with $\bar{S}$, and since S' is $\mathcal{T}$-disconnected, it is $\mathcal{T}$-compatible with itself by Proposition 1. It follows that $\mathcal{T} \cup P \equiv_s \bar{S} \cup S'$.

If $\mathcal{T}$ is a combination of theories, that is, $\mathcal{T} = \mathcal{T}_1 \cup \mathcal{T}_2$, the scheme of Fig. 1 can be used again, under the assumption that $\mathcal{T}_2$ is $\mathcal{T}_1$-disconnected. Indeed, $\mathcal{T}_2$ is then contained in S', and the sets $\mathcal{T}_1 \cup \mathcal{T}_2 \cup P$ and $\bar{S} \cup S'$ are equisatisfiable. This is especially useful when $\mathcal{T}_2$ is a presentation that $\mathcal{SP}$ cannot handle, such as the (infinite) axiomatization of linear arithmetic: the theory is *ignored by the prover* and dealt with by the specialized procedure of the SMT solver. On the

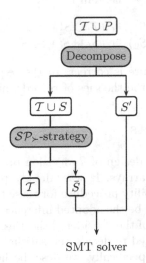

SMT solver

Fig. 1. $\mathcal{T}$-decision procedures based on $\mathcal{SP}$

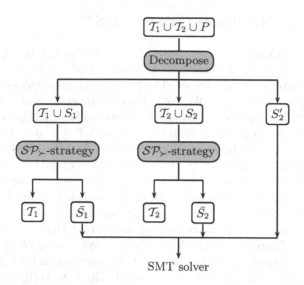

Fig. 2. $\mathcal{T}$-decision procedure in a combination of theories

other hand, if the inference system can handle both theories, the more specialized scheme of Fig. 2 applies:

The 2-theories scheme. Assume that a fair $\mathcal{SP}_\succ$-strategy is also a $\mathcal{T}_2$-satisfiability procedure and $\bar{S}$ is $\mathcal{T}_2$-disconnected. The set of clauses P is decomposed into S_1 and $\mathcal{T}_2 \cup S_1'$, in such a way that S_1 only contains flat unit $\mathcal{T}_1$-clauses. In turn, S_1' is decomposed into S_2 and S_2', in such a way that S_2 only contains flat unit $\mathcal{T}_2$-clauses. The $\mathcal{SP}_\succ$-strategy applied to $\mathcal{T}_1 \cup S_1$ generates the limit $\mathcal{T}_1 \cup \bar{S}_1$, and, by hypothesis, $\bar{S}_1$ is $\mathcal{T}_2$-disconnected. The $\mathcal{SP}_\succ$-strategy applied to $\mathcal{T}_2 \cup S_2$ generates the limit $\mathcal{T}_2 \cup \bar{S}_2$. By Theorem 1,

$$\mathcal{T}_1 \cup \mathcal{T}_2 \cup P \equiv_s (\mathcal{T}_1 \cup S_1) \cup (\mathcal{T}_2 \cup S_1') \equiv_s \bar{S}_1 \cup [(\mathcal{T}_2 \cup S_2) \cup S_2']$$
$$\equiv_s (\mathcal{T}_2 \cup S_2) \cup (\bar{S}_1 \cup S_2') \equiv_s \bar{S}_1 \cup \bar{S}_2 \cup S_2',$$

so that the resulting procedure is correct. In the sequel, we shall see that the 2-theories scheme applies to the theories of records, integer offsets and arrays.

5   Some $\mathcal{T}$-Stable Sets

In this section we apply our design of $\mathcal{T}$-decision procedures to the theories of records, integer offsets and arrays. It was already proved in [3,2] that a fair $\mathcal{SP}_\succ$-strategy is a $\mathcal{T}$-satisfiability procedure for these theories. We first define an inference system $\mathcal{U}_\succ$ that will be the adopted inference system when determining $\mathcal{T}$-stable sets. Then for each of the considered theories, we prove that the scheme described above can be applied to decide the satisfiability of $\mathcal{T} \cup P$, for all sets of ground clauses P. More specifically, we describe how P is decomposed into $S \uplus S'$, and then prove there exists a $\mathcal{T}$-stable set for $\mathcal{U}_\succ$ that contains S and S'.

5.1 The Inference System $\mathcal{U}_\succ$

Superposition and paramodulation in $\mathcal{SP}$ are restricted in such a way that only maximal sides of maximal literals are paramodulated from and into. We define an $\mathcal{SP}$-based supported strategy that relaxes this restriction to some extent:

Definition 12. *Let $\mathcal{U}_\succ$ be the strategy that works on pairs of sets $(\mathcal{T}, S)$, contains all the contraction rules of $\mathcal{SP}_\succ$, and such that $(\mathcal{T}, S) \vdash_{\mathcal{U}_\succ} (\mathcal{T}, S \cup \{D\})$, if D is generated by:*

- *a unary inference rule of $\mathcal{SP}_\succ$ applied to a clause in S,*
- *a binary inference rule of $\mathcal{SP}_\succ$ applied from a clause in $\mathcal{T}$ into one in S,*
- *a binary inference rule of $\mathcal{SP}_\succ$ applied to two clauses in S, with the relaxation that if $u \simeq v \vee D$ paramodulates into $C = l[u'] \bowtie r \vee C'$, neither $l[u'] \bowtie r$ is required to be a maximal literal in C nor $l[u']$ is required to be maximal in this literal.*

Proposition 4. *Let $\mathcal{T}$ be a presentation. For all sets of flat literals S, if $S_\infty = \mathcal{T} \cup \bar{S}$ is the limit generated by a fair $\mathcal{SP}_\succ$-strategy from $\mathcal{T} \cup S$, then S is $\mathcal{T}$-compatible with $\bar{S}$ for $\mathcal{U}_\succ$. Furthermore, if no $\mathcal{SP}_\succ$-inference applies from a clause C into a clause in $\mathcal{T}$, then C is $\mathcal{T}$-disconnected for $\mathcal{U}_\succ$.*

5.2 The Theory of Records

The theory of records with n fields assumes a signature Σ that contains, for all i, $1 \leq i \leq n$, the function symbol rstore_i, which stores a value in the ith-field of a record, and rselect_i, which extracts a value from the ith-field of a record. It is defined by the following (saturated) presentation, denoted by $\mathcal{R}$:

$$\forall x, v. \qquad \text{rselect}_i(\text{rstore}_i(x, v)) \simeq v \qquad \text{for all } 1 \leq i \leq n, \tag{1}$$

$$\forall x, v. \ \text{rselect}_j(\text{rstore}_i(x, v)) \simeq \text{rselect}_j(x) \quad \text{for all } 1 \leq i \neq j \leq n. \tag{2}$$

The theory of records with extensionality is axiomatized by the (saturated) presentation $\mathcal{R}^e$, which consists of the previous axioms together with:

$$\forall x, y. \ (\textstyle\bigwedge_{i=1}^n \text{rselect}_i(x) \simeq \text{rselect}_i(y)) \rightarrow x \simeq y.$$

An $\mathcal{R}^e$-satisfiability problem can be reduced to an $\mathcal{R}$-satisfiability problem:

Lemma 2 (Lemma 1 of [2]). *Let $S = S_1 \uplus S_2$ be a set of ground flat literals, such that S_2 contains the literals of the form $l \not\simeq r$, where l and r are records. For all $L = l \not\simeq r \in S_2$ let C_L denote the clause $\bigvee_{i=1}^n \text{rselect}_i(l) \not\simeq \text{rselect}_i(r)$. Then $\mathcal{R}^e \cup S \equiv_s \mathcal{R} \cup S_1 \cup \{C_L \mid L \in S_2\}$.*

Since an $\mathcal{R}^e$-decision problem can be reduced to an $\mathcal{R}^e$-satisfiability problem by reduction to disjunctive normal form, this reduction holds also for $\mathcal{R}^e$-decision problems. A given set of ground clauses P is decomposed into S and S' as follows: P is flattened; among the resulting clauses, the unit clauses of the form rstore$_i(a, e) \simeq b$ go into S and all other clauses go into S'. Indeed, the decomposition scheme of Fig. 1 only requires that S is made of flat unit clauses, so that decomposition does not coincide with flattening. It is simple to check that S' is $\mathcal{R}$-disconnected for $\mathcal{U}_\succ$.

Definition 13. *Let $\mathcal{B}_\mathcal{R}$ denote the set of ground clauses consisting of:*

   i) all strictly flat clauses,
   ii) all clauses of the form rstore$_i(a, e) \simeq b \vee B$ *where $1 \le i \le n$ and B is ground and strictly flat,*
   iii) all clauses of the form rselect$_i(a) \simeq e \vee B$ *where $1 \le i \le n$ and B is ground and strictly flat,*
   iv) all clauses of the form rselect$_i(a) \simeq$ rselect$_i(b) \vee B$, *where $1 \le i \le n$ and B is ground and strictly flat.*

Theorem 2. *$\mathcal{B}_\mathcal{R}$ is $\mathcal{R}$-stable for $\mathcal{U}_\succ$.*

Since $\mathcal{B}_\mathcal{R}$ contains $S \uplus S'$ and is $\mathcal{R}$-stable for $\mathcal{U}_\succ$, the scheme of Fig. 1 applies to $\mathcal{R}$. Since $\mathcal{B}_\mathcal{R}$ only contains ground clauses and is $\mathcal{T}$-closed under $\mathcal{U}_\succ$, not only S and S', but also $\bar{S}$ is ground. Thus, $\bar{S} \cup S'$ is ground, and its satisfiability can be decided by a decision procedure for the theory of Equality with Uninterpreted Function symbols (EUF).

5.3   The Theory of Integer Offsets

The theory of integer offsets is a fragment of the theory of integers. Its signature Σ contains two unary function symbols s and p, that represent the successor and predecessor functions, respectively. This theory is presented by the following (infinite) set of axioms $\mathcal{I}$:

$$\forall x.\ \mathsf{s}(\mathsf{p}(x)) \simeq x,$$
$$\forall x.\ \mathsf{p}(\mathsf{s}(x)) \simeq x,$$
$$\forall x.\ \ \mathsf{s}^i(x)\ \not\simeq x \text{ for } i > 0,$$

where $\mathsf{s}^0(x) = x$ and $\mathsf{s}^{i+1}(x) = \mathsf{s}(\mathsf{s}^i(x))$ for $i \ge 0$. For the sake of convenience, we also define for all $n \in \mathbb{N}$

$$A_\mathcal{I} = \{\mathsf{s}(\mathsf{p}(x)) \simeq x,\ \mathsf{p}(\mathsf{s}(x)) \simeq x\},$$
$$Ac(n) = \{\mathsf{s}^i(x) \not\simeq x \mid 0 < i \le n\},$$
$$Ac = \bigcup\nolimits_{n \ge 0} Ac(n).$$

It was proved in [5] that if S is a set of flat ground literals, then for all n greater or equal to the number of occurrences of the function symbols s and p in S, $A_\mathcal{I} \cup Ac \cup S \equiv_s A_\mathcal{I} \cup Ac(n) \cup S$. We deduce a similar result for $\mathcal{I}$-decision problems:

Proposition 5. *Let P be an $\mathcal{I}$-decision problem containing n occurrences of the function symbols s and p. Then $A_\mathcal{I} \cup Ac \cup P \equiv_s A_\mathcal{I} \cup Ac(n) \cup P$.*

Given $n \in \mathbb{N}$, let $A_s(n)$ denote the set $\{s^i(x) \not\simeq p^j(x) \mid 1 \le i + j \le n\}$. The saturated limit of $A_{\mathcal{I}} \cup Ac(n)$ has the form $A_{\mathcal{I}} \cup A_s(n)$. Let $\mathcal{I}_s[n]$ denote this saturated set. A set of ground clauses P is decomposed as follows: P is flattened; all the resulting unit clauses go into S and all strictly flat clauses go into S'. Thus, in this case, decomposition coincides with flattening.

Definition 14. *Let $\mathcal{B}_{\mathcal{I}_s[n]}$ denote the set consisting of:*

i) *all strictly flat clauses,*
ii) *all clauses of the form $p(a) \simeq b \vee B$ where B is ground and strictly flat,*
iii) *all clauses of the form $s(a) \simeq b \vee B$ where B is ground and strictly flat,*
iv) *all clauses of the form $s^i(a) \not\simeq p^j(b) \vee B$, where $0 \le i + j \le n - 1$ and B is ground and strictly flat.*

Theorem 3. $\mathcal{B}_{\mathcal{I}_s[n]}$ *is $\mathcal{I}_s[n]$-stable for $\mathcal{U}_\succ$.*

Since $\mathcal{B}_{\mathcal{I}_s[n]}$ only contains ground clauses, by the same observation made for the theory of records, the satisfiability of $\bar{S} \cup S'$ can be decided by a decision procedure for EUF.

5.4 The Theory of Arrays

The theory of arrays is defined by the following (saturated) presentation $\mathcal{A}$:

$$\forall x, z, v. \; \text{select}(\text{store}(x, z, v), z) \simeq v, \tag{3}$$

$$\forall x, z, w, v. \; (z \simeq w \vee \text{select}(\text{store}(x, z, v), w) \simeq \text{select}(x, w)). \tag{4}$$

The theory of arrays with extensionality $\mathcal{A}^e$ is defined by axioms (3) and (4), along with the following extensionality axiom:

$$\forall x, y. \; (\forall z. \; \text{select}(x, z) \simeq \text{select}(y, z) \to x \simeq y). \tag{5}$$

It was proved in [3] that satisfiability of sets of ground literals in $\mathcal{A}^e$ can be reduced to satisfiability of sets of ground literals in $\mathcal{A}$ by replacing every negative literal of the form $a \not\simeq a'$, where a and a' are arrays, by a literal $\text{select}(a, sk) \not\simeq \text{select}(a', sk)$, where sk is a fresh (Skolem) constant. Such a reduction also holds for sets of ground clauses. A set of ground clauses P is decomposed as follows: P is flattened; S contains all the unit clauses of the form $\text{store}(a, i, e) \simeq a'$, and S' contains all the other clauses.

Definition 15. *Consider the set $\mathcal{B}_{\mathcal{A}}$ consisting of:*

i) *all strictly flat clauses,*
ii) *all clauses of the form $\text{store}(a, i, e) \simeq a' \vee B$ where B is strictly flat,*
iii) *all clauses of the form $\text{select}(a, i) \simeq e \vee B$ where B is strictly flat,*
iv) *all clauses of the form $\text{select}(a, x) \simeq \text{select}(a', x) \vee x \simeq i_1 \vee \ldots \vee x \simeq i_n \vee B$, where the i_j's are constants and B is strictly flat.*

Theorem 4. $\mathcal{B}_{\mathcal{A}}$ *is $\mathcal{A}$-stable for $\mathcal{U}_\succ$.*

Note that the set $\mathcal{B}_A$ does not contain only ground clauses, and testing the satisfiability of the set $\bar{S} \cup S'$ requires to rely on the ability of SMT-solvers to handle quantifiers (cf. Section 5 in [11]). The non-ground clauses in this set have the form

$$\mathrm{select}(a, x) \simeq \mathrm{select}(a', x) \vee x \simeq i_1 \vee \ldots \vee x \simeq i_n \vee B,$$

where B is strictly flat and ground. Borrowing the notation of [17, Definition 2] for so-called *partial equations*, this clause can be rewritten as $a \approx_D a' \vee B$, where D denotes the set $\{i_1, \ldots, i_n\}$. Such a clause states that under the guard $\neg B$, the *uninterpreted* terms $\mathrm{select}(a, x)$ and $\mathrm{select}(a', x)$ are identical for all $x \notin D$. Since arrays can be regarded as representing functions, and a term $\mathrm{select}(a, x)$ has the same intuitive meaning of $apply(a, x)$, the *uninterpreted* functions a and a' agree for all values of x except those in D.

5.5   Combination of Records, Integer Offsets and Arrays

We conclude by showing how the 2-theories scheme applies to combine these theories. In [2], the termination of $\mathcal{SP}$ on $\mathcal{T}$-satisfiability problems $\mathcal{T} \cup S$, where S is a set of flat unit clauses, is proved by analyzing all possible kinds of clauses in the limit $\mathcal{T} \cup \bar{S}$, generated by a fair derivation from $\mathcal{T} \cup S$. Let $\mathcal{T} \cup S$ be a problem in one of these three theories, either records, or integer offsets or arrays, and let $\mathcal{T} \cup \bar{S}$ be the corresponding limit. Based on those analyses, no clause in $\bar{S}$ paramodulates into a clause of either one of the two other presentations. In other words, $\bar{S}$ is disconnected from either one of the two other presentations[4]. We deduce that:

Theorem 5. *The 2-theories scheme is correct for any combination of the theories of records, integer offsets and arrays.*

6   Discussion

In this paper we introduced a decomposition framework that consists in using a generic theorem prover to "compile a theory away" from a $\mathcal{T}$-decision problem, before invoking an SMT-solver on the resulting problem. After presenting a set of sufficient conditions collectively termed $\mathcal{T}$-*stability*, that guarantee the correctness of this scheme, we showed how it applies to the superposition calculus and the theories of *records*, *integer offsets* and *arrays*. This rewrite-based approach to $\mathcal{T}$-decision problems is more efficient than one based on feeding the entire formula to theorem provers, that are not designed to handle its Boolean part efficiently, and it is simpler than a lazy approach that would require a tight integration of a theorem prover and a SAT-solver. The compilation stage can be viewed also as a *reduction*: in essence, our results *reduce* the theories of records and integer offsets to that of equality with uninterpreted functions (EUF). Thus,

---

[4] Technically, this follows from the fact that the theories are variable-inactive and share no function symbols.

concrete $\mathcal{T}$-decision procedures can be implemented simply by interfacing a theorem prover implementing $\mathcal{SP}$, such as E [16], with a decision procedure for EUF, such as DPLL($=$) (e.g., [13]). Similarly, the theory of arrays is reduced, as expected, to a theory of *partial functions*, with axioms stating that some uninterpreted functions are equal everywhere except on a given domain.

We also showed that this framework can be used to deal with combinations of theories under the $\mathcal{T}$-*disconnection* condition: if the theorem prover can handle all the theories in the problem, they can all be compiled away; if it cannot handle some of them, as it would be the case, for instance, with linear arithmetic or the theory of bitvectors (e.g., [9]), these are simply passed on to the SMT solver. In this scheme, the theorem prover plays the role of a procedure that reduces the SMT problems in a *uniform* manner. After such a *sifting* process, the SMT-solver only needs to solve "simpler" problems that are equisatisfiable to the original ones.

We are currently investigating how to adapt the techniques of [8] to devise a generic theory reasoner for a theory of *partial functions*, that may be generated by $\mathcal{SP}$ from a problem involving the theory of arrays. After integrating such a theory reasoner into an SMT-solver and interfacing the resulting tool with a theorem prover implementing $\mathcal{SP}$, we intend to run experiments to evaluate the efficiency of the system thus obtained.

For future work, we plan to investigate which other theories or inference systems satisfy the requirements of the decomposition framework. Indeed, the framework was presented in such a way to be as abstract as possible, so that it does not depend on a particular inference system. Thus, it is likely that more theories can be captured, with $\mathcal{SP}$ or other inference systems. Another direction for future research is to explore how to integrate automated model building methods into this framework, with the goal of designing SMT-tools capable of constructing both proofs and counterexamples, a highly desirable feature in applications. To this end, we intend to study how *hybrid* model building techniques (e.g., [15]), that try simultaneously to prove unsatisfiability or compute a model of a formula, could be applied within our approach.

References

1. Armando, A., Bonacina, M.P., Ranise, S., Schulz, S.: On a rewriting approach to satisfiability procedures: Extension, combination of theories and an experimental appraisal. In: Gramlich, B. (ed.) Frontiers of Combining Systems. LNCS (LNAI), vol. 3717, pp. 65–80. Springer, Heidelberg (2005)
2. Armando, A., Bonacina, M.P., Ranise, S., Schulz, S.: New results on rewrite-based satisfiability procedures. ACM Transactions on Computational Logic, Accepted pending revision, February 2007, full version of [1] (2007) available at http://profs.sci.univr.it/~bonacina/rewsat.html
3. Armando, A., Ranise, S., Rusinowitch, M.: A rewriting approach to satisfiability procedures. Inf. Comput. 183(2), 140–164 (2003)
4. Bonacina, M.P.: A taxonomy of theorem-proving strategies. In: Veloso, M.M., Wooldridge, M.J. (eds.) Artificial Intelligence Today. LNCS (LNAI), vol. 1600, pp. 43–84. Springer, Heidelberg (1999)

5. Bonacina, M.P., Echenim, M.: On variable-inactivity and polynomial T-satisfiability procedures (submitted)
6. Bonacina, M.P., Echenim, M.: Rewrite-based satisfiability procedures for recursive data structures. In: Cook, B., Sebastiani, R. (eds.) Proc. 4th PDPAR Workshop, FLoC 2006, ENTCS, Elsevier, Amsterdam (to appear)
7. Bonacina, M.P., Echenim, M.: Theory decision by decomposition. Technical Report RR 50/2007 Dipartimento di Informatica, Università degli Studi di Verona (2007) Available at http://profs.sci.univr.it/~echenim
8. Bradley, A.R., Manna, Z., Sipma, H.B.: What's decidable about arrays? In: Emerson, E.A., Namjoshi, K.S. (eds.) VMCAI 2006. LNCS, vol. 3855, pp. 427–442. Springer, Heidelberg (2005)
9. Cyrluk, D., Möller, O., Rueß, H.: An efficient decision procedure for a theory of fixed-sized bitvectors with composition and extraction. Technical Report UIB96-08, Fakultät für Informatik, Universität Ulm, Ulm, Germany (1996)
10. Dershowitz, N., Plaisted, D.A.: Rewriting. In: Robinson, J., Voronkov, A. (eds.) Handbook of Automated Reasoning, vol. I, pp. 535–610. Elsevier, Amsterdam (2001)
11. Detlefs, D.L., Nelson, G., Saxe, J.B.: Simplify: a theorem prover for program checking. J. ACM 52(3), 365–473 (2005)
12. Nelson, G., Oppen, D.C.: Simplification by cooperating decision procedures. ACM TOPLAS 1(2), 245–257 (1979)
13. Nieuwenhuis, R., Oliveras, A., Tinelli, C.: Solving SAT and SAT Modulo Theories: from an Abstract Davis-Putnam-Logemann-Loveland Procedure to DPLL(T). J. ACM 53(6), 937–977 (2006)
14. Nieuwenhuis, R., Rubio, A.: Paramodulation-based theorem proving. In: Robinson, J.A., Voronkov, A. (eds.) Handbook of Automated Reasoning, pp. 371–443. Elsevier and MIT Press (2001)
15. Peltier, N.: A calculus combining resolution and enumeration for building finite models. Journal of Symbolic Computation 36(1-2), 49–77 (2003)
16. Schulz, S.: E – a brainiac theorem prover. J. of AI Communications 15(2–3), 111–126 (2002)
17. Stump, A., Barrett, C.W., Dill, D.L., Levitt, J.R.: A decision procedure for an extensional theory of arrays. In: LICS, pp. 29–37 (2001)
18. Zhang, L., Malik, S.: The quest for efficient boolean satisfiability solvers. In: Voronkov, A. (ed.) Automated Deduction - CADE-18. LNCS (LNAI), vol. 2392, pp. 295–313. Springer, Heidelberg (2002)

Towards Efficient Satisfiability Checking for Boolean Algebra with Presburger Arithmetic

Viktor Kuncak[1] and Martin Rinard[2]

[1] Ecole Politechnique Fédérale de Lausanne, Lausanne, VD, Switzerland
[2] Massachusetts Institute of Technology, Cambridge, MA, USA

Abstract. Boolean Algebra with Presburger Arithmetic (BAPA) is a decidable logic that combines 1) Boolean algebra of sets of uninterpreted elements (BA) and 2) Presburger arithmetic (PA). BAPA can express relationships between integer variables and cardinalities of unbounded sets. In combination with other decision procedures and theorem provers, BAPA is useful for automatically verifying quantitative properties of data structures. This paper examines QFBAPA, the quantifier-free fragment of BAPA. The computational complexity of QFBAPA satisfiability was previously unknown; previous QFBAPA algorithms have non-deterministic exponential time complexity due to an explosion in the number of introduced integer variables.

This paper shows, for the first time, how to avoid such exponential explosion. We present an algorithm for checking satisfiability of QFBAPA formulas by reducing them to formulas of quantifier-free PA, with only O(n log(n)) increase in formula size. We prove the correctness of our algorithm using a theorem about sparse solutions of integer linear programming problems. This is the first proof that QFBAPA satisfiability is in NP and therefore NP-complete. We implemented our algorithm in the context of the Jahob verification system. Our preliminary experiments suggest that our algorithm, although not necessarily better for proving formula unsatisfiability, is more effective in detecting formula satisfiability than previous approaches.

1 Introduction

This paper considers the satisfiability problem for a logic that allows reasoning about sets and their cardinalities. We call this logic quantifier-free Boolean Algebra with Presburger Arithmetic and denote it QFBAPA. Our motivation for QFBAPA is proving the validity of formulas arising from program verification [12,13,14], but QFBAPA constraints also occur in mechanized set theory [7], constraint data bases [24,25], as a fragment of other logics [19,21,1] and in the semantic analysis of natural language [16]. Figure 1 shows the syntax of QFBAPA. The logic contains 1) arbitrary boolean algebra (BA) expressions denoting sets, supporting operations such as union, intersection and complement, 2) arbitrary quantifier-free Presburger arithmetic (PA) expressions, supporting addition of integers and multiplication by constants, and 3) a cardinality operator $|B|$ for

F. Pfenning (Ed.): CADE 2007, LNAI 4603, pp. 215–230, 2007.
© Springer-Verlag Berlin Heidelberg 2007

computing the the size of a BA expression B and treating it as a PA expression. The constant MAXC denotes the size of the finite universal set $\mathcal{U}$, so $|\mathcal{U}| = $ MAXC. The expression K dvd T means that an integer constant K divides an integer expression T, whereas B^c denotes the complement of the set B.

$$F ::= A \mid F_1 \wedge F_2 \mid F_1 \vee F_2 \mid \neg F$$
$$A ::= B_1 = B_2 \mid B_1 \subseteq B_2 \mid T_1 = T_2 \mid T_1 < T_2 \mid K \text{ dvd } T$$
$$B ::= x \mid \emptyset \mid \mathcal{U} \mid B_1 \cup B_2 \mid B_1 \cap B_2 \mid B^c$$
$$T ::= k \mid K \mid \text{MAXC} \mid T_1 + T_2 \mid K \cdot T \mid |B|$$
$$K ::= \ldots -2 \mid -1 \mid 0 \mid 1 \mid 2 \ldots$$

Fig. 1. Quantifier-Free Boolean Algebra with Presburger Arithmetic (QFBAPA)

Using QFBAPA in software verification. We implemented the algorithm described in this paper in the Jahob data structure verification system [12]. Figure 2 shows some of the verification conditions expressible in QFBAPA that we encountered and proved using our decision procedure. In these verification conditions, sets such as content, C, and C_1 represent the contents of dynamically allocated data structures. (For more examples, see [14, Chapters 2 and 7].) The formulas in Figure 2 are in HOL syntax, where cardinality of a set is denoted by card. Jahob soundly maps such formulas into stronger BAPA, using a simple syntactic translation that represents individual variables as singleton sets and approximates constructs unsupported by BAPA. Section 5 describes our preliminary experience with using our algorithm on formulas such as those in Figure 2, showing that the new algorithm is promising for detecting formula satisfiability.

QFBAPA and BAPA. The logic QFBAPA is the quantifier-free fragment of Boolean Algebra with Presburger Arithmetic (BAPA). In addition to the constructs in Figure 1, full BAPA supports arbitrary set and integer quantifiers. Feferman and Vaught [9, Section 8, Page 90] showed the decidability of a variant of BAPA and used it to show the decidability of generalized products of first-order structures. In [13,14] we formalize a decision procedure for BAPA and show that BAPA has the same complexity as the complexity of Presburger arithmetic (PA), namely alternating doubly exponential time with a linear number of alternations, denoted $\text{STA}(*, 2^{2^{n^{O(1)}}}, n)$ in [4], [11, Lecture 24].

BAPA admits quantifier elimination, which implies that QFBAPA formulas define the same class of relations on sets and integers as BAPA formulas, so they essentially have the same expressive power. Quantifier elimination also makes BAPA interesting as a potential shared language for combining multiple reasoning procedures [10].

1.1   Challenges in Checking QFBAPA Satisfiability

QFBAPA satisfiability is clearly NP-hard, because QFBAPA supports arbitrary propositional operators. Moreover, QFBAPA contains Boolean algebra of sets,

VC#	verification condition	property being checked
1	$x \notin$ content $\wedge$ size $=$ card content $\longrightarrow$ (size $= 0 \leftrightarrow$ content $= \emptyset$)	using invariant on size to prove correctness of an efficient emptiness check
2	$x \notin$ content $\wedge$ size $=$ card content $\longrightarrow$ size $+ 1 =$ card($\{x\} \cup$ content)	maintaining correct size when inserting fresh element
3	size $=$ card content $\wedge$ size1 $=$ card($\{x\} \cup$ content) $\longrightarrow$ size1 $\leq$ size $+ 1$	maintaining size after inserting any element
4	content $\subseteq$ alloc $\wedge$ $x_1 \notin$ alloc $\wedge$ $x_2 \notin$ alloc $\cup \{x_1\}$ $\wedge$ $x_3 \notin$ alloc $\cup \{x_1\} \cup \{x_2\}$ $\longrightarrow$ card (content $\cup \{x_1\} \cup \{x_2\} \cup \{x_3\}$) $=$ card content $+ 3$	allocating and inserting three objects into a container data structure
5	content $\subseteq$ alloc0 $\wedge$ $x_1 \notin$ alloc0 $\wedge$ alloc0 $\cup \{x_1\} \subseteq$ alloc1 $\wedge$ $x_2 \notin$ alloc1 $\wedge$ alloc1 $\cup \{x_2\} \subseteq$ alloc2 $\wedge$ $x_3 \notin$ alloc2 $\longrightarrow$ card (content $\cup \{x_1\} \cup \{x_2\} \cup \{x_3\}$) $=$ card content $+ 3$	allocating and inserting at least three objects into a container data structure
6	$x \in C \wedge C_1 = (C \setminus \{x\}) \wedge$ card(alloc1 $\setminus$ alloc0) $\leq 1 \wedge$ card(alloc2 $\setminus$ alloc1) $\leq$ card $C_1 \longrightarrow$ card (alloc2 $\setminus$ alloc0) $\leq$ card C	bound on the number of allocated objects in a recursive function that incorporates container C into another container

Fig. 2. Examples proved using our QFBAPA decision procedure

which has its own propositional structure, so even the satisfiability of individual atomic formulas is NP-hard. The challenge is therefore proving the membership in NP. Membership in NP means that there are short certificates for satisfiability of QFBAPA formulas, or, dually, that invalid QFBAPA formulas have short counterexamples. Despite the widespread occurrence of QFBAPA constraints, this result was not known until now. To understand why existing approaches fail to establish membership in NP, consider the following example QFBAPA formula:

$$|\mathcal{U}| = 100 \ \wedge \bigwedge_{0 \leq i < j \leq 10} |x_i \cup x_j| = 30 \wedge \bigwedge_{0 \leq i \leq 10} |x_i| = 20 \qquad (E)$$

Explicitly specifying set contents. The formula (E) has 10 set variables. Each of these variables represents a subset of the universe of 100 elements. Therefore, a straightforward certificate of satisfiability of this QFBAPA formula requires 100 bits for each set to indicate whether each element is in the set. Such certificate is therefore exponential in the size of the formula (we assume that 100 is represented using $\log_2 100$ bits). Such certificates therefore yield merely a membership of QFBAPA in NEXPTIME. Note that, even if we restrict the constants K in QFBAPA language to be 0 and 1, Presburger arithmetic expressions such as $k_1 = 1$, $k_{i+1} = k_i + k_i$ can efficiently encode large constants. Fundamentally, the reason we are interested in large set cardinalities is because they arise from small model theorem for Presburger arithmetic [20]; supporting them is necessary for verifying symbolic cardinality bounds and constraints such as $|x \cap y| = |z|$.

Abstraction using sizes of partitions. An alternative to examining set interpretations up to a certain size is to consider a complete partitioning of sets into disjoint Venn regions $x_1^c \cap \ldots \cap x_{10}^c$, $x_1^c \cap \ldots \cap x_{10}$, $\ldots$, $x_1 \cap \ldots \cap x_{10}$, and introduce one integer variable for the size each of these partitions, yielding 2^{10} variables $l_{0,\ldots,0}, l_{0,\ldots,1}, \ldots, l_{1,\ldots,1}$. We can then represent cardinality of any set expression as a sum of finitely many of these integer variables. This approach is widely known [19], [7, Chapter 11] and is often used to illustrate the very idea of Venn diagrams. It has the advantage of not being exponential in the cardinalities of sets, because it reasons about these cardinalities symbolically. It also naturally integrates with the PA structure of QFBAPA and allows reducing QFBAPA to quantifier-free PA, as we explain below. Unfortunately, its direct use introduces a number of integer variables that is exponential in the number of sets. This approach is the essence of previous algorithms for QFBAPA [29,24,19] and appears as a special case of our algorithm for quantified BAPA [13,14]. All these algorithms would yield exponentially large certificates for satisfiability of QFBAPA, specifying the values of exponentially many integer variables.

1.2   Our Results

We can summarize the results of this paper as follows:

1. The key contribution of this paper is an encoding of QFBAPA formulas into polynomially-sized quantifier-free PA formulas. Instead of using exponentially many Venn region cardinality variables $l_{0,\ldots,0}, l_{0,\ldots,1}, \ldots, l_{1,\ldots,1}$, we use polynomially many "generic" variables along with polynomially many indices that determine the region that each generic variable represents. In the example (E) above, which has 56 equations, we would introduce $N = g(56) = 502$ generic integer variables $l_{p_1^i,\ldots,p_{10}^i}$ for $1 \le i \le N$ that are a function of propositional variables $(p_1^i, \ldots, p_{10}^i) \in \{0,1\}^{10}$ for $1 \le i \le N$. The polynomially bounded function g is given by the equation (6) below. We assume that the remaining $2^{10} - g(56)$ Venn regions are all empty, which allows us to express any set expression b as a sum of those of the N integer variables $l_{p_1^i,\ldots,p_{10}^i}$ whose indices $p_1^i, \ldots, p_{10}^i$ identify Venn regions that belong to b.

2. The computation of a sufficient polynomial value for N is the second contribution of this paper. We start with the result [8] that if an element is in an integer cone generated by a set of vectors X of dimension d, then it is also in an integer cone generated by a "small" subset of X of size $N(d)$. This result implies that a system of equations with bounded coefficients, if satisfiable, has a *sparse solution* with only polynomially many non-zero variables, even if the number of variables in the system is exponential. As a consequence,

every satisfiable QFBAPA formula has a witness of polynomial size, which indicates the values of integer variables in the original QFBAPA formula, lists the Venn regions that are non-empty, and indicates the cardinalities of these non-empty regions. This application of [8] gives the membership of QFBAPA in NP, but, given the NP-hardness of satisfiability of the generated formulas, it is desirable to obtain as tight a bound on $N(d)$ as possible. We make the following steps towards the computation of a precise bound: 1) we compute the exact bound $N(d) = d$ for $d \leq 3$; 2) we identify a lower bound $N(d) \geq d + \lfloor \frac{d}{4} \rfloor$ for $d \geq 4$; 3) we provide several equivalent characterizations of vectors that achieve the optimal bound for any d; 4) we provide a more precise bound in the presence of cardinality constraints of the form $|b| \leq c$ and $|b| = c$ for a small constant c.

3. We describe our implementation of the algorithm in the context of the Jahob verification system and present preliminary experiments on the examples of Figure 2 and their variations.

Our previously reported results. We suggested the possibility of the existence of sparse solutions in the final version of [14], where we also established the complexity of quantified BAPA. In a previous technical report [17] we identified a PSPACE algorithm for QFBAPA, but the techniques used there are different and not needed for the results of this paper. A preliminary version of the current result is described in [12, Section 7.9].

2   Constructing Small Presburger Arithmetic Formulas

Given a QFBAPA formula, this section shows how to construct an associated polynomially larger quantifier-free PA formula. Section 3 then proves that the constructed formula is equisatisfiable with the original one.

Consider an arbitrary QFBAPA formula in the syntax of Figure 1. To analyze the problem, we first separate PA and BA parts of the formula by replacing $b_1 = b_2$ with $b_1 \subseteq b_2 \land b_2 \subseteq b_1$, replacing $b_1 \subseteq b_2$ with $|b_1 \cap b_2^c| = 0$, and then introducing integer variables k_i for all cardinality expressions $|b_i|$ occurring in the formula. With a linear increase in size, we obtain an equisatisfiable QFBAPA formula of the form $G \land F$ where G is a quantifier-free PA formula and F is of the form

$$\bigwedge_{i=0}^{p} |b_i| = k_i \tag{1}$$

We assume $b_0 = \mathcal{U}$ and $k_0 = \text{MAXC}$, i.e., the first constraint is $|\mathcal{U}| = \text{MAXC}$.

Let $y_1, \ldots, y_e$ be the set variables in $b_1, \ldots, b_p$. If we view each Boolean algebra formula b_i as a propositional formula, then for $\beta = (p_1, \ldots, p_e)$ where $p_i \in \{0, 1\}$ let $\llbracket b_i \rrbracket_\beta \in \{0, 1\}$ denote the truth value of b_i under the propositional valuation assigning the truth value p_i to the variable y_i. Let further s_β denote the Venn region associated with β, given by $s_\beta = \cap_{j=1}^{e} y_j^{p_j}$ where $y_j^0 = y_j^c$ is set complement and $y_j^1 = y_j$. Because b_i is a disjoint union of its corresponding Venn regions, we have $|b_i| = \sum_{\beta \models b_i} |s_\beta|$. For the sake of analysis, for each $\beta \in \{0,1\}^e$ introduce a non-negative integer variable l_β denoting $|s_\beta|$. Then (1) is equisatisfiable with the exponentially larger PA formula

$$\bigwedge_{i=0}^{p} \sum \{l_\beta \mid \beta \in \{0,1\}^e \wedge [\![b_i]\!]_\beta{=}1\} = k_i \qquad (2)$$

Instead of this exponentially large formula where β ranges over all 2^e propositional assignments, the idea of our paper is to check the satisfiability of an asymptotically smaller formula

$$\bigwedge_{i=0}^{p} \sum \{l_\beta \mid \beta \in \{\beta_1, \ldots, \beta_N\} \wedge [\![b_i]\!]_\beta{=}1\} = k_i \qquad (3)$$

where β ranges over a set of N assignments $\beta_1, \ldots, \beta_N$ for $\beta_i = (p_{i1}, \ldots, p_{ie})$ and p_{ij} are fresh free variables ranging over $\{0,1\}$. Let $d = p + 1$. We are interested in the best upper bound $N(d)$ on the number of non-zero Venn regions over all possible systems of equations. In the sequel we show that $N(d)$ is polynomial in d and therefore polynomial in the size of the original QFBAPA formula. This result implies that QFBAPA is in NP and gives an effective bound on how to construct a quantifier-free PA formula for checking the satisfiability of a given QFBAPA formula.

Encoding generic cardinality variables in PA. Formula (3) uses some PA constructs along with some meta-notation. We next explain how to write (3) as a polynomially large quantifier-free PA formula. Because there are only N distinct assignments β_j considered, we introduce one variable l_j for each $1 \leq j \leq N$, for a total of N integer variables. Let $c_{ij} = [\![b_i]\!]_{\beta_j}$ for $1 \leq i \leq p$ and $1 \leq j \leq N$. Then each conjunct of (3) becomes $\sum_{j=1}^{N} c_{ij}l_j = k_i$. It therefore suffices to show how to efficiently express sums with boolean variable (as opposed to constant) coefficients. For this we can use the standard conditional expression $\text{ite}(p, t_1, t_2)$, where p is a propositional formula and t_1, t_2 are integer terms. The $\text{ite}(p, t_1, t_2)$ expression evaluates to t_1 when p evaluates to true, and evaluates to t_2 when p evaluates to false. It can be efficiently eliminated by flattening the formula to contain no nested terms and then replacing $t = \text{ite}(p, t_1, t_2)$ with the formula $(p \rightarrow t = t_1) \wedge (\neg p \rightarrow t = t_2)$. (It is also directly available in the SMT-LIB format [23].) Using ite, we can express $c_{ij}l_j$ as $\text{ite}(c_{ij}, l_j, 0)$. Then (3) becomes $\bigwedge_{i=0}^{p} \sum_{j=1}^{N} \text{ite}([\![b_i]\!]_{\beta_j}, l_j, 0) = k_i$. Note that we can substitute the values k_i back into the original PA formula G, so there is no need to perform the separation into $G \wedge F$ in practice. We obtain the following simple summary of our algorithm: substitute each expression $|b_i|$ with $\sum_{j=1}^{N} \text{ite}([\![b_i]\!]_{\beta_j}, l_j, 0)$. Note that this translation of QFBAPA into PA is parameterized by N. Sufficiently large values of N guarantee soundness and are the subject of the following sections, which show that a polynomial value suffices. However, any value of N can be used to try to prove the existence of a satisfying assignment for QFBAPA formulas. because a satisfying assignment for N_0 implies the existence of satisfying assignments for all $N \geq N_0$, letting $l_j = 0$ for $N_0 + 1 \leq j \leq N$. This suggests an iterative algorithm of Figure 3 that starts with $N = 0$ and increases N until a counterexample is found or a provably sufficient bound is reached. 'break_symmetry' is a symmetry breaking predicate that imposes a lexicographical order on propositional variables β_j. 'set_expressions_into_card' transforms all boolean algebra expressions into form $|b_i| = 0$.

let findN$(f : \mathsf{QFBAPA})$: bool =
  let $d = \#$atomic_formulas(f)
  let $s_0 = \#$formulas_with_0_rhs(f)
  let $s_1 = \#$formulas_with_1_rhs(f)
  let $d_1 = d - s_0 - s_1$
  let $N_1 = $ **if** $(d_1 \leq 3)$ d_1
        else $\max\{n \mid 2^n \leq (n+1)^{d_1}\}$
  return $N_1 + s_1$
let makePA$(f : \mathsf{QFBAPA}, N : \text{int})$: QFPA =
  let $f_1 = f[|b_i| \mapsto \sum_{j=1}^{N} \mathtt{ite}([\![b_i]\!]_{\beta_j}, l_j, 0)]_i$
  return
  $((\bigwedge_j l_j \geq 0) \wedge$ break_symmetry$) \rightarrow f_1$

let valid$(f_0 : \mathsf{QFBAPA})$: bool =
  let $f = $ negation_normal_form(
    set_expressions_into_card(f_0))
  let $N_0 = $ findN(f);
  $N := 0$;
  while$(N \leq N_0)$ **do**
    let $f_{PA} = $ makePA(f, N)
    if $\neg$validPA(f_{PA}) **return** false;
    else $N := N + 1$;
  return true;

Fig. 3. Our algorithm for deciding QFBAPA formulas

3   Upper Bound on the Number of Non-zero Regions

We next prove that the number $N(d)$ of non-zero Venn regions can be assumed to be polynomial in d. Let $\mathbb{Z}$ denote the set of integers and $\mathbb{Z}_{\geq 0}$ denote the set of non-negative integers. We write $\sum X$ for $\sum_{y \in X} y$.

Definition 1. *For $X \subseteq \mathbb{Z}^d$ a set of integer vectors, let*

$$\text{int\_cone}(X) = \{\lambda_1 x_1 + \ldots + \lambda_t x_t \mid t \geq 0 \wedge x_1, \ldots, x_t \in X \wedge \lambda_1, \ldots, \lambda_n \in \mathbb{Z}_{\geq 0}\}$$

The following result is established as Theorem 1(ii) in [8].

Fact 1 (Eisenbrand, Shmonina (2005)). *Let $X \subseteq \mathbb{Z}^d$ be a finite set of integer vectors and $M = \max\{(\max_{i=1}^d |x_j^i|) \mid (x_j^1, \ldots, x_j^d) \in X\}$ be the bound on the coordinates of vectors in X. If $b \in \text{int\_cone}(X)$, then there exists a subset $\tilde{X} \subseteq X$ such that $b \in \text{int\_cone}(\tilde{X})$ and $|\tilde{X}| \leq 2d \log_2(4dM)$.*

To apply Fact 1 to formula (2), let $X = \{x_\beta \mid \beta \in \{0,1\}^e\}$ where $x_\beta \in \{0,1\}^e$ is given by

$$x_\beta = ([\![b_0]\!]_\beta, [\![b_1]\!]_\beta, \ldots, [\![b_e]\!]_\beta).$$

Fact 1 implies is that if $(k_0, k_1, \ldots, k_p) \in \text{int\_cone}(X)$ where k_i are as in formula (2), then $(k_0, k_1, \ldots, k_p) \in \text{int\_cone}(\tilde{X})$ where $|\tilde{X}| = 2d \log_2(4d)$ (note that

$M = 1$ because x_β are $\{0,1\}$-vectors). The subset $\tilde{X}$ corresponds to selecting a polynomial subset of N Venn region cardinality variables l_β and assuming that the remaining ones are zero. This implies that formulas (2) and (3) are equisatisfiable.

A direct application of Fact 1 yields $N = 2d \log_2(4d)$ bound, which is sufficient to prove that QFBAPA is in NP. However, because this bound is not tight, in the sequel we prove results that slightly strengthen the bound and provide additional insight into the problem.

4   Bounds and Nonredundant Integer Cone Generators

Definition 2. *Let* $X \subseteq \mathbb{Z}^d$. *We say that* X *is a* nonredundant integer cone generator *for* b, *and write* $NICG(X, b)$, *if both 1)* $b \in \text{int\_cone}(X)$, *and 2)* $b \notin \text{int\_cone}(X \setminus \{y\})$ *for every* $y \in X$.

In the sequel we consider only vectors of *non-negative* integers, so $X \subseteq \mathbb{Z}_{\geq 0}^d$.

Lemma 1 says that if $NICG(X, b)$ for some b, then the sums of vectors $\sum Y$ for $Y \subseteq X$ are uniquely generated elements of $\text{int\_cone}(X)$.

Lemma 1. *Suppose* $NICG(X, b)$ *for* $X \subseteq \mathbb{Z}_{\geq 0}^d$. *If* $\lambda_1, \lambda_2 : X \to \mathbb{Z}_{\geq 0}$ *such that*

$$\sum_{x \in X} \lambda_1(x)x = \sum_{x \in X} \lambda_2(x)x \tag{4}$$

and $\lambda_1(x) \in \{0, 1\}$ *for all* $x \in X$, *then* $\lambda_2 = \lambda_1$.

Proof. Suppose $NICG(X, b)$. Then $(0, \ldots, 0) \notin X$. Let $\lambda_1, \lambda_2 : X \to \mathbb{Z}_{\geq 0}$ such that (4) holds and $\lambda_1(x) \in \{0, 1\}$ for all $x \in X$, but $\lambda_2 \neq \lambda_1$. If there are vectors x on the left-hand side of (4) that also appear on the right-hand side, we can cancel them. We obtain an equality of the form (4) for distinct λ_1', λ_2' with the additional property that $\lambda_1'(x) = 1$ implies $\lambda_2'(x) = 0$. Moreover, not all $\lambda_1'(x)$ are equal to zero (otherwise the left-hand side would be zero vector and the right-hand side a vector with a strictly positive coordinate since $(0, \ldots, 0) \notin X$). By $b \in \text{int\_cone}(X)$, let $\lambda : X \to \mathbb{Z}_{\geq 0}$ such that $b = \sum_{x \in X} \lambda(x)x$. Let x_0 be such that $\lambda_1'(x_0) = 1$ and $\lambda(x_0) = \min\{\lambda(x) \mid \lambda_1'(x) = 1\}$. By construction, $\lambda_1'(x_0) = 1$ and $\lambda_2'(x_0) = 0$. We then have, with x in sums ranging over X:

$$
\begin{aligned}
b &= \sum_{\lambda_1'(x)=1} \lambda(x)x + \sum_{\lambda_1'(x)=0} \lambda(x)x \\
&= \sum_{\lambda_1'(x)=1} (\lambda(x) - \lambda(x_0))x + \lambda(x_0) \sum_{\lambda_1'(x)=1} x + \sum_{\lambda_1'(x)=0} \lambda(x)x \\
&= \sum_{\lambda_1'(x)=1} (\lambda(x) - \lambda(x_0))x + \lambda(x_0) \sum \lambda_2'(x)x + \sum_{\lambda_1'(x)=0} \lambda(x)x
\end{aligned}
$$

In the last sum, the coefficient next to x_0 is zero in all three terms. Because all coefficients are non-negative, we conclude $b \in \text{int\_cone}(X \setminus \{x_0\})$, contradicting $NICG(X, b)$. ∎

We write $NICG(X)$ as a shorthand for $NICG(X, \sum X)$. Theorem 1 gives several equivalent characterizations of $NICG(X)$. The equivalence of 1) and 4) is interesting because it justifies the use of $NICG(X)$ independently of the generated vector b.

Theorem 1. *Let $X \subseteq \mathbb{Z}_{\geq 0}^d$. The following statements are equivalent:*

1) *there exists a vector $b \in \mathbb{Z}_{\geq 0}^d$ such that $NICG(X, b)$;*
2) *If $\lambda_1, \lambda_2 : X \to \mathbb{Z}_{\geq 0}$ are non-negative integer coefficients for vectors in X such that*

$$\sum_{x \in X} \lambda_1(x)x = \sum_{x \in X} \lambda_2(x)x$$

   and $\lambda_1(x) \in \{0, 1\}$ for all $x \in X$, then $\lambda_2 = \lambda_1$.
3) *For $\{x_1, \ldots, x_n\} = X$ (for $x_1, \ldots, x_n$ distinct), the system of d equations expressed in vector form as*

$$\lambda(x_1)x_1 + \ldots + \lambda(x_n)x_n = \sum X \tag{5}$$

   has $(\lambda(x_1), \ldots, \lambda(x_n)) = (1, \ldots, 1)$ as the unique solution in $\mathbb{Z}_{\geq 0}^n$.
4) *$NICG(X)$.*

Proof. 1) $\to$ 2): This is Lemma 1.

2) $\to$ 3): Assume 2) and let $\lambda_1(x_i) = 1$ for $1 \leq i \leq n$. For any solution λ_2 we then have $\sum_{x \in X} \lambda_1(x)x = \sum_{x \in X} \lambda_2(x)x$, so $\lambda_2 = \lambda_1$. Therefore, λ_1 is the unique solution.

3) $\to$ 4): Assume 3). Clearly $\sum X \in \text{int\_cone}(X)$; it remains to prove that X is minimal. Let $y \in X$. For the sake of contradiction, suppose $\sum X \in \text{int\_cone}(X \setminus \{y\})$. Then there exists a solution $\lambda(x)$ for (5) with $\lambda(y) = 0 \neq 1$, a contradiction with the uniqueness of the solution.

4) $\to$ 1): Take $b = \sum X$. ∎

Corollary 1 is used in [8] to establish the bound on the size of X with $NICG(X)$. We obtain it directly from Lemma 1 taking $\lambda_2(x) \in \{0, 1\}$.

Corollary 1. *If $NICG(X)$ then for $Y_1, Y_2 \subseteq X$, $Y_1 \neq Y_2$ we have $\sum Y_1 \neq \sum Y_2$.*

Every set contains a NICG subset that generates a given element. To establish the existence of sparse solutions, it therefore suffices to establish bounds on the cardinality of X such that $NICG(X)$.

Lemma 2. *If $b \in \text{int\_cone}(X)$, then there exists $\tilde{X} \subseteq X$ with $b \in \text{int\_cone}(\tilde{X})$ and $NICG(\tilde{X}, b)$.*

Proof. If $b \in \text{int\_cone}(X)$ then by definition $b \in \text{int\_cone}(X_0)$ for a finite $X_0 \subseteq X$. If not $NICG(X_0, b)$, then $b \in \text{int\_cone}(X_1)$ where X_1 is a proper subset of X_0. Continuing in this fashion we obtain a finite maximal sequence $X_0 \supset X_1 \supset \ldots \supset X_k$ where $NICG(X_k, b)$, so we let $\tilde{X} = X_k$. ∎

Lemma 3. *If $NICG(X)$ and $Y \subseteq X$, then $NICG(Y)$.*

Define
$$g(d) = \max\{n \mid 2^n \le (n+1)^d\} \tag{6}$$

Theorem 2. *Let $X \subseteq \{0,1\}^d$, NICG(X), and $N = |X|$. Then for $d \ge 2$,*

$$N \le g(d) \le (1 + \varepsilon(d))(d \log_2 d) \tag{7}$$

where $\varepsilon(d) \le 1$ and $\lim_{d \to \infty} \varepsilon(d) = 0$.

Proof. Let $X \subseteq \{0,1\}^d$, NICG(X) and $N = |X|$. We prove $2^N \le (N+1)^d$. Suppose that, on the contrary, $2^N > (N+1)^d$. If $\sum Y = (x^1, \ldots, x^d)$ for $Y \subseteq X$, then $0 \le x^j \le N$ because $Y \subseteq \{0,1\}^d$ and $|Y| \le N$. Therefore, there are only $(N+1)^d$ possible sums $\sum Y$. Because there are 2^N subsets $Y \subseteq X$, there exist two distinct subsets $U, V \in 2^X$ such that $\sum U = \sum V$. This contradicts Corollary 1. Therefore, $2^N \le (N+1)^d$. We next show that any n for which $2^n \le (n+1)^d$ is bounded by $(1 + \varepsilon(d))(d \log_2 d)$. Using elementary reasoning, from $2^n \le (n+1)$ we obtain $n \le 2d \log_2(2n)$ (see [8], [12, Section 7.9.3] for details). Substituting this bound on n back into $n \le d \log_2(n+1)$ we obtain

$$n \le d \log_2(n+1) \le d \log_2(2d \log_2(2d) + 1) = d \log_2(2d(\log_2(2d) + \tfrac{1}{2d}))$$

$$= d(1 + \log_2 d + \log_2(\log_2(2d) + \tfrac{1}{2d})) = d \log_2 d(1 + \tfrac{1 + \log_2(\log_2(2d) + \frac{1}{2d})}{\log_2 d})$$

so we can let $\varepsilon(d) = (1 + \log_2(\log_2 d + 1 + \tfrac{1}{2d}))/\log_2 d$.   ∎

Define $N(d) = \max\{|X| \mid X \subseteq \{0,1\}^d \wedge \text{NICG}(X)\}$. We have shown $N(d) \le g(d)$. Thanks to the monotonicity of g, we can compute $g(d)$ efficiently using binary search.

4.1 Lower Bounds

Although we currently do not have tight bounds for $N(d)$, in this section we show several observations about lower bounds for $N(d)$.

We first show $d \le N(d)$.

Lemma 4. *Let $X = \{(x_i^1, \ldots, x_i^d) \mid 1 \le i \le n\}$ and*

$$X^+ = \{(x_i^1, \ldots, x_i^d, 0) \mid 1 \le i \le n\} \cup \{(0, \ldots, 0, 1)\}$$

Then NICG(X) if and only if NICG(X^+).

Corollary 2. $N(d) + 1 \le N(d+1)$ *for all $d \ge 1$.*

Proof. Let $X \subseteq \{0,1\}^d$, NICG(X), and $|X| = N(d)$. Then NICG(X^+) by Lemma 4 and $|X^+| = N(d) + 1$, which implies $N(d+1) \ge N(d) + 1$.   ∎

Lemma 5. $d \le N(d)$. *Specifically, NICG($\{e_1, \ldots, e_d\}$) where e_i are unit vectors.*

Note that for $X = \{e_1, \ldots, e_d\}$ we have $\text{int\_cone}(X) = \mathbb{Z}_{\geq 0}^d$, which implies that X is a *maximal* NICG, in the sense that no proper superset $W \supset X$ has the property $\text{NICG}(W)$.

$N(d) = d$ for $d \in \{1, 2, 3\}$. We next show that for $d \in \{1, 2, 3\}$ not only $d \leq N(d)$ but also $N(d) \leq d$.

Lemma 6. $N(d) = d$ for $d \in \{1, 2, 3\}$.

Proof. By Corollary 2, if $N(d + 1) = d + 1$, then $N(d) + 1 \leq d + 1$ so $N(d) \leq d$. Therefore, $N(3) = 3$ implies $N(2) = 2$ as well, so we can take $d = 3$.

If $N(d) > d$, then there exists a set X with $\text{NICG}(X)$ and $|X| > d$. From Lemma 3, a subset $X_0 \subseteq X$ with $|X_0| = d + 1$ also satisfies $\text{NICG}(X_0)$. Therefore, $N(3) = 3$ is equivalent to showing that there is no set $X \subseteq \{0, 1\}^3$ with $\text{NICG}(X)$ and $|X| = 4$.

Consider a possible counterexample $X = \{x_1, x_2, x_3, x_4\} \subseteq \{0, 1\}^3$ with $b \in \text{int\_cone}(X)$. By previous argument on real-valued relaxation, $N_R(3) = 3$, so b is in convex cone of some three vectors from X, say $b \in \text{cone}(\{x_1, x_2, x_3\})$. On the other hand, $b \notin \text{int\_cone}(\{x_1, x_2, x_3\})$. If we consider a system $\lambda_1 x_1 + \lambda_2 x_2 + \lambda_3 x_3 = b$ this implies that such system has solution over non-negative reals, but not over non-negative integers. This can only happen if the absolute value of the determinant of the matrix $[x_1, x_2; x_3]$ is greater than 1. The only set of three vectors for which this can occur is $X_1 = \{(0, 1, 1), (1, 0, 1), (1, 1, 0)\}$. We then consider all possibilities for the fourth vector in X, which, modulo permutations of coordinates, are $(0, 0, 0)$, $(1, 1, 1)$, $(1, 1, 0)$, and $(1, 0, 0)$. However, adding any of these vectors violates the uniqueness of the solution to $\lambda_1 x_1 + \lambda_2 x_2 + \lambda_3 x_3 + \lambda_4 x_4 = \sum X$, so $\text{NICG}(X)$ does not hold by Theorem 1, condition 3). ∎

$N = \frac{5}{4}d - \frac{3}{4}$ lower bound. We next show that there exists an example $X_5 \subseteq \{0, 1\}^4$ with $\text{NICG}(X_5)$ and $|X_5| = 5$. From this it follows that $N(d) > d$ for all $d \geq 4$.

Consider the following system of 4 equations with 5 variables, where all variable coefficients are in $\{0, 1\}$. (We found this example by narrowing down the search using the observations on minimal counterexamples in the proof of Lemma 6.)

$$
\begin{aligned}
\lambda_1 + \lambda_2 + \lambda_3 \qquad\qquad &= 3 \\
\lambda_2 + \lambda_3 + \lambda_4 \quad\; &= 3 \\
\lambda_1 \qquad + \lambda_3 + \lambda_4 + \lambda_5 &= 4 \\
\lambda_1 + \lambda_2 \qquad + \lambda_4 + \lambda_5 &= 4
\end{aligned}
\tag{8}
$$

It is easy to see that the system has $(1, 1, 1, 1, 1)$ as *the only solution* in the space of non-negative integers. Note that all variables are non-zero in this solution. The five columns of the system (8) correspond to the set of vectors $X_5 = \{(1, 0, 1, 1), (1, 1, 0, 1), (1, 1, 1, 0), (0, 1, 1, 1), (0, 0, 1, 1)\}$ such that $\text{NICG}(X_5)$. The set X_5 is also a maximal NICG, because adding any of the remaining 9 non-zero vectors in $\{0, 1\}^4 \setminus X_5$ results in a set that is not NICG.

This argument shows that there exist maximal NICG of size larger than d for $d \geq 4$. As we have remarked before, the set of d unit vectors is a maximal NICG for every d, which means that, unlike linearly independent sets of vectors over a field or other independent sets in a matroid [28], there are maximal NICG sets of different cardinality. Nevertheless, Lemma 2 and Lemma 3 show that some of the properties of independent sets do hold for vectors in X where $\text{NICG}(X)$.

Note also that X_5 is not a Hilbert basis [26]. Namely, we have that $(1,1,1,1) \in \text{cone}(X_5) \setminus \text{int\_cone}(X_5)$ because $(1,1,1,1) = 1/3((1,0,1,1) + (1,1,0,1) + (1,1,1,0) + (0,1,1,1))$. This illustrates why previous results on Hilbert bases do not directly apply to the notion of NICG.

Using k identical copies of X_5 (with 4 equations in a group mentioning a disjoint set of 5 variables) we obtain systems of $4k$ equations with $5k$ variables such that the only solution is a vector $(1, \ldots, 1)$ of all ones. By adding p unit vector columns for $1 \leq p \leq 3$, we also obtain systems of $4k + p$ equations with $5k + p$ variables, with $N = \frac{5}{4}d - \frac{p}{4} = d + \lfloor \frac{d}{4} \rfloor \geq \frac{5}{4}d - \frac{3}{4}$, which, in particular, shows that $N = d$ upper bound is invalid for all $d \geq 4$.

4.2   Better Upper Bounds for Small Cardinalities

Consider a QFBAPA formula in separated form $G \wedge F$ as in Section 2, where G is a PA formula and F is given by (2). Our bounds on N so far are a function of d alone. For many formulas arising in practice we can reduce N using bounds on the values that k_i can take, as explained in this section. In our experience, this improvement significantly reduced the overall running time of our algorithm.

Improved bound. Suppose that we can conclude that if the formula $F \wedge G$ is satisfiable, then there exists a satisfying assignment for variables where $0 \leq k_i \leq c_i$ (if we do not have a bound for some i, we let $c_i = \infty$). We can often obtain such a bound c_i by transforming G to negation-normal form and checking if k_i occurs in literals such as $k_i = 0$ or $k_i < c_i$. Given the bounds c_i, we have the following inequality that generalizes the one in Theorem 2:

$$2^N \leq \prod_{i=1}^{d}(1 + \min(c_i, N)) \tag{9}$$

The reasoning follows the proof of Theorem 2.

Consequences for common cases. Two common cases that we can easily take advantage of are bounds $c_i = 0$ and $c_i = 1$. Suppose that for $i \in I_0$ we have $c_i = 0$ and for $i \in I_1$ (where $I_1 \cap I_0 = \emptyset$) we have $c_i = 1$. Let $|I_0| = s_0$ and $|I_1| = s_1$. Letting $c_i = \infty$ for $i \notin I_0 \cup I_1$, from (9) we obtain $2^N \leq 2^{s_1}(N + 1)^{d-s_0-s_1}$. For $c_i = 0$ and $c_i = 1$ we can in fact obtain a slightly stronger bound from the condition $2^N \leq 2^{s_1}(N-s_1+1)^{d-s_0-s_1}$, which can be justified as follows. Consider a satisfying assignment for $G \wedge F$. When $i \in I_0$, we can eliminate the equation $|b_i| = k_i$ in (2) and remove all l_β such that $[\![b_i]\!]_\beta = 1$ from the remaining equations, while preserving the property that all vectors in the matrix corresponding to (2) are in $\{0, 1\}$. The bound on non-zero variables for the resulting system with $d - s_0$ equations therefore applies to the original system as well. Similarly, if $i \in I_1$ and the right-hand side $k_i = 1$, then we know that in the satisfying assignment there is exactly one β_1 such that $[\![b_i]\!]_{\beta_1} = 1$, so we can remove the equation $|b_i| = 1$, and for all j such that $[\![b_j]\!]_{\beta_1} = 1$ subtract 1 from k_j and remove l_{β_1}. The result is again a system with $\{0, 1\}$ coefficients, but one less equation. Increasing the bound for the resulting system by one (to account for $l_{\beta_1} = 1$) we obtain the bound for the original system, which proves our claim.

These observations are important in practice because they imply that pure boolean algebra expressions (such as $b_1 \subseteq b_2$ and $b_1 = b_2$) do not increase N when they occur positively, since for them $c_i = 0$. The bound $c_i = 1$ also frequently occurs in our examples because we encode elements as singleton sets.

5   Preliminary Experiments

Figure 4 shows formula sizes and running times for the original BAPA algorithm and our new QFBAPA algorithm (Figure 3) on formulas of Figure 2 and their variations.[1]

VC# (*=invalid)	BAPA		QFBAPA		
	PA size(nodes)	total time(s)	PA size(nodes)	iteration of N	total time(s)
1	39	< 0.1	190	3	< 0.1
2	57	< 0.1	220	4	0.1
2a	1049	1.8	840	5	15.4
*2b	946	1.4	87	1	< 0.1
3	51	< 0.1	131	3	< 0.1
3a	532	0.4	688	5	7.3
*3b	532	0.4	92	1	< 0.1
4	546	0.5	1328	8	> 100.0
*4b	554	0.5	284	2	0.1
5	2386	13.6	1750	8	> 100.0
*5b	2318	13.4	570	3	0.4
6	442	0.4	2613	18	> 100.0
6a	10822	> 100.0	8401	23	> 100.0
*6b	10822	> 100.0	1021	3	0.8
*6c	10563	> 100.0	990	3	0.9

Fig. 4. Results for variations of formulas in Figure 2

The examples $2a$, $3a$, $6a$ are more realistic versions of examples 2, 3, 6 because they contain some unnecessary assumptions that would normally appear in an automatically generated verification condition. Syntactically determining which assumptions are useful is a difficult problem [6], so it is reasonable to leave this

---

[1] The examples are available from http://lara.epfl.ch/~kuncak/cade07examples

task to the the decision procedure. Formulas $1-6$, $2a$, $3a$, $6a$ are all valid. Formulas $2b$, $3b$, $4b$, $5b$, $6b$, $6c$ are obtained from $2a$, $3a$, 4, 5, $6a$, $6a$, respectively, by dropping one of the necessary assumptions or changing the relation between integers to make the formula invalid. All invalid formulas are marked by $*$ in Figure 4. In addition to the running time, the figure shows the number of abstract syntax tree nodes in the generated quantifier-free Presburger arithmetic formulas. For the QFBAPA algorithm, the "iteration of N" column indicates the number of non-empty Venn regions for which a counterexample was found, in the case when the formula is invalid. For valid formulas this column indicates the bound that was computed as being sufficient to establish formula validity; this bound is actually explored whenever validity checking terminates in the given timeout. In any case, the size of the generated PA formula corresponds to this value of N. The running time for QFBAPA is the sum of running times over all iterations, corresponding to the overall running time of the algorithm. We ran the experiments on 3GHz, 1MB cache, 2GB RAM workstation. As a decision procedure for quantifier-free PA we used CVC3 version 20070217 [3].

Discussion. These results suggest that our new algorithm is more effective than the previous algorithm for finding counterexamples of invalid formulas. On large valid formulas our algorithm generates more compact quantifier-free PA formulas than the introduction of exponentially many variables, but the complexity of generated formulas makes them difficult to solve, leading to worse overall performance. Nevertheless, on small formulas our new algorithm terminates, reaching the computed upper bound on N and thus establishing formula validity.

6   Related Work

We have presented the the first decision procedure for a logic with sets and cardinality constraints that does not explicitly construct all set partitions. Using a new form of small model representation property, the "small number of non-zero variables" property, we obtained a non-deterministic polynomial-time algorithm that can be solved by producing polynomially large quantifier-free Presburger arithmetic formulas. A polynomial bound sufficient for NP membership can be derived from [8]. In addition to improvements in the bounds that take into account small cardinalities, we introduced the notion of non-redundant integer cone generators and established their properties. Previous results, such as [26], consider matroids and Hilbert bases. As we remark in Section 4.1, the sets of vectors X with $\mathrm{NICG}(X)$ do not form a matroid, and maximal $\mathrm{NICG}(X)$ need not be a Hilbert basis. The equations generated from QFBAPA problems are more difficult than set packing and set partitioning problems [2], because our partition cardinality variables are not restricted to $\{0, 1\}$.

Relationship to counting SAT. Although similarly looking, QFBAPA satisfiability is different from the #SAT problem [27]. Solving QFBAPA formula differs from counting the number of satisfying assignments of propositional formulas because set partitions may possibly be empty. An immediate consequence of our results is that there is no QFBAPA formula of size polynomial in n that would express the property "all 2^n partitions of n sets are non-empty".

Reasoning about sets. The quantifier-free fragment of BA is shown NP-complete in [18]; see [15] for a generalization of this result using the parameterized complexity of the Bernays-Schönfinkel-Ramsey class of first-order logic [5, Page 258]. The decision procedure for quantifier-free fragment with cardinalities in [7, Chapter 11] introduces exponentially many integer variables to reduce the problem to PA.

Using first-order provers. With appropriate axioms and decision procedures, first-order provers can also be used to reason about QFBAPA-like constraints, as shown, for example, by SPASS+T [22]. Our decision procedure by itself is not nearly as widely applicable as SPASS+T, but is complete for its domain (for example, it proves a formulation of problem number (73) from [22] in 0.1 seconds whereas SPASS+T is reported to time out in [22]).

Acknowledgements. Alexandr Andoni suggested using binary search instead of an analytical expression to compute the inverse of $N/\log(N + 1)$. Stefan Andrei and Bruno Marnette made remarks about result [17]. Emina Torlak used her Kodkod constraint solver to search for counterexamples of the conjecture $N(3) = 3$ (Section 4.1 shows that this conjecture is true). We thank Zoran Džunić, Michael Sipser, and the anonymous reviewers for useful feedback.

References

1. Baader, F., Calvanese, D., McGuinness, D., Nardi, D., Patel-Schneider, P. (eds.): The Description Logic Handbook: Theory, Implementation and Applications. CUP (2003)
2. Balas, E., Padberg, M.W.: Set partitioning: A survey. SIAM Review 18(4), 710–760 (1976)
3. Barrett, C., Berezin, S.: CVC Lite: A new implementation of the cooperating validity checker. In: Alur, R., Peled, D.A. (eds.) CAV 2004. LNCS, vol. 3114, pp. 515–518. Springer, Heidelberg (2004)
4. Berman, L.: The complexity of logical theories. Theoretical Computer Science 11(1), 71–77 (1980)
5. Börger, E., Grädel, E., Gurevich, Y.: The Classical Decision Problem. Springer, Heidelberg (1997)
6. Bouillaguet, C., Kuncak, V., Wies, T., Zee, K., Rinard, M.: Using first-order theorem provers in a data structure verification system. In: Cook, B., Podelski, A. (eds.) VMCAI 2007. LNCS, vol. 4349, Springer, Heidelberg (2007)
7. Cantone, D., Omodeo, E., Policriti, A.: Set Theory for Computing. Springer, Heidelberg (2001)
8. Eisenbrand, F., Shmonina, G.: Carathéodory bounds for integer cones. Operations Research Letters 34(5), 564–568 (2006),
   http://dx.doi.org/10.1016/j.orl.2005.09.008
9. Feferman, S., Vaught, R.L.: The first order properties of products of algebraic systems. Fundamenta Mathematicae 47, 57–103 (1959)

10. Ghilardi, S.: Model theoretic methods in combined constraint satisfiability. Journal of Automated Reasoning 33(3-4), 221–249 (2005)
11. Kozen, D.: Theory of Computation. Springer, Heidelberg (2006)
12. Kuncak, V.: Modular Data Structure Verification. PhD thesis, EECS Department, Massachusetts Institute of Technology (February 2007)
13. Kuncak, V., Nguyen, H.H., Rinard, M.: An algorithm for deciding BAPA: Boolean Algebra with Presburger Arithmetic. In: Nieuwenhuis, R. (ed.) Automated Deduction – CADE-20. LNCS (LNAI), vol. 3632, Springer, Heidelberg (2005)
14. Kuncak, V., Nguyen, H., Rinard, M.: Deciding Boolean Algebra with Presburger Arithmetic. J. of Automated Reasoning (2006),
    http://dx.doi.org/10.1007/s10817-006-9042-1
15. Kuncak, V., Rinard, M.: Decision procedures for set-valued fields. In: 1st International Workshop on Abstract Interpretation of Object-Oriented Languages (AIOOL 2005) (2005)
16. Lev, I.: Precise understanding of natural language. Stanford Univeristy PhD dissertation draft (February 2007)
17. Marnette, B., Kuncak, V., Rinard, M.: On algorithms and complexity for sets with cardinality constraints. Technical report, MIT CSAIL (August 2005)
18. Marriott, K., Odersky, M.: Negative boolean constraints. Technical Report 94/203, Monash University (August 1994)
19. Ohlbach, H.J., Koehler, J.: How to extend a formal system with a boolean algebra component. In: Bibel, W., Schmidt, P.H. (eds.) Automated Deduction. A Basis for Applications, vol. III, Kluwer Academic Publishers, Dordrecht (1998)
20. Papadimitriou, C.H.: On the complexity of integer programming. J. ACM 28(4), 765–768 (1981)
21. Pratt-Hartmann, I.: Complexity of the two-variable fragment with counting quantifiers. Journal of Logic, Language and Information 14(3), 369–395 (2005)
22. Prevosto, V., Waldmann, U.: SPASS+T. In: ESCoR: Empirically Successful Computerized Reasoning, vol. 192 (2006)
23. Ranise, S., Tinelli, C.: The SMT-LIB Standard: Version 1.2. Technical report, Department of Computer Science, The University of Iowa (2006) Available at http://www.SMT-LIB.org
24. Revesz, P.: Quantifier-elimination for the first-order theory of boolean algebras with linear cardinality constraints. In: Benczúr, A.A., Demetrovics, J., Gottlob, G. (eds.) ADBIS 2004. LNCS, vol. 3255, Springer, Heidelberg (2004)
25. Revesz, P.Z.: The expressivity of constraint query languages with boolean algebra linear cardinality constraints. In: Eder, J., Haav, H.-M., Kalja, A., Penjam, J. (eds.) ADBIS 2005. LNCS, vol. 3631, pp. 167–182. Springer, Heidelberg (2005)
26. Sebö, A.: Hilbert bases, Caratheodory's theorem and combinatorial optimization. In: Kannan, R., Pulleyblank, W. (eds.) Integer Programming and Combinatorial Optimization I, University of Waterloo Press (1990)
27. Toda, S.: PP is as hard as the polynomial-time hierarchy. SIAM Journal on Computing 20(5), 865–877 (1991)
28. Whitney, H.: On the abstract properties of linear independence. American Journal of Mathematics 57, 509–533 (1935)
29. Zarba, C.G.: Combining sets with cardinals. J. of Automated Reasoning 34(1) (2005)

Improvements in Formula Generalization

Markus Aderhold

Fachgebiet Programmiermethodik, Technische Universität Darmstadt, Germany
aderhold@pm.tu-darmstadt.de

Abstract. For proofs by induction it is often necessary to generalize statements to strengthen the induction hypotheses. This paper presents improved heuristics to generalize away subterms, unnecessary conditions and function symbols in a formula. This resolves shortcomings that we encountered within an experimental evaluation of generalization heuristics from the literature. Our generalization method has been implemented in the verification tool √eriFun. An evaluation with examples from the literature as well as several case studies of our own demonstrates the success of our development.

1 Introduction

When proving statements within a first-order theory that includes induction, one frequently needs to invent and prove auxiliary statements to obtain a proof of the original statement. This process is known as *lemma discovery* [7]. A special case of lemma discovery is *generalization*. This is the process of deriving a statement φ_{gen} from a proof obligation φ such that φ_{gen} entails φ and—in contrast to φ—the generalization φ_{gen} can be proved by induction. Here we consider heuristics that aim at computing such generalizations automatically.

Formally, a generalization can be obtained by applying first-order inference rules in the *inverse* direction [14]. In this paper, we consider the generalization rules *inverse substitution*, *inverse weakening*, and *inverse functionality*. We resolve the indeterminism of this rule system by developing heuristics for when and how to apply these rules. The challenge in the design of such heuristics is to avoid over-generalizations (where φ_{gen} is false) and at the same time not to be overly cautious and miss useful generalizations. We improve upon existing heuristics [4,5,8,9] by making our heuristics more liberal and by using a *disprover* [3] to detect over-generalizations. The disprover tries to find an instance of φ_{gen} that renders the formula false. Despite its incompleteness, the disprover helps to find over-generalizations that slipped through the heuristics.

Our generalization heuristics have been integrated and proved successful in √eriFun [1,16,17], an interactive system for verifying statements about programs written in the functional programming language $\mathcal{L}$ [15]. This language consists of definition principles for freely generated polymorphic data types, for procedures operating on these data types based on recursion, case analyses, let-expressions and functional composition, and for statements (called "lemmas") about the data types and procedures. Lemmas are defined by universally quantified Boolean

F. Pfenning (Ed.): CADE 2007, LNAI 4603, pp. 231–246, 2007.
© Springer-Verlag Berlin Heidelberg 2007

```
structure bool <= true, false
structure ℕ <= 0, ⁺(⁻ : ℕ)
structure list[@A] <= ε, [infix] ::(hd : @A,  tl : list[@A])
function [infix] >(x, y : ℕ) : bool <=
if x = 0 then false else if y = 0 then true else ⁻(x) > ⁻(y) end end
function [infix] <>(k, l : list[@A]) : list[@A] <=
if k = ε then l else hd(k) :: (tl(k) <> l) end
function rev(k : list[@A]) : list[@A] <=
if k = ε then ε else rev(tl(k)) <> hd(k) :: ε end
lemma rev_rev <= ∀k : list[@A] rev(rev(k)) = k
```

Fig. 1. A simple $\mathcal{L}$-program

terms using case analyses and truth values to represent connectives. We use the functional notation $if\{B, A_1, A_2\}$ instead of *if B then A_1 else A_2 end* in lemma definitions; e. g., $if\{B, A, true\}$ represents the implication $B \rightarrow A$.

Figure 1 shows an example of an $\mathcal{L}$-program that defines a polymorphic data type $list[@A]$, list concatenation $<>$, and list reversal *rev*. In this program, the symbols *true* and *false* are *constructors* of type *bool*. ℕ denotes the data type of natural numbers with constructors 0 and $^+(\ldots)$ (denoting the successor function). Likewise, ε and :: construct lists. Each argument position of a constructor is assigned a *selector* function. For example, $^-(\ldots)$ (denoting the predecessor function) is the only selector of $^+(\ldots)$, and *hd* and *tl* are the selectors of constructor :: for lists. Expressions of the form $?cons(t)$ for a constructor *cons* and corresponding selectors sel_i are used as shorthand notation for $t = cons(sel_1(t), \ldots, sel_n(t))$, so $?::(k)$ holds if $k \neq \varepsilon$, for example.

Subsequently, we let $\Sigma(P)$ denote the signature of all function symbols defined by an $\mathcal{L}$-program P. An operational semantics for $\mathcal{L}$-programs P is defined by an interpreter $eval_P : \mathcal{T}(\Sigma(P)) \mapsto \mathcal{T}(\Sigma(P))$ which either maps a ground term[1] to a constructor ground term or returns a so-called *stuck computation* (e. g., $eval_P(hd(\varepsilon)) = hd(\varepsilon)$), using the definitions of the procedures and data types in P, cf. [13,15,18]. A lemma **lemma** *name* $<= \forall x_1 : \tau_1, \ldots, x_n : \tau_n \; b$ is *true* if each constructor ground instance of the lemma body b is evaluated to *true* by $eval_P$, see [13,15,18] for formal details.

In ✓eriFun, lemmas are proved using a sequent calculus, called the *HPL-calculus* [17]. A *sequent* of the form $\langle H, IH \mapsto goal \rangle$ consists of a finite set H of literals[2] (defining the base or step case of an induction), a finite set IH of induction hypotheses (given by Boolean terms), and a Boolean goal term *goal*. A sequent is *true* if each constructor ground instance of *goal* is evaluated to *true* whenever the corresponding instances of H and IH are evaluated to *true*. A proof is represented by a finite *proof tree* whose nodes are labeled with sequents. For a lemma with body b, the root node is given by the *initial sequent* $\langle \emptyset, \emptyset \mapsto b \rangle$.

---

[1] As usual, $\mathcal{T}(\Sigma(P), \mathcal{V})$ denotes the set of all terms over $\Sigma(P)$ and a set $\mathcal{V}$ of variables. We write $\mathcal{T}(\Sigma(P))$ instead of $\mathcal{T}(\Sigma(P), \emptyset)$ for the set of all ground terms over $\Sigma(P)$.

[2] An *atom* is an *if*-free Boolean term. A *literal* is an atom A or a negated atom $\neg A$, where the latter abbreviates $if\{A, false, true\}$.

Child nodes are obtained by applying a proof rule of the HPL-calculus to a sequent. Each proof rule is *sound* in the sense that the truth of all child sequents entails the truth of the parent sequent. If each leaf of the proof tree is of the form $\langle \dots, \dots \mapsto true \rangle$, the proof tree is *closed*, and we thus have a proof of the lemma.

In our context, the following proof rules are of particular interest (for further proof rules see [13, 17]): *Induction* creates the base and step sequents for an initial sequent wrt. an induction axiom. *Simplification* symbolically evaluates the goal term *goal* of a sequent by pure first-order reasoning, yielding an equivalent goal term *s-eval$_P$(goal)*. *Use Lemma* applies a lemma or induction hypothesis to a sequent, and *Apply Equation* replaces a subterm of *goal* with an equal term.

√eriFun's *Verify Tactic* builds a proof tree by heuristically applying some proof rules. A proof typically starts with *Induction* wrt. an induction axiom suggested by the system's *induction heuristic*. Then the tactic tries to close the proof tree by applying *Simplification* to the child nodes. It also employs *Use Lemma* and *Apply Equation* to use heuristically helpful induction hypotheses if they have not already been used by the previous *Simplification*. If it fails to close the proof tree, it is usually beneficial to *generalize* the sequent of a leaf node before trying to prove the remaining proof obligation by another induction.

A proof by induction without prior generalization can fail if some subterm blocks the application of an induction hypothesis. For instance, when trying to prove $\forall n, y, z : \mathbb{N}\ fac(n) + (y + z) = (fac(n) + y) + z$ by induction on either n, y or z, it is impossible to apply the induction hypothesis if procedure "+" is defined recursively in its first argument [14]. The solution is to use the generalization rule *inverse substitution* to replace the occurrences of $fac(n)$ with a fresh variable x, yielding $\forall x, y, z : \mathbb{N}\ x + (y + z) = (x + y) + z$. This is a goal-directed generalization: For a procedure f we define $\mathcal{RP}(f)$ as the set of *recursion position sets* of f. The elements of each recursion position set $I \in \mathcal{RP}(f)$ denote the indices of the formal parameters of f that are relevant to prove termination of f; e.g., $\mathcal{RP}(+) = \{\{1\}\}$ and $\mathcal{RP}(>) = \{\{1\}, \{2\}\}$.[3] A subterm t_i of $f(t_1, \dots, t_n)$ occurs in a *recursion position* if there is some $I \in \mathcal{RP}(f)$ such that $i \in I$. Variables in recursion positions are good candidates for induction [4, 14], because this allows for the application of the definitions of procedures. As $fac(n)$ occupies a recursion position in the above formula, generalizing $fac(n)$ to a fresh variable x offers the new possibility to induct on x. We will develop separate heuristics for *inverse substitution* to generalize selector terms (e.g., $^-(n)$), other non-variable terms (e.g., $fac(n)$), or variables. As a proof can also fail if the formula contains unnecessary (pre-)conditions or function symbols, we will furthermore design heuristics for *inverse weakening* and *inverse functionality*, respectively.

Section 2 describes our generalization heuristics in detail. We compare the approach with other proposals in Sect. 3 and evaluate our heuristics on numerous examples in Sect. 4. Section 5 concludes with an outlook on future work.

---

[3] $\mathcal{RP}(f)$ is computed by the system's algorithm for termination analysis.

2   Generalization Heuristics

If the sequent $\langle H, IH \mapsto goal \rangle$ to be generalized contains helpful induction hypotheses, we assume that ✔eriFun's *Verify Tactic* or some user interactions have already used them to modify the goal term. Therefore, our heuristics ignore the set IH and start with $\langle H, \emptyset \mapsto goal \rangle$, which is a common first generalization step [5, 8, 9]. The rationale behind this is that unused induction hypotheses are heuristically useless.

We apply *inverse substitution* to eliminate selectors (Sect. 2.1) and get a new sequent $\langle H', \emptyset \mapsto goal' \rangle$. Then we iteratively consider the other generalization heuristics for the formula $\varphi := s\text{-}eval_P(\bigwedge H' \to goal')$. In each iteration we apply the first heuristic to φ that succeeds:

1. *inverse weakening* to remove unnecessary conditions (Sect. 2.4)
2. *inverse substitution* to generalize apart variable occurrences (Sect. 2.3)
3. *inverse substitution* for common non-variable subterms (Sect. 2.2)
4. *inverse functionality* to remove unnecessary function symbols (Sect. 2.5)

When one of these heuristics has transformed φ into another formula φ_{gen}, we use $\varphi := s\text{-}eval_P(\varphi_{gen})$ for the next iteration. If none of the heuristics has found a generalization, we return formula φ and terminate the generalization process.

The motivation for the order of the heuristics is that selector elimination first tidies up the result of a previous destructor style induction. As unnecessary conditions may mislead the remaining heuristics (e. g., they change the number of subterm occurrences), they should be removed as early as possible by *inverse weakening*. *Inverse substitution* prefers generalizing apart variable occurrences to generalizing away non-variable subterms, so that $k <> (k <> k) = (k <> k) <> k$ is generalized to $k' <> (k <> k) = (k' <> k) <> k$ without considering the over-generalization $k <> l = l <> k$ first. *Inverse functionality* is not needed too often and tends to suggest over-generalizations, so we assign it the lowest priority.

2.1   Inverse Substitution: Selector Elimination

In destructor style induction [6, 14], induction hypotheses are basically formed by replacing the induction variable(s) with selector terms (e. g., n with $^-(n)$ or k with $tl(k)$). When the proof of a step case fails, we typically have a goal term left that involves many selector calls stemming from an attempt of applying the induction hypotheses. *Selector elimination* is the first step towards a generalized formula that is ready for a subsequent proof by induction.

Example 1. During a proof of $\forall n : \mathbb{N}, k : list[\mathbb{N}]$ $if\{n \in isort(k), n \in k, true\}$ (i. e., that insertion sort does not add new elements to the input list), in the induction step we eventually get a sequent $\langle \{\neg k = \varepsilon\}, \{\ldots\} \mapsto goal \rangle$, where $goal$ is

$$if\{n = hd(k), true,$$
$$if\{n \in tl(k), true,$$
$$if\{n \in isort(tl(k)), true, \neg\, n \in insert(hd(k), isort(tl(k)))\}\}\} \ .$$

Algorithm *eliminateSelectors*($\langle H, \emptyset \mapsto goal \rangle$)

while there is a variable $v : \alpha$ that does not occur in a recursion position in *goal*
  and $H \vdash ?cons(v)^5$ for some constructor $cons(sel_1{:}\beta_1, \dots, sel_n{:}\beta_n) : \beta$

  $\theta := matchTypes(\beta, \alpha)$
  $\sigma := \{v/cons(x_1, \dots, x_n)\}$ for fresh variables x_i of type $\theta(\beta_i)$
  $H := s\text{-}eval_P(\sigma(H)); \; goal := s\text{-}eval_P(\sigma(goal))$

return $\langle H, \emptyset \mapsto goal \rangle$

Fig. 2. Selector elimination

As the set of hypotheses ensures that k is non-empty, we can safely replace $hd(k)$ and $tl(k)$ with fresh variables m and l, respectively. "Safe" means that this replacement preserves equivalence. If there were occurrences of k in other subterms than $hd(k)$ or $tl(k)$, we could replace those with $m :: l$. This eliminates all occurrences of k, so we drop the hypothesis $\neg k = \varepsilon$ and get the new goal term

$$if\{n = m, true, if\{n \in l, true, if\{n \in isort(l), true, \neg n \in insert(m, isort(l))\}\}\}.$$

This formula is not yet general enough to be provable by induction. However, m and l are two fresh variables that we could in principle use for induction. Furthermore, the replacement of $hd(k)$ and $tl(k)$ with fresh variables will make it easier to identify unnecessary conditions in subsequent generalization steps.

Example 2. Consider the simplified induction step for the proof of the formula $\forall n : \mathbb{N} \; dbl(n) = n + n$: $\langle \{\neg n = 0\}, \{\dots\} \mapsto {}^+({}^-(n) + {}^-(n)) = {}^-(n) + n \rangle$. Replacing n with ${}^+(m)$ and subsequent simplification yields ${}^+(m + m) = m + {}^+(m)$.

The next example shows that elimination of selectors is not always desirable.

Example 3. In the following sequent $\langle \{\neg k = \varepsilon\}, \{\dots\} \mapsto goal \rangle$, resulting from the induction step of $\forall n : \mathbb{N}, k : list[\mathbb{N}] \; n \# k = n \# bsort(k)$ for a bubble sort procedure *bsort*, the selectors for k should *not* be eliminated, because the subgoal can be directly proved by another induction on k:[4]

$$if\{n = hd(k), if\{n = last(bubble(k)),$$
$$n \# tl(k) = n \# but\_last(bubble(k)),$$
$${}^+(n \# tl(k)) = n \# but\_last(bubble(k))\}, \dots\}$$

In general, we should *not* replace selector calls $sel(v)$ if variable v directly occurs in a recursion position in *goal*. For instance, the occurrence of variable k in $bubble(k)$ should inhibit the replacement of $hd(k)$ and $tl(k)$. This leads to the algorithm shown in Fig. 2. As $s\text{-}eval_P(?cons(cons(x_1, \dots, x_n))) = true$ and $s\text{-}eval_P(sel_i(cons(x_1, \dots, x_n))) = x_i$, this effectively eliminates selector calls $sel_i(v)$ and removes hypotheses that are no longer necessary when they have been simplified to *true*.

---

[4] $n \# k$ denotes the number of occurrences of n in k.

[5] $H \vdash ?cons(v)$ is true if $?cons(v) \in H$ or if $\neg ?cons'(v) \in H$ for all constructors $cons' \neq cons$ of the same type as $cons$. E. g., we can infer $\{\neg k = \varepsilon\} \vdash ?{::}(k)$.

Algorithm $generateProposals(t, \varphi)$
$P := \emptyset$
if $t = f(t_1, \ldots, t_n)$ for some function symbol $f \neq$ = and some terms t_i **then**
    for each $I \in \mathcal{RP}(f)$ **do**
        $S := \{ t_i \mid i \in I \}$
        if $seemsSuitable(S, \varphi)$ **then** $P := P \circ \langle S \rangle$
    for each $i \in \{1, \ldots, n\}$ **do**
        $P := P \circ generateProposals(t_i, \varphi)$
if $t = t_1 = t_2$ for some terms t_1, t_2 **then**
    for each $i \in \{1, 2\}$ **do**
        $P_i := generateProposals(t_i, \varphi)$
        if $seemsSuitable(\{t_i\}, \varphi)$ **then** $P_i := P_i \circ \langle \{t_i\} \rangle$
        $P := P \circ \langle S' \in P_i \mid \exists t' \in S'. \ t' \text{ occurs in } t_{3-i} \text{ or at least twice in } t_i \rangle$
return P

Fig. 3. Finding common non-variable subterms to generalize

2.2   Inverse Substitution: Common Non-Variable Subterms

If a term $t \notin \mathcal{V}$ occupies a recursion position of a procedure call in a formula, generalizing all occurrences of t to a fresh variable x_t offers the possibility to prove the formula by induction on x_t. The following terms are considered *generalizable*:

Definition 1. *A term t is* generalizable *if the following holds:*

(1) *t has a recursively defined type (as there is no induction principle for non-recursively defined types such as bool),*
(2) *t is not a variable (we deal with this case in Sect. 2.3),*
(3) *t does not contain constructors (as these generate only a subset of a type),*
(4) *t does not contain selectors (we use selector elimination instead).*

Generating proposals. Intuitively, a *proposal* S for a formula φ is a set of some generalizable subterms of φ. To generate proposals, we examine formula φ recursively as depicted in Fig. 3.[6] Proposals are stored in a list P so that we can count how often a proposal was suggested later on. If the current subterm t of φ is of the form $f(t_1, \ldots, t_n)$, we propose the simultaneous generalization of the subterms t_i in recursion positions with respect to some $I \in \mathcal{RP}(f)$ if this seems to be a "suitable proposal" with respect to formula φ:

Definition 2. *A set S of terms is called a* suitable proposal *for some formula φ if each $t' \in S$ is a generalizable subterm of φ and if there is some $t' \in S$ that occurs at least twice in φ.*

This definition avoids many over-generalizations of single occurrences of subterms. For equations, the algorithm only adds those proposals S' that include a term t' that also occurs on the other side of the equation or that occurs more than once on one side.

---

[6] $\circ$ denotes list concatenation, and $\langle S_1, \ldots, S_n \rangle$ represents a list of n elements.

Example 1 (continued). The singleton $\{isort(l)\}$ is proposed twice, which leads to $\varphi_{gen} = if\{n = m, true, if\{n \in l, true, if\{n \in l', true, \neg n \in insert(m, l')\}\}\}$ for a fresh variable l'. Although $insert(m, isort(l))$ occurs in a recursion position, $\{insert(m, isort(l))\}$ is not a suitable proposal, because this subterm occurs only once in the formula.

Example 4. The following formula results after eliminating the selectors for k in the induction step of $\forall n : \mathbb{N}, k : list[\mathbb{N}]$ $if\{n \succcurlyeq k, n \succcurlyeq qsort(k), true\}$ to ascertain that the quicksort procedure $qsort$ preserves upper bounds:

$if\{m > n, true, if\{n \succcurlyeq l,$
$\quad if\{n \succcurlyeq larger(m, l),$
$\quad\quad if\{n \succcurlyeq qsort(larger(m, l)),$
$\quad\quad\quad if\{n \succcurlyeq smaller(m, l),$
$\quad\quad\quad\quad if\{n \succcurlyeq qsort(smaller(m, l)),$
$\quad\quad\quad\quad\quad n \succcurlyeq qsort(smaller(m, l)) <> m :: qsort(larger(m, l)), true\},$
$\quad\quad\quad\quad n \succcurlyeq qsort(smaller(m, l)) <> m :: qsort(larger(m, l))\}, true\},$
$\quad\quad\quad if\{n \succcurlyeq smaller(m, l),$
$\quad\quad\quad\quad if\{n \succcurlyeq qsort(smaller(m, l)),$
$\quad\quad\quad\quad\quad n \succcurlyeq qsort(smaller(m, l)) <> m :: qsort(larger(m, l))\}, true\},$
$\quad\quad\quad n \succcurlyeq qsort(smaller(m, l)) <> m :: qsort(larger(m, l))\}, true\}$

P contains eight proposals $\{smaller(m, l)\}$, six proposals $\{larger(m, l)\}$ and $\{qsort(smaller(m, l))\}$ each, and one proposal $\{qsort(larger(m, l))\}$.

Example 5. For $x + y * z = y * z + x$, we get one proposal $\{y * z\}$, because this subterm occurs on both sides of the equation and occupies one recursion position. The generalization is the commutativity law for addition.

Example 6. For $(y * z + x) - y * z = x$, the single proposal $\{y * z\}$ leads to the easily provable formula $(n + x) - n = x$.

Proposals for recursive calls. Boyer and Moore's motivation for generalizing subterms is that some subterms have often already "played their role" and now are merely "place holders for arbitrary objects" [5]. We found that *recursive calls* frequently are such arbitrary leftovers from a previous induction [2]. Therefore we add proposals to directly generalize recursive calls, which can significantly speed up the generalization process: The additional proposals may either be "better" (e. g., combined) proposals or can support existing proposals. In either case, this may reduce the number of calls to the disprover to check for over-generalizations.

If the substitution σ that summarizes the preceding generalization steps is one-to-one, we check for each proposal $S = \{f(t_1, \ldots, t_n)\}$ in P if $\sigma(f(t_1, \ldots, t_n))$ is an instance of a recursive call in f's body, and if so, we propose the simultaneous generalization of all instantiated (and by σ^{-1} generalized) recursive calls. We illustrate this process with an example; the precise algorithm is given in [2].

Example 4 (continued). Substitution $\sigma = \{m/hd(k), l/tl(k)\}$ (determined by the preceding selector elimination for k) is one-to-one, and $\sigma(qsort(smaller(m, l)))$

is one of the two recursive calls of the quicksort procedure *qsort*. This leads to six proposals $\{qsort(smaller(m,l)),\ qsort(larger(m,l))\}$ (one for each proposal $\{qsort(smaller(m,l))\}$). As we can similarly trace back the single proposal $\{qsort(larger(m,l))\}$, we get a seventh proposal of the recursive calls.

Organizing the proposals. The proposals in P are organized into a new list P' so that each proposal occurs exactly once in the resulting list. Furthermore, P' is sorted lexicographically wrt. the following priority list of criteria:

1. proposals that pass the *induction test* (see below),
2. proposals that have been suggested more often,
3. proposals S with more occurrences of the subterms $t \in S$ of φ,
4. some more tie-breaking criteria that favour less complex proposals and produce a deterministic ranking of the proposals, see [2] for details.

The *induction test* for a proposal S checks if the induction heuristic suggests an induction on at least one of the fresh variables x_t after tentatively replacing the occurrences of each $t \in S$ in φ with x_t. In this case the proposal receives a boost so that it is considered before proposals that fail the induction test. As the induction heuristic is used as a black box, our algorithm can be easily integrated in various theorem provers. (Note that our algorithm does not *require* an induction heuristic, but may *profit* if one is present.)

Example 4 (continued). The only proposal that passes the induction test is $\{qsort(smaller(m,l)),\ qsort(larger(m,l))\}$, because the induction heuristic suggests induction on the fresh variable that replaces $qsort(smaller(m,l))$. So this proposal is considered first and yields a useful generalization which states that *smaller*, *larger*, and $<>$ preserve upper bounds, see [2] for details. Without the induction test, we would examine the over-generalization of $smaller(m,l)$ first. Without the proposals for recursive calls, we would consider the over-generalizations of $smaller(m,l)$ and $larger(m,l)$ first. Avoiding these over-generalizations leads to a speed-up factor of about 3 (depending on the disprover configuration).

Figure 4 summarizes the overall algorithm that tries to replace generalizable subterms of a formula φ. The generalization itself is carried out by applying the inverse substitution σ_{gen}^{-1} (which replaces each occurrence of $t \in S$ in φ with x_t, see [2] for technical details on inverse substitutions). The first generalization φ_{gen} that is not rejected by the disprover is returned as result, along with the substitution σ_{gen} indicating how to use the generalization.

2.3   Inverse Substitution: Generalizing Apart Variables

In some formulas, e. g., $x + (x + x) = (x + x) + x$, it is necessary to generalize apart the occurrences of a variable to facilitate an inductive proof. Generally, it is beneficial to separate the occurrences in recursion positions from occurrences in non-recursion positions [4].[7]

---

[7] For the sake of brevity, we also use some artificial examples to illustrate our algorithm. However, formulas such as $(x + {}^-(y) * x) + x = x + (x + {}^-(y) * x)$ may actually occur in realistic examples (e. g., when proving the distributivity of $*$ over $+$).

Algorithm $generalizeCommonSubterms(\varphi, \sigma)$

$P := generateProposals(\varphi, \varphi)$
if σ is one-to-one **then** $P := P \circ recCallProposals(\varphi, \sigma, P)$
$P' := organizeProposals(\varphi, P)$
for each $S \in P'$ **do**
$\quad \sigma_{gen} := \bigcup_{t \in S} \{x_t/t\}$ for fresh variables x_t
$\quad \varphi_{gen} := \sigma_{gen}^{-1}(\varphi)$
$\quad$ **if** disprover does not find a counter-example for φ_{gen} **then return** $(\varphi_{gen}, \sigma_{gen})$
return $\bot$

Fig. 4. Generalizing common non-variable subterms

The first two lines of the algorithm in Fig. 5 form a heuristic filter to predict whether generalizing apart is necessary. The algorithm fails if it cannot find values for f, I, i, and j. Hence, although variables k and m occur in recursion and non-recursion positions in Examples 3 and 4, the algorithm correctly fails at this early stage, while allowing the generalization in the above formula. If formula φ passes this filter, we use the values for f, I, i, and j to generalize apart in a goal-directed way, thus improving upon existing heuristics [4, 9].

The subalgorithms *separate* and *replace* share the meta-variables f, v, ρ, and *all-rpos*. Function $\rho : \Sigma(P) \to 2^{\mathbb{N}}$ maps each function symbol to a set of (recursion) positions and thus controls which occurrences of v are to be replaced with the fresh variable v'. The algorithm first tries to generalize apart the occurrences of variable v in recursion positions of a procedure f from the other occurrences:

Example 2 (continued). In $\varphi = {}^+(m+m) = m + {}^+(m)$ we generalize apart wrt. $v := m$ and $f := +$. Assuming that $+$ is defined recursively in its first parameter, we have $\rho(+) = \{\{1\}\}$ and generalize to $\varphi_{gen} = {}^+(m'+m) = m' + {}^+(m)$. Similarly, we generalize $\varphi = x + (x + x) = (x + x) + x$ to $\varphi_{gen} = x' + (x + x) = (x' + x) + x$.

Example 7. In $\varphi = x * (x + x) = x * x + x * x$, we generalize apart wrt. $v := x$ and $f := *$. Assuming $\mathcal{RP}(*) = \{\{1\}\}$, on the left-hand side we replace the first occurrence of x with x'. On the right-hand side, we recurse into both arguments of $+$ and get $\varphi_{gen} = x' * (x + x) = x' * x + x' * x$.

Example 8. In $\varphi = (x + x) - x = x$, we generalize apart wrt. $v := x$, $f := +$, and $\rho(+) = \{\{1\}\}$. This leads to $(x' + x) - x = x'$, which can be proved with a single induction on x using the commutativity of $+$.

We say that a term t was *generalized apart successfully* if $t = v'$ or if at least one, but not all occurrences of v in t were replaced with v'. For equations, we additionally demand that both sides be generalized apart successfully. Formula φ_{gen} is considered a *useful generalization* if (1) it was generalized apart successfully, (2) each equation in φ was either left unchanged or generalized apart successfully, and (3) the disprover did not find a counter-example for φ_{gen}.

If φ_{gen} is *not* considered a useful generalization, we also allow the replacement of v in recursion positions of procedure calls $g(\ldots)$ with $g \neq f$ (*all-rpos* := *true*).

Algorithm *generalizeApart*(φ)

find a procedure f, some set $I \in \mathcal{RP}(f)$, some procedure calls $f(t_1, \ldots, t_n)$ and $f(t'_1, \ldots, t'_n)$ in φ, and $i, j \in \{1, \ldots, n\}$ such that $t_i = t'_j \in \mathcal{V}$, $i \in I$ and $j \notin I$

all-rpos := *false*; $v := t_i$; $\rho(f) := I$; $\varphi_{gen} := separate(\varphi)$

if φ_{gen} is considered a useful generalization **then return** φ_{gen}

for each ρ with $\rho(f) = I$, $\rho(g) \in \mathcal{RP}(g)$ for all procedures g and
$\qquad\qquad\quad \rho(h) = \mathbb{N}$ for all other function symbols h **do**

$\quad$ *all-rpos* := *true*; $\varphi_{gen} := separate(\varphi)$

$\quad$ if φ_{gen} is considered a useful generalization **then return** φ_{gen}

return $\bot$

Subalgorithm *separate*(t), sharing variables f, ρ, and *all-rpos*

if *all-rpos* and $t = g(t_1, \ldots, t_m)$ for some terms t_i **then**
$\quad$ **return** $g(replace(t_1, 1 \in \rho(g)), \ldots, replace(t_m, m \in \rho(g)))$
else if $t = t_1 = t_2$ **then**
$\quad$ **return** $replace(t_1, true) = replace(t_2, true)$
else if $t = f(t_1, \ldots, t_n)$ for some terms t_i **then**
$\quad$ **return** $f(replace(t_1, 1 \in \rho(f)), \ldots, replace(t_n, n \in \rho(f)))$
else if $t = g(t_1, \ldots, t_m)$ for some terms t_i **then**
$\quad$ **return** $g(separate(t_1), \ldots, separate(t_m))$
else return t

Subalgorithm *replace*$(t, rpos)$, sharing variable v

if $\neg\, rpos$ **then return** t
else if $t = v$ **then return** v'
else return $separate(t)$

Fig. 5. Generalizing apart variable occurrences

Therefore we need to choose recursion position sets $\rho(g)$ for these procedures. For constructors, selectors, *if*, and =, $\rho(h) = \mathbb{N}$ lets the algorithm recursively examine all argument positions. Looking for an appropriate ρ leads to at most $\prod_{g \in \Sigma^{proc}(\varphi) \setminus \{f\}} |\mathcal{RP}(g)|$ further iterations, which is usually a very small number, because only few procedures have more than one set of recursion positions.

Example 9. In $\varphi = |k <> k| = |k| + |k|$, we successfully generalize apart wrt. $v := k$, $f := <>$, and $\rho(<>) = \{\{1\}\}$ on the left-hand side, yielding $|k' <> k|$. The right-hand side remains unchanged and thus is *not* generalized apart successfully at first. Using the only choice $\rho(+) := \rho(|) := \{\{1\}\}$ we successfully generalize both sides on the second attempt, which leads to $\varphi_{gen} = |k' <> k| = |k'| + |k|$.

Note that our heuristic solves all these examples with just a single disprover call. We are not aware of a heuristic in the literature that is equally goal-directed. For instance, Aubin's heuristic requires "a few attempts" [4] to solve Example 7. Our heuristic could be improved further by trying some more experimental alternatives to generalize formulas such as $rev(k <> k) = rev(k) <> rev(k)$. However, we did not find "naturally occurring" examples that would need such an extension and therefore do not consider additional arbitrary choices of variable occurrences for replacement.

2.4 Inverse Weakening

Generalization by *inverse weakening* allows us to remove an unnecessary condition B from a formula $if\{B, A_1, A_2\}$ by generalizing the conditional to the conjunction of A_1 and A_2, i. e., $if\{A_1, A_2, false\}$.

In Example 1 (p. 237), the information that n does not occur in l is irrelevant, so it would be useful to drop the condition $n \in l$. The isolated occurrence of variable l gives us a hint that this condition might be unnecessary:

Definition 3. *A variable v occurs* insignificantly *in a literal ℓ if no other variable occurs in ℓ (i. e., $\mathcal{V}(\ell) = \{v\}$) and if no procedure is used in ℓ. A condition B in a subterm $if\{B, A_1, A_2\}$ of a term t is* probably unnecessary *if all occurrences of a variable v in B, in the conditions on the path in t to B, and in the literals in A_1 and A_2 are insignificant. Condition B is deemed* possibly unnecessary *if*

(1) *there exists a variable $v \in \mathcal{V}(B)$ such that all further occurrences of v (if any) in the conditions on the path in t to B and in the literals in A_1 and A_2 are insignificant, and*

(2) *neither A_1 nor A_2 is equal to "false".*

We remove *probably unnecessary* conditions right away, whereas after the removal of a *possibly unnecessary* condition the result is checked by the disprover.

Example 1 (continued). Condition $n \in l$ is deemed possibly unnecessary, giving the final touch to the formula: $if\{n = m, true, if\{n \in l', true, \neg\, n \in insert(m, l')\}\}$.

Example 10. Our heuristic is liberal enough to iteratively remove the two probably unnecessary conditions in $if\{?::(k), if\{?::(tl(k)), A, true\}, true\}$ if k does not occur in A. For instance, this happens in a generalization with merge sort, where $A = if\{ordered(l_1), if\{ordered(l_2), ordered(merge(l_1, l_2)), true\}, true\}$.

2.5 Inverse Functionality

We adopt the heuristic for inverse functionality presented in [14] in the following way: For each equation $f(t_1, \ldots, t_n) = f(t'_1, \ldots, t'_n)$ in formula φ that does not occur as condition of some conditional statement, we check whether the argument lists differ in only one position, i. e., if $t_j \neq t'_j$ for some $j \in \{1, \ldots, n\}$ and $t_i = t'_i$ for all $i \neq j$. In this case we replace the equation with $t_j = t'_j$. If the disprover finds a counter-example for the resulting formula, we try to generalize another equation instead (if there is one); otherwise the heuristic fails.

Example 11. Formula $|rev(rev(k))| = |k|$ is generalized to $rev(rev(k)) = k$, while the over-generalization $isort(k) = k$ of $isort(isort(k)) = isort(k)$ is rejected by the disprover. (Section 4 gives examples for this heuristic in more realistic proofs.)

3 Related Work

Even though some generalization heuristics were proposed about 30 years ago [4, 5], these techniques are still used in today's theorem provers. Therefore we will discuss their features before describing the modifications that more recent implementations added to them.

The Nqthm system (and its current successor ACL2)[8] features generalization heuristics without a disprover [5]. Its destructor elimination allows more sophisticated generalizations than pure selector elimination. However, the user then needs to assist the system by providing so-called *elimination lemmas* for destructors such as *quotient* and *remainder*. The heuristic does not prevent the counterproductive selector elimination from Example 3. Nqthm generalizes common *minimal* subterms. In Example 4, this would delete $qsort(smaller(m, l))$ and $qsort(larger(m, l))$ from further consideration, since these terms properly contain $smaller(m, l)$ and $larger(m, l)$, which unfortunately lead to non-theorems. The heuristic also fails to generalize equations such as $(y * z + x) - y * z = x$, because $y * z$ occurs on one side only. Nqthm's heuristic to "eliminate irrelevance" removes disconnected, probably falsifiable literals from a clause. Literals are connected if they share variables. In Example 1, this heuristic is too weak to remove the unnecessary condition $n \in l$, because all of the literals share variable n. Generalizing apart and inverse functionality are not supported.

Aubin's search strategy for inverse substitution focuses on subterm occurrences in recursion positions [4]. This heuristic is unable to produce the generalization from Examples 5 and 6, because it would require $y * z$ to occur in recursion positions on *both* sides of the equation.[9] Aubin's heuristic can generalize apart variable occurrences and identifies wrong choices of variable occurrences by a disprover. His system does not support inverse weakening, while inverse functionality is basically the same heuristic that we use. Aubin presents a heuristic for *inverse replacement* called *indirect generalization* for statements about procedures with *accumulator parameters* that occur in recursive formulations of iterative algorithms. For instance, it generalizes $fac(n) = it\_fac(n, 1)$ to $fac(n) * m = it\_fac(n, m)$ if the lemma $fac(n) * 1 = fac(n)$ has been proved before.

Hummel extends Aubin's heuristics for the INKA system [9]. Her heuristic for inverse substitution also considers whether a subterm is able to "generate" all possible values of the domain. While $x + y$ can represent any natural number, $^+(x)$ does not have this property. We do not generalize constructor terms anyway and leave the check for over-generalization of subterms to the disprover. Hummel generalizes $y * z$ in $(y * z + x) - y * z = x$, because it does not share variables with other subterms of the formula. However, this fails on $(y * z + y) - y * z = y$, which our heuristic handles successfully. Inverse weakening in INKA is an improved version of Boyer and Moore's "elimination of irrelevance" that allows the removal of $n \in l$ in Example 1, but fails if no variable occurs in just a single literal, cf. Example 10. Inverse functionality also works for implications in INKA. As this

---

[8] Personal communication with J S. Moore.

[9] Aubin gives the example $(n + m * n) * p = n * p + (m * n) * p$ in [4], where his heuristic fails to generalize $m * n$ in contrast to our heuristic.

produces fairly strong generalizations and in our experience does not occur too often, we do not generalize in implications.[10]

Dixon developed an inductive theorem prover for Isabelle within his proof planning framework [8]. It supports generalization by inverse substitution, based on Boyer and Moore's heuristic, and inverse functionality. His system does not use a disprover, so it may produce over-generalizations. In contrast to Nqthm, Dixon chooses a *maximal* generalization with more than one occurrence. While this works for Example 4, it simply ignores smaller subterms and would for instance over-generalize in a proof of $\forall n : \mathbb{N}, k : list[\mathbb{N}] \; n \in k \rightarrow n \in isort(k)$.

Bundy et al. use generalization as a subsidiary algorithm in an approach to lemma discovery in CLAM [7] that builds upon *rippling*, a heuristic to guide an inductive proof. Proof critics analyze the failure of rippling. To discover a lemma, unknown term structures are represented by second-order meta variables and instantiated during subsequent rewrite steps. A disprover checks for invalid instantiations. The final generalization step involves inverse replacement and generalizing apart (cf. Aubin) as well as inverse substitution in the Nqthm style.

The RRL system follows a similar approach and uses term schemes that are instantiated by attempting to prove the generalized schema [10, 11]. It avoids second-order unification by more specialized heuristics. To generalize formulas, it employs inverse substitution and inverse weakening in conjunction with a disprover. As RRL's heuristic for inverse substitution requires occurrences of the subterm on both sides of an equation, it cannot generalize Example 6 as well as formulas that need generalizing apart variable occurrences. Like CLAM, RRL is particularly strong at generalizations with accumulators but has less sophisticated heuristics (if at all) for inverse substitution, inverse weakening, and inverse functionality compared to our approach.

The generalization command in PVS [12] is basically just a text processing feature without any heuristic support. It replaces all occurrences of a user-defined subterm in a sequent with a fresh variable.

4   Evaluation of the Generalization Heuristics

To evaluate our generalization heuristics, we integrated them into the ✓eriFun system.[11] The user can now invoke the tactic by simply clicking a button. Without any user interaction, the system will try to generalize the current sequent. In order to check for over-generalizations, ✓eriFun's disprover [3] is used.

The quality of a generalization feature is determined by both its success rate and the number of proposed over-generalizations. Table 1 shows a selection of 20 formulas that ✓eriFun could prove using our generalization heuristics. Out

---

[10] E. g., in the proof of $even(|k <> k|)$, $even(|tl(k) <> tl(k)|) \rightarrow even(^+(|tl(k) <> k|))$ would be over-generalized to $|tl(k) <> tl(k)| = {}^+(|tl(k) <> k|)$.

[11] An experimental version of ✓eriFun that includes our generalization heuristics (along with example files) can be downloaded from http://www.inferenzsysteme.informatik.tu-darmstadt.de/~aderhold/. Our improvements will be available in the next official release of the system.

Table 1. Selected examples for the generalization heuristics. A reference " [7]:Tnn" indicates that this is example Tnn from [7], Table 3.1.

No.	Formula	Sequence	Checks	Reference
1	$dbl(n) = n + n$	SV	1 (0)	[7]:T1
2	$|rev(k)| = |k|$	SC	1 (0)	[7]:T5
3	$|rev(k <> l)| = |k| + |l|$	SCC	2 (0)	[7]:T6
4	$nth(nth(nth(k, w), x), y) = nth(nth(nth(k, y), x), w)$	ScF	2 (1)	[7]:T9
5	$rev(rev(k)) = k$	SC	1 (0)	[7]:T10
6	$rev(rev(k) <> rev(l)) = l <> k$	SCC	2 (0)	[7]:T11
7	$half(x + x) = x$	SVF	2 (0)	[7]:T13
8	$half(|k <> l|) = half(|l <> k|)$	Ff	2 (1)	[7]:T23
9	$x \in A \rightarrow x \in A \cup B$	SW	1 (0)	[7]:T42
10	$A \cup (B \cup C) = (A \cup B) \cup C$	SWWWc	4 (1)	
11	$|isort(k)| = |k|$	SC	1 (0)	[7]:T48
12	$n \in isort(k) \rightarrow n \in k$	SCW	2 (0)	[7]:T49
13	$n \in k \rightarrow n \in isort(k)$	SCWc	3 (1)	
14	$n \# k = n \# isort(k)$	SCf	2 (1)	[7]:T50
15	$n \succcurlyeq k \rightarrow n \succcurlyeq qsort(k)$	SCc	2 (1)	
16	$ordered(mergesort(k))$	CWW	1 (0)	
17	$(x + y) * z = x * z + y * z$	SC	1 (0)	[10]
18	$x * (y * z) = (x * y) * z$	SC	1 (0)	[4]
19	$rev(k <> l) = rev(l) <> rev(k)$	SCC	2 (0)	[4]
20	$k \subset k$	SV	1 (0)	[4]

of 50 examples in [7], **✔eriFun** could prove 11 formulas even without generalization. With our generalization heuristics, this number almost tripled to 32 proved examples. 5 examples (e. g., T25, $even(|k <> l|) \leftrightarrow even(|l| + |k|)$) could easily be solved by inverse functionality for implications (but do not look as though they occured in everyday examples). The remaining 13 examples are specific to CLAM's proof critics for rippling and its heuristic for inverse replacement that we did not consider.

In the selection of examples, we were especially interested in "naturally occurring" generalization problems: The formulas we focused on state correctness properties of common sorting algorithms (e. g., insertion sort, bubble sort, merge sort, quicksort) and properties of common arithmetic or list operations (e. g., monotonicity of + and $*$, associativity of $\cap$ and $\cup$). A collection of case studies that we also use as motivating examples in graduate and undergraduate courses can be found in [1, 17]. Table 1 contains some examples from our case studies and some further examples from the literature. In total, we investigated 40 generalization examples.

Letters S, C, V, W, and F denote applications of our heuristics for **S**elector elimination, inverse substitution for **C**ommon non-variable subterms or **V**ariables, inverse **W**eakening, and inverse **F**unctionality, respectively. Capital letters represent successful applications, lower-case letters denote attempts that were rejected by the disprover. We also include the number of generalization conjectures that were checked by the disprover. The number in parentheses gives the number of rejected conjectures.

The results show that our heuristics rarely suggest an over-generalization. Less than 12 % of the suggestions were rejected by the disprover. In particular, our heuristic for inverse weakening successfully removes unnecessary conditions and never attempts to over-generalize in these examples.

5   Conclusion

We presented improved heuristics for a generalization algorithm that uses the generalization rules *inverse substitution, inverse weakening*, and *inverse functionality* in a goal-directed way.

For *inverse substitution*, we eliminate selectors to tidy up the result of a previous destructor style induction *only if* this does not heuristically impede a subsequent inductive proof. For common non-variable subterms, our heuristic is more liberal than other techniques and does not commit to only minimal or maximal subterms. By using recursion information about the involved procedures, we typically find the correct subterms to be generalized at once. We also generalize apart variable occurrences in many naturally occurring generalization problems without having to try out many different combinations. Similarly, we made *inverse weakening* more widely applicable in order to remove unnecessary conditions and get easily reusable generalizations. For *inverse functionality*, we selected a compromise that does not attempt to over-generalize often.

The evaluation within the √eriFun system shows that our improvements in fact pay off and solve many examples we found in the literature as well as in our case studies. Although we relaxed the preconditions for *inverse substitution* and *inverse weakening* in comparison to other approaches, the disprover rarely has to reject a generalization attempt.

To our knowledge, √eriFun now offers the best performing heuristics for these generalization rules among publicly available theorem provers. Since our approach is flexible—it does not rely on a specific induction selection or rewriting strategy (e. g., rippling)—, other verification systems can benefit from the improved heuristics as well.

As a next step in our development, we are experimenting with an automatic invocation of our generalization algorithm. The goal is to suggest a generalization only when this seems beneficial and not in all cases where the verification tactic fails. Preliminary experiments with suggesting only "substantial" generalizations (that is, generalizations that involve more than selector elimination) have been quite promising.

Acknowledgment. I am grateful to Christoph Walther and the anonymous CADE referees for constructive feedback on earlier versions of this paper.

References

1. http://www.verifun.org
2. Aderhold, M.: Formula generalization in ✓eriFun. Diploma thesis, Technische Universität Darmstadt (2004)
3. Aderhold, M., Walther, C., Szallies, D., Schlosser, A.: A fast disprover for ✓eriFun. In: Ahrendt, W., Baumgartner, P., de Nivelle, H. (eds.) Proc. of the 3rd Workshop on Disproving, pp. 59–69 (2006)
4. Aubin, R.: Mechanizing Structural Induction. PhD thesis, University of Edinburgh (1976)
5. Boyer, R.S., Moore, J S.: A Computational Logic. Academic Press, San Diego (1979)
6. Bundy, A.: The automation of proof by mathematical induction. In: Robinson, A., Voronkov, A. (eds.) Handbook of Automated Reasoning (chapter 13), vol. I, pp. 845–911. Elsevier, Amsterdam (2001)
7. Bundy, A., Basin, D., Hutter, D., Ireland, A.: Rippling: Meta-Level Guidance for Mathematical Reasoning (chapter 3). In: Cambridge Tracts in Theoretical Computer Science, no. 56, Cambridge University Press, Cambridge (2005)
8. Dixon, L.: A Proof Planning Framework For Isabelle. PhD thesis, University of Edinburgh (2005)
9. Hummel, B.: Generierung von Induktionsformeln und Generalisierung beim automatischen Beweisen mit vollständiger Induktion. Doctoral dissertation, Universität Karlsruhe (1990)
10. Kapur, D.: Theorem proving support for hardware verification. In: Third Intl. Workshop on First-Order Theorem Proving, (2000) Invited talk, paper available at http://www.cs.unm.edu/~kapur/myabstracts/tphardware00.html
11. Kapur, D., Subramaniam, M.: Lemma discovery in automating induction. In: McRobbie, M.A., Slaney, J.K. (eds.) Automated Deduction – CADE-13. LNCS, vol. 1104, pp. 538–552. Springer, Heidelberg (1996)
12. Owre, S., Rushby, J., Shankar, N.: PVS: A prototype verification system. In: Kapur, D. (ed.) Automated Deduction – CADE-11. LNCS, vol. 607, pp. 748–752. Springer, Heidelberg (1992)
13. Schweitzer, S.: Symbolische Auswertung und Heuristiken zur Verifikation funktionaler Programme. Doctoral dissertation, TU Darmstadt (2007)
14. Walther, C.: Mathematical induction. In: Gabbay, D.M., Hogger, C.J., Robinson, J.A. (eds.) Handbook of Logic in Artificial Intelligence and Logic Programming, vol. 2, pp. 127–228. Oxford University Press, Oxford (1994)
15. Walther, C., Aderhold, M., Schlosser, A.: The $\mathcal{L}$ 1.0 Primer. Technical Report VFR 06/01, Technische Universität Darmstadt (2006)
16. Walther, C., Schweitzer, S.: About ✓eriFun. In: Baader, F. (ed.) Automated Deduction – CADE-19. LNCS (LNAI), vol. 2741, pp. 322–327. Springer, Heidelberg (2003)
17. Walther, C., Schweitzer, S.: Verification in the classroom. Journal of Automated Reasoning 32(1), 35–73 (2004)
18. Walther, C., Schweitzer, S.: Reasoning about incompletely defined programs. In: Sutcliffe, G., Voronkov, A. (eds.) LPAR 2005. LNCS (LNAI), vol. 3835, pp. 427–442. Springer, Heidelberg (2005)

On the Normalization and Unique Normalization Properties of Term Rewrite Systems[*]

Guillem Godoy[1] and Sophie Tison[2]

[1] Technical University of Catalonia
Jordi Girona 1, Barcelona, Spain
ggodoy@lsi.upc.edu
[2] Universit des Sciences et Technologies de Lille
59655 Villeneuve d'Ascq CEDEX, France
tison@lifl.fr

Abstract. Computation with a term rewrite system (TRS) consists of
the application of rules from a given starting term until a normal form
is reached. Two natural questions arise from this the definition: whether
all terms can reach at least one normal form (normalization property),
and whether all terms can reach at most one normal form (unique normalization property).

We study the decidability of these properties for two syntactically
restricted classes of TRS: for (i) shallow right-linear TRS, and for (ii)
linear right-shallow TRS.

We show that the normalization property is decidable for both cases
(i) and (ii), and that the unique normalization property is undecidable for
case (ii), whereas for case (i) remains unknown. Nevertheless, for case (i),
if the normalization property is satisfied, then the unique normalization
property becomes decidable. Hence, whether all terms reach exactly one
normal form for TRS of kind (i) is decidable.

These results are based on known constructions of tree automata with
constraints and rewrite closure, and on reducing the normalization property to normalization from a concrete finite set of terms.

1   Introduction

Term rewriting is a Turing-complete model of computation that specifies rules
for replacing certain patterns in terms by equivalent, in some cases simpler, other
terms. Computation with a rewrite system consists of the application of rules
from a given starting term until a normal form is reached, i.e. a term that can
not be rewritten any more.

Two natural questions arise from this the definition: whether all terms can
reach at least one normal form (normalization property, sometimes called weak
normalization) for a given TRS, and whether all terms can reach at most one
normal form (unique normalization property).

[*] The first author is supported by Spanish Min. of Educ. and Science by the LogicTools
project (TIN2004-03382).

F. Pfenning (Ed.): CADE 2007, LNAI 4603, pp. 247–262, 2007.
© Springer-Verlag Berlin Heidelberg 2007

These properties are difficult to deal with, but often can be obtained as a consequence of other properties. For example, termination (sometimes called strong normalization) is a much studied property of TRS. It states that no infinite rewrite derivation exists, and in particular implies normalization. Another well known property is confluence, which states that any two terms derived from a common one can also be derived into another common one term. Confluence implies in particular unique normalization, and in fact, when a TRS is normalizing, confluence and unique normalization are equivalent properties.

The normalization and unique normalization properties are undecidable in general. In [16] a polynomial-time algorithm for checking whether a ground rewrite system has the unique normalization property is presented. In [13] it is shown that normalization is decidable for left-linear growing TRS.

In this paper we study the decidability of these properties for two syntactically restricted classes of TRS. On the one hand, for (i) shallow right-linear TRS, i.e., for TRS where the variables occur at depth 0 or 1 in the rules, and such that the variables occur at most once in the right-hand sides of the rules. On the other hand, for (ii) linear right-shallow TRS, i.e., for TRS where the variables occur at most once in every side of the rules, and such that the variables occur at depth 0 or 1 in the right-hand sides of the rules.

For the normalization property we obtain decidability in both cases (i) and (ii), but for unique normalization the answer is negative for case (ii), and we give a reduction proving its undecidability, whereas for case (i) (un)decidability remains unknown. Nevertheless, for case (i), if the normalization property is satisfied, then the unique normalization property becomes decidable, as a consequence of the fact that confluence is known to be decidable [7] for TRS of kind (i).

These results are obtained by proving, on the one hand, that normalization is equivalent to normalization restricted to a finite set of terms, and on the other hand, that normalization from a given starting term is decidable. The latter is proved by making an adequate use of already known constructions on tree automata with constraints.

The paper is structured as follows. In Section 2 we introduce some basic notions and notations. In Section 3 we present normalization-preserving transformations that replace the shallow terms by flat terms, and allow us to simplify the arguments in the rest of the paper. In Sections 4 and 5 we show how to reduce normalization of linear right-flat, and flat right-linear TRS, respectively, to normalization from a given finite set of terms. In Section 6 we use the previous characterizations and tree automata techniques for deciding the normalization property for both cases. Finally, in Section 7 we show that unique normalization is undecidable for linear right-shallow TRS.

2   Preliminaries

We use standard notation from the term rewriting literature. A signature Σ is a (finite) set of function symbols, which is partitioned as $\cup_i \Sigma_i$ such that $f \in \Sigma_n$ if the arity of f is n. Symbols in Σ_0, called *constants*, are denoted by a, b, c, d, with possible subscripts. The elements of a set $\mathcal{V}$ of variable symbols are denoted by x, y, z with possible subscripts. The set $\mathcal{T}(\Sigma, \mathcal{V})$ of *terms* over Σ and $\mathcal{V}$, *position* p in a term, *subterm* $t|_p$ of term t at position p, and the term $t[s]_p$ obtained by replacing $t|_p$ by s are defined in the standard way. For example, if t is $f(a, g(b, h(c)), d)$, then $t|_{2.2.1} = c$, and $t[d]_{2.2} = f(a, g(b, d), d)$. The empty sequence, denoted by λ, corresponds to the root position. By $Pos(t)$ we denote the set of all positions p such that $t|_p$ is defined. We write $p_1 > p_2$ (equivalently, $p_2 < p_1$) and say p_1 is below p_2 (equivalently, p_2 is above p_1) if p_2 is a proper prefix of p_1, that is, $p_1 = p_2.p_2'$ for some nonempty p_2'. Positions p and q are *disjoint* if $p \not\geq q$ and $q \not\geq p$. When p_1 is of the form $p_2.p_2'$, $p_1 - p_2$ denotes p_2'. By $Vars(t)$ we denote the set of all variables occurring in t. Usually we will denote a term $f(t_1, \ldots, t_n)$ by the simplified form $ft_1 \ldots t_n$, and $t[s]_p$ by $t[s]$ when p is clear by the context or not important. The *height* of a term s is 0 if s is a variable or a constant, and $1 + \mathtt{Max}_i(\mathtt{height}(s_i))$ if $s = fs_1, \ldots, s_m$. The *depth* of an occurrence at position p of a term t in a term s, i.e. $s = s[t]_p$, is $|p|$. The *size* of a term $s = fs_1 \ldots s_m$, denoted by $|s|$, is $1 + \Sigma_{i=1}^m |s_i|$, and the size of a constant or a variable is 1.

A substitution σ is sometimes presented explicitly as $\{x_1 \mapsto t_1, \ldots, x_n \mapsto t_n\}$. Let $\mathcal{V}_n$ be a set of n variables. A linear term $C \in \mathcal{T}(\Sigma, \mathcal{V}_n)$ is called a *context* and the expression $C[t_1, \ldots t_n]$ denotes the term in $\mathcal{T}(\Sigma)$ obtained from C by replacing variable x_i by t_i for each $1 \leq i \leq n$. We assume standard definitions for a *rewrite rule* $l \rightarrow r$, a *rewrite system* R, the *one step rewrite relation at position* p *induced by* R $\rightarrow_{R,p}$, or $\rightarrow_{l \rightarrow r, p, \sigma}$ if we make explicit the used rule $l \rightarrow r$ and substitution σ, and the *one step rewrite relation induced by* R (at any position) $\rightarrow_R$. For a rule $l \rightarrow r$, l is the left-hand side (lhs for short) and r is the right-hand side (rhs). If $p = \lambda$, then the rewrite step $\rightarrow_{R,p}$ is said to be applied *at the topmost position* (at the root); and it is denoted by $s \rightarrow_{R, > \lambda} t$ otherwise. We make the usual assumptions for the rules $l \rightarrow r$ of a rewrite system R, i.e. l is not a variable, and all variables occurring in r also occur in l. The *size* of a TRS R, denoted by $|R|$, is the sum of all the terms in their rules.

The notations $\leftrightarrow$, $\rightarrow^+$, and $\rightarrow^*$, are standard [4]. R is terminating if no infinite derivation $s_1 \rightarrow_R s_2 \rightarrow \cdots$ exists. A term t is *reachable* from s by R (or, R-reachable) if $s \rightarrow_R^* t$. A term t is *reachable* from a set of terms S by R if t is reachable from all terms in S. A term t is a *descendant* of a set of terms S by R if t is reachable from at least one term in S. A term s is R-*irreducible* (or, in R-normal form) if there is no term t such that $s \rightarrow_R t$. A term s is R-normalizing if s R-reaches a normal form, and in this case we also say that s has a normal form. It is R-uniquely normalizing if it R-reaches at most one normal form.

A *(rewrite) derivation* (from s) is a sequence of rewrite steps (starting from s), that is, a sequence $s \rightarrow_R s_1 \rightarrow_R s_2 \rightarrow_R \ldots$. With $s \rightarrow_R^* t$ we will denote that t is R-reachable from s, or a concrete derivation from s to t, depending on the context.

A term t is called *ground* if t contains no variables. It is called *shallow* if all variable positions in t are at depth 0 or 1. It is *flat* if its height is at most 1. It is called linear if every variable occurs at most once in t.

A rule $l \rightarrow r \in R$ is called *shallow* (*flat*, *linear*) if both l, r are shallow (flat, linear). It is called *right-shallow* (*right-flat*, *right-linear*) if r is shallow (flat, linear). It is called *left-shallow* (*left-flat*, *left-linear*) if l is shallow (flat, linear). It is called *collapsing* if r is a variable.

A rule $l \rightarrow r$ is called *decreasing* if $\mathtt{height}(l) > \mathtt{height}(r)$, *increasing* if $\mathtt{height}(l) < \mathtt{height}(r)$, and *preserving* if $\mathtt{height}(l) = \mathtt{height}(r)$. A rewrite step application $s \rightarrow_{l \rightarrow r} t$ is *decreasing* (*increasing*, *preserving*) if $l \rightarrow r$ is.

A TRS R satisfies the normalization property, or, equivalently, R is normalizing, if all terms are R-normalizing. It satisfies the unique normalization property, or, equivalently, R is uniquely normalizing, if all terms are R-uniquely normalizing. Note that unique normalization does not imply normalization.

A tree automaton -fta in short- over Σ is a tuple $\mathcal{A} = (Q, \Sigma, Q_f, \Delta)$ where Q is a set of states, $Q_f \subseteq Q$ is a set of final states, and Δ is a set of transition rules of the form $f(q_1, ..., q_n) \rightarrow q$. The set of rules define a ground TRS and the move relation in the fta can be viewed as the corresponding rewrite relation which will be denoted $\rightarrow_{\mathcal{A}}^*$. $L(\mathcal{A}) = \{t \in \mathcal{T}(\Sigma) | t \rightarrow_{\mathcal{A}}^* q, q \in Q_f\}$ is the language recognized by $\mathcal{A}$. A deterministic automaton (dfta in short) is an automaton where no two rules share the same left-hand side.

3   Simplifying Assumptions

In this section we comment on some simplifying assumptions on the signature and the rewrite system, and possible transformations of them in order to satisfy the assumptions when initially this is not the case. Similar transformations have appeared in other previous works [10,8]. We just comment them and give sketched proofs in the appendix showing that they preserve the normalization property.

We will always assume that all terms are constructed over a given fixed signature Σ that contains several constants and only one non-constant function symbol f. If this was not the case, we can define a transformation T from terms over Σ into terms over a new signature Σ' as follows. Let m be the maximum arity of a symbol in Σ plus 1. We choose a new function symbol f with arity m and define the new signature $\Sigma' = \Sigma_0' \cup \Sigma_m'$ as $\Sigma_0' = \Sigma$ and $\Sigma_m' = \{f\}$. Note that all symbols of Σ appear also in Σ' but with arity 0. Now, we recursively define $T : \mathcal{T}(\Sigma, \mathcal{V}) \rightarrow \mathcal{T}(\Sigma', \mathcal{V})$ as $T(c) = c$ and $T(x) = x$ for constants $c \in \Sigma_0$ and variables $x \in \mathcal{V}$, and $T(gt_1 \ldots t_k) = f(T(t_1), \ldots, T(t_k), g, \ldots, g)$ for terms headed with $g \in \Sigma_k$, for $k > 0$. Given a TRS R, by $T(R)$ we denote $\{T(l) \rightarrow T(r) | l \rightarrow r \in R\}$.

Lemma 1. *R is normalizing if and only if $T(R)$ is normalizing.*

For the case where the TRS R is left-shallow we will assume that R is indeed left-flat. If this was not the case, we can modify R by applying the following transformation whenever it is possible.

- If there is a non-constant ground term t that is a subterm at depth 1 of a left-hand side of a rule in R, then create a new constant c, replace all occurrences of t in the left-hand sides of the rules of R by c, and add the rule $t \rightarrow c$ to R. If it is the case that t is not a normal form, then add also the rule $c \rightarrow t$.

Lemma 2. *Let R be a left-shallow TRS and R^∞ be the resulting TRS obtained from R by the above transformation*
Then R is normalizing if and only if R^∞ is normalizing.

Finally, we will also assume that all right-hand sides in R are flat. If this was not the case, but R is right-shallow, we can modify R by applying the following transformation whenever it is possible.

- If there is a non-constant ground term t that is a subterm at depth 1 of a right-hand side of a rule in R, then create a new constant c, replace all occurrences of t at depth 1 in the right-hand sides of the rules of R by c, and add the rule $c \rightarrow t$ to R.

Note that the previous transformation converts right-shallow TRS's into right-flat TRS's, but also preserves the possible left-flatness obtained by the previous transformation. The proof of the following lemma is analogous to the previous one, and even simpler.

Lemma 3. *Let R be a right-shallow TRS and R^∞ the resulting TRS of the above transformation.*
Then R is normalizing if and only if R^∞ is normalizing.

4 Characterizing Normalization of Linear Right-Flat TRS

In this section we show that normalization of a linear right-flat TRS R is equivalent to the R-normalization of all ground terms of height 0 or 1. To this end, we first obtain a rewrite closure presentation of R, which is only necessary for simplification purposes in the argumentation, but not for the decision procedure of normalization.

4.1 Rewrite Closure

We present a rewrite closure transformation for linear right-flat TRS that is a straightforward variation of others presented before, like for the special case of ground TRS [14], for rule-linear shallow TRS [15], and for flat linear TRS [9]. The process of saturation, in this context, can be interpreted as asymmetric completion [12].

A linear right-flat TRS can be saturated under the following ordered chaining inference rule to give an enlarged linear right-flat TRS with some nice properties.

$$\text{Ordered Chaining:} \quad \frac{l \rightarrow r \quad s[u] \rightarrow t}{s[l]\sigma \rightarrow t\sigma}$$

where this inference rule is only applied if $l \to r$ is either an increasing or preserving rule, $s[u] \to t$ is a decreasing rule, σ is the most general unifier of r and u, and neither r nor u is a variable.

Note that these restrictions ensure that ordered chaining preserves linearity and right-flatness. Note also that $\text{height}(s[l]\sigma) \leq \text{height}(s[u])$, and hence, the saturation process terminates, since only a finite number of rules can be generated.

Application of ordered chaining preserves the normalization property, since it just adds new rules that can be emulated by several applications of the original ones. In fact, it preserves the rewrite relation $\to_R^+$.

Lemma 4. *Let R be a linear right-flat TRS saturated under the ordered chaining inference rules. If $s \to_R^* t$, then there is a derivation of the form $s \to_R^* u \to_R^* t$ where the subderivation $s \to_R^* u$ contains only applications of decreasing rules, and the subderivation $u \to_R^* t$ contains only application of preserving or increasing rules.*

Lemma 4 can be easily established using proof simplification arguments [1].

4.2 Characterization

In this subsection we assume that R is now the linear right-flat TRS resulting from the previous rewrite closure transformation.

We need a definition for depth 1 positions, that are then denoted as natural numbers i, j. Recall that m is the arity of the only non-constant function symbol f.

Definition 1. *We define that position i goes to position j in a derivation $s \to_R^* t$, where all rewrite rules $l \to r$ applied at position λ satisfy $|l|, |r| > 0$, recursively as follows:*

- *if $s \to_R^* t$ has 0 steps then every position i in $\{1 \ldots m\}$ goes to i.*
- *if $s \to_R^* t$ is of the form $s \to_R^* t' \to_{R, > \lambda} t$ and i goes to j in $s \to_R^* t'$, then i goes to j in $s \to_R^* t$.*
- *if $s \to_R^* t$ is of the form $s \to_R^* t' \to_{f l_1 \ldots l_m \to f r_1 \ldots r_m, \lambda} t$, i goes to j in $s \to_R^* t'$, and $l_j = r_k$ is a variable, then i goes to k in $s \to_R^* t$.*

The following lemma is straightforward from the previous definition.

Lemma 5. *Let R be a linear right-flat TRS resulting from the previous rewrite closure transformation. If i goes to j in $s \to_R^* t$, then $t|_j$ is reachable from $s|_i$ and $s[u]_i \to_R^* t[u]_j$ for any term u.*

Lemma 6. *Let R be a linear right-flat TRS resulting from the previous rewrite closure transformation. If s satisfies that $s|_i$ is a variable x that occurs only once in s, and $s \to_R^* t$, then the variable x occurs at most once in t. Moreover, if x occurs just once in t and the rewrite steps at λ in $s \to_R^* t$ are always preserving, then there exists a depth 1 position j such that $t|_j = x$ and i goes to j in $s \to_R^* t$.*

Definition 2. *A rewrite step $s \to_{l \to r, \lambda} t$ eats position i if $\text{height}(l) > 1$ and $\text{height}(l|_i) > 1$*

Note that, in particular, if a rewrite step eats some position, then it uses a decreasing rule.

Lemma 7. *Let R be a linear right-flat TRS resulting from the previous rewrite closure transformation. If i goes to j in a derivation $s \to_R^* t$ where only preserving and increasing rules are used, the rewrite step $t \to_{l \to r, \lambda} u$ eats position j, and no height 0 term is reachable from $s|_i$, then, there exists a rewrite rule application $s \to_{R, \lambda} s'$ that eats position i.*

Lemma 8. *Let R be a linear right-flat TRS resulting from the previous rewrite closure transformation, and suppose that all constants and height 1 terms can reach a normal form. Then all terms can reach a normal form by R.*

Proof. Let t be the minimal term in size that can not reach any normal form. By the assumptions of the lemma, the height of t is at least 2. We write t of the form $ft_1 \ldots t_m$. For every t_i we define t_i' to be as t_i if it is a constant, or to be a new variable x_i if t_i is not a constant. Note that the t_i's of the second case can not reach a constant, by the minimality of t. The term $t' = ft_1' \ldots t_m'$ is flat, and hence, by the assumptions of the lemma, it can reach a normal form u. By Lemma 4 there exists a derivation $t' \to_R^* u$, with a first part with only decreasing rules and a second part without them. The only possible decreasing rewrite step in $t' \to_R^* u$ can occur then at the beginning. But in fact it can not occur, since the rule would also be applicable on t producing a smaller term than t, which can not reach a normal form since t can not, and this is a contradiction with the minimality of t. Hence, all the rewrite steps in $t' \to_R^* u$ are either preserving or increasing, and the ones at position λ are preserving.

Now, for every t_i that is not a constant we define t_i'' to be a normal form reachable from t_i. Note that such a t_i'' must exist since t is the minimal term having no normal form reachable from it. Moreover, a derivation $t_i \to_R^* t_i''$ with a first part with decreasing rules and a second part without them, can only have preserving and increasing rewrite steps, again by the minimality of t. We define a substitution σ on the previously new introduced variables x_i as $x_i \sigma = t_i''$. The derivation $t' \to_R^* u$ instantiated with σ gives a derivation $t'' = ft_1'' \ldots t_m'' \to_R^* u\sigma$, and we have also the derivation $t \to_R^* t''$ with no rewrite steps at λ. Both derivations have preserving and increasing rewrite steps. Combining the two derivations we have a derivation $t \to_R^* u\sigma$, such that a position i goes to j in it if and only if i goes to j in $t'' \to_R^* u\sigma$. By Lemma 6 applied on the derivation $t' \to_R^* u$, if one of the new variables x_i occurs in u, then it occurs at a depth 1 position j such that i goes to j. Since u is a normal form and $u\sigma$ can not be a normal form, there exists a rewrite step at position λ on $u\sigma$ such that eats some of these positions j. On the other hand, instantiation of a derivation does not affect the goes to property, and hence, if a position i goes to j in $t' \to_R^* u$, then i also goes to j in $t'' \to_R^* u\sigma$, but also in $t \to_R^* u\sigma$. From all these facts we conclude that there exists a depth 1 position i in t that goes to a depth 1 position j in $u\sigma$, such that a rewrite step at position λ in $u\sigma$ eats position j. Moreover, $t|_i$ can not reach a constant. By Lemma 7 it follows that then there exists a rewrite rule application in t that eats position i. But this rewrite step is then decreasing, and contradicts the minimality of t.   □

5   Characterizing Normalization of Flat Right-Linear TRS

In this section we show that normalization of a flat right-linear TRS R is equivalent to the R-normalization of a finite set of terms. These terms are constructed over other sets of terms that we describe as follows.

Let $S \subseteq \Sigma_0$. We define $N(S)$ to be the set of all non-constant normal forms reachable from S and not reachable from any constant in $\Sigma_0 - S$. We assume that we have computed sets $N'(S)$ for every $S \subseteq \Sigma_0$ satisfying that $N'(S) \subseteq N(S)$ and $|N'(S)| = min(m, |N(S)|)$ (the computation of a concrete $N'(S)$ for every S is postponed to Section 6). Recall that m is the arity of the only non-constant function symbol f. The idea is that only a small subset $N'(S)$ of examples of normal forms reachable from S suffices to decide normalization.

We assume also that there are at least m new constants not occurring in R (note that the addition of new constants preserves normalization).

Lemma 9. *If there exists a term from which no normal form is reachable, then there exists one ground term t' that is either a constant or of the form $ft'_1 \ldots t'_m$, where all t'_i are either constants or terms in some $N'(S)$, such that no normal form is reachable from t'.*

Proof. Assume that for every ground term t' that is either a constant or of the form $ft'_1 \ldots t'_m$, where all t'_i are either constants or terms in some $N'(S)$, some normal form is reachable from t'. Assume also that t is a minimal term in height from which no normal form is reachable. Then t is of the form $ft_1 \ldots t_m$, and all t_i have at least one normal form. Replacing every t_i by a corresponding normal form we get a term reachable from t, and hence, a term from which no normal form is reachable. Hence, we can assume directly that all t_i's are normal forms (at this point we lose the minimality assumption for t).

Before continuing we need a technical definition based on the t_i's. We consider the set $T = \{t_i | i \in \{1 \ldots m\}\}$ and define a function $F : T \to \mathcal{T}(\Sigma, \mathcal{V})$ as follows. For every constant $u \in T$ we define $F(u) := u$. For every $u \in T$ that is not a constant, let S be the set containing just all the constants that reach u. If S is empty then we choose $F(u)$ to be a constant not occurring in R and different from all the rest of $F(u')$'s for $u \neq u' \in T$ (this is always possible since there exist at least m constants not occurring in R). Otherwise, if S is not empty, then either $u \in N'(S)$ or $u \notin N'(S)$. In the first case we define $F(u) := u$. In the second case we know that $N'(S)$ contains at least m elements, and we chose $F(u)$ to be one element in $N'(S)$ different from all the rest of $F(u')$'s for $u \neq u' \in T$. With this definition, F is injective, and $F(u) \neq u$ implies $F(u) \notin T$. Hence, considering F^{-1} as its inverse on the image $F(T)$, it holds that $F' = F \cup F^{-1}$ is a bijective function from $T \cup F(T)$ to $T \cup F(T)$. Now, we consider F' extended to all terms by the identity for the ones not in $T \cup F(T)$.

We comment some properties of F'. First note that F' is its own inverse, i.e. $F'(F'(v)) = v$ for all terms v. Moreover, if v is a normal form, then $F'(v)$ is also a normal form. Finally, if a constant reaches a term v, then it also reaches $F'(v)$. But also note that for the depth 1 subterms t_i of t, $F'(t_i)$ is either a constant or a term in some $N'(S)$,

We show now that any derivation starting from $s = fF'(t_1)\ldots F'(t_m)$ into a term $v = fv_1\ldots v_m$ and such that all the rewrite steps at λ are preserving can be converted into a derivation from t into $fF'(v_1)\ldots F'(v_m)$. We write the original derivation as $s = s_1 \to^*_{>\lambda} s'_1 \to_\lambda s_2 \to^*_{>\lambda} s'_2 \to_\lambda s_3 \ldots s'_{n-1} \to_\lambda s_n \to^*_{>\lambda} s'_n = v$, and use it for constructing a new derivation of the form $u = u_1 \to^*_{>\lambda} u'_1 \to_\lambda u_2 \to^*_{>\lambda} u'_2 \to_\lambda u_3 \ldots u'_{n-1} \to_\lambda u_n \to^*_{>\lambda} u'_n$. We define the explicit terms starting from u'_n and going backwards. The term u'_n is obtained from s'_n by replacing every subterm at depth 1 by its image by F'. Formally, $u'_n = fF'(s'_n|_1),\ldots,F'(s'_n|_m)$. Now, every u_i is obtained from s_i and u'_i as follows. Let $\{j_1 \ldots j_k\}$ be the positions at depth 1 in s_i that are not constants. Then $u_i = s_i[u'_i|_{j_1}]_{j_1} \ldots [u'_i|_{j_k}]_{j_k}$. Every u'_{i-1} is obtained from u_i as follows. Let $l \to r$ be the applied rule at λ and σ the used substitution for obtaining s_i from s'_{i-1}. Let σ' be the substitution defined only on $\mathtt{Vars}(r)$ and such that $r\sigma = u_i$. We extend σ' to the variables x occurring in l and not in r as $x\sigma' = F'(x\sigma)$, and define $u'_{i-1} = l\sigma'$.

It is not difficult to prove inductively on the previous construction that, for every i in $\{1\ldots n\}$ and every depth 1 position j, it holds that $s_i|_j \to^*_R F'(u_i|_j)$ and that $s'_i|_j \to^*_R F'(u'_i|_j)$. To this end the important fact is that F' is its own inverse, and that if a constant reaches a term v, then it also reaches $F'(v)$. Moreover, the previous derivation is a correctly defined derivation.

Now we look at the term $u = u_1$. It has been defined from $s = s_1$ and from u'_1. By this definition, if $s|_j$ is a constant, then $u|_j = s|_j$, and in particular, $F'(s|_j) = u|_j$. If $s|_j$ is not a constant, then, by the original definition of s, $s|_j$ is a normal form. But we have also the property stating that $s|_j \to^*_R F'(u|_j)$, and since $s|_j$ is a normal form, it is exactly $F'(u|_j)$, which implies that $F'(s|_j) = F'(F'(u|_j)) = u|_j$. Therefore, for any depth 1 position j, $F'(s|_j) = u|_j$ holds. This and the original definition of s implies $u = t$.

We come back to analyze $t = ft_1 \ldots t_m$ and note that $s = fF'(t_1)\ldots F'(t_m)$ satisfies that all the $F'(t_i)$'s are either constants or terms in some $N'(S)$. Hence, by the initial assumptions, there exists a derivation from s into a normal form. Assume first that there is no decreasing rewrite step at λ in this derivation. Then, if $fv_1\ldots v_m$ is the reached normal form, it holds that $fF'(v_1)\ldots F'(v_m)$ is also a normal form, and it is reachable from t, which contradicts our initial assumption. Hence, assume that there is at least one decreasing rewrite step at λ in the derivation from s into a normal form. We write this derivation making explicit the first of such rewrite decreasing steps at λ as $s \to^*_R fv_1\ldots v_m \to_\lambda v \to^*_R u$, where either v is a constant or v is in $\{v_1 \ldots v_m\}$, depending on whether the applied rule has a constant as right-hand side or is collapsing. Note that all rewrite steps at position λ in $s \to^*_R fv_1\ldots v_m$ are preserving. Again we have $t \to^*_R fF'(v_1)\ldots F'(v_m)$, but also $fF'(v_1)\ldots F'(v_m) \to_\lambda F'(v)$. If v is a normal form then $F'(v)$ is also a normal form, and hence t reaches a normal form, contradicting the initial assumption. If v is not a normal form, then $F'(v) = v$, and hence, t reaches v, and v reaches u, which is a normal form, contradicting again our initial assumption. □

6 Deciding with Automata

6.1 The Right-Flat Linear Case

By Lemma 8, for deciding normalization for right-flat linear TRSs, we have just to decide whether a given constant or height 1 term can reach a normal form in a right-flat linear TRS. We will see that this can be done by using tree automata.

First, it is well known that the set of normal forms of a left-linear TRS is recognizable by a finite tree automaton. Let $\mathcal{V}$ be a finite set of variables and $NF(R, \mathcal{V})$ be the set of irreducible terms of $\mathcal{T}(\Sigma, \mathcal{V})$ w.r.t. R:

Lemma 10. *Let R be a right-flat linear TRS. A dfta whose number of states is $O(2^{|R|})$ which recognizes $NF(R, \mathcal{V})$ can be computed. Furthermore, if the signature is fixed, it can be computed in time $O(|R| * m * 2^{|R| * m})$ where m is the maximal arity of the signature.*

Proof. Let $P = \{(i, p) \mid p \in Pos(l_i), (l_i, r_i) \in R\}$. It is easy to compute for $NF(R, \mathcal{V})$ a dfta where the set of states is 2^P and the set of final states is $\{S \subset P | \forall i, (i, \lambda) \notin S\}$. Furthermore, let us note that if the TRS is also left-flat, the number of states can be reduced to $O(|R|)$. □

It is also well known that for a fta $\mathcal{A}$ and a right-flat linear TRS R, the set of descendants of $L(A)$ by R is recognizable [6,11,3]. Indeed, for computing from $\mathcal{A}$ a fta for the set of descendants by R of $L(\mathcal{A})$, we saturate the rules of $\mathcal{A}$ as follows: for any rewrite rule $l \to r$ of R, for any substitution σ from $\mathcal{V}$ to Q (restricted to accessible states) s.t. $\sigma l \to_{\mathcal{A}}^* q$, we add rules for enabling $\sigma r \to_{\mathcal{A}}^* q$. We can suppose w.l.o.g. that for any constant c occurring in a rhs of R, there is one state q_c which accepts exactly $\{c\}$. Then, as R is right-flat, for enabling $\sigma r \to_{\mathcal{A}}^* q$, just one rule has to be added: e.g. let $g((h(a, x), h(y, a)) \to f(a, y, b, x)$ be a rule of R and q_1, q_2, q states of $\mathcal{A}$ s.t. $g(h(a, q_1), h(q_2, a)) \to_{\mathcal{A}}^* q$; for enabling $f(a, q_2, b, q_1) \to_{\mathcal{A}}^* q$, the rule $f(q_a, q_1, q_b, q_2) \to q$ is added. Let us note that the construction works also for non-ground terms (with $\mathcal{V}$ finite). If $L(\mathcal{A})$ is included in $\mathcal{T}(\Sigma, \mathcal{V})$, the set of terms reachable from at least one term of $L(\mathcal{A})$ is also included in $\mathcal{T}(\Sigma, \mathcal{V})$, as each variable occurring in a rhs of a rule occurs in the corresponding lhs, and we can consider variables as new constants. Therefore, adapting the precise complexity analysis of [5] we obtain:

Lemma 11. *Let R be a right-flat linear TRS, and let t be a constant or term of height 1. Then, L_t, the set of terms reachable from t is recognizable and a fta recognizing it can be computed in $O(|R|^2 * (|R| + m)^{4|R|})$ where m is the maximal arity of the signature. Furthermore its number of states is $O(|R| + m)$.*

Hence, let t be a constant or term of height 1 in $\mathcal{T}(\Sigma, \mathcal{V})$. By the preceding lemmas, we can compute ftas for L_t and $NF(R, \mathcal{V})$. Then, by intersecting them and testing emptiness, we can decide whether a normal form can be reached from t. Therefore, by Lemma 8, we can decide whether R is normalizing.

Theorem 1. *Normalization of a linear right-shallow TRS is decidable.*

6.2   The Flat Right-Linear Case

Whereas the set of normal forms of a left-linear TRS is recognizable by a fta, it is of course no more the case when the TRS is not left-linear. Hence, in order to represent the set of normal forms of a flat TRS, we will need more powerful class of automata which enable to test equality or disequality between sibling subterms.

Tree automata with disequality and equality constraints between brothers. An elementary equality constraint (resp. disequality constraint) between brothers is a predicate on $\mathcal{T}(\Sigma)$ written $i = j$ (resp. $i \neq j$) where $i, j \in \mathbb{N}^*$. Such a predicate is satisfied on a term t, which we write $t \models i = j$, if $i, j \in Pos(t)$ and $t|_i = t|_j$ (resp. $i \neq j$ is satisfied on t if $i = j$ is not satisfied on t).

The satisfaction relation $\models$ is extended as usual to any Boolean combination of equality and disequality constraints. The empty conjunction and disjunction are respectively written $\top$ (true) and $\bot$ (false). A constraint will be such a boolean combination. Let π be a partition of $[1..n]$ and $\equiv_\pi$ the associated equivalence relation. It defines a constraint $\wedge_{i \equiv_\pi j} i = j \wedge \wedge_{i \not\equiv_\pi j} i \neq j$. A constraint definable by a partition is called *strong*. Two constraints are said compatible if they can simultaneously be satisfied. Two constraints are equivalent if they have the same models. A constraint is said compatible with a partition if it is compatible with (actually implied by) the constraint defined by the partition.

An automaton with disequality and equality constraints between brothers (a.w.c.b.b. in short) is a tuple (Q, Σ, Q_f, Δ) where Σ is a finite ranked alphabet, Q is a finite set of states, Q_f is a subset of Q of finite states and Δ is a set of transition rules of the form $f(q_1, \ldots, q_n) \xrightarrow{c} q$ where $f \in \Sigma$, $q_1, \ldots, q_n, q \in Q$, and c is a Boolean combination of equality (and disequality) constraints between brothers.

Let $A = (Q, \Sigma, Q_f, \Delta)$. The move relation $\rightarrow_A$ is defined as for fta modulo the satisfaction of equality and disequality constraints: let $t, t' \in F(\Sigma \cup Q, X)$, then $t \rightarrow_A t'$ if and only if:

. there is a context $C \in \mathcal{C}(\Sigma \cup Q)$ and some terms $u_1, \ldots, u_n \in \mathcal{T}(\Sigma)$
. there exists a rule $f(q_1, \ldots, q_n) \xrightarrow{c} q \in \Delta$ s.t.

$\quad t = C[f(q_1(u_1), \ldots, q_n(u_n))]$ and $t' = C[q(f(u_1, \ldots, u_n))]$
$\quad f(u_1, \ldots, u_n) \models c$

$\xrightarrow{*}_A$ is the reflexive and transitive closure of $\rightarrow_A$. A term t is accepted iff $t \rightarrow_A q$ for some q in Q_f.

An a.w.c.b.b. is *deterministic* if there are no two rules $f(q_1, \ldots, q_n) \xrightarrow{c} q$, $f(q_1, \ldots, q_n) \xrightarrow{c'} q'$, with c and c' compatible and $q \neq q'$. If an automaton is deterministic, we can suppose for any rule $f(q_1, \ldots, q_n) \xrightarrow{c} q$, that if c implies $i = j$, then $q_i = q_j$.

A *normalized* a.w.c.b.b. is an automaton where all constraints are strong. Note that, we can always normalize an a.w.c.b.b.: one rule $f(q_1, \ldots, q_n) \xrightarrow{c} q$ will correspond to all the rules $f(q_1, \ldots, q_n) \xrightarrow{c_p} q$ with c_p strong and compatible with c. This transformation can multiply the number of rules by B_n the number of partitions of $[1 \ldots n]$. A normalized automaton can be determinized by the usual subset construction.

An a.w.c.b.b. recognizing the intersection of two languages recognized by a.w.c.b.b.s can be computed by a standard product construction: the constraint associated with the by-product of two rules is the conjunction of the constraints of the two rules. Emptiness of the language recognized by an a.w.c.b.b. is decidable and polynomial for normalized deterministic automata [2]. Let us note that if the automaton is normalized but not deterministic, the complexity of the problem becomes EXPTIME-complete. If the automaton is deterministic but not normalized, the problem is polynomial for fixed signature, (as the normalization explained above is polynomial), NP-complete otherwise. Here, we will need a stronger result:

Lemma 12. *Let $\mathcal{A}$ be a deterministic normalized a.w.c.b.b. and m greater or equal to the maximal arity. Deciding whether $L(\mathcal{A})$ is of cardinality greater or equal to m and computing $min(|L(\mathcal{A})|, m)$ terms of $L(\mathcal{A})$ can be done in time complexity $O(m^3 * |\Delta| * |Q|)$.*

Proof. The idea is just to memorize for each state q, $Ex(q)$ a set of at most m terms reaching q. The $Ex(q)$ are initialized to the empty sets. At each iteration, we compute for every state q a new set $Ex(q)$ from the previous sets $Ex(s)$: let q be a state, r a rule $f(q_1, \ldots, q_n) \xrightarrow{c} q$, with c expressed by a partition π, $[i]_\pi$ denoting the class of i in the equivalence relation defined by π. For each s in Q, let $need_r(s) = |\{[i]_\pi | s = q_i\}|$: $need_r(s)$ is the number of different terms reaching s you need to apply the rule and is bounded by the maximal arity, so by m. If $nex(s)$ denotes the cardinality of $Ex(s)$, the rule r produces $\Pi_{s \in Q} P_{need_r(s)}^{nex(s)}$ examples, where $P_{k_2}^{k_1}$ expresses permutations of k_2 elements chosen from a set of k_1 elements without repetition.

Hence let R_q be the set of rules whose target state is q: the number of examples available at this step for q is $\sum_{r \in R_q} \Pi_{q' \in Q} P_{need_r(q')}^{nex(q')}$ and you build $min(m, \sum_{r \in R_q} \Pi_{q' \in Q} P_{need_r(q')}^{nex(q')})$ terms reaching q. Computation stops when one iteration keeps unchanged the cardinality of the $Ex(q)$.

Therefore there are at most $m * |Q|$ iterations, with each iteration in $O(|\Delta| * m^2)$. $\qquad \square$

Ground normal forms of a left-flat TRS. An a.w.c.b.b. can be used for representing the set of ground normal forms of a left-flat TRS:

Lemma 13. *Let R be a left-flat TRS; we can compute a deterministic normalized a.w.c.b.b. which recognizes $NF(R)$. Its number of states will be in $O(|R|)$, its size in $O(|\Sigma| * |R|^{m+1} * B_m)$ where B_m is the number of partitions of $\{1..m\}$. The computation can be done in time $O(|\Sigma| * |R|^{m+2} * B_m)$.*

Proof. Let Sub be the set of ground irreducible constants occurring in lhs of R; $Q = Sub \cup \{OK, \bot\}$ will be the set of states. Every state except $\bot$ is final. The rules are defined as follows:

for any constant a, $a \to a$ is a rule if a is irreducible, otherwise $a \to \bot$ is a rule.

$f(q_1, \ldots, q_n) \overset{c}{\to} q$ with c a constraint defined by a partition π is a rule iff one of the following conditions is satisfied:

(1) some $q_i = \bot$ and $q = \bot$.
(2) All q_i are different from $\bot$, q is either $\bot$ or OK, and for all i, j, $c \models i = j$ implies $q_i = q_j$. Moreover, q is $\bot$ iff there exists a rule $f l_1 \ldots l_m \to r$ satisfying that, if l_i is a constant then $l_i = q_i$, and if $l_j = l_k$ are the same variable then $c \models j = k$.

The number of states is $|Sub| + 2$, so in $O(|R|)$. Let us note that the number of rules is $O(|\Sigma| * |R|^{m+1} * B_m)$ as here we require- in order to simplify the proof- the automaton to be normalized. However, this restriction can be weakened which would decrease the number of rules. $\qquad\square$

Preservation of recognizability for right-linear right-shallow TRS has been proved by Nagaya and Toyama [5,13]. The construction is a little more critical than in the linear case as you have to ensure determinism of the automaton along the construction. E.g., when you saturate the rules for taking in account the rewrite rule $f(x, x) \to g(x)$, determinism ensures that you can consider only the rules whose lhs are of the form $f(q, q)$. Once more, a precise analysis of the construction can be found in [5]. We adapt here the construction to our particular necessities:

Lemma 14. *Let R be a right-linear flat TRS, and $S \subseteq \Sigma_0$ a set of constants. We can compute a dfta which recognizes the set of terms reachable from S by R and not reachable from any constant in $\Sigma_0 - S$ by R. The number of states is in $O(2^{|\Sigma_0|})$. The computation can be done in $O(|\Sigma| * |R|^2 * 2^{(|\Sigma_0| * O(m))})$ time.*

Proof. We will build a complete dfta $\mathcal{A} = (Q, \Sigma, Q_f, \Delta)$ with $Q = 2^{\Sigma_0}$, $Q_f = \{S\}$.

The set of transitions is initialized by $\Delta = \{s \to \{s\}/s \in \Sigma_0\} \cup \{f(q_1, ..., q_n) \to \emptyset / f \in \Sigma - \Sigma_0\}$..

Then, the rules are saturated in order to simulate rewriting by R. The objective is to get, for any set of constants B, $t \overset{*}{\to}_{\mathcal{A}} B$ Iff t is reachable from B by R and not reachable from any constant in $\Sigma_0 - B$. More precisely, let $l \to r$ be a rule of R, σ a substitution from $Vars(l) \cup Vars(r)$ into Q (restricted to the accessible states), and B the state s.t. $l\sigma \xrightarrow{*}_A B$; $r\sigma = f(r_1, ..., r_p)$ with r_i either a state or a constant. Let $A_1 ... A_p$ be accessible states satisfying that $A_i = r_i$, if r_i is a state, A_i containing r_i if r_i is a constant. The rule $f(A_1, ..A_p) \to A$, will be transformed into $f(A_1, ..A_p) \to A \cup B$.

As saturation increases cardinality of the rhs of rules (considered as a set of constants), the process clearly terminates, the number of iterations being bounded by $|\Sigma_0| * 2^{|\Sigma_0|*(1+m)} * |\Sigma|$.

Then, it can be proven by induction that the language accepted by $\mathcal{A}$ in the state C, i.e. the set of terms t s.t. $t \xrightarrow{*}_A C$,is the set of terms reachable from C, not reachable from any constant in $\Sigma_0 - C$. In particular, as $Q_f = \{S\}$, the automaton recognizes the set of terms reachable from S by R and not reachable from any constant in $\Sigma_0 - S$ by R.

As each iteration is in time $O(|R|^2 * 2^{|\Sigma_0|*2m})$, the algorithm is in time $O(|\Sigma| * |R|^2 * 2^{|\Sigma_0|*O(m)})$.   □

The preceding lemmas provide us tools for computing for each subset S of constants a set $N'(S)$ of non-constant normal forms reachable from S and not reachable from any other constant, whose cardinality is $min(m, |N(S)|)$.

Lemma 15. *Let R be a flat right-linear TRS, m a positive integer and S a set of constants. We can compute a subset $N'(S)$ of $N(S)$ whose cardinality is $min(m, |N(S)|)$. Furthermore, this can be done in polynomial time for a fixed signature.*

Proof. We first compute by Lemma 14 a dfta for the terms reachable from S and not reachable from any constant in $\Sigma_0 - S$; Then we intersect it with the normalized deterministic automaton with constraints recognizing the set of non constant normal forms obtained from Lemma 10 (this can be done by the product construction as for fta). We obtain a deterministic normalized automaton with constraints whose number of states is $O(|R| * 2^{|\Sigma_0|})$ and then we apply Lemma 12 to compute $N'(S)$. For a fixed signature, it can be done in polynomial time.   □

Once the $N(S')$ have been computed, we can generate all the ground terms t that are either constant or of the form $ft_1 ... t_m$, where all t_i are either constants or terms in some $N'(S)$. Then, for each such t, we can check whether there is a normal form reachable from t, by computing the set of terms reachable from t (with a similar construction to the one in the proof of Lemma 13, but for a term t instead of for a set of constants S), intersecting with the set of ground normal forms and testing emptiness. Therefore, by Lemma 9, and by applying simplification lemmas 2 and 3, we get:

Theorem 2. *Normalization of a shallow right-linear TRS is decidable.*

We have also the following result, as a consequence of the previous theorem, the fact that confluence is known decidable for shallow right-linear TRS [7], and the fact that, when a TRS is normalizing, confluence and unique normalization are equivalent properties.

Theorem 3. *It is decidable to determine if a given shallow right-linear TRS satisfies both the normalization and the unique normalization properties simultaneously.*

7 Undecidability of Unique Normalization in the Linear Right-Shallow Case

Lemma 16. *Unique normalization is undecidable for linear right-shallow TRSs.*

We will associate with a PCP problem a linear right-shallow TRS which is uniquely normalizing iff the problem has no solution. Let $PCP = \{(u_i, v_i)|1 \leq i \leq n\}$ a Post Correspondence problem over $\{a, b\}$. Let R the TRS defined by:

$$pcp(x, y) \rightarrow eq(x, y), pcp(x, y) \rightarrow pair(x, y),$$
$$eq(a(x), a(y)) \rightarrow eq(x, y), eq(b(x), b(y)) \rightarrow eq(x, y)$$
$$eq(c, c) \rightarrow nf1$$
$$pair(u_i(x), v_i(y)) \rightarrow pair(x, y), 1 \leq i \leq n,$$
$$pair(u_i(c), v_i(c)) \rightarrow nf2, 1 \leq i \leq n,$$
$$a(x) \rightarrow loop, b(x) \rightarrow loop, c \rightarrow loop$$
$$pair(x, y) \rightarrow loop, eq(x, y) \rightarrow loop, pcp(x, y) \rightarrow loop$$
$$loop \rightarrow loop$$

Then, as any term different from $nf1, nf2$ can be rewritten to $loop$, the only two irreducible terms are $nf1, nf2$. It can be easily proven by induction on the length of the derivation that $t \rightarrow_R^* nf1$ iff $t = nf1$ or $t = eq(u, u)$ or $t = pcp(u, u)$ with u in $(a + b)^*(c)$. Similarly, $t \rightarrow_R^* nf2$ iff $t = nf2$ or $t = pair(u, v)$ or $t = pcp(u, v)$ with $u = u_{i_1}...u_{i_p}c$ and $v = v_{i_1}...v_{i_p}c$ for some $i_1, ...i_p$ with $p > 0$. Hence, there is some t such that $t \rightarrow_R^* nf1$ and $t \rightarrow_R^* nf2$ iff there is a solution to the PCP problem, i.e. R is not uniquely normalizing iff there is a solution to the PCP problem.

References

1. Bachmair, L.: Canonical Equational Proofs. Birkhäuser, Boston (1991)
2. Bogaert, B., Tison, S.: Equality and disequality constraints on direct subterms in tree automata. In: International Symposium on Theoretical Aspects of Computer Science, pp. 161–171 (1992)
3. Comon, H., Dauchet, M., Gilleron, R., Jacquemard, F., Lugiez, D., Tison, S., Tommasi, M.: Tree automata techniques and applications (1997) Available on http://www.grappa.univ-lille3.fr/tata
4. Dershowitz, N., Jouannaud, J.P.: Rewrite systems. In: van Leeuwen, J. (ed.) Handbook of Theoretical Computer Science (Vol. B: Formal Models and Semantics), pp. 243–320, Amsterdam, North-Holland (1990)
5. Durand, I.: Call by need computations in orthogonal term rewriting systems, 07, Habilitation diriger des recherches de l'université de Bordeaux (2005)

262   G. Godoy and S. Tison

6. Gilleron, R., Tison, S.: Regular tree languages and rewrite systems. Fundam. Inform. 24(1/2), 157–174 (1995)
7. Godoy, G., Tiwari, A.: Confluence of shallow right-linear rewrite systems. In: Luke, C.-H. (ed.) CSL 2005. LNCS, vol. 3634, pp. 541–556. Springer, Heidelberg (2005)
8. Godoy, G., Tiwari, A.: Termination of rewrite systems with shallow right-linear, collapsing, and right-ground rules. In: Nieuwenhuis, R. (ed.) Automated Deduction – CADE-20. LNCS (LNAI), vol. 3632, pp. 164–176. Springer, Heidelberg (2005)
9. Godoy, G., Tiwari, A., Verma, R.: On the confluence of linear shallow term rewrite systems. In: Alt, H., Habib, M. (eds.) STACS 2003. LNCS, vol. 2607, pp. 85–96. Springer, Heidelberg (2003)
10. Godoy, G., Tiwari, A., Verma, R.: Deciding confluence of certain term rewriting systems in polynomial time. Annals of Pure and Applied Logic 130(1-3), 33–59 (2004)
11. Jacquemard, F.: Decidable approximations of term rewriting systems. In: Rewriting Techniques and Applications, 7th International Conference, pp. 362–376 (1996)
12. Levy, J., Agusti, J.: Bi-rewriting, a term rewriting technique for monotone order relations. In: Kirchner, C. (ed.) Rewriting Techniques and Applications. LNCS, vol. 690, pp. 17–31. Springer, Heidelberg (1993)
13. Nagaya, T., Toyama, Y.: Decidability for left-linear growing term rewriting systems. Inf. Comput. 178(2), 499–514 (2002)
14. Tiwari, A.: Rewrite closure for ground and cancellative AC theories. In: Hariharan, R., Mukund, M., Vinay, V. (eds.) FST TCS 2001: Foundations of Software Technology and Theoretical Computer Science. LNCS, vol. 2245, pp. 334–346. Springer, Heidelberg (2001)
15. Tiwari, A.: On the combination of equational and rewrite theories induced by certain term rewrite systems. Menlo Park, CA 94025 (2002) Available at: www.csl.sri.com/~tiwari/combinationER.ps
16. Verma, R., Hayrapetyan, A.: A new decidability technique for ground term rewriting systems. ACM Trans. Comput. Log. 6(1), 102–123 (2005)

Handling Polymorphism in Automated Deduction

Jean-François Couchot[1,2] and Stéphane Lescuyer[1,2]

[1] INRIA Futurs, ProVal, Parc Orsay Université, F-91893
[2] LRI, Univ Paris-Sud, CNRS, Orsay, F-91405
{couchot,lescuyer}@lri.fr

Abstract. Polymorphism has become a common way of designing short and reusable programs by abstracting generic definitions from type-specific ones. Such a convenience is valuable in logic as well, because it unburdens the specifier from writing redundant declarations of logical symbols. However, top shelf automated theorem provers such as Simplify, Yices or other SMT-LIB ones do not handle polymorphism. To this end, we present efficient reductions of polymorphism in both unsorted and many-sorted first order logics. For each encoding, we show that the formulas and their encoded counterparts are logically equivalent in the context of automated theorem proving. The efficiency keynote is to disturb the prover as little as possible, especially the internal decision procedures used for special sorts, e.g. integer linear arithmetic, to which we apply a special treatment. The corresponding implementations are presented in the framework of the Why/Caduceus toolkit.

1 Introduction

Polymorphism allows a single definition to be used with different types of data: a polymorphic function's definition generalizes several type-specific ones. Obviously, polymorphism is not reduced to the foundation of basic arithmetic operators (e.g. + deals naturally with integers, reals, vectors, ...), but it is a common feature of object-oriented and functional languages. For instance, a function **append** which concatenates two lists of elements of the same type can be constructed without taking care of the elements' type: let α be any type and let α LIST denote the type of lists with elements of type α. **append** can then be typed α LIST $\times$ α LIST $\rightarrow$ α LIST.

In the context of program verification by analysis of assertions and generation of proof obligations, formalizing the features of a programming language involves a large collection of definitions and axioms, some of them being polymorphic. Even when the language, like C, does not have polymorphism, memory modelization makes use of polymorphic types and definitions. In these cases, polymorphism becomes critical since it allows specifications to be both typed and short: types can be used to guide the prover and avoid ill-sorted deductions, which often pollute the proof search of unsorted provers.

F. Pfenning (Ed.): CADE 2007, LNAI 4603, pp. 263–278, 2007.

Then, it is definitely a challenge to automatically discharge the verification conditions expressed in a polymorphic first order language: only interactive higher-order proof assistants like Isabelle/Hol [1] or Coq [2] are amenable to such polymorphic logic goals. Among automated provers, some deal with unsorted First Order Logic (FOL), e.g. Simplify [3] or haRVey [4] and others treat many-sorted FOL, e.g. SMT-LIB [5] provers and among them Yices [6] or CVC-lite [7], but none of them allows the definition of uninterpreted polymorphic symbols.

The main contribution of this work is a correct and complete reduction of polymorphic many-sorted FOL to unsorted FOL that preserves the sorting informations (Sect. 3). The second contribution is an equally powerful reduction targeting many-sorted FOL (Sect. 4), which takes advantage of sorted provers to provide an *ad hoc* translation for interpreted terms, e.g. arithmetic terms. The third contribution is an implementation of both approaches and their application on a full scale benchmark (Sect. 5). Section 2 presents some formal preliminaries about polymorphism, gives a running example and shows how inefficient some coarse techniques of polymorphism reduction are. Section 6 discusses works related to our study, concludes and presents future work. Note that proofs are sketched in this paper to fit within the space constraints. An extended version [8] details them.

2   Preliminaries

Our polymorphic logic is built on classical first order logic and its usual connectives $\vee, \neg, \exists, \ldots$ Atoms are built on a signature $\Sigma = (\mathcal{S}, \mathcal{F}_s, \mathcal{X}_s, \mathcal{X}, \mathcal{F})$ where $\mathcal{S}$ is the set of constant sorts, $\mathcal{F}_s$ is the set of sort functions (e.g. LIST or ARRAY), $\mathcal{X}_s$ is the set $\{\alpha, \beta, \ldots\}$ of type variables, $\mathcal{X}$ is the set of term variables and $\mathcal{F}$ is the set of all functional and predicative symbols (including constant symbols).

Each symbol in $\mathcal{F}_s$ comes with an integer number n of parameters and the set of all sorts Ω is the smallest set containing type variables and constant sorts such that if $f \in \mathcal{F}_s$ is a sort function of arity n and $s_1, \ldots, s_n \in \Omega$, then $f(s_1, \ldots, s_n) \in \Omega$.

Similarly, each functional symbol in $\mathcal{F}$ comes with an arity $s_1 \times \ldots \times s_n \to s$ where each s_i, $1 \leqslant i \leqslant n$, is in Ω and s is either in Ω or the special propositional sort o. When $n = 0$, the symbol is a constant of type s. Variables from $\mathcal{X}$ and functional symbols from $\mathcal{F}$ are then used to build terms in the usual manner. Among these terms, those of type o form the atoms of our propositional language.

Since we are only interested in well-typed atoms and well-typed formulas, we define a well-typing relation $\Gamma \vdash e : \tau$ where Γ is a typing context (i.e. a mapping from $\mathcal{X}$ to Ω) and τ is a sort. Inference rules for this typing system are given in Fig. 1. The rules for $\forall, \neg$ and $\wedge$ are similar to rules (EXISTS) and (OR) and are not shown. In the following, unless we specify otherwise, we only consider well-typed formulas ϕ, that is, such that $\vdash \phi : o$. Finally, type variables that appear in formulas are implicitly universally quantified.

$$
\begin{array}{cc}
\dfrac{\Gamma(x) = \tau}{\Gamma \vdash x : \tau} \quad (\text{VAR}) &
\dfrac{\begin{array}{c} \sigma \text{ substitution from } \mathcal{X}_s \text{ to } \Omega \\ f : s_1 \times \ldots \times s_n \to s \\ \text{for all } i, \Gamma \vdash e_i : s_i\sigma \end{array}}{\Gamma \vdash f(e_1, \ldots, e_n) : s\sigma} \quad (\text{APP}) \\[3em]
\dfrac{x \in \mathcal{X} \quad \Gamma, x : s \vdash e : o}{\Gamma \vdash \exists x : s.e : o} \quad (\text{EXISTS}) &
\dfrac{\Gamma \vdash \phi : o \quad \Gamma \vdash \psi : o}{\Gamma \vdash \phi \vee \psi : o} \quad (\text{OR})
\end{array}
$$

Fig. 1. Typing system

Let us now explain why the simplest encodings that come to mind for removing typing information are not adequate. First of all, instead of dealing with sorts, one may think that we can omit sorting information, but unfortunately, this method is unsound. For instance, consider the following formula: $\forall x : unit . x = void$. It states that sort $unit$ is a singleton whose only member is $void$. Removing sorts in this formula gives $\forall x . x = void$ which states that *every* term is equal to $void$, and in turn easily yields things like $1 = 2$.

Secondly, the reader who is familiar with polymorphism can think that a polymorphic theory can be reduced to a many-sorted one by instantiating the type variables in polymorphic symbols according to the contexts they are applied to, and generating as many instances as necessary to "monomorphize" the original theory.

However, the computation of these mandatory monomorphic instances can be an infinite process: for instance, consider the symbol $cons : \alpha \times \alpha\,\text{LIST} \to \alpha\,\text{LIST}$, which adds an element in front of a list, and $nested : \text{INT} \to \alpha\,\text{LIST}$, which is axiomatized by:

$$nested(0) = cons(0, nil)$$
$$\forall x : \text{INT} . nested(x + 1) = cons(nested(x), nil)$$

If $nested$ is then applied to some arithmetic function f whose result is not statically predictable, one can see that there is no way to adequately monomorphize this theory since a potentially infinite number of instantiations of $cons$ (on INT LIST, (INT LIST) LIST, and so on) may be required. Even if this shortcoming does not appear often in practical cases, monomorphization always returns theories that are much bigger than the original ones, which dramatically slows down provers. Therefore, this approach is not satisfactory in our context.

Finally, a potentially good reduction of polymorphic logic to unsorted logic is suggested by a reduction from many-sorted logic to unsorted logic developed in [9, p. 277]: it suffices to take a language with the same symbols as in the many-sorted language being translated, augmented with a predicate symbol P used to ensure the type of variables. P has two parameters: the first one is the term being sorted and the second one is its sort, given as a term. For instance, the formula $\forall l : \alpha\,\text{LIST} . append(l, nil) = l$ would be translated to $\forall \alpha, l . P(l, list(\alpha)) \Rightarrow append(l, nil) = l$.

Similarly, sorts in existentially quantified formulae are replaced by a conjunction and axioms are added for all symbols so that $P(t, \tau)$ is provable iff t has type τ. For instance, the following axioms are added for lists:

$$\forall \alpha . P(nil, list(\alpha))$$
$$\forall \alpha, x, l . (P(x, \alpha) \land P(l, list(\alpha))) \Rightarrow P(cons(x, l), list(\alpha))$$

Altogether, this new typing predicate P and the axioms ensure soundness and completeness. However, this translation cannot be used in our context since it strongly modifies the boolean structure of formulas, especially by introducing useless disjunctions, that are often inefficiently handled by SMT solvers (see benchmarks in Sect. 5).

Notice that this encoding is not a solution for many-sorted logic with built-in types: we cannot give a type for P that is compliant both with terms of built-in sorts and user ones. Adding one predicate p_t for each sort t is not a solution either since it does not allow one to deal with polymorphism.

We now present the running example, used in the following to illustrate non-obvious steps. Let $acc : \alpha\, \text{ARRAY} \times \text{INT} \rightarrow \alpha$ and $upd : \alpha\, \text{ARRAY} \times \text{INT} \times \alpha \rightarrow \alpha\, \text{ARRAY}$ be the functional symbols of an array theory [10], axiomatized by:

$$\forall a : \alpha\, \text{ARRAY}, i : s\text{INT}, e : \alpha . acc(upd(a, i, e), i) = e \tag{1}$$
$$\forall a : \alpha\, \text{ARRAY}, i : \text{INT}, j : \text{INT}, e : \alpha . i \neq j$$
$$\Rightarrow acc(upd(a, i, e), j) = acc(a, j). \tag{2}$$

Intuitively, a being an INT-indexed array and i an integer, $acc(a, i)$ represents the ith element of a while $upd(a, i, e)$ represents the array a where the ith element has been changed to an (α-sorted) element e.

Running example. We want to check whether the formula

$$acc(upd(k, 3, x), 3) + 2 = 7 \tag{3}$$

is satisfiable modulo the theory built as the union of $\{(1), (2)\}$ and a theory of linear arithmetic, where x (resp. k) has the sort INT (resp. INT ARRAY).

3   Reduction to Unsorted Logic

Unsorted FOL is a special case of polymorphic FOL where there is only one constant sort U (for Unsorted elements) and neither sort functions, built-in types nor type variables. We now present an encoding from a polymorphic logic with built-in types to an unsorted logic: the idea behind this encoding is to syntactically type expressions by adding the sort information directly in terms and rely on the fact that unification will guide the prover and ensure that instantiations remain well-typed. We also illustrate how to deal with interpreted symbols, as we consider the case of arithmetic terms.

3.1   Translation

In the polymorphic signature $\Sigma = (\mathcal{S}, \mathcal{F}_s, \mathcal{X}_s, \mathcal{X}, \mathcal{F})$ we translate, we assume $\mathcal{F}$ contains an *equality* predicate $=$ of arity $\alpha \times \alpha \to o$. We also consider a built-in sort INT $\in \mathcal{S}$ and $\mathcal{F}_{\mathcal{A}} \subset \mathcal{F}$ the set of arithmetic symbols (i.e. built-in operations and predicates on integers, but not $=$). The translation of signature Σ is the monosorted signature $\Sigma^* = (\{U\}, \emptyset, \emptyset, \mathcal{X}^*, \mathcal{F}^*)$ defined by:

- $\mathcal{X}^* = \mathcal{X} \cup \{t_\alpha \mid \alpha \in \mathcal{X}_s\}$ where the t_α are fresh term variables
- $\mathcal{F}^* = \mathcal{F} \cup \mathcal{S} \cup \mathcal{F}_s \cup \widehat{\mathcal{F}_{\mathcal{A}}} \cup \{\mathsf{sort}\}$ where this union is supposed disjoint and
  - symbols from $\mathcal{F}$ have the same arity as before where all sorts from Ω have been replaced by U (e.g. *cons* : U $\times$ U $\to$ U)
  - symbols from $\mathcal{S}$ have arity U
  - symbols from $\mathcal{F}_s$ with n parameters have arity $\underbrace{\text{U} \times \ldots \times \text{U}}_{n \text{ times}} \to \text{U}$

  - $\widehat{\mathcal{F}_{\mathcal{A}}} = \{\hat{f} \mid f \in \mathcal{F}_{\mathcal{A}}\}$ where each symbol $\hat{f}$ is fresh in $\mathcal{F}$, has the same arity as f and where INT has been replaced by U (e.g. $\hat{+}$: U $\times$ U $\to$ U)
  - the new special symbol sort has arity U $\times$ U $\to$ U

The idea behind this new function symbol sort is that it is used to associate a term with its type: the first argument is a syntactic sort and the second a term whose type is the first argument in the context. Unlike the P-predicate of Enderton ([9]), it is a function symbol and not a predicate symbol. Also, treating arithmetic symbols in a special way is mandatory to ensure completeness and is discussed below.

The translation $(.)^*$ of sorts from Ω into terms of Σ^* is inductively defined on the structure of a sort:

$$
\begin{aligned}
s \in \mathcal{S} &\quad \rightsquigarrow \quad s^* = s \in \mathcal{F}^* \\
\alpha \in \mathcal{X}_s &\quad \rightsquigarrow \quad \alpha^* = t_\alpha \in \mathcal{X}^* \\
f(s_1, \ldots, s_n) \in \Omega &\quad \rightsquigarrow \quad f(s_1^*, \ldots, s_n^*) \text{ a term on } \Sigma^*.
\end{aligned}
$$

The propositional structure of formulas is not affected by our encoding: merely, sorts in quantifiers are all replaced by U since our signature is monosorted, and we will omit these sorts hereafter. Thus, we are left to define the translation of an atom t. Since a translation of a term depends on its type and since a term may have many different types in a polymorphic logic, we have to be careful as to the choice of the type. To translate a well-typed formula, we consider the most general typing derivation of this formula: such a derivation always exists and is unique up to a renaming of type variables (see [11, p. 33 – 35]). A subterm t of the formula is then translated with respect to its type τ: in other words, the translation is inductively defined on the most-general typing derivation of the formula.

Since the well-typing rules are syntax-directed, the different cases can be described by the following rules, where τ is the type on the right-hand side of the sequent:

1. If t is a variable x, then $t^* = \mathsf{sort}(\tau^*, x)$
2. If t is a functional term $f(t_1, \ldots, t_n)$ and $f \in \mathcal{F}_{\mathcal{A}}, t^* = \mathsf{sort}(\text{INT}, \hat{f}(t_1^*, \ldots, t_n^*))$

3. If t is a functional term $f(t_1, \ldots, t_n)$ and $f \notin \mathcal{F}_\mathcal{A}$, $t^* = \mathsf{sort}(\tau^*, f(t_1^*, \ldots, t_n^*))$
4. If t is a predicative term $p(t_1, \ldots, t_n)$ and $p \in \mathcal{F}_\mathcal{A}$, $t^* = \hat{p}(t_1^*, \ldots, t_n^*)$
5. Otherwise, t is an atom $p(t_1, \ldots, t_n)$ with $p \notin \mathcal{F}_\mathcal{A}$ and $t^* = p(t_1^*, \ldots, t_n^*)$

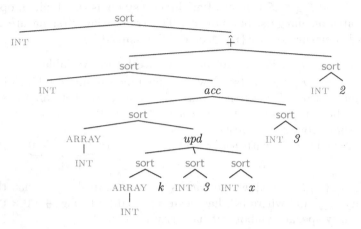

Fig. 2. Syntactic tree view of the translation of $acc(upd(k, 3, x), 3) + 2$

For instance, Fig. 2 represents the translation of $acc(upd(k, 3, x), 3) + 2$ as a syntactic tree. In that tree the term is globally unchanged, except that layers of sorts (in gray) have been introduced at each junction in the original syntactic tree, which is why we say this is a *stratified* encoding.

There are a couple of things to note about this translation. First, translated formulas are not necessarily closed because type variables that were implicitly universally quantified are now free term variables, and this can be accounted for by universally quantifying over these variables as well (which we will do in the next section when we describe the translation of a theory). Second, arithmetic expressions were encoded with new special symbols and are not interpreted expressions anymore, so we need axioms to define the meaning of these new symbols.

Each arithmetic symbol in $\mathcal{F}_\mathcal{A}$ is defined by one of the following axioms depending on whether it is a functional symbol f or a predicative symbol p:

$$\phi_f \equiv \forall x_1 \ldots x_n . \hat{f}(\mathsf{sort}(\mathrm{INT}, x_1), \ldots, \mathsf{sort}(\mathrm{INT}, x_n)) = f(x_1, \ldots, x_n)$$
$$\phi_p \equiv \forall x_1 \ldots x_n . \hat{p}(\mathsf{sort}(\mathrm{INT}, x_1), \ldots, \mathsf{sort}(\mathrm{INT}, x_n)) \Leftrightarrow p(x_1, \ldots, x_n).$$

They aim at stripping away type information from encoded arithmetic expressions. Simiarly, there is also a need for an instance of ϕ_p where p is the equality on integers, i.e.

$$\forall x_1, x_2 . \mathsf{sort}(\mathrm{INT}, x_1) = \mathsf{sort}(\mathrm{INT}, x_2) \Leftrightarrow x_1 = x_2 \tag{4}$$

This axiom corresponds to the injectivity of the function $x \mapsto \mathsf{sort}(\mathrm{INT}, x)$. We write $\mathcal{P}$ (as *prelude*) for the set of all these axioms and we will later add this prelude to the solvers' context when trying to prove a translated formula.

The introduction of rules 2., 4. together with axioms ϕ_f and ϕ_p accounts for the completeness of the encoding: for arithmetic expressions, provers usually have dedicated decision procedure. Therefore, we need a logical link between encoded and original arithmetic expressions in order for a prover to be able to dispatch them to the decision procedure. This is not a solution specific to arithmetic : the same method could be used for other built-in types.

Without these axioms, a prover might for instance conclude that the formula sort(INT, 2) $\geqslant$ sort(INT, 3) is satisfiable whereas it is not. Another obvious alternative would be to add the axiom $\forall x$. sort(INT, x) = x, but this results in a dramatic loss of efficiency for provers based on ground instantiation of quantifiers (which is currently the rule for SMT solvers), because they could instantiate this equality everytime an integer term is encountered, although there are many integers that do not require this because they are not applied on a symbol from $\mathcal{F}_A$.

Running example. The translation of (3) is

$$
\begin{aligned}
&\mathsf{sort}(\mathrm{INT}, \mathsf{sort}(\mathrm{INT},\\
&\quad acc(\mathsf{sort}(\mathrm{ARRAY}(\mathrm{INT}),\\
&\qquad upd(\mathsf{sort}(\mathrm{ARRAY}(\mathrm{INT}), k), \mathsf{sort}(\mathrm{INT}, 3), \mathsf{sort}(\mathrm{INT}, x)), \mathsf{sort}(\mathrm{INT}, 3))))\\
&\quad \hat{+}\, \mathsf{sort}(\mathrm{INT}, 2)) = \mathsf{sort}(\mathrm{INT}, 7).
\end{aligned} \tag{5}
$$

By instantiating the counterpart of axiom (1), i.e.

$$
\begin{aligned}
&\forall \alpha, a, i, e\,.\\
&\mathsf{sort}(\alpha, acc(\mathsf{sort}(\mathrm{ARRAY}(\alpha),\\
&\qquad\qquad upd(\mathsf{sort}(\mathrm{ARRAY}(\alpha), a), \mathsf{sort}(\mathrm{INT}, i), \mathsf{sort}(\alpha, e)), \mathsf{sort}(\mathrm{INT}, i))))\\
&= \mathsf{sort}(\alpha, e)
\end{aligned}
$$

with $\alpha = $ INT, $a = k$, $i = 3$ and $e = x$, the formula (5) simplifies to
$$\mathsf{sort}(\mathrm{INT}, \mathsf{sort}(\mathrm{INT}, x)\hat{+}\mathsf{sort}(\mathrm{INT}, 2)) = \mathsf{sort}(\mathrm{INT}, 7)$$
which is again reduced to sort(INT, $x + 2$) = sort(INT, 7) thanks to the axiom ϕ_f and to $x + 2 = 7$ thanks to (4).

3.2   Translation Proofs

To prove results about our encoding, we use the natural deduction system for polymorphic FOL described in [13]. We slightly adapt this formalism by considering a theory $\mathcal{T} = (\Sigma, \mathcal{A}x, \Gamma)$ as the tuple of a signature Σ, a set of axioms $\mathcal{A}x$ and a typing context Γ. When ϕ is a monomorphic formula[1], the sequent $\mathcal{T} \models \phi$ expresses the fact that ϕ is a formula on Σ which is well-typed in Γ and valid given the axioms in $\mathcal{A}x$. Finally, axioms in $\mathcal{A}x$ are written $\forall \overline{\alpha}[P]$ where P is a formula and $\overline{\alpha}$ its polymorphic parameters. Figure 3 recalls rules of [13] which are used in the following proofs.

---

[1] Which is not a restriction, since a polymorphic goal can be monomorphized by replacing each type variable by a fresh uninterpreted sort, without loss of generality.

$$\frac{T \vdash t : \tau}{T \models t = t}(\mathsf{Eq_1}) \qquad \frac{T \models x = y \quad T \models Q[x/z]}{T \models Q[y/z]}(\mathsf{Eq_2}) \qquad \frac{T \models P \wedge Q}{T \models P}(\mathsf{And_2})$$

$$\frac{\mathbf{axiom} \ \forall \overline{\alpha} \, [P] \in T}{T \models \sigma(P)}(\mathsf{Ax}) \qquad \frac{T \models \forall x : \tau . P \quad T \vdash t : \tau}{T \models P[t/x]}(\mathsf{Forall_2})$$

$$\frac{x_1, \dots, x_n \models_A P}{T \models \forall x_1 : \mathrm{INT} . \ \dots \ \forall x_n : \mathrm{INT} . P}(\mathsf{Arith})$$

In rule (Ax), σ is a ground substitution from $\overline{\alpha}$ to sorts. In rule (Arith), the formula P is exclusively built with variables and constants of sort INT, symbols from $\mathcal{F}_A$ and equality. If $x_1, \dots, x_n$ are the free variables in P, we write $x_1, \dots, x_n \models_A P$ as soon as P is valid (this is decidable, cf. for instance by the Omega test in [12]).

Fig. 3. Natural deduction system for polymorphic FOL (excerpt from [13])

The encoded version T^* of such a theory T is the tuple $(\Sigma^*, \mathcal{A}x^*, \Gamma^*)$ where:

- $\mathcal{A}x^* = \{[\forall t_{\alpha_1} : \mathrm{U} . \ \dots \ \forall t_{\alpha_k} : \mathrm{U} . P^*] \mid \forall \alpha_1 \dots \alpha_k [P] \in \mathcal{A}x\} \cup \mathcal{P}$
- Γ^* is Γ where all bindings are replaced by the unique sort U

Note that $\mathcal{A}x^*$ is made out of closed monomorphic encoded versions of the earlier axioms, and also contains the prelude we described in the previous section. Thanks to the axioms in this prelude, we can show the following results on arithmetic terms and their encoded versions:

Lemma 1 (Arithmetic terms). *Let t be an arithmetic term on Σ, that is, a term built exclusively with arithmetic symbols, integer constants and variables. Then $T^* \models \mathsf{sort}(\mathrm{INT}, t) = t^*$.*

PROOF. The proof proceeds by structural induction on t. The case of a variable is obviously handled by the reflexivity rule $(\mathsf{Eq_1})$. A functional term $f(t_1, \dots, t_n)$ is treated by first applying the induction hypothesis to all the $t_i, 1 \leq i \leq n$, which transforms $\hat{f}(t_1^*, \dots, t_n^*)$ to $\hat{f}(\mathsf{sort}(\mathrm{INT}, t_1), \dots, \mathsf{sort}(\mathrm{INT}, t_n))$, and next by instantiating the additional axiom ϕ_f to transform this term to $f(t_1, \dots, t_n)$, which is the desired result. □

Lemma 2 (Arithmetic predicates). *Let P be an arithmetic formula in a theory T, that is, an atom built exclusively with arithmetic symbols, equality and arithmetic terms. Then, $T^* \models P \Leftrightarrow P^*$.*

PROOF. The proof is done by induction on the structure of a formula. The only non-trivial case is for an arithmetic atom $p(t_1, \dots, t_n)$. By applying the previous lemma to all the $t_i, 1 \leq i \leq n$, we transform the encoded predicate $\hat{p}(t_1^*, \dots, t_n^*)$ to $\hat{p}(\mathsf{sort}(\mathrm{INT}, t_1), \dots, \mathsf{sort}(\mathrm{INT}, t_n))$, which is equivalent to $p(t_1, \dots, t_n)$ by virtue of the added axiom ϕ_p. □

Theorem 1 (Completeness). *Let T be a theory and P a monomorphic formula on T. Then, $T \models P$ implies $T^* \models P^*$.*

PROOF. We proceed by structural induction on the proof derivation of $T \models P$ and we only present non obvious cases.

Rule (Ax): An application of the rule (Ax) can be translated in the following derivation where the application of the substitution σ is replaced by k applications of the rule (Forall$_2$), one for each type variable:

$$\dfrac{\text{axiom } \forall t_{\alpha_1} : \text{U} \ldots \forall t_{\alpha_k} : \text{U} . P^* \in T^*}{} \text{(Ax)}$$

$$\dfrac{\begin{array}{c}\vdots \qquad\qquad\qquad\qquad\qquad T^* \vdash \sigma(\alpha_k)^* : \text{U}\end{array}}{T^* \models P^*[\sigma(\alpha_1)^*/t_{\alpha_1}] \ldots [\sigma(\alpha_k)^*/t_{\alpha_k}]} \text{(Forall}_2)_{(6)}$$

Rule (Forall$_2$): By definition, we clearly have $(P[t/x])^* = P^*[e/x]$ where $t^* = \text{sort}(\tau^*, e)$. This property makes the translation of the rules (Forall$_2$) straightforward:

$$\dfrac{T^* \models \forall x : \text{U} . P^* \qquad T^* \vdash e : \text{U} \quad \text{where} \quad t^* = \text{sort}(\tau^*, e)}{T^* \models P^*[e/x]} \text{(Forall}_2)$$

Rule (Arith): In this rule, P is only composed of arithmetic symbols (including integer constants) and integer variables. Therefore, P is true in the theory of arithmetic and is true in T^*. The lemma 2 about the encoding of arithmetic atoms tells us that P is equivalent to P^* in T^*, therefore it is obvious to build a proof for P^*. □

The soundness of the encoding is expressed by the fact that $T^* \models P^*$ implies $T \models P$.

Since we have erased type from quantifiers, a prover may *a priori* make ill-typed substitutions of the variables in translated formulae. Indeed, we emphasized in Sect. 2 that erasing types was not sound at all. Now, solvers do not instantiate a variable by *any* term but rather try to find an existing term that matches the context around the variable. Since our encoding ensures that the context around a variable contains its sort information, only terms with the same sort can be used for the instantiation. For instance, if a variable x was quantified over a sort τ in the original formula, every occurrence of x in the encoded formula is actually an occurrence of $\text{sort}(\tau^*, x)$: when trying to intanstantiate x, solvers will *match* ground terms with that pattern and will only substitute x by a certain term e if the term $\text{sort}(\tau^*, e)$ has already been encountered. If the ground terms have not been obtained by ill-typed instantiations (which is the case at first), this term e corresponds to a term t of type τ such that $t^* = \text{sort}(\tau^*, e)$. The substitution of x by e in the encoded formula then corresponds to the substitution of x by t in the original formula, and this ensures that the property that all ground terms are well-formed is preserved when new instantiations are made by the solver. A formalization of that *matching* process and a proof of that result are presented in [11, p. 53 – 58].

The conclusion of that discussion is that we can consider a restriction of the deduction system $\models$, later called $\models^*$, where instantiations of variables in rules for quantifiers are correct with respect to the types in the original formulas: if x appears as $\mathsf{sort}(\tau^*, x)$ in the formula, it can only be replaced with the translation of a ground term of sort τ, and otherwise it must be replaced with the translation τ^* of a ground sort τ. Therefore, our soundness theorem takes the following form:

Theorem 2 (Soundness). *Let T be a theory and P a monomorphic formula on T. Then, $T^* \models^* P^*$ implies $T \models P$.*

PROOF. We proceed by induction on a minimal proof derivation for $T^* \models^* P^*$ but it is less straightforward than completeness. Indeed, consider elimination rules for logical connectives, like (And_2). When trying to reason by induction, we cannot apply the induction hypothesis to the second premise Q if it is not of the form Q_0^*. By taking a minimal proof, in particular without cuts, we ensure the connective $\wedge$ cannot come from an introduction rule, but only from an axiom in the theory, which means that the conjunction $P^* \wedge Q$ is a – possibly instantiated – subformula of an axiom in the theory. There are two cases to distinguish there: if the axiom comes from $\mathcal{P}$, the result is straightforward (either the connective does not appear in these axioms, or the proof of P is trivial); otherwise, the axiom comes from $\mathcal{A}x^*$ and since they are translations of axioms in $\mathcal{A}x$, $P^* \wedge Q$ is a subterm of an instantiation of a translated axiom, and that implies that Q has the expected form Q_0^*.

All introduction rules are straightforward and rely only on applying the induction hypothesis to all premises. We have also discussed elimination rules above. Among the remaining rules, we only detail the non obvious ones:

Rule (Forall_2): We have $P^* = Q[t/x]$ and $\dfrac{T^* \models^* \forall x : \mathrm{U}.Q \qquad T^* \vdash t : \mathrm{U}}{T^* \models^* Q[t/x]}$ (Forall_2)

As argued above, the universal quantifier comes from an axiom rule and corresponds either to a quantification on a type variable, or to a quantification on a variable x of type τ in the original formula. In the first case, P can be proved in T by replacing the instantiations of type variables by a type substitution in the premises of the rule (Ax). In the second case, $Q = Q_0^*$ and $P^* = (Q_0[u/x])^*$ for some u of type τ, hence the following derivation: $\dfrac{T \models \forall x : \tau.Q_0 \qquad T \vdash u : \tau}{T \models Q_0[u/x]}$.

Rule (Eq_2): Since the proof is minimal, the equality $x = y$ comes from an axiom and has the form $t^* = u^*$. Also, $Q[y/z]$ is a translated formula $P^* = (P_0[u/z])^*$, so $Q[x/z] = P_0[t/z]^*$ is also a translated formula and we can apply the induction hypothesis to create the following derivation $\dfrac{T \models t = u \qquad T \models P_0[t/z]}{T \models P_0[u/z]}$.

4   Reduction to Many-Sorted Logic

In this section, we address the case of a prover that works in many-sorted logic. One may think that there is no need to do so since we have already presented an encoding to unsorted FOL and it is obvious that unsorted FOL is a special case of many-sorted FOL. Unfortunately, trying to use the previous encoding with a many-sorted prover raises the issue of how to type the new symbol sort and the built-in symbols $+, <$, etc. Indeed, built-in symbols and integer constants have the sort INT and cannot be considered as being of sort U. Taking $U = INT$ would be a solution, but this would not be easily adaptable to a case with several different built-in types and decision procedures (arithmetic + lists + ...).

Such a solution should not only translate polymorphic formulas to many-sorted logics in a generic way, but should also take advantage of the many-sorted logic to avoid to encode linear arithmetic as we did in the previous section, since it is a source of inefficiency. In the following, we present an encoding that solves this issue by only encoding integer expressions when they are used in a polymorphic context.

In addition to INT, there are three sorts S, T, U whose meaning is as follows: each term, except those of sort INT, is translated into a term $sort(\_, \_)$ which has the sort S (for Syntactically sorted terms). The function sort has arity $T \times U \to S$ where T is the sort of Type and where U is the sort of terms not built with sort.

4.1   Translation

The polymorphic signature is translated into the monomorphic many-sorted signature $\Sigma^* = (S^*, \emptyset, \emptyset, \mathcal{X}^*, \mathcal{F}^*)$ defined by:

- S^* is $\{U, S, T, INT\}$,
- $\mathcal{X}^*$ is $\mathcal{X} \cup \{t_\alpha \mid \alpha \in \mathcal{X}_s\}$ as in the unsorted case,
- $\mathcal{F}^*$ is $\mathcal{F} \cup \mathcal{F}_s \cup \{sort\} \cup \mathcal{F}_{cast} \cup S \setminus \{INT\}$ where
  - a symbol from $\mathcal{F}$ with arity $s_1 \times \ldots \times s_n \to s$ now has the arity $s'_1 \times \ldots \times s'_n \to s'$ where s' is INT if s is INT and U otherwise and where $s'_i, 1 \leqslant i \leqslant n$, is INT if s_i is INT and S otherwise (e.g the function $upd : \alpha ARRAY \times INT \times \alpha \to \alpha ARRAY$ now has the arity $S \times INT \times S \to U$),
  - symbols from $\mathcal{F}_s$ with n parameters have arity $\underbrace{T \times \ldots \times T}_{n \text{ times}} \to T$,
  - $\mathcal{F}_{cast}$ is $\{int2u : INT \to U, s2int : S \to INT\}$,
  - each symbol of $S \setminus \{INT\}$ is now a constant of sort T.

The translation t^* of a term t of type τ depends on the context.

1. If t is a predicate term $p(t_1, \ldots, t_n)$, $t^* = p(t_1^*, \ldots, t_n^*)$
2. if t is a functional term or a variable, then it is the ith parameter of some symbol g: $g(\ldots, t, \ldots)$. We call τ_i the type of the ith argument in g's arity and the translation depends on τ and τ_i being INT or not:
   (a) if neither τ nor τ_i are INT, then
       - if t is a variable x, $t^* = sort(\tau^*, x)$

- if t is a term $f(t_1, \ldots, t_n)$, $t^* = \mathsf{sort}(\tau^*, f(t_1^*, \ldots, t_n^*))$

(b) if τ and τ_i are INT,

    - if t is a variable x, $t^* = x$

    - if t is a term $f(t_1, \ldots, t_n)$, $t^* = f(t_1^*, \ldots, t_n^*)$

(c) if τ is not INT but τ_i is INT, then

    - if t is a variable x, $t^* = s2int(\mathsf{sort}(\tau^*, x))$

    - if t is a term $f(t_1, \ldots, t_n)$ then $t^* = s2int(\mathsf{sort}(\tau^*, f(t_1^*, \ldots, t_n^*)))$

(d) finally, if τ is INT but τ_i is not INT, then

    - if t is a variable x, $t^* = \mathsf{sort}(\mathrm{INT}, int2u(\tau^*, x))$

    - if t is a term $f(t_1, \ldots, t_n)$ then $t^* = \mathsf{sort}(\mathrm{INT}, int2u(f(t_1^*, \ldots, t_n^*))))$

It is straightforward to check that encoded expressions are still well-typed in Σ^*. Compared to the previous translation, exploiting sorts unburdens the terms sort INT from being encoded (rule 2b). However, rules 2c and 2d use casting functions $int2u$ and $s2int$ which have to be defined by the axioms

$$\forall x : \mathrm{B} . \; s2int(\mathsf{sort}(\mathrm{INT}, int2u(x))) = x \tag{7}$$

$$\forall x : \mathrm{U} . \; int2u(s2int(\mathsf{sort}(\mathrm{INT}, x))) = x. \tag{8}$$

In this section, the prelude is defined by $\mathcal{P} = \{(7), (8)\}$.

Running example. By encoding (3) we obtain

$$s2int(\mathsf{sort}(\mathrm{INT}, acc(\mathsf{sort}(\mathrm{ARRAY}(\mathrm{INT}),$$
$$upd(\mathsf{sort}(\mathrm{ARRAY}(\mathrm{INT}), k), 3, \mathsf{sort}(\mathrm{INT}, int2u(x)))), 3)))$$
$$+ 2 = 7$$

which reduces to $s2int(\mathsf{sort}(\mathrm{INT}, int2u(x))) + 2 = 7$, by applying the translation of the axiom (1) and to $x + 2 = 7$ thanks to the axiom (7).

4.2   Translation Proofs

We prove in this section the same theorems with the same notations as in Sect. 3.

PROOF OF THEOREM 1. With this encoding, the proof is again achieved by structural induction on the proof derivation. The only non-obvious cases are the axiom rule and rules which infer a substitution: a term that appears in two hypotheses of an inference rule can generate two distinct translations according to its sort and its position in a logical symbol. Notice that unlike the proof detailed in Sect. 3.2, the arithmetic rule is obviously obtained since this encoding preserves pure arithmetic terms by definition.

An application of the rule (Ax) is replaced by a derivation similar to (6) where sort U is replaced by T.

For rules (Forall$_2$) and (Exists$_1$), if τ is not INT or if τ is INT and t^* has the sort INT, then the result is straightforward. Otherwise, τ is INT, $t^* = \mathsf{sort}(\mathrm{INT}, e)$, and we have the following inference:

$$
\frac{
  \begin{array}{c} \vdots \\ \mathcal{T}^* \models \forall x : \text{INT} . P^* \end{array}
  \qquad
  \frac{
    \begin{array}{c} \vdots \\ \Sigma^* \vdash \mathsf{sort}(\text{INT}, e) : \mathrm{S} \end{array}
    \qquad
    s2int : \mathrm{S} \to \text{INT}
  }{
    \Sigma^* \vdash s2int(t^*) : \text{INT}
  } \; (\mathsf{T_2})
}{
  \mathcal{T}^* \models P^*[s2int(\mathsf{sort}(\text{INT}, e))/x]
} \; (\mathsf{Forall_2})
$$

However, if the generated predicate $P^*[s2int(\mathsf{sort}(\text{INT}, e))/x]$ contains some $int2u(s2int(\mathsf{sort}(\text{INT}, e)))$, it can be simplified by applying axiom (8) through rules ($\mathsf{Forall_2}$) and ($\mathsf{Eq_2}$).

For the rule ($\mathsf{Eq_2}$), the proof is similar. If τ is not INT or if τ is INT and x^* has the sort INT, then the result is direct. Otherwise, τ is INT and the counterpart of $x = y$ is $\mathsf{sort}(\text{INT}, int2u(x^*)) = y^*$; it suffices to deduce the equality $s2int(\mathsf{sort}(\text{INT}, int2u(x))) = s2int(y^*)$ by applying ($\mathsf{Eq_2}$) which is then simplified into $x^* = s2int(y^*)$ by applying axiom (7) through ($\mathsf{Forall_2}$) and ($\mathsf{Eq_2}$). □

PROOF OF THEOREM 2. The proof, which relies on the same arguments than those of the proof of soundness in Sect. 3.2, is omitted. □

5   Experiments

All the encodings presented in this work are implemented as modules in the Why [14] tool. The benchmark we exploit has 1272 valid proof obligations (PO). They are built by the Caduceus tool [15] from 55 annotated C programs. They aim at certifying that each function implementation is consistent with its specification and that the program is free of null pointer dereferencing and out-of-bounds array access. To do so, it widely relies on linear arithmetic and polymorphism coming from the memory model axiomatization.

Results of benchmarks for several provers and several different encodings are summarized in the tables represented in Fig. 4. More precisely, Figure 4(a) shows experiments with the unsorted prover Simplify [3] whereas figure 4(b) shows experiments with many-sorted ones: Yices [6] and CVC-lite [7]. Rows labeled "Without encoding", "With typing predicates" and "With monomorphization" are the coarse ones detailed in Sect. 2 and "Stratified encoding" of the Fig. 4(a) and of the Fig. 4(b) correspond to encodings given in section 3 and 4 respectively.

Each prover got 10 seconds for each obligation, on an Intel Xeon 3.20GHz with 2Gb of Memory. The results represent the percentage of obligations proved valid within these 10 seconds. Also, the average time only takes proved obligations into account and not timeouts.

The first observation for unsorted provers is that the best results are obtained without any encoding (by just removing types), but we have seen that this method is unsound. Among the other encodings, differences are pretty important: the encoding with typing predicates is pretty poor (as we discussed in section 2) while our stratified encoding proves almost as many obligations as the prover without encoding.

Another remark is that the difference between the average times in benchmarks with and without encoding is really significant, whereas only a very small

		Simplify
Without encoding	Percentage	99.6%
(no types at all)	Avg Time	60ms
With	Percentage	66.2%
typing predicates	Avg Time	171ms
Stratified	Percentage	98.8%
encoding	Avg Time	243ms

(a) Unsorted Encodings

		Yices	CVCLite
With mono-	Percentage	49. %	36.9 %
-morphization	Avg Time	772ms	752ms
Stratified	Percentage	99.1%	69.8%
encoding	Avg Time	430ms	1312ms

(b) Many-Sorted Encodings

Fig. 4. Benchmarks of different encodings

percentage of the obligations cannot actually be proved within the 10 seconds. Of course, encoded formulas are slightly longer to prove because they are bigger and arithmetic requires more steps of instantiation than without encoding. But another possible and less obvious source of inefficiency (and even incompleteness) is that the encoding can disrupt other specificities of the inner mechanism of a prover, namely *triggers* (see for instance the description of Simplify triggers in [3]). Triggers are patterns used to trigger the instantiation of axioms in the theory, by matching them to existing ground terms. They can be declared by the user (e.g. Simplify) or automatically determined by some heuristics (in Simplify or Yices). In the latter case, nothing guarantees that the inferred triggers will be the same before and after encoding. For instance, an axiom like $\forall x : \text{T} . pred(x)$ would have $pred(x)$ as unique trigger; the encoded version $\forall x . pred(\text{sort}(\text{T}, x))$ may have the trigger $\text{sort}(\text{T}, x)$ which would be instantiated much more often than the original since it is smaller and matches more terms than the bigger one, resulting in inefficiencies.

Concerning sorted provers, the monomorphization, does not terminate for 6 problems (corresponding to 625 POs). The percentage of proven obligations and the corresponding average time show that the stratified encoding allows Yices to discharge about twice as many proof obligations with the monomorphization. Furthermore, each of them is faster discharged than when encoded by the monomorphization. Note, though, that this encoding suffers from the same inherent inefficiencies than the first one (bigger theories, slower arithmetics, problems with triggers) but this is not visible on the benchmark because the monomorphized theories are already many times bigger than the original theories.

6   Related Works and Conclusion

Translating polymorphic logic to first order logic has been previously presented, but as far as we know, without considering dedicated cases for interpreted functional symbols as we do.

Encoding with predicates has been studied in [16,17]. A generic translation from Mizar Mathematical Library [18] into first order logic is studied in the former. In the latter, the authors show how they integrate a first-order intuitionistic prover into the Nuprl [19] proof assistant.

In [20], Joe Hurd proposes the Metis tactic to discharge subgoals from higher-order logic (HOL4) into first order proof procedures. This task is achieved by firstly omitting sort information and trying to find an untyped proof. Such a proof is then checked to be typable by HOL. In the case of a failure, a complete translation is done, which corresponds to our unsorted stratified encoding without any optimization. Similarly, the authors of [21,22] address the task of proving higher-order formulas using first order resolution provers [23,24] and rely on Isabelle to check the proof's soundness.

In [25], L.C. Paulson introduces the Isabelle `Blast` tactic which integrates a tableau-based procedure. This procedure internally stores types of some symbols to avoid ill-sorted deductions whereas the approach we developped is applicable to a broad range of SMT solvers. In [26], the considered proof obligations are expressed in a specific many-sorted first order language, reduced to contain only two disjoint sorts. In such a context, the authors prove that sorts can be omitted without loosing soundness. This reduced context is not directly applicable here since we claim to present a generic approach.

To conclude, we have presented in this paper two close efficient reductions of polymorphism in unsorted logic and many-sorted logic. In both cases, the main idea is to syntactically type expressions by adding the sorts information directly into terms. Soundness is ensured by the way solvers produce ground instantiations of quantified variables, as argued in Sect. 3.2. The fact that our method depends on the intricacies of the solver's procedure is definitely a shortcoming. However, judging by the number of provers it applies to, we believe that the advantages of our method over other encodings, both performance-wise and flexibility-wise, sufficiently outweigh its shortcoming for this encoding to be of practical interest to others in the community.

In order to exploit as much as possible the decision procedures dedicated to linear arithmetic, the encodings also have special cases for arithmetic terms. Our large experiments show that the method is very efficient in the context of a representative panel of POs issued from software verification. An extension to several constant sorts should be straightforward, because we were as generic as possible. It is planned as a future work. That way, we could also benefit from decision procedures dedicated to other constant sorts (e.g. for reals, arrays, WS1S).

Acknowledgements

We are grateful to S. Conchon, E. Contejean, J.-C. Filliâtre, A. Giorgetti, C. Marché for stimulating discussions and suggestions on this topic, and to the anonymous referees for their comments which greatly helped to improve the final version of this paper.

References

1. Nipkow, T., Paulson, L.C., Wenzel, M.: Isabelle/HOL - A Proof Assistant for Higher-Order Logic. LNCS, vol. 2283. Springer, Heidelberg (2002)
2. Bertot, Y., Castéran, P.: Interactive Theorem Proving and Program Development. In: Coq'Art: the Calculus of Inductive Constructions, Springer, Heidelberg (2004)
3. Detlefs, D., Nelson, G., Saxe, J.B.: Simplify: a Theorem Prover for Program Checking. J. ACM 52(3), 365–473 (2005)
4. Déharbe, D., Ranise, S.: BDD-driven First-Order Satisfiability Procedures (extended version). Technical Report 4630, LORIA (2002)

5. Ranise, S., Tinelli, C.: The Satisfiability Modulo Theories Library (SMT-LIB) (2006) http://www.SMT-LIB.org
6. Dutertre, B., de Moura, L.: The YICES SMT Solver (2006) avaliable at http://yices.csl.sri.com/tool-paper.pdf
7. Barrett, C.W., Berezin, S.: CVC Lite: A New Implementation of the Cooperating Validity Checker Category B. In: Alur, R., Peled, D.A. (eds.) CAV 2004. LNCS, vol. 3114, pp. 515–518. Springer, Heidelberg (2004)
8. Couchot, J.F., Lescuyer, S.: Handling Polymorphism in Automated Deduction (2007) Available at http://lri.fr/~couchot/ftp/publis/CL07t.ps
9. Enderton, H.B.: A Mathematical Introduction to Logic. Ac. Press, Inc. (1972)
10. Armando, A., Ranise, S., Rusinowitch, M.: A Rewriting Approach to Satisfiability Procedures. Journal of Information and computation 183, 140–164 (2003)
11. Lescuyer, S.: Codage de la logique du premier ordre polymorphe multi-sortée dans la logique sans sortes. Master's thesis (in english) pp. 28–58 (2006)
12. Pugh, W.: The Omega Test: a fast and practical integer programming algorithm for dependence analysis. Communications of the ACM 35(8), 102–114 (1992)
13. Ayache, N., Filliâtre, J.C.: Combining the Coq Proof Assistant with First-Order Decision Procedures. Unpublished (March 2006)
14. Filliâtre, J.C.: Why: a multi-language multi-prover verification tool. Research Report 1366, LRI, Université Paris Sud (March 2003)
15. Filliâtre, J.C., Marché, C.: Multi-Prover Verification of C Programs. In: Davies, J., Schulte, W., Barnett, M. (eds.) ICFEM 2004. LNCS, vol. 3308, pp. 15–29. Springer, Heidelberg (2004)
16. Dahn, I.: Interpretation of a mizar-like logic in first-order logic. In: Selected Papers from Automated Deduction in Classical and Non-Classical Logics, pp. 137–151. Springer, London (2000)
17. Schmitt, S., Lorigo, L., Kreitz, C., Nogin, A.: Jprover: Integrating connection-based theorem proving into interactive proof assistants. In: Goré, R.P., Leitsch, A., Nipkow, T. (eds.) IJCAR 2001. LNCS (LNAI), vol. 2083, pp. 421–426. Springer, Heidelberg (2001)
18. Rudnicki, P.: An overview of the Mizar project. In: Workshop on Types for Proofs and Programs, pp. 311–330 (1992)
19. Allen, S.F., Constable, R.L., Eaton, R., Kreitz, C., Lorigo, L.: The nuprl open logical environment. In: McAllester, D. (ed.) Automated Deduction - CADE-17. LNCS, vol. 1831, pp. 170–176. Springer, Heidelberg (2000)
20. Hurd, J.: First-Order Proof Tactics in Higher-Order Logic Theorem Provers. Technical Report NASA/CP-2003-212448, NASA (2003)
21. Meng, J., Paulson, L.C.: Translating Higher-Order Problems to First-Order Clauses. In: ESCoR (CEUR Workshop Proceedings), vol. 192, pp. 70–80 (2006)
22. Meng, J., Quigley, C., Paulson, L.C.: Automation for interactive proof: first prototype. Inf. Comput. 204(10), 1575–1596 (2006)
23. Schulz, S.: System Description: E 0.81. In: Basin, D., Rusinowitch, M. (eds.) IJCAR 2004. LNCS (LNAI), vol. 3097, pp. 223–228. Springer, Heidelberg (2004)
24. Riazanov, A., Voronkov, A.: The design and Implementation of VAMPIRE. AI Commun. 15(2-3), 91–110 (2002)
25. Paulson, L.C.: A generic tableau prover and its integration with Isabelle. J.UCS: Journal of Universal Computer Science 5(3), 73 (1999)
26. Bouillaguet, C., Kuncak, V., Wies, T., Zee, K., Rinard, M.: Using first-order theorem provers in the Jahob data structure verification system. In: Cook, B., Podelski, A. (eds.) VMCAI 2007. LNCS, vol. 4349, pp. 74–88. Springer, Heidelberg (2007)

Automated Reasoning in Kleene Algebra

Peter Höfner and Georg Struth

Department of Computer Science, University of Sheffield, United Kingdom
{p.hoefner,g.struth}@dcs.shef.ac.uk

Abstract. It has often been claimed that model checking, special purpose automated deduction or interactive theorem proving are needed for formal program development. We demonstrate that off-the-shelf automated proof and counterexample search is an interesting alternative if combined with the right domain model. We implement variants of Kleene algebras axiomatically in Prover9/Mace4 and perform proof experiments about Hoare, dynamic, temporal logics, concurrency control and termination analysis. They confirm that a simple automated analysis of some important program properties is possible. Particular benefits of this approach include "soft" model checking in a first-order setting, cross-theory reasoning between standard formalisms and full automation of some (co)inductive arguments. Kleene algebras might therefore provide light-weight formal methods with heavy-weight automation.

1 Introduction

Formal systems verification and computer mathematics requires the integration of domain-specific knowledge. This is usually achieved through higher-order theorem proving at the expense of computational power or through model checking at the expense of expressive power. For automated deduction, however, this task is still a challenge. Over the last decades, considerable effort has been put into the development of special purpose calculi for automated deduction with algebraic theories, but the practical impact of this approach on formal methods has been rather limited. Nevertheless, the specific balance of expressive and computational power and the user-friendliness of automated deduction could considerably increase the practical applicability of formal software verification.

This paper proposes an alternative approach to automated deduction for systems verification: domain-specific algebras for standard provers instead of domain-specific provers for standard algebras. More concretely, we investigate the potential of automated reasoning in Kleene algebra with the resolution- and paramodulation-based Prover9 and the counterexample generator Mace4 [2].

Over the last few years, variants of Kleene algebras emerged as fundamental structures in computing. They found widespread applications ranging from program analysis and semantics to combinatorial optimisation and concurrency control. Kleene algebras seem particularly suitable for our task: They offer a concise syntax for modelling actions, programs or state transitions under non-deterministic choice, sequential composition and iteration. They provide a uniform semantics for various program analysis tasks that supports cross-theory

F. Pfenning (Ed.): CADE 2007, LNAI 4603, pp. 279–294, 2007.

reasoning with modal, relational, trace-based, language-based and event-based approaches. They come with a simple first-order equational calculus that yields particularly short and abstract proofs, and they are supported by powerful automata-based decision procedures. Kleene algebras have already been integrated into higher-order theorem provers [22,15,3] and their applicability as a formal method has successfully been demonstrated in that setting. But their potential for automated deduction has not yet been explored.

At first sight, feeding an automated prover with the Kleene algebra axioms and some meaningful conjecture might seem hopeless: Kleene algebras contain a commutative idempotent additive monoid and a multiplicative monoid that interact via distributivity. So one would rather expect the prover to get lost in term rearrangements and complex unifications. But our proof experiments on program verification, logics of programs and modal correspondence theory support the opposite, and perhaps surprising conclusion: The combination of Kleene algebra and state-of-the-art theorem proving technology makes it often possible to prove theorems of considerable complexity and practical relevance.

Our main contributions are as follows: First, we specify Kleene algebras [16], omega algebras [6] and their modal extensions [9,19] in Prover9 and Mace4. We chose this particular tool primarily because it integrates automated deduction with counterexample search. Any other paramodulation-based theorem prover should lead us to similar conclusions. We can automatically verify the standard calculus of these structures. We can prove more than 100 theorems, most of them from scratch, and fail on a very small number of statements. Second, we apply our approach to a number of program analysis and computer mathematics tasks: Proof automation of separation and reduction theorems in concurrency control; automated program verification in Hoare logic; automated verification of the axioms of propositional dynamic logic and linear temporal logic; an automated modal correspondence proof of Löb's formula.

These experiments confirm the feasibility of our approach. Many proofs were fully automatic, interaction (introduction of lemmas) was only needed for some more complex statements. The example tasks, which are rather advanced, have been chosen for particular reasons: The concurrency control examples show some (co)inductive arguments and termination analysis within first-order logic. The examples from Hoare, dynamic and temporal logic demonstrate the versatility and practical relevance of the approach. The correspondence proof shows that some non-trivial mathematics (viz. a second-order frame property) can be automated and that abstraction is often a key to success. We believe that the approach can be extended to a light-weight formal method with a particularly high degree of automation.

Our experiments also pose some interesting research questions for automated deduction and formal methods. A further discussion can be found in the conclusion and the respective sections.

The emphasis of this paper is rather on the universality of Kleene algebra than on a detailed particular application. We will therefore only survey the specifications and concrete proofs with Prover9 and Mace4. The complete input and output files for each proof discussed can be found at a web-site [1].

Also, to further underpin the applicability for non-experts in automated deduction, we consistently use a rather naïve black-box approach to theorem proving and avoid sophisticated encodings, refined proof orderings, hints or proof planning, and excessive running times. Much stronger results could therefore be obtained with reasonable additional effort.

2   Idempotent Semirings

Idempotent semirings form the algebraic basis for the proof experiments of this paper. They provide the appropriate level of abstraction for modelling actions, programs or state transitions under non-deterministic choice and sequential composition in a first-order equational calculus. This makes them very suitable for resolution-based and paramodulation-based theorem proving.

A *semiring* is a structure $(S, +, ;, 0, 1)$ such that $(S, +, 0)$ is a commutative monoid, $(S, ;, 1)$ is a monoid, multiplication distributes over addition from the left and right and 0 is a left and right zero of multiplication. A semiring S is *idempotent* (an *i-semiring*) if $(S, +)$ is a semilattice with $x + y = \sup(x, y)$. We usually omit the multiplication symbol. The semilattice-order $\leq$ on S has 0 as its least element; addition and multiplication are isotone with respect to it.

The specification for Prover9/Mace4 is

```
x+y = y+x.                  % additive commutative monoid
x+0 = x.
x+(y+z) = (x+y)+z.
x;1 = x & 1;x = x.          % multiplicative monoid
x;(y;z) = (x;y);z.
x+x = x.                    % additive idempotence
0;x = 0 & x;0 = 0.          % multiplicative zeroes
x;(y+z) = x;z+x;y.          % distributivity laws
(x+y);z = x;z+y;z.
```

The definition of $\leq$ can be added, x<=y <-> x+y=y, but we usually work with equations to profit from the rewrite-based simplification techniques of Prover9. In contrast, human reasoning with i-semiring is largely order-based.

Every semiring comes with an *opposite* semiring in which the order of multiplication is swapped. The associated duality gives theorems for free.

Tests of a program or sets of states of a transitions system can also be modelled in this setting. Such objects are needed, e.g., for expressing conditions in if-then-else statements or loops, or the propositions of modal logics. It is natural to assume that these objects form a Boolean algebra. They can be integrated into i-semirings as follows: A *test* in an i-semiring S is an element of a Boolean subalgebra test$(S) \subseteq S$ (the *test algebra* of S) such that test(S) is bounded by 0 and 1 and multiplication coincides with lattice meet. We will write $x, y \ldots$ for arbitrary semiring elements and $p, q, \ldots$ for tests. Idempotent semirings admit at least the test algebra $\{0, 1\}$ and can have different test algebras. We use predicates for embedding tests; c(p) represents the complement $\neg p$ in Prover9.

```
test(p) -> p;c(p) = 0 & p+c(p) = 1.
test(0) & test(1).
test(p) -> c(c(p)) = p.
test(p) & test(q) -> c(p+q) = c(p);c(q).
test(p) & test(q) -> c(p;q) = c(p)+c(q).
test(p) -> test(c(p)).
```

The first line expresses existence and uniqueness of complements. The remaining lines induce the Boolean algebra of tests from a given set of tests. This can be verified with Prover9.

Idempotent semirings with tests are expressive enough for (indirectly) encoding Hoare logic without the assignment and the loop-rule [17]. Validity of a Hoare triple $\{p\}x\{q\}$ is captured by $px\neg q = 0$: no action x transforms a precondition p into a postcondition $\neg q$. We will discuss an automation of Hoare logic and the associated weakest liberal precondition semantics in Section 5 and 7.

The standard calculus of i-semirings and tests can automatically be verified with Prover9. A non-trivial example is the equivalence of

$$px\neg q = 0, \qquad px \le xq, \qquad x\neg q \le \neg px, \qquad px = pxq.$$

This equivalence is important, e.g., for reasoning in Hoare logic and with modal Kleene algebras.

3   Iteration Algebras

More interesting behaviours of programs and transition systems arise from finite and infinite iteration.

A *Kleene algebra* [16] is an i-semiring S extended by an operation $* : S \to S$ that satisfies the *star unfold* and the *star induction* axiom

$$1 + xx^* = x^*, \qquad y + xz \le z \Rightarrow x^*y \le z$$

and their duals with respect to opposition. The induction axioms are encoded as equations, e.g, `(y+x;z)+z = z -> x*;y+z = z`. The expression x^* abstractly represents the reflexive transitive closure of x. The transitive closure of x is defined as $x^+ = xx^*$.

An *omega algebra* [6] is a Kleene algebra S extended by an operation $^\omega : S \to S$ that satisfies the *omega unfold* and the *omega coinduction* axiom

$$x^\omega \le xx^\omega, \qquad z \le y + xz \Rightarrow z \le x^\omega + x^*y.$$

By these definitions, x^*y and $x^\omega + x^*y$ are the least and greatest fixed points of $\lambda z.y + xz$. The elements x^* and x^ω arise as special cases.

The following facts are interesting for automated deduction: First, the induction axioms act as star and omega elimination rules that simplify expressions. Second, these axioms formalise (co)induction without external measures (e.g.

length of a sequence) in first-order equational logic. Third, there are strong connections with standard automata-based decision procedures: While the equational theory of Kleene algebra is that of regular expressions [16], the uniform word problem is undecidable. Similar results hold for omega algebras and ω-regular expressions [6].

The following identities, e.g., can be proved automatically: $0^* = 1 = 1^*$, $1 \leq x^*$, $xx^* \leq x^*$, $x^*x^* = x^*$, $x \leq x^*$, $x^*x = xx^*$, $x^{**} = x^*$, $1 + xx^* = x^* = 1 + x^*x$, $x(yx)^* = (xy)^*x$ and $(x+y)^* = x^*(yx^*)^*$. $0^\omega = 0$, $x \leq 1^\omega$, $x^\omega = x^\omega 1^\omega$, $x^\omega = xx^\omega$, $x^\omega y \leq x^\omega$, $x^*x^\omega = x^\omega$, $x^{+\omega} = x^\omega$ and $(x+y)^\omega = (x^*y)^\omega + (x^*y)^*x^\omega$.

While these identities could as well be decided by automata, automated deduction can also verify implications such as

$$x \leq y \Rightarrow x^* \leq y^*, \qquad x \leq y \Rightarrow x^\omega \leq y^\omega, \qquad xz \leq zy \Rightarrow x^*z \leq zy^*.$$

We sometimes need some simple intermediate lemmas, obtained from proofs by hand, for proving more complex statements, but nothing beyond.

We can also detect some non-theorems, e.g. $x^{\omega*} = x^\omega$, with the model generation tool Mace4, but only one statement considered, $x^\omega x^\omega = x^\omega$, could neither be proved nor refuted (automatically or by hand); Mace4 can generate all idempotent semirings, Kleene algebras and omega algebras with < 20 elements. This conjecture and refutation game with Prover9 and Mace4 is very helpful in general. Table 1 shows that the number of Kleene algebras grows very fast with the number of elements.

Table 1. Enumeration of Kleene algebras

#elements	#KAs	#KAs (up to iso.)	#KAs with test (up to iso.)
1	1	1	1
2	1	1	1
3	3	3	3
4	39	20	21
5	753	149	149
6	23357	1488	1491
7	1052475	18554	
8	69199211		

Mace4 can check all Kleene algebras with less than 15 elements in a few minutes on a desktop PC[1]. It takes, for example, ~ 20s to check that $px\neg q = 0$ and $px + xq = xq$ are equivalent in all Kleene algebras with 15 elements.

Generation of Kleene algebras with Mace4 requires isomorphism checking and therefore storing models (7 elements need > 2GB RAM). Interestingly, Conway's classical book on regular algebras [7] lists 21 Kleene algebras with four elements. We found that his examples (5.) and (7.) are flawed and another one is missing. According to the Mace4 manual, the integrated isomorphism checking should be

---

[1] We used a Pentium 4 CPU, 1.6GHz, 384MB RAM.

taken with a grain of salt. But our numbers for < 7 elements are confirmed by Jipsen's computations with the GAP system [14].

4   Automating Concurrency Control

In this and the following sections we only aim at illustrating the main ideas, achievements and difficulties of the approach. All technical details of all proofs in this paper, including the Prover9 and Mace4 input and output files, that provide complete information about the the proof search and the time and memory used, can be found at a web-site [1]. All proofs have been done from scratch, i.e., with the full sets of axioms plus isotonicity of addition, multiplication, star and omega, but without any further assumptions, unless otherwise stated.

The expressions $(x + y)^*$ or $(x + y)^\omega$ can be interpreted as the repeated concurrent execution of two processes x and y. In this context, *reduction laws* such as $(x + y)^* = x^*(yx^*)^*$ connect concurrency with interleaving while *separation laws* infer global system properties from those of the particular processes. Kleene algebras are very useful for deriving such laws [6,23]. We present two examples that show how such derivations can be automated.

Our first example is the reduction law

$$y^*x^* \leq x^*y^* \Rightarrow (x + y)^* \leq x^*y^*$$

which says that repeated concurrent executions of x and y can be reduced to an x-sequence followed by a y-sequence (both possibly void) if all x-sequences have priority over y-sequences. This statement abstracts the relational encoding of the Church-Rosser theorem for abstract reduction systems.

The Church-Rosser theorem is usually proved by induction over the number of y^*x^*-peaks that arise from $(x + y)^*$, i.e., with an external induction measure (cf. [24]). However, equational proofs with the internal induction provided by Kleene algebra can also be given [23]. We can automatically prove the reduction law in about 3s; we can also automate an abstraction of the proof by induction on the number of peaks.

This result is a first step towards further proof automation that seems now feasible, viz. an automated proof of (the abstract part of) the Church-Rosser theorem of the λ-calculus. Equational proofs in Kleene algebra have already been given [23]. An essential feature of the proof method is abstraction. Properties about λ-terms are proved separately (e.g. in a higher-order prover [20]) and represented abstractly as *bridge lemmas* within Kleene algebra. These are then used as hypotheses at the algebraic level that is suitable for automation.

Reasoning about abstract reduction systems is traditionally diagrammatic. Kleene algebra provides a semantics for a considerable part of diagrammatic reasoning [10] which can therefore be verified by using a theorem prover in the background.

Our second example is a separation theorem due to Bachmair and Dershowitz [4]. It states that, in the presence of a suitable commutation condition, concurrent processes terminate iff individual processes do. The theorem can be specified and proved by hand in omega algebra [23]. In this setting, termination of a process x can be expressed as $x^\omega = 0$ (absence of infinite iteration). The separation theorem can therefore be stated as

$$yx \leq x(x+y)^* \Rightarrow (x^\omega + y^\omega = 0 \Leftrightarrow (x+y)^\omega = 0). \tag{1}$$

The implication $(x+y)^\omega = 0 \Rightarrow x^\omega + y^\omega = 0$ does not depend on the hypothesis. It can be proved in less than one second.

The converse direction requires a series of lemmas, at least with our naïve approach. Our search for automation lead us to a simpler proof than that in [23]. First, we can prove automatically that the hypothesis is equivalent to $y^+ x \leq x(x+y)^*$ and to $y^* x \leq x(x+y)^*$. We then attempted to prove that

$$x^\omega = 0 \wedge yx \leq x(x+y)^* \Rightarrow y^* x \leq x^+ y^*, \tag{2}$$

but failed. The essential part is proving $x(x+y)^* \leq x^+ y^* (= x^\omega + x^+ y^*)$ from the hypotheses. By omega coinduction, it suffices to show that $x(x+y)^* \leq xy^* + xx(x+y)^*$, which can be done automatically, but using the identity $(x+y)^* = y^* + y^* x(x+y)^*$, which itself can be done automatically. The coinduction step, however, let the search explode.

This proof is essentially a step-wise replay of a proof by hand. The main problem of proving is that applications of isotonicity, which are trivial in an inequational context, require intricate unifications in the equational case. A combination of equational and inequational reasoning would be very beneficial here. Equation (2) allows us to replace the hypothesis $yx \leq x(x+y)^*$ by the computationally simpler $y^* x \leq x^+ y^*$ whenever x terminates.

The remaining lemmas for (1), $x^*(x^* y)^\omega = (x^* y)^\omega$, and that $x^\omega = 0$ and $yx \leq x(x+y)^*$ imply $(y^* x)^\omega = 0$, are again automatic. Our separation theorem is then immediate from the lemmas.

This second example shows that it is possible to reason automatically about program termination in a first-oder setting, although finiteness cannot be expressed within first-order logic. The proofs are essentially coalgebraic and use the coinduction axiom of omega algebra. Explicit (bi)simulation is not needed.

These two proof experiments show that in many cases, despite the associativity and commutativity laws involved, Prover9 can prove some impressive facts. Some proofs, however, require an amount of interaction that is similar to higher-order proof checkers: proving individual lemmas automatically first and then using them as hypotheses for the main goal in a second round.

5   Automating Hoare Logic: A First Attempt

It is well-known that the programming constructs of Dijkstra's guarded command language can be encoded in Kleene algebra [17]. In particular,

if p then x else $y = px + \neg py$ \qquad and \qquad while p do $x = (px)^* \neg p$.

Using the above encoding of Hoare triples, validity of the rules of Hoare logic (except assignment) can then be expressed—although quite indirectly—and verified in Kleene algebra [17]. Validity of the while-rule

$$\frac{\{p \wedge q\}\ x\ \{q\}}{\{q\}\ \text{while}\ p\ \text{do}\ x\ \{\neg p \wedge q\}}$$

for instance, is expressed as $pqx\neg q = 0 \Rightarrow q(px)^*\neg(p+q) = 0$. We could not prove from scratch that this implication is a theorem of Kleene algebra. However, we can immediately prove that $qyq = qy \Rightarrow qy^*q = qy^*$, from which the above implication follows by isotonicity and substitution. Again, an encoding based on inequalities and in particular a theorem prover that can handle chaining rules for transitive relations might resolve this problem.

This negative result illustrates the fact that choosing the right algebra and the appropriate level of abstraction is important for a successful automation. First, the rules of Hoare logic are superfluous for verifying programs with Kleene algebra, but they are sound with respect to the algebraic semantics. Therefore, we don't even need to bother about verifying them. Second, the difficulty with proving validity of the while-rule reflects the general problems with verifying programs in this setting. In the following sections, we will show that a modal extension of Kleene algebra considerable simplifies this purpose.

6   Modal Semirings

The scope of Kleene algebras can be considerably extended by adding modalities. As we will see, the resulting formalism is similar to propositional dynamic logic but also strongly related to temporal logics.

An i-semiring S is called *modal* [19] if it can be endowed with a total (forward) diamond operation $|x\rangle : \text{test}(S) \rightarrow \text{test}(S)$, for each $x \in S$, that satisfies

$$|x\rangle p \leq q \Leftrightarrow xp \leq qx \quad \text{and} \quad |xy\rangle p = |x\rangle|y\rangle p.$$

Intuitively, $|x\rangle p$ characterises the set of states with at least one x-successor in p, i.e., the preimage of set p under the action x. According to the aforementioned property $xp \leq qx \Leftrightarrow xp = qxp$ and the fact that xp models the right-restriction of an action (e.g. a relation) by a set p, $|x\rangle p$ is the least set from which every element of p can be reached via action x. Therefore, the above definition of diamonds captures the usual Kripke semantics with the modal syntax at the left-hand side and the relational semantics at the right-hand side of the equivalence.

A *domain* operation $\text{dom} : S \rightarrow \text{test}(S)$ is obtained from the diamond operator as $\text{dom}(x) = |x\rangle 1$. Alternatively, domain can be axiomatised on i-semirings, even equationally, from which diamonds are defined as $|x\rangle p = \text{dom}(xp)$. By this axiomatisation, $\text{dom}(x)$ is the least set that does not restrict action x from the left, which is indeed a natural condition for a domain operation.

Dually, backward diamond operators can be defined via semiring opposition, $\langle x|p \leq q \Leftrightarrow px \leq xq$ and $\langle xy|p = \langle y|\langle x|p$, and related with a notion of codomain.

Modal boxes can be defined, as usual, via de Morgan duality: $|x]p = \neg|x\rangle\neg p$ and $[x|p = \neg\langle x|\neg p$. Modal semirings can be extended to modal Kleene algebras without any further modal axioms.

The equational axioms of (co)domain can easily be implemented in Prover9, boxes and diamonds can be defined relative to them. Modal operators must be totalised to functions of type $S \times S \to \mathsf{test}(S)$ by setting, e.g., $|x\rangle y = 0$ if $y \notin \mathsf{test}(S)$.

Modalities enjoy a rich calculus and symmetries that are expressed by Galois connections and conjugations [19], for instance, $|x\rangle p \le q \Leftrightarrow p \le [x|q$ and $p|x\rangle q = 0 \Leftrightarrow q\langle x|p = 0$. These and further standard laws can be proved automatically from the axioms. While dualities transform theorems, Galois connections and conjugations generate them. We therefore need not prove statements that follow generically from Galois connections or that are duals of other statements. This particular advantage of the algebraic approach saves a lot of work in practice.

Our experiments confirm that the number of axioms introduced through the different layers considerably inhibits proof search. Particular sources of complexity are the complementation axioms of the test algebra and the domain axioms that are computationally not sufficiently meaningful. In contrast, the following laws for modalities are very useful in practice.

$$|x\rangle(p + q) = |x\rangle p + |x\rangle q, \quad |x + y\rangle p = |x\rangle p + |y\rangle p, \quad |xy\rangle p = |x\rangle|y\rangle p, \quad |x\rangle 0 = 0,$$
$$p + |x\rangle|x^*\rangle p = |x^*\rangle p \quad |x\rangle p \le p \Rightarrow |x^*\rangle p \le p.$$

They can be automatically verified; only the last implication requires a simple intermediate lemma. The relevance of this alternative approach to modalities over Kleene algebras has further been explored in [11]. Essentially, the above laws define a *Kleene module*, a two-sorted structure over a Kleene algebra and a Boolean algebra in which the diamond operator acts as a scalar product. By using Kleene modules, we can completely dispense with domain (and even with Boolean complements, if necessary) and thereby considerably guide the proof search.

7   Automating Hoare Logic

We will now use modal Kleene algebra—instead of the previous non-modal approach—to show that the rules of Hoare logic (except the assignment rule) are theorems of modal Kleene algebra that can easily be automated. We also argue that the rules of the weakest liberal precondition calculus come for free by dualising the calculus of modal diamonds, which has to a large extent been automated. Finally, we show how partial correctness proofs of concrete programs can be automated in Kleene algebra up to domain specific calculations.

Encodings of validity of the Hoare rules in modal Kleene algebras can be found in [19]. In particular, validity of the while-rule is encoded as

$$\langle x|pq \le q \Rightarrow \langle(px)^*|\neg p|q \le \neg pq. \tag{3}$$

Dualisation yields $|xp\rangle q \le q \Rightarrow \neg p|(xp)^*\rangle q \le \neg pq$ and we can now apply the rules of our forward diamond calculus for Prover9. Obviously, there is almost nothing to prove. (3) follows immediately and automatically from the diamond induction law of Kleene modules and isotonicity of multiplication in an inequational encoding.

Validity of the remaining rules (except assignment) follows immediately from the Kleene module laws, too. The weakening rule, for instance, reduces to an isotonicity property. Up to a trivial induction over proofs in Hoare logic, this yields an automation of the soundness proof of Hoare logic with respect to the Kleene algebra semantics given in [19].

The standard completeness proof uses Hoare's weakest liberal precondition semantics. For each postcondition p and terminating action x it computes the weakest precondition (or the greatest set) for which each x-transition leads to p. This is precisely captured by $|x]p$. The calculus of weakest liberal preconditions therefore is just the calculus of forward box operators. It can be obtained without proof by dualising the diamond calculus. Based on these results, a simple calculational completeness proof of Hoare logic has been given, but it uses structural induction with respect to the programming constructs [19]. A partial automation is certainly possible. While the induction is schematic, the base case and the induction step are entirely equational and can be automated.

The previous considerations about Hoare logic abstracted from the assignment rule $\{p[e/x]\}\ x := e\ \{p\}$ which can be encoded as $\langle\{x := e\}|\ p[e/x] \leq p$ or, by the Galois connection, as

$$p[e/x] \leq |\{x := e\}]p.$$

Using this rule, we will now completely verify an algorithm for division of a non-negative integer n by a positive integer m in modal Kleene algebra. We will use abstraction for the Kleene algebra part and the assignment rule at the leaves of the proof tree as an interface to the specific calculations with integers.

> funct Div $\equiv k := 0;\ l := n;$
>   while $m \leq l$ do $k := k + 1;\ l := l - m;$

We will consistently write arithmetic expressions in brackets and therefore overload arithmetic notation. Setting

$$x_1 \hateq \{k := 0\},\quad x_2 \hateq \{l := n\},\quad y_1 \hateq \{k := k+1\},\quad y_2 \hateq \{l := l - m\},\quad r \hateq \{m \leq l\}$$

and using the precondition and the postconditions

$$p \hateq \{0 \leq n\},\quad q_1 \hateq \{n = km + l\},\quad q_2 \hateq \{0 \leq l\},\quad q_3 \hateq \{l < m\} = \neg r$$

yields the Hoare triple $\{p\}\ x_1 x_2 (r y_1 y_2)^* \neg r\ \{q_1 q_2 \neg r\}$. Its translation to modal Kleene algebra obliges us to prove

$$\langle x_1 x_2 (r y_1 y_2)^* \neg r | p \leq q_1 q_2 \neg r.$$

This can easily be done automatically from the hypotheses

$$p \leq |x_1]|x_2](q_1 q_2) \qquad \text{and} \qquad q_1 q_2 r \leq |y_1]|y_2](q_1 q_2).$$

The assumptions themselves have precisely the form of the assignment rule; they cannot be further analysed by Prover9. We give a proof by hand, but a full automation could be achieved by integrating a solver for a suitable fragment of arithmetics. For the first hypothesis we calculate

$$|x_1||x_2](q_1 q_2) = |\{k := 0\}| \, |\{l := n\}](q_1 q_2) \geq (\{n = km + l\}\{0 \leq l\})[k/0][l/n]$$
$$= \{n = 0m + n\}\{0 \leq n\} = \{0 \leq n\} = p.$$

For the second hypothesis we calculate

$$|y_1||y_2](q_1 q_2) \geq (\{n = km + l\}\{0 \leq l\})[l/(l - m)][k/(k + 1)]$$
$$= \{n = (k + 1)m + (l - m)\}\{0 \leq (l - m)\}$$
$$\geq \{n = km + l\}\{0 \leq l\}\{m \leq r\}.$$

This shows that partial correctness proofs can be fully automated in modal Kleene algebra in the presence of domain-specific solvers. This particular case would require a solver for simple arithmetics. Other proofs might require solvers, e.g., for data structures like lists, arrays or stacks or for more complex numeric domains. Integrating such solvers into state of the art theorem provers would therefore have immediate practical relevance for program analysis and verification. The special syntax and the specific inference rules of the Hoare calculus are not at all needed.

8   Automating Dynamic Logics

Modal Kleene algebras are very similar to propositional dynamic logics. More precisely, they are strongly related to variants of dynamic algebras developed by Kozen, Parikh and Pratt (cf. [12]). The axioms of dynamics algebras look like those of Kleene modules, but the induction axiom of Kleene modules is replaced by Segerberg's induction axiom

$$|x^*\rangle p - p \leq |x^*\rangle(|x\rangle p - p), \tag{4}$$

with $p - q$ defined as $p \neg q$. However, while dynamic algebras use a Boolean algebra in the second argument of diamonds, there is no Kleene algebra in the first argument, only a term algebra of Kleenean signature (cf. [11,19]).

It has been shown that (4) is a theorem of modal Kleene algebra, which means that propositional dynamic logic is subsumed by modal Kleene algebra. We can give a step-wise automated proof of (4). We can prove that

$$p \leq |x^*\rangle q + p, \qquad |x\rangle|x^*\rangle q \leq |x^*\rangle q + p, \qquad q \leq |x^*\rangle q$$

where q replaces $|x\rangle p - p$. With these hypotheses we can show that (4) follows from distributivity, the induction law of Kleene modules and the Galois connection $p - q \leq r \Leftrightarrow p \leq q + r$, which holds in Boolean algebra.

Another variant of dynamic algebra uses the additional axiom $|p?\rangle q = pq$ where $? : B \to K$ embeds tests into actions. In Kleene algebra, the embedding of tests is left implicit and this axiom reduces to $|p\rangle q = pq$. The proof can be automated from scratch as well.

Automated deduction with propositional dynamic logic is now available via modal Kleene algebras. This treatment of modal logic is completely axiomatic whereas previous approaches usually translate the Kripke semantics for modal logics more indirectly into first-order logic (cf. [21,8]). These translational approaches therefore reason in one particular model whereas ours, beyond relations, also covers models based on traces, paths and languages. Finally, an extension to first-order dynamic logics seems feasible.

9   Automating Linear Temporal Logics

It is well known that the operators of linear temporal logics can be expressed in propositional dynamic logics. The operators of next-step and until can be defined by $\mathsf{X}p = |x\rangle p$ and $p\mathsf{U}q = |(px)^*\rangle q$; the operators for finally and globally are $\mathsf{F}p = |x^*\rangle p$ and $\mathsf{G}p = |x^*]p$, where x stands for an arbitrary action. We can also define the initial state by $\mathsf{init}_x = [x|0$; it is the set of states with no x-predecessors. A set of axioms has been proposed by Manna and Pnueli [18] and further been adapted and explained by von Karger [25] to a setting of second-order quantales. However, von Karger's axioms can easily be translated to the first-order setting of modal Kleene algebras.

$$|(px)^*\rangle q = q + p|x\rangle|(px)^*\rangle q, \qquad \langle(xp)^*|q = q + p\langle(xp)^*|\langle x|q,$$
$$|(px)^*\rangle 0 \le 0, \qquad \langle x|0 = 1,$$
$$|x^*](p \to q) \le |x^*]p \to |x^*]q, \qquad [x^*|(p \to q) \le [x^*|p \to [x^*|q,$$
$$|x^*]p \le p|x]|x^*]p, \qquad |x^*](p \to |x]p) \le |x^*](p \to |x^*]p),$$
$$p \le [x||x\rangle p, \qquad p \le |x]\langle x|p,$$
$$\mathsf{init}_x \le |x^*](p \to [x|q) \to |x^*](p \to [x^*|q), \qquad \mathsf{init}_x \le |x^*]p \to |x^*][x|p,$$
$$|x](p \to q) = |x]p \to |x]q, \qquad [x|(p \to q) = [x|p \to [x|q,$$
$$\langle x|p \le [x|p, \qquad |x\rangle p = |x]p.$$

These axioms split into two groups. Those in the first five lines are theorems of modal Kleene algebra; the remaining ones express the particular properties of the underlying model and therefore need not be proved. But also for the first five lines there is nothing to prove: a closer inspection shows that they are instances of general theorems of Kleene algebras that have already been automated, e.g, $|x\rangle p - |x\rangle q \le |x\rangle(p-q)$. The axioms in the fifth line, in particular, are instances of generic cancellation laws of Galois connections. The second axiom in the fourth line is a dual variant of Segerberg's induction axiom (4).

Adding the axioms in the three last lines to those of modal Kleene algebras allows one to perform automated proofs in linear temporal logics in this setting with Prover9. These axioms encode relational properties in the sense of modal correspondence theory. Those in the sixth line encode confluence of x, the remaining ones encode linearity of x and the fact that there is no upper endpoint.

We did not attempt to further automate this analysis. Instead we will provide a more significant correspondence result in the next section.

Since variants of Dijkstra's guarded command language can also be specified in Kleene algebra, our approach could provide a kind of "soft model checking" in a first-order setting. System specifications can be written in the guarded command language, system properties can be specified in linear temporal logic. Proofs or refutations can then be attempted in Prover9 and Mace4. Again, our approach seems to allow an extension to first-order linear temporal logic.

10   Automating Modal Correspondence Theory

We will now consider an example from modal logics to further demonstrate the balance between expressive and computational power of modal Kleene algebras.

We will automate a modal correspondence proof of Löb's formula (cf. [5]), which in modal logic expresses well-foundedness of a transitive relation. In its usual form Löb's formula is written as $\Box(\Box p \rightarrow p) \rightarrow p$. To represent it algebraically, we first replace $\Box$ by $|x]$ and then dualise the result to forward diamonds. This yields

$$|x\rangle p \le |x\rangle (p - |x\rangle p). \tag{5}$$

We must express transitivity and well-foundedness. An element x is *transitive* if $xx \le x$, which implies that $|x\rangle|x\rangle p \le |x\rangle p$. Furthermore, x is *well-founded* if

$$p - |x\rangle p = 0 \Rightarrow p = 0. \tag{6}$$

This notion coincides with the usual set-theoretic notion. The expression $p - |x\rangle p$ abstractly represents the x-maximal elements of a set p, i.e., the set of elements of p from which no further x-transition is possible. Formula (6) therefore says that only the empty set has no x-maximal element, whence x is well-founded (with respect to increasing chains).

A deeper discussion of these notions and a proof by hand can be found in [9]. The proof has two steps. The first one shows that a transitive element is equal to its transitive closure. We can automatically prove $|x\rangle|x\rangle p \le |x\rangle p \Rightarrow |x^+\rangle p \le |x\rangle p$. The second one shows that well-foundedness of x is equivalent to

$$|x\rangle p \le |x^+\rangle (p - |x\rangle p). \tag{7}$$

Equivalence of (6) and (5) for transitive elements is then obvious.

While the proof that (7) implies (6) is immediate with Prover9, the converse implication is more complex. First, note that the antecedent of (6) is equivalent to $p \le |x\rangle p$. So if we can show that

$$|x\rangle p - |x^+\rangle (p - |x\rangle p) \le |x\rangle (|x\rangle p - |x^+\rangle (p - |x\rangle p)) \tag{8}$$

then (7) follows from (6). We can do a step-wise proof from the Kleene module axioms in which $p - q$ is consistently replaced by $p\neg q$. The arising difficulties show that we do not work at the right level of abstraction.

Since a modal operator $|a\rangle$ operates on the Boolean algebra of tests, we can lift our considerations to the function space. As usual, this is done by stipulating, for all $f, g : \text{test}(S) \to \text{test}(S)$, that $f \leq g$ iff $\forall p \in \text{test}(S).f(p) \leq g(p)$. The operations of Kleene algebras can be lifted as well, e.g., $(f+g)(p) = f(p)+g(p)$, $(fg)(p) = f(g(p))$ and $1(p) = p$. It can be shown that the structure induced on the function space is again a Kleene algebra (except for one induction axiom) [19]. The structure induced is even richer. In particular, we obtain $(f - g)(p) = f(p) - g(p)$. Lifting (8) and setting $f = |a\rangle$ yields

$$f - f^+(1 - f) \leq f(f - f^+(1 - f)).$$

We can now prove automatically that $f - f^+(1-f) \leq f((1-(1-f))-f^+(1-f))$. The remaining step requires an application of the inequality $1 - (1 - f) \leq f$, which we can prove automatically in Boolean algebra. However, this isotonicity step requires an intricate matching in our equational encoding, which could not be done by the prover in a reasonable amount of time.

This experiment illustrates the benefits of the abstraction and lifting techniques that come with the algebraic approach. It also illustrates the limitations of our naïve equational encoding that cannot sufficiently cope with isotonicity.

The standard correspondence result for Löb's formula is model-theoretic; it strongly uses implicit set theory and infinite chains and its frame property is second-order. In contrast, our approach is entirely calculational and therefore more suitable for automation. In particular, modal Kleene algebra allows us to express syntax and semantics in one and the same formalism. Beyond this example, further modal correspondence results can easily be automated.

11   Conclusion

We implemented variants of Kleene algebras in the automated deduction system Prover9 and the associated counterexample generator Mace4. We automatically verified the standard calculus of these algebras and proved some non-trivial statements that are relevant to systems verification and modal correspondence theory. We used the theorem-proving technology in a rather naïve way and did not put much effort into tuning syntactic orderings or using the selection and hint mechanisms provided. We usually stopped the prover after searching for a few minutes and introduced step-wise proofs when proofs from scratch were not successful with this approach. The immediate benefit of the black-box approach is that it yields a very conservative estimation of the possibilities and limitations of the approach, which is very valuable with respect to industrial applicability.

Compared to our initial expectations, the number and difficulty of the theorems we could prove came as a surprise. The Church-Rosser proof from scratch in a few seconds, for instance, seems quite impressive. We chose our experiments due to their practical relevance for computer mathematics and formal methods as well as due to their complexity. They support our claim that domain-specific algebras can successfully be combined with general purpose theorem provers; a direction that certainly deserves further investigation.

For mathematicians, our experiments underpin that automated deduction with complex algebraic structures is feasible, sometimes surprisingly simple and fast. Routine proofs can often be fully automated even by non-experts in automated deduction. In the context of formal methods, automated proof support, e.g. for B or Z, is still a challenge. Our approach has the potential to improve this situation. Our experiments suggest that modal Kleene algebras provide the appropriate level of abstraction to formalise and reason about programs and systems in a simple, concise and efficient way. While special purpose theorem provers have often been deemed necessary this task, our experiments suggest that off the shelf theorem proving technology can be very successful if combined with the appropriate algebra. The approach therefore seems very promising as a light-weight formal method with heavy-weight automation. In particular, the interplay of conjectures and refutations—a kind of "soft model checking"—seems very useful in practice.

Our experiments also pose some interesting research questions for automated deduction. First, equational reasoning should be complemented by reasoning with inequalities (viz. chaining calculi), an issue that has so far rather been neglected in implementations. During the submission phase of this paper, we have encoded inequalities as predicate in Prover9 together with the obvious axioms. Using this alternative approach, we could automatically verify some key refinement laws for concurrent systems, which are far more sophisticated than the examples treated in this paper [13]. The equational coding failed on most of these examples. Second, an integration of domain-specific solvers and decision procedures promises a full automation of partial correctness analysis of programs and beyond. Third, we cannot sufficiently exploit the symmetries and dualities of Kleene algebra within Prover9, and, although some forms of (co)induction are supported by Kleene algebra, structural induction is not possible. A combination of other tools that support these tasks would be very helpful.

In this paper we could only outline the first steps of our new approach to automated program analysis. In the future, we plan to build up a library of automatically verified theorems of Kleene algebra. The development of a tool that combines diagrammatic reasoning about transition systems with formal verification through automated deduction seems very interesting. We will also further pursue the specification and automated verification of programs and protocols via the guarded command language and the modal apparatus provided by Kleene algebra. And, last but not least, we are planning to continue transforming our approach into an applicable and strongly automated formal method.

Acknowledgements. We are grateful to the anonymous referee of a previous paper [23] for challenging us to automate Kleene algebras. We would also like to thank Peter Jipsen, Wolfram Kahl, Dexter Kozen and Renate Schmidt for inspiring discussions on deduction with these structures.

References

1. http://www.dcs.shef.ac.uk/~georg/ka
2. Prover9 and Mace4. http://www.cs.unm.edu/~mccune/mace4

3. Aboul-Hosn, K., Kozen, D.: KAT-ML: An interactive theorem prover for Kleene algebra with tests. Journal of Applied Non-Classical Logics 16(1-2), 9–33 (2006)
4. Bachmair, L., Dershowitz, N.: Commutation, transformation, and termination. In: Siekmann, J.H. (ed.) 8th International Conference on Automated Deduction. LNCS, vol. 230, pp. 5–20. Springer, Heidelberg (1986)
5. Blackburn, P., de Rijke, M., Venema, Y.: Modal Logic. Cambridge University Press, Cambridge (2001)
6. Cohen, E.: Separation and reduction. In: Backhouse, R., Oliveira, J.N. (eds.) MPC 2000. LNCS, vol. 1837, pp. 45–59. Springer, Heidelberg (2000)
7. Conway, J.H.: Regular Algebra and Finite Machines. Chapman & Hall, Sydney (1971)
8. De Nivelle, H., Schmidt, R.A., Hustadt, U.: Resolution-based methods for modal logics. Logic Journal of the IGPL 8(3), 265–292 (2000)
9. Desharnais, J., Möller, B., Struth, G.: Kleene algebra with domain. ACM Trans. Computational Logic 7(4), 798–833 (2006)
10. Ebert, M., Struth, G.: Diagram chase in relational system development. In: Minas, M. (ed.) 3rd IEEE workshop on Visual Languages and Formal Methods (VLFM'04), ENTCS, vol. 127, pp. 87–105. Elsevier, Amsterdam (2005)
11. Ehm, T., Möller, B., Struth, G.: Kleene modules. In: Berghammer, R., Möller, B., Struth, G. (eds.) Relational and Kleene-Algebraic Methods in Computer Science. LNCS, vol. 3051, pp. 112–123. Springer, Heidelberg (2004)
12. Harel, D., Kozen, D., Tiuryn, J.: Dynamic Logic. MIT Press, Cambridge (2000)
13. Höfner, P., Struth, G.: Can refinement be automated? Technical Report CS-07-08, Department of Computer Science, University of Sheffield (2007)
14. Jipsen, P.: Personal communication
15. Kahl, W.: Calculational relation-algebraic proofs in Isabelle/Isar. In: Berghammer, R., Möller, B., Struth, G. (eds.) Relational and Kleene-Algebraic Methods in Computer Science. LNCS, vol. 3051, pp. 179–190. Springer, Heidelberg (2004)
16. Kozen, D.: A completeness theorem for Kleene algebras and the algebra of regular events. Information and Computation 110(2), 366–390 (1994)
17. Kozen, D.: On Hoare logic and Kleene algebra with tests. ACM Trans. Computational Logic 1(1), 60–76 (2000)
18. Manna, Z., Pnueli, A.: The Temporal Logic of Reactive and Concurrent Systems—Specification. Springer, Heidelberg (1991)
19. Möller, B., Struth, G.: Algebras of modal operators and partial correctness. Theoretical Computer Science 351(2), 221–239 (2006)
20. Nipkow, T.: More Church-Rosser proofs (in Isabelle/HOL). J. Automated Reasoning 26(1), 51–66 (2001)
21. Ohlbach, H.J., Nonnengart, A., de Rijke, M., Gabbay, D.: Encoding Two-Valued Nonclassical Logics in Classic Logic. In: Robinson, A., Voronkov, A. (eds.) Handbook of Automated Reasoning (chapter 21), pp. 1403–1485. Elsevier, Amsterdam (2001)
22. Struth, G.: Calculating Church-Rosser proofs in Kleene algebra. In: de Swart, H. (ed.) RelMiCS 2001. LNCS, vol. 2561, pp. 276–290. Springer, Heidelberg (2002)
23. Struth, G.: Abstract abstract reduction. Journal of Logic and Algebraic Programming 66(2), 239–270 (2006)
24. Terese (ed.): Term Rewriting Systems. Cambridge University Press, Cambridge (2003)
25. von Karger, B.: Temporal algebra. Mathematical Structures in Computer Science 8(3), 277–320 (1998)

SRASS - A
Semantic Relevance Axiom Selection System

Geoff Sutcliffe and Yury Puzis

University of Miami, USA
geoff@cs.miami.edu

Abstract. This paper describes the design, implementation, and testing of a system for selecting necessary axioms from a large set also containing superfluous axioms, to obtain a proof of a conjecture. The selection is determined by semantics of the axioms and conjecture, ordered heuristically by a syntactic relevance measure. The system is able to solve many problems that cannot be solved alone by the underlying conventional automated reasoning system.

1 Introduction

In recent years the ability of systems to reason over large theories – theories in which there are many functors and predicates, many axioms of which typically only a few are required for the proof of a theorem, and many theorems to be proved from the same set of axioms – has become more important. Large theory problems are becoming more prevalent as large knowledge bases, e.g., ontologies and large mathematical knowledge bases, are translated into forms suitable for automated reasoning [14,28,16], and mechanical generation of automated reasoning problems becomes more common, e.g., [3,10]. Over the years there have been regular investigations into techniques for the a priori selection of the necessary axioms, e.g., [11,23,9,27,13], and the use of externally provided lemmas, e.g., [30,5,6,32,27,12]. Performances on large theory problems in the TPTP library [25] and the associated CADE ATP System Competition [22] show that automated reasoning systems have improved their ability to select and use the necessary axioms.

The work described in this paper addresses the issue of selecting necessary axioms, from a large set also containing superfluous axioms, to obtain a proof of a conjecture. It is based on the idea in Petr Pudlak's PhD research [13] (which he attributes to Jiří Vyskočil), to iteratively select axioms using semantics to guide the selection. This work diverges from that of Pudlak in that it focuses on extensions that improve the implemented performance of the basic idea, while Pudlak extends the basic idea towards finding a minimal adequate set of axioms.

The use of semantics to select axioms is in contrast to previous work (see the citations above) that uses syntactic characteristics both to estimate the potential usefulness of axioms, and to select which axioms to use in a proof attempt. While this work does use a syntactic relevance measure to determine

F. Pfenning (Ed.): CADE 2007, LNAI 4603, pp. 295–310, 2007.
© Springer-Verlag Berlin Heidelberg 2007

the order in which axioms are considered, semantics is used to select axioms. Further, no proof attempts need be made until the semantic selection of axioms is completed, at which point theoremhood of the conjecture has probably already been established.

The results obtained by the implementation show that the system is able to solve problems that cannot be solved alone by the underlying automated reasoning system. Additionally, in some cases where the underlying considered automated reasoning system is able to find a proof from the full axiom set, the axiom selection improves performance in terms of time taken and proof size.

This paper is organized as follows: Section 2 explains the semantic selection technique. Section 3 describes the syntactic relevance evaluation. Section 4 provides details of the implementation. Section 5 gives test results, with commentary. Section 6 concludes and discusses possible future research. In this paper all semantic statuses are given in terms of the SZS ontology [26].[1]

2   Semantic Relevance Axiom Selection

2.1   The Basic Process

The definition of logical consequence provides the intuitive basis for the semantic relevance axiom selection technique:

> A conjecture is a logical consequence of a set of axioms (i.e., a theorem of the axioms) iff every model of the axioms is a model of the formula.

The selection starts with an empty set of selected axioms. At each iteration the process looks for a model of the selected axioms and the negation of the conjecture. If no such model exists then the conjecture is a logical consequence of the selected axioms. If such a model exists then an unselected axiom that is false in the model is moved to the set of selected axioms. The newly selected axiom excludes the model (and possibly other models) from the models of the selected axioms and negated conjecture, eventually leading to the situation where there are no models of the selected axioms and the negated conjecture. Figure 1 shows the idea.[2] The plane represents the space of interpretations, the rectangle encompasses the models of the conjecture C, and an oval encompasses the models of the corresponding axiom A_i. In the first iteration, when the set of selected axioms is empty, the model M_0 of the negation of the conjecture, $\neg C$, is found. That leads to the selection of the axiom A_1, which is false in the model. Iteratively, the model M_1 of $\{A_1, \neg C\}$ is found, leading to the selection of A_2, the model M_2 of $\{A_1, A_2, \neg C\}$ is found, leading to the selection of A_3, at which point there is no model of $\{A_1, A_2, A_3, \neg C\}$, proving that C is a logical consequence of $\{A_1, A_2, A_3\}$. In the last part of the figure this is seen by the intersection of the axiom ovals lying within the conjecture rectangle. Note that the model may be finite or infinite, provided that formulae can be evaluated with respect to the

---

[1] See the most recent version online at http://www.tptp.org/TSTP/
[2] This way of representing the idea was taken from Petr Pudlak's PhD [13].

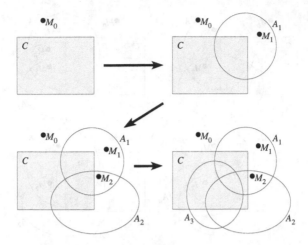

Fig. 1. The Basic Process

model. (In the implementation described in Section 4 a finite model builder is used, but this is not an "in principle" limitation.)

Example.[3] Consider the simple propositional problem, to prove the conjecture $C = b$ from the axioms $E_1 = a \mid b$, $E_2 = b \Rightarrow a$, $E_3 = (\neg a \And (b \mid c)) \mid (a \And \neg b \And \neg c)$. and $E_4 = b \mid (a \Leftrightarrow c)$. The conjecture C can be proved from E_3 and E_4, i.e., E_1 and E_2 are superfluous. The following table shows a possible sequence of models and selected axioms. Note how E_1, E_2, and E_3 are true in the first model, so only E_4 can be selected. E_1 and E_3 are false in the second model, but E_1 is found first. E_2 is true in every model of $\neg C$, and thus can never be selected. If the model $\{a, \neg b, c\}$ had been used in the second iteration, then E_3 would have been selected, leading to immediate success.

	Selected set	Model	Axiom
1	$\{\ \}$	$\{a, \neg b, \neg c\}$	$E_4 = b \mid (a \Leftrightarrow c)$
2	$\{E_4\}$	$\{\neg a, \neg b, \neg c\}$	$E_1 = a \mid b$
3	$\{E_1, E_4\}$	$\{a, \neg b, c\}$	$E_3 = (\neg a \And (b \mid c)) \mid (a \And \neg b \And \neg c)$
4	$\{E_1, E_3, E_4\}$	-	-

The basic process described above assumes that the axioms are consistent and non-redundant, and that the conjecture is a logical consequence of (some subset of) the axioms.

Inconsistent Axioms. If the axioms are inconsistent, then a situation such as that shown in the upper left of Figure 2 exists, There is no model of the selected axioms $\{A_1, A_2, A_3\}$. In this case the conjecture is a logical consequence of the selected axioms, and the process described above still reports logical consequence.

---

[3] Thanks to Josef Urban for his Prolog program that cooked up this illustrative example.

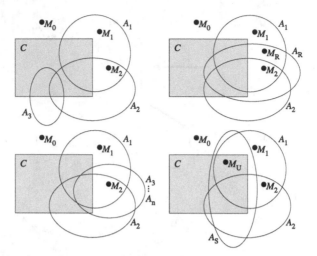

Fig. 2. Exceptional Cases

Redundant Axioms. If the axioms are redundant (i.e., some can proved from others, which is worse than being superfluous), then a situation such as that shown in the upper right of Figure 2 exists. A_R is selected because it is false in M_1, but is redundant after the selection of A_2. Retaining redundant axioms is (typically) deleterious to subsequent processing of the selected axiom set. This situation can be detected by attempting to prove any axiom that is not selected (because it is found to be true in the current model) from the selected axioms, and after selecting an axiom, by attempting to prove each previously selected axiom from the remaining selected axioms. A negative aspect of this approach to detecting redundant axioms is that it requires an "expensive" proof attempt on each unselected axiom that is true in each model.

CounterSatisfiable Conjecture. If the conjecture is not a logical consequence of the axioms, then a situation such as that shown in the lower left of Figure 2 exists. All the unselected axioms $A_3 \ldots A_n$ are true in the current model M_2. This situation is detected in the above process when looking for an unselected axiom that is false in the current model, by noticing that all the unselected axioms are true in the current model.

2.2   The Extended Process

While the basic process described in Section 2.1 provides a complete solution to the axiom selection problem, it does not (and cannot in general) ensure that each selected axiom is not superfluous, and it ignores implementation issues. In this section the basic process is extended to improve performance, and to cope with practical issues that arise in implementation. All these extensions have been implemented, as described in Section 4.

Initial Proof Attempt. While axiom selection is a useful technique, there are many problems with superfluous axioms that can be easily solved using conventional automated reasoning. It is possible that the overhead of axiom selection may even prevent the solution of such problems in a resource limited environment. In order to detect such easily solved problems, an initial proof attempt may be made using conventional automated reasoning. If this is successful then no further processing is required.

Relevance Ordering. At each iteration of the basic process it is necessary to search through the unselected axioms to find one that is false in the current model (and similar searches turn out to be necessary in other situations described below). The chances of selecting a useful axiom are increased if the unselected axioms are considered in decreasing order of potential usefulness. This is necessarily a heuristic ordering. The implementation described in Section 4 uses a syntactic relevance score to order the unselected axioms. The details of the relevance scoring system are given in Section 3. The heuristic ordering also has the practical effect of increasing the chances of finding a false axiom early in each search through the unselected axioms, resulting in faster progress. The results in Section 5 show that the syntactic relevance ordering is a key to the success of the implemented system.

Efficient Termination. The basic process terminates when it determines that there is no model of the selected axioms and negated conjecture. This can be more efficiently established by testing if the selected axioms and negated conjecture are unsatisfiable (although these two are logically the same, different techniques may be used to establish the two conditions). As this will be the case only when sufficient axioms have been selected, i.e., the test will normally fail, it is prudent to first check if the selected axioms and negated conjecture are satisfiable - if they are, then the unsatisfiability test is unnecessary.

Greedy Termination. A greedy approach may be taken to detect the situation when only one more axiom needs to be selected, by looking for an unselected axiom whose negation can be proved from the selected axioms and negated conjecture, i.e., the axiom is a *counter theorem* of the selected axioms and negated conjecture. This situation is seen in the last part of Figure 1 (and in the case of inconsistent axioms, in the upper left of Figure 2), with A_3 being the final axiom. Note how A_3's oval does not intersect with any part of the area containing the models of the selected axioms and negated conjecture (the area containing M_2). In the example in Section 2.1, at the start of the second iteration, greedy termination detects that $\neg E_3$ can be proved from $\{E_4, \neg C\}$. Greedy termination is reminiscent of the unit conflict strategy found in some automated reasoning systems, e.g., Otter [8]. A negative aspect of using greedy termination is that it fails until an adequate set of axioms has been selected, so that at each iteration before the last one there is an expensive wasted proof attempt for each unselected axiom.

Incomplete Models. In practice, the model found at each iteration might be able to interpret only the symbols found in the selected axioms and negated conjecture. If so, it might be impossible to evaluate unselected axioms that use other symbols. In the example in Section 2.1, given only the negated conjecture $C = \neg b$ in the first iteration, the model $\{\neg b\}$ might be found. Axiom E_2 might be evaluated as true in the model, but the other three axioms cannot be evaluated. To deal with this situation the basic process is extended: If no unselected axiom is evaluated as false in the model, then look for an unselected axiom that cannot be evaluated as true in the model. Such an axiom is called a *not-true* axiom.

Inadequate Models. In practice, it might not be possible to find a model for a given set of selected axioms and negated conjecture, even if one exists, because of resource limits, or because a finite model builder is used and only infinite models exist. If this occurs then the unselected axioms cannot be evaluated as false or not-true. Remedial steps, e.g., increasing the resources assigned to model finding, may optionally be taken. Even if a model can be found, it may still not be possible to evaluate an unselected axiom as false or not-true, because of resource limits, or because the model is incomplete. To deal with situations in which axioms cannot be evaluated with respect to a model, the process is further extended: If no unselected axiom is evaluated as false or not-true, then look for an unselected axiom that cannot be proved from the selected axioms and the negated conjecture, i.e., the axiom is *counter satisfiable* with respect to the selected axioms and negated conjecture. This is implemented by looking for a model of the selected axioms, the negated conjecture and the negation of an unselected axiom. This extension is thus a converse of the basic process – the basic process finds a model and then looks for a false axiom, while this extension selects an axiom and then looks for a model in which the axiom is false. This extension can be used alone, but is less successful alone because it allows the axioms to determine the models rather than vice versa. The following table shows a possible sequence of models and selected axioms for the example in Section 2.1, with incomplete models, and no evaluation if the model is incomplete for the formula. Note how in the first and second iteration none of the unselected axioms can be evaluated as false or not-true in the model. In the second iteration E_2 cannot be selected as counter satisfiable because there is no model of $\{E_1, \neg C, \neg E_2\}$.

Selected set	Model	False Axiom	Not-true Axiom	CSA Model	CSA Axiom
1 { }	$\{\neg b\}$	-	-	$\{\neg a, \neg b\}$	$E_1 = a \mid b$
2 $\{E_1\}$	$\{a, \neg b\}$	-	-	$\{a, \neg b, c\}$	$E_3 = (\neg a \,\&\, (b \mid c)) \mid$ $(a \,\&\, \neg b \,\&\, \neg c)$ $= b \mid (a \Leftrightarrow c)$
3 $\{E_1, E_3\}$	$\{a, \neg b, \neg c\}$	E_4			
4 $\{E_1, E_3, E_4\}$	-	-	-	-	

This extension can be efficiently implemented because it is not necessary to actually build a model of the selected axioms, the negated conjecture, and the negation of an unselected axiom. It is merely necessary to establish the existence of such a model, i.e., to establish that selected axioms, the negated conjecture, and the negation of the unselected axiom are satisfiable. However, this again might not be possible. To deal with this situation the process is finally extended: If no unselected axiom is evaluated as false or not-true, and no unselected axiom is counter satisfiable with respect to the selected axioms and negated conjecture, then select the axiom that has the highest syntactic relevance.

Aggressive Selection. The goal of the process is to select a set of axioms so that every model of the axioms is a model of the conjecture, or, put another way, the intersection of the sets of models of the axioms is a subset of the set of models of the conjecture. This is shown in the last part of Figure 1. When selecting an axiom at each iteration, an axiom for which there is a model of its negation, the selected axioms, and the conjecture, might be preferred over an axiom that is true in every model of the selected axioms and the conjecture. The intuitive reason is that the former axiom reduces the size of the intersection (of the sets of models of the selected axioms) within the set of models of the conjecture. This is shown in the lower right of Figure 2, where the axiom A_S is necessarily superfluous if used with A_1, while axiom A_2 is seen to be potentially useful due to the existence of the model M_U. In the example in Section 2.1, in the second iteration both E_1 and E_3 are false in the model, but aggressive selection prefers E_3 over E_1 because there is a model of $\{\neg E_3, E_4, C\}$ (e.g., $\{a, b, c\}$) but no model of $\{\neg E_1, E_4, C\}$. Of course an M_U does not necessarily exist for every selected axiom, e.g., in the first iteration of the example there is no model of $\{C, \neg E_4\}$. If there are axioms that meet the semantic requirements for selection, but all are rejected by aggressive selection, then aggressive selection can no longer be used.

Batch Selection. The extended process described so far selects a single axiom at each iteration. The effort required to make the selection in each iteration may be quite significant. In order to make faster progress it is possible to select multiple axioms at each iteration, by selecting muliple axioms that are false in the model, and then, if more are required, multiple not-true axioms, and so on. This reduces the effort-per-axiom selected, and is particularly useful when large numbers of axioms are necessary for a proof of the conjecture. The disadvantage of batch selection is that the selection is less focussed, because the set of selected axioms and model upon which decisions are predicated are not updated for the second and subsequent axioms of each batch.

Limited Selection. For each of the alternative methods of selecting an axiom (false in the model, not-true in the model, ...), in the default process each method considers all of the unselected axioms before progressing to the next method. This might lead to an axiom of low syntactic relevance being selected by an earlier method, while it may be preferable to select a more syntactically relevant axiom by a later method. In order to balance these alternatives the number of unselected axioms that is considered by each method can be limited. Limiting the number of axioms considered by methods with high resource requirements also produces faster progress.

Final Proof Attempt. The selection terminates normally when it is established that the conjecture is a logical consequence of the selected axioms – theoremhood has been established but no proof has been generated. It is also possible for all axioms to be selected without theoremhood being established, because of resource limits on the tests, or because all axioms are necessary. Therefore, when the axiom selection process terminates, a final proof attempt is made using conventional automated reasoning, to build a proof. If this succeeds then theoremhood is established and the proof can be output.

3   Syntactic Relevance Ordering

A *syntactic relevance measure* uses the syntax of axiom formulae to gauge the extent to which the formulae may contribute to a proof of a given conjecture. Syntactic relevance measurement, like semantic axiom selection, is necessarily heuristic. The syntactic relevance measure described here is a measure of the extent to which the formulae use the same predicates and functors. The notion of using the language of formulae to gauge connections between the formulae has also been used to guide the use of formulae as parents of inferences, e.g., in partition-based reasoning [7], in axiom selection, e.g., [9], and more generally in information retrieval applications, e.g., web queries [17].

The *direct relevance* between two formulae is the ratio of how many predicates and/or functors they have in common to how many predicate and/or functors they use overall. Let $sym(F)$ be the set of predicates and/or functors that occur in the formula F. The direct relevance between two formulae F_a and F_c is

$$\frac{|sym(F_a) \cap sym(F_c)|}{|sym(F_a) \cup sym(F_c)|}$$

The *contextual direct relevance* between two formulae replaces the intersection in the numerator by *contextual intersection*, which places the two formulae in the context of a set of formulae. The contextual intersection $\sqcap$ of two formulae F_a and F_c in the context of the set of all formulae (all the axioms and the conjecture) S is

$$\sum_{s \in (sym(F_a) \cap sym(F_c))} \left(1 - \frac{|\{f : f \in S, s \in sym(f)\}|}{|S|} \right)$$

and the contextual direct relevance is

$$\frac{|sym(F_a) \sqcap sym(F_c)|}{|sym(F_a) \cup sym(F_c)|}$$

Contextual relevance captures the intuitive notion that if a symbol occurs in many formulae, then the fact that it appears in two given formulae does not indicate any special connection between the two formulae.

In addition to (contextual) direct relevance between two formulae, there may be (contextual) *indirect relevance*, by virtue of both being relevant to some other formula. The (contextual) indirect relevance between two formulae F_a and F_c is determined by examining the (contextual) direct relevances between intermediate formulae F_i and F_{i+1}, in all paths $F_a = F_1 \cdot F_2 \cdot \ldots \cdot F_n = F_c$ from F_a to

F_c. The relevance measure for such a path is the smallest relevance on the path divided by the length of the path. This reflects the idea that a path is only as strong as its weakest link, and that relevance decreases with distance. The (contextual) indirect relevance between two formulae is the maximal (contextual) indirect relevance over all paths connecting the two formulae.

4   Implementation

The processes described in Sections 2 and 3 have been implemented as the system SRASS. The various tests required by the process are all implemented using conventional automated reasoning systems: a theorem prover to test for (counter)theoremhood, test for unsatisfiability, and to find explicit proofs; a finite model builder to test for (counter)satisfiability and build models; and a saturating system to further test for (counter)satisfiability in cases where the finite model builder fails and it is necessary only to establish the existence of a model, e.g., for selecting counter satisfiable axioms. Contextual indirect syntactic relevance is used to order the axioms. This implementation places SRASS alongside other work based around a combination of component reasoning systems, e.g., [34,33,20].

The evaluation of an unselected axiom with respect to a model is done by representing the model as a set of formulae [24], and the unselected axiom (or its negation) as a conjecture. An axiom is evaluated as false in the model if its negation can be proved from the model (the axiom is a counter theorem of the model), evaluated as not-true in the model if its negation and the model are satisfiable (the axiom is counter satisfiable with respect to the model), and is evaluated as true in the model if it can be proved from the model (the axiom is a theorem of the model). This method of evaluation is slightly resource intensive, but allows consistent use of automated reasoning for all tests.

The implementation is in C, built on top of the JJParser library of TPTP compliant functions, and using the SystemOnTPTP harness [21] for calling the component automated reasoning systems. The various features of SRASS are parameterized, thus allowing the various features of the process to be enabled and disabled, different resource limits to be imposed, different forms of output to be reported, and different automated reasoning systems to be used. The implementation algorithm is shown in Figure 3.

5   Results

SRASS has been tested on several problem sets. The first problem set is in the domain of logical calculi – the 132 TPTP problems LCL448+1 to LCL578+1. The problems come from research into mechanically proving relationships between different axiomatizations of various modal logic systems [19,15]. The modal logic formulae are encoded as first-order terms, and modal inference rules as first-order implications. The problems include equivalence definitions for all the modal axioms in the problem suite, in the form $axiom\_name \Leftrightarrow encoded\_form$, which are

```
 1 Sort axioms into descending order of syntactic relevance;
 2 if Initial Proof Attempt is successful then
 3     Report "Theorem";
 4     Report proof;
 5     exit;
 6 end
 7 while SZS status not established & Some axioms are unselected do
 8     if Theoremhood established by Efficient Termination then
 9         break;
10     else if Theoremhood established by Greedy Termination then
11         break;
12     else if Can find model of {¬C} ∪ Selected then
13         Select axioms that are counter theorems of the model;
14         if CounterSatisfiable Conjecture then
15             break;
16         end
17         if Batch Selection is not complete then
18             Select axioms that are counter satisfiable wrt the model;
19         end
20     else
21         Optionally increase resources for finding models;
22     end
23     if Batch Selection is not complete then
24         Select axioms that are counter satisfiable wrt {¬C} ∪ Selected;
25     end
26     if Batch Selection is not complete then
27         if An axiom was rejected by Aggressive Selection then
28             Select that axiom;
29             Cancel Aggressive Selection;
30         else
31             Select most syntactically relevant axioms;
32         end
33     end
34 end
35 if Problem not solved & All axioms are selected then
36     Check if conjecture proved by Efficient Termination;
37 end
38 if Theoremhood established then
39     Report "Theorem";
40 end
41 if Final Proof Attempt is successful then
42     Report proof;
43 end
44 if Countersatisfiability established then
45     Report "CounterSatisfiable";
46 end
```

Fig. 3. SRASS Algorithm

"activated" by asserting or conjecturing the *axiom_name*. Many of the definitions are not relevant to a given problem, and hence not asserted or conjectured, and within each problem it is typically the case that many of the modal axioms (and hence their encoded forms) are superfluous. The second problem set is in the domain of set theory – the 253 TPTP problems SET866+1 to SEU118+1. The problems come from a first-order encoding of theorems in the Mizar library [28]. The problems are generated by a process that attempts to automatically detect what background knowledge in the Mizar library is relevant to the conjecture, and then encodes the Mizar form into first-order logic. The process of accumulating background information cannot be precise, and therefore conservatively adds background so that problems have superfluous axioms. The third problem set is in the domain of software verification – the 109 TPTP problems SWV022+1 to SWV130+1. The problems come from certification of auto-generated aerospace software [3]. The certification approach uses Hoare-style techniques that produce safety obligations in the form of first-order problems that are provable if and only if the software is safe. The safety obligations have superfluous axioms as a result of their mechanical production. Problems that E 0.99 cannot solve in 20s were used, giving 75 logical calculi problems, 103 set theory problems, and 61 software verification problems. Of these 239 problems, either E 0.99 or SRASS could solve 71: 22 logical calculi problems, 28 set theory problems, and 21 software verification problems. The results for these 71 problems are reported below.

For the testing SRASS was configured conservatively: no Initial Proof Attempts were made[4], no tests for CounterSatisfiable Conjectures were done, Greedy Termination and Aggressive Selection were disabled, and no Batch Selection or Limited Selection was used. The automated reasoning systems used were: E 0.99 [18] to test for (counter)theoremhood and unsatisfiability, EP 0.99 to find explicit proofs, FM-Darwin 1.3g [1] to build models, Paradox 2.0b [2] to test for (counter)satisfiability, and SPASS 2.2 [31] to further test for (counter) satisfiability. The CPU limits imposed were 600s overall, 10s for (counter)theoremhood tests, 120s for unsatisfiability tests, 600s for finding explicit proofs, 10s for building models, and 2s for (counter)satisfiability tests. The testing was done on a 2.8GHz Intel Xeon computer with 1GB memory, and running Linux 2.6.

Table 1 summarizes the results. The columns provide the TPTP problem name, the number of axioms in the problem, the time taken by EP to find a proof (or, if no proof is found, the time taken by E to establish theoremhood), the number of axioms used in EP's proof, the time taken by SRASS to find a proof (or, if no proof is found, the time taken to establish theoremhood), the number of axioms selected, the time taken by EP to find the proof from the selected axioms, and the number of axioms in the proof from the selected axioms. There are 71 problems. EP finds proofs for 18 problems, and E establishes theoremhood for a further 21, for a total of 39. SRASS finds proofs for 47 problems, and establishes

---

[4] The manual selection of problems that E 0.99 cannot solve in 20s could be replaced by making Initial Proof Attempts with a 20s CPU limit. Thus for black-box testing, add 20s to all the SRASS times in the results table below.

theoremhood for a further 7, for a total of 54. SRASS and EP both find proofs for 15 problems, and SRASS is faster than EP in 11 of these 15 cases. SRASS and E both establish theoremhood for 22 problems (including the cases where both find proofs), and SRASS is faster than E in 12 of these 22 cases.

For 9 of the 15 problems for which SRASS and EP both find proofs, the proofs use a different number of axioms. Of particular interest are LCL524+1, where SRASS uses 17 axioms and EP uses 36, and the four SWV problems where SRASS uses no axioms while EP uses 2 axioms. Generally SRASS outperforms EP on the SWV problems because SRASS finds that a proof is possible with just a few axioms (often none).

As mentioned in Section 2.2, the syntactic relevance ordering is a key to the success of SRASS. Without syntactic relevance ordering SRASS solves only 36 of the problems (compared to the 54 solved with syntactic relevance ordering). Interestingly, there are five problems that are solved without the relevance ordering that are not solved with the relevance ordering. Aggressive selection, on the other hand, is of less utility – SRASS solves 52 of the problems with aggressive selection enabled. However there are some cases where use of aggressive selection results in fewer axioms being selected.

In order to confirm the utility of building and using models to guide axiom selection, SRASS was configured to simply take the best axiom according to the syntactic relevance ordering, at each iteration. Efficient termination remained in use, i.e., at each iteration a test was made for the satisfiability of the selected axioms and negated conjecture, and if that failed a test for unsatisfiability was made. In this configuration only 37 problems were solved. Two problems were solved that could not be solved by the model guided configuration. In all of the 35 problems solved by both configurations, the model guidance resulted in selection of fewer axioms. For 21 problems the absence of model guidance resulted in lower solution times (as might be expected), but typically the time saved was not significant. For 14 problems the failed unsatisfiability tests resulted in higher solution times, often an order of magnitude greater than the model guided times.

In addition to the three problem sets described above for which SRASS obtained positive results, SRASS was also tested in the conservative configuration on three other problem sets: problems from Art Quaife's development of NBG set theory [14] – the 52 TPTP problems SET016+1 to SET122+1, number theory problems that simulate human arithmetic – the 84 TPTP problems NUM290+1 to NUM373+1, and software creation problems regarding software component retrieval [4] – the 586 TPTP problems SWC001+1 to SWC423+1. These tests give less impressive results, with SRASS and EP solving similar numbers of problems, although not always the same problems.

SRASS was tested in a less conservative configuration on the MPTP Challenge problems [29]. The challenge is divided into two divisions: the bushy division, and the chainy division, each of which has 252 problems. The bushy problems have from 6 to 340 axioms - average 76, some of which are superfluous due to the way in which background axioms are added. The chainy problems are the bushy problems augmented by lemmas that are superfluous but sometimes

Table 1. SRASS Results

Problem	Ax	EP.t	.ax	S.t	S.axs	SP.t	.ax	Problem	Ax	EP.t	.ax	S.t	S.axs	SP.t	.ax
LCL461+1	52	305	—	—	—	—	—	LCL462+1	42	444	—	—	—	—	—
LCL466+1	42	188	—	—	—	—	—	LCL467+1	42	187	—	—	—	—	—
LCL468+1	42	447	—	—	—	—	—	LCL473+1	42	23	—	210	21	—	—
LCL476+1	42	102	—	479	28	—	—	LCL480+1	42	187	—	—	—	—	—
LCL481+1	42	188	—	—	—	—	—	LCL485+1	44	21	—	98	15	4	15
LCL486+1	44	—	—	86	15	0	9	LCL489+1	44	35	—	164	24	—	—
LCL495+1	44	88	—	—	—	—	—	LCL496+1	44	—	—	90	15	0	9
LCL498+1	44	74	15	244	26	3	17	LCL502+1	42	86	—	—	—	—	—
LCL504+1	42	30	—	—	—	—	—	LCL519+1	42	107	—	184	20	—	—
LCL524+1	81	44	36	411	33	1	17	LCL528+1	87	434	—	599	51	—	—
LCL533+1	87	52	45	—	—	—	—	LCL541+1	94	493	—	—	—	—	—
SET946+1	11	—	—	26	5	—	—	SET964+1	12	—	—	159	6	1	3
SET973+1	25	50	9	—	—	—	—	SET982+1	7	84	3	—	—	—	—
SET992+1	35	—	—	21	2	0	2	SET994+1	31	241	—	41	11	0	8
SEU003+1	36	106	3	54	14	1	3	SEU005+1	40	—	—	19	6	1	4
SEU012+1	38	—	—	589	14	0	3	SEU013+1	34	—	—	36	10	3	5
SEU017+1	39	460	—	—	—	—	—	SEU024+1	40	0	4	33	8	0	3
SEU027+1	36	—	—	15	4	0	3	SEU028+1	44	—	—	119	11	0	8
SEU029+1	40	0	4	28	6	0	3	SEU031+1	42	37	4	11	4	0	4
SEU043+1	41	—	—	21	5	—	—	SEU048+1	34	—	—	29	7	0	4
SEU049+1	35	—	—	24	3	5	2	SEU055+1	39	—	—	211	13	0	4
SEU064+1	33	—	—	58	9	0	3	SEU065+1	39	—	—	256	9	160	4
SEU076+1	33	—	—	38	8	0	3	SEU077+1	35	—	—	36	10	0	3
SEU078+1	42	209	—	—	—	—	—	SEU105+1	47	—	—	22	11	0	4
SEU110+1	33	170	6	22	4	0	3	SEU114+1	35	590	—	—	—	—	—
SWV025+1	99	233	2	15	0	0	0	SWV026+1	99	271	2	10	0	0	0
SWV027+1	99	247	2	10	0	0	0	SWV028+1	91	199	0	10	0	0	0
SWV034+1	91	79	2	10	0	0	0	SWV036+1	84	—	—	175	9	91	3
SWV038+1	84	—	—	10	1	0	1	SWV089+1	84	—	—	41	4	0	4
SWV090+1	84	—	—	68	2	17	2	SWV091+1	84	—	—	75	2	18	2
SWV093+1	101	—	—	10	0	0	0	SWV094+1	101	—	—	10	0	0	0
SWV095+1	101	125	0	10	0	0	0	SWV096+1	101	123	0	10	0	0	0
SWV097+1	91	—	—	10	0	0	0	SWV099+1	91	113	0	10	0	0	0
SWV103+1	84	—	—	27	2	9	2	SWV109+1	101	—	—	10	0	0	0
SWV115+1	101	—	—	10	0	0	0	SWV116+1	101	—	—	10	0	0	0
SWV122+1	93	—	—	10	0	0	0								

useful. The chainy problems have from 12 to 1233 axioms - average 403. The conservative configuration of SRASS was extended to make an Initial Proof Attempt with a CPU limit of 30s, to Batch Select 3 axioms in each iteration, and to have a Limited Selection from the 10 most syntactically relevant axioms in each iteration. An overall CPU limit of 300s was imposed. The testing aimed only to establish theoremhood for each problem, without proofs being found. In the bushy division, E establishes theoremhood for 141 problems, and SRASS establishes theoremhood for 171. SRASS and E both establish theoremhood for 138 problems, E establishes theoremhood for 3 problems that SRASS does not, and SRASS establishes theoremhood for 33 problems that E does not. In the chainy division, E establishes theoremhood for 91 problems, and SRASS establishes theoremhood for 127. SRASS and E both establish theoremhood for 83 problems, E establishes theoremhood for 8 problems that SRASS does not, and SRASS establishes theoremhood for 44 problems for E does not.

6   Conclusion

This paper has shown how semantics can be used to determine the selection of necessary axioms from a large set also containing superfluous axioms, to obtain a proof of a conjecture. While the selection is a fairly resource intensive process, the results show that benefits can often be obtained. Axiom selection is appropriate when it is known that the axiom set contains superfluous axioms. Axiom selection cannot help when the axiom set is already minimal, and the difficulty of the problem stems from a deep proof or highly explosive search space.

Future work will be to determine appropriate configurations with respect to problem characteristics, investigating the practical options for using both finite and infinite models, and examining the performance in the face of axioms sets that are orders of magnitude larger than those used in the testing so far – for such axiom sets it is possible that further extensions to the basic process will need to be devised and implemented.

SRASS is available for use online through the SystemOnTPTP interface ...

http://www.tptp.org/cgi-bin/SystemOnTPTP.

References

1. Baumgartner, P., Fuchs, A., Tinelli, C.: Darwin - A Theorem Prover for the Model Evolution Calculus. In: Sutcliffe, G., Schulz, S., Tammet, T. (eds.) Proceedings of the Workshop on Empirically Successful First Order Reasoning, 2nd International Joint Conference on Automated Reasoning (2004)
2. Claessen, K., Sorensson, N.: New Techniques that Improve MACE-style Finite Model Finding. In: Baumgartner, P., Fermueller, C. (eds.) Proceedings of the CADE-19 Workshop: Model Computation - Principles, Algorithms, Applications Miami, USA (2003)
3. Denney, E., Fischer, B., Schumann, J.: Using Automated Theorem Provers to Certify Auto-generated Aerospace Software. In: Basin, D., Rusinowitch, M. (eds.) IJ-CAR 2004. LNCS (LNAI), vol. 3097, pp. 198–212. Springer, Heidelberg (2004)
4. Fischer, B., Schumann, J., Snelting, G.: Deduction-Based Software Component Retrieval. In: Bibel, W., Schmitt, P. (eds.) Automated Deduction - A Basis for Applications. Applied Logic Series, vol. 3, pp. 265–292. Kluwer, Dordrecht (1998)
5. Fuchs, M.: System Description: Similarity-Based Lemma Generation for Model Elimination. In: Kirchner, C., Kirchner, H. (eds.) Automated Deduction - CADE-15. LNCS (LNAI), vol. 1421, pp. 33–37. Springer, Heidelberg (1998)
6. Fuchs, M.: Controlled Use of Clausal Lemmas in Connection Tableau Calculi. Journal of Symbolic Computation 29(2), 299–341 (2000)
7. MacCartney, B., McIlraith, S., Amir, E., Uribe, T.: Practical Partition-Based Theorem Proving for Large Knowledge Bases. In: Gottlob G., Walsh, T. (eds.) Proceedings of the 18th International Joint Conference on Artificial Intelligence, pp. 89–96 (2003)

8. McCune, W.W.: Otter 3.0 Reference Manual and Guide. Technical Report ANL-94/6, Argonne National Laboratory, Argonne, USA (1994)
9. Meng, J., Paulson, L.: Lightweight Relevance Filtering for Machine-Generated Resolution Problems. In: Sutcliffe, G., Schmidt, R., Schulz, S. (eds.) Proceedings of the FLoC'06 Workshop on Empirically Successful Computerized Reasoning, 3rd International Joint Conference on Automated Reasoning, CEUR Workshop Proceedings, vol. 192, pp. 53–69 (2006)
10. Meng, J., Paulson, L.: Translating Higher-Order Problems to First-Order Clauses. In: Sutcliffe, G., Schmidt, R., Schulz, S. (eds.) Proceedings of the FLoC'06 Workshop on Empirically Successful Computerized Reasoning, 3rd International Joint Conference on Automated Reasoning, CEUR Workshop Proceedings, vol. 192, pp. 70–80 (2006)
11. Plaisted, D.A., Yahya, A.: A Relevance Restriction Strategy for Automated Deduction. Artificial Intelligence 144(1-2), 59–93 (2003)
12. Pudlak, P.: Search for Faster and Shorter Proofs using Machine Generated lemmas. In: Sutcliffe, G., Schmidt, R., Schulz, S. (eds.) Proceedings of the FLoC'06 Workshop on Empirically Successful Computerized Reasoning, 3rd International Joint Conference on Automated Reasoning, CEUR Workshop Proceedings, vol. 192, pp. 34–52 (2006)
13. Pudlak, P.: Draft Thesis: Verification of Mathematical Proofs (2007)
14. Quaife, A.: Automated Development of Fundamental Mathematical Theories. Kluwer Academic Publishers, Boston (1992)
15. Rabe, F.: Towards Determining the Subset Relation between Propositional Modal Logics. In: Sutcliffe, G., Schmidt, R., Schulz, S. (eds.) Proceedings of the FLoC'06 Workshop on Empirically Successful Computerized Reasoning, 3rd International Joint Conference on Automated Reasoning, CEUR Workshop Proceedings, vol. 192 (2006)
16. Ramachandran, D., Reagan, P., Goolsbey, K.: First-orderized ResearchCyc: Expressiveness and Efficiency in a Common Sense Knowledge Base. In: Shvaiko P. (ed.) Proceedings of the Workshop on Contexts and Ontologies: Theory, Practice and Applications (2005)
17. Sahami, M.: Mining the Web to Determine Similarity Between Words, Objects, and Communities. In: Sutcliffe, G., Goebel, R. (eds.) Proceedings of the 19th International FLAIRS Conference, pp. 14–19. AAAI Press, Stanford (2006)
18. Schulz, S.: E: A Brainiac Theorem Prover. AI Communications 15(2-3), 111–126 (2002)
19. Shen, W.: Automated Proofs of Equivalence of Modal Logic Systems. Master's thesis, Department of Computer Science, University of Miami, Miami, USA (2006)
20. Sorge, V., Meier, A., McCasland, R., Colton, S.: Automatic Construction and Verification of Isotopy Invariants. In: Furbach, U., Shankar, N. (eds.) IJCAR 2006. LNCS (LNAI), vol. 4130, pp. 36–51. Springer, Heidelberg (2006)
21. Sutcliffe, G.: SystemOnTPTP. In: McAllester, D. (ed.) Automated Deduction - CADE-17. LNCS, vol. 1831, pp. 406–410. Springer, Heidelberg (2000)
22. Sutcliffe, G.: The 3rd IJCAR Automated Theorem Proving Competition. AI Communications (to appear)
23. Sutcliffe, G., Dvorsky, A.: Proving Harder Theorems by Axiom Reduction. In: Russell, I., Haller, S. (eds.) Proceedings of the 16th International FLAIRS Conference, pp. 108–112. AAAI Press, Stanford (2003)

24. Sutcliffe, G., Schulz, S., Claessen, K., Van Gelder, A.: Using the TPTP Language for Writing Derivations and Finite Interpretations. In: Furbach, U., Shankar, N. (eds.) IJCAR 2006. LNCS (LNAI), vol. 4130, pp. 67–81. Springer, Heidelberg (2006)

25. Sutcliffe, G., Suttner, C.B.: The TPTP Problem Library: CNF Release v1.2.1. Journal of Automated Reasoning 21(2), 177–203 (1998)

26. Sutcliffe, G., Zimmer, J., Schulz, S.: TSTP Data-Exchange Formats for Automated Theorem Proving Tools. In: Zhang, W., Sorge, V. (eds.) Distributed Constraint Problem Solving and Reasoning in Multi-Agent Systems, number 112 in Frontiers in Artificial Intelligence and Applications, pp. 201–215. IOS Press, Amsterdam (2004)

27. Urban, J.: MizarMode - An Integrated Proof Assistance Tool for the Mizar Way of Formalizing Mathematics. Journal of Applied Logic 4(4), 414–427 (2006)

28. Urban, J.: MPTP 0.2: Design, Implementation, and Initial Experiments. Journal of Automated Reasoning 37(1-2), 21–43 (2007)

29. Urban, J., Sutcliffe, G.: The MPTP $100 Challenges (2006)
    http://www.tptp.org/MPTPChallenge/

30. Veroff, R.: Using Hints to Increase the Effectiveness of an Automated Reasoning Program: Case Studies. Journal of Automated Reasoning 16(3), 223–239 (1996)

31. Weidenbach, C., Brahm, U., Hillenbrand, T., Keen, E., Theobald, C., Topic, D.: SPASS Version 2.0. In: Voronkov, A. (ed.) Automated Deduction - CADE-18. LNCS (LNAI), vol. 2392, pp. 275–279. Springer, Heidelberg (2002)

32. Zhang, Y., Sutcliffe, G.: Lemma Management Techniques for Automated Theorem Proving. In: Konev, B., Schulz, S., (eds.) Proceedings of the 5th International Workshop on the Implementation of Logics, pp. 87–94 (2005)

33. Zimmer, J., Autexier, S.: The MathServe System for Semantic Web Reasoning Services. In: Furbach, U., Shankar, N. (eds.) IJCAR 2006. LNCS (LNAI), vol. 4130, pp. 17–20. Springer, Heidelberg (2006)

34. Zimmer, J., Meier, A., Sutcliffe, G., Zhang, Y.: Integrated Proof Transformation Services. In: Benzmüller, C., Windsteiger, W. (eds.) Proceedings of the Workshop on Computer-Supported Mathematical Theory Development, 2nd International Joint Conference on Automated Reasoning, Electronic Notes in Theoretical Computer Science (2004)

Labelled Clauses

Tal Lev-Ami[1,*], Christoph Weidenbach[2], Thomas Reps[3,**], and Mooly Sagiv[1]

[1] School of Comp. Sci., Tel Aviv University
{tla,msagiv}@post.tau.ac.il
[2] Max-Planck-Institut für Informatik, Saarbrücken
weidenbach@mpi-inf.mpg.de
[3] Comp. Sci. Dept., University of Wisconsin, Madison
reps@cs.wisc.edu

Abstract. We add labels to first-order clauses to simultaneously apply superpositions to several proof obligations inside one clause set. From a theoretical perspective, the approach unifies a variety of deduction modes. These include different strategies such as set of support, as well as explicit case analysis, e.g., splitting. From a practical perspective, labelled clauses offer advantages in the case of related proof obligations resulting from multiple conjectures over the same axiom set or from a single conjecture that is a large conjunction. Here we can share clauses (e.g., the axioms and clauses deduced from them, share Skolem symbols), share deduced clause variants, and transfer lemmas between the different obligations. Motivated by software verification, we have created a prototype implementation of labelled clauses that supports multiple conjectures, and we provide convincing experiments for the benefits.

1 Introduction

Our work in program analysis and software verification using the TVLA system [10] has led us to explore the use of theorem provers for computing the effects of program statements [25]. Recently, we explored the possibility of using first-order automated theorem provers for the task [9]. A major obstacle in using existing automated theorem provers, such as E [18], SPASS [21] and VAMPIRE [16], is that of performance. TVLA requires many calls to the theorem prover to compute the effect of a single program statement. Therefore, the overall time required for analyzing even a simple program is prohibitive. This situation is common in other program analysis methods such as Cartesian Abstraction [1].

In the process of computing the effect of a program statement, TVLA generates multiple conjectures that share a common axiom set. However, current theorem provers can only attempt to prove a single conjecture at a time. Running the theorem prover multiple times, once for each conjecture, has three problems:

* Supported by an Adams Fellowship through the Israel Academy of Sciences and Humanities.
** Supported by ONR under grant N00014-01-1-0796 and by NSF under grants CCF-0540955 and CCF-0524051.

F. Pfenning (Ed.): CADE 2007, LNAI 4603, pp. 311–327, 2007.
© Springer-Verlag Berlin Heidelberg 2007

(1) if the conjectures are proven sequentially, any inferences/reductions made between clauses from the axiom set are reconstructed and no synergies between the proof attempts can be exploited, (2) because not all the conjectures are valid and first-order logic is only semi-decidable, we are required to use time-outs, which may cause us to give up on valid conjectures, (3) if a conjecture is validated by a proof attempt, there is no automatic way inside the prover to transfer the result to other proof attempts.

To overcome these obstacles, we devised algorithms to prove different conjectures simultaneously inside one proof attempt. We chose to modify the calculus used by the theorem prover to support deduction in parallel, i.e., for multiple conjectures, via a methodology of labelled clauses. The idea is to label each clause with the conjectures for which it is relevant, and update these labels during deduction. As a consequence, we solved the above problems: (1) inferences on axiom clauses are no longer duplicated but are shared — as are variant clauses derived from separate conjectures and reductions, (2) a fair strategy among all proof attempts (with one global timeout parameter) replaces the use of separate timeouts, and (3) valid conjectures can be naturally transferred to other proof attempts.

We have created a prototype implementation of labelled clauses for the purpose of proving multiple conjectures within the automated theorem prover SPASS, and report on convincing experimental results in the context of our original application.

After having seen the success of labelled clauses for multiple conjectures, we believe that the methodology of labelled clauses has more potential in the context of first-order theorem proving. Labelled deductive systems (see e.g., [2]) as have been pushed forward by Dov Gabbay in the last fifteen years and have become recognized as a significant component of the logic culture, in particular in the context of non-classical logics. There labels are used on the one hand to bring the semantics into the syntax by naming possible worlds using labels (e.g., a Kripke structure) and on the other hand they can act as proof-theoretic resource labels. Our motivation of using labels is different. We suggest to use labels to study and implement variants of classical first-order-logic (superposition-based) theorem-proving calculi to eventually improve automation. We show that the methodology of labels carries over beyond proving multiple conjectures by instantiating the methodology for clausal splitting (see e.g., [20]), slicing (see e.g., [23]), and the set-of-support strategy (see e.g., [24]).

We use labels to summarize the derivation tree of a clause. For example, when using labelled clauses for clausal splitting, the labels represent the splits the clause depends on, and when using labelled clauses for multiple conjectures, the labels represent the conjectures for which the clause is valid. The purpose of the abstract framework described in Sect. 2 is to generalize the different applications of labelled clauses and give a common presentation for all of them. We believe that the abstract framework has interesting properties of its own, which we plan to investigate as future work.

1.1 Related Work

For the general methodology of labelled clauses there is a huge literature related to our approach in the sense that the work can be reformulated and explored via a labelled-clause discipline. A discussion of this general aspect is beyond the scope of this paper. Therefore, we concentrate on work related to our approach of proving multiple conjectures via labelled clauses.

Similar techniques for enhancing a theorem prover (for classical logic) to work with multiple goals have been developed by A. Voronkov, and are being incorporated into Vampire [19]. However, his approach is based on an extension of splitting, as described in [15].

A logical candidate for proving conjectures in parallel is to use additional predicates [6]. In our setting, this would mean replacing each negated conjecture $\neg\varphi_i$ with the disjunction $b_i \vee \neg\varphi_i$ where b_i is a fresh propositional variable (i.e., nullary relation). Now if the prover deduces the unit clause b_i, the conjecture φ_i is valid. The main problem with this approach is that it will also explore disjunctions between different b_i's, i.e., between different conjectures, which unnecessarily increases the search space by an exponential factor. Furthermore, the literals added to the clauses block any reductions from (derived) conjecture clauses in the axioms' clauses.

Symbolic decision procedures [8] are a technique for finding all possible disjunctions of conjectures for a given axiom set. The technique is limited to specific theories, such as uninterpreted functions and difference logic. Furthermore, because it is described in the context of the Nelson-Oppen method [13] for combining decision procedures, its usability in the case of quantifiers is limited.

In the Boolean satisfiability community there is a related idea of incremental solvers (see e.g., [22]). There, it is possible to add and remove clauses from the theorem prover without restarting it. On the other hand, labelled clauses allow us to attempt to prove multiple conjectures simultaneously.

1.2 Contributions

The main contributions of this paper are as follows:

- We introduce a deduction technique for working on multiple related proof attempts simultaneously. We have successfully created a first prototype implementation within SPASS.
- We describe applications of the method in software verification, and provide experimental results to demonstrate the improvement.
- We propose the concept of superposition with labels as a general framework for the study of deduction techniques and their combination.
- We demonstrate several instantiations of this general framework for implementing different ideas, including clause splitting and slicing.

In Sect. 2, we present a labelled superposition calculus as an extension of the standard superposition calculus. In Sect. 3, we present several instantiations of the general calculus including one for multiple conjectures. In Sect. 4, we present applications of multiple conjectures in software verification and present experimental results from using our extension of SPASS for handling multiple conjectures. We conclude in Sect. 5.

The tool as well as the input files used for the experiments are available at [11].

2   Superposition with Labels

For the presentation of the superposition calculus, we refer to the notation and notions of [20]. We write clauses in implication form $\Gamma \to \Delta$ where comma to the left means conjunction and comma to the right disjunction. Upper Greek letters denote sequences of atoms (Γ, Δ), lower Greek letter substitutions (σ, τ), lower Latin characters terms (s, r, t) and upper Latin characters atoms (A, B, E) where $\approx$ is used as the equality symbol. The notations $s[l]_p$ $(E[l]_p)$ expresses that the term s (the atom E) contains the term l at position p. Replacing a subterm at position p with a term r is denoted by $s[p/r]$ $(E[p/r])$.

We distinguish inference from reduction rules, where the clause(s) below the bar, the conclusions, of an inference rule are added to the current clause set, while the clause(s) below the bar of a reduction rule replace the clause(s) above the bar, the premises. For example,

$$\mathcal{I} \frac{\Gamma_1 \to \Delta_1 \quad \Gamma_2 \to \Delta_2}{\Gamma_3 \to \Delta_3} \qquad \mathcal{R} \frac{\Gamma_1' \to \Delta_1' \quad \Gamma_2' \to \Delta_2'}{\Gamma_3' \to \Delta_3'}$$

an application of the above inference adds the clause $\Gamma_3 \to \Delta_3$ to the current clause set, while the above reduction replaces the clauses $\Gamma_1' \to \Delta_1'$, $\Gamma_2' \to \Delta_2'$ with the clause $\Gamma_3' \to \Delta_3'$. Note that reductions can actually be used to delete clauses, if there are no conclusions.

For the introduction and proofs of the properties of our label discipline, sorts, ordering or selection restrictions are not of importance. Therefore, we leave them out of the presentation of the superposition inference and reduction rules. They can all be added in a straightforward way.

To each superposition clause $\Gamma \to \Delta$ we add a label m resulting in $m : \Gamma \to \Delta$. Then the standard calculus rules are extended by conditions and operations on the labels. We use a binary operation $\circ$ to combine labels for inferences, and a binary operation $\bullet$ to combine labels for reductions. Both operations are commutative and associative. We use $\ominus$ as a special label to indicate when an inference or a reduction should be blocked.[1] Finally, a preorder, $\leq$, is used to define when labels are compatible for clause deletion.

The interpretation of the labels and label operators depends on the instantiation of the superposition-with-labels calculus. We will give examples in Section 3. In particular, the standard superposition calculus is obtained if all clauses are labelled by the set $\{1\}$ and $\circ$, $\bullet$, $\leq$, and $\ominus$ are instantiated by the standard set operations $\cap$, $\cap$, $\subseteq$, and $\emptyset$, respectively.

---

[1] We require that, for any label m, $\ominus \circ m = \ominus$ and $\ominus \bullet m = \ominus$.

Below we present the extended inference rule superposition right. The missing binary inference rules superposition left, merging paramodulation, and ordered resolution are defined accordingly.

Definition 1 (Superposition Right). *The inference*

$$\mathcal{I} \frac{m_1 \,:\, \Gamma_1 \to \Delta_1, l \approx r \qquad m_2 \,:\, \Gamma_2 \to \Delta_2, s[l']_p \approx t}{(m_1 \circ m_2 \,:\, \Gamma_1, \Gamma_2 \to \Delta_1, \Delta_2, s[p/r] \approx t)\sigma}$$

where
1. *$m_1 \circ m_2 \neq \ominus$*
2. *σ is the mgu of l' and l*
3. *l' is not a variable*
and the usual ordering/selection restrictions apply is called a superposition right inference.

For the unary inference rules equality resolution, ordered factoring, and equality factoring on a clause labelled with m, the resulting clause is labelled with $m \circ m$, and the rule has an extra condition that $m \circ m \neq \ominus$. For inference rules with multiple premises, such as hyper resolution, the label computations are straightforward extensions of the binary case.

Definition 2 (Ordered Hyper Resolution). *The inference*

$$\mathcal{I} \frac{m_1 \,:\, E_1, \ldots, E_n \to \Delta \qquad m_{2,i} \,:\, \to \Delta_i, E_i' \quad (1 \le i \le n)}{(m_1 \circ m_{2,1} \circ \ldots \circ m_{2,n} \,:\, \to \Delta, \Delta_1, \ldots, \Delta_n)\sigma}$$

where
1. *$m_1 \circ m_{2,1} \circ \ldots \circ m_{2,n} \neq \ominus$*
2. *σ is the simultaneous mgu of $E_1, \ldots, E_n, E_1', \ldots, E_n'$,*
and the usual ordering restrictions apply is called an ordered hyper resolution inference.

Below we present matching replacement resolution, weak contextual rewriting, and subsumption deletion as examples of how to extend reduction rules by labels. In contrast to the standard superposition calculus, one or more premises of a reduction rule are typically retained.

The reason for this is illustrated by the application of labelled clauses to splitting (see Sect. 3.2), where the label describes the clause splittings on which a given clause depends. Here it is clear that when a reduction is performed from a clause C_1 to a clause C_2 that depends on fewer splittings, we must keep C_1.

Definition 3 (Matching Replacement Resolution). *The reduction*

$$\mathcal{R} \frac{m_1 \,:\, \Gamma_1 \to \Delta_1, E_1 \qquad m_2 \,:\, \Gamma_2, E_2 \to \Delta_2}{\begin{array}{c} m_1 \,:\, \Gamma_1 \to \Delta_1, E_1 \\ m_2 \,:\, \Gamma_2, E_2 \to \Delta_2 \\ m_1 \bullet m_2 \,:\, \Gamma_2 \to \Delta_2 \end{array}}$$

where

1. $m_1 \bullet m_2 \neq \ominus$
2. $E_1 \sigma = E_2$
3. $(\Gamma_1 \rightarrow \Delta_1)\sigma$ *subsumes* $\Gamma_2 \rightarrow \Delta_2$, *where all variables in the co-domain of σ are treated as constants for both clauses*

is called matching replacement resolution.

This presentation of the matching replacement resolution rule is non-standard, because the parent clause $m_2 : \Gamma_2, E_2 \rightarrow \Delta_2$ is kept. However, in many applications it can then be subsequently deleted by subsumption deletion (see below). For example, in the case of simulating the standard calculus where all labels are identical to $\{1\}$, the clause $\{1\} : \Gamma_2, E_2 \rightarrow \Delta_2$ is always subsumed by $\{1\} \cap \{1\} : \Gamma_2 \rightarrow \Delta_2$, yielding the standard rule.

We present a variant of the rewriting rule; other variants are modified similarly. Two versions of the rule are supplied. The first one is a reduction that can be used when the resulting label is smaller than the parent clause to be deleted. In the second version, the clause is simplified, but the parent clause is not deleted.

Definition 4 (Weak Contextual Rewriting). *The reductions*

$$\mathcal{R} \frac{m_1 : \Gamma_1 \rightarrow \Delta_1, s \approx t \qquad m_2 : \Gamma_2 \rightarrow \Delta_2, E[s']_p}{m_1 : \Gamma_1 \rightarrow \Delta_1, s \approx t}$$
$$m_1 \bullet m_2 : \Gamma_2 \rightarrow \Delta_2, E[p/t\sigma]$$

and

$$\mathcal{R} \frac{m_1 : \Gamma_1 \rightarrow \Delta_1, s \approx t \qquad m_2 : \Gamma_2 \rightarrow \Delta_2, E[s']_p}{m_1 : \Gamma_1 \rightarrow \Delta_1, s \approx t}$$
$$m_2 : \Gamma_2 \rightarrow \Delta_2, E[s']_p$$
$$m_1 \bullet m_2 : \Gamma_2 \rightarrow \Delta_2, E[p/t\sigma]$$

where

1. $m_1 \bullet m_2 \neq \ominus$
2. $s\sigma = s'$
3. $\Gamma_1 \sigma \subseteq \Gamma_2$, $\Delta_1 \sigma \subseteq \Delta_2$
4. *For the first variant, $m_1 \bullet m_2 \leq m_2$*
5. *For the second variant $m_1 \bullet m_2 \not\leq m_2$*

and the usual ordering restrictions apply are called weak contextual rewriting.

The unary simplification rules, such as trivial literal elimination or condensation, are handled similarly to unary inference rules; i.e., given a clause labelled with m, the resulting clause is labelled with $m \bullet m$ and the rule has an extra condition that $m \bullet m \neq \ominus$.

For rules that actually delete clauses, such as tautology deletion and subsumption deletion, we need to guarantee the compatibility of labels, as shown for subsumption deletion below. Tautology deletion is never blocked by the labels because $\leq$ is reflexive.

Definition 5 (Subsumption Deletion). *The reduction*

$$\mathcal{R}\frac{m_1 : \Gamma_1 \to \Delta_1 \qquad m_2 : \Gamma_2 \to \Delta_2}{m_1 : \Gamma_1 \to \Delta_1}$$

where

1. $m_2 \leq m_1$
2. $\Gamma_2 \to \Delta_2$ *is subsumed by* $\Gamma_1 \to \Delta_1$

is called subsumption deletion.

3 Instantiations

3.1 Multiple Labelled Conjectures

The starting point are n different proof obligations $\Psi_1, \ldots, \Psi_n$ (dependent or independent) with respect to a theory Φ. We want to check for which i $\Phi \models \Psi_i$ holds. Labels are subsets of $\{1, \ldots, n\}$. All clauses resulting from Φ receive the label $\{1, \ldots, n\}$, and all clauses resulting from Ψ_i receive the label $\{i\}$. The label indicates for which proof obligations the clause may be used. The operations $\circ$, $\bullet$, $\leq$, and $\ominus$ are instantiated by the standard set operations $\cap$, $\cap$, $\subseteq$, and $\emptyset$, respectively.

Proposition 1. *From $\Phi \wedge \neg \Psi_i$ we can derive $\to \square$ by superposition iff we can derive $\{i\} : \to \square$ by labelled superposition.*

Proof. (Sketch) By induction on the length of the superposition derivation doing a case analysis over the different rules. For all labelled inference and simplification rules it holds that the conclusion of a rule is labelled with a number i iff all premises are labelled with i. If a clause can be removed by labelled subsumption deletion, there exists a more general clause labelled with a superset, i.e., subsumption deletion can be applied to the standard subproofs.

3.1.1 Refinements

Labelled subsumption deletion is actually weaker than subsumption deletion. For example, in the form shown in Definition 5 it does not enable subsumption of axiom clauses by conjecture clauses. Furthermore, the calculus considered so far for multiple labelled conjectures does not consider sharing of clauses resulting (from inferences) from different conjectures. Both problems can be overcome by adding the following rules to the calculus.

Definition 6 (Join). *The reduction*

$$\mathcal{R}\frac{m_1 : \Gamma_1 \to \Delta_1 \qquad m_2 : \Gamma_2 \to \Delta_2}{m_1 \cup m_2 : \Gamma_1 \to \Delta_1}$$

where

1. $m_1 \neq \emptyset$ and $m_2 \neq \emptyset$
2. $\Gamma_2 \to \Delta_2$ and $\Gamma_1 \to \Delta_1$ are variants[2]

is called join.

---

[2] Equal with respect to variable renaming.

Definition 7 (Subsumption Separation). *The reduction*

$$\mathcal{R}\frac{m_1 \,:\, \Gamma_1 \to \Delta_1 \qquad m_2 \,:\, \Gamma_2 \to \Delta_2}{\begin{array}{c} m_1 \,:\, \Gamma_1 \to \Delta_1 \\ m_2 \setminus m_1 \,:\, \Gamma_2 \to \Delta_2 \end{array}}$$

where

1. $m_1 \cap m_2 \neq \emptyset$
2. $m_2 \not\subseteq m_1$
3. $\Gamma_2 \to \Delta_2$ *is subsumed by* $\Gamma_1 \to \Delta_1$

is called subsumption separation.

Subsumption separation can be built into other reduction rules that rely on subsumption. For example, when $m_2 \not\subseteq m_1$ we can turn matching replacement resolution, Definition 3, into a reduction, keeping the first parent clause and reducing the second parent clause to $m_2 \setminus m_1 \,:\, \Gamma_2, E_2 \to \Delta_2$.

Note that using labels allow us to perform reductions of the axiom clauses using conjecture clauses. This would not be possible when using extra predicates for handling multiple conjectures.

When adding the Join rule, the correctness claim needs to be refined as well.

Proposition 2. *From* $\Phi \wedge \neg\Psi_i$ *we can derive* $\to \square$ *by superposition iff we can derive* $m \,:\, \to \square$ *by labelled superposition for some label* m *that contains* i.

When deriving an empty clause with a label that contains a certain conjecture, we know that the conjecture is valid given the axiom set. It is sometimes useful to then clausify the conjecture and add the result as new axioms to the axiom set so that it can be used by the other conjectures not yet proven.

Reusing Skolem Functions. We can use the labels to devise a better Skolemization process for our setting that results in more clauses being shared between the different proof obligations and thereby avoids duplicate work. Our experimental results is Sect. 4.3 show that this is valuable in practice. The idea is that two Skolem functions of the same arity can be merged if all the clauses they appear in have disjoint labels: any inference between such clauses is blocked, and thus the terms containing the merged functions will never be unified.

In general, we would want to merge Skolem functions in a way that allows the Join rule to share the most active clauses. Lacking a way to predict this, we use a heuristic that ensures that at least some clauses will be shared as a result of the process. The heuristic searches for clauses that will be variants after Skolem functions are merged. The heuristic guarantees that the merge is allowed by maintaining for each symbol the set of conjectures it is currently used in.

Example 1. *Let conjecture 1 be* $\forall v \,.\, p(v) \vee q(v)$ *and conjecture 2 be* $\forall v \,.\, p(v) \vee \neg q(v)$. *The usual Skolemization of the negated conjectures would result in the following four clauses:* $\{1\} \,:\, p(c_1) \to, \{1\} \,:\, q(c_1) \to, \{2\} \,:\, p(c_2) \to, \{2\} \,:\, \to q(c_2)$. *However, by sharing Skolem constants the following clauses suffice:* $\{1,2\} \,:\, p(c_1) \to, \{1\} \,:\, q(c_1) \to, \{2\} \,:\, \to q(c_1)$.

Note that although $\{1\} : q(c_1) \rightarrow$ *and* $\{2\} :\rightarrow q(c_1)$ *are resolvable if labels were ignored (resulting in the empty clause), they will never be resolved because their labels are disjoint. As the number and complexity of the conjectures increases, more of the shared structures can be used.*

Conjunction Conjectures. When trying to prove a conjecture composed of a large conjunction of formulas, the standard practice of negation and then Skolemization creates large clauses and is typically intractable. Instead, the conjunction can be split into a conjecture per conjunct and processed using the refined calculus above. Now, proving a contradiction for *all* the labels is equivalent to proving the validity of the original formula.

Proposition 3. *From* $\Phi \wedge \neg(\bigwedge_{1 \leq i \leq n} \Psi_i)$ *we can derive* $\rightarrow \square$ *by superposition iff we can derive* $\{1, \ldots, n\} :\rightarrow \square$ *by labelled superposition for multiple labelled conjectures.*

Theory Consistency. When proving that $\Phi \rightarrow \Psi$ is valid, it is possible that the reason for the validity is that Φ is inconsistent. In the framework of the standard superposition calculus we cannot distinguish between the two cases without inspecting proofs. However, it is easy to support such a consistency check in the context of labelled superposition. We simply add to the label of the axioms a new number 0 resulting in the extended set $\{0, \ldots, n\}$ for n conjectures. Then the theory is inconsistent iff we can derive $m :\rightarrow \square$ for some label m that contains 0.

3.1.2   Implementation

We have a prototype implementation of the labelled clauses calculus for multiple conjectures within the SPASS theorem prover (available at [11]). Labels were implemented using bit-vectors attached to each clause. The inference and reduction rules were modified to correctly maintain the labels during derivations. The Join rule and Skolem function reuse were also implemented.

The most challenging part in modifying SPASS to support labelled clauses is updating the forward reduction rules, which can now generate many clauses instead of only reducing the given clause. We used a naive approach for implementing these reductions and yet the result is still effective, as can be seen in Sect. 4.3. Backward reduction rules were modified to perform separation to correctly handle, for example, reduction of axiom clauses by conjecture clauses.

We can prevent one conjecture from starving the rest by once in a while selecting a clause from a conjecture that was missing from the labels of the recently selected given clauses. We have implemented this idea as a runtime option in the new version, but do not yet have experimental results concerning its effectiveness.

3.2   Labelled Splitting

Let us consider how labels can be used to model splitting with a single conjecture. For splitting we use a different type of label: sequences of (overlined) clauses with an extra label $\ominus$. We use the labels to record the path in the derivation tree of splits required to generate the clause. We say that $m_1 \leq m_2$ when m_2 is a prefix of m_1, or $m_1 = \ominus$. The combine operations are simply the greatest lower bound of $\leq$, i.e., $m_1 \circ m_2 = m_1$ if $m_1 \leq m_2$, $m_1 \circ m_2 = m_2$ if $m_2 \leq m_1$, and $m_1 \circ m_2 = \ominus$ otherwise (we define $\bullet$ to be the same is $\circ$). Initially, all clauses are labelled with the empty sequence, denoted by ϵ.

In addition to the labelled superposition rules the extra rules implementing labelled splitting are:

Definition 8 (Splitting). *The inference*

$$\mathcal{I} \frac{m \,:\, \Gamma_1, \Gamma_2 \to \Delta_1, \Delta_2}{\begin{array}{c} m.\Gamma_1, \Gamma_2 \to \Delta_1, \Delta_2 \,:\, \Gamma_1 \to \Delta_1 \\ m.\overline{\Gamma_1}, \Gamma_2 \to \Delta_1, \Delta_2 \,:\, \Gamma_2 \to \Delta_2 \end{array}}$$

where
  1. $vars(\Gamma_1 \to \Delta_1) \cap vars(\Gamma_2 \to \Delta_2) = \emptyset$
  2. $\Delta_1 \neq \emptyset$ and $\Delta_2 \neq \emptyset$
is called splitting.

Definition 9 (Branch Closing). *The inference*

$$\mathcal{I} \frac{m.C \,:\, \to \square \qquad m.\overline{C} \,:\, \to \square}{m \,:\, \to \square}$$

is called branch closing.

Proposition 4. *From a clause set N we can derive a contradiction by superposition with splitting iff we can derive $\epsilon \,:\, \to \square$ by labelled superposition with splitting.*

Proof. (Sketch) By induction on the length of the superposition derivation, via a case analysis over the different rules. The Splitting rule needs special consideration: we have to show that no inference (reduction) between two clauses $m.C.m_1 \,:\, \Gamma_1 \to \Delta_1$ and $m.\overline{C}.m_2 \,:\, \Gamma_2 \to \Delta_2$ is possible. This holds by the definitions of the two combination operations ($\circ$ and $\bullet$): combining any two sequences $m.C.m_1$ and $m.\overline{C}.m_2$ results in $\ominus$. On the other hand, the combination of $m.C$ (or $m.\overline{C}$) and any prefix of m results in $m.C$ ($m.\overline{C}$), which corresponds to the standard clause set copy and separation of the standard splitting rule.

3.2.1 Refinements
Once the labels are available and the different branches of the derivation tree spanned by the splitting rule can be investigated simultaneously, it is easy to define and employ the well-known refinements for splitting and tableau proofs. By studying the labels of clauses used in the derivation of an empty clause, refinements like branch condensing (implemented in SPASS, splittings from the most recent backtracking empty clause that did not contribute to the current

empty clause can be removed from the label) or the generation of more suitable "backtracking clauses" (see e.g., [14]) are straightforward to integrate. The lemma-generation rules invented in the context of tableau [7], for example, the *folding up rule* can also be integrated.

An obvious refinement of splitting is to add the negation of the first clause part $\Gamma_1 \rightarrow \Delta_1$ to the second part, labelled with the second part (or the other way round). For example, applying this refined version of splitting to the clause $C = m : \rightarrow A, B$ yields $m.C : \rightarrow A$, $m.\overline{C} : \rightarrow B$, and $m.\overline{C} : A \rightarrow$.

3.2.2 Implementation

In addition to the above mentioned refinements, implementing Splitting via labelled clauses seems to be less effort and as efficient as a standard implementation via a depth-first search and clause copy, as it is done, e.g., in SPASS. For example, branch closing becomes a standard inference/reduction rule application of the calculus while in the context of the depth-search algorithm implemented in SPASS it is a procedure running orthogonal to the standard saturation process, complicating the overall implementation.

3.3 Strategies

Labelled clauses can also be used to model well-known strategies and new strategies. For example, the set-of-support strategy forbids inferences between axiom clauses. This can be easily established by the labelled superposition framework using the label set $\{0, 1, \ominus\}$ and labelling all axiom clauses with 0, all conjecture clauses with 1. We instantiate $m_1 \leq m_2$ to always be true and use the following combination operations:

Thus any inferences between clauses for the axiom set are blocked, but reductions are allowed, keeping the 0 label.

3.4 Slicing

When trying to prove a conjecture in a given time limit, it can be a good heuristic to try different strategies for a fixed period of time. For example, strategies might differ in the selection strategy for negative literals (no selection, always select a negative literal, etc.) or the heuristic to pick the next clauses for inferences (lightest weight, heaviest weight, lowest age). Labelled superposition offers here a framework where these runs can be done simultaneously and benefit from each other.

We simply run the same conjecture simultaneously with different labels for the different strategies. Given n strategies, we give each one a number from $\{1, \ldots, n\}$.

Initially we label all clauses with $\{1, \ldots, n\}$. We extend the labelled superposition calculus of Section 2 to also consider the strategy label, say m' for inference computation. Then the newly generated clause gets the label $m_1 \circ m_2 \circ m'$ and we have to check the condition $m_1 \circ m_2 \circ m' \neq \ominus$. Nevertheless, common clauses can be shared via the Join rule as in the case of multiple labelled conjectures.

Because the reduction (and simplification) combinator • is different from the inference combinator, it can be used to implement different strategies concerning reductions and simplifications between clauses generated by different strategies. This provides a high potential for synergy between the different proof attempts. Note that because different strategies may use different orderings, by considering the strategy label at inference rule level, the ordering used by the rule conditions can also be chosen by that label.

4 Applications in Software Verification

We present two applications that motivated our interest in labelled clauses. Both concern the application of *abstract interpretation* [4] in software verification. Abstract interpretation provides a way to obtain information about the possible states that a program reaches, without actually running the program on specific inputs; instead, the program is "run abstractly", using descriptors that represent collections of many states. Each different family of descriptors (or "abstract domain") that is used can typically be characterized by means of a restricted class of formulas (presented in some normal form). Abstract interpretation provides a way to synthesize loop invariants (albeit only ones expressible in a given class of formulas), and hence sidesteps the need for a user to supply loop invariants.

4.1 Cartesian Abstraction

Predicate abstraction [5] abstracts a program into a Boolean program that conservatively simulates (i.e., overapproximates) all potential executions of the original program. Thus, every safety property that holds for the Boolean program is guaranteed to hold for the original program. A predicate p in predicate abstraction is defined by a closed formula ψ_p that evaluates to true or false for each concrete program state. An *abstract state* is a conjunction of (possibly negated) predicates; it represents the set of concrete states that satisfy each (possibly negated) predicate. A set of abstract states corresponds to a disjunction of the individual abstract states. The best approximation of a set of concrete states C is the strongest set of abstract states such that every $c \in C$ is satisfied (or, equivalently, the strongest Boolean combination of predicates that holds for every $c \in C$).

The operational semantics of a statement st in a program can be defined using a formula τ_{st} over the pre-state and the post-state. A post-state S' can be the result of a given pre-state S if τ_{st} holds for $S \uplus S'$. The predicate p' defined using formula ψ_p, but applied to the post-state, is called the *primed version* of p. The effect of st on an abstract pre-state A can be computed using a theorem prover by checking which combinations of primed-predicate formulas are satisfiable when conjoined with $A \wedge \tau_{st}$.

A less-costly, but less-precise, variant of predicate abstraction is called Cartesian Abstraction [1]. Instead of using a Boolean combination of predicates to represent a set of states C, this uses a single conjunction of (possibly negated) predicates. Thus, a predicate p should appear in abstract state A_C (i) positively when ψ_p holds for every $c \in C$; (ii) negatively when ψ_p does not hold for any $c \in C$; and (iii) otherwise should not appear.

With Cartesian Abstraction, it is possible to compute the effect of a statement via a set of validity queries to a theorem prover. In each query, the axiom set contains the pre-state A, the transformer τ_{st}, and any background theory we have. The conjecture is either a primed predicate or a negated primed predicate. This makes computing transformers for Cartesian Abstraction a good target for our method. All the primed predicates and their negations can be added as conjectures to the same axiom set, and the effect of the statement can be computed using a single call to the theorem prover; any shared structure between the different predicates or similarities among the proofs of the different conjectures will be exploited by the theorem prover.

4.2   Shape Analysis and Canonical Abstraction

Shape analysis aims to discover information (in a conservative way) about the possible "shapes" of heap-allocated data structures to which a program's pointer variables can point. The method of Canonical Abstraction [17] provides a family of abstract domains for capturing certain classes of memory configurations. Canonical Abstraction uses first-order (FO) logic with transitive closure (TC), in which individuals are heap-cells and predicate symbols of the vocabulary are interpreted via relations on heap-cells. A background theory is used to formalize the properties of these predicates (e.g. a pointer variable can point to at most one location). TVLA [10] is a parametric framework for building analyzers for canonical-abstraction-based abstract domains.

In Canonical Abstraction, the heap is partitioned according to conjunctions of unary predicates. Only universal information about these partitions is saved; that is, if formulas such as $node_1(v)$, $node_2(v)$, etc. are conjunctions of unary predicates that characterize the various subsets that partition the heap-cells, and p is a binary predicate symbol from the vocabulary, we can only record information of the form

$$\forall v_1, v_2.node_i(v_1) \wedge node_j(v_2) \Rightarrow [\neg]p(v_1, v_2). \tag{1}$$

To control the abstraction, the designer of an abstraction (or an automatic tool for discovering abstractions [12]) can define auxiliary unary predicates with FO+TC formulas that are added to the background theory.

Similar to Sect. 4.1, the operational semantics of a statement is defined using a formula over the pre-state and the post-state; to determine the effect of a statement, we need to determine which formulas in form Eq. (1) hold for the primed predicates.[3] In this setting, it is again possible to compute the effect of

---

[3] See [9] for methods that can be used to handle formulas that involve the TC operator.

a statement via a set of validity queries, which may be answered *en masse* by a theorem prover using our method.[4] This allows the theorem prover to exploit similarities among the proofs of the different conjectures.

4.3   Experiments

We have integrated the prototype implementation of labelled clauses for multiple conjectures in SPASS into TVLA, i.e., the validity queries required to compute the result of applying a transformer are performed by SPASS. In this section, we present a comparison between the performance of the improved version and running the original SPASS version 2.2 on each conjecture sequentially. The results presented here are from the queries generated by the analysis of several heap-manipulating programs, including reversal of a singly-linked list, insert sort of a singly-linked list, insertion into a doubly-linked list, and the mark phase of a simple mark-and-sweep garbage collector.

   To make the comparison fair, we removed three types of queries: (i) any conjecture that is not valid, (ii) queries in which the common axioms are inconsistent, and (iii) queries in which there is only one valid conjecture. When also considering invalid conjectures, the advantage of the labelled-clauses method is even more apparent because the sequential approach has to wait for a timeout for each invalid conjecture. Similarly, when considering queries with an inconsistent axiom set, the improved version can detect that the original axioms are inconsistent, while the sequential approach will have to prove it again and again for each conjecture. Finally, for a single conjecture the labelled-clauses version behaves almost exactly the same as the original version, both in terms of the clauses generated and the time required.

   The test set includes 125 queries, with a minimum of 2 conjectures, a maximum of 32 conjectures, and an average of 9.3 conjectures per query. To improve the statistical significance of the results, we took to the test set only queries in which the total time taken by the sequential prover was less than one second. We compare the provers according to three criteria: the number of derived clauses, the number of kept clauses (i.e., which were not forward subsumed), and the time. Table 1 has a comparison of the maximum, minimum, and average values for these three criteria for the two provers.

   Fig. 1 presents a histogram for each criterion showing the values of the labelled-clauses prover as a percentage of the appropriate value for the sequential prover. In most cases we have a least 2-fold improvement in all criteria. The number of kept clauses never increases. The number of derived clauses increases in one case, but only by 6%. There are three examples in which the sequential version was faster; we believe that this is a result of the quality of the current prototype implementation, because the number of derived and kept clauses in these cases is lower in the labelled-clauses version.

---

[4] One technical point: case splits are performed externally to the theorem prover (and before the theorem prover is called), by the "focus" operation of [17], hence we do not have to be concerned about disjunctions of the different conjectures.

Table 1. Comparison between the labelled-clauses SPASS and running the original SPASS sequentially

Criteria	Sequential			Labelled Clauses		
	Min.	Max.	Avg.	Min.	Max.	Avg.
Derived	3569	408837	83657.1	1408	140679	33088.5
Kept	3882	70463	22672.1	1366	26238	7357.2
Time (sec)	1.0	74.0	8.1	0.2	29.0	3.8

Because our conjectures are based on formulas in the normal form shown in Eq. (1), the negated conjectures are sets of ground unit clauses. This makes the technique of reusing Skolem constants between conjectures very lucrative. We have checked the improvements brought about by the Join rule and by reusing the Skolem constants. Introducing the Join rule to a vanilla implementation of the labelled-clauses approach makes it run 1.7 times faster. Reusing Skolem constants added, on average, an extra speedup of 1.7, which produced about a 3-fold speedup in total. When considering only cases in which 10 or more conjectures are used, the average speedup is 7-fold.

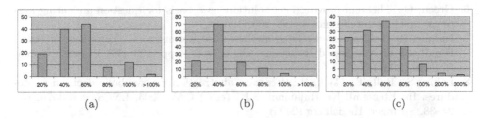

Fig. 1. Histograms for each criterion showing the percentage of the values for the labelled-clauses version compared with the sequential version: (a) derived clauses, (b) kept clauses, (c) running time

5   Conclusion

We suggested the methodology of labelled clauses for the study and implementation of superposition-based classical first-order-logic calculi. We believe that using labelled clauses as an extension of ordinary ones will become as fruitful for advances in automated theorem proving as it is in the context of non-classical logics.

Our work on labelled clauses offers new possibilities to study saturation and tableau-like calculi in a common framework. This might also be fruitful for advances in theorem-proving search strategies, as, e.g., suggested by Bonacina [3].

We have shown how to instantiate the general framework of labelled clauses for several interesting cases, including clause splitting and slicing. For the case of proving multiple conjectures simultaneously, we have also implemented the calculus as an extension of the SPASS theorem prover and report on convincing experimental results in the context of software verification.

We believe that there are other techniques in the world of theorem proving that can benefit from the idea of labelled clauses. Investigating them is the subject of future work. In particular, the combination of theorem proving techniques represented in the labelling methodology simplifies to the combination of the labelling disciplines.

References

1. Ball, T., Podelski, A., Rajamani, S.K.: Boolean and cartesian abstraction for model checking C programs. In: Margaria, T., Yi, W. (eds.) ETAPS 2001 and TACAS 2001. LNCS, vol. 2031, pp. 268–283. Springer, Heidelberg (2001)
2. Basin, D., D'Agostino, M., Gabbay, D.M., Matthews, S., Viganò, L.: Labelled Deduction. Applied Logic Series, vol. 17. Kluwer, Dordrecht (2000)
3. Bonacina, M.P.: Towards a unified model of search in theorem-proving: subgoal-reduction strategies. J. Symb. Comput. 39(2), 209–255 (2005)
4. Cousot, P., Cousot, R.: Abstract interpretation: A unified lattice model for static analysis of programs by construction of approximation of fixed points. In: POPL, pp. 238–252 (1977)
5. Graf, S., Saïdi, H.: Construction of abstract state graphs with PVS. In: Grumberg, O. (ed.) CAV 1997. LNCS, vol. 1254, pp. 72–83. Springer, Heidelberg (1997)
6. Green, C.: Theorem-proving by resolution as a basis for question-answering systems. Machine Intelligence 4, 183–205 (1969)
7. Hähnle, R.: Tableaux and related methods. In: Robinson, A., Voronkov, A. (eds.) Handbook of Automated Reasoning, ch. 6, vol. 1, pp. 103–177. Elsevier, North-Holland (2001)
8. Lahiri, S., Ball, T., Cook, B.: Predicate abstraction via symbolic decision procedures. In: Etessami, K., Rajamani, S.K. (eds.) CAV 2005. LNCS, vol. 3576, pp. 24–38. Springer, Heidelberg (2005)
9. Lev-Ami, T., Immerman, N., Reps, T.W., Sagiv, M., Srivastava, S., Yorsh, G.: Simulating reachability using first-order logic with applications to verification of linked data structures. In: Nieuwenhuis, R. (ed.) Automated Deduction – CADE-20. LNCS (LNAI), vol. 3632, pp. 99–115. Springer, Heidelberg (2005)
10. Lev-Ami, T., Sagiv, M.: TVLA: A system for implementing static analyses. In: Palsberg, J. (ed.) SAS 2000. LNCS, vol. 1824, Springer, Heidelberg (2000)
11. Lev-Ami, T., Weidenbach, C., Reps, T., Sagiv, M.: Experimental version of SPASS for multiple conjectures (2007) Available at
http://www.cs.tau.ac.il/~tla/SPASS
12. Loginov, A., Reps, T., Sagiv, M.: Abstraction refinement via inductive learning. In: Etessami, K., Rajamani, S.K. (eds.) CAV 2005. LNCS, vol. 3576, pp. 519–533. Springer, Heidelberg (2005)
13. Nelson, C.G., Oppen, D.C.: A simplifier based on efficient decision algorithms. In: POPL, pp. 141–150 (1978)
14. Nieuwenhuis, R., Oliveras, A.: Decision procedures for SAT, SAT modulo theories and beyond. The BarcelogicTools. In: Sutcliffe, G., Voronkov, A. (eds.) LPAR 2005. LNCS (LNAI), vol. 3835, pp. 23–46. Springer, Heidelberg (2005)
15. Riazanov, A., Voronkov, A.: Splitting without backtracking. In: IJCAI, pp. 611–617 (2001)
16. Riazanov, A., Voronkov, A.: The design and implementation of VAMPIRE. AI Communications 15(2-3), 91–110 (2002)

17. Sagiv, M., Reps, T., Wilhelm, R.: Parametric shape analysis via 3-valued logic. TOPLAS 217–298 (2002)
18. Schulz, S.: E – A Brainiac Theorem Prover. Journal of AI Communications 15(2/3), 111–126 (2002)
19. Voronkov, A.: Personal communication (2007)
20. Weidenbach, C.: Combining superposition, sorts and splitting. In: Robinson, A., Voronkov, A. (eds.) Handbook of Automated Reasoning, ch. 27, vol. 2, pp. 1965–2012. Elsevier, North-Holland (2001)
21. Weidenbach, C., Brahm, U., Hillenbrand, T., Keen, E., Theobald, C., Topic, D.: SPASS version 2.0. In: Voronkov, A. (ed.) Automated Deduction - CADE-18. LNCS (LNAI), vol. 2392, pp. 275–279. Springer, Heidelberg (2002)
22. Whittemore, J., Kim, J., Sakallah, K.A.: SATIRE: A new incremental satisfiability engine. In: DAC, pp. 542–545 (2001)
23. Wolf, A.: Strategy selection for automated theorem proving. In: Giunchiglia, F. (ed.) AIMSA 1998. LNCS (LNAI), vol. 1480, pp. 452–465. Springer, Heidelberg (1998)
24. Wos, L., Robinson, G.A., Carson, D.F.: Efficiency and completeness of the set of support strategy in theorem proving. J. ACM 12(4), 536–541 (1965)
25. Yorsh, G., Reps, T., Sagiv, M.: Symbolically computing most-precise abstract operations for shape analysis. In: Jensen, K., Podelski, A. (eds.) TACAS 2004. LNCS, vol. 2988, pp. 530–545. Springer, Heidelberg (2004)

Automatic Decidability and Combinability Revisited

Christopher Lynch[1] and Duc-Khanh Tran[2]

[1] Clarkson University, USA
[2] LORIA & INRIA-Lorraine, France

Abstract. We present an inference system for clauses with ordering constraints, called *Schematic Paramodulation*. Then we show how to use Schematic Paramodulation to reason about decidability and stable infiniteness of finitely presented theories. We establish a close connection between the two properties: if Schematic Paramodulation for a theory halts then the theory is decidable; and if, in addition, Schematic Paramodulation does not derive the trivial equality $X = Y$ then the theory is stably infinite. Decidability and stable infiniteness of component theories are conditions required for the Nelson-Oppen combination method. Schematic Paramodulation is loosely based on Lynch-Morawska's meta-saturation but it differs in several ways. First, it uses ordering constraints instead of constant constraints. Second, inferences into constrained variables are possible in Schematic Paramodulation. Finally, Schematic Paramodulation uses a special deletion rule to deal with theories for which Lynch-Morawska's meta-saturation does not halt.

1 Introduction

Satisfiability procedures for theories of data types such as lists, arrays or integers are at the core of many state-of-the-art verification tools. The task of designing, proving correct, and implementing such procedures is far from simple. One of the main problems is proving their correctness. To overcome this difficulty, an approach to flexibly build satisfiability procedures based on saturation has been proposed in [2]. The key idea is that proving correctness of the procedure for a theory T reduces to showing the termination of the fair and exhaustive application of the rules of the paramodulation calculus [8] on an axiomatization of T plus an arbitrary set S of (ground) literals. An automated method to check the termination of paramodulation for a theory T is given in [6] by using a meta-saturation calculus simulating the inferences of the standard paramodulation calculus relevant to solve the satisfiability problem of T.

The idea of using meta-saturation to automatically check decidability is highly original, however contrary to what was advocated in [6], there are theories for which meta-saturation cannot always simulate every inference in the saturation process. Therefore the decidability and complexity results stated in [6] do not hold for every theory (cf. Example 1, Section 4). The first contribution of this paper is a Schematic Paramodulation inference system using ordering constraints

F. Pfenning (Ed.): CADE 2007, LNAI 4603, pp. 328–344, 2007.
© Springer-Verlag Berlin Heidelberg 2007

to simulate the inferences of the standard paramodulation calculus. Schematic Paramodulation differs from meta-saturation in the following ways. First, inferences into constrained variables are possible in Schematic Paramodulation, unlike meta-saturation which excludes every inference into variables, no matter whether the variables are constrained or unconstrained. As a consequence, Schematic Paramodulation is now capable of simulating every inference in the saturation process, in contrast with meta-saturation. Another interesting feature of Schematic Paramodulation is the use of a special *deletion* rule to prove decidability of theories for which meta-saturation fails (cf. Example 2, Section 4). Finally, we can also derive an upper bound on the number of clauses generated in paramodulation by using Schematic Paramodulation.

Since most verification problems require reasoning in a combination of theories, there is a need to modularly build decision procedures for combined theories by re-using available procedures for the component theories. To this end, we can adopt the general and flexible method for combining decision procedures given by Nelson-Oppen in [7]. It is well known that the Nelson-Oppen combination method is correct if the component theories are *stably infinite*. In [5], the authors give an automatic method using meta-saturation for checking stable infiniteness of finitely presented theories.

The second contribution of this paper concerns the generalization of the results of [5] to automatically check stable infiniteness. In [5], the authors define the notion of variable-active clause so that if, for given a theory T, meta-saturation halts, and does not infer any variable-active clauses, then T is stably infinite. Basically, a variable-active clause is a clause containing a maximal equality in which there is a maximal variable. However, it turns out that the absence of variable-active clauses in meta-saturation is too strong a requirement because there exist theories not satisfying this requirement which are stably infinite (cf. Example 3, Section 5). In this paper, we prove a stronger result: if Schematic Paramodulation for a theory halts and does not derive the trivial equality $X = Y$ then that theory is stably infinite (cf. Section 5). Moreover, all the results stated in this paper do not assume any restrictions on the selection function used in the paramodulation calculus, but fairness. This is contrary to [5], in which it is required to use a negative selection strategy, i.e. negative literals are always selected first by the selection function.

2 Preliminaries

We assume the usual first-order syntactic notions of signature, term, position, and substitution, as defined, e.g., in [4]. If l and r are two terms, then $l = r$ is an *equality* and $\neg(l = r)$ (also written as $l \neq r$) is a *disequality*. A *literal* is either an equality or a disequality. A first-order *formula* is built in the usual way over the universal and existential quantifiers, Boolean connectives, and symbols in a given first-order signature. We call a formula *ground* if it has no variables. A *clause* is a disjunction of literals. A *unit* clause is a clause with only one disjunct, equivalently a literal. The *empty* clause is the clause with no disjunct, equivalently an unsatisfiable formula. For a term t, $depth(t) = 0$, if t is a constant or a variable, and $depth(f(t_1, \ldots, t_n)) = 1 + max\{depth(t_i) \mid 1 \le i \le n\}$. A term is *flat* if its depth is 0 or 1. For a literal, $depth(l \bowtie r) = depth(l) + depth(r)$, where $\bowtie \in \{=, \neq\}$. A positive literal is *flat* if its depth is 0 or 1. A negative literal is *flat* if its depth is 0.

We also assume the usual first-order notions of model, satisfiability, validity, logical consequence. A *first-order theory* (with finite signature) is a set of first-order formulae with no free variables. When T is a finitely axiomatized theory, $Ax(T)$ denotes the set of axioms of T. All the theories in this paper are first-order theories *with equality*, which means that the equality symbol $=$ is always interpreted as the equality relation. A formula is *satisfiable in a theory* T if it is satisfiable in a model of T. The *satisfiability problem* for a theory T amounts to establishing whether any given finite conjunction of literals (or equivalently, any given finite set of literals) is T-satisfiable or not. A *satisfiability procedure* for T is any algorithm that solves the satisfiability problem for T (the satisfiability of any quantifier-free formula can be reduced to the satisfiability of sets of literals by converting to disjunctive normal form and then splitting on disjunctions).

3   Paramodulation-Based Satisfiability Procedure

Below, $=$ is (unordered) equality, $\equiv$ is identity, l, r, u, t are terms, v, w, x, y, z are variables, all other lower case letters are constant or function symbols. A fundamental feature of $\mathcal{PC}$ is the usage of a *reduction ordering* $\succ$ which is total on ground terms, for example the lexicographic path ordering [4]. We also assume that if a term t is not a variable or constant, then for any constant c we have that $t \succ c$. The ordering $\succ$ is extended to positive literals by considering them as multisets of terms, and then to the clauses by considering them as multisets of positive literals.

The inference system $\mathcal{PC}$ uses a selection function sel such that for each clause C, $sel(C)$ contains a negative literal in C or all maximal literals in C wrt. $\succ$. A clause C is *redundant* with respect to a set S of clauses if either $C \in S$ or S can be obtained from $S \cup \{C\}$ by a sequence of application of the contraction rules of Figure 2. An inference is *redundant* with respect to a set S of clauses if its conclusion is redundant with respect to S. A set S of clauses is *saturated* with respect to $\mathcal{PC}$ if every inference of $\mathcal{PC}$ with a premise in S is redundant with respect to S. A *derivation* is a sequence $S_0, S_1, \ldots, S_i, \ldots$ of sets of clauses where at each step an inference of $\mathcal{PC}$ is applied to generate and add a clause (cf. expansion rules in Figure 1) or to delete or reduce a clause (cf. contraction rules in Figure 2). A derivation is characterized by its *limit*, defined as the set of persistent clauses $S_\infty = \bigcup_{j \ge 0} \bigcap_{i > j} S_i$. A derivation $S_0, S_1, \ldots, S_i, \ldots$ with limit S_∞ is *fair* with respect to $\mathcal{PC}$ if for every inference in $\mathcal{PC}$ with premises in S_∞, there is some $j \ge 0$ such that the inference is redundant in S_j.

Theorem 1 ([8]). *If $S_0, S_1, \ldots$ is a fair derivation of $\mathcal{PC}$, then (i) its limit S_∞ is saturated with respect to $\mathcal{PC}$, (ii) S_0 is unsatisfiable iff the empty clause is in*

Right paramodulation	$\dfrac{\Gamma \Rightarrow \Delta, l[u'] = r \quad \Pi \Rightarrow \Sigma, u = t}{\sigma(\Gamma, \Pi \Rightarrow \Delta, \Sigma, l[t] = r)}$	*(i), (ii), (iii), (iv)*
Left paramodulation	$\dfrac{\Gamma, l[u'] = r \Rightarrow \Delta \quad \Pi \Rightarrow \Sigma, u = t}{\sigma(l[t] = r, \Gamma, \Pi \Rightarrow \Delta, \Sigma)}$	*(i), (ii), (iii), (iv)*
Reflection	$\dfrac{\Gamma, u' = u \Rightarrow \Delta}{\sigma(\Gamma \Rightarrow \Delta)}$	*(v)*
Eq. Factoring	$\dfrac{\Gamma \Rightarrow \Delta, u = t, u' = t'}{\sigma(\Gamma, t = t' \Rightarrow \Delta, u = t')}$	*(i), (vi)*

where a clause $\neg A_1 \vee \cdots \vee \neg A_n \vee B_1 \vee \cdots \vee B_n$ is written in sequent style as $\{A_1, \ldots, A_n\} \Rightarrow \{B_1, \ldots, B_m\}$ (where the A_i's and B_j's are equalities), equality is the only predicate symbol, σ is the most general unifier of u and u', u' is not a variable in *Left paramodulation* and *Right paramodulation*, L is a literal, and:

(i) $\sigma(u) \not\preceq \sigma(t)$, *(ii)* $u = t$ is selected in its clause, *(iii)* $\sigma(l[u']) \not\preceq \sigma(r)$, *(iv)* $l = r$ is selected in its clause, *(v)* $u' = u$ is selected in its clause, *(vi)* $u = t$ is selected in its clause and $\sigma(t) \not\preceq \sigma(t')$ and $\sigma(u') \not\preceq \sigma(t')$.

Fig. 1. Expansion Inference Rules of $\mathcal{PC}$

Subsumption	$\dfrac{S \cup \{C, C'\}}{S \cup \{C\}}$	if for some substitution θ, $\theta(C) \subseteq C'$
Simplification	$\dfrac{S \cup \{C[l'], l = r\}}{S \cup \{C[\theta(r)], l = r\}}$	if $l' \equiv \theta(l)$, $\theta(l) \succ \theta(r)$, and $C[l'] \succ$ $(\theta(l) = \theta(r))$
Tautology Deletion	$\dfrac{S \cup \{\Gamma \Rightarrow \Delta, t = t\}}{S}$	

where C and C' are clauses and S is a set of clauses.

Fig. 2. Contraction Inference Rules of $\mathcal{PC}$

S_j for some j, and *(iii)* if such a fair derivation is finite, i.e. it is of the form $S_0, \ldots, S_n$, then S_n is saturated and logically equivalent to S_0.

The paramodulation-based methodology [2] for satisfiability modulo a theory T (or T-satisfiability) consists of two phases:

1. *Flattening:* all ground literals are flattened by introducing new constants, yielding an equisatisfiable *flat* problem.
2. *Ordering selection and termination:* any fair derivation of $\mathcal{PC}$ is shown to be finite when applied to a flat problem together with the axioms of T, provided that $\succ$ satisfies a few properties depending on T.

If T is a theory for which the paramodulation-based methodology applies, a T-satisfiability procedure can be built by implementing the flattening (this can be done once and for all), and by using a prover mechanizing $\mathcal{PC}$ with a suitable ordering $\succ$. If the final set of clauses returned by the prover contains the empty clause, then the T-satisfiability procedure returns unsatisfiable; otherwise, it returns satisfiable.

4   Automatic Decidability

Like meta-saturation [6], Schematic Paramodulation works by saturating the axioms $Ax(T)$ of a theory T together with the set G_0^T schematizing any finite set of ground flat literals built out of symbols in the signature of T, with respect to the inference system $\mathcal{SPC}$ (see Figures 3 and 4). Therefore if Schematic Paramodulation halts for the theory T, then any saturation of $Ax(T) \cup S$ is finite and consequently the T-satisfiability problem is decidable. Below, we give the formal concepts underlying the Schematic Paramodulation approach with ordering constraints.

Definition 1 (Constraint). *An atomic constraint is of the form $t \preceq t'$ or $t \npreceq t'$. A constraint is a conjunction of atomic constraints.*

A substitution λ satisfies a constraint ϕ if $\lambda(\phi)$ is true. A constraint ϕ is satisfiable if there exists a substitution λ satisfying ϕ. In the sequel, by $c^\top$, we mean the biggest constant wrt. $\succ$. For example, a constraint of the form $t \preceq c^\top$ is true if t is a constant, it is false if t is a term of depth at least 1 (i.e. containing a function symbol) and it is satisfiable if t is a variable.

Definition 2 (Constrained clause). *A constrained clause is of the form $C \parallel \phi$, where C is a (unconstrained) clause and ϕ is a constraint.*

We say that $\lambda(C)$ is an *instance* of $C \parallel \phi$ if λ is a substitution satisfying ϕ.

Definition 3 (Constrained variable). *A variable x is constrained in a constrained clause $C \parallel \phi$ if ϕ contains $x \preceq c^\top$, otherwise it is unconstrained.*

Definition 4 (Constrained variant). *Let $C \parallel \phi$ and $C' \parallel \phi'$ be two constrained clauses. We say that C is a constrained variant of C' if there exists a renaming λ such that $\lambda(C) = \lambda(C')$ and the domain of λ only contains constrained variables.*

Definition 5 (Constraint instance). *We say that $\lambda(C)$ is a constraint instance of $C \parallel \phi$ if the domain of λ contains all the constrained variables in $C \parallel \phi$, the range of λ contains only contains constants and $\lambda(\phi)$ is satisfiable.*

Ordering on constrained clauses can be defined so that a clause C is bigger than a clause D if all constraint instances of C are bigger than all constraint instances of D.

For a given theory T with the signature Σ_T, we define G_0^T as follows:

$$G_0^T = \{x = y \parallel x \preceq c^\top \wedge y \preceq c^\top\} \cup \{x \neq y \parallel x \preceq c^\top \wedge y \preceq c^\top\} \cup$$

$$\bigcup_{f \in \Sigma_T} \{f(x_1, \ldots, x_n) = x_0 \parallel \bigwedge_{i=0}^{n} x_i \preceq c^\top\}$$

Right paramodulation	$$\frac{\Gamma \Rightarrow \Delta, l[u'] = r \parallel \phi \;\; \Pi \Rightarrow \Sigma, u = t \parallel \varphi}{\sigma(\Gamma, \Pi \Rightarrow \Delta, \Sigma, l[t] = r \parallel \phi \wedge \varphi \wedge u \not\preceq t \wedge l[u'] \not\preceq r)}$$	(i), (ii), (iii), (iv)
Left paramodulation	$$\frac{\Gamma, l[u'] = r \Rightarrow \Delta \parallel \phi \;\; \Pi \Rightarrow \Sigma, u = t \parallel \varphi}{\sigma(l[t] = r, \Gamma, \Pi \Rightarrow \Delta, \Sigma \parallel \phi \wedge \varphi \wedge u \not\preceq t \wedge l[u'] \not\preceq r)}$$	(i), (ii), (iii), (iv)
Reflection	$$\frac{\Gamma, u' = u \Rightarrow \Delta \parallel \phi}{\sigma(\Gamma \Rightarrow \Delta \parallel \phi)}$$	(v)
Eq. Factoring	$$\frac{\Gamma \Rightarrow \Delta, u = t, u' = t' \parallel \phi}{\sigma(\Gamma, t = t' \Rightarrow \Delta, u = t' \parallel \phi \wedge u \not\preceq t \wedge u' \not\preceq t')}$$	(i), (vi)

where σ is the most general unifier of u and u', u' is not an unconstrained variable in *Left paramodulation* and *Right paramodulation*, L is a literal, and:

(i) $\sigma(u) \not\preceq \sigma(t)$, **(ii)** $u = t$ is selected in its clause, **(iii)** $\sigma(l[u']) \not\preceq \sigma(r)$, **(iv)** $l = r$ is selected in its clause, **(v)** $u' = u$ is selected in its clause, **(vi)** $u = t$ is selected in its clause and $\sigma(t) \not\preceq \sigma(t')$ and $\sigma(u') \not\preceq \sigma(t')$.

Fig. 3. Constrained Expansion Inference Rules of $\mathcal{SPC}$

Subsumption	$$\frac{S \cup \{C, C' \parallel \phi'\}}{S \cup \{C\}}$$	if $C \in Ax(T)$ and for some substitution θ, $\theta(C) \subseteq C'$, or if C and $C' \parallel \phi'$ are renamings of each other.
Simplification	$$\frac{S \cup \{C[l'] \parallel \phi, l = r\}}{S \cup \{C[\theta(r)] \parallel \phi, l = r\}}$$	if $l = r \in Ax(T)$, $l' \equiv \theta(l)$, $\theta(l) \succ \theta(r)$, and $C[l'] \succ (\theta(l) = \theta(r))$
Tautology Deletion	$$\frac{S \cup \{\Gamma \Rightarrow \Delta, t = t \parallel \phi\}}{S}$$	
Schematic Deletion	$$\frac{S \cup \{\Gamma \Rightarrow \Delta \parallel \phi\}}{S}$$	if ϕ is unsatisfiable
	$$\frac{S \cup \{C\}}{S}$$	(i)

where C and C' are clauses and S is a set of clauses, and:

(i) if $C \equiv D \vee l_1 \vee \ldots \vee l_n \parallel \phi$ where $n \geq 0$, D is a constrained variant of D' of some clause $D' \parallel \phi'$ in S, and

- either for $i = 1, \ldots, n$ l_i is a constrained variant of some non maximal literal in D,
- or $D \vee l_1 \vee \ldots \vee l_n$ is a non-unit clause containing only equalities or disequalities between constrained variable.

Fig. 4. Constrained Contraction Inference Rules of $\mathcal{SPC}$

The inference system $\mathcal{SPC}$ (see Figures 3 and 4) is almost identical to $\mathcal{PC}$, except that all clauses now have constraints (unconstrained clauses have empty constraints) and applicability conditions are slightly different. Constraints of clauses contain two parts. The first part aims to constrain variables to be instantiated with constants and the second part captures the ordered selection of terms and literals in a saturation of $Ax(T) \cup S$. Obviously constraints are inherited by the conclusions of an inference. Also, an atomic constraint not containing any variables in the clause part will be deleted from its constrained clause. Notice that inferences into constrained variables are now allowed in some constrained expansion rules in order to simulate inferences into constants. Constrained contraction rules have different applicability conditions. This is because we cannot simulate every subsumption, deletion or simplification since we cannot assume that ground literals are always present in a saturation of $Ax(T) \cup S$, on which such contraction inferences depend.

For the sake of simplicity, we sometimes omit the second part of constraints of persisting constrained clauses, which is not important because a constrained clause persisting actually means that the second part of its constraint is always satisfiable.

Schematic Paramodulation is heavily based on the meta-saturation of [6]. Meta-saturation inference system uses constraints of the form $const(t_1) \wedge \ldots \wedge const(t_n)$ to constrain variables to be instantiated with constants, and it excludes every inference into variables, no matter they are constrained or unconstrained. However excluding every inference into constrained variables implies that meta-saturation cannot simulate every inference into constants anymore. The following example illustrate this problem.

Example 1. Let T be a theory with the presentation

$$X = Y \vee Y = Z \vee Z = X$$
$$f(X) = g(X)$$

Following [6], G_0^T contains the following clauses

$$x = y \parallel const(x) \wedge const(y)$$
$$x \neq y \parallel const(x) \wedge const(y)$$
$$f(x) = y \parallel const(x) \wedge const(y)$$
$$g(x) = y \parallel const(x) \wedge const(y)$$

Since no inference into variables is possible in meta-saturation, it is easy to see that G_∞^T is exactly $Ax(T) \cup G_0^T$. Now let us consider the set $S = \{f(c) = c'\}$. The saturation of $Ax(T) \cup S$ by $\mathcal{PC}$ generates the clause

$$f(Y) = c' \vee Y = Z \vee Z = c$$

which is neither subsumed by any other clause nor schematized by any clause in G_∞^T.

We have experimented on this example with Spass [10]. The saturation process of $Ax(T) \cup S$ not only generates clauses not schematized by the meta-saturation but also it seems to diverge (actually we do not know if it will halt). And the number of persisting clauses (at the moment we stop the saturation process) is by far greater than the bound $2^{|S|^2}$ given in [6]. The problem is that in meta-saturation, paramodulations between variables are excluded, no matter whether they are constrained or unconstrained, but in a saturation of $Ax(T) \cup S$ there might be paramodulations between a constant and a variable.

In our settings, Schematic Paramodulation for this example will not halt because of paramodulations between constrained variables.   □

Contrary to meta-saturation Schematic Paramodulation allows inferences into constrained variables. One might think this kind of inferences is rather prolific but in fact this is not the case. Whenever a term with a function at the top position paramodulates into a constrained variable, the conclusion of the inference will be immediately deleted because the constraint of the conclusion is unsatisfiable. Also, if a constrained variable x in a clause $x = f(y) \vee C \parallel x \preceq c^\top \wedge y \preceq c^\top \wedge \phi$ is used in an inference, then the constraint of the conclusion contains $x \preceq c^\top \wedge y \preceq c^\top \wedge x \npreceq f(y)$, which is clearly unsatisfiable.

Schematic Paramodulation also differs from meta-saturation by the second case of the *Schematic Deletion* rule. The key idea is the following. We would like to schematize every clause generated in paramodulation but we do not know in advance how many constants there are in the input. On the other hand we would like to avoid inferences introducing new constrained variables because that might render Schematic Paramodulation non terminating. This happens when inferences introduce unlimited duplications of literals obtained by renaming constrained variables within the same clause. Therefore, we use the second case of *Schematic Deletion* to contract them. However if contracting a clause is performed carelessly, we may loose literals on which inferences may apply; and thereby we may loose track of the conclusion of such inferences. That is the reason why we use a disjunction of a clause in Schematic Paramodulation and non maximal literals in this clause or (dis)equalities between constant to schematize clauses generated in paramodulation. To have a better idea about how it works, let us consider the following example.

Example 2. The theory T of arrays is axiomatized by the following finite set $Ax(T)$ of axioms, where A, I, J, E are implicitly universally quantified variables:

$$select(store(A, I, E), I) = E$$
$$I = J \vee select(store(A, I, E), J) = select(A, J)$$

It is shown in [2] that for every set S of ground flat Σ_T-literals, any saturation of $Ax(T) \cup S$ by $\mathcal{PC}$ is finite. But meta-saturation generates the clause

$$select(x, I) = select(z, I) \vee y = I \parallel const(x) \wedge const(y) \wedge const(z)$$

which will paramodulate with a renamed version of itself, i.e.

$$select(x', I') = select(z', I') \vee y' = I' \parallel const(x') \wedge const(y') \wedge const(z')$$

to generate a clause of a new form, namely

$$select(x, I) = select(z, I) \vee y = I \vee w = I \parallel const(x) \wedge const(y) \wedge const(z) \wedge const(w)$$

The process continues so on and meta-saturation will diverge.

In our settings, clauses generated by self-paramodulations, i.e. clauses of the form

$$select(x_1, I) = select(x_2, I) \vee x_3 = I \vee \ldots \vee x_n = I \parallel x_1 \preceq c^\top \wedge \ldots \wedge x_n \preceq c^\top$$

will be deleted by applying the second case of *Schematic Deletion*. This is so because the clause $select(x, I) = select(z, I) \vee y = I \parallel x \preceq c^\top \wedge y \preceq c^\top \wedge z \preceq c^\top$ already persists and the literals $x_3 = I, \ldots, x_n = I$ are actually constrained variants of the non maximal literal $y = I$.

Also the clause $x = y \vee x' = y' \parallel x \preceq c^\top \wedge y \preceq c^\top \wedge x' \preceq c^\top \wedge y' \preceq c^\top$, generated by a *Right paramodulation* inference of Figure 3 between $select(x, I) = z \vee y = I \parallel x \preceq c^\top \wedge y \preceq c^\top \wedge z \preceq c^\top$ and $select(x, I) = y \parallel x \preceq c^\top \wedge y \preceq c^\top$, will be deleted

Finally, Schematic Paramodulation will contain $Ax(T) \cup G_0^T$ and the following clauses:

$$select(x, I) = select(z, I) \vee y = I \parallel x \preceq c^\top \wedge y \preceq c^\top \wedge z \preceq c^\top$$
$$select(x, I) = z \vee y = I \parallel x \preceq c^\top \wedge y \preceq c^\top \wedge z \preceq c^\top$$

□

We are now in a position to show that Schematic Paramodulation can be used to automatically check decidability of finitely presented theories.

Theorem 2. *Let T be a theory axiomatized by a finite set $Ax(T)$ of clauses, which is saturated with respect to $\mathcal{PC}$. Let G_∞^T be the set of all clauses in a finite saturation of $Ax(T) \cup G_0^T$ by $\mathcal{SPC}$. Then for every set S of ground flat Σ_T-literals, every clause in a saturation $Ax(T) \cup S$ by $\mathcal{PC}$ is a clause of the form*

$$C \vee l_1 \vee \ldots \vee l_n$$

where $n \geq 0$, C is a constraint instance of some clause C' in G_∞^T, and for $i = 1, \ldots, n$

- *either l_i is non maximal, and is a constraint instance of some literal in C' or a (dis)equality between constant,*
- *or l_i is a (dis)equality between constant, and C contains an equality between constant.*

Proof (Sketch). The proof is by induction on the length of saturation inferences by $\mathcal{PC}$. For the base case, it is true because all the clauses in $Ax(T) \cup S$ satisfy the theorem. For the inductive case, we need to show three facts:

1. each clause added in the process of saturation of $Ax(T) \cup S$ is of the mentioned form, and
2. if a clause is deleted by *Subsumption* or by *Tautology Deletion* of Figure 4 from (resp. simplified by *Simplification* of Figure 4 in) the saturation of $Ax(T) \cup G_0^T$ by $\mathcal{SPC}$, then all clauses containing a constraint instances of the latter will also be deleted from (resp. simplified in) the saturation of $Ax(T) \cup S$ by $\mathcal{PC}$, and

3. if a clause is deleted by *Schematic Deletion* of Figure 4 from the saturation of $Ax(T) \cup G_0^T$ by $\mathcal{SPC}$, then each clause in the process of saturation of $Ax(T) \cup S$ is still in the form mentioned in the theorem.

For the first case, consider *Right paramodulation* of Figure 1. Assume that $\Gamma \Rightarrow \Delta, l[u'] = r$ and $\Pi \Rightarrow \Sigma, u = t$ have the mentioned form. Then there are some clause D in G_∞^T and a substitution θ such that $\theta(D \vee l_1 \vee \ldots \vee l_n) \equiv \Gamma \Rightarrow \Delta, l[u'] = r$, and some clause D' in G_∞^T such that $\theta(D' \vee l_1' \vee \ldots \vee l_m') \equiv \Pi \Rightarrow \Sigma, u = t$. If the *Right paramodulation* inference of Figure 1 is performed at $\theta(D)$ part and the $\theta(D')$ part, then there must exist a *Right paramodulation* inference of Figure 3 in the saturation of $Ax(T) \cup G_0^T$ by $\mathcal{SPC}$, whose premises are D, D' and conclusion D'' such that we can then extend θ so that $\theta(D'' \vee l_1 \vee \ldots \vee l_n \vee l_1' \vee \ldots \vee l_m') \equiv \sigma(\Gamma, \Pi \Rightarrow \Delta, \Sigma, l[t] = r)$. And hence the conclusion of the *Right paramodulation* inference of Figure 1 is still in the form mentioned in the theorem. If the *Right paramodulation* inference of Figure 1 is performed at $\theta(l_1 \vee \ldots \vee l_n)$ and $\theta(l_1' \vee \ldots \vee l_m')$, then $\theta(D \vee l_1 \vee \ldots \vee l_n)$ and $\theta(l_1' \vee \ldots \vee l_m')$ must only contain constants or variables (no function symbols). We must have that $D \equiv D_1 \vee x_1 = y_1$ and $D' \equiv D_1' \vee x_1' = y_1'$, where x_1, x_2, x_1', x_2' are constrained variables. There must exist a *Right paramodulation* inference of Figure 3 in the saturation of $Ax(T) \cup G_0^T$ by $\mathcal{SPC}$, whose premises are D, D' and conclusion $(D_1 \vee D_1')[x_1' \rightarrow x_1] \vee y_1 = y_1'$. But then, the conclusion of the *Right paramodulation* inference of Figure 1 between $\theta(D \vee l_1 \vee \ldots \vee l_n)$ and $\theta(D' \vee l_1' \vee \ldots \vee l_m')$ is still in the form mentioned in the theorem. If the inference is performed at $\theta(l_1 \vee \ldots \vee l_n)$ and $\theta(D')$, then $D \equiv D_1 \vee x_1 = y_1$. If D contains an unconstrained variable, G_∞^T will be infinite because of inferences from constrained variables into constrained variables, which introduce new unconstrained variables. If D does not contains any unconstrained variable, then $\theta(D \vee l_1 \vee \ldots \vee l_n)$ only contains constants, which means that the conclusion of the *Right paramodulation* inference of Figure 1 inference is still in the right form.

The rule *Left paramodulation* of Figure 1 is handled exactly in the same way as *Right paramodulation* of Figure 1.

For *Reflection* of Figure 1, if the inference is performed in the C part then it is simulated by a *Reflection* inference of Figure 3 applied to C'. If the inference is performed at the $l_1 \vee \ldots \vee l_n$ part, then the conclusion is still in the right form.

Eq. Factoring of Figure 1 can be handled similarly to *Right paramodulation* of Figure 1.

For the second case, let us consider *Subsumption* of Figure 4. The second case of *Subsumption* is just a matter of deleting duplicates. For the first case, assume that there is a clause A deleted from the saturation of $Ax(T) \cup G_0^T$ by $\mathcal{SPC}$ and there is a clause B in the saturation of $Ax(T) \cup S$ by $\mathcal{PC}$, which contains a constraint instance of A. Then there must exist a clause $C \in Ax(T)$ and some substitution θ such that $\theta(C) \subseteq A$. Since all the clauses in $Ax(T)$ persist, there must be a substitution θ' such that $\theta'(C) \subseteq B$. Thereby B must also be deleted from the saturation of $Ax(T) \cup S$ by $\mathcal{PC}$. A similar argument can be given for *Simplification* of Figure 4. For the *Tautology Deletion* rule of Figure 4, it is easy to see that a constraint instance of a tautology is also a tautology.

For the third case it is sufficient to argue that the deleted clause has no constraint instance, or contains exactly a constrained variant of a clause in G_∞^T, or contain exactly a constrained variant a clause C in G_∞^T and constrained variants of non maximal literals or constrained variants of maximal (dis)equalities between constrained variables in C. Therefore all clauses in a saturation of $Ax(T) \cup S$ still have one of the forms mentioned in the theorem.   □

We can also determine, by Schematic Paramodulation, an upper bound on the number of clauses generated in paramodulation by simply counting the number of possible ground instantiations of constrained variables, given a finite set of constants. We have that the number of possible instantiations polynomially depends on the number of constants in the input set of ground flat literals. This quickly leads us to the following result.

Theorem 3. *Let T be a theory axiomatized by a finite set $Ax(T)$ of clauses, which is saturated with respect to $\mathcal{PC}$. Let G_∞^T be the set of all clauses in a finite saturation of $Ax(T) \cup G_0^T$ by $\mathcal{SPC}$. Then for every set S of ground flat Σ_T-literals, the number of clauses in a saturation $Ax(T) \cup S$ by $\mathcal{PC}$ is bounded by*

- $|G_\infty^T| \times |S|^V$ *if $Ax(T)$ only contains unit clauses, and*
- $2^{|G_\infty^T| \times |S|^V}$ *if $Ax(T)$ contains non-unit clauses,*

where $|S|$ is the number of constants in S, $|G_\infty^T|$ is the number of literals in G_∞^T and V is the number of constrained variables in G_∞^T.

Proof. Since there are $|S|^V$ ways to instantiate constrained variables in G_∞^T. There are at most $|G_\infty^T| \times |S|^V$ literals in a saturation of $Ax(T) \cup S$ by $\mathcal{PC}$. We can conclude following Theorem 2 that there are at most $|G_\infty^T| \times |S|^V$ unit clauses and $2^{|G_\infty^T| \times |S|^V}$ non-unit clauses built out of $|G_\infty^T| \times |S|^V$ literals.   □

5   Automatic Combinability

The Nelson-Oppen combination method [7] allows us to combine satisfiability procedures for the class of stably infinite theories (cf. Definition 6 below) in a modular way. Although stable infiniteness is undecidable in general (see, e.g., [3] for more details), it is interesting to develop automated techniques to prove it for a subclass of first order theories, in particular those admitting paramodulation-based satisfiability procedures.

Definition 6 (Stably infinite theory). *Let T be a consistent theory. T is stably infinite iff every T-satisfiable conjunction φ of ground literals is T-satisfiable in an infinite model.*

In [5], the authors define the notion of variable-active clause so that if, for given a theory T, any saturation of $Ax(T) \cup S$ halts, and does not infer any variable-active clauses, then T is stably infinite. In essence, a variable-active clause is a clause containing a maximal equality in which there exists a maximal variable.

However, the absence of variable-active clauses in any saturation is rather too strong a requirement because there exist theories not satisfying this requirement but which are stably infinite. Let us consider the following example.

Example 3. The theory presented by the clause

$$f(X) = a \vee X = Y \vee f(Y) = a$$

is stably infinite, but we cannot detect it by using the method of [5] because the given clause is variable-active.   □

Moreover, the method of [5] needs to assume that the paramodulation inference system uses a negative selection function. This is again a rather strong requirement, which narrows the applicability scope of the method because there exist theories where Schematic Paramodulation halts with one special ordering but not with others. Let us consider the following example.

Example 4. The theory presented by the clause

$$Nat(X) \neq True \vee Nat(s(X)) = True$$

is stably infinite. However if we consider negative selection, then the clause $Nat(x) = y \parallel x \preceq c^\top \wedge y \preceq c^\top$ will paramodulate with the theory axiom to generate the clause $y \neq True \vee Nat(s(x)) = True \parallel x \preceq c^\top \wedge y \preceq c^\top$ to which *Reflection* applies to yield $Nat(s(x)) = True \parallel x \preceq c^\top$. The new clause will again paramodulate with the axiom and the process continue so on. Consequently, the Schematic Paramodulation will not halt.   □

We now develop a much more general technique for automatically checking stable infiniteness by using Schematic Paramodulation. Our technique is not based on variable-inactivity condition anymore and it does not require using negative selection.

Definition 7 (Finite cardinality clause). *A clause is a* finite cardinality clause *if it has the form*

$$\bigvee_{0 \leq j \neq k \leq n} (x_j = x_k)$$

where n is a positive integer and x_i (for $i = 0, \dots, n$) is a variable.

Definition 8 (Elementary clause). *An elementary clause is a a clause of the form $x_1 = y_1 \vee \dots \vee x_n = y_n$, where x_i, y_i are distinct constants or variables for $i = 1, \dots, n$. A constrained clause is elementary if one of its constraint instance is elementary.*

The following result follows from the compactness of first order logic (see, e.g., [9]).

Lemma 1. *Let T be a satisfiable set of formulae. If T has no infinite models then T entails a finite cardinality clause.*

The following result applies to paramodulation calculi, which are *stable under signature extension*[1], for instance $\mathcal{PC}$, meaning that extending the initial signature with new symbols does not destroy completeness.

Lemma 2. *Let T be a consistent theory axiomatized by a finite set $Ax(T)$ of clauses and S be a finite T-satisfiable set of ground literals. If $T \cup S$ entails a finite cardinality clause, then any saturation of $Ax(T) \cup S$ by $\mathcal{PC}$ contains a non-ground elementary clause.*

Proof. The proof uses the *model generation* technique (see, e.g., [8] for more details). Let S bet a set of ground clauses and C be a clause in S. Then $Gen(C) = \{l \to r\}$, and C is said to *generate* the rule $\{l \to r\}$, if and only if, C is of the form $\Gamma \Rightarrow \Delta, l = r$ and the following conditions hold:

1. $R_C^* \not\models C$,
2. $l \succ r$ and $l \succ \Gamma$ and $l = r \succ^{mul} u = v$ for all $u = v \in \Delta$, where $\succ^{mul}$ is the multiset extension of $\succ$ (see, e.g., [8] for more details),
3. l is irreducible by R_C,
4. $R_C^* \not\models r = t'$ for every $l = t' \in \Delta$,

where $R_C = \bigcup_{C \succ D} Gen(D)$, and R_C^* is the congruence induced by R_C. In all other cases, $Gen(C) = \emptyset$. Finally, R denotes the set of all rules generated by clauses of S, that is $R = \bigcup_{D \in S} Gen(D)$.

Now assume that $T \cup S$ entails a finite cardinality clause with n distinct variables. Let S' be the saturation of $Ax(T) \cup S$ by $\mathcal{PC}$. Since S' and $Ax(T) \cup S$ are logically equivalent, we have that S' entails the same finite cardinality clause. This also means that $S' \cup \bigcup_{1 \le j \ne k \le n+1} \{c_j \ne c_k\}$ is also unsatisfiable, where c_j, c_k are new constants. Let $R_{S'}$ be the set of all rules generated by all the clauses in $grd(S')$, where $grd(S')$ denotes the set of all ground instances of all the clauses in S'. Then, $S' \cup \bigcup_{1 \le j \ne k \le n+1} \{c_j \ne c_k\}$ is unsatisfiable only if there exists a smallest constant c_i such that c_i is reducible by $R_{S'}$.

Assume that c_i is reduced by a rule $c_i \to r$ in $R_{S'}$. Then $c_i \to r$ must be in a clause C which generates $c_i \to r$. Since c_i is a constant r must also be constants and thereby C must be a disjunction of equalities or disequalities between constants. Assume that C is a ground instance of some clause C' in S'. Because c_i is a fresh constant and hence it is not in S', C generates the rule $c_i \to r$ only if C' contains an equality of the form $x = y$, where at least x must be a variable. Therefore, C' must have the form $x = y \vee x_1 \bowtie y_1 \vee \ldots \vee x_n \bowtie y_n$, where $n \ge 0$, $x, y, x_1, y_1, \ldots, x_n, y_n$ are constants or variables, at least x is a variable, and $\bowtie \; \in \{=, \ne\}$.

We prove that C' is a non-ground elementary clause. To this end, we only need to show that C' does not contain any disequalities. Since c_i is the smallest reducible constant, C' must not contain any disequalities containing a constant

---

[1] This is not restrictive because most of state of the art paramodulation-based provers enjoy this property, except those which interpret ordering constraints as symbolic constraint solving problems in the original signature (see [8,3] for a more detailed discussion).

(occurring in S'), otherwise the condition 2 of model generation would not be satisfied and thereby $c_i \to r$ would not be generated. Assume that C' contains a disequality between variable, says $x_i \neq y_i$ ($i \in \{1, \ldots, n\}$). If $x_i \equiv x$ or $y_i \equiv x$ then C contains both $c_i = r$ and $c_i \neq r'$. In this case, the condition 2 of model generation would again not be satisfied and consequently C could not generate $c_i \to r$. So x_i, y_i are different from x. But then *Reflection* applies to C' to infer a smaller clause C'' containing $x = y$. This means that C could not generate $c_i \to r$ because a ground instance of C'' will generate $c_i \to r$. Summing up, in all cases C' must not contain any disequalities and this completes the proof of the lemma. $\qquad\square$

Since any saturation of a set S of ground flat literal together with $Ax(T)$ can be simulated by Schematic Paramodulation, we have an automatic method for checking stable infiniteness of finitely presented theories, as stated in the following theorem.

Theorem 4. *Let T be a consistent theory axiomatized by a finite set $Ax(T)$ of clauses, which is saturated with respect to $\mathcal{PC}$. Let G_∞^T be the set of all clauses generated in a finite saturation of $Ax(T) \cup G_0^T$ by $\mathcal{SPC}$. If G_∞^T does not contain $X = Y$, then T is stably infinite.*

Proof. Assume by contradiction that T is not stably infinite. Then there exists a T-satisfiable set S of ground flat Σ_T-literals such that $T \cup S$ has no infinite models. By Lemma 1, $T \cup S$ must entail a finite cardinality constraint. Let S' be the saturation of $Ax(T) \cup S$ by $\mathcal{PC}$. By Lemma 2, S' contains a non-ground elementary clause C. We consider two cases:

1. C is a unit clause, i.e. $C \equiv x = y$ where x is a variable and y is a variable or a constant. If y is a variable then $x = y$ is a trivial equality. But then, by Theorem 2, $x = y$ must be a constraint instance of some clause in G_∞^T, which must be a trivial equality. Now, consider that case where y is a constant. Then again by Theorem 2, $x = y$ is a constraint instance of the clause $X = y \parallel y \preceq c^\top$. But $X = y \parallel y \preceq c^\top$ will paramodulate with a renamed version of itself to generate the trivial equality $X = X'$ in G_∞^T. And the theorem is proved.

2. C is a non-unit clause. By Theorem 2, C is a clause of the form $D \vee l_1 \vee \ldots \vee l_n$, where D is a constraint instance of some clause D' in G_∞^T, and (for $i = 1, \ldots, n$ and $n \geq 0$) either l_i is constraint instance of some literal in D' or a (dis)equality between constant. We argue that D' is non-ground elementary (i.e. containing an unconstrained variable) because otherwise D will be ground. We can assume wlog. that every equality in D' is non-ground, because otherwise it will paramodulate with $x \neq y \parallel x \preceq c^\top \wedge y \preceq c^\top$ to infer a clause in the desired form. If D' is an unit clause, then we are in the case 1. Let us consider D' to be non-unit, then D' has one of the following forms, where X, Y, Z are unconstrained variables:

    (a) $X = x \vee X = y \vee D_1 \parallel x \preceq c^\top \wedge y \preceq c^\top \wedge \phi$: then D' will paramodulate with a renamed version of itself, i.e. $X' = x' \vee X' = y' \vee D_1' \parallel x' \preceq$

$c^\top \wedge y' \preceq c^\top \wedge \phi'$, to infer the clause $X = X' \vee Y = y \vee Y' = y' \vee (D_1[x \to x']) \vee D_1' \parallel ((x \preceq c^\top \wedge y \preceq c^\top \wedge \phi \wedge \phi')[x \to x'])$. This new clause will again paramodulate with a renamed version of itself to generate a clause of yet another new form. And *Schematic Deletion* cannot apply to the new clause since it contains new unconstrained variables. The process continues so on and G_∞^T will be infinite.

(b) $X = x \vee X = Z \vee D_1 \parallel x \preceq c^\top \wedge \phi$: then D' will paramodulate with $x' = y' \parallel x' \preceq c^\top \wedge y' \preceq c^\top$ to infer the clause $X = x \vee X = y' \vee (D_1[Z \to x']) \parallel ((x \preceq c^\top \wedge x' \preceq c^\top \wedge y' \preceq c^\top \wedge \phi)[Z \to x'])$, which is in the first form. By a similar argument G_∞^T will be infinite.

(c) $X = Y \vee X = Z \vee D_1 \parallel \phi$: then D' will paramodulate with $x = y \parallel x \preceq c^\top \wedge y \preceq c^\top$ to generate the clause $X = y \vee X = Z \vee (D_1[Y \to x]) \parallel ((x \preceq c^\top \wedge y \preceq c^\top \wedge \phi)[Y \to x])$, which is in the second form. But then G_∞^T will also be infinite.

Summing up, in all cases if T is not stably infinite, then either the trivial equality $X = Y$ is in G_∞^T or G_∞^T is infinite, which will contradict the hypothesis of the theorem. And this completes the proof of the theorem. □

Now, considering again Example 3, it is easy to see that Schematic Paramodulation contains the axiom clause, G_0^T and the following set of clauses

$$X \neq x \vee f(y) = a \vee f(X) = a \parallel x \preceq c^\top \wedge y \preceq c^\top$$
$$f(x) = a \parallel x \preceq c^\top$$
$$f(x) = a \vee f(y) = a \parallel x \preceq c^\top \wedge y \preceq c^\top$$
$$X = y \vee x = a \vee f(X) = a \parallel x \preceq c^\top \wedge y \preceq c^\top \wedge f(x) \npreceq y$$
$$X = y \vee x = a \vee f(X) = a \vee f(z) = a \parallel x \preceq c^\top \wedge y \preceq c^\top \wedge z \preceq c^\top$$

The saturated set is finite and does not contain the trivial equality $X = Y$. By Theorem 4, the theory is stably infinite.

For Example 4, since we do not assume any restriction on the selection function but fairness, we can freely consider an ordered selection such that

$$sel(Nat(X) \neq True \vee Nat(s(X)) = True) = \{Nat(s(X)) = True\}$$

It is easy to see that Schematic Paramodulation will contain the theory axiom, G_0^T and the following set of clauses

$$Nat(x) \neq True \parallel x \preceq c^\top$$
$$Nat(x) = True \parallel x \preceq c^\top$$
$$Nat(x) = True \vee Nat(y) \neq True \parallel x \preceq c^\top \wedge y \preceq c^\top$$

The saturated set is finite and does not contain the trivial equality $X = Y$. Thus the theory is stably infinite by Theorem 4.

6   Conclusion

We consider our work as an improvement and an extension of previous work. Our Schematic Paramodulation improves the meta-saturation of [6] in several ways. First, Schematic Paramodulation simulates every paramodulation inference unlike meta-saturation (cf. Example 1). Second, the *Schematic Deletion* rule makes Schematic Paramodulation halt more often than meta-saturation, and therefore allows us to prove decidability and stable infiniteness of theories for which meta-saturation fails (cf. Example 2). In [1] the authors define the class of variable-inactive theories so that modular termination of saturation holds. The work of [5] provides an automatic check of variable-inactivity condition of finitely presented theories and goes beyond that by showing that variable-inactive theories are actually stably infinite. The result about stable infiniteness of this paper generalizes the one of [5]. Theorem 4 demonstrates that it is, in fact, sufficient to only check whether the trivial equality $X = Y$ persists. Therefore, even when some theories are not variable-inactive we might still combine them using the Nelson-Oppen method because they might be stably infinite, as shown in Example 3. Furthermore, we could observe that no requirement is made on the selection function, but fairness. This should make clear that our method for automatically checking stable infiniteness is definitely much more general than the one proposed in [5].

Acknowledgments. We would like to thank Hélène Kirchner, Silvio Ranise, Christophe Ringeissen, Michaël Rusinowitch and the anonymous referees for their helpful comments and suggestions.

References

1. Armando, A., Bonacina, M.P., Ranise, S., Schulz, S.: On a Rewriting Approach to Satisfiability Procedures: Extension, Combination of Theories and an Experimental Appraisal. In: Gramlich, B. (ed.) Frontiers of Combining Systems. LNCS (LNAI), vol. 3717, pp. 65–80. Springer, Heidelberg (2005)
2. Armando, A., Ranise, S., Rusinowitch, M.: A Rewriting Approach to Satisfiability Procedures. Info. and Comp. 183(2), 140–164 (2003)
3. Bonacina, M.P., Ghilardi, S., Nicolini, E., Ranise, S., Zucchelli, D.: Decidability and Undecidability Results for Nelson-Oppen and Rewrite-Based Decision Procedures. In: Furbach, U., Shankar, N. (eds.) IJCAR 2006. LNCS (LNAI), vol. 4130, pp. 513–527. Springer, Heidelberg (2006)
4. Dershowitz, N., Jouannaud, J.-P.: Handbook of Theoretical Computer Science. In: Rewrite Systems, ch. 6, vol. B, pp. 244–320. Elsevier, North-Holland (1990)
5. Kirchner, H., Ranise, S., Ringeissen, C., Tran, D.-K.: Automatic Combinability of Rewriting-Based Satisfiability Procedures. In: Hermann, M., Voronkov, A. (eds.) LPAR 2006. LNCS (LNAI), vol. 4246, pp. 542–556. Springer, Heidelberg (2006)
6. Lynch, C., Morawska, B.: Automatic decidability. In: Proc. of 17th IEEE Symposium on Logic in Computer Science, Copenhagen, Copenhagen, Denmark, pages 7, IEEE Computer Society Press, Los Alamitos (2002)

7. Nelson, G., Oppen, D.C.: Simplification by cooperating decision procedures. ACM Trans. on Programming Languages and Systems 1(2), 245–257 (1979)
8. Nieuwenhuis, R., Rubio, A.: Paramodulation-based theorem proving. In: Robinson, A., Voronkov, A. (eds.) Handbook of Automated Reasoning, ch. 7, vol. I, pp. 371–443. Elsevier, North-Holland (2001)
9. van Dalen, D.: Logic and Structure, 2nd edn. Springer, Heidelberg (1989)
10. Weidenbach, C.: Spass version 0.49. Journal of Automated Reasoning 14(2), 247–252 (1997)

Designing Verification Conditions for Software

K. Rustan M. Leino

Microsoft Research, Redmond, WA, USA
leino@microsoft.com

Abstract. Software verification technology has the potential to improve the quality of software. The basic technique is to generate verification conditions for a given program and to discharge these proof obligations using a theorem prover. Encoding the verification conditions is a delicate process, not just because it must capture the intended programming semantics, but also because it must yield formulas that a theorem prover can process effectively.

In this talk, I will discuss the process of generating verification conditions in the program verifier for the object-oriented language Spec#. I will highlight design decisions we have made in modeling programs and targeting SMT solvers, lessons we have learned, and challenges that remain ahead.

F. Pfenning (Ed.): CADE 2007, LNAI 4603, p. 345, 2007.
© Springer-Verlag Berlin Heidelberg 2007

Encodings of Bounded LTL Model Checking in Effectively Propositional Logic

Juan Antonio Navarro-Pérez and Andrei Voronkov

The University of Manchester
School of Computer Science
{navarroj,voronkov}@cs.manchester.ac.uk

Abstract. We present an encoding of LTL bounded model checking problems within the Bernays-Schönfinkel fragment of first-order logic. This fragment, which also corresponds to the category of effectively propositional problems (EPR) of the CASC system competitions, allows a natural and succinct representation of both a software/hardware system and the property that one wants to verify.

The encoding for the transition system produces a formula whose size is linear with respect to its original description in common component description languages used in the field (e.g. smv format) preserving its modularity and hierarchical structure. Likewise, the LTL property is encoded in a formula of linear size with respect to the input formula, plus an additional component, with a size of $O(\log k)$ where k is the bound, that represents the execution flow of the system.

The encoding of bounded model checking problems by effectively propositional formulae is the main contribution of this paper. As a side effect, we obtain a rich collection of benchmarks with close links to real-life applications for the automated reasoning community.

1   Introduction

Model checking is a technique suitable for verifying that a hardware or software component works according to some formally specified expected behaviour. This is usually done by building a description of the system, often modelled as a finite state machine in a formal language suitable for further deployment, and using a temporal logic to specify properties that the system is expected to satisfy.

One of the first advances in model checking consists of the use of symbolic model checkers [9], where the transition system of the finite state machine is represented symbolically. These symbolic representations, which usually take the form of a binary decision diagram (BDD), provide significant improvements over previous techniques; but some formulae are still hard to encode succinctly using BDDs and, moreover, the encoding itself is often highly sensitive to the variable order used to create the representation.

Another significant achievement in the state of the art of model checking came when Biere et al. [1] proposed a technique now widely known as bounded model checking (BMC). In bounded model checking instead of trying to prove

F. Pfenning (Ed.): CADE 2007, LNAI 4603, pp. 346–361, 2007.
© Springer-Verlag Berlin Heidelberg 2007

the correctness of the given property, one searches for counterexamples within executions of the system of a bounded length. A propositional formula is created and a decision procedure for propositional logic, such as DPLL [5], is used to find models which in turn represent bugs in the system. When no models are found the bound is increased trying to search for longer counterexamples.

Although the basic method is not complete by itself, i.e. it can only disprove properties, it has been found as a useful tool for finding simple bugs in systems [1, 4, 11] and a good complement to other BDD based techniques. A significant amount of research has been spent recently on extending this technique to more expressive temporal logics [6], obtaining better propositional encodings [7], and proposing termination checks to regain completeness [10]. A recent survey on the state of the art is found in the work of Biere et al. [2].

Bounded model checking has been largely focused on generating and solving problems encoded in propositional logic. We observe, however, that BMC problems can also be easily and naturally encoded within the Bernays-Schönfinkel class of formulae. One of our motivations is to obtain a new source of problems for first-order reasoners able to decide the class. Problems in this class are also known as EPR (effectively propositional) problems in the CASC competition [12]. These problems are non-propositional but have a finite Herbrand Universe.

Moreover, we believe that the EPR encoding has several advantages over the propositional approach. First, it gives a more succinct and natural description of both the system and the property to verify. It is not needed, for example, to replicate copies of the temporal formula for every step of the execution trace. Furthermore, it is possible to directly translate systems descriptions written in a modular way, without requiring to flatten or expand module definitions before the encoding. A prover could potentially use this information to better organise the search for a proof or counterexample.

On the other hand, our encoding may also turn out to be useful for propositional, SAT-based, approaches to bounded model checking. Indeed, it preserves the structure of the original bounded model checking problem in the obtained effectively propositional formula and reduces the problem of finding an optimised propositional encoding to the problem of finding an optimised propositional instantiation of the EPR description.

After introducing a number of formal definitions in Section 2, we present in Section 3 two different encodings of linear temporal logic (LTL) into effectively propositional formulae. The first encoding takes an LTL formula and a bound k, and produces a set of constraints that captures the execution paths satisfying the temporal property. The second encoding is an improvement that produces two sets of constraints: one that depends on the LTL formula only (i.e. not the bound) and its output is linear with respect to its input; and another, with a size of $O(k)$, that depends on the bound k only. Compare with propositional encodings where, if n is the size of the LTL formula, the output is typically of size $O(nk)$ instead of $O(n + k)$ with our approach. Furthermore, with a binary encoding of states, the size of the later component can be reduced to $O(\log^2 k)$.

We also present, in Section 4, an approach to the encoding of modular descriptions of model checking problems preserving their modularity and hierarchical representation. We show in particular how several features of a software/hardware description language such as smv [3] can be easily represented within the effectively propositional fragment. Using the ideas depicted here, it is also possible to develop a tool to automatically translate system descriptions in industry standard formats (e.g. smv or verilog) into a format such as tptp [13] suitable for consumption by first order theorem provers.

2   Background

In this section we introduce the main formal definitions that are used throughout this paper. We first define the linear temporal logic (LTL) in a way that closely follows the standard definitions found in literature but with a few modifications to better represent the notion of bounded executions.

Definition 1. Let $\mathcal{V} = \{p_1, \ldots, p_n\}$ be a set of elements called *state variables*. A subset $s \subseteq \mathcal{V}$ is known as a *state*.

A *path* $\pi = s_0 s_1 \ldots$ is a, finite or infinite, sequence of states. The *length* of a finite path $\pi = s_0 \ldots s_k$, denoted by $|\pi|$, is $k + 1$; while, for an infinite path, we define $|\pi| = \omega$, where $\omega > k$ for every number k.

A *k-path* is either a finite path of the form $\pi = s_0 \ldots s_k$, or an infinite path with a loop of the form $\pi = s_0 \ldots s_{l-1} s_l \ldots s_k s_l \ldots s_k \ldots$, in the sequel also written as $\pi = s_0 \ldots s_{l-1} (s_l \ldots s_k)^\omega$.   □

We will assume that system executions are always infinite paths, i.e. there are no deadlock states. Finite paths, however, are also needed to represent the prefix of an execution of the system up to a bounded length. With this intuition in mind we now define the semantics of LTL formulae in negation normal form; these are formulae built using propositional and temporal connectives, but negation is only allowed in front of atomic propositions.

Definition 2. A path $\pi = s_0, s_1, \ldots$ is a *model* of an LTL formula ϕ at a state s_i, where $i < |\pi|$, denoted by $\pi \models_i \phi$, if

$$
\begin{aligned}
&\pi \models_i p &&\text{iff} &&p \in s_i, \\
&\pi \models_i \neg p &&\text{iff} &&p \notin s_i, \\
&\pi \models_i \psi \wedge \phi &&\text{iff} &&\pi \models_i \psi \text{ and } \pi \models_i \phi, \\
&\pi \models_i \psi \vee \phi &&\text{iff} &&\pi \models_i \psi \text{ or } \pi \models_i \phi, \\
&\pi \models_i \mathbf{X}\phi &&\text{iff} &&i + 1 < |\pi| \text{ and } \pi \models_{i+1} \phi, \\
&\pi \models_i \mathbf{F}\phi &&\text{iff} &&\exists j, i \leq j < |\pi|, \pi \models_j \phi, \\
&\pi \models_i \psi \mathbf{W}\phi &&\text{iff} &&\text{either: } \pi \text{ is infinite and } \forall j, i \leq j, \pi \models_j \psi, \\
& && &&\text{or: } \exists j', i \leq j' < |\pi|, \pi \models_{j'} \phi \text{ and } \forall j, i \leq j < j', \pi \models_j \psi.
\end{aligned}
$$

Also π is a model of $\top$ for every state s_i with $i < |\pi|$, and of $\bot$ for no state. We write $\pi \models \phi$ to denote $\pi \models_0 \phi$.   □

Note that we introduced the *weak until*, $\mathbf{W}$, as a primary connective of our temporal logic. Other standard temporal connectives —such as *until*, *release* and *globally*— can be introduced as abbreviations of the other existing connectives: $\psi \mathbf{U} \phi = \mathbf{F} \phi \wedge (\psi \mathbf{W} \phi)$, $\psi \mathbf{R} \phi = \phi \mathbf{W} (\psi \wedge \phi)$, and $\mathbf{G} \phi = \phi \mathbf{W} \bot$.

If we consider infinite paths only, then the definition given matches the standard definition of LTL that can be found in literature; in particular dualities such as $\neg \mathbf{F} \phi \equiv \mathbf{G} \neg \phi$ do hold. Since we assume that system executions are always infinite, one can make use of these identities to put formulae into negation normal form without any loss of generality.

The finite case is defined so that if $\pi \models_i \phi$ then, for all possible infinite paths π' extending π, it is also the case that $\pi' \models_i \phi$. Here we deviate a little from usual definitions of LTL and dualities such as the above-mentioned do not hold anymore. For example, neither $\mathbf{F} \phi$ nor $\mathbf{G} \neg \phi$ hold in a finite path where $\neg \phi$ holds at all states. In particular, since finite paths in the temporal logic defined are interpreted as prefixes of longer paths, one cannot write a formula to test for the end of a path.

Definition 3. A *Kripke structure* over a set of state variables $\mathcal{V}$ is a tuple $M = (S, I, T)$ where $S = 2^{\mathcal{V}}$ is the set of all states, $I \subseteq S$ is a set whose elements are called *initial states*, and T is a binary relation on states, $T \subseteq S \times S$, called the *transition relation* of the system. We also make the assumption that the transition relation is total, i.e. for every state $s \in S$ there is a state $s' \in S$ such that $(s, s') \in T$.

A *path* $\pi = s_0 s_1 \ldots$ *is in the structure* M if $s_0 \in I$ and for every $0 < i < |\pi|$ we have $(s_{i-1}, s_i) \in T$. We say that a path π in M is a *prefix path* if it is finite, and a *proper path* otherwise.

An LTL formula ϕ is *satisfiable* in a Kripke structure M if there is a proper path π in M such that $\pi \models \phi$. Similarly, a formula ϕ is *valid* in M if, for every proper path π in M, $\pi \models \phi$. □

Note that, if π is a prefix path in M and $\pi \models \phi$, then for every extension π' of π we also have $\pi' \models \phi$, thus prefix paths are enough for testing satisfiability. Observe, however, that formulae such as $\mathbf{G} \psi$ or $\psi \mathbf{W} \phi$ (where ϕ never holds) are never satisfied by (finite) prefix paths.

We proceed now to formally introduce the fragment of quantifier free predicate logic which is the target language of our main translation. This fragment, also known as the Bernays-Schönfinkel class of formulae, does not allow the use of function symbols or arbitrary quantification. Only variables and constant symbols are allowed as terms, and variables are assumed to be universally quantified. We also define its semantics using Herbrand interpretations.

Definition 4. We assume given a set of *predicate symbols* $\mathcal{P}$, a finite set of *constant symbols* $\mathcal{D} = \{\mathsf{s}_0, \ldots, \mathsf{s}_k\}$, and a set of *variables* which we will usually denote by uppercase letters: $X, Y, \ldots$. The set $\mathcal{D}$ is sometimes referred to as the *domain* of the logic. A *term* is either a variable or a constant symbol. An *atom* is an expression of the form $\mathsf{p}(t_1, \ldots, t_n)$ where $\mathsf{p} \in \mathcal{P}$ and each t_i is a term. A *ground atom* is an atom all whose terms are constant symbols.

Quantifier-free predicate formulae are built from atoms using the standard propositional connectives ($\top$, $\bot$, $\wedge$, $\vee$, $\neg$). Other connectives can be introduced as abbreviations: $F \rightarrow G \equiv \neg F \vee G$. A *ground formula* is a formula built using only ground atoms. A *ground instance* of a formula F is any ground formula obtained by uniformly replacing the variables in F with constant symbols.

A *Herbrand interpretation* is a set of ground atoms. The notion of whether a Herbrand interpretation $\mathcal{I}$ is a *model* of a ground formula F, denoted by $\mathcal{I} \models F$, is defined in the usual way:

$$\begin{array}{llll}
\mathcal{I} \models A & \text{iff} \quad A \in \mathcal{I}, & \mathcal{I} \models F \wedge G & \text{iff} \quad \mathcal{I} \models F \text{ and } \mathcal{I} \models G, \\
\mathcal{I} \models \neg F & \text{iff} \quad \mathcal{I} \not\models F, & \mathcal{I} \models F \vee G & \text{iff} \quad \mathcal{I} \models F \text{ or } \mathcal{I} \models G.
\end{array}$$

Also $\mathcal{I}$ is always a model of $\top$ and never of $\bot$. Now a Herbrand interpretation $\mathcal{I}$ is said to be a *model of a non-ground formula* F if it is a model of every ground instance of F, and a model of a set of formulae if it is a model of every formula in the set. A set of formulae, also referred to as a *set of constraints*, is called *satisfiable* if it has at least one model.   □

Since we will only be dealing with quantifier-free formulae and Herbrand interpretations, we will often simply say *predicate formula* when we refer to a quantifier-free predicate formula and *interpretation* when we refer to a Herbrand interpretation. Also note that, while the symbol s_i represents a state in a path, s_i represents a constant symbol in a predicate formulae. The similar notation was chosen intentionally since a constant s_i will be used as a symbolic representation of a state s_i. The intended meaning should always be clear by context, but a different typeface is also used as a hint to distinguish the two possibilities.

Similarly, it is assumed throughout this paper that $\mathcal{P}$ contains a unary predicate symbol p for every state variable $p \in \mathcal{V}$. The atom $\mathsf{p}(\mathsf{s}_i)$ symbolically represents the fact that a variable p is true at the state s_i of a path (i.e. $p \in s_i$), and the symbol $\mathcal{P}_\mathcal{V}$ denotes the set of predicates representing state variables. Our next aim is to define a notion of symbolic representation of Kripke structures along the lines of representations commonly used in the propositional case.

Let us define the *canonical first-order structure* for $\mathcal{P}_\mathcal{V}$, denoted by $C_\mathcal{V}$. This structure is an interpretation which, instead of the symbolic representations s_i used elsewhere, draws constant symbols from the domain $2^\mathcal{V}$, its signature the set of predicate symbols $\mathcal{P}_\mathcal{V}$, and the interpretation of every predicate $\mathsf{p} \in \mathcal{P}_\mathcal{V}$ is defined as $C_\mathcal{V} \models \mathsf{p}(s)$ iff $p \in s$.

Definition 5. Let $I(X)$ and $T(X, Y)$ be predicate formulae of variables X and X, Y, respectively, using predicate symbols $\mathcal{P}_\mathcal{V}$ and no constants. We say that this pair of formulae *symbolically represents* a Kripke structure M if

1. a state s is an initial state of M iff $C_\mathcal{V} \models I(s)$.
2. a pair (s, s') belongs to the transition relation of M iff $C_\mathcal{V} \models T(s, s')$.   □

The idea used in this definition extends to represent paths in a Kripke structure M by Herbrand interpretations as follows.

Definition 6. Given an interpretation $\mathcal{I}$ over the domain $\mathcal{D} = \{s_0, \ldots, s_k\}$, we define *the k-path induced by* $\mathcal{I}$, denoted by $\pi^{\mathcal{I}}$, by $\pi^{\mathcal{I}} = s_0^{\mathcal{I}} \ldots s_k^{\mathcal{I}}$, where $s_i^{\mathcal{I}} = \{p \in \mathcal{V} \mid \mathcal{I} \models p(s_i)\}$, for all $0 \leq i \leq k$. We will rather informally refer to the states $s_i^{\mathcal{I}}$ as *induced states*. For the induced k-path $\pi^{\mathcal{I}}$ we will often omit the superscripts on the induced states and simply write $\pi^{\mathcal{I}} = s_0 \ldots s_k$.

Given a value l with $0 \leq l \leq k$, we also introduce the notation $\pi^{l,\mathcal{I}}$ to denote the infinite k-path $s_0 \ldots s_{l-1}(s_l \ldots s_k)^{\omega}$ with a loop starting at s_l. □

In the sequel we will assume that the set of initial states I and the transition relation T of our Kripke structures are always symbolically described in this way. Also, we will normally consider only interpretations $\mathcal{I}$ over the domain $\mathcal{D} = \{s_0, \ldots, s_k\}$. Then $s_i^{\mathcal{I}}$ means the induced state along the k-path $s_0^{\mathcal{I}}, \ldots, s_k^{\mathcal{I}}$ induced by $\mathcal{I}$. Definition 6 immediately implies the following fact.

Lemma 1. *Let $M = (S, I, T)$ be a Kripke structure and $\mathcal{I}$ an interpretation.*

1. *$\mathcal{I} \models I(s_i)$ iff $s_i^{\mathcal{I}}$ is an initial state of M.*
2. *$\mathcal{I} \models T(s_i, s_j)$ iff $(s_i^{\mathcal{I}}, s_j^{\mathcal{I}})$ belongs to the transition relation of M.* □

3 Encoding of Temporal Properties

In this section we present a translation that allows one to encode an LTL formula as a quantifier free predicate formula. Following the results from Biere et al. [1], it has been shown that, if one wants to check the satisfiability of an LTL formula, it is enough to search for k-paths that satisfy this formula.

Theorem 1 (Biere et al. [1]). *An LTL formula ϕ is satisfiable in a Kripke structure M iff, for some k, there is a k-path π in M with $\pi \models \phi$.* □

Our translation makes use of this result by creating, for a given value k and a Kripke structure M, a predicate formula whose models correspond to k-paths of the system satisfying the original LTL formula (the details of such correspondence are given later in Proposition 2). We give a set of constraints that characterise the k-paths of Kripke structures and define some auxiliary symbols, which are used later in the translation.

Definition 7. Let $M = (S, I, T)$ be a Kripke structure, and also let $k \geq 0$. The *predicate encoding of k-paths*, denoted by $\|[\,k\,]\|$, is defined as the set of constraints:

$$\mathsf{succ}(s_0, s_1)$$
$$\mathsf{succ}(s_1, s_2)$$
$$\ldots$$
$$\mathsf{succ}(s_{k-1}, s_k)$$
$$\mathsf{succ}(X, Y) \rightarrow \mathsf{less}(X, Y)$$
$$\mathsf{succ}(X, Y) \wedge \mathsf{less}(Y, Z) \rightarrow \mathsf{less}(X, Z)$$
$$\mathsf{succ}(X, Y) \rightarrow \mathsf{trans}(X, Y)$$
$$\mathsf{hasloop} \rightarrow \mathsf{trans}(s_k, s_0) \vee \cdots \vee \mathsf{trans}(s_k, s_k)$$

And the *predicate encoding* of the structure M, denoted by $\|[M]\|$, is defined as:

$$\mathsf{trans}(X, Y) \to T(X, Y)$$
$$I(\mathsf{s_0})$$

We also define $\|[M, k]\| = \|[M]\| \cup \|[k]\|$. Note that the predicates $\mathsf{succ}(X, Y)$, $\mathsf{less}(X, Y)$, $\mathsf{trans}(X, Y)$ and $\mathsf{hasloop}$ are fresh new predicates not in $\mathcal{P_V}$. $\qquad \square$

The intuition behind the predicates introduced in the previous definition is to model paths in the Kripke structure. It easily follows, for example, that if an interpretation $\mathcal{I}$ satisfies $\mathsf{trans}(\mathsf{s}_i, \mathsf{s}_j)$ then the pair $(s_i^{\mathcal{I}}, s_j^{\mathcal{I}})$ is in the transition relation of the structure. The encoding of temporal formulae can then use the $\mathsf{hasloop}$ predicate as a trigger to enforce paths accepted as models to be infinite, since it would make $\mathsf{trans}(\mathsf{s}_k, \mathsf{s}_l)$ true for some l. The following proposition summarises important properties of the models of $\|[M, k]\|$.

Proposition 1. *Let M be a Kripke structure, and let $\mathcal{I}$ be a model of the set of constraints $\|[M, k]\|$. Then for every $0 \leq i, j, l \leq k$:*

1. *If $i < j$ then $\mathcal{I} \models \mathsf{less}(\mathsf{s}_i, \mathsf{s}_j)$.*
2. *The induced k-path $\pi^{\mathcal{I}} = s_0 \ldots s_k$ is a finite path in M.*
3. *If $\mathcal{I} \models \mathsf{trans}(\mathsf{s}_k, \mathsf{s}_l)$ then the induced k-path $\pi^{l, \mathcal{I}} = s_0 \ldots s_{l-1}(s_l \ldots s_k)^{\omega}$ is an infinite path in M.* $\qquad \square$

The following two definitions give the translation of an LTL formula ϕ into a predicate encoding following an approach similar to structural clause form translations: a new predicate symbol is first introduced to represent each subformula, here denoted by $\Theta_\phi(X)$ in Definition 8, and then a set of constraints, given in Definition 9, are added to give $\Theta_\phi(X)$ its intended meaning.

Definition 8. We define the *symbolic representation* of an LTL formula γ, a predicate formula $\Theta_\gamma(X)$, as follows:

$$\Theta_\top(X) = \top \qquad\qquad \Theta_\bot(X) = \bot$$
$$\Theta_p(X) = \mathsf{p}(X) \qquad\qquad \Theta_{\neg p}(X) = \neg \mathsf{p}(X)$$
$$\Theta_{\psi \wedge \phi}(X) = \Theta_\psi(X) \wedge \Theta_\phi(X) \qquad\qquad \Theta_{\psi \vee \phi}(X) = \Theta_\psi(X) \vee \Theta_\phi(X)$$
$$\Theta_{\mathbf{X}\phi}(X) = \mathsf{next}_\phi(X) \qquad\qquad \Theta_{\mathbf{F}\phi}(X) = \mathsf{evently}_\phi(X)$$
$$\Theta_{\psi \mathbf{W} \phi}(X) = \mathsf{weak}_{\psi, \phi}(X)$$

where $\mathsf{next}_\phi(X)$, $\mathsf{evently}_\phi(X)$ and $\mathsf{weak}_{\psi, \phi}(X)$ are fresh new predicates, not already in $\mathcal{P_V}$, introduced as needed for subformulae of γ. $\qquad \square$

Definition 9. For every pair of LTL formulae ψ, ϕ and a value $k \geq 0$, we define the following sets of constraints:

$\Phi_{\mathbf{X}\phi}^k$: x1: $\mathsf{next}_\phi(X) \wedge \mathsf{trans}(X, Y) \to \Theta_\phi(Y)$
$\qquad$ x2: $\mathsf{next}_\phi(\mathsf{s}_k) \to \mathsf{hasloop}$

$\Phi^k_{\mathbf{F}\phi}$:   f1: $\mathsf{evently}_\phi(X) \rightarrow \mathsf{event}_\phi(X, \mathsf{s}_0) \vee \cdots \vee \mathsf{event}_\phi(X, \mathsf{s}_k)$
     f2: $\mathsf{event}_\phi(X, Y) \rightarrow \Theta_\phi(Y)$
     f3: $\mathsf{event}_\phi(X, Y) \wedge \mathsf{less}(Y, X) \rightarrow \mathsf{hasloop}$
     f4: $\mathsf{event}_\phi(X, Y) \wedge \mathsf{less}(Y, X) \wedge \mathsf{trans}(\mathsf{s}_k, L) \wedge \mathsf{less}(Y, L) \rightarrow \bot$

$\Phi^k_{\psi\mathbf{W}\phi}$: w1: $\mathsf{weak}_{\psi,\phi}(X) \rightarrow \Theta_\phi(X) \vee \mathsf{xweak}_{\psi,\phi}(X)$
     w2: $\mathsf{xweak}_{\psi,\phi}(X) \wedge \mathsf{trans}(X, Y) \rightarrow \mathsf{weak}_{\psi,\phi}(Y)$
     w3: $\mathsf{xweak}_{\psi,\phi}(X) \rightarrow \Theta_\psi(X)$
     w4: $\mathsf{xweak}_{\psi,\phi}(\mathsf{s}_k) \rightarrow \mathsf{hasloop}$

Again $\mathsf{event}_\phi(X, Y)$ and $\mathsf{xweak}_{\psi,\phi}(X)$ are fresh new predicates not in $\mathcal{P_V}$.

We finally introduce the set of *structural definitions* of an LTL formula γ (with depth k), denoted by $\|[\gamma, k]\|$, as the union of the sets Φ^k_ϕ for every temporal subformula ϕ of the original γ.   □

Later in Proposition 2 we show how the models of such formulae relate to the k-paths satisfying an LTL formula. We need first to introduce the concept of a *rolling function* which will be used as a tool in the proof of such proposition.

Definition 10. Given a k-path π we define its *rolling function* δ, a function defined for every $0 \leq i < |\pi|$ and with range $\{0, \ldots k\}$, as follows:

– If π is of the form $s_0 \ldots s_{l-1}(s_l \ldots s_k)^\omega$, then

$$\delta(i) = \begin{cases} i & i \leq k \\ l + [(i - l) \bmod (k + 1 - l)] & \text{otherwise} . \end{cases}$$

– Otherwise, if $\pi = s_0 \ldots s_k$, then $\delta(i) = i$ for every $0 \leq i < |\pi|$.   □

The rolling function is a notational convenience used to unfold an infinite k-path $\pi = s_0 \ldots s_{l-1}(s_l \ldots s_k)^\omega$ as the sequence $\pi = s_{\delta(0)} s_{\delta(1)} \ldots$, without explicitly showing the loop. We emphasise the fact that the rolling function is defined only when $0 \leq i < |\pi|$; in particular, if π is finite, the function is not defined for indices outside of the path. Also notice that, for both finite and infinite paths, the rolling function acts as the identity for all i with $0 \leq i \leq k$. Moreover, for $0 \leq i < |\pi|$, it is always the case that $s_i = s_{\delta(i)}$; in fact, the following stronger result holds.

Lemma 2. *Let π be a k-path, ϕ an LTL formula, $i < |\pi|$ and δ the rolling function of π. Then it follows that $\pi \models_i \phi$ if and only if $\pi \models_{\delta(i)} \phi$.*   □

We can now prove one of the main propositions, which shows how from models of the encoded formula, one can obtain a k-path in the given Kripke structure that, moreover, satisfies the original LTL formula at a particular state.

Proposition 2. *Let M be a Kripke structure, γ an LTL formula, and $\mathcal{I}$ a model of the formula $\|[M, k]\| \cup \|[\gamma, k]\|$ with domain $D = \{s_0, \ldots, s_k\}$. We define a path π according to the following two cases:*

1. If $\mathcal{I} \models \mathsf{trans}(\mathsf{s}_k, \mathsf{s}_l)$, for some $0 \leq l \leq k$, then let $\pi = \pi^{l,\mathcal{I}}$ for any such l.
2. If $\mathcal{I} \not\models \mathsf{trans}(\mathsf{s}_k, \mathsf{s}_l)$, for every $0 \leq l \leq k$, then let $\pi = \pi^{\mathcal{I}}$.

Let $i < |\pi|$, and let δ be the rolling function of π. If $\mathcal{I} \models \Theta_\gamma(\mathsf{s}_{\delta(i)})$ then $\pi \models_i \gamma$.
□

The previous proposition shows that, under the given assumptions, if we have $\mathcal{I} \models \Theta_\phi(\mathsf{s}_{\delta(i)})$ then there is a path π, determined by $\mathcal{I}$, such that $\pi \models_i \phi$. Note, however, that the converse is not always true, e.g. $\mathcal{I} \not\models \Theta_\phi(\mathsf{s}_{\delta(i)})$ does not necessarily imply $\pi \not\models_i \phi$ for the possible induced paths.

Additional constraints could be added to the set $\|[\phi, k]\|$ in order to make the converse hold but, since we are mostly interested in satisfiability of the LTL formulae, this is not required for the correctness of our main result. Whether the addition of such constraints would be helpful for the solvers to find solutions more quickly, is an interesting question for further research.

What we do need to show is that, if there is a path that satisfies an LTL formula, we can also find an interpretation that satisfies its symbolic representation. The following definition shows how to build such an interpretation and later in Proposition 3 we prove that it serves the required purpose.

Definition 11. Let π be a k-path and δ its rolling function. We define an interpretation $\mathcal{I}^\pi$ with domain $D = \{\mathsf{s}_0, \ldots, \mathsf{s}_k\}$, for every $\mathsf{s}_i, \mathsf{s}_j \in D$ and pair of LTL formulae ψ, ϕ, as follows:

$$
\begin{aligned}
\mathcal{I}^\pi &\models \mathsf{p}(\mathsf{s}_i) & &\text{iff} & &p \in s_i, \text{ for } p \in \mathcal{V}. \\
\mathcal{I}^\pi &\models \mathsf{less}(\mathsf{s}_i, \mathsf{s}_j) & &\text{iff} & &i < j. \\
\mathcal{I}^\pi &\models \mathsf{succ}(\mathsf{s}_i, \mathsf{s}_j) & &\text{iff} & &i + 1 = j. \\
\mathcal{I}^\pi &\models \mathsf{trans}(\mathsf{s}_i, \mathsf{s}_j) & &\text{iff} & &\delta(i + 1) = j. \\
\mathcal{I}^\pi &\models \mathsf{hasloop} & &\text{iff} & &\pi \text{ is an infinite path.} \\
\mathcal{I}^\pi &\models \mathsf{next}_\phi(\mathsf{s}_i) & &\text{iff} & &\pi \models_i \mathbf{X}\phi. \\
\mathcal{I}^\pi &\models \mathsf{evently}_\phi(\mathsf{s}_i) & &\text{iff} & &\pi \models_i \mathbf{F}\phi. \\
\mathcal{I}^\pi &\models \mathsf{event}_\phi(\mathsf{s}_i, \mathsf{s}_j) & &\text{iff} & &\pi \models_j \phi \text{ and there is a } j' \geq i \text{ with } \delta(j') = j. \\
\mathcal{I}^\pi &\models \mathsf{weak}_{\psi,\phi}(\mathsf{s}_i) & &\text{iff} & &\pi \models_i \psi\mathbf{W}\phi. \\
\mathcal{I}^\pi &\models \mathsf{xweak}_{\psi,\phi}(\mathsf{s}_i) & &\text{iff} & &\pi \models_i \psi\mathbf{W}\phi \wedge \neg\phi.
\end{aligned}
$$
□

Proposition 3. Let π be a k-path in a Kripke structure M, and δ its rolling function. Also let γ be an arbitrary LTL formula, and let $i < |\pi|$.

1. $\mathcal{I}^\pi \models \Theta_\gamma(\mathsf{s}_{\delta(i)})$ iff $\pi \models_i \gamma$,
2. $\mathcal{I}^\pi \models \|[M, k]\| \cup \|[\gamma, k]\|$.
□

With this results being put in place we can now show, in Theorem 2, how the problem of testing the satisfiability of an LTL formula in a Kripke structure can be translated into the problem of checking satisfiability of predicate formulae.

Definition 12. Let M be a Kripke structure, ϕ an LTL formula and $k \geq 0$. The *predicate encoding* of M and ϕ (with depth k), denoted by $\|[M, \phi, k]\|$, is defined as the set of constraints $\|[M, k]\| \cup \|[\phi, k]\| \cup \{\Theta_\phi(\mathsf{s}_0)\}$.
□

Theorem 2. *Let ϕ be an LTL formula, and M a Kripke structure.*

1. ϕ is satisfiable in M iff $\|[\,M, \phi, k\,]\|$ is satisfiable for some $k \geq 0$.
2. ϕ is valid in M iff $\|[\,M, \mathsf{NNF}(\neg\phi), k\,]\|$ is unsatisfiable for every $k \geq 0$.   □

3.1 Implicit Bound Encoding

As can be seen in Definition 9, the encoding just presented makes explicit use of the bound k in order to build the symbolic representation of an LTL formula. Notice that, in particular, a constraint of size $O(k)$ is created for every subformula of the form $\mathbf{F}\phi$ of the property to be checked. In this section we present an alternate encoding, which only uses the bound in an implicit way.

Definition 13. Given pair of LTL formulae ψ, ϕ, we define the following sets of constraints:

$\Phi'_{\mathbf{F}\phi}$: f1': $\mathsf{evently}_\phi(X) \rightarrow \Theta_\phi(X) \vee \mathsf{xevently}_\phi(X)$
       f2': $\mathsf{xevently}_\phi(X) \wedge \mathsf{succ}(X,Y) \rightarrow \mathsf{evently}_\phi(Y)$
       f3': $\mathsf{xevently}_\phi(X) \wedge \mathsf{last}(X) \rightarrow \mathsf{hasloop}$
       f4': $\mathsf{xevently}_\phi(X) \wedge \mathsf{last}(X) \wedge \mathsf{trans}(X,Y) \rightarrow \mathsf{evently2}_\phi(Y)$

       f5': $\mathsf{evently2}_\phi(X) \rightarrow \Theta_\phi(X) \vee \mathsf{xevently2}_\phi(X)$
       f6': $\mathsf{xevently2}_\phi(X) \wedge \mathsf{succ}(X,Y) \rightarrow \mathsf{evently2}_\phi(Y)$
       f7': $\mathsf{xevently2}_\phi(X) \wedge \mathsf{last}(X) \rightarrow \bot$

The sets $\Phi'_{\mathbf{X}\phi}$ and $\Phi'_{\psi\mathbf{W}\phi}$ are identical to $\Phi^k_{\mathbf{X}\phi}$ and $\Phi^k_{\psi\mathbf{W}\phi}$, except for the following constraints which replace x2 and w4 respectively.

$\Phi'_{\mathbf{X}\phi}$: x2': $\mathsf{next}_\phi(X) \wedge \mathsf{last}(X) \rightarrow \mathsf{hasloop}$

$\Phi'_{\psi\mathbf{W}\phi}$: w4': $\mathsf{xweak}_{\psi,\phi}(X) \wedge \mathsf{last}(X) \rightarrow \mathsf{hasloop}$

   We finally introduce the set of *implicit structural definitions* of an LTL formula γ, denoted simply by $\|[\,\gamma\,]\|$, as the union of the sets Φ'_ϕ for every temporal subformula ϕ of the original γ.   □

Note that the newly defined sets Φ'_ϕ, do not explicitly use the value of the bound k anymore. We replaced the explicit references to s_k with a predicate $\mathsf{last}(X)$ which should be made true for the constant symbol representing the last state. Moreover, since the size of $\Phi'_{\mathbf{F}\phi}$ is constant, the size of the encoding $\|[\,\gamma\,]\|$ is now linear with respect to the size of γ.

   The k-paths that satisfy an LTL formula ϕ can therefore now be captured with the set of constraints $\|[\,k\,]\| \cup \{\mathsf{last}(\mathsf{s}_k)\} \cup \|[\,\phi\,]\| \cup \{\Theta_\phi(\mathsf{s}_0)\}$. This representation is convenient since it breaks the encoding in two independent parts, one depending on the bound only and the other on the LTL formula only. Moreover it has a size of $O(n + k)$ where n is the size of the original temporal formula.

   A complete instance of the bounded model checking problem would be then represented, analogous to Definition 12, as

$$\|[\,M, \phi, k\,]\|^* = \|[\,M\,]\| \cup \|[\,k\,]\| \cup \{\mathsf{last}(\mathsf{s}_k)\} \cup \|[\,\phi\,]\| \cup \{\Theta_\phi(\mathsf{s}_0)\}$$

and, for such set of constraints, the statement of Theorem 2 also holds.

This encoding is particularly useful when searching for counterexamples in an incremental setting, since both the system description and the temporal formula have to be encoded only once. Just the small set $\|[k]\| \cup \{\mathsf{last}(\mathsf{s}_k)\}$ needs to be updated while testing for increasing bounds. If we are using a model finder that supports incremental solving features, then one only needs to add $\mathsf{succ}(\mathsf{s}_k, \mathsf{s}_{k+1})$ and replace $\mathsf{last}(\mathsf{s}_k)$ with $\mathsf{last}(\mathsf{s}_{k+1})$.

3.2 Logarithmic Encoding of States

As can be seen in the previous section, the only part of the translation where there is an increase of size with respect to the input is in $\|[k]\|$, because of the series of facts of the form $\mathsf{succ}(\mathsf{s}_i, \mathsf{s}_{i+1})$ and the constraint

$$\mathsf{hasloop} \rightarrow \mathsf{trans}(\mathsf{s}_k, \mathsf{s}_0) \vee \cdots \vee \mathsf{trans}(\mathsf{s}_k, \mathsf{s}_k) \ . \tag{1}$$

This group of constraints, which is of size $O(k)$, can be more compactly encoded by representing the names of states in binary notation. For this we introduce a pair of constant symbols $\{\mathsf{b0}, \mathsf{b1}\}$ so that we can write, for example when $k = 2^4$, the following definition for the succ predicate:

$$\mathsf{succ}(\,X_3, X_2, X_1, \mathsf{b0}\,,\,X_3, X_2, X_1, \mathsf{b1}\,)$$
$$\mathsf{succ}(\,X_3, X_2, \mathsf{b0}\,, \mathsf{b1}\,,\,X_3, X_2, \mathsf{b1}\,, \mathsf{b0}\,)$$
$$\mathsf{succ}(\,X_3, \mathsf{b0}\,, \mathsf{b1}\,, \mathsf{b1}\,,\,X_3, \mathsf{b1}\,, \mathsf{b0}\,, \mathsf{b0}\,)$$
$$\mathsf{succ}(\,\mathsf{b0}\,, \mathsf{b1}\,, \mathsf{b1}\,, \mathsf{b1}\,,\,\mathsf{b1}\,, \mathsf{b0}\,, \mathsf{b0}\,, \mathsf{b0}\,)$$

In general we only need $w = \lceil \log k \rceil$ constraints, with a total size of $O(\log^2 k)$. On the other hand, the constraint (1) can be rewritten as:

$$\mathsf{hasloop} \rightarrow \mathsf{loopafter}(\overline{\mathsf{b0}})$$
$$\mathsf{loopafter}(\overline{X}) \wedge \mathsf{last}(\overline{Y}) \rightarrow \mathsf{trans}(\overline{Y}, \overline{X}) \vee \mathsf{xloopafter}(\overline{X})$$
$$\mathsf{xloopafter}(\overline{X}) \wedge \mathsf{succ}(\overline{X}, \overline{Y}) \rightarrow \mathsf{loopafter}(\overline{Y})$$
$$\mathsf{xloopafter}(\overline{X}) \wedge \mathsf{last}(\overline{X}) \rightarrow \bot$$

where $\overline{\mathsf{b0}}$ is a string of w symbols $\mathsf{b0}$, $\overline{X} = X_{w-1}, \dots, X_0$ and similarly for $\overline{Y}$.

One also has to replace everywhere else occurrences of s_0 with $\overline{\mathsf{b0}}$, the constant symbol s_k with its binary representation (e.g. for $k = 13$ use $\mathsf{b1}, \mathsf{b1}, \mathsf{b0}, \mathsf{b1}$), and variables such as X and Y with the corresponding $\overline{X}$ or $\overline{Y}$. The resulting set of constraints, which we denote by $\|[M, k, \phi]\|^b$, is of size $O(n \log k + \log^2 k)$, where n is the compound size of M and ϕ, and satisfies the statement of Theorem 2.

4   Encoding of the System Description

Generating an instance of the bounded model checking problem requires three parameters as input: a system description M, a temporal formula ϕ and a bound k. In the previous section we showed how to encode an LTL formula as a predicate formula (w.r.t. the bound), but we generally assumed that the system (a Kripke structure M) was already symbolically described.

In this section we deal with how a system, which is originally given in some industry standard format suitable to describe software/hardware components, can be also be encoded in the form of a predicate formula. An advantage of using a predicate rather than a propositional encoding is that important features for component development, such as the ability to describe systems in a modular and hierarchical way, can be directly represented in the target language. There is no need, for example, to perform a flattening phase to create and instantiate all modules of a system description before doing the actual encoding.

We will show now, by means of an example, how a system described in the smv language can be succinctly and naturally encoded within the effectively propositional fragment. Although we would prefer to formally define the fragment of smv considered here, the number of different smv variants and the lack of documentation on the formal semantics in existing implementations made this task particularly difficult. Anyway, the explanation of the ideas presented in this section is always general enough so that they can be applied to other arbitrary systems, not only the one in the example, and even implemented to be performed in an automated way.

For our running example we consider a distributed mutual exclusion (DME) circuit first described by Martin [8] and then made available in the smv format with the distribution of the NuSMV model checker [3]. The system description is fragmented in a number of modules, each being a separate unit specifying how a section of the system works. The DME, for example, organises modules in a hierarchical way: the most basic modules are *gates* which perform simple logical operations, then a number of gate modules are replicated and assembled together to form the module of a *cell*, finally a number of cells are also replicated and linked together in the *main* module which represents the entire system.

4.1 Module Variables

A module usually defines a number of variables and describe how their values change in time. In the DME example, a typical gate module looks like:

```
module and−gate(in1,in2)
var
   out: boolean;
assign
   init(out) := 0;
   next(out) := (in1 & in2) union out;
```

This is a module named 'and−gate' which defines two boolean variables as input ('in1' and 'in2') and an output boolean variable ('out'). The initialisation part causes the output of all 'and−gate' instances to hold the value zero (i.e. false) when the system starts to execute. At each step the module nondeterministically chooses to compute the logical and of its inputs and update the output, or keep the output from the last clock cycle.[1] Note that this is the model of

---

[1] The '**union**' operator in smv effectively creates a set out of its two operands and nondeterministically chooses an element of the set as the result of the expression.

an asynchronous logic gate; fairness constraints (which can also be encoded as LTL formulae) could be added to ensure, for example, that the gate eventually computes the required value.

In the symbolic description we represent each of these variables with a predicate symbol such as, in this particular example, $and\_gate\_in1(I_1, I_2, X)$. The variable name is prefixed with the module name so that variables of different modules do not interfere with each other. Since, moreover, several instances of the 'and−gate' can be created, the first arguments I_1, I_2 serve to distinguish among such instances, the following section explains this in more detail. The last argument X represents a time step within the execution trace. Using this naming convention, the module can then be described as follows:

$\neg and\_gate\_out(I_1, I_2, s_0)$
$trans(X, Y) \rightarrow$
    $(and\_gate\_out(I_1, I_2, Y) \leftrightarrow and\_gate\_in1(I_1, I_2, X) \wedge and\_gate\_in2(I_1, I_2, X))$
    $\vee (and\_gate\_out(I_1, I_2, Y) \leftrightarrow and\_gate\_out(I_1, I_2, X))$

Note that, although the original smv description distinguishes between inputs and outputs of the module, our proposed encoding does not need to.

4.2 Submodel Instances

Modules can also create named instances of other modules and specify how its own variables and the variables of the its submodule instances relate to each other. There is also one designated 'main' module, an instance of which represents the entire system to verify. One has to distinguish between the notions of a module (the abstract description of a component) and its possibly many module instances, which actually conform the complete system. In our running example, the DME circuit, part of the definition of a cell module looks like:

```
module  cell ( left , right , token )
var
   ack :  boolean ;
   c :  and−gate ( a . out ,  ! left . ack );
   d :  and−gate ( b . out ,  !u . ack )
   ⋮
```

Here two submodule instances 'c' and 'd' are created, both instances of the 'and−gate' module. The elements 'a, b: mutex_half' and 'u: user' are instances of other modules also created within the cell, with definitions of other internal variables such as 'out' and 'ack'. The elements ' left ' and 'right' are references to other ' cell ' instances, these are explained later in the following section.

Symbolically, we can describe the relations between the inputs and outputs of these modules using the constraints:

$$cell\_left(I, J) \rightarrow \begin{array}{l} and\_gate\_in1(I, c, X) \leftrightarrow mutex\_half\_out(I, a, X) \\ and\_gate\_in2(I, c, X) \leftrightarrow \neg cell\_ack(J, X) \\ and\_gate\_in1(I, d, X) \leftrightarrow mutex\_half\_out(I, b, X) \\ and\_gate\_in2(I, d, X) \leftrightarrow \neg user\_ack(I, u, X) \end{array} \qquad (2)$$

Here the variable I stands for a particular cell instance, the second argument of the predicates is now filled in with the instance names of the different modules.

In general, if a module M_1 creates instances of a module M_2, we say that M_2 is a *submodule* of M_1. The submodule relation must then create a directed acyclic graph among the modules of a system; and the *submodule depth* of a module is the length of the longest path that can reach it from the designated 'main' module. The depth of the 'main' module, for example, is always 0; and the depth of a module is strictly less than the depth of its submodules.

In a module of depth d we will therefore use $d+1$ arguments in the predicates that represent the module's boolean variables. The last argument always denotes time, and the interpretation of the other d arguments is the string of names that represent each created instance in a chain of submodules. Consider for example the 'out' variable of a module 'some$-$gate' which corresponds to an instance with the fully qualified name of 'main.sub1.sub2.sub3.sub4.out'; symbolically we would represent such variable with the predicate

$$\mathsf{some\_gate\_out}(\mathsf{sub1}, \mathsf{sub2}, \mathsf{sub3}, \mathsf{sub4}, X)\,.$$

Finally note that instances of the same module could be reached from the main module by paths of different lengths.[2]. Consider for example a module of depth d that creates an instance named 'sub' of another module of depth d'; if a sequence of constant symbols $\mathsf{m}_1, \ldots, \mathsf{m}_d$ is used to identify an instance of the first module, then the sequence of d' constant symbols $\mathsf{m}_1, \ldots, \mathsf{m}_d, \ldots, \mathsf{o}, \ldots, \mathsf{sub}$ —where a number of dummy constant symbols 'o' (unused anywhere else) serve as padding to get the required length— is used to identify the second.

4.3   Module References

Another feature of the smv language is that modules can receive references to other modules as parameters (e.g. ' left ' and 'right' in the cell example). This feature is encoded introducing a new predicate, c.f. $\mathsf{cell\_left}(I, J)$ in (2), that establishes these relation between the two modules. References are used in our running example to communicate three different cells 'e$-$1', 'e$-$2' and 'e$-$3':

module main
var
   e$-$3: **process** cell (e$-$1,e$-$2,1);
   ⋮

which is encoded as: $\{\mathsf{cell\_left}(\mathsf{e\_3}, \mathsf{e\_1}), \mathsf{cell\_right}(\mathsf{e\_3}, \mathsf{e\_2}), \mathsf{cell\_token}(\mathsf{e\_3}, X)\}$. In general, the reference from a 'module1' to another 'module2' is encoded as:

$$\mathsf{module1\_link}(\overline{I}, \overline{J}) \rightarrow (\mathsf{module1\_var1}(\overline{I}, X) \leftrightarrow \mathsf{module2\_var2}(\overline{J}, X)),$$

where $\overline{I}$ and $\overline{J}$ are sequences of variables of appropriate lengths according to the depths of each module, and 'link' is the local name which the first module uses to reference the second. Compare this with the relevant constraint in (2).

---

[2] Consider a module 'm1' that creates instances of 'm2' and 'm3', but 'm2' also creates instances of 'm3'. As long as the *submodule* relation is acyclic, this is possible.

4.4   Enumerated Types

Finally, another common feature of component description languages is the use of enumerated types, e.g. 'colour: {red, green, blue}'. Using standard encodings, such variables are represented with an additional argument to denote the value currently hold. Also, a number of constraints have to be added in order to ensure that one (and only one) value of an enumerated variable holds at a time.

5   Conclusions and Future Work

In this paper we presented different strategies to encode instances of the bounded model checking problem as a predicate formula in the Bernays-Schönfinkel class. We showed a translation which, given a linear temporal logic formula and a bound k, produces a set of constraints whose models represent all the possible paths (of bounded length k) which satisfy the given property. We also discussed how to further improve this translation and generate an output of size $O(n + k)$ where n is the size of the input LTL formula. The translation is also further improved by using a binary representation to denote the states.

We then proceeded to show how to efficiently describe transition systems as effectively propositional formulae, and demonstrated how many features commonly found in software/hardware description languages are succinctly and naturally encoded within our target language. Most significantly, modular and hierarchical system descriptions are directly encoded without a significant increase in the size; unlike propositional encodings where a preliminary, and potentially exponential, flattening phase needs to be applied to the system description.

We are also currently working in the development of a tool that —taking as input a smv description, an LTL formula, and a bound k— produces an EPR formula in the tptp format suitable for use with effectively propositional and first-order reasoners.[3] Directions for future work include the extension to more general forms of temporal logics (such as μTL), the inclusion of more features to describe systems (such as arrays and arithmetic) and the application of similar encoding techniques to other suitable application domains.

References

[1] Biere, A., Cimatti, A., Clarke, E.M., Zhu, Y.: Symbolic model checking without BDDs. In: Cleaveland, W.R. (ed.) ETAPS 1999 and TACAS 1999. LNCS, vol. 1579, Springer, Heidelberg (1999)
[2] Biere, A., Heljanko, K., Junttila, T., Latvala, T., Schuppan, V.: Linear encodings of bounded LTL model checking. Logical Methods in Computer Science 2(5:5) (2006)
[3] Cimatti, A., Clarke, E., Giunchiglia, F., Pistore, M., Roveri, M., Sebastiani, R., Tacchella, A.: NuSMV 2: An opensource tool for symbolic model checking. In: Brinksma, E., Larsen, K.G. (eds.) CAV 2002. LNCS, vol. 2404, pp. 359–364. Springer, Heidelberg (2002)

---

[3] The developed tool and a number of generated benchmarks are publicly available at http://www.cs.man.ac.uk/~navarroj/eprbmc.

[4] Copty, F., Fix, L., Fraer, R., Giunchiglia, E., Kamhi, G., Tacchella, A., Vardi, M.Y.: Benefits of bounded model checking at an industrial setting. In: Berry, G., Comon, H., Finkel, A. (eds.) CAV 2001. LNCS, vol. 2102, pp. 436–453. Springer, Heidelberg (2001)

[5] Davis, M., Logemann, G., Loveland, D.: A machine program for theorem-proving. Communications of the ACM 5, 394–397 (1962)

[6] Jehle, M., Johannsen, J., Lange, M., Rachinsky, N.: Bounded model checking for all regular properties. Electr. Notes Theor. Comput. Sci. 144(1), 3–18 (2006)

[7] Latvala, T., Biere, A., Heljanko, K., Junttila, T.: Simple bounded LTL model checking. In: Hu, A.J., Martin, A.K. (eds.) FMCAD 2004. LNCS, vol. 3312, pp. 186–200. Springer, Heidelberg (2004)

[8] Martin, A.J.: The design of a self-timed circuit for distributed mutual exclusion. In: Fuchs, H. (ed.) Proceedings of the 1985 Chapel Hill Conference on Very Large Scale Integration (1985)

[9] McMillan, K.L.: Symbolic Model Checking: An Approach to the State Explosion Problem. Kluwer Academic Publishers, Dordrecht (1993)

[10] Prasad, M.R., Biere, A., Gupta, A.: A survey of recent advances in SAT-based formal verification. International Journal on Software Tools for Technology Transfer (STTT) 7, 156–173 (2005)

[11] Strichman, O.: Accelerating bounded model checking for safety properties. Formal Methods in System Design 24(1), 5–24 (2004)

[12] Sutcliffe, G., Suttner, C.: The state of CASC. AI Communications 19(1), 35–48 (2006)

[13] Sutcliffe, G., Suttner, C.B.: The TPTP problem library: CNF release v1.2.1. Journal of Automated Reasoning 21(2), 177–203 (1998)

Combination Methods for Satisfiability and Model-Checking of Infinite-State Systems

Silvio Ghilardi[1], Enrica Nicolini[2], Silvio Ranise[2], and Daniele Zucchelli[1,2]

[1] Dipartimento di Informatica, Università degli Studi di Milano, Italia
[2] LORIA & INRIA-Lorraine, Nancy, France

Abstract. Manna and Pnueli have extensively shown how a mixture of first-order logic (FOL) and discrete Linear time Temporal Logic (LTL) is sufficient to precisely state verification problems for the class of reactive systems. Theories in FOL model the (possibly infinite) data structures used by a reactive system while LTL specifies its (dynamic) behavior. In this paper, we derive undecidability and decidability results for both the satisfiability of (quantifier-free) formulae and the model-checking of safety properties by lifting combination methods for (non-disjoint) theories in FOL. The proofs of our decidability results suggest how decision procedures for the constraint satisfiability problem of theories in FOL and algorithms for checking the satisfiability of propositional LTL formulae can be integrated. This paves the way to employ efficient Satisfiability Modulo Theories solvers in the model-checking of infinite state systems. We illustrate our techniques on two examples.

1 Introduction

In [12] and many other writings, Manna and Pnueli have extensively shown how a mixture of first-order logic (FOL) and discrete Linear time Temporal Logic (LTL) is sufficient to precisely state verification problems for the class of reactive systems. Theories in FOL model the (possibly infinite) data structures used by a reactive system while LTL specifies its (dynamic) behavior. The combination of LTL and FOL allows one to specify infinite state systems and the subtle ways in which their data flow influences the control flow. Indeed, the capability of automatically solving satisfiability and model-checking problems is of paramount importance to support the automation of verification techniques using this framework. In this paper, our approach is to reduce both problems to first-order combination problems over non-disjoint theories.

Preliminarily, we describe our framework for *integrating LTL operators with theories in FOL* (cf. Section 2.1): we fix a theory T in a first-order signature Σ and consider as a temporal model a sequence $\mathcal{M}_1, \mathcal{M}_2, \ldots$ of standard (first-order) models of T and assume such models to share the same carrier (or, equivalently, the domain of the temporal model is 'constant'). Following [15], we consider symbols from a subsignature Σ_r of Σ to be *rigid*, i.e. in a temporal model $\mathcal{M}_1, \mathcal{M}_2, \ldots$, the Σ_r-restrictions of the $\mathcal{M}_i$'s must coincide. The symbols in $\Sigma \setminus \Sigma_r$ are called 'flexible' and their interpretation is allowed to change

F. Pfenning (Ed.): CADE 2007, LNAI 4603, pp. 362–378, 2007.

over time (free variables are similarly divided into 'rigid' and 'flexible'). For model-checking, the *initial states* and the *transition relation* are represented by first-order formulae, whose role is that of (non-deterministically) restricting the temporal evolution of the model (cf. Section 4).

The *first contribution* (cf. Theorem 3.1 in Section 3) of the paper is a reduction of the satisfiability problem for quantifier-free LTL formulae modulo the background theory T to an instance of the Nelson-Oppen combination problem for first-order theories (the combination being disjoint if the rigid subsignature is empty). More precisely, we consider a theory T whose constraint satisfiability problem consists of non-deterministically solving one of the (decidable) constraint satisfiability problem of two signature-disjoint theories T_1, T_2. Although the satisfiability problem of T is decidable, it is possible to write a quantifier-free LTL formula which is equisatisfiable to a constraint of $T_1 \cup T_2$, whose satisfiability problem turns out to be undecidable if T_1 and T_2 are chosen as shown in [1]. The undecidability of the safety model-checking problem follows (under mild hypotheses) from a well-known reduction to the reachability problem for Minsky machines [13].

Since the satisfiability problem for quantifier-free LTL formulae modulo a background theory T looks very much like a non-disjoint combination problem, the hope is that the same (or similar) requirements yielding the decidability of the constraint satisfiability problem in unions of theories [8], will also give decidability here. The *second contribution* (cf. Theorem 3.2 in Section 3) of the paper is to show that this is indeed the case: we derive the decidability of the satisfiability problem for quantifier-free LTL formulae modulo T, in case T has decidable universal fragment and is T_r-compatible [8], where T_r is the restriction of the universal fragment of T to the rigid subsignature. For termination, one must also assume T_r to be locally finite [8].

The *third* (and main) *contribution* (Theorem 4.1 in Section 4) of the paper is that (under the same hypotheses of T_r-compatibility and local finiteness) the model-checking problem for quantifier-free safety properties is also decidable. The proof of this result suggests how decision procedures for the constraint satisfiability problem of theories in FOL and algorithms for checking the satisfiability of propositional LTL formulae can be integrated. This paves the way to employ efficient *Satisfiability Modulo Theories* (SMT) solvers in the model-checking of infinite state systems, as previous proposals have suggested their use for bounded model-checking [4]. Finally, we illustrate our techniques on two examples.

For lack of space, the proofs of our results are omitted: they can be found in the on-line version of the paper and also in the Technical Report [9].

2 Background

We assume the usual first-order syntactic notions of signature, term, position, atoms, formula, and so on. Let Σ be a first-order signature; we assume the equality symbol '=' to be part of the language ('equality is a logical constant'), so that it can be used to build formulae, but it is not explicitly displayed in a signature. A Σ-*constraint* is a set of Σ-literals (intended conjunctively). A positive Σ-clause is a disjunction of Σ-atoms. A Σ-theory T is a set of sentences in the signature Σ; the sentences in T are also called *axioms*. A theory is *universal* iff it has universal closures of open formulas as axioms. We also assume the usual first-order notions of interpretation, satisfiability, validity, and logical consequence. The equality symbol '=' is interpreted as the identity. If $\Sigma_0 \subseteq \Sigma$ is a subsignature of Σ and if $\mathcal{M}$ is a Σ-structure, the Σ_0-*reduct* of $\mathcal{M}$ is the Σ_0-structure $\mathcal{M}_{|\Sigma_0}$ obtained from $\mathcal{M}$ by forgetting the interpretation of function and predicate symbols from $\Sigma \setminus \Sigma_0$. A Σ-structure $\mathcal{M}$ is a *model* of a Σ-theory T (in symbols, $\mathcal{M} \models T$) iff all the sentences of T are true in $\mathcal{M}$. A Σ-theory T admits *elimination of quantifiers* iff for every formula $\varphi(\underline{x})$ there is a quantifier-free formula $\varphi'(\underline{x})$ such that $T \models \varphi(\underline{x}) \leftrightarrow \varphi'(\underline{x})$. Standard versions of Linear Arithmetics, Real Arithmetics, acyclic lists, and any theory axiomatizing enumerated datatypes admit elimination of quantifiers. Let Σ be a finite signature; an *enumerated datatype theory* in the signature Σ is the theory consisting of the set of sentences which are true in a finite given Σ-structure $\mathcal{M} = (M, \mathcal{I})$; we also require that for every $m \in M$ there is $c \in \Sigma$ such that $c^{\mathcal{M}} = m$. It is easy to see that an enumerated datatype theory has a finite set of universal axioms and admits elimination of quantifiers.

The *(constraint) satisfiability problem* for the theory T is the problem of deciding whether a Σ-sentence (Σ-constraint, resp.) is satisfiable in a model of T. We will use free constants instead of variables in constraint satisfiability problems, so that we (equivalently) redefine a constraint satisfiability problem for the theory T as the problem of *establishing the satisfiability of* $T \cup \Gamma$ (or, equivalently, the T-satisfiability of Γ) *for a finite set* Γ of ground $\Sigma^{\underline{a}}$-*literals* (where $\Sigma^{\underline{a}} := \Sigma \cup \{\underline{a}\}$, for a finite set of new constants $\underline{a}$). For the same reason, from now on, *by a 'Σ-constraint' we mean a 'ground $\Sigma^{\underline{a}}$-constraint'*, where the free constants $\underline{a}$ should be clear from the context.

A Σ-*embedding* (or, simply, an embedding) between two Σ-structures $\mathcal{M} = (M, \mathcal{I})$ and $\mathcal{N} = (N, \mathcal{J})$ is any mapping $\mu : M \longrightarrow N$ among the corresponding support sets satisfying the condition

$$(*) \qquad \mathcal{M} \models \varphi \text{ iff } \mathcal{N} \models \varphi,$$

for all Σ^M-atoms φ (here $\mathcal{M}$ is regarded as a Σ^M-structure, by interpreting each additional constant $a \in M$ into itself and $\mathcal{N}$ is regarded as a Σ^M-structure by interpreting each additional constant $a \in M$ into $\mu(a)$). If $M \subseteq N$ and if the embedding $\mu : M \longrightarrow \mathcal{N}$ is just the identity inclusion $M \subseteq N$, we say that $\mathcal{M}$ is a *substructure* of $\mathcal{N}$ or that $\mathcal{N}$ is an *extension* of $\mathcal{M}$. In case condition (*) holds for all first order formulas, the embedding μ is said to be *elementary*. Correspondingly, in case μ is also an inclusion, we say that $\mathcal{M}$ is an elementary substructure of $\mathcal{N}$ or that $\mathcal{N}$ is an elementary extension of $\mathcal{M}$.

The T_0-compatibility notion is crucial for the completeness of combination schemas [8].

Definition 2.1 (T_0-compatibility [8]). *Let T be a theory in the signature Σ and T_0 be a universal theory in a subsignature $\Sigma_0 \subseteq \Sigma$. We say that T is T_0-*

compatible *iff* $T_0 \subseteq T$ and there is a Σ_0-theory $T_0^\star$ such that (1) $T_0 \subseteq T_0^\star$; (2) $T_0^\star$ has quantifier elimination; (3) every model of T_0 can be embedded into a model of $T_0^\star$; and (4) every model of T can be embedded into a model of $T \cup T_0^\star$.

If T_0 is the empty theory over the empty signature, then $T_0^\star$ is the theory axiomatizing an infinite domain and (4) above can be shown equivalent to the stably infinite requirement of the Nelson-Oppen schema [14,19].

Local finiteness yields termination of combination schemas [8].

Definition 2.2 (Local Finiteness [8]). *A Σ_0-theory T_0 is locally finite iff Σ_0 is finite and, for every finite set of free constants $\underline{a}$, there are finitely many ground $\Sigma_0^{\underline{a}}$-terms $t_1, \ldots, t_{k_{\underline{a}}}$ such that for every further ground $\Sigma_0^{\underline{a}}$-term u, we have that $T_0 \models u = t_i$ (for some $i \in \{1, \ldots, k_{\underline{a}}\}$). If such $t_1, \ldots, t_{k_{\underline{a}}}$ are effectively computable from $\underline{a}$ (and t_i is computable from u), then T_0 is effectively locally finite.*

If T_0 is effectively locally finite, for any finite set of free constants $\underline{a}$ it is possible to compute finitely many $\Sigma_0^{\underline{a}}$-atoms $\psi_1(\underline{a}), \ldots, \psi_m(\underline{a})$ such that for any $\Sigma_0^{\underline{a}}$-atom $\psi(\underline{a})$, there is some i such that $T_0 \models \psi_i(\underline{a}) \leftrightarrow \psi(\underline{a})$. These atoms $\psi_1(\underline{a}), \ldots, \psi_m(\underline{a})$ are the *representatives* (modulo T_0-equivalence) and they can replace arbitrary $\Sigma_0^{\underline{a}}$-atoms for computational purposes. For example, any theory in a purely relational signature is locally finite (this will be used in Example 4.1).

The following technical Lemma is the key combination result allowing us to reduce satisfiability in first-order LTL to satisfiability in first-order logic.

Lemma 2.1. *Let $\Sigma_i^{\underline{c}, \underline{a}_i}$ (here i ranges over a given set I of indexes) be signatures expanded with free constants $\underline{c} \cup \underline{a}_i$, whose pairwise intersections are all equal to a certain signature $\Sigma_r^{\underline{c}}$ (i.e. $\Sigma_i^{\underline{c}, \underline{a}_i} \cap \Sigma_j^{\underline{c}, \underline{a}_j} = \Sigma_r^{\underline{c}}$, for all distinct $i, j \in I$). Suppose we are also given Σ_i-theories T_i which are all T_r-compatible, where $T_r \subseteq \bigcap_i T_i$ is a universal Σ_r-theory; let finally $\{\mathcal{N}_i = (N_i, \mathcal{I}_i)\}_{i \in I}$ be a sequence of $\Sigma_i^{\underline{c}, \underline{a}_i}$-structures which are models of T_i and satisfy the same $\Sigma_r^{\underline{c}}$-atoms. Under these hypotheses, there exists a $\bigcup_i(\Sigma_i^{\underline{c}, \underline{a}_i})$-structure $\mathcal{M} \models \bigcup_i T_i$ such that $\mathcal{N}_i$ has a $\Sigma_i^{\underline{c}, \underline{a}_i}$-embedding into $\mathcal{M}$, for each $i \in I$.*

2.1 Temporal Logic

We assume the standard syntactic and semantic notions concerning Propositional LTL (PLTL), such as PLTL-formula and PLTL-Kripke model. Following [12], we fix a first-order signature Σ and we consider formulae obtained by applying temporal and Boolean operators (but no quantifiers) to first-order Σ-formulae.

Definition 2.3 (LTL($\Sigma^{\underline{a}}$)-Sentences). *Let Σ be a signature and $\underline{a}$ be a (possibly infinite) set of free constants. The set of LTL($\Sigma^{\underline{a}}$)-sentences is inductively defined as follows: (i) if φ is a first-order $\Sigma^{\underline{a}}$-sentence, then φ is an LTL($\Sigma^{\underline{a}}$)-sentence and (ii) if ψ_1, ψ_2 are LTL($\Sigma^{\underline{a}}$)-sentences, so are $\psi_1 \wedge \psi_2$, $\neg\psi_1$, $X\psi_1$, $\psi_1 U \psi_2$.*

We abbreviate $\neg(\neg\psi_1 \wedge \neg\psi_2)$, $\top U\psi$, $\neg\Diamond\neg\psi$, $\neg(\neg\psi_1 U\neg\psi_2)$ as $\psi_1 \vee \psi_2$, $\Diamond\psi$, $\Box\psi$, and $\psi_1 R\psi_2$, respectively. Notice that free constants are allowed in the definition of a LTL($\Sigma^{\underline{a}}$)-sentence.

Definition 2.4. *Given a signature Σ and a set $\underline{a}$ of free constants, an LTL($\Sigma^{\underline{a}}$)-structure (or simply a structure) is a sequence $\mathcal{M} = \{\mathcal{M}_n = (M, \mathcal{I}_n)\}_{n\in\mathbb{N}}$ of $\Sigma^{\underline{a}}$-structures. The set M is called the domain (or the universe) and $\mathcal{I}_n$ is called the n-th level interpretation function of the LTL($\Sigma^{\underline{a}}$)-structure.*

So, an LTL($\Sigma^{\underline{a}}$)-structure is a family of $\Sigma^{\underline{a}}$-structures indexed over the naturals. When considering a background Σ-theory T, these structures will also be models of T. What should the various $\Sigma^{\underline{a}}$-structures of the family share? Our answer (according to Definition 2.4) is that they should share their domains or, equivalently, we assume M_n to be *constant*.

Definition 2.5. *Given an LTL($\Sigma^{\underline{a}}$)-sentence φ and $t \in \mathbb{N}$, the notion of "φ being true in the LTL($\Sigma^{\underline{a}}$)-structure $\mathcal{M} = \{\mathcal{M}_n = (M, \mathcal{I}_n)\}_{n\in\mathbb{N}}$ at the instant t" (in symbols $\mathcal{M} \models_t \varphi$) is inductively defined as follows:*

- *if φ is a first-order $\Sigma^{\underline{a}}$-sentence, $\mathcal{M} \models_t \varphi$ iff $\mathcal{M}_t \models \varphi$;*
- *$\mathcal{M} \models_t \neg\varphi$ iff $\mathcal{M} \not\models_t \varphi$;*
- *$\mathcal{M} \models_t \varphi \wedge \psi$ iff $\mathcal{M} \models_t \varphi$ and $\mathcal{M} \models_t \psi$;*
- *$\mathcal{M} \models_t X\varphi$ iff $\mathcal{M} \models_{t+1} \varphi$;*
- *$\mathcal{M} \models_t \varphi U\psi$ iff there exists $t' \geq t$ such that $\mathcal{M} \models_{t'} \psi$ and for each t'', $t \leq t'' < t' \Rightarrow \mathcal{M} \models_{t''} \varphi$.*

We say that φ is true in $\mathcal{M}$ or, equivalently, that $\mathcal{M}$ satisfies φ (in symbols $\mathcal{M} \models \varphi$) iff $\mathcal{M} \models_0 \varphi$.

Which is the relationship between the interpretations $\mathcal{I}_n$ in an LTL($\Sigma^{\underline{a}}$)-structure? Following [15], our answer is that certain symbols are declared *rigid* (i.e. their interpretation is time independent) while the remaining are considered *flexible* (i.e. time dependent). There are various reasons supporting this choice. The most important is that our framework allows us more flexibility in solving certain problems: actions from the environment on a reactive systems are somewhat unpredictable and can be better modelled by flexible function symbols, as demonstrated by the following Example.

Example 2.1. Suppose we want to model a a water level controller. To this aim, we need two functions symbols in(flow)/out(flow) expressing the water level variations induced by the environment and by the opening action of the valve, respectively: these functions depend both on the current water level and on the time instant, thus the natural choice is to model them by just *unary* function symbols, which are then *flexible* because the time dependency becomes in this way implicit. On the other hand, the constants expressing the alarm and the overflow level should not depend on the time instant, hence they are modeled as *rigid* constants; for obvious reasons, the arithmetical binary comparison symbol $<$ is also time-independent, hence *rigid* too. Having chosen these (flexible and rigid) symbols, we can express constraints on the behavior of our system by introducing a suitable theory (see Example 4.1 below for details).

There is also a more technical (but still crucial) reason underlying our distinction between rigid and flexible symbols: we can avoid some undecidability problems by carefully choosing problematic function or predicates to be flexible. In fact, if we succeed to keep the rigid part relatively simple (e.g., a locally finite theory), then we usually do not lose decidability.

Definition 2.6. *An* LTL-theory *is a 5-tuple* $\mathcal{T} = \langle \Sigma, T, \Sigma_r, \underline{a}, \underline{c} \rangle$ *where* Σ *is a signature,* T *is a* Σ-theory *(called the underlying theory of* $\mathcal{T}$ *),* Σ_r *is a subsignature of* Σ, *and* $\underline{a}, \underline{c}$ *are sets of free constants.*

Σ_r is the *rigid subsignature* of the LTL-theory; the constants $\underline{c}$ will be rigidly interpreted, whereas the constants $\underline{a}$ will be interpreted in a time-dependant way. The constants $\underline{a}$ are also (improperly) called the *system variables* of the LTL-theory, and the constants $\underline{c}$ are called its *system parameters*. The equality symbol will always be considered as rigid. A LTL-theory $\mathcal{T} = \langle \Sigma, T, \Sigma_r, \underline{a}, \underline{c} \rangle$ is *totally flexible* iff Σ_r is empty and is *totally rigid* iff $\Sigma_r = \Sigma$.

3   The Satisfiability Problem

We formally state the satisfiability problem for LTL($\Sigma^{\underline{a}}$)-sentences.

Definition 3.1. *An* $LTL(\Sigma^{\underline{a},\underline{c}})$-structure $\mathcal{M} = \{\mathcal{M}_n = (M, \mathcal{I}_n)\}_{n \in \mathbb{N}}$ *is appropriate for an* LTL-theory $\mathcal{T} = \langle \Sigma, T, \Sigma_r, \underline{a}, \underline{c} \rangle$ *iff we have*

$$\mathcal{M}_n \models T, \quad \mathcal{I}_n(f) = \mathcal{I}_m(f), \quad \mathcal{I}_n(P) = \mathcal{I}_m(P), \quad \mathcal{I}_n(c) = \mathcal{I}_m(c).$$

for all $m, n \in \mathbb{N}$, *for each function symbol* $f \in \Sigma_r$, *for each relational symbol* $P \in \Sigma_r$, *and for all constants* $c \in \underline{c}$. *The* satisfiability problem *for* $\mathcal{T}$ *is the following: given an* $LTL(\Sigma^{\underline{a},\underline{c}})$-sentence φ, *decide whether there is an* $LTL(\Sigma^{\underline{a},\underline{c}})$-structure $\mathcal{M}$ *appropriate for* $\mathcal{T}$ *such that* $\mathcal{M} \models \varphi$. *When* φ *is ground, we speak of* ground satisfiability problem *for* $\mathcal{T}$.

In the following, it is useful to distinguish two classes of LTL-theories.

Definition 3.2. *An* LTL-theory $\mathcal{T} = \langle \Sigma, T, \Sigma_r, \underline{a}, \underline{c} \rangle$ *is*

1. finite state *iff it is totally rigid and* T *is an enumerated datatype theory;*
2. locally finite compatible *iff there is a* Σ_r-universal *and effectively locally finite theory* T_r *such that* T *is* T_r-compatible;

Enumerated datatype theories are locally finite, but not conversely (for instance, the theory of dense linear orders is locally finite but cannot be the theory of a single finite structure, because finite linear orders are not dense).

In the hope to derive decidability results for the satisfiability of first-order LTL formulae, we restrict ourselves to consider only ground formulae and assume the decidability of the constraint satisfiability problem of the theory underlying any LTL-theory (cf. Assumption 1 in Figure 1). Unfortunately, this assumption alone is not sufficient to guarantee the decidability of the ground satisfiability problem (cf. Definition 3.1).

Assumptions

1. We assume the underlying theory T of an LTL-theory $\mathcal{T} = \langle \Sigma, T, \Sigma_r, \underline{a}, \underline{c} \rangle$ to have decidable constraint satisfiability problem.
2. For any LTL-system specification $(\mathcal{T}, \delta, \iota)$, the transition relation δ and the initial state description ι in a system specification $(\mathcal{T}, \delta, \iota)$ are assumed to be ground sentences. Furthermore, we assume all our LTL-systems specifications to be serial.

Fig. 1. The main assumptions of the paper

Theorem 3.1. *There exists a totally flexible LTL-theory $\mathcal{T}$ whose ground satisfiability problem is undecidable.*

There are two key observations underlying the proof of our undecidability result. First, we build a theory T whose constraint satisfiability problem consists of non-deterministically solving the constraint satisfiability problem among two signature-disjoint theories T_1, T_2. It is easy to see that the decidability of the constraint satisfiability problem transfer from T_1, T_2 to T. The second observation is that for every constraint Γ it is possible to write an LTL($\Sigma^{\underline{a}}$)-sentence whose satisfiability is equivalent to the satisfiability of Γ in $T_1 \cup T_2$. In [1], it is shown that such a problem is undecidable for suitable T_1 and T_2.

These arguments suggest that the undecidability of the ground satisfiability problem for a given LTL-theory $\mathcal{T} = \langle \Sigma, T, \Sigma_r, \underline{a}, \underline{c} \rangle$ arises precisely for the same reasons leading to the undecidability of combined constraint satisfiability problems in the first-order framework. It turns out that the requirements yielding the decidability of the constraint satisfiability problem in unions of theories will also give the decidability of the ground satisfiability problem for $\mathcal{T}$.

Theorem 3.2. *The ground satisfiability problem for a locally finite compatible LTL-theory is decidable.*

Below, we give two constructive proofs of this Theorem (cf. Proposition 3.1 and Corollary 3.1).

For the rest of this Section, we fix a locally finite compatible LTL-theory $\mathcal{T} = \langle \Sigma, T, \Sigma_r, \underline{a}, \underline{c} \rangle$. A syntactic relationship between (ground) first-order and propositional LTL-formulae can be introduced as follows.

Definition 3.3 (PLTL-Abstraction). *Given a signature $\Sigma^{\underline{a}}$ and a set $\mathcal{L}$ of propositional letters (of the same cardinality as the set of ground $\Sigma^{\underline{a}}$-atoms), let $[\![\cdot]\!]$ be a bijection from the set of ground $\Sigma^{\underline{a}}$-atoms into $\mathcal{L}$. By translating identically Boolean and temporal connectives, the map is inductively extended to a bijective map (also denoted with $[\![\cdot]\!]$) from the set of LTL($\Sigma^{\underline{a}}$)-sentences onto the set of propositional $\mathcal{L}$-formulae.*

Given a ground LTL($\Sigma^{\underline{a}}$)-sentence φ, we call $[\![\varphi]\!]$ the *PLTL-abstraction* of φ; if Θ is a set of ground LTL($\Sigma^{\underline{a}}$)-sentences, then $[\![\Theta]\!] := \{ [\![\varphi]\!] \mid \varphi \in \Theta \}$.

Eager Reduction to Propositional LTL-Satisfiability. The key of our reduction to the satisfiability problem in PLTL is guessing.

Definition 3.4 (Guessing). *Let Σ be a signature Σ and S be a finite set of Σ-atoms. A S-guessing $\mathcal{G}$ is a Boolean assignment to members of S. We also view $\mathcal{G}$ as the set $\{\varphi \mid \varphi \in S$ and $\mathcal{G}(\varphi)$ is assigned to true$\} \cup \{\neg\varphi \mid \varphi \in S$ and $\mathcal{G}(\varphi)$ is assigned to false$\}$.*

Indeed, guessing must take into account rigid constants. Since $\mathcal{T}$ is locally finite compatible, there must exist a Σ_r-theory T_r such that $T_r \subseteq T$ is effectively locally finite. So, given a finite subset $\underline{c}_0$ of $\underline{c}$, it is possible to compute a finite set S of ground $\Sigma_r^{\underline{c}_0}$-atoms which are representative modulo T-equivalence: for this choice of S, an S-guessing is called a *rigid $\underline{c}_0$-guessing*. Now, let $\tilde{S}$ be any finite set of $\Sigma^{\underline{a},\underline{c}}$-atoms and let $\mathcal{G}$ be a rigid $\underline{c}_0$-guessing: an $\tilde{S}$-guessing $\tilde{\mathcal{G}}$ is $\mathcal{G}$-compatible iff $\mathcal{G} \cup \tilde{\mathcal{G}}$ is T-satisfiable. The set of $\mathcal{G}$-compatible $\tilde{S}$-guessing is denoted by $C(\tilde{S}, \mathcal{G})$. Theorem 3.2 is an immediate consequence of the fact that PLTL-satisfiability is decidable and the following Proposition.

Proposition 3.1. *Let $\mathcal{T} = \langle \Sigma, T, \Sigma_r, \underline{a}, \underline{c} \rangle$ be a locally finite compatible LTL-theory. Let $\mathcal{L}$ be a set of propositional letters and $[\![\cdot]\!]$ be a PLTL-abstraction function mapping ground $LTL(\Sigma^{\underline{a},\underline{c}})$-sentences into propositional $\mathcal{L}$-formulae. A ground $LTL(\Sigma^{\underline{a},\underline{c}})$-sentence φ is satisfiable in an $LTL(\Sigma^{\underline{a},\underline{c}})$-structure $\mathcal{M}$ appropriate for $\mathcal{T}$ iff there exists a rigid $\underline{c}_0$-guessing $\mathcal{G}$ such that the propositional formula*

$$[\![\varphi]\!] \wedge \square \bigwedge_{\psi \in \mathcal{G}} [\![\psi]\!] \wedge \square \left(\bigvee_{\tilde{\mathcal{G}} \in C(At(\varphi), \mathcal{G})} \bigwedge_{\psi \in \tilde{\mathcal{G}}} [\![\psi]\!] \right) \tag{1}$$

is satisfiable in a PLTL-Kripke model (here $\underline{c}_0 \subseteq \underline{c}$ is the set of system parameters occurring in φ and $At(\varphi)$ is the set of $\Sigma^{\underline{a},\underline{c}}$-atoms occurring in φ).

To prove this Proposition, we use Lemma 2.1 with $I := \mathbb{N}$, $T_i := T$ (symbols from $\Sigma \setminus \Sigma_r$ are disjointly renamed when building the signature Σ_i for the i-th copy of T). The Σ_i-structures $\mathcal{M}_i$ required to build a temporal model are obtained by signature restrictions from the model of $\bigcup T_i$ which is provided by Lemma 2.1.

The main advantage of the *eager reduction algorithm* suggested by Proposition 3.1 is that decision procedures for the constraint satisfiability problem of the underlying locally finite theory and PLTL-decision procedures (based on tableau, automata, or temporal resolution) can be used 'off-the-shelf'. Its main drawback is that the resulting PLTL-satisfiability problem may be quite large.

A Lazy Tableau Procedure. Avoiding the up-front generation of possibly very large PLTL-formulae should allow one to scale up more smoothly. The price to pay is a finer grain integration between the constraint reasoner for the underlying locally finite theory and the PLTL satisfiability solver.

A ground $LTL(\Sigma^{\underline{a},\underline{c}})$-sentence is in *Negation Normal Form* (NNF) iff it is built up from $LTL(\Sigma^{\underline{a},\underline{c}})$-literals by using $\vee, \wedge, X, R, U$. It can be shown that every ground $LTL(\Sigma^{\underline{a},\underline{c}})$-sentence is logically equivalent to one in NNF. If φ is a ground $LTL(\Sigma^{\underline{a},\underline{c}})$-sentence in NNF, then the *closure* of φ is the set $cl(\varphi)$ containing: (i) all subformulae of φ and all negations of atoms occurring in φ; (ii) the formulae $X(\psi U \chi)$, where $\psi U \chi$ is a subformula of φ; (iii) the formulae $X(\psi R \chi)$, where $\psi R \chi$ is a subformula of φ and, most importantly, (iv) a *representative set (modulo*

T-equivalence) of $\Sigma_r^{c_0}$-literals, where c_0 is the finite set of system parameters occurring in φ.

Definition 3.5. *Given a ground $LTL(\Sigma^{a,c})$-sentence φ in NNF, a* Hintikka set *for φ is a subset $H \subseteq cl(\varphi)$ such that: (i) H contains a maximal T-satisfiable set of literals from $cl(\varphi)$; (ii) if $\psi_1 \wedge \psi_2 \in H$, then $\psi_1, \psi_2 \in H$; (iii) if $\psi_1 \vee \psi_2 \in H$, then $\psi_1 \in H$ or $\psi_2 \in H$; (iv) if $\psi_1 U \psi_2 \in H$, then $\psi_2 \in H$ or ($\psi_1 \in H$ and $X(\psi_1 U \psi_2) \in H$); (v) if $\psi_1 R \psi_2 \in H$, then $\psi_1, \psi_2 \in H$ or $\psi_2, X(\psi_1 R \psi_2) \in H$.*

To design the lazy reduction procedure, we extend the tableaux-based approach to PLTL-satisfiability by lifting the definition of Hintikka sets to take into account ground $LTL(\Sigma^{a,c})$-sentences in NNF.

Definition 3.6. *The* Hintikka graph $\mathcal{H}(\varphi)$ *of φ is the directed graph having as nodes the Hintikka sets for φ and as edges the pairs $H \to H'$ such that (i) $H' \supseteq \{\psi \mid X\psi \in H\}$ and (ii) H and H' contain the same ground $\Sigma_r^{c_0}$-literals.*

A *strongly connected subgraph* (scs) of $\mathcal{H}(\varphi)$ is a set $\mathcal{C}$ of nodes of $\mathcal{H}(\varphi)$ such that for every $H, H' \in \mathcal{C}$ there is a (non-empty) $\mathcal{H}(\varphi)$-path from H to H' whose nodes belong to $\mathcal{C}$. An scs $\mathcal{C}$ is *fulfilling* [12] iff for every $\psi_1 U \psi_2 \in cl(\varphi)$ there is $H \in \mathcal{C}$ such that either $\psi_1 U \psi_2 \notin H$ or $\psi_2 \in H$. A node H in $\mathcal{H}(\varphi)$ is *initial* iff $\varphi \in H$.

Corollary 3.1. *A ground $LTL(\Sigma^{a,c})$-formula φ in NNF is satisfiable in an $LTL(\Sigma^{a,c})$-structure $\mathcal{M}$ appropriate for T iff there is an $\mathcal{H}(\varphi)$-path leading from an initial node into a fulfilling scs.*

This Corollary is a consequence of Proposition 3.1 and basic properties of Tableaux (see, e.g., Section 5.5 of [12]). When the set of representative $\Sigma_r^{c_0}$-atoms has polynomial size, the decision procedure derived from Corollary 3.1 is in PSPACE (provided that the T-constraint satisfiability problem is in PSPACE too): the key to achieve this is to explore the Hintikka graph 'on-the-fly' by using well-known techniques of the PLTL literature without explicitly constructing it.

4 The Model-Checking Problem

Given two signatures Σ_r and Σ such that $\Sigma_r \subseteq \Sigma$, we define the *one-step signature* as $\Sigma \oplus_{\Sigma_r} \Sigma := ((\Sigma \setminus \Sigma_r) \uplus (\Sigma \setminus \Sigma_r)) \cup \Sigma_r$, where $\uplus$ denotes disjoint union. In order to build the one-step signature $\Sigma \oplus_{\Sigma_r} \Sigma$, we first consider two copies of the symbols in $\Sigma \setminus \Sigma_r$; the two copies of $r \in \Sigma \setminus \Sigma_r$ are denoted by r^0 and r^1, respectively. Notice that the symbols in Σ_r are not renamed. Also, arities in the one-step signature $\Sigma \oplus_{\Sigma_r} \Sigma$ are defined in the obvious way: the arities of the symbols in Σ_r are unchanged and if n is the arity of $r \in \Sigma \setminus \Sigma_r$, then n is the arity of both r^0 and r^1. The one-step signature $\Sigma \oplus_{\Sigma_r} \Sigma$ will be also written as $\bigoplus_{\Sigma_r}^2 \Sigma$; similarly, we can define the *n-step signature* $\bigoplus_{\Sigma_r}^{n+1} \Sigma$ for $n > 1$ (our notation for the copies of $(\Sigma \setminus \Sigma_r)$-symbols extends in the obvious way, that is we denote by $r^0, r^1, \dots, r^n$ the $n+1$ copies of r).

Definition 4.1. *Given two signatures Σ_r and Σ such that $\Sigma_r \subseteq \Sigma$, two Σ-structures $\mathcal{M}_0 = \langle M, \mathcal{I}_0 \rangle$ and $\mathcal{M}_1 = \langle M, \mathcal{I}_1 \rangle$ whose Σ_r-reducts are the same, the* one-step $(\Sigma \oplus_{\Sigma_r} \Sigma)$-structure $\mathcal{M}_0 \oplus_{\Sigma_r} \mathcal{M}_1 = \langle M, \mathcal{I}_0 \oplus_{\Sigma_r} \mathcal{I}_1 \rangle$ *is defined as follows:*

- *for each function or predicate symbol $s \in \Sigma \setminus \Sigma_r$, $(\mathcal{I}_0 \oplus_{\Sigma_r} \mathcal{I}_1)(s^0) := \mathcal{I}_0(s)$ and $(\mathcal{I}_0 \oplus_{\Sigma_r} \mathcal{I}_1)(s^1) := \mathcal{I}_1(s)$;*
- *for each function or predicate symbol $r \in \Sigma_r$, $(\mathcal{I}_0 \oplus_{\Sigma_r} \mathcal{I}_1)(r) := \mathcal{I}_0(r)$.*

If φ is a Σ-formula, the $\Sigma \oplus_{\Sigma_r} \Sigma$ formulae φ^0, φ^1 are obtained from φ by replacing each symbol $r \in \Sigma \setminus \Sigma_r$ by r^0 and r^1, respectively. The one-step theory $T \oplus_{\Sigma_r} T$ is taken to be the combination of the theory T with a partially renamed copy of itself:

Definition 4.2. *Given two signatures Σ_r and Σ such that $\Sigma_r \subseteq \Sigma$, the $(\Sigma \oplus_{\Sigma_r} \Sigma)$-theory $T \oplus_{\Sigma_r} T$ is defined as $\{\varphi^0 \wedge \varphi^1 \mid \varphi \in T\}$.*

We will write $\bigoplus_{\Sigma_r}^2 T$ instead of $T \oplus_{\Sigma_r} T$; the n-step theories $\bigoplus_{\Sigma_r}^{n+1} T$ (for $n > 1$) are similarly defined.

Let now $\mathcal{T} = \langle \Sigma, T, \Sigma_r, \underline{a}, \underline{c} \rangle$ be an LTL-theory with *finitely* many parameters and system variables. A *transition relation* for the LTL-theory $\mathcal{T}$ is a $(\Sigma^{\underline{a},\underline{c}} \oplus_{\Sigma_r^{\underline{c}}} \Sigma^{\underline{a},\underline{c}})$-sentence δ: we write such formula as $\delta(\underline{a}^0, \underline{a}^1)$ to emphasize that it contains the two copies of the system variables $\underline{a}$ (on the other hand, the system parameters $\underline{c}$ are not duplicated and will never be displayed). An *initial state description* for the LTL-theory $\mathcal{T} = \langle \Sigma, T, \Sigma_r, \underline{a}, \underline{c} \rangle$ is simply a $\Sigma^{\underline{a},\underline{c}}$-sentence $\iota(\underline{a})$ (again, the system parameters $\underline{c}$ will not be displayed).

Definition 4.3 (LTL-System Specification and Model-Checking). *An LTL-system specification is a LTL-theory $\mathcal{T} = \langle \Sigma, T, \Sigma_r, \underline{a}, \underline{c} \rangle$ (with finitely many system variables and parameters) endowed with a transition relation $\delta(\underline{a}^0, \underline{a}^1)$ and with an initial state description $\iota(\underline{a})$. An $LTL(\Sigma^{\underline{a},\underline{c}})$-structure $\mathcal{M} = \{\mathcal{M}_n = (M, \mathcal{I}_n)\}_{n \in \mathbb{N}}$ is a* run *for such an LTL-system specification iff it is appropriate for $\mathcal{T}$ and moreover it obeys the initial state description ι and the transition δ, i.e. (1) $\mathcal{M}_0 \models \iota(\underline{a})$, and (2) $\mathcal{M}_n \oplus_{\Sigma_r^{\underline{c}}} \mathcal{M}_{n+1} \models \delta(\underline{a}^0, \underline{a}^1)$, for every $n \geq 0$. The* model-checking problem *for the system specification $(\mathcal{T}, \delta, \iota)$ is the following: given an $LTL(\Sigma^{\underline{a},\underline{c}})$-sentence φ, decide whether there is a run for $(\mathcal{T}, \delta, \iota)$ such that $\mathcal{M} \models \varphi$.[1] The* ground model-checking *problem for $(\mathcal{T}, \delta, \iota)$ is similarly defined for a ground φ.*

The (syntactic) *safety model-checking problem* is the model-checking problem for formulae of the form $\Diamond v$, where v is a $\Sigma^{\underline{a},\underline{c}}$-sentence. Since v is intended to describe the set of *unsafe* states, we say that the system specification $(\mathcal{T}, \delta, \iota)$ is *safe for v* iff the model-checking problem for $\Diamond v$ has a negative solution. This implies that $\Box \neg v$ is true for all runs of $(\mathcal{T}, \delta, \iota)$.

---

[1] In the literature, the model-checking problem is the complement of ours, i.e. it is the problem of deciding whether a given sentence is true in all runs.

In the literature about model-checking (especially, for finite-state systems), it is usually assumed the seriality of the transition relation: every state of the system must have at least one successor state (see, e.g., [3] for more details).

Definition 4.4. *An LTL-system specification* $(\mathcal{T}, \delta, \iota)$, *based on the LTL-theory* $\mathcal{T} = \langle \Sigma, T, \Sigma_r, \underline{a}, \underline{c} \rangle$, *is said to be* serial *iff for every* $\Sigma^{\underline{a}, \underline{c}}$*-structure* $\mathcal{M}_0 = (M, \mathcal{I}_0)$ *which is a model of* T, *there is another* $\Sigma^{\underline{a}, \underline{c}}$*-structure* $\mathcal{M}_1 = (M, \mathcal{I}_1)$ *(still a model of* T*) such that* $(\mathcal{M}_0)_{|\Sigma_r} = (\mathcal{M}_1)_{|\Sigma_r}$ *and* $\mathcal{M}_0 \oplus_{\Sigma_r^{\underline{c}}} \mathcal{M}_1 \models \delta(\underline{a}^0, \underline{a}^1)$.

Although the notion of seriality defined above is non-effective, there exist simple and effective conditions ensuring it. For example, if the transition relation δ consists of the conjunction of (possibly guarded) assignments of the form $P(\underline{a}^0) \rightarrow a^1 = t^0(\underline{a}^0)$ where P is the condition under which the assignment is executed, then δ is serial (see, e.g., Example 4.1). The standard trick [3] of ensuring seriality by a 0-ary predicate describing error states works in our framework too.

Definition 4.5. *An LTL-system specification* $(\mathcal{T}, \delta, \iota)$, *based on the LTL-theory* $\mathcal{T} = \langle \Sigma, T, \Sigma_r, \underline{a}, \underline{c} \rangle$, *is* finite state *or* locally finite compatible *iff so is* $\mathcal{T}$.

Finite state system specifications are investigated by traditional symbolic model-checking methods [3]. Since we are interested in ground safety model-checking problems we assume Assumption 2 in Figure 1, besides Assumption 1. Unfortunately, these two hypotheses are not sufficient to guarantee the decidability, even in the case the underlying LTL-theory is totally rigid. In fact, it is possible to reduce the ground safety model-checking problem to the the reachability problem of Minsky machines, which is known to be undecidable (see, e.g., [9]).

Fortunately, the safety model-checking problem is decidable for locally finite compatible LTL-system specifications. In the rest of this Section, let $\mathcal{T} = \langle \Sigma, T, \Sigma_r, \underline{a}, \underline{c} \rangle$ be a locally finite compatible LTL-theory, $(\mathcal{T}, \delta, \iota)$ be an LTL-system specification based on $\mathcal{T}$, and $\upsilon(\underline{a})$ be a ground $\Sigma^{\underline{a}, \underline{c}}$-sentence. The related safety model-checking problem amounts to checking whether there exists a run $\mathcal{M} = \{\mathcal{M}_n\}_{n \in \mathbb{N}}$ for $(\mathcal{T}, \delta, \iota)$ such that $\mathcal{M} \models_n \upsilon(\underline{a})$ for some $n \geq 0$: if this is the case, we say that the system is *unsafe* since there is a *bad run of length* n.

We can ignore bad runs of length $n = 0$, because the existence of such runs can be preliminarily decided by checking the ground sentence $\iota(\underline{a}) \wedge \upsilon(\underline{a})$ for T-satisfiability. So, for $n \geq 1$, taking into account the seriality of the transition, a bad run of length $n + 1$ exists iff the ground $(\bigoplus_{\Sigma_r^{\underline{c}}}^{n+2} \Sigma^{\underline{a}, \underline{c}})$-sentence

$$\iota^0(\underline{a}^0) \wedge \delta^{0,1}(\underline{a}^0, \underline{a}^1) \wedge \delta^{1,2}(\underline{a}^1, \underline{a}^2) \wedge \cdots \wedge \delta^{n,n+1}(\underline{a}^n, \underline{a}^{n+1}) \wedge \upsilon^{n+1}(\underline{a}^{n+1}) \quad (2)$$

is $\bigoplus_{\Sigma_r^{\underline{c}}}^{n+2} T$-satisfiable, where $\iota^0(\underline{a}^0)$ is obtained by replacing each flexible symbol $r \in \Sigma \setminus \Sigma_r$ with r^0 in $\iota(\underline{a})$ (the system variables $\underline{a}$ are similarly renamed as $\underline{a}^0$); $\delta^{i,i+1}(\underline{a}^i, \underline{a}^{i+1})$ is obtained by replacing in $\delta(\underline{a}^0, \underline{a}^1)$ the copy r^0 and r^1 of each flexible symbol $r \in \Sigma \setminus \Sigma_r$ with r^i and r^{i+1} respectively (the two copies $\underline{a}^0, \underline{a}^1$ of the system variables $\underline{a}$ are similarly renamed as $\underline{a}^i, \underline{a}^{i+1}$); and $\upsilon^{n+1}(\underline{a}^{n+1})$ is obtained by replacing each flexible symbol $r \in \Sigma \setminus \Sigma_r$ with r^{n+1} in $\upsilon(\underline{a})$ (the system variables $\underline{a}$ are similarly renamed as $\underline{a}^{n+1}$). For the sake of simplicity, we will write formula (2) by omitting the superscripts of ι, δ, and υ (but we maintain those of the system variables $\underline{a}$).

Now, for a given $n + 1$, an iterated application of the main combination result in [8] and the fact that T_0-compatibility is a modular property (see again [8]) yield the decidability of the satisfiability of formula (2). Unfortunately, this is not sufficient to solve the model-checking problem for LTL-system specifications since the length of a bad run is not known apriori. To solve this problem, we reduce the existence of a satisfiable formula of the form (2) to a reachability problem in a safety graph (see Definition 4.7 below).

Definition 4.6. *A ground $(\Sigma^{\underline{a},\underline{c}} \oplus_{\Sigma_r^{\underline{c}}} \Sigma^{\underline{a},\underline{c}})$-sentence δ is said to be purely left (purely right) iff for each symbol $r \in \Sigma \setminus \Sigma_r$, we have that r^1 (r^0, resp.) does not occur in δ. We say that δ is pure iff it is a Boolean combination of purely left or purely right atoms.*

Given a formula $\delta(\underline{a}^0, \underline{a}^1)$, it is always possible (see, e.g., [8]) to obtain an equisatisfiable formula $\tilde{\delta}(\underline{a}^0, \underline{a}^1, \underline{d}^0)$ which is pure by introducing "fresh" constants that we call $\underline{d}^0$ (i.e., $\underline{d}^0 \cap (\underline{a}^0 \cup \underline{a}^1) = \emptyset$) to name "impure" subterms. Usually, $\tilde{\delta}$ is called the purification of δ. Let $A_1, \ldots, A_k$ be the atoms occurring in $\tilde{\delta}(\underline{a}^0, \underline{a}^1, \underline{d}^0)$. A $\tilde{\delta}$-assignment is a conjunction $B_1 \wedge \cdots \wedge B_k$ (where B_i is either A_i or $\neg A_i$, for $1 \leq i \leq k$), such that $B_1 \wedge \cdots \wedge B_k \to \tilde{\delta}$ is a propositional tautology. Since $\tilde{\delta}$ is pure, we can represent a $\tilde{\delta}$-assignment V in the form $V^l(\underline{a}^0, \underline{a}^1, \underline{d}^0) \wedge V^r(\underline{a}^0, \underline{a}^1, \underline{d}^0)$, where V^l is a purely left conjunction of literals and V^r is a purely right conjunction of literals. As a consequence, a bad run of length $n + 1$ exists iff the ground sentence

$$\iota(\underline{a}^0) \wedge \bigwedge_{i=0}^{n} (V_{i+1}^l(\underline{a}^i, \underline{a}^{i+1}, \underline{d}^i) \wedge V_{i+1}^r(\underline{a}^i, \underline{a}^{i+1}, \underline{d}^i)) \wedge \upsilon(\underline{a}^{n+1}) \qquad (3)$$

is $\bigoplus_{\Sigma_r}^{n+2} T$-satisfiable, where $\underline{d}^0, \underline{d}^1, \ldots, \underline{d}^n$ are $n + 1$ copies of the fresh constants $\underline{d}^0$ and $V_1, \ldots, V_{n+1}$ range over the set of $\tilde{\delta}$-assignments. Since T_r is locally finite, there are finitely many ground $\Sigma_r^{\underline{c}, \underline{a}^0, \underline{a}^1, \underline{d}^0}$-literals which are representative (modulo T_r-equivalence) of all $\Sigma_r^{\underline{c}, \underline{a}^0, \underline{a}^1, \underline{d}^0}$-literals. A guessing $G(\underline{a}^0, \underline{a}^1, \underline{d}^0)$ (cf. Definition 3.4) over such literals will be called a *transition Σ_r-guessing*.

Definition 4.7. *The safety graph associated to the LTL-system specification $(\mathcal{T}, \delta, \iota)$ based on the locally finite compatible LTL-theory $\mathcal{T}$ is the directed graph defined as follows:*

- *the nodes are the pairs (V, G) where V is a $\tilde{\delta}$-assignment and G is a transition Σ_r-guessing;*
- *there is an edge $(V, G) \to (W, H)$ iff the ground sentence*

$$G(\underline{a}^0, \underline{a}^1, \underline{d}^0) \wedge V^r(\underline{a}^0, \underline{a}^1, \underline{d}^0) \wedge W^l(\underline{a}^1, \underline{a}^2, \underline{d}^1) \wedge H(\underline{a}^1, \underline{a}^2, \underline{d}^1) \qquad (4)$$

is $\mathcal{T}$-satisfiable.

The initial nodes *of the safety graph are the nodes* (V, G) *such that* $\iota(\underline{a}^0) \wedge V^l(\underline{a}^0, \underline{a}^1, \underline{d}^0) \wedge G(\underline{a}^0, \underline{a}^1, \underline{d}^0)$ *is* T-*satisfiable; the* terminal nodes *of the safety graph are the nodes* (V, G) *such that* $V^r(\underline{a}^0, \underline{a}^1, \underline{d}^0) \wedge v(\underline{a}^1) \wedge G(\underline{a}^0, \underline{a}^1, \underline{d}^0)$ *is* T-*satisfiable.*

The decision procedure for safety model-checking relies on the following fact.

Proposition 4.1. *The system is unsafe iff either* $\iota(\underline{a}) \wedge v(\underline{a})$ *is* T-*satisfiable or there is a path in the safety graph from an initial to a terminal node.*

The idea behind the proof is the following: by contradiction, assume there is a path from an initial to a terminal node and the system is safe. Repeatedly, compute Σ_r-ground interpolants of (3) between T and $\bigoplus_{\Sigma_r}^{j} T$, for $j = n+1, \ldots, 1$ (an argument based on Lemma 2.1 guarantees they exist). This yields the T-unsatisfiability of the final node (formula) in the graph; a contradiction.

Theorem 4.1. *The ground safety model-checking problem for a locally finite compatible LTL-system specification is decidable.*

For complexity, the same remarks after Corollary 3.1 apply here too.

Example 4.1 ([18]). Consider a water level controller such that (i) changes in the water level by in(flow)/out(flow) depend on the water level l and on the time instant; (ii) if $l \geq l_{\text{alarm}}$ at a given state (where l_{alarm} is a fixed value), then a valve is opened and, at the next observable instant, $l' = in(out(l))$; and (iii) if $l < l_{\text{alarm}}$ then the valve is closed and, at the next observable instant, $l' = in(l)$.

Let us now consider the LTL-theory $\mathcal{T} = \langle \Sigma, T, \Sigma_r, \underline{a}, \underline{c} \rangle$ where l is the only system variable ($\underline{a} := \{l\}$) and there are no system parameters ($\underline{c} := \emptyset$); $\Sigma_r = \{l_{\text{alarm}}, l_{\text{overflow}}, <\}$, $l_{\text{alarm}}, l_{\text{overflow}}$ are two constant symbols and $<$ is a binary predicate symbol; $\Sigma := \Sigma_r \cup \{in, out\}$; T_r is the theory of dense linear orders without endpoints endowed with the additional axiom $l_{\text{alarm}} < l_{\text{overflow}}$; and

$$T := T_r \cup \left\{ \begin{array}{l} \forall x \, (x < l_{\text{alarm}} \rightarrow in(x) < l_{\text{overflow}}), \\ \forall x \, (x < l_{\text{overflow}} \rightarrow out(x) < l_{\text{alarm}}) \end{array} \right\}$$

It can be shown that the constraint satisfiability problem for T is decidable, T_r admits quantifier elimination, and T_r is effectively locally finite. From these, it follows that $\mathcal{T}$ is a locally finitely compatible LTL-theory. We consider now the LTL-system specification $(\mathcal{T}, \delta, \iota)$ where $\iota := l < l_{\text{alarm}}$ and

$$\delta := \left(l_{\text{alarm}} \leq l^0 \rightarrow l^1 = in^0(out^0(l^0)) \right) \wedge \left(l^0 < l_{\text{alarm}} \rightarrow l^1 = in^0(l^0) \right).$$

Notice that δ is a purely left $(\Sigma^{\underline{a}} \oplus_{\Sigma_r} \Sigma^{\underline{a}})$-formula.

We consider the safety model-checking problem specified by the LTL-system above and whose unsafe states are described by $v := l_{\text{overflow}} < l$. Using the procedure suggested by Theorem 4.1 we can prove that the system is safe, i.e. that there is no run $\mathcal{M}$ for $(\mathcal{T}, \delta, \iota)$ such that $\mathcal{M} \models \Diamond v$. We can observe that the task in practice is not extremely hard computationally. It is sufficient to consider just 50 nodes (modulo T-equivalence) of the safety graph that are T-satisfiable (i.e. the nodes (V, G) such that $V \wedge G$ is T-satisfiable). Also, instead of considering all the edges of the safety graph, it is sufficient to build just the paths starting from the initial nodes or ending in a terminal node (namely to apply a forward/backward search strategy). In the first case, only 26 nodes of the safety graph are reachable from an initial node. In the latter, just 12 nodes are backward reachable from a terminal node. Hence the the problem is clearly amenable to automatic analysis by combining a decision procedure for T with a SAT-solver which is able to enumerate the $\tilde{\delta}$-assignments needed to traverse the safety graph.

Example 4.2. The aim of this example is to use our techniques to analyze the safety of the well-known Lamport's mutual exclusion "Bakery" algorithm. If the number of involved processes is unknown, we can build for the problem an appropriate LTL-system specification T which violates our assumptions in Figure 1 because it has universal (instead of ground) transition relation and initial state description. More in detail, we use a language with two sorts, one for the individuals (i.e the involved processes), the other for the tickets. The tickets are ruled by the theory of dense total order with named distinct (rigid) endpoints 0 and 1; moreover, a (flexible) function for the ticket assignment is constrained by an "almost-injectivity" axiom (i.e., people cannot have the same ticket with the exception of the ticket 1 that means being out of the queue). Finally, a flexible constant models the current ticket bound and a flexible predicate captures the served individuals. The transition says the following: (i) the values of the current ticket bound are strictly increasing; (ii) every individual is removed from the queue immediately after being served; (iii) if an individual is in the queue and is not served, then its ticket is preserved; (iv) if an individual is not the first in the queue, it cannot be served; (v) if an individual is not in the queue, either remains out of the queue or takes a ticket lying in the interval between two consecutive values of the current ticket bound (without being immediately served). The initial state description says that no one is in the queue and the current ticket bound is set to 0, whereas the unsafe states are the ones in which at least two people are served at the same time.

By Skolemization and instantiation, we produce out of T a locally finite compatible LTL-system specification T' which is safe iff T is safe. Safety of T' can then be easily checked through our techniques (see [9] for details). We point out that the features of T that make the whole construction to work are *purely syntactic* in nature: they basically consist of the finiteness of the set of terms of certain sorts in the skolemized Herbrand universe.

5 Discussion

The undecidability of quantified modal logics over a discrete flow was discovered by D. Scott already in the sixties. Recent works isolated quite interesting fragments of quantified LTL which are computationally better behaved (see [7] for a survey). However such fragments are often insufficient for verification; in this respect, a more promising restriction is to prohibit the interplay between quantifiers and temporal operators [12]. In this paper, we have taken a similar approach by enriching the extensional part of the language so to be able to model infinite data structures manipulated by systems. This lead us to consider satisfiability of quantifier-free LTL formulae built up from a first-order signature Σ and models with constant domain consisting of a sequence $\{\mathcal{M}_i\}_i$ of first-order models of a Σ-theory T. Furthermore, symbols in Σ and free variables were divided into two groups. The former are interpreted rigidly whereas the latter flexibly in the $\mathcal{M}_i$'s. This approach was already taken in the seminal paper [15] by Plaisted, who established a decidability result when the quantifier-free fragment of T is decidable and the flexible symbols are considered as free symbols by the theory T. By using recent techniques and results from the combination literature, we were able to attack the problem in its full generality and derive both the undecidability in the unrestricted case and the decidability under the 'combinability' hypotheses for T of [8]. Such hypotheses, besides decidability of the universal first-order fragment, were compatibility over a locally finite subtheory in the rigid subsignature (local finiteness may be replaced by the weaker requirement of Noetherianity, but this result has been omitted in the paper for lack of space and can be found in [9]).

In the second part of the paper we considered model-checking problems under the same 'combinability' hypotheses on T. We were able to derive positive decidability results for the safety properties and we plan to extend our results to different kinds of properties (such as liveness) as well as to full LTL model-checking. Our framework generalizes finite state model-checking in two respects. First, the rigid symbols are constrained by a locally finite theory, not just by an enumerated datatype theory. Second, we do not impose limitations on the flexible symbols, whose interpretation is only constrained by the axioms of T.

The literature on infinite state model-checking is extremely vast (see [20,16,2] to name but a few approaches). For lack of space, we consider works which are closely related to ours. The paper [5] extensively reviews constrained LTL, which can be the basis for model checking of infinite state systems but it does not allow for flexible symbols (apart from system variables). Furthermore, fixed purely relational structures play there the same role of the models of the theory T in our approach. However, [5] is not limited to safety properties. If our results can be extended beyond safety (as it seems likely), *some* of the results in [5] could be seen as specializations of our work to totally rigid system specifications. Other results and techniques from [5] (and also from the recent [6]) should be taken into account for integration in our framework so to be able to handle richer underlying theories such as Linear Arithmetic.

An integration of classic tableaux and automated deduction techniques is presented in [17,11]. While using a similar approach, [17] only provides a uniform framework for such an integration with no guarantee of full automation, whereas [11] focuses on the decidability of the model-checking problem of particular classes of parametrized systems. Both works do not use combination techniques. The approach in [4] proposes the reduction of bounded model-checking problems to SMT problems. Theorem 4.1 identifies precise conditions under which our reduction yields a decision procedure: our safety graph is not just an approximation of the set of reachable states. With [4], we share the focus on using SMT solvers, which is also a common feature of the "abstract-check-refine" approach to infinite-state model-checking (see the seminal work in [10]). However, our work is foundational whereas abstract-check-refine techniques focus more on practical usability.

References

1. Bonacina, M.P., Ghilardi, S., Nicolini, E., Ranise, S., Zucchelli, D.: Decidability and undecidability results for Nelson-Oppen and rewrite-based decision procedures. In: Furbach, U., Shankar, N. (eds.) IJCAR 2006. LNCS (LNAI), vol. 4130, Springer, Heidelberg (2006)
2. Burkart, O., Caucal, D., Moller, F., Steffen, B.: Verification of infinite state structures. In: Handbook of Process Algebras (2001)
3. Clarke, E.M., Grumberg, O., Peled, D.A.: Model Checking. MIT Press, Cambridge (2000)
4. de Moura, L., Rueß, H., Sorea, M.: Lazy theorem proving for bounded model checking over infinite domains. In: Voronkov, A. (ed.) Automated Deduction - CADE-18. LNCS (LNAI), vol. 2392, Springer, Heidelberg (2002)
5. Demri, S.: Linear-time temporal logics with Presburger constraints: An overview. Journal of Applied Non-Classical Logics 16(3-4) (2006)
6. Demri, S., Finkel, A., Goranko, V., van Drimmelen, G.: Towards a model-checker for counter systems. In: Graf, S., Zhang, W. (eds.) ATVA 2006. LNCS, vol. 4218, Springer, Heidelberg (2006)
7. Gabbay, D.M., Kurucz, A., Wolter, F., Zakharyaschev, M.: Many-Dimensional Modal Logics: Theory and Applications. North-Holland Publishing Co. (2003)
8. Ghilardi, S.: Model theoretic methods in combined constraint satisfiability. Journal of Automated Reasoning 33(3-4) (2004)
9. Ghilardi, S., Nicolini, E., Ranise, S., Zucchelli, D.: Combination methods for satisfiability and model-checking of infinite-state systems. Technical Report RI313-07, Università degli Studi di Milano (2007) Available at http://homes.dsi.unimi.it/ zucchell/publications/techreport/ GhiNiRaZu-RI313-07.pdf
10. Graf, S., Saïdi, H.: Construction of abstract state graphs with PVS. In: Grumberg, O. (ed.) CAV 1997. LNCS, vol. 1254, Springer, Heidelberg (1997)
11. Maidl, M.: A unifying model checking approach for safety properties of parameterized systems. In: Berry, G., Comon, H., Finkel, A. (eds.) CAV 2001. LNCS, vol. 2102, Springer, Heidelberg (2001)
12. Manna, Z., Pnueli, A.: Temporal Verification of Reactive Systems: Safety. Springer, Heidelberg (1995)
13. Minsky, M.L.: Recursive unsolvability of Post's problem of "tag" and other topics in the theory of Turing machines. Annals of Mathematics 74(3) (1961)
14. Nelson, G., Oppen, D.C.: Simplification by cooperating decision procedures. ACM Transaction on Programming Languages and Systems 1(2) (1979)
15. Plaisted, D.A.: A decision procedure for combination of propositional temporal logic and other specialized theories. Journal of Automated Reasoning 2(2) (1986)
16. Pnueli, A., Ruath, S., Zuck, L.D.: Automatic deductive verification with invisible invariants. In: Margaria, T., Yi, W. (eds.) ETAPS 2001 and TACAS 2001. LNCS, vol. 2031, Springer, Heidelberg (2001)

17. Sipma, H.B., Uribe, T.E., Manna, Z.: Deductive model checking. Formal Methods in System Design 15(1) (1999)
18. Sofronie-Stokkermans, V.: Interpolation in local theory extensions. In: Furbach, U., Shankar, N. (eds.) IJCAR 2006. LNCS (LNAI), vol. 4130, Springer, Heidelberg (2006)
19. Tinelli, C., Harandi, M.T.: A new correctness proof of the Nelson-Oppen combination procedure. In: Proc. of FroCoS 1996 (1996)
20. Vardi, M.Y.: Verification of concurrent programs: the automata-theoretic framework. Annals of Pure and Applied Logic 51(1-2) (1991)

The KeY System 1.0
(Deduction Component)

Bernhard Beckert, Martin Giese, Reiner Hähnle, Vladimir Klebanov,
Philipp Rümmer, Steffen Schlager, and Peter H. Schmitt

www.key-project.org

Abstract. The KeY system is a development of the ongoing KeY project, whose aim is to integrate formal specification and deductive verification into the industrial software engineering processes. The deductive component of the KeY system is a novel interactive/automated prover for first-order Dynamic Logic for Java. The KeY prover features a user-friendly graphical interface, a backtracking-free free-variable sequent calculus, a simple and powerful theory formalization language called "taclets," solution procedures for linear and non-linear integer arithmetic, external theorem prover integration, and facilities for proof reuse, among other aspects. The system is publicly available.

Introduction. The KeY system is the main software product of the KeY project, a joint effort between the University of Karlsruhe, Chalmers University of Technology in Göteborg, and the University of Koblenz. The KeY system is a formal software development tool that aims to integrate design, implementation, formal specification, and formal verification of object-oriented software as seamlessly as possible. At the core of the system is a deductive verification component, which also can be used as a stand-alone prover. It employs a free-variable sequent calculus for first-order Dynamic Logic for JAVA. The calculus is proof-confluent, i.e., no backtracking is necessary during proof search.

While we constantly strive to increase the degree of automation, user interaction remains indispensable in deductive program verification. The main design goal of the KeY prover is thus a seamless integration of automated and interactive proving. Efficiency must be measured in terms of user plus prover, not just prover alone. Therefore, a combination of a good user interface for proof state presentation and rule application, a high level of automation, extensibility of the rule base, and a calculus without backtracking is the strong point of KeY.

In this paper we concentrate on the description of the KeY prover and the reasoning techniques it employs. The prover consists of ca. 124,000 lines[1] of JAVA code. The standard rule base consists of 1,725 rules that are written in about 15,000 lines of KeY's "taclet" rule description language. About 1,300 of these formalize the semantics of the JAVA programming language. The system has been created by 14 implementors since 1999, who spent a total of about

---

[1] Not counting comments. These numbers are based on our estimates and the results of the SLOCCount tool (www.dwheeler.com/sloccount).

F. Pfenning (Ed.): CADE 2007, LNAI 4603, pp. 379–384, 2007.
© Springer-Verlag Berlin Heidelberg 2007

30 person years. Recently, version 1.0 of the KeY system has been released in connection with the KeY book [2]. The KeY tool is available under GPL and can be downloaded from www.key-project.org.

The KeY Program Verification System. The architecture of the KeY system is shown in Fig. 1. Optional plugins to the popular Eclipse IDE and to the Borland Together CASE tool suite have been developed to lower the entry hurdle for users with no or little training in formal methods. KeY supports several languages for specifying properties of object-oriented models. Many people working with UML or model-driven development have familiarity with the specification language OCL (Object Constraint Language), a part of UML 2.0. Another supported specification language, which enjoys popularity among JAVA developers, is JML (Java Modeling Language). KeY can also translate OCL expressions to natural language (English and German).

The target programming language for verification in KeY is JAVA CARD 2.2.1. KeY is the only publicly available verification tool that supports the full JAVA CARD standard including the persistent/transient memory model of the card devices and the atomic transactions. Rich specifications of the JAVA CARD API are available both in OCL and JML. JAVA 1.4 programs that respect the limitations of JAVA CARD (no floats, no reflection, no dynamic class loading) can be verified as well. A first prototype for verifying (restricted) multi-threaded programs is also available.

The system is not a classical verification condition generator (VCG), but a theorem prover for program logic that combines a variety of automated reasoning techniques. The KeY prover is distinguished from most other deductive verification systems in that symbolic execution of programs, first-order reasoning, arithmetic simplification, external decision procedures, and symbolic state

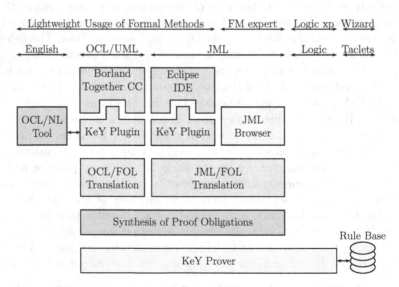

Fig. 1. Architecture and interfaces of the KeY system

simplification are interleaved. For loop- and recursion-free programs, symbolic execution typically is performed in a fully automated manner.

Syntax and Semantics of the KeY Logic. The foundation of the KeY logic is a typed first-order predicate logic with subtyping. This foundation is extended with parameterized modal operators $\langle p \rangle$ and $[p]$, where p can be any sequence of legal JAVA CARD statements. The resulting multi-modal program logic is called JAVA CARD Dynamic Logic or, for short, JAVA CARD DL [2, Chapt. 3].

As is typical for dynamic logic, JAVA CARD DL integrates programs and formulas within a single language. The modal operators refer to the final state of program p and can be placed in front of any formula. The formula $\langle p \rangle \phi$ expresses that the program p terminates in a state in which ϕ holds, while $[p]\phi$ does not demand termination and expresses that *if* p terminates, then ϕ holds in the final state. For example, "when started in a state where x is zero, x++; terminates in a state where x is one" can be expressed as $x \doteq 0 \rightarrow \langle x++; \rangle (x \doteq 1)$. The states used to interpret formulas are first-order structures sharing a common universe.

The type system of the KeY logic is designed to match the JAVA type system but can be used for other purposes as well. The logic includes *type casts* (changing the static type of a term) and *type predicates* (checking the dynamic type of a term) in order to reason about inheritance and polymorphism [2, Chapter 2]. The type hierarchy contains the types such as boolean, the root reference type Object, and the type Null, which is a subtype of all reference types. It contains a set of user-defined types, which are usually used to represent the interfaces and classes of a given JAVA CARD program. Finally, it contains several integer types, including both the range-limited types of JAVA and the infinite integer type $\mathbb{Z}$.

Beside built-in symbols (such as type-cast functions, equality, and operations on integers), user-defined functions and predicates can be added to the signature. They can be either *rigid* or *non-rigid*. Intuitively, rigid symbols have the same meaning in all program states (e.g., the addition on integers), whereas the meaning of non-rigid symbols may differ from state to state.

Finally, there is another kind of modal operators called *updates*. They can be seen as a language for describing program transitions. There are simple function updates corresponding to assignments in an imperative programming language, which in turn can be composed sequentially and used to form parallel or quantified updates. Updates play a central role in KeY: the verification calculus transforms JAVA CARD programs into updates. KeY contains a powerful and efficient mechanism for simplifying updates and applying them to formulas.

Rule Formalization and Application. The user can easily interleave the automated proof search implemented in KeY and interactive rule application. For interactive rule application, the KeY prover has an easy to use graphical user interface that is built around the idea of direct manipulation (Fig. 2). To apply a rule, the user first selects a *focus of application* by highlighting a (sub-)formula or a (sub-)term in the goal sequent. The prover then offers a choice of rules applicable at this focus. This choice remains manageable even for very large rule bases. Rule schema variable instantiations are mostly inferred by matching.

Another simple way to apply rules and give instantiations is by drag and drop. If the user drags an equation onto a term the system will try to rewrite the term with the equation. If the user drags a term onto a quantifier the system will try to instantiate the quantifier with this term.

The interaction style is closely related to the way rules are formalized in the KeY prover. There are no hard-coded rules; all rules are defined in the *taclet language* instead. Besides the conventional declarative semantics, taclets have a clear operational semantics, as the following example shows—a "modus ponens" rule in textbook notation (left) and as a taclet (right):

$$\frac{\phi, \psi, \Gamma \vdash \Delta}{\phi, \phi \rightarrow \psi, \Gamma \vdash \Delta}$$

```
\find (p -> q ==>)        // implication in antecedent
\assumes (p ==>)          // side condition
\replacewith(q ==>)       // action on found focus
\heuristics(simplify)     // strategy information
```

The **find** clause specifies the potential application focus. The taclet will be offered to the user on selecting a matching focus and if the formula mentioned in the **assumes** clause is present in the sequent. The action clauses **replacewith** and **add** allow modifying (or deleting) the formula in focus, as well as adding additional formulas (not present here). The **heuristics** clause provides priority information to the parameterized automated proof search strategy.

The taclet language is quickly mastered and makes the rule base easy to maintain and extend. Taclets can be proven correct against a set of base taclets. A full account of the taclet language is given in [2].

Confluent Calculus. In order to simplify the proof construction, which is typically partly automated and partly interactive, we have developed and employ a proof confluent sequent calculus. This means that automated proof search does

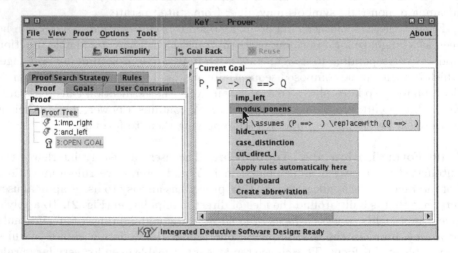

Fig. 2. Screenshot of the KeY prover user interface

not require backtracking over rule applications, which is advantageous for analyzing failed proof attempts. The automated search for quantifier instantiations uses rigid free variables (called meta variables) like in a free-variable tableau calculus. Instead of backtracking over meta-variable instantiations, instantiations are postponed to the point where the whole proof can be closed, and an incremental global closure check is used. To minimize the confusion of novice users, meta variables are not visible in normal interactive use, if the user provides all required instantiations. Rule applications requiring particular instantiations (unifications) of meta variables are handled by attaching unification constraints to the resulting formulas [2, Sects. 4.3 and 10.2.2]. Equations are handled by ordered rewriting (currently in an incomplete way, which we have not, however, found to be a limiting factor so far).

The taclet language is designed in such a way that the user can only write rules with local effects on sequents, and the handling of meta variables, skolemization, constraints, etc. is taken care of automatically, to reduce the risk of inadvertently introducing rules that are unsound or damage confluence.

Handling Arithmetics. As the theory of integer arithmetic is omnipresent in program verification, KeY directly provides a number of automatic solution and simplification procedures for different fragments of arithmetic. All procedures are formulated in terms of taclets, which have been verified against a small set of base axioms. The implemented methods target both proving (showing that equations are unsolvable) and construction of counterexamples (finding solutions of equations) for ground integer formulas.

The most basic method is a sequent calculus formulation of integer Gaussian elimination, which is a complete method for solving linear equations. As a prerequisite of the procedure, integer expressions are always fully expanded and sorted. Linear inequalities are handled by Fourier-Motzkin variable elimination, which we combine with systematic case distinctions in order to obtain a complete procedure over the integers.

Reasoning in non-linear integer arithmetic is mainly carried out by heuristic cross-multiplication of inequalities, similar to the approach of the ACL2 prover. In order to reduce expressions as far as possible and handle non-linear equations more efficiently, KeY also computes Gröbner bases over the integers.

The KeY system also features a component for easy integration of external automated theorem provers and (semi-)decision procedures. Proof goals are translated into the standardized input format SMT-LIB and discharged by calling any tool that understands this format, such as Yices or CVC Lite. A similar connector for the theorem prover Simplify is also available. The user benefits from the particular abilities of these tools to decide fragments of arithmetics, heuristically instantiate quantifiers, etc.

Applications. The main application of the KeY prover is to support program verification in the KeY system. Among the major achievements in this field so far are the treatment of the Demoney case study (an electronic purse application provided by Trusted Logic S.A.) and the verification of a JAVA implementation of the Schorr-Waite graph marking algorithm. This algorithm, originally developed for garbage collectors, has recently become a popular benchmark for program verification tools. Chapters 14 and 15 of the KeY book [2] are devoted to a detailed description of these case studies. A case study [6] performed within the HIJA project has verified with KeY the lateral module of the flight management system, a part of the on-board control software from Thales Avionics.

Lately we have applied the KeY system also to issues of security analysis [3], and in the area of model-based test case generation [1,4] where, in particular, the prover is used to compute path conditions and to identify infeasible paths. The flexibility of KeY w.r.t. the used logic and calculus further manifests itself in the fact that the prover has been chosen as a reasoning engine for a variety of other purposes. These include the mechanization of a logic for Abstract State Machines [7] and the implementation of a calculus for simplifying OCL constraints [5].

KeY is also very useful for teaching logic, deduction, and formal methods. Its graphical user interface makes KeY easy to use for students. They can step through proofs with different degrees of automation (using the full verification calculus or just the first-order core rules). The authors have been successfully teaching courses for several years using the KeY system. An overview and course materials are available at www.key-project.org/teaching.

References

1. Beckert, B., Gladisch, C.: White-box testing by combining deduction-based specification extraction and black-box testing. In: Gurevich, Y. (ed.) Proceedings, Testing and Proofs, Zürich, Switzerland. LNCS, Springer, Heidelberg (2007)
2. Beckert, B., Hähnle, R., Schmitt, P.H. (eds.): Verification of Object-Oriented Software. LNCS (LNAI), vol. 4334. Springer, Heidelberg (2007)
3. Darvas, Á., Hähnle, R., Sands, D.: A theorem proving approach to analysis of secure information flow. In: Hutter, D., Ullmann, M. (eds.) SPC 2005. LNCS, vol. 3450, pp. 193–209. Springer, Heidelberg (2005)
4. Engel, C., Hähnle, R.: Generating unit tests from formal proofs. In: Gurevich, Y. (ed.) Proceedings, Testing and Proofs, Zürich, Switzerland. LNCS, Springer, Heidelberg (2007)
5. Giese, M., Larsson, D.: Simplifying transformations of OCL constraints. In: Briand, L.C., Williams, C. (eds.) MoDELS 2005. LNCS, vol. 3713, Springer, Heidelberg (2005)
6. Hunt, J.J., Jenn, E., Leriche, S., Schmitt, P., Tonin, I., Wonnemann, C.: A case study of specification and verification using JML in an avionics application. In: Rochard-Foy, M., Wellings, A. (eds.) Proc. of the 4th Workshop on Java Technologies for Real-time and Embedded Systems (JTRES), ACM Press, New York (2006)
7. Nanchen, S., Schmid, H., Schmitt, P., Stärk, R.F.: The ASMKeY prover. Technical Report 436, Department of Computer Science, ETH Zürich (2004)

KeY-C: A Tool for Verification of C Programs

Oleg Mürk, Daniel Larsson, and Reiner Hähnle

Chalmers University of Technology, Dept. of Computer Science and Engineering
S-412 96 Gothenburg, Sweden
oleg.myrk@gmail.com, danla@chalmers.se, reiner@chalmers.se

Abstract. We present KeY-C, a tool for deductive verification of C programs. KeY-C allows to prove partial correctness of C programs relative to pre- and postconditions. It is based on a version of KeY that supports JAVA CARD. In this paper we give a glimpse of syntax, semantics, and calculus of C Dynamic Logic (CDL) that were adapted from their JAVA CARD counterparts, based on an example. Currently, the tool is in an early development stage.

1 Introduction

We present KeY-C, a variant of the software verification tool KeY [1] that supports a subset of C as its target language. KeY is an interactive theorem proving environment and allows one to prove properties of imperative/object-oriented sequential programs. The central concept is an axiomatization of the operational semantics of the target language in the form of a sequent calculus for dynamic logic, i.e., a program logic. The rules of the calculus that axiomatize program formulae define a symbolic execution engine for C. The system provides heuristics and proof strategies that automate large parts of proof construction, for example, first-order reasoning, arithmetic simplification, and symbolic execution of loop-free non-recursive programs is performed mostly automatically. The remaining user input typically consists of occasional existential quantifier instantiations. The main creative part is to specify a program including loop (in)variants. KeY was designed to ease interactive proof construction (see screenshot Fig. 1) and to lower the gradient of the learning curve. For example, JAVA/C Dynamic Logic formulae contain executable source code, not a logic encoding or abstraction.

The existing KeY system can handle JAVA CARD and most of sequential JAVA, allowing verification of complex programs [1, Part IV]. Its calculus contains over 1000 rules of which about half are language-independent Dynamic Logic (DL) rules. We are working on adding gradual support for a portable type-safe subset of C, axiomatized in C Dynamic Logic (CDL). As a side-product of this work we expect to generalize the KeY architecture such that support for further programming languages can be easily added.

In Section 2 we give a taste of CDL and illustrate some of the problems that had to be solved during its design by working through a simple, but non-trivial, example that computes the sum of integer elements in a linked list (see Fig. 2). Section 3 describes the current status and further work, and in Section 4 we conclude with related work and a summary.

F. Pfenning (Ed.): CADE 2007, LNAI 4603, pp. 385–390, 2007.
© Springer-Verlag Berlin Heidelberg 2007

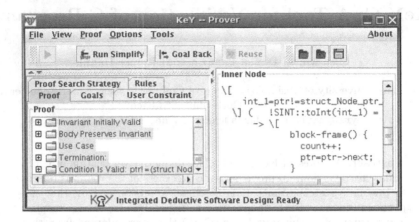

Fig. 1. KeY graphical user interface

```
struct Node {
    struct Node* next;
    int elem;
};
```

```
int sum(register struct Node* first) {
    register struct Node* ptr = first;
    int psum = 0;
    while (ptr != 0) {
        psum = psum + ptr->elem;
        ptr = ptr->next;
    }
    return psum;
}
```

Fig. 2. Example C program

2   C Dynamic Logic by Example

Dynamic Logic (DL) is based on First-Order Logic (FOL) extended with a *type system*—function and predicate arguments and function results are equipped with a type. In order to arrive at a reasonable calculus, the subtyping relationship ⊑ must form a lattice. In the formal semantics all elements of the semantic domain also receive a type. In order to represent different states during program execution, function and predicate symbols are split into *rigid* and *non-rigid* symbols. Rigid symbols behave the same as in FOL, while non-rigid symbols can have different values in different execution states.

CDL is a modal logic with a parametric modality [P] for every (compilable) C program P. The semantics is defined in terms of deterministic Kripke structures, where states (worlds) are determined by the values of non-rigid symbols and transitions are defined by the semantics of C programs. A formula is *valid* iff it is true in all possible states. The formula [P]ϕ is true in a state s iff ϕ holds in the final state reached when P is started in s provided that P terminates at all. In other words, [P]ϕ asserts *partial correctness* of [P] w.r.t. postcondition ϕ.

Locations are special non-rigid functions that can have an arbitrary value in different states of the Kripke structure and are used to model modifiable memory locations of the program. I.e., there exists a state for every combination of the values of the locations, while the value of other non-rigid symbols in some state may, for instance, depend on the values of some locations in this state.

The type system and the signature of CDL reflect the peculiarities of the C language. To represent integer *rvalues* we introduce an integer type int with the signature and semantics of mathematical integers $\mathbb{Z}$. Further, we need a supertype of all *object* types Void. Objects are memory locations that hold values and can be referenced by pointers (and consequently are *lvalues*). Symbols representing pointer rvalues will have a type which is either Void or one of its subtypes. To represent pointer null rvalues we introduce the subtype of all object types Null. The semantics of this type consists of exactly one element represented by the constant null. All concrete object types are a subtype of Void and a supertype of Null. All types T are equipped with a *scalar* object type T@ and value location T@::value : T@ → T. In the example, these are int@ and \$Node@, where \$Node is a *structure* object type with rigid member accessor functions \$Node::next : \$Node → \$Node@ and \$Node::elem : \$Node → int@. In the following we use the more compact notation *i*.value, *n*.next, etc.

Program variables are represented by location symbols. In the example, their types are ptr : \$Node and psum : int@. We use the storage class **register** of variable ptr to denote that it cannot be referenced by a pointer and consequently can have an rvalue type as opposed to an lvalue type. We left the variable psum without this storage class to illustrate the challenge of having to prove non-aliasing of arbitrary object references of the same type, e.g., psum and ptr.elem. Otherwise, the type of psum would simply be int.

We create a proof obligation expressing that function sum actually computes the sum of the elements in a linked list. In general, proof obligations for (partial) correctness have the form *pre* ⇒ [F]*post*, where *pre* specifies assumptions about the initial state and *post* specifies the requirements for the state if function body F terminates. In order to express the precondition that the function argument first refers to a linked list we need to introduce two fresh rigid functions *len* : int and *list* : int → \$Node. A possible precondition is now

$$len \geq 0 \ \wedge \ list(0) = \text{first} \ \wedge$$
$$\forall \text{ int } i; ((0 \leq i) \wedge (i < len) \Rightarrow list(i).\text{next.value} = list(i+1)) \ \wedge$$
$$\forall \text{ int } i; ((0 \leq i) \wedge (i < len) \Rightarrow list(i) \neq \text{null}) \ \wedge \ list(len) = \text{null}$$

and the postcondition becomes psum.value $= sumSpec(len)$, where $sumSpec$: int → int is a fresh rigid function and $sumSpec(i)$ gives the sum of the first i elements of *list*. Its properties are axiomatised in the precondition:

$$sumSpec(0) = 0 \ \wedge$$
$$\forall \text{ int } i; (i > 0 \Rightarrow sumSpec(i) = sumSpec(i-1) + list(i-1).\text{elem.value}) \ .$$

A *sequent calculus* is used for performing deduction. A sequent is of the form $\Gamma \vdash \Delta$, where Γ and Δ are sets of formulae. The semantics of a sequent is the same as that of the formula $\bigwedge \Gamma \Rightarrow \bigvee \Delta$. The CDL calculus builds upon standard FOL with equality and arithmetic. DL calculus rules that work on program modalities always modify the first active statement of the programs in the modalities.

The main principle of CDL is to reduce program modalities to so-called *updates*. An *atomic update* has the form $\mathcal{U} = \{loc := val\}$, where *loc* is a *location* expression and *val* is its new value term. Semantically, the validity of $\mathcal{U}\phi$ in state s is defined as the validity of ϕ in state s', which is state s where the values of locations are modified according to the update $\mathcal{U}$. There are operations for sequential and parallel composition of updates as well as for quantification, where the update is quantified by a free variable satisfying some condition. An update applied to a pure FOL formula can be automatically transformed into a pure FOL formula without an update. Typically, most loop- and recursion-free sequences of program statements can be turned into updates fully automatically.

For instance, symbolic execution of the first two lines of the function body in the sequent *pre* ⊢ [F]*post* results in *pre* ⊢ $\mathcal{U}$[W]*post*, where W is the remaining program starting with the while-loop and $\mathcal{U}$ is the following update:

{ ptr := first; psum := int@::⟨lookup⟩(next); next := next + 1; psum.value = 0 } .

This update illustrates *object allocation* in CDL: psum is assigned int@::⟨lookup⟩(next) (the object lookup function ⟨lookup⟩ is rigid) and the non-rigid object counter next, pointing to the non-allocated object with lowest index, is incremented. As explained above, the value location of the scalar object type int@ is accessed with the function value.

When a loop or a recursive function call is encountered, one must perform induction or use a loop invariant. In our case a suitable invariant $\mathcal{I}$ is:

$$\exists \text{ int } i; (0 \leq i \wedge i \leq len \wedge \text{ptr} = list(i) \wedge \text{psum.value} = sumSpec(i)) .$$

To establish partial correctness of our loop using an invariant rule for imperative languages [2] one proves that the invariant holds initially, i.e., *pre* ⊢ $\mathcal{U}\mathcal{I}$, as well as formulae

$$pre \vdash \mathcal{U}\mathcal{V}(\mathcal{I} \Rightarrow [\textbf{register int } \text{b} = \text{ptr} \mathrel{!=} 0](\text{b} = 1 \Rightarrow [\text{B}]\mathcal{I})) ,$$
$$pre \vdash \mathcal{U}\mathcal{V}(\mathcal{I} \Rightarrow [\textbf{register int } \text{b} = \text{ptr} \mathrel{!=} 0](\text{b} = 0 \Rightarrow post)) ,$$

where statement B is the loop body. $\mathcal{V}$ is a so called *anonymous* parallel update { ptr = c_1 ‖ psum.value = c_2 } that resets the variables modified within the loop body B to unknown values represented by fresh skolem symbols. To ensure soundness one is generally required to reset *all* locations as the loop body must preserve the invariant $\mathcal{I}$ for any initial state satisfying $\mathcal{I}$. This requirement can be relaxed in a sound manner to those locations that are modifiable in the loop body, resulting in easier proof obligations.

The resulting program modalities are unrolled into updates over modality-free FOL formulae, which can be reduced into pure FOL formulae. The latter are proven using the rules of typed FOL sequent calculus and the rules expressing the properties of the particular Kripke structure. For instance, we need axioms expressing the C heap's forest-like structure, such as:

$$\forall \, \$\mathsf{Node} \; n; \forall \, \mathsf{int} \; i; (n.\mathsf{elem} \neq \mathsf{int@}::\langle\mathsf{lookup}\rangle(i)),$$
$$\forall \, \$\mathsf{Node} \; n_1, n_2; (n_1 = n_2 \Leftrightarrow n_1.\mathsf{elem} = n_2.\mathsf{elem}),$$
$$\forall \, \$\mathsf{Node} \; n_1, n_2; (n_1.\mathsf{elem} \neq n_2.\mathsf{next}) \; .$$

3   Current Status and Further Work

At this time, the type system, the signature, and the calculus outlined above are implemented in KeY-C and we are at the stage of debugging the calculus and improving its usability. In essence, we can work with a large subset of C variable declarations, expressions, and we support **while** and **if** statements. However, recall that we restrict ourselves to a type-safe, portable subset of C with no raw memory access.

Compared to the presentation used in our example the actually implemented CDL calculus is somewhat more complicated. First, C specification introduces the concept of *undefined* behavior. Further, there are *unspecified* behavior and values: the C language specification lists the possible options for interpretation, but does not tell which one is actually used. Finally, we need to model *trap* values. These are invalid values whose attempted access leads to undefined behavior. For instance, a pointer to a deleted object is a trap value, but there can also be integer trap values. Our approach requires to prove, before reducing statements to updates, that conditions leading to undefined behavior cannot occur. Unspecified behavior and values are modeled by introducing fresh skolem symbols. The order of evaluation of some C expressions is undefined. Our approach requires ensuring by external means (for example, by static analysis) that the result of an expression evaluation does not depend on the order.

C integer types cannot be represented in CDL by the type int, because the same integer value can have multiple bit representations (e.g., negative zero). In reality, we have for each C integer type (e.g., **signed int**) a corresponding logic type (e.g., SINT) with corresponding conversion functions (e.g., SINT::toInt and SINT::fromInt). Note that SINT::toInt might not be injection.

Creating a calculus for C pointer expressions contains many technical challenges. In C, objects can be deleted and C pointers may point to local variables that eventually go out of scope. C allows arithmetic operations on pointers to the elements of the same array or to the element past the last element. Finally, C supports *deep* value assignments o1 = o2 of objects, where all member values of o2 are copied into o1. Such assignments can be modeled by just rewriting them into a sequence of scalar assignments, but we reduce them to an update.

Supporting full C of course, requires a lot more work to model numerous minor and major features of the C language: **for** loops, **const** and **volatile** modifiers, string literals, typedefs, enumerations, const expressions, unions, bit-fields, varargs, and different forms of jump statements just to name a few.

Another conceptual extension is introducing modularity: translation units, extern and static variables, function calls, and function pointers. Luckily the

C module system can be viewed as a special case of the JAVA module system, so taking over the calculus from the KeY for JAVA should be straightforward, although laborious. Calling function pointers can be implemented in the same way as polymorphic method calls in JAVA which is fully realized in KeY.

4   Related Work and Summary

There are several automatic and interactive verification tools for C including approaches based on abstraction and model checking. In addition, tools such as SLAM (research.microsoft.com/slam) concentrate on bug finding. For lack of space we only mention the most relevant. In the Caduceus tool [3] correctness assertions over C programs are compiled into an intermediate programming language for which verification condition generators and FOL prover backends are available. Interleaving of symbolic execution and first-order reasoning is not possible and interaction takes place on the level of intermediate code, not C source code. As part of the Verisoft project (www.verisoft.de) a Hoare calculus and formal semantics of the C subset C0 on top of Isabelle/HOL were developed [5], however, verification of C programs is less automated than in KeY.

In this paper we briefly described the ongoing effort to develop KeY-C, the C target version of the verification system KeY. The implementation is done in JAVA and we are using the Cetus framework [4] for parsing and analysing C programs. As a side-product of this work we expect to generalize KeY architecture for easily adding the support for new programming languages. The JAVA target version of KeY is available from www.key-project.org. KeY-C is available from the authors on request.

Acknowledgements. We benefited from many discussions with the members of the KeY project. The remarks of the reviewers led to several clarifications.

References

1. Beckert, B., Hähnle, R., Schmitt, P.H. (eds.): Verification of Object-Oriented Software. LNCS (LNAI), vol. 4334. Springer, Heidelberg (2007)
2. Beckert, B., Schlager, S., Schmitt, P.H.: An improved rule for while loops in deductive program verification. In: Lau, K.-K., Banach, R. (eds.) ICFEM 2005. LNCS, vol. 3785, pp. 315–329. Springer, Heidelberg (2005)
3. Filliâtre, J.-C., Marché, C.: Multi-prover verification of C programs. In: Davies, J., Schulte, W., Barnett, M. (eds.) ICFEM 2004. LNCS, vol. 3308, pp. 15–29. Springer, Heidelberg (2004)
4. Lee, S.I., Johnson, T.A., Eigenmann, R.: Cetus—an extensible compiler infrastructure for source-to-source transformation. In: Rauchwerger, L. (ed.) LCPC 2003. LNCS, vol. 2958, pp. 539–553. Springer, Heidelberg (2004)
5. Schirmer, N.: Verification of Sequential Imperative Programs in Isabelle/HOL. PhD thesis, Technische Universität München (2006)

The Bedwyr System for Model Checking over Syntactic Expressions

David Baelde[1], Andrew Gacek[2], Dale Miller[1], Gopalan Nadathur[2], and Alwen Tiu[3]

[1] INRIA & LIX, École Polytechnique
[2] Digital Technology Center and Dept of CS, University of Minnesota
[3] Australian National University and NICTA

1 Overview

Bedwyr is a generalization of logic programming that allows model checking directly on syntactic expressions possibly containing bindings. This system, written in OCaml, is a direct implementation of two recent advances in the theory of proof search. The first is centered on the fact that both finite success and finite failure can be captured in the sequent calculus by incorporating inference rules for *definitions* that allow *fixed points* to be explored. As a result, proof search in such a sequent calculus can capture simple model checking problems as well as may and must behavior in operational semantics. The second is that higher-order abstract syntax is directly supported using term-level λ-binders and the ∇ quantifier. These features allow reasoning directly on expressions containing bound variables.

2 Foundations

The logical foundation of Bedwyr is the logic called LINC [12], an acronym for "lambda, induction, nabla, and co-induction" that is an enumeration of its major components. LINC extends intuitionistic logic in two directions.

Fixed points via definitions. Clauses such as $A \overset{\triangle}{=} B$ are used to provide (mutually) recursive definitions of atoms. Once a set $\mathcal{D}$ of such definition clauses has been fixed, LINC provides inference rules for introducing atomic formulas based on the idea of unfolding definitions. Unfolding on the right of the sequent arrow is specified by the following *definition-right* rule:

$$\frac{\Sigma : \Gamma \vdash B\theta}{\Sigma : \Gamma \vdash A} \text{, provided } A' \overset{\triangle}{=} B \in \mathcal{D} \text{ and } A'\theta = A.$$

This rule resembles backchaining in more conventional logic programming languages. The *definition-left* rule is a case analysis justified by a closed-world reading of a definition.

$$\frac{\{\Sigma\theta : \Gamma\theta, B\theta \vdash G\theta \mid A' \overset{\triangle}{=} B \in \mathcal{D} \text{ and } \theta \in csu(A, A')\}}{\Sigma : \Gamma, A \vdash G}$$

F. Pfenning (Ed.): CADE 2007, LNAI 4603, pp. 391–397, 2007.

Notice that this rule uses unification: the eigenvariables of the sequent (stored in the signature Σ) are instantiated by θ, which is a member of a complete set of unifiers (csu) for atoms A and A'. Bedwyr implements a subset of this rule that is restricted to *higher-order pattern unification* and, hence, to a case where *csu* can be replaced by *mgu*. If an atom on the left fails to unify with the head of any definition, the premise set of this inference rule is empty and, hence, the sequent is proved: thus, a unification *failure* is turned into a proof search *success*.

Notice that this use of definitions as fixed points implies that logic specifications are not treated as part of a *theory* from which conclusions are drawn. Instead, the proof system itself is parametrized by the logic specification. In this way, definitions remain fixed during proof search and the *closed world assumption* can be applied to the logic specification. For earlier references to this approach to fixed points see [3,11,4].

Nabla quantification. Bedwyr supports the λ-*tree syntax* [6] approach to higher-order abstract syntax [9] by implementing a logic that provides (i) terms that may contain λ-bindings, (ii) variables that can range over such terms, and (iii) equality (and unification) that follows the rules of λ-conversion. Bedwyr shares these attributes with systems such as λProlog. However, it additionally includes the ∇-quantifier that is needed to fully exploit the closed-world aspects of LINC. This quantifier can be read informally as "for a new variable" and is accommodated easily within the sequent calculus with the introduction of a new kind of local context scoped over formulas. We refer the reader to [7] for more details. We point out here, however, that ∇ can always be given minimal scope by using the equivalences $\nabla x.(Ax * Bx) \equiv (\nabla x.Ax) * (\nabla x.Bx)$ where $*$ may be $\supset$, $\wedge$ or $\vee$ and the fact that ∇ is self-dual: $\nabla x.\neg Bx \equiv \neg \nabla x.Bx$. When ∇ is moved under $\forall$ and $\exists$, it *raises* the type of the quantified variable: in particular, in the equivalences $\nabla x \forall y.Fxy \equiv \forall h \nabla x.Fx(hx)$ and $\nabla x \exists y.Fxy \equiv \exists h \nabla x.Fx(hx)$, the variable y is replaced with a functional variable h. Finally, when ∇ is scoped over equations, the equivalence $\nabla x(Tx = Sx) \equiv (\lambda x.Tx) = (\lambda x.Sx)$ allows it to be completely removed. As a result, no fundamentally new ideas are needed to implement ∇ in a framework where λ-term equality is supported.

3 Architecture

Bedwyr implements a fragment of LINC that is large enough to permit interesting applications of fixed points and ∇. In this fragment, *all* the left rules are invertible. Consequently, we can use a simple proof strategy that alternates between left and right-rules, with the left-rules taking precedence over the right rules.

Two provers. The fragment of LINC implemented in Bedwyr is given by the following grammar:

$$L0 ::= \top \mid A \mid L0 \wedge L0 \mid L0 \vee L0 \mid \nabla x.\ L0 \mid \exists x.\ L0$$
$$L1 ::= \top \mid A \mid L1 \wedge L1 \mid L1 \vee L1 \mid \nabla x.\ L1 \mid \exists x.\ L1 \mid \forall x.\ L1 \mid L0 \supset L1$$

The formulas in this fragment are divided into *level-0* formulas, given by $L0$ above, and *level-1* formulas, given by $L1$. Implicit in the above grammar is the partition of atoms into level-0 atoms and level-1 atoms. Restrictions apply to goal formulas and definitions: goal formulas can be level-0 or level-1 formulas, and in a definition $A \overset{\triangle}{=} B$, A and B can be level-0 or level-1 formulas, provided that the level of A is greater than or equal to the level of B.

Level-0 formulas are essentially a subset of goal formulas in λProlog (with ∇ replacing $\forall$). Proof search for a defined atom of level-0 is thus the same as in λProlog (and Bedwyr implements that fragment following the basic ideas described in [2]). We can think of a level-0 definition, say, $p\,x \overset{\triangle}{=} B\,x$, as defining a set of elements x satisfying $B\,x$. A successful proof search for $p\,t$ means that t is in the set characterized by B. A level-1 statement like $\forall x.p\,x \supset R\,x$ would then mean that R holds for all elements of the set characterized by p. That is, this statement captures the enumeration of a *model* of p and its verification can be seen as a form of model checking. To reflect this operational reading of level-1 implications, the proof search engine of Bedwyr uses two subprovers: the Level-0 prover (a simplified λProlog engine), and the Level-1 prover. The latter is a usual depth-first goal-directed prover but with a novel treatment of implication. When the Level-1 prover reaches the implication $A \supset B$, it calls the Level-0 prover on A and gets in return a stream of answer substitutions: the Level-1 prover then checks that, for every substitution θ in that stream, $B\theta$ holds. In particular, if Level-0 finitely fails with A, the implication is proved.

As with most depth-first implementations of proof search, Bedwyr suffers from some aspects of incompleteness: for example, the prover can easily loop during a search although different choices of goal or clause ordering can lead to a proof, and certain kinds of unification problems should be delayed instead of attempted eagerly. For a more detailed account on the incompleteness issues, we refer the reader to [14]. Bedwyr does not currently implement static checking of types and the stratification of definitions (which is required in the cut-elimination proof for LINC). This allows us to experiment with a wider range of examples than those allowed by LINC.

Higher-order pattern unification. We adapt the treatment of higher-order pattern unification due to Nadathur and Linnell [8]. This implementation uses the *suspension calculus* representation of λ-terms. We avoid explicit raising, which is expensive, by representing ∇-bound variables by indices and associating a *global* and a *local* level annotation with other quantified variables. The global level replaces raising over existential and universal variables. The local level replaces raising over ∇-bound variables. For example, the scoping in $\forall x.\exists y.\nabla n.\forall z.F x y n z$ is represented by the following annotation: $F x^{0,0} Y^{1,0} \#_0 z^{2,1}$ (we use lowercase letters for universal variables, uppercase for existentials, the index $\#_n$ for the n-th ∇-bound variable, and write in superscript the annotation $(global, local)$). Using this annotation scheme, the scoping aspects of ∇ quantifiers are reflected into new conditions on local levels but the overall structure of the higher-order pattern unification problem and its mgu properties are preserved.

Tabling. We introduced tabling in Bedwyr to cut-down exponential blowups caused by redundant computations and to detect loops during proof-search. The first optimization is critical for applications such as weak bisimulation checking. The second one proves useful when exploring reachability in a cyclic graph.

Tabling is currently used in Bedwyr to experiment with proof search for inductive and co-inductive predicates. A loop over an inductive predicate that would otherwise cause a divergence can be categorized using tabling as a failure. Similarly, in the co-inductive case, loops yield success. This interpretation of loops as failure or success is not part of the meta-theory of LINC. Its soundness is currently conjectured, although we do not see any inconsistency of this interpretation on the numerous examples that we tried.

Inductive proof-search with tabling is implemented effectively in provers like XSB [10] using, for example, suspensions. The implementation of tables in Bedwyr fits simply in the initial design of the prover but is much weaker. We only table a goal in Level-1 when it does not have free occurrences of variables introduced by an existential quantifier; and in Level-0 when it does not have any free variable occurrence. Nevertheless, this implementation of tabling has proved useful in several cases, ranging from graph examples to bisimulation.

4   Examples

We give here a brief description of the range of applications of Bedwyr. We refer the reader to `http://slimmer.gforge.inria.fr/bedwyr` and the user manual for Bedwyr [1] for more details about these and other examples.

Finite failure. Let *false* be an atom that has no definition. Negation of a level-0 formula G can then be written as the level-1 formula $G \supset false$ and this negation is provable in the level-1 prover if all attempts to prove G in the level-0 prover fail. For example, the formula $\forall y[\lambda x.x = \lambda x.y \supset false]$ is a theorem: *i.e.*, the identity abstraction is always different from a constant-valued abstraction.

Model-checking. If the two predicates P and Q are defined using Horn clauses, then the Level-1 prover is capable of attempting a proof of $\forall x. \ P \ x \supset Q \ x$. This covers most (un)reachability checks common in model-checking. Related examples in the Bedwyr distribution include the verification of a 3 bits addition circuit and graph cyclicity checks.

Games and strategies. Assuming that a transition in a game from position P to position P' can be described by a level-0 formula *step P P'* then proving the level-1 atom *win P* defined by

$$win \ P \overset{\triangle}{=} \forall P'. \ step \ P \ P' \supset \exists P''. \ step \ P' \ P'' \wedge win \ P''$$

will determine if there is a winning strategy from position P. If all *win*-atoms are tabled during proof search, the resulting table contains an actual winning strategy.

Simulation in process calculi. If the level-0 atom $P \xrightarrow{A} Q$ specifies a one-step transition (process P does an A-action and results in process Q), then simulation can be written in Bedwyr as follows [5].

$$sim\ P\ Q \triangleq \forall A \forall P'.\ P \xrightarrow{A} P' \supset \exists Q'.\ Q \xrightarrow{A} Q' \wedge sim\ P'\ Q'$$

In dealing with the π-calculus, where bindings can occur within one-step transitions, there are two additional transitions that need to be encoded: in particular, $P \xrightarrow{\downarrow X} P'$ and $P \xrightarrow{\uparrow X} P'$, for bound input and bound output transitions on channel X. In both of these cases, P is a process but P' is a name abstraction over a process. The full specification of (late, open) simulation for the π-calculus can be written using the following [7].

$$
\begin{aligned}
sim\ P\ Q \triangleq\ &[\forall A \forall P'.\ P \xrightarrow{A} P' \supset \exists Q'.\ Q \xrightarrow{A} Q' \wedge sim\ P'\ Q'] \wedge \\
&[\forall X \forall P'.\ P \xrightarrow{\downarrow X} P' \supset \exists Q'.\ Q \xrightarrow{\downarrow X} Q' \wedge \forall w.sim\ (P'w)\ (Q'w)] \wedge \\
&[\forall X \forall P'.\ P \xrightarrow{\uparrow X} P' \supset \exists Q'.\ Q \xrightarrow{\uparrow X} Q' \wedge \nabla w.sim\ (P'w)\ (Q'w)]
\end{aligned}
$$

Notice that the abstracted continuation resulting from bound input and bound output actions are treated by the $\forall$-quantifier and the ∇-quantifier, respectively. In a similar way, modal logics for the π-calculus can be captured [13]. If *sim*-atoms are tabled during proof search, the resulting table contains an actual simulation. Bisimulation is easily captured by simply adding the symmetric clauses for all those used to define *sim*.

Meta-level reasoning. Because Bedwyr uses the ∇ quantifier and the λ-tree approach to encoding syntax, it is possible to specify provability in an object logic and to reason to some extent about what is and is not provable. Consider the tiny fragment of intuitionistic logic with the universal quantifier $\bar{\forall}$ and the implication $\Rightarrow$ in which we only allow atoms to the left of implications. If the formula $\bar{\forall}x.\ (p\ x\ r \Rightarrow \bar{\forall}y.\ (p\ y\ s \Rightarrow p\ x\ t))$ is provable in this logic then one would expect r and t to be syntactically equal terms. In searching for a proof of this formula, the quantified variables are replaced by distinct eigenvariables: therefore, the only way the formula could have been proved is for $p\ x\ t$ to match $p\ x\ r$, hence $r = t$. Provability of a formula B from a list of atomic formulas L can be specified by the following meta-level (Bedwyr-level) judgment $pv\ L\ B$:

$$
\begin{aligned}
pv\ L\ B &\triangleq memb\ B\ L. & pv\ L\ (\bar{\forall}B) &\triangleq \nabla x.\ pv\ L\ (B\ x). \\
pv\ L\ (A \Rightarrow B) &\triangleq pv\ (A :: L)\ B.
\end{aligned}
$$

Here, *memb* and :: are the usual predicate for list membership and the non-empty list constructor. Object-level eigenvariables are specified using the meta-level ∇-quantifier. The above observation about object-logic provability can now be stated in the meta-logic as the following formula, which is provable in Bedwyr:

$$\forall r \forall s \forall t.\ pv\ nil\ (\bar{\forall}x.\ (p\ x\ r \Rightarrow \bar{\forall}y.\ (p\ y\ s \Rightarrow p\ x\ t))) \supset r = t.$$

5 Future Work

We are working on several improvements to Bedwyr, including more sophisticated tabling and allowing the suspension of goals containing non-higher-order-pattern unification (rescheduling them when instantiations change them into higher-order pattern goals). We will also explore using tables as proof certificates: for example, when proving that two processes are bisimilar, the table stores an actual bisimulation, the existence of which proves the bisimilarity. Bedwyr is an open source project: more details about it can be found at http://slimmer.gforge.inria.fr/bedwyr/.

Acknowledgments. Support has been obtained for this work from the following sources: from INRIA through the "Equipes Associées" Slimmer, from the ACI grant GEOCAL, from the NSF Grants OISE-0553462 (IRES-REUSSI) and CCR-0429572 and from a grant from Boston Scientific.

References

1. Baelde, D., Gacek, A., Miller, D., Nadathur, G., Tiu, A.: A User Guide to Bedwyr (November 2006)
2. Elliott, C., Pfenning, F.: A semi-functional implementation of a higher-order logic programming language. In: Lee, P. (ed.) Topics in Advanced Language Implementation, pp. 289–325. MIT Press, Cambridge (1991)
3. Girard, J.-Y.: A fixpoint theorem in linear logic. An email posting to the mailing list linear@cs.stanford.edu (February 1992)
4. McDowell, R., Miller, D.: A logic for reasoning with higher-order abstract syntax. In: Proc. LICS 1997, pp. 434–445. IEEE Comp. Soc. Press, Los Alamitos (1997)
5. McDowell, R., Miller, D., Palamidessi, C.: Encoding transition systems in sequent calculus. Theoretical Computer Science 294(3), 411–437 (2003)
6. Miller, D.: Abstract syntax for variable binders: An overview. In: Palamidessi, C., Moniz Pereira, L., Lloyd, J.W., Dahl, V., Furbach, U., Kerber, M., Lau, K.-K., Sagiv, Y., Stuckey, P.J. (eds.) CL 2000. LNCS (LNAI), vol. 1861, pp. 239–253. Springer, Heidelberg (2000)
7. Miller, D., Tiu, A.: A proof theory for generic judgments. ACM Trans. on Computational Logic 6(4), 749–783 (2005)
8. Nadathur, G., Linnell, N.: Practical higher-order pattern unification with on-the-fly raising. In: Gabbrielli, M., Gupta, G. (eds.) ICLP 2005. LNCS, vol. 3668, pp. 371–386. Springer, Heidelberg (2005)
9. Pfenning, F., Elliott, C.: Higher-order abstract syntax. In: Proceedings of the ACM-SIGPLAN Conference on Programming Language Design and Implementation, pp. 199–208. ACM Press, New York (1988)
10. Sagonas, K., Swift, T., Warren, D.S., Freire, J., Rao, P., Cui, B., Johnson, E., de Castro, L., Marques, R.F., Dawson, S., Kifer, M.: The XSB Version 3.0, vol. 1: Programmer's Manual (2006)
11. Schroeder-Heister, P.: Rules of definitional reflection. In: Proc. LICS 1993, pp. 222–232. IEEE Comp. Soc. Press, Los Alamitos (1993)

12. Tiu, A.: A Logical Framework for Reasoning about Logical Specifications. PhD thesis, Pennsylvania State University (May 2004)
13. Tiu, A.: Model checking for π-calculus using proof search. In: Abadi, M., de Alfaro, L. (eds.) CONCUR 2005. LNCS, vol. 3653, pp. 36–50. Springer, Heidelberg (2005)
14. Tiu, A., Nadathur, G., Miller, D.: Mixing finite success and finite failure in an automated prover. In: Proc. of ESHOL'05: Empirically Successful Automated Reasoning in Higher-Order Logics, pp. 79–98 (December 2005)

System for Automated Deduction (SAD): A Tool for Proof Verification

Konstantin Verchinine[1], Alexander Lyaletski[2], and Andrei Paskevich[3]

[1] Université Paris 12, IUT Sénart/Fontainebleau,
77300 Fontainebleau, France
verko@capet.iut-fbleau.fr
[2] Kyiv National Taras Shevchenko University, Faculty of Cybernetics,
03680 Kyiv, Ukraine
lav@unicyb.kiev.ua
[3] Université Paris 12, Laboratoire d'Algorithmique, Complexité et Logique,
94010 Créteil, France
andrei@capet.iut-fbleau.fr

Abstract. In this paper a proof assistant called SAD is presented. SAD deals with mathematical texts that are formalized in the ForTheL language (a brief description of which is also given) and checks their correctness. We give a short description of SAD and a series of examples that show what can be done with it. Note that abstract notion of correctness on which the implementation is based, can be formalized with the help of a calculus (not presented here).

1 Introduction

The idea to use a formal language along with formal symbolic manipulations to solve complex "common" problems has a long history. We only mention G.W. Leibniz's writings (1685) and the pioneering paper of Hao Wang [1]. It is worth noting the ambitious title of Wang's article! Numerous attempts to "mechanize" mathematics have led to the less ambitious and more realistic idea of "computer aided" mathematics as well as to the notion of "proof assistant" — a piece of software that is able to do complex deductions for you.

The mathematical text SAD deals with is a complex object that contains axioms, definitions, theorems, and proofs of various kinds (by contradiction, by induction, by case analysis, etc). The formal semantics of a text can be given by packing the whole text in a single statement and transforming it to the corresponding logical formula (which we call the *formula image* of the text). Then the text is declared correct whenever its formula image is deducible in the underlying logic. This approach would be simple and theoretically transparent but obviously impractical. The SAD system implements a more intricate notion of text correctness which is formalized with the help of a logical calculus and can serve as a formal specification of a "correctness verifier".

The SAD project is the continuation of a project initiated by academician V. Glushkov at the Institute for Cybernetics in Kiev more than 30 years ago

F. Pfenning (Ed.): CADE 2007, LNAI 4603, pp. 398–403, 2007.

[2]. Its original title was "Evidence Algorithm". Three main components had to be developed: an inference engine (we call it *prover* below) that implements the basic level of evidence, an extensible collection of tools (we call it *reasoner*) to reinforce the basic engine, and a formal input language which must be close to natural mathematical language and easy to use. A working version of SAD is implemented [3,4,5] and available online at `http://ea.unicyb.kiev.ua`.

In a general setting, SAD may be positioned as a declarative style proof assistant/verifier that accepts input texts written in the formal language ForTheL [6,5], uses an automated first-order prover as the basic inference engine and possesses an original reasoner. The closest to our approach is the Mizar system [7] — the oldest and most well-known proof assistant working with proofs of declarative style.

2 ForTheL Language

Like usual mathematical text, a ForTheL text consists of definitions, axioms, hypotheses, conjectures, proofs. ForTheL is a controlled natural language: its syntax follows the rules of English grammar. ForTheL sentences are of three kinds: assumptions ("`Let S be a finite set.`", "`Assume that m is less than n.`"), selections ("`Take an even prime number X.`"), and affirmations ("`If p divides n-p then p divides n.`"). Series of transformations which convert a ForTheL statement to its *formula image* determine the semantics of the statement. For example, the formula image of the statement "`all closed subsets of any compact set are compact`" is: $\forall$A ((A is a set $\wedge$ A is compact) $\supset$ $\forall$B ((B is a subset of A $\wedge$ B is closed) $\supset$ B is compact)). Sentences, compound sections and a ForTheL text itself are given formula images, too.

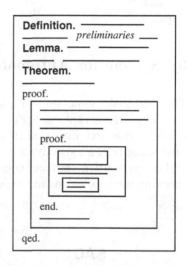

Fig. 1. ForTheL text's structure

Affirmations and selections can be accompanied with a proof. ForTheL supports various proof schemes like proof by contradiction, by case analysis, and by general induction. Proofs need not to be ultimately detailed: reasoning "steps" can be as large as the deductive facilities of a verifier (e.g. SAD) can manage. Consider for example an excerpt of a verified formalization of the Tarski's fixed point theorem:

```
Definition DefCLat. A complete lattice is a set S such that
    every subset of S has an infimum in S and a supremum in S.

Definition DefIso.  f is isotone iff for all x,y << Dom f
    x <= y  =>  f(x) <= f(y).
```

```
Theorem Tarski.
  Let U be a complete lattice and f be an isotone function on U.
  Let S be the set of fixed points of f. S is a complete lattice.
Proof.
  Let T be a subset of S.
  Let us show that T has a supremum in S.
    Take P = { x << U | f(x) <= x and x is an upper bound of T in U }.
    Take an infimum p of P in U.
    f(p) is a lower bound of P in U and an upper bound of T in U.
    Hence p is a fixed point of f and a supremum of T in S.
  end.
  Let us show that T has an infimum in S.
    Take Q = { x << U | f(x) >= x and x is a lower bound of T in U }.
    Take a supremum q of Q in U.
    f(q) is an upper bound of Q in U and a lower bound of T in U.
    Hence q is a fixed point of f and an infimum of T in S.
  end.
qed.
```

3   System for Automated Deduction

The principal components of SAD are shown in Figure 2.

The *parser* accepts a ForTheL text, checks its syntactical correctness and converts the text into a normalized form that will be convenient for further processing (e.g. all synonyms are replaced with their canonical representatives).

The *verification manager* goes through the normalized text section by section, checking the ontological and logical correctness. If a section (say, $\mathbb{A}$) is a sentence,

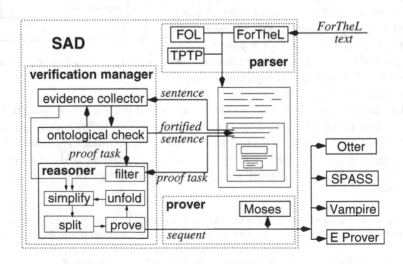

Fig. 2. Architecture of SAD

then it is first sent to the *evidence collector* that accumulates so called term properties for the term occurrences in the formula image of A.

Term properties are literals that tell us something important about a given term occurrence. A literal (i.e. an atomic formula or its negation) L is considered to be a property of a term t in a context Γ, whenever t is a subterm of L and L is deducible in Γ. The most important purpose of term properties is to hold information about term "types", which is usually expressed by an atomic statement of the form "t is a $\langle class \rangle$". Some simple properties, like non-emptiness, are highly useful, too.

Fortified with the found properties, occurrences of terms and atoms are passed to the *ontological checker*. For each symbol occurrence, the checker looks through the text processed so far for an appropriate definition or signature extension. The deductive core of the system, the so-called *reasoner*, is used to prove the instantiated guards. The results of ontological checking (the applicable definitions) together with the collected properties are used in evidence collection for outer occurrences.

Then the verification manager processes the section A according to the rules of the special Calculus of Text Correctness, **CTC**, which we do not describe in this paper. Generally, if A contains a statement to prove, then a new verification cycle is started to verify the submitted proof, possibly empty. This statement becomes the initial *thesis* of the new cycle. The thesis may be gradually simplified as the proof proceeds: when the thesis is an implication and we assume its antecedent, or when it is a conjunction and we affirm its part. At the end of the proof (i.e. immediately, if there was no proof in the text), the current thesis is sent to the *reasoner*. In other words, a ForTheL proof provides hints to the verification manager on how to split the statement being proved into several proof tasks and the rules of thesis transformation guarantee the soundness of splitting.

The *reasoner* deals with proof tasks of the form $\Gamma \vdash F$. This module can be viewed as a kind of automated heuristic based prover, supplied with a collection of proof task transformation rules. This collection is not intended to form a complete logic calculus. The purpose of the reasoner is not to find the entire proof on its own, but rather to simplify inference search for the *background prover*.

At present, the capabilities of the reasoner are as follows: propositional goal splitting, formula simplification with respect to accumulated term properties, simple filtering of premises according to explicit references in the text, incremental definition expansion.

The reasoner of SAD uses term properties to simplify goal formulas and formulas which arise from definition expansion: any literal that appears to hold as a property of some of its subterms can be replaced by logical constant "truth" (indeed, it can be deduced from the current context and, hence, is redundant). Similarly, a literal can be replaced by "false", if its complement occurs among the properties of its subterms.

The *background prover* is a combinatorial automated prover in classical first-order logic, whose duty is to complete the proofs started by the reasoner. If the background prover fails to find the inference at some instant, the reasoner may continue the proof task transformation or try an alternative way, or reject the text.

The background prover is independent from SAD by design, so that an external theorem prover can be used. Our experiments (see below) were performed with Otter [8], SPASS [9], Vampire [10], and E [11]. Note that this feature of SAD provides us with a (yet another) scale to compare automated theorem provers: trying them on relatively simple problems in complex and heavily redundant contexts rather than on hard problems with a pre-adjusted set of relevant premises (mostly the case for problems in the famous TPTP library [12]).

Also there exists the native background prover of SAD, called Moses. It is based on an original goal-driven sequent calculus [4,5].

4   Experiments

In the course of development of SAD, we have conducted a number of experiments in the formalization and verification of non-trivial mathematical results:

- Ramsey's Finite and Infinite theorems.
- Stability of a refinement relation over a number of operations on program specifications [13].
- Cauchy-Bouniakowsky-Schwarz inequality.
- The square root of a prime number is irrational: 30 statements in preliminaries (integer numbers), 5 definitions, 7 lemmas, about 50 sentences in the proof of the main lemma (any prime dividing a product divides one of the factors), 10 sentences in the proof of the theorem (see [5] for detailed explanation of this experiment).
- Chinese remainder theorem and Bezout's identity in terms of abstract rings: 25 statements in preliminaries (ring axioms, operations on sets), 7 definitions (ideal, principal ideal, greatest common divisor, etc), 3 lemmas, 8 sentences in the proof of CRT, about 30 sentences in the proof of Bezout's identity.
- Tarski's fixed point theorem (cited above): 11 statements in preliminaries (ordered sets), 7 definitions (upper and lower bounds, supremum, infimum, complete lattice, isotone function, fixed point), 2 lemmas, 18 sentences in the proof of the theorem.

The texts listed above were written in ForTheL and automatically verified in SAD using different background provers. The best results were obtained with SPASS. This is due, in particular, to its original technique of handling sort-like information, which abounds in mathematical texts.

5   Conclusion

SAD is a powerful system and its power lies in its reasoning facility. Experiments show that, for example, the specific strategy of definition processing contributes a lot to the success of the whole verification process. If we use definitions

straightforwardly — convert them into formula images and add the corresponding premises to the sequent that goes into a prover — we have no chance to
verify the proof of Tarski fixed-point theorem as it is formulated above, even
when the winner of CASC competitions is chosen as the background prover.

SAD is not a perfect system (if any!). One can easily see how it may be
improved and developed. Our research and implementation plans with respect
to SAD are: extend ForTheL and SAD with some means to talk and reason
about second-order objects (functions, vectors, sequences) and operations on
them; develop and implement a mathematical library of SAD to accumulate
verified portions of mathematical knowledge and to support further (deeper)
advances in formalization.

References

1. Wang, H.: Towards mechanical mathematics. IBM J. of Research and Development 4, 2–22 (1960)
2. Glushkov, V.M.: Some problems of automata theory and artificial intelligence (in
   Russian). Kibernetika 2, 3–13 (1970)
3. Lyaletski, A., Verchinine, K., Paskevich, A.: On verification tools implemented
   in the System for Automated Deduction. In: Proc. 2nd CoLogNet Workshop on
   Implementation Technology for Computational Logic Systems (ITCLS' 2003), Pisa,
   Italy, pp. 3–14 (2003)
4. Lyaletski, A., Paskevich, A., Verchinine, K.: Theorem proving and proof verification
   in the system SAD. In: Asperti, A., Bancerek, G., Trybulec, A. (eds.) MKM 2004.
   LNCS, vol. 3119, pp. 236–250. Springer, Heidelberg (2004)
5. Lyaletski, A., Paskevich, A., Verchinine, K.: SAD as a mathematical assistant —
   how should we go from here to there? Journal of Applied Logic 4(4), 560–591 (2006)
6. Vershinin, K., Paskevich, A.: ForTheL — the language of formal theories. International Journal of Information Theories and Applications 7(3), 120–126 (2000)
7. Trybulec, A., Blair, H.: Computer assisted reasoning with Mizar. In: Proc. 9th
   International Joint Conference on Artificial Intelligence, pp. 26–28 (1985)
8. McCune, W.: Otter 3.0 reference manual and guide. Tech. Report ANL-94/6, Argonne National Laboratory, Argonne, USA (1994)
9. Weidenbach, C., Brahm, U., Hillenbrand, T., Keen, E., Theobald, C., Topic, D.:
   SPASS version 2.0. In: Voronkov, A. (ed.) Automated Deduction - CADE-18. LNCS
   (LNAI), vol. 2392, pp. 275–279. Springer, Heidelberg (2002)
10. Riazanov, A., Voronkov, A.: The design and implementation of VAMPIRE. AI
    Communications 15(2–3), 91–110 (2002)
11. Schulz, S.: System Description: E 0.81. In: Basin, D., Rusinowitch, M. (eds.) IJCAR
    2004. LNCS (LNAI), vol. 3097, pp. 223–228. Springer, Heidelberg (2004)
12. Sutcliffe, G., Suttner, C.B., Yemenis, T.: The TPTP problem library. In: Bundy,
    A. (ed.) Automated Deduction - CADE-12. LNCS, vol. 814, pp. 252–266. Springer,
    Heidelberg (1994)
13. Mammar, A.: Un environnement formel pour le développement d'application bases
    de données. PhD thesis, Conservatoire National des Arts et Métiers, France (2002)

Logical Engineering with Instance-Based Methods

Peter Baumgartner

NICTA and
Australian National University
Canberra, Australia
Peter.Baumgartner@nicta.com.au

1 Instance Based Methods

The term "instance based methods" (IMs) refers to a certain family of methods for first-order logic theorem proving. IMs share the principle of carrying out proof search by maintaining a set of instances of input clauses and analyzing it for satisfiability until completion. IMs are conceptually essentially different to well established methods like resolution or free-variable analytic tableaux. (See [Pla94] for a comparison of various calculi and strategies, including an instance based method.) Also, IMs exhibit a search space and termination behaviour (in the satisfiable case) different from those methods, which makes them attractive from a practical point of view as a complementary method.

The idea behind IMs is already present in a rudimentary way in the work by Davis, Putnam, Logemann and Loveland, and others, in the early sixties of the last century [DP60, DLL62b, DLL62a, Dav63, CDHM64]. The contemporary stream of research on IMs was initiated with the Lee and Plaisted's Hyperlinking calculus [PL90, LP92] Since then, other methods have been developed by Plaisted and his coworkers [CP94, PZ97, PZ00]; Billon's disconnection calculus [Bil96] was picked up by Letz and Stenz and has been significantly developed further since then [LS01, LS02, SL04, LS07]. New methods have been described in [Bau98, BEF99], by Hooker [HRCS02], and by Ganzinger and Korovin [GK03, GK04, GK06]. See [JW07] for a thorough comparison of some of these IMs.

The author introduced a first-order version of the propositional DPLL procedure, FDPLL [Bau00, Bau02], which is now subsumed by the Model Evolution (ME) calculus [BT03, BT05, BFT06b]. The model representation formalism in the ME calculus has been studied in [FP05].

Some quite sophisticated implementations are available, two of which, Darwin [BFT06a] and DCTP [Ste02], regularly participate in the CASC competition.

Open research questions concern, for example, better understanding of theoretical properties and comparison with other methods, implementation techniques, extensions for reasoning modulo fixed background theories, variants for deciding more fragments of first-order logic than currently known, and adaption for specific applications, as outlined in the following section.

F. Pfenning (Ed.): CADE 2007, LNAI 4603, pp. 404–409, 2007.
© Springer-Verlag Berlin Heidelberg 2007

2   Logical Engineering

The term *logical engineering* is meant to refer to the strategy to exploit the properties of the logical calculus or proof procedure at hand to solve a given problem or class of problems. This may involve translating the problem into a suitable logical language and also specific tailoring the calculus or tuning the proof procedure.

For example, in the context of IMs, the ME calculus when applied to *range-restricted* [MB88] clause sets can be used as a bottom-up model-generation method similar to hyper tableau [BFN96] or hyper resolution (with splitting). This setup has applications, e.g., for reasoning in modal logics (in conjunction with certain translations into first-order clause logic) [GHS02, SH05, e.g.]. Any such application is thus amenable to Model Evolution, too.

An interesting property of *all* (known) instance based methods is that they provide natural decision procedures for the Bernays-Schönfinkel fragment of first-order logic, or, more precisely, function-free clause logic (FFCL).[1] In contrast, most other first-order methods, including free-variable tableau and resolution methods cannot be used as decision procedures for FFCL.[2] This suggests to capitalize on this distinguishing property of IMs and to investigate reduction of application problems into FFCL.

For instance, the optimized functional translation of modal logics [OS97] leads directly to FFCL [Sch99]. Many benchmark problems obtained this way are contained in the TPTP problem library [SS98], and implementations of instance based methods consistently score very well on them. In the description logic context, [MSS04] show how to translate the expressive description logic $\mathcal{SHIQ}(\mathrm{D})$ to FFCL (with a different motivation, though).

Another "generic" application area is *finite model computation*. Most approaches for finite model computation essentially work by stepwise reduction to formulas in propositional logic [Sla92, McC94, ZZ95, CS03, e.g.].[3] In [BF+07] we have shown how the MACE-style model computation paradigm can be rooted in the Model Evolution calculus instead of a SAT solver, which can lead to space advantages.

In a similar spirit, IMs might be usable within a SMT architecture (satisfiability modulo theories, see [RT06] for a recent overview). For instance, one could design a DPLL(T) solver [Tin02, NOT06] based on the ME calculus, which would thus be equipped with a first-order variant of a DPLL solver instead of a propositional one. The then available native first-order reasoning capabilities could turn out to be useful for various purposes, such as guiding the search for a candidate model by adding (redundant) theory axioms to the clause set, solving problems over an extended background theory, or going beyond quantifier-free problems. The latter will typically require an heuristic approach, though, as no complete

---

[1] i.e., first-order clause logic without function symbols of arity > 0.

[2] Not counting approaches that are based on reduction to ground clause logic. See [BS06] for recent improvements of that approach.

[3] But see [FL96, BT98, Pel03b, Pel03a, BS06, dNM06, e.g.] for direct first-order methods; [FLHT01] is a more general overview.

calculus can exist already for rather simple decidable arithmetic theories when extended with free predicate symbols [MHM98].

Other (potential) applications of the FFCL fragment and IMs lie within the *constraint programming* area. Perhaps IMs are not the preferred choice as solvers for search problems (in NP), as this is the domain of the traditional constraint programming paradigm. More appropriate seems the application to, e.g., model expansion problems [MTHM06] (with NEXPTIME combined query/data complexity), which can be reduced to FFCL in a way similar to finite model computation mentioned above. Another application is to reason *about* constraint specifications for the purpose to prove "interesting" properties, like functional dependencies and symmetries [CM05, CM04]. Quite often, the resulting proof obligations lie within FFCL.

References

[Bau98]   Baumgartner, P.: Hyper Tableaux — The Next Generation. In: de Swart, H. (ed.) TABLEAUX 1998. LNCS (LNAI), vol. 1397, pp. 60–76. Springer, Heidelberg (1998)

[Bau00]   Baumgartner, P.: FDPLL – A First-Order Davis-Putnam-Logeman-Loveland Procedure. In: McAllester, D. (ed.) Automated Deduction - CADE-17. LNCS, vol. 1831, pp. 200–219. Springer, Heidelberg (2000)

[Bau02]   Baumgartner, P.: A First-Order Logic Davis-Putnam-Logemann-Loveland Procedure. In: Lakemeyer, G., Nebel, B. (eds.) AI in the new Millenium, Morgan Kaufmann, Seattle (2002)

[BEF99]   Baumgartner, P., Eisinger, N., Furbach, U.: A confluent connection calculus. In: Ganzinger, H. (ed.) Automated Deduction - CADE-16. LNCS (LNAI), vol. 1632, pp. 329–343. Springer, Heidelberg (1999)

[BF+07]   Baumgartner, P., Fuchs, A., de Nivelle, H., Tinelli, C.: Computing finite models by reduction to function-free clause logic. Journal of Applied Logic (to appear)

[BFN96]   Baumgartner, P., Furbach, U., Niemelä, I.: Hyper Tableaux. In: Orłowska, E., Alferes, J.J., Moniz Pereira, L. (eds.) JELIA 1996. LNCS, vol. 1126, Springer, Heidelberg (1996)

[BFT06a]   Baumgartner, P., Fuchs, A., Tinelli, C.: Implementing the model evolution calculus. International Journal of Artificial Intelligence Tools 15(1), 21–52 (2006)

[BFT06b]   Baumgartner, P., Fuchs, A., Tinelli, C.: Lemma learning in the model evolution calculus. In: Hermann, M., Voronkov, A. (eds.) LPAR 2006. LNCS (LNAI), vol. 4246, pp. 572–586. Springer, Heidelberg (2006)

[Bil96]   Billon, J.-P.: The Disconnection Method. In: Miglioli, P., Moscato, U., Ornaghi, M., Mundici, D. (eds.) TABLEAUX 1996. LNCS, vol. 1071, pp. 110–126. Springer, Heidelberg (1996)

[BS06]   Baumgartner, P., Schmidt, R.: Blocking and other enhancements for bottom-up model generation methods. In: Furbach, U., Shankar, N. (eds.) IJCAR 2006. LNCS (LNAI), vol. 4130, Springer, Heidelberg (2006)

[BT98]   Bry, F., Torge, S.: A Deduction Method Complete for Refutation and Finite Satisfiability. In: Proc. 6th European Workshop on Logics in AI (JELIA). LNCS (LNAI), Springer, Heidelberg (1998)

[BT03]   Baumgartner, P., Tinelli, C.: The Model Evolution Calculus. In: Baader, F. (ed.) Automated Deduction – CADE-19. LNCS (LNAI), vol. 2741, pp. 350–364. Springer, Heidelberg (2003)

[BT05]   Baumgartner, P., Tinelli, C.: The model evolution calculus with equality. In: Nieuwenhuis [Nie05], pp. 392–408

[Bun94]   Bundy, A. (ed.): Automated Deduction - CADE-12. LNCS, vol. 814. Springer, Heidelberg (1994)

[CDHM64]   Chinlund, T.J., Davis, M., Hinman, P.G., McIlroy, M.D.: Theorem-Proving by Matching. Technical report, Bell Laboratories (1964)

[CM04]   Cadoli, M., Mancini, T.: Exploiting functional dependencies in declarative problem specifications. In: Alferes, J.J., Leite, J.A. (eds.) JELIA 2004. LNCS (LNAI), vol. 3229, pp. 628–640. Springer, Heidelberg (2004)

[CM05]   Cadoli, M., Mancini, T.: Using a theorem prover for reasoning on constraint problems. In: AI*IA, pp. 38–49 (2005)

[CP94]   Chu, H., Plaisted, D.A.: Semantically Guided First-Order Theorem Proving using Hyper-Linking. In: Bundy [Bun94], pp. 192–206

[CS03]   Claessen, K., Sörensson, N.: New techniques that improve mace-style finite model building. In: Baader, F. (ed.) Automated Deduction – CADE-19. LNCS (LNAI), vol. 2741, Springer, Heidelberg (2003)

[Dav63]   Davis, M.: Eliminating the irrelevant from mechanical proofs. In: Proceedings of Symposia in Applied Amthematics – Experimental Arithmetic, High Speed Computing and Mathematics, vol. XV, pp. 15–30. American Mathematical Society (1963)

[DLL62a]   Davis, M., Logemann, G., Loveland, D.: A machine program for theorem proving. Communications of the ACM 5(7) (1962)

[DLL62b]   Davis, M., Logemann, G., Loveland, D.: A machine program for theorem proving. Communications of the ACM 5(7), 394–397 (1962)

[dNM06]   de Nivelle, H., Meng, J.: Geometric resolution: A proof procedure based on finite model search. In: Furbach, U., Shankar, N. (eds.) IJCAR 2006. LNCS (LNAI), vol. 4130, Springer, Heidelberg (2006)

[DP60]   Davis, M., Putnam, H.: A computing procedure for quantification theory. Journal of the ACM 7(3), 201–215 (1960)

[EF02]   Egly, U., Fermüller, C.G. (eds.): TABLEAUX 2002. LNCS (LNAI), vol. 2381. Springer, Heidelberg (2002)

[FL96]   Fermüller, C., Leitsch, A.: Hyperresolution and automated model building. J. Log. Comput. 6(2), 173–203 (1996)

[FLHT01]   Fermüller, C.G., Leitsch, A., Hustadt, U., Tammet, T.: Resolution decision procedures. In: Robinson, A., Voronkov, A. (eds.) Handbook of Automated Reasoning (ch. 25), 25th edn., vol. II, pp. 1791–1849. Elsevier, North-Holland (2001)

[FP05]   Fermüller, C.G., Pichler, R.: Model representation via contexts and implicit generalizations. In: Nieuwenhuis [Nie05], pp. 409–423

[GHS02]   Georgieva, L., Hustadt, U., Schmidt, R.A.: Hyperresolution for guarded formulae. Journal of Symbolic Computation (2002)

[GK03]   Ganzinger, H., Korovin, K.: New directions in instance-based theorem proving. In: LICS - Logics in Computer Science (2003)

[GK04]   Ganzinger, H., Korovin, K.: Integrating equational reasoning into instantiation-based theorem proving. In: Marcinkowski, J., Tarlecki, A. (eds.) CSL 2004. LNCS, vol. 3210, pp. 71–84. Springer, Heidelberg (2004)

[GK06]   Ganzinger, H., Korovin, K.: Theory Instantiation. In: Hermann, M.,
            Voronkov, A. (eds.) LPAR 2006. LNCS (LNAI), vol. 4246, Springer, Hei-
            delberg (2006)
[HRCS02]   Hooker, J.N., Rago, G., Chandru, V., Shrivastava, A.: Partial Instantia-
            tion Methods for Inference in First Order Logic. Journal of Automated
            Reasoning 28(4), 371–396 (2002)
[JW07]   Jacobs, S., Waldmann, U.: Comparing instance generation methods for
            automated reasoning. J. Autom. Reason. 38(1-3), 57–78 (2007)
[LP92]   Lee, S.-J., Plaisted, D.: Eliminating Duplicates with the Hyper-Linking
            Strategy. Journal of Automated Reasoning 9, 25–42 (1992)
[LS01]   Letz, R., Stenz, G.: Proof and Model Generation with Disconnection
            Tableaux. In: Nieuwenhuis, R., Voronkov, A. (eds.) LPAR 2001. LNCS
            (LNAI), vol. 2250, Springer, Heidelberg (2001)
[LS02]   Letz, R., Stenz, G.: Integration of Equality Reasoning into the Discon-
            nection Calculus. In: Egly and Fermüller [EF02], pp. 176–190
[LS07]   Letz, R., Stenz, G.: The disconnection tableau calculus. J. Autom. Rea-
            son. 38(1-3), 79–126 (2007)
[MB88]   Manthey, R., Bry, F.: SATCHMO: a theorem prover implemented in Pro-
            log. In: Lusk, E., Overbeek, R. (eds.) CADE-9. LNCS, vol. 310, pp. 415–
            434. Springer, Heidelberg (1988)
[McC94]   McCune, W.: A davis-putnam program and its application to finite first-
            order model search: Qusigroup existence problems. Technical report, Ar-
            gonne National Laboratory (1994)
[MHM98]   Mesnard, F., Hoarau, S., Maillard, A.: CLP(χ) for automatically proving
            program properties. J. Log. Program 37(1-3), 77–93 (1998)
[MSS04]   Motik, B., Sattler, U., Studer, R.: Query answering for owl-dl with rules.
            In: Dubois, D., Welty, C.A., Williams, M.-A. (eds.) International Semantic
            Web Conference, pp. 549–563. AAAI Press, Stanford (2004)
[MTHM06]   Mitchell, D., Ternovska, E., Hach, F., Mohebali, R.: Model expansion as
            a framework for modelling and solving search problems. Technical Report
            TR 2006-24 (December 2006)
[Nie05]   Nieuwenhuis, R. (ed.): Automated Deduction – CADE-20. LNCS (LNAI),
            vol. 3632. Springer, Heidelberg (2005)
[NOT06]   Nieuwenhuis, R., Oliveras, A., Tinelli, C.: Solving SAT and SAT Mod-
            ulo Theories: from an Abstract Davis-Putnam-Logemann-Loveland Pro-
            cedure to DPLL(T). Journal of the ACM 53(6), 937–977 (2006)
[OS97]   Ohlbach, H.J., Schmidt, R.A.: Functional translation and second-order
            frame properties of modal logics. Journal of Logic and Computation 7(5),
            581–603 (1997)
[Pel03a]   Peltier, N.: A calculus combining resolution and enumeration for building
            finite models. Journal of Symbolic Computation 36(1-2), 49–77 (2003)
[Pel03b]   Peltier, N.: A more efficient tableaux procedure for simultaneous search
            for refutations and finite models. In: Mayer, M.C., Pirri, F. (eds.)
            TABLEAUX 2003. LNCS, vol. 2796, pp. 181–195. Springer, Heidelberg
            (2003)
[PL90]   Plaisted, D.A., Lee, S.-J.: Inference by clause matching. In: Ras, Z.W.,
            Zemankova, M. (eds.) Intelligent Systems: State of the Art and Future
            Directions, pp. 200–235. Ellis Horwood, New York (1990)
[Pla94]   Plaisted, D.: The Search Efficiency of Theorem Proving Strategies. In:
            Bundy [Bun94]

[PZ97]   Plaisted, D.A., Zhu, Y.: Ordered Semantic Hyper Linking. In: Proceedings
           of Fourteenth National Conference on Artificial Intelligence (AAAI-97)
           (1997)
[PZ00]   Plaisted, D.A., Zhu, Y.: Ordered Semantic Hyper Linking. Journal of
           Automated Reasoning 25(3), 167–217 (2000)
[RT06]   Ranise, S., Tinelli, C.: Satisfiability modulo theories. Trends and Contro-
           versies - IEEE Intelligent Systems Magazine 21(6), 71–81 (2006)
[Sch99]   Schmidt, R.A.: Decidability by resolution for propositional modal logics.
           J. Autom. Reason. 22(4), 379–396 (1999)
[SH05]   Schmidt, R.A., Hustadt, U.: The axiomatic translation principle for modal
           logic. ACM Transactions on Computational Logic (to appear)
[SL04]   Stenz, G., Letz, R.: Generlized handling of variables in disconnection
           tableaux. In: Basin, D., Rusinowitch, M. (eds.) IJCAR 2004. LNCS
           (LNAI), vol. 3097, pp. 289–306. Springer, Heidelberg (2004)
[Sla92]   Slaney, J.: Finder (finite domain enumerator): Notes and guide. Tech-
           nical Report TR-ARP-1/92, Australian National University, Automated
           Reasoning Project, Canberra (1992)
[SS98]   Sutcliffe, G., Suttner, C.B.: The TPTP Problem Library: CNF Release
           v1.2.1. Journal of Automated Reasoning 21(2), 177–203 (1998)
[Ste02]   Stenz, G.: DCTP 1.2 - System Abstract. In: Egly and Fermüller [BF02],
           pp. 335–340
[Tin02]   Tinelli, C.: A DPLL-based calculus for ground satisfiability modulo the-
           ories. In: Flesca, S., Greco, S., Leone, N., Ianni, G. (eds.) JELIA 2002.
           LNCS (LNAI), vol. 2424, Springer, Heidelberg (2002)
[ZZ95]   Zhang, J., Zhang, H.: Sem: a system for enumerating models. In: IJCAI-
           95 — Proceedings of the 14th International Joint Conference on Artificial
           Intelligence, Montreal, pp. 298–303 (1995)

Predictive Labeling with Dependency Pairs Using SAT

Adam Koprowski[1] and Aart Middeldorp[2],[*]

[1] Department of Computer Science
Eindhoven University of Technology
P.O. Box 513, 5600 MB Eindhoven, The Netherlands
[2] Institute of Computer Science
University of Innsbruck
6020 Innsbruck, Austria

Abstract. This paper combines predictive labeling with dependency pairs and reports on its implementation. Our starting point is the method of proving termination of rewrite systems using semantic labeling with infinite models in combination with lexicographic path orders. We replace semantic labeling with predictive labeling to weaken the quasi-model constraints and we combine it with dependency pairs (usable rules and argument filtering) to increase the power of the method. Encoding the resulting search problem as a propositional satisfiability problem and calling a state-of-the-art SAT solver yields a powerful technique for proving termination automatically.

1 Introduction

Termination is an important topic in term rewriting and over the years many techniques have been developed for proving termination. Recently the emphasis in the field is on automation and since 2004 an annual termination competition is being organized in which automatic termination provers compete on a set of termination problems.

One of the techniques for proving termination is a transformational method of *semantic labeling* due to Zantema [20]. The idea of this method is to give semantics to function symbols and use the semantics to label the function symbols in order that simpler termination methods become applicable. At first in automatic termination provers this method was used, if at all, with finite (typically two elements) model. In [14] the method of automating semantic labeling over infinite domains has been worked out and implemented in the termination prover TPA [13]. The approach was to find a quasi-model for the given rewrite system, transform it to a labeled rewrite system, and apply the recursive path order using the information in the labels to distinguish different occurrences of function symbols depending on their context.

The recent development of *predictive labeling* [11] aims at improving semantic labeling by weakening the quasi-model constraints—it allows to consider only

---

[*] Partially supported by FWF (Austrian Science Fund) project P18763.

F. Pfenning (Ed.): CADE 2007, LNAI 4603, pp. 410–425, 2007.

usable rules instead of all rules of the rewrite system under consideration when checking the quasi-model condition and it requires semantics only for the relevant part of the signature.

The first contribution of this paper is to increase the power of predictive labeling with natural numbers by incorporating it in the framework of *dependency pairs* [1,6]. This requires an extension of the theory of predictive labeling which in [11] was presented for ordinary termination only. Furthermore, since labeling with natural numbers produces infinite systems over infinite signatures, powerful ingredients of the dependency pair method like usable rules with argument filterings are not directly applicable.

The second contribution is to extend the approach of automatically proving termination using semantic labeling with natural numbers, as in [14], to incorporate the improvement of predictive labeling. This is not completely straightforward due to the fact that apart from choosing semantics for function symbols one now also needs to decide which symbols to label which in turn influences the set of usable rules. This greatly enlarges the search space.

The third contribution is the presentation of insights used in the implementation of this approach in TPA. This is the first implementation of the predictive labeling method ever. It uses the increasingly popular method of encoding the search problems resulting from an application of a termination technique as propositional formulas and handing them over to a SAT solver.

The remainder of this paper is organized as follows. In the next section we recall basic notions and starting points of this paper. In Section 3 we present the combination of predictive labeling with dependency pairs. Section 4 describes the SAT encoding of the combination. In Section 5 we present experimental results and we conclude in Section 6.

2   Preliminaries

We begin by briefly recalling a few basic notions and refer to [2] for further details on term rewriting. This is followed by a presentation of dependency pairs in Section 2.1 and semantic and predictive labeling in Section 2.2.

We assume a signature $\mathcal{F}$ and a set of variables $\mathcal{V}$ and denote by $\mathcal{T}(\mathcal{F}, \mathcal{V})$ the set of terms over $\mathcal{F}$ and $\mathcal{V}$. By $\mathcal{F}un(t)$ we denote the set of function symbols and by $\mathcal{V}ar(t)$ the set of variables occurring in a term t. The root symbol of a term t is denoted by $\text{root}(t)$. A *rewrite rule* is a pair (l, r), written $l \to r$, with $l, r \in \mathcal{T}(\mathcal{F}, \mathcal{V})$, $l \notin \mathcal{V}$, and $\mathcal{V}ar(r) \subseteq \mathcal{V}ar(l)$. A *term rewriting system* (TRS for short) is a set of rewrite rules. Given a TRS $\mathcal{R}$ and a function symbol f, the subset of $\mathcal{R}$ consisting of those rules that have f as root of the left-hand side is denoted by $\mathcal{R}_f$: $\mathcal{R}_f = \{l \to r \in \mathcal{R} \mid \text{root}(l) = f\}$. The subterm relation on terms is denoted by $\trianglelefteq$. The *rewrite relation* $\to_{\mathcal{R}}$ of a TRS $\mathcal{R}$ is defined as follows: $s \to_{\mathcal{R}} t$ if there exists a rewrite rule $l \to r \in \mathcal{R}$, a substitution σ, and a context C such that $s = C[l\sigma]$ and $t = C[r\sigma]$. A TRS $\mathcal{R}$ is called *terminating* if there is no infinite reduction $t_1 \to_{\mathcal{R}} t_2 \to_{\mathcal{R}} \cdots$.

We write $\mathcal{SN}$ for the subset of $\mathcal{T}(\mathcal{F}, \mathcal{V})$ consisting of all terminating terms and $\mathcal{T}_\infty$ for the set of minimal non-terminating terms, that is, non-terminating terms all of whose arguments are terminating. For a TRS $\mathcal{R}$ and a relation $\succ$ we define $\mathcal{R}_\succ = \{s \to t \in R \mid s \succ t\}$.

Example 1. We will use the following TRS from [17] (AProVE/rta1.trs in TPDB [21]) to illustrate various developments throughout this paper:

(1) $\mathsf{plus}(0, y) \to y$ (5) $\mathsf{plus}(\mathsf{s}(\mathsf{s}(x)), y) \to \mathsf{s}(\mathsf{plus}(x, \mathsf{s}(y)))$

(2) $\mathsf{plus}(\mathsf{s}(0), y) \to \mathsf{s}(y)$ (6) $\mathsf{plus}(x, \mathsf{s}(\mathsf{s}(y))) \to \mathsf{s}(\mathsf{plus}(\mathsf{s}(x), y))$

(3) $\mathsf{ack}(0, y) \to \mathsf{s}(y)$ (7) $\mathsf{ack}(\mathsf{s}(x), \mathsf{s}(y)) \to \mathsf{ack}(x, \mathsf{plus}(y, \mathsf{ack}(\mathsf{s}(x), y)))$

(4) $\mathsf{ack}(\mathsf{s}(x), 0) \to \mathsf{ack}(x, \mathsf{s}(0))$

2.1 Dependency Pairs

The dependency pair method [1] is a powerful approach for proving termination of TRSs. The dependency pair framework [6] is a modular reformulation and improvement of this approach. We present a simplified version which is sufficient for our purposes. For further information on dependency pairs and more detailed explanations of the concepts introduced below the reader is referred to [1,6,7,12]. Let $\mathcal{R}$ be a TRS over a signature $\mathcal{F}$. The set of *defined* symbols is defined as $\mathcal{D}_\mathcal{R} = \{\mathrm{root}(l) \mid l \to r \in \mathcal{R}\}$. The signature $\mathcal{F}$ is extended with symbols $f^\sharp$ for every symbol $f \in \mathcal{D}_\mathcal{R}$, resulting in the signature $\mathcal{F}^\sharp$. If $t \in \mathcal{T}(\mathcal{F}, \mathcal{V})$ with $\mathrm{root}(t)$ defined then $t^\sharp$ denotes the term that is obtained from t by replacing its root symbol with $\mathrm{root}(t)^\sharp$. If $l \to r \in \mathcal{R}$ and $t \trianglelefteq r$ with $\mathrm{root}(t)$ defined then the rule $l^\sharp \to t^\sharp$ is a *dependency pair* of $\mathcal{R}$. The set of dependency pairs of $\mathcal{R}$ is denoted by $\mathrm{DP}(\mathcal{R})$. A *DP problem* is a pair of TRSs $(\mathcal{P}, \mathcal{R})$. The problem is said to be *finite* if there is no infinite sequence $t_1 \to_\mathcal{R}^* s_1 \xrightarrow{\epsilon}_\mathcal{P} t_2 \to_\mathcal{R}^* s_2 \xrightarrow{\epsilon}_\mathcal{P} \cdots$ such that all terms $t_1, t_2, \ldots$ are terminating with respect to $\mathcal{R}$. Here ϵ in $\xrightarrow{\epsilon}_\mathcal{P}$ denotes that the application of the rule in $\mathcal{P}$ takes place at the root position. The main result underlying the dependency pair approach states that a TRS $\mathcal{R}$ is terminating iff the DP problem $(\mathrm{DP}(\mathcal{R}), \mathcal{R})$ is finite.

Example 2. For the TRS presented in Example 1 there are six dependency pairs:

(8) $\mathsf{ack}^\sharp(\mathsf{s}(x), 0) \to \mathsf{ack}^\sharp(x, \mathsf{s}(0))$

(9) $\mathsf{plus}^\sharp(\mathsf{s}(\mathsf{s}(x)), y) \to \mathsf{plus}^\sharp(x, \mathsf{s}(y))$

(10) $\mathsf{plus}^\sharp(x, \mathsf{s}(\mathsf{s}(y))) \to \mathsf{plus}^\sharp(\mathsf{s}(x), y)$

(11) $\mathsf{ack}^\sharp(\mathsf{s}(x), \mathsf{s}(y)) \to \mathsf{ack}^\sharp(x, \mathsf{plus}(y, \mathsf{ack}(\mathsf{s}(x), y)))$

(12) $\mathsf{ack}^\sharp(\mathsf{s}(x), \mathsf{s}(y)) \to \mathsf{plus}^\sharp(y, \mathsf{ack}(\mathsf{s}(x), y))$

(13) $\mathsf{ack}^\sharp(\mathsf{s}(x), \mathsf{s}(y)) \to \mathsf{ack}^\sharp(\mathsf{s}(x), y)$

In order to prove finiteness of a DP problem a number of so-called *DP processors* have been developed. DP processors are functions that take a DP problem as input and return a set of DP problems as output. In order to be employed to prove termination they need to be sound, that is, if all DP problems in a set returned by a DP processor are finite then the initial DP problem is finite.

Below we shortly introduce three key concepts of the dependency pair method that are important for our approach: reduction pairs, argument filtering, and usable rules [1,7].

A reduction pair $(\gtrsim, >)$ consists of a preorder $\gtrsim$ which is closed under contexts and substitutions and a well-founded order $>$ which is closed under substitutions such that the inclusion $\gtrsim \cdot > \subseteq >$ or the inclusion $> \cdot \gtrsim \subseteq >$ holds. We say that a reduction pair $(\gtrsim, >)$ is $\mathcal{C}_\mathcal{E}$-compatible iff $\mathsf{c}(x,y) \gtrsim x$ and $\mathsf{c}(x,y) \gtrsim y$, where c is a new binary function symbol.

An argument filtering is a mapping π that assigns to every n-ary function symbol f an argument position $i \in \{1, \ldots, n\}$ or a (possibly empty) list $[i_1, \ldots, i_m]$ of argument positions with $1 \leqslant i_1 < \cdots < i_m \leqslant n$. Every argument filtering π induces a mapping on terms:

$$\pi(t) = \begin{cases} t & \text{if } t \text{ is a variable,} \\ \pi(t_i) & \text{if } t = f(t_1, \ldots, t_n) \text{ and } \pi(f) = i, \\ f(\pi(t_{i_1}), \ldots, \pi(t_{i_m})) & \text{if } t = f(t_1, \ldots, t_n) \text{ and } \pi(f) = [i_1, \ldots, i_m]. \end{cases}$$

Given a binary relation $\succ$ and an argument filtering π, we write $s \succ^\pi t$ iff $\pi(s) \succ \pi(t)$.

Next we introduce the concept of usable rules modulo argument filtering. Let $(\mathcal{P}, \mathcal{R})$ be a DP problem and π an argument filtering. We define the set of usable rules for $(\mathcal{P}, \mathcal{R})$ modulo π as

$$\mathcal{U}_\pi(\mathcal{P}, \mathcal{R}) = \bigcup_{s \to t \in \mathcal{P}} \mathcal{U}_\pi(t, \mathcal{R})$$

with $\mathcal{U}_\pi(t, \mathcal{R}) = \varnothing$ if t is a variable and

$$\mathcal{U}_\pi(t, \mathcal{R}) = \mathcal{R}_f \cup \bigcup_{l \to r \in \mathcal{R}_f} \mathcal{U}_\pi(r, \mathcal{R} \setminus \mathcal{R}_f) \cup \bigcup_{i:\, \pi(f) = i \,\vee\, i \in \pi(f)} \mathcal{U}_\pi(t_i, \mathcal{R} \setminus \mathcal{R}_f)$$

if $t = f(t_1, \ldots, t_n)$. We illustrate usable rules on our leading example.

Example 3. Consider the TRS $\mathcal{R}$ from Example 1 and its dependency pairs $\mathcal{P}$, as presented in Example 2. Given argument filtering $\pi(\mathsf{ack}^\sharp) = 1$ and $\pi(f) = [1, \ldots, n]$ for the remaining symbols $f \in \mathcal{F}^\sharp$, where n is the arity of f. Then applying the above definition yields $\mathcal{U}_\pi(\mathcal{P}, \mathcal{R}) = \{3, 4, 7\}$.

Theorem 4 (Reduction Pair Processor). *Let $\mathcal{P}$ and $\mathcal{R}$ be (possibly infinite) TRSs. Let $(\gtrsim, >)$ be a $\mathcal{C}_\mathcal{E}$-compatible reduction pair and let π be an argument filtering. If $\mathcal{R}$ is finitely branching, $\mathcal{P} = \mathcal{P}_{\gtrsim^\pi} \cup \mathcal{P}_{>^\pi}$, and $\mathcal{U}_\pi(\mathcal{P}, \mathcal{R}) \subseteq \gtrsim^\pi$ then the DP processor $(\mathcal{P}, \mathcal{R}) \mapsto \{(\mathcal{P} \setminus \mathcal{P}_{>^\pi}, \mathcal{R})\}$ is sound.* $\square$

In [7] the above theorem is stated and proved for finite TRSs $\mathcal{P}$ and $\mathcal{R}$. In our setting we deal with infinite TRSs obtained by labeling finite TRSs. So finiteness of $\mathcal{R}$ is too restrictive. A careful inspection of the proof in [7] as well as the proofs of related statements in [12,18] reveals that it is sufficient that $\mathcal{R}$ is finitely branching. The reason is that then the sets $\{t \mid s \to_{\mathcal{R}}^* t\}$ of reducts of terminating terms s are still guaranteed to be finite.

2.2   Semantic and Predictive Labeling

We start by presenting semantic labeling [20] in the setting of monotone algebras. Let $\mathcal{R}$ be a TRS over signature $\mathcal{F}$ and let $\mathcal{A} = (A, \{f_A\}_{f \in \mathcal{F}}, >, \gtrsim)$ be a well-founded weakly monotone $\mathcal{F}$-algebra, that is a quadruple consisting of

- a non-empty carrier set A,
- a set of algebra operations on A that are weakly monotone in all coordinates: $f_A(a_1, \ldots, a_i, \ldots, a_n) \gtrsim f_A(a_1, \ldots, b, \ldots, a_n)$ for all n-ary $f \in \mathcal{F}$, $a_1, \ldots, a_n, b \in A$, and $i \in \{1, \ldots, n\}$ with $a_i \gtrsim b$,
- a well-founded order $>$ on A, and
- a relation $\gtrsim$ such that $> \cdot \gtrsim \subseteq >$ or $\gtrsim \cdot > \subseteq >$.

A weakly monotone *labeling* ℓ for $\mathcal{A}$ consists of a set of labels $L_f \subseteq A$ together with a mapping $\ell_f : A^n \to L_f$ for every n-ary function symbol $f \in \mathcal{F}$ such that ℓ_f is weakly monotone in all coordinates. The labeled signature $\mathcal{F}_{\mathsf{lab}}$ consist of n-ary function symbols f_a for every n-ary function symbol $f \in \mathcal{F}$ and every label $a \in L_f$ together with all function symbols $f \in \mathcal{F}$ such that $L_f = \varnothing$. We extend an assignment of variables $\alpha: \mathcal{V} \to A$ to the mapping $\mathsf{lab}_\alpha : \mathcal{T}(\mathcal{F}, \mathcal{V}) \to \mathcal{T}(\mathcal{F}_{\mathsf{lab}}, \mathcal{V})$ in the following way:

$$\mathsf{lab}_\alpha(t) = \begin{cases} t & \text{if } t \text{ is a variable,} \\ f(\mathsf{lab}_\alpha(t_1), \ldots, \mathsf{lab}_\alpha(t_n)) & \text{if } t = f(t_1, \ldots, t_n) \text{ and } L_f = \varnothing, \\ f_a(\mathsf{lab}_\alpha(t_1), \ldots, \mathsf{lab}_\alpha(t_n)) & \text{if } t = f(t_1, \ldots, t_n) \text{ and } L_f \neq \varnothing \end{cases}$$

where a denotes the label $\ell_f([\alpha]_\mathcal{A}(t_1), \ldots, [\alpha]_\mathcal{A}(t_n))$. We extend the relation $>$ on A to $>_\mathcal{A}$ on $\mathcal{T}(\mathcal{F}, \mathcal{V})$ as follows: $s >_\mathcal{A} t$ if $[\alpha]_\mathcal{A}(s) > [\alpha]_\mathcal{A}(t)$ for all variable assignments α; $\gtrsim$ is similarly extended to $\gtrsim_\mathcal{A}$. We say that $\mathcal{A}$ is a quasi-model for $\mathcal{R}$ if $\mathcal{R} \subseteq \gtrsim_\mathcal{A}$. We define the TRS $\mathcal{D}ec$ to consist of all rewrite rules $f_a(x_1, \ldots, x_n) \to f_b(x_1, \ldots, x_n)$ with $f \in \mathcal{F}$ an n-ary function symbol, $a, b \in L_f$ with $a > b$, and pairwise different variables $x_1, \ldots, x_n$.

The following is the straightforward generalization of the result for ordinary termination from [20] to DP problems. The only observation is that interpretations of dependency pair symbols do not contribute to labels so by choosing them to be the same constant we get the quasi-model constraints for DP rules for free. We omit the easy proof.

Theorem 5. *Let $\mathcal{R}$ be a TRS, $\mathcal{A}$ a weakly monotone quasi-model for $\mathcal{R}$, and ℓ a weakly monotone labeling for $\mathcal{A}$. The DP problem $(\mathrm{DP}(\mathcal{R}), \mathcal{R})$ is finite iff the DP problem $(\mathrm{DP}(\mathcal{R})_{\mathsf{lab}}, \mathcal{R}_{\mathsf{lab}} \cup \mathcal{D}ec)$ is finite.* $\square$

In the remainder of this subsection we recall some definitions pertinent to predictive labeling that are needed for the developments in the next section. Let $\mathcal{R}$

be a TRS. For function symbols f and g we write $f \rhd_d g$ if there exist a rewrite rule $l \to r \in \mathcal{R}$ such that $f = \text{root}(l)$ and g is a function symbol in $\mathcal{F}\text{un}(r)$. Let ℓ be a labeling and t a term. We define

$$\mathcal{G}_\ell(t) = \begin{cases} \varnothing & \text{if } t \text{ is a variable,} \\ \mathcal{F}\text{un}(t_1)^* \cup \cdots \cup \mathcal{F}\text{un}(t_n)^* & \text{if } t = f(t_1,\ldots,t_n) \text{ and } L_f \neq \varnothing, \\ \mathcal{G}_\ell(t_1) \cup \cdots \cup \mathcal{G}_\ell(t_n) & \text{if } t = f(t_1,\ldots,t_n) \text{ and } L_f = \varnothing \end{cases}$$

where F^* denotes the set $\{g \mid f \rhd_d^* g \text{ for some } f \in F\}$. Furthermore we define

$$\mathcal{G}_\ell(\mathcal{R}) = \bigcup_{l \to r \in \mathcal{R}} \mathcal{G}_\ell(l) \cup \mathcal{G}_\ell(r)$$

and the set of *usable rules* for ℓ is defined as $\mathcal{U}(\ell) = \{l \to r \in \mathcal{R} \mid \text{root}(l) \in \mathcal{G}_\ell(\mathcal{R})\}$. Typically, $\mathcal{U}(\ell)$ is a proper subset of $\mathcal{R}$. The point of predictive labeling is to replace the condition $\mathcal{R} \subseteq \gtrsim_\mathcal{A}$ in semantic labeling by the easier to satisfy condition $\mathcal{U}(\ell) \subseteq \gtrsim_\mathcal{A}$. We illustrate this on an example.

Example 6. Consider the TRS R from Example 1. Suppose $L_s \neq \varnothing$ and $L_{\text{plus}} = L_{\text{ack}} = \varnothing$. Then applying the above definition gives $\mathcal{G}_\ell(\mathcal{R}) = \{\text{plus}, \text{s}\}$ and $\mathcal{U}(\ell) = \{1, 2, 5, 6\}$.

The weakly monotone algebras $\mathcal{A} = (A, \{f_A\}_{f \in \mathcal{F}}, >, \gtrsim)$ used to determine the labeling and to satisfy the quasi-model constraints in connection with predictive labeling (i.e., $\mathcal{U}(\ell) \subseteq \gtrsim_\mathcal{A}$), must satisfy the additional property that for every finite subset $X \subseteq A$ there exists a least upper bound $\bigsqcup X$ of X in A (with respect to $\gtrsim$). Such algebras are called $\sqcup$-*algebras* in [11]. The main result of [11] can now be stated.

Theorem 7. *Let $\mathcal{R}$ be a finitely branching TRS, $\mathcal{A}$ a weakly monotone $\sqcup$-algebra, and ℓ a weakly monotone labeling for $\mathcal{A}$ such that $\mathcal{U}(\ell) \subseteq \gtrsim_\mathcal{A}$. If $\mathcal{R}_{\text{lab}} \cup \text{Dec}$ is terminating then $\mathcal{R}$ is terminating.* $\square$

Due to the restriction to $\sqcup$-algebras, predictive labeling is less powerful than semantic labeling in theory. However, since the algebras used in current termination tools are $\sqcup$-algebras, in practice predictive labeling is to be preferred as it has the clear advantage of weakening the quasi-model condition; instead of all rules only the usable rules need to be oriented, which brings improvements in proving power as well as efficiency.

3 Predictive Labeling and Dependency Pairs

The following theorem constitutes the main theoretical result of this paper.

Theorem 8. *Let $\mathcal{R}$ and $\mathcal{P} \subseteq \text{DP}(\mathcal{R})$ be TRSs. Let $\mathcal{A}$ be a weakly monotone $\sqcup$-algebra and ℓ a weakly monotone labeling for $\mathcal{A}$ such that $\mathcal{U}(\ell) \subseteq \gtrsim_\mathcal{A}$. If $\mathcal{R}$ is finitely branching then the DP processor $(\mathcal{P}, \mathcal{R}) \mapsto \{(\mathcal{P}_{\text{lab}}, \mathcal{R}_{\text{lab}} \cup \text{Dec})\}$ is sound.*

Before presenting a proof sketch, we make some clarifying remarks. The condition $\mathcal{P} \subseteq \mathrm{DP}(\mathcal{R})$ ensures that the root symbols of the rules in $\mathcal{P}$ are dependency pair symbols that occur nowhere else. This implies that we do not have to worry about the semantics of the rules $\mathcal{P}$ and thus $\mathcal{U}(\ell)$ will be a subset of $\mathcal{R}$. Nevertheless, dependency pair symbols in $\mathcal{P}$ can be labeled and this may influence the usable rules. It follows that the definition of $\mathcal{U}(\ell)$ given in the preceding section has to be slightly modified: $\mathcal{U}(\ell) = \{l \to r \in \mathcal{R} \mid \mathrm{root}(l) \in \mathcal{G}_\ell(\mathcal{P} \cup \mathcal{R})\}$. The $\mathcal{D}ec$ rules are computed for all labeled symbols in $\mathcal{F}^\sharp$, where $\mathcal{F}$ is the signature of $\mathcal{R}$.

Proof (sketch). Suppose the DP processor $(\mathcal{P}, \mathcal{R}) \mapsto \{(\mathcal{P}_{\mathrm{lab}}, \mathcal{R}_{\mathrm{lab}} \cup \mathcal{D}ec)\}$ is not sound. So the DP problem $(\mathcal{P}_{\mathrm{lab}}, \mathcal{R}_{\mathrm{lab}} \cup \mathcal{D}ec)$ is finite whereas $(\mathcal{P}, \mathcal{R})$ is not. Hence there exists an infinite sequence

$$t_1 \to_\mathcal{R}^* u_1 \overset{\epsilon}{\to}_\mathcal{P} t_2 \to_\mathcal{R}^* u_2 \overset{\epsilon}{\to}_\mathcal{P} \cdots$$

such that the terms t_1, t_2, ... are terminating with respect to $\mathcal{R}$. Let α be an arbitrary assignment. We recall the following definitions from [11].

- Let $t \in \mathcal{SN}$. The interpretation $[\alpha]_\mathcal{A}^*(t)$ is inductively defined as follows:

$$[\alpha]_\mathcal{A}^*(t) = \begin{cases} \alpha(t) & \text{if } t \text{ is a variable,} \\ f_\mathcal{A}([\alpha]_\mathcal{A}^*(t_1), \ldots, [\alpha]_\mathcal{A}^*(t_n)) & \text{if } t = f(t_1, \ldots, t_n) \text{ and } f \in \mathcal{G}_\ell, \\ \bigsqcup\{[\alpha]_\mathcal{A}^*(u) \mid t \to_\mathcal{R}^+ u\} & \text{if } t = f(t_1, \ldots, t_n) \text{ and } f \notin \mathcal{G}_\ell. \end{cases}$$

- Let $t \in \mathcal{SN} \cup \mathcal{T}_\infty$. The labeled term $\mathrm{lab}_\alpha^*(t)$ is inductively defined as follows:

$$\mathrm{lab}_\alpha^*(t) = \begin{cases} t & \text{if } t \text{ is a variable,} \\ f(\mathrm{lab}_\alpha^*(t_1), \ldots, \mathrm{lab}_\alpha^*(t_n)) & \text{if } L_f = \varnothing, \\ f_a(\mathrm{lab}_\alpha^*(t_1), \ldots, \mathrm{lab}_\alpha^*(t_n)) & \text{if } L_f \neq \varnothing \end{cases}$$

where $a = \ell_f([\alpha]_\mathcal{A}^*(t_1), \ldots, [\alpha]_\mathcal{A}^*(t_n))$.
- Given a substitution σ such that $\sigma(x) \in \mathcal{SN}$ for all variables x, the assignment α_σ^* is defined as $[\alpha]_\mathcal{A}^* \circ \sigma$ and the substitution $\sigma_{\mathrm{lab}_\alpha^*}$ as $\mathrm{lab}_\alpha^* \circ \sigma$.

We will apply $\mathrm{lab}_\alpha^*(\cdot)$ to the terms in the above sequence. Fix $i \geqslant 1$. Repeated application of Lemma 17 in [11] yields $\mathrm{lab}_\alpha^*(t_i) \to_{\mathcal{R}_{\mathrm{lab}} \cup \mathcal{D}ec}^* \mathrm{lab}_\alpha^*(u_i)$. We have $u_i = l\sigma$ and $t_{i+1} = r\sigma$ for some $l \to r \in \mathcal{P}$. We use Lemma 15 in [11] to obtain

$$\mathrm{lab}_\alpha^*(l\sigma) \to_{\mathcal{D}ec}^* \mathrm{lab}_{\alpha_\sigma^*}(l)\sigma_{\mathrm{lab}_\alpha^*}.$$

Since $\mathrm{lab}_{\alpha_\sigma^*}(l) \to \mathrm{lab}_{\alpha_\sigma^*}(r) \in \mathcal{P}_{\mathrm{lab}}$, $\mathrm{lab}_{\alpha_\sigma^*}(l)\sigma_{\mathrm{lab}_\alpha^*} \overset{\epsilon}{\to}_{\mathcal{P}_{\mathrm{lab}}} \mathrm{lab}_{\alpha_\sigma^*}(r)\sigma_{\mathrm{lab}_\alpha^*}$. A variation of Lemma 16 in [11] gives $\mathrm{lab}_{\alpha_\sigma^*}(r)\sigma_{\mathrm{lab}_\alpha^*} = \mathrm{lab}_\alpha^*(r\sigma)$. Putting things together yields $\mathrm{lab}_\alpha^*(t_i) \to_{\mathcal{R}_{\mathrm{lab}} \cup \mathcal{D}ec}^* \cdot \overset{\epsilon}{\to}_{\mathcal{P}_{\mathrm{lab}}} \mathrm{lab}_\alpha^*(t_{i+1})$. Hence, the above infinite sequence is transformed into

$$\mathrm{lab}_\alpha^*(t_1) \to_{\mathcal{R}_{\mathrm{lab}} \cup \mathcal{D}ec}^* \cdot \overset{\epsilon}{\to}_{\mathcal{P}_{\mathrm{lab}}} \mathrm{lab}_\alpha^*(t_2) \to_{\mathcal{R}_{\mathrm{lab}} \cup \mathcal{D}ec}^* \cdot \overset{\epsilon}{\to}_{\mathcal{P}_{\mathrm{lab}}} \cdots$$

If we can show that the terms $\mathsf{lab}^*_\alpha(t_1)$, $\mathsf{lab}^*_\alpha(t_2)$, $\cdots$ are terminating with respect to $\mathcal{R}_{\mathsf{lab}} \cup \mathcal{D}ec$ then the DP problem $(\mathcal{P}_{\mathsf{lab}}, \mathcal{R}_{\mathsf{lab}} \cup \mathcal{D}ec)$ is not finite, providing the desired contradiction. Suppose $\mathsf{lab}^*_\alpha(t_i)$ for some i admits an infinite reduction with respect to $\mathcal{R}_{\mathsf{lab}} \cup \mathcal{D}ec$. Because $\mathcal{D}ec$ is a terminating TRS, there must be infinitely many $\mathcal{R}_{\mathsf{lab}}$-steps in this sequence. If we remove all labels, the $\mathcal{D}ec$-steps disappear and the $\mathcal{R}_{\mathsf{lab}}$-steps are turned into $\mathcal{R}$-steps. It follows that t_i is not terminating with respect to $\mathcal{R}$. This completes the proof.   □

4   SAT Encoding

We start this section by giving an outline of the main steps of our termination proving procedure. Afterwards we explain which parts are encoded in SAT and how this is actually achieved.

1. First the dependency pairs of $\mathcal{R}$ are computed. Then the strongly connected components (SCCs) in an over-approximation of the dependency graph of $\mathcal{R}$ are determined.
2. In the next step the subterm criterion [12] is applied in connection with the recursive SCC algorithm [10]. The purpose of this step is to quickly remove components which do not pose a challenge for the termination proof.
3. At this point we deal with a number of problems of the form $(\mathcal{P}, \mathcal{R})$ where $\mathcal{P}$ is a set of dependency pairs of the original TRS $\mathcal{R}$. Both $\mathcal{P}$ and $\mathcal{R}$ are finite systems over a finite signature. Each of these problems is subjected to the following steps.
4. Predictive labeling (Theorem 8) transforms $(\mathcal{P}, \mathcal{R})$ into $(\mathcal{P}_{\mathsf{lab}}, \mathcal{R}_{\mathsf{lab}} \cup \mathcal{D}ec)$. This new problem generally consists of infinite systems over infinite signatures.
5. Next we apply the reduction pair processor with argument filtering (Theorem 4). In our implementation this step is specialized by taking LPO as the underlying reduction order. In order to make progress, there must be at least one rule in $\mathcal{P}$ with the property that all its labeled versions in $\mathcal{P}_{\mathsf{lab}}$ are strictly decreasing.
6. In the next step we return to the problem $(\mathcal{P}, \mathcal{R})$ and remove those rules from $\mathcal{P}$ that were identified in the preceding step. Then we repeat the algorithm on the resulting problem from step 2 onward.

We illustrate this procedure on an example.

Example 9. We continue with our leading example. The estimated dependency graph has two SCCs: $\{(8), (11), (13)\}$ and $\{(9), (10)\}$. The former is taken care of by two applications of the subterm criterion, first with projection $\pi(\mathsf{ack}^\sharp) = 1$ and then with $\pi(\mathsf{ack}^\sharp) = 2$. So in step 3 the problem $(\mathcal{P}, \mathcal{R})$ with $\mathcal{P} = \{(9), (10)\}$ and $\mathcal{R} = \{(1), \ldots, (7)\}$ remains. We will label function symbol $\mathsf{plus}^\sharp$, so $\mathcal{G}_\ell(\mathcal{P} \cup \mathcal{R}) = \{\mathsf{s}\}$ and thus $\mathcal{U}_\ell(\mathcal{R}) = \varnothing$. Taking the successor function as semantics for s together with the labeling function $\ell_{\mathsf{plus}^\sharp}(x, y) = x + y$ produces in step 4 the DP problem $(\mathcal{P}_{\mathsf{lab}}, \mathcal{R}_{\mathsf{lab}} \cup \mathcal{D}ec)$ with $\mathcal{P}_{\mathsf{lab}}$ consisting of the rules

$$\mathsf{plus}^{\sharp}_{i+j+2}(\mathsf{s}(\mathsf{s}(x)), y) \rightarrow \mathsf{plus}^{\sharp}_{i+j+1}(x, \mathsf{s}(y))$$

$$\mathsf{plus}^{\sharp}_{i+j+2}(x, \mathsf{s}(\mathsf{s}(y))) \rightarrow \mathsf{plus}^{\sharp}_{i+j+1}(\mathsf{s}(x), y)$$

for all $i, j \geqslant 0$, $\mathcal{R}_{\mathsf{lab}} = \mathcal{R}$, and $\mathcal{D}ec = \{\mathsf{plus}^{\sharp}_{i}(x, y) \rightarrow \mathsf{plus}^{\sharp}_{j}(x, y) \mid i > j \geqslant 0\}$. The DP problem $(\mathcal{P}_{\mathsf{lab}}, \mathcal{R}_{\mathsf{lab}} \cup \mathcal{D}ec)$ is taken care of in step 5 by the argument filtering $\pi(\mathsf{plus}^{\sharp}_{i}) = [\,]$ for all i in combination with the well-founded LPO precedence $\mathsf{plus}^{\sharp}_{i} \succ \mathsf{plus}^{\sharp}_{j}$ whenever $i > j$. Note that the rules in $\mathcal{R}_{\mathsf{lab}}$ are ignored as they are not usable. Since all rules in $\mathcal{P}_{\mathsf{lab}}$ are strictly decreasing, there is nothing left to do in step 6.

We use SAT for steps 4 and 5 of our algorithm. The starting point of our encoding is the approach to semantic labeling with natural numbers and LPO from [14] and the encoding of specific instances of Theorem 4 in [3,19]. The main challenges are the encoding of

- the search for interpretations f_A and labeling functions ℓ_f,
- the choice of function symbols to be labeled and the corresponding computation of usable rules,
- the induced quasi-model constraints,
- the precedence constraints over the infinite signature of the labeled system, and
- the finite branching condition in Theorem 4.

For the first problem, we adopt the SAT encoding of matrix interpretations [5].

To address the second problem we introduce a new propositional variable L_f for every function symbol f that will indicate whether $L_f \neq \varnothing$. Given those variables we need to compute the set of usable rules for predictive labeling according to the definitions at the end of Section 2.2. To this end we introduce propositional variables U_f for every defined symbol f of $\mathcal{R}$ indicating whether the rewrite rules defining f are usable. For a DP problem $(\mathcal{P}, \mathcal{R})$ the encoding of usable rules is expressed as:

$$\omega_{\mathrm{UR}}(\mathcal{P}, \mathcal{R}) = \bigwedge_{f \in \mathcal{F}^{\sharp}} \left(\mathsf{L}_f \implies \bigwedge_{g \in \Delta_f(\mathcal{P}, \mathcal{R})^*} \mathsf{U}_g \right)$$

where

$$\Delta_f(\mathcal{P}, \mathcal{R}) = \bigcup_{l \rightarrow r \in \mathcal{P} \cup \mathcal{R}} \{g \in \mathcal{F}un(t) \mid \mathrm{root}(t) = f \text{ and } t \trianglelefteq l \text{ or } t \trianglelefteq r\}.$$

Now the encoding of quasi-model constraints can easily be expressed as

$$\omega_{\mathrm{QM}}(\mathcal{R}) = \bigwedge_{f \in \mathcal{D}_{\mathcal{R}}} \left(\mathsf{U}_f \implies \bigwedge_{l \rightarrow r \in \mathcal{R}_f} \ulcorner [l]_A \gtrsim_A [r]_A \urcorner \right).$$

Here $\ulcorner \ldots \urcorner$ converts inequalities into formulas. For that we need to be able to compute term interpretations in the algebra A and compare them by $\gtrsim_A$.

To that end we can use any technique following the weakly monotone algebra approach from Section 2.2, like polynomial interpretations [15] or matrix interpretations [5]. In our implementation we use matrix interpretations with dimensions 1 (which correspond to linear polynomial interpretations) and 2. The reader is referred to [5] for details on how the corresponding constraints can be encoded. We note that both polynomial and matrix interpretations give ⊔-algebras, which is required for the soundness of predictive labeling (Theorem 8).

Note that we encode quasi-model constraints for $\mathcal{R}$ but not for $\mathcal{P}$. The reason is that every DP problem $(\mathcal{P}, \mathcal{R})$ encountered during the execution of our algorithm has the property that the root symbols of the left- and right-hand sides of rules in $\mathcal{P}$ are dependency pair symbols, which do not occur elsewhere in the problem. Hence they are not part of $\mathcal{G}_\ell(\mathcal{P} \cup \mathcal{R})$ and consequently no rule from $\mathcal{P}$ is usable.

The next question is how to restrict the spectrum of possible precedence relations for infinite labeled TRSs in such a way that they have finite representation, can be searched for easily, and ensuring their well-foundedness is feasible. With every (unlabeled) function symbol f we associate a pair of natural numbers (f_L, f_{SL}), the *level* and *sublevel* of f. Such an assignment induces a precedence $\succ_{\mathcal{F}_{lab}}$ on labeled function symbols in the following way. Firstly, no matter what the labels are, if the level of f is greater than the level of g then $f \succ_{\mathcal{F}_{lab}} g$. If two symbols have the same level but the label of f is greater (with respect to $>_{\mathcal{A}}$) than that of g then again $f \succ_{\mathcal{F}_{lab}} g$. Finally, if the levels and labels of f and g are equal but the sublevel of f is bigger than the sublevel of g then again $f \succ_{\mathcal{F}_{lab}} g$. Note that $\succ_{\mathcal{F}_{lab}}$ is well-founded since it is obtained as the lexicographic comparison of three well-founded orders.

The straightforward encoding of the (strict) precedence comparisons is presented below. For the computation of labels and their comparison with $>_{\mathcal{A}}$ and $\gtrsim_{\mathcal{A}}$ we may use any approach following the weakly monotone algebra framework.

$$\ulcorner f_i \succ_{\mathcal{F}_{lab}} g_j \urcorner = \ulcorner f_L >_N g_L \urcorner \vee \left(\ulcorner f_L =_N g_L \urcorner \wedge L_f \wedge L_g \wedge \left(\ulcorner i >_{\mathcal{A}} j \urcorner \vee \right. \right.$$
$$\left. \left. (\ulcorner i \gtrsim_{\mathcal{A}} j \urcorner \wedge \ulcorner f_{SL} >_N g_{SL} \urcorner) \right) \right)$$
$$\ulcorner f_i \succ_{\mathcal{F}_{lab}} f_j \urcorner = L_f \wedge \ulcorner i >_{\mathcal{A}} j \urcorner$$

The use of sublevels allows us to represent more precedences on the signatures of infinite labeled TRSs, which increases the termination proving power with only a small reduction in efficiency.

A natural question is how this setting for precedences compares to the one from [14]. It is easy to observe that every precedence in our setting has a counterpart in the setting of [14]. The converse is also true. More precisely, for every well-founded precedence $\succ_{\mathcal{F}_{lab}}$ from [14] there exists a precedence $\succ'_{\mathcal{F}_{lab}}$ in our setting (well-founded by definition), such that $\succ_{\mathcal{F}_{lab}} \subseteq \succ'_{\mathcal{F}_{lab}}$. So the expressive power of the two approaches is the same.

The last challenge that we address is the requirement of Theorem 4 that the TRS $\mathcal{R}_{lab}$ is finitely branching. For the type of infinite but well structured, parameterized TRSs obtained by labeling finite TRSs this is easy to check. The only source of violation may be a parameterized (labeled) rule where a single labeled instance of a left-hand sides has infinitely many corresponding labeled right-hand sides. In the case of weakly monotone polynomial interpretations this means that a variable must be present in some labels in the right-hand side but not in any label in the corresponding left-hand side. So we define

$$\omega_{\mathrm{FB}}(\mathcal{R}) = \bigwedge_{l \to r \in \mathcal{R}} \bigwedge_{x \in \mathcal{V}ar(r)} (\varPhi_x(r) \implies \varPhi_x(l))$$

with

$$\varPhi_x(t) = \bigvee_{f(t_1, \ldots, t_n) \trianglelefteq t} \mathsf{L}_f \wedge a > 0$$

Here a is the coefficient of x when (symbolically) computing the label of f in $f(t_1, \ldots, t_n)$. So $\varPhi_x(t)$ evaluates to true when the variable x occurs in some label in term t. Thus $\omega_{\mathrm{FB}}(\mathcal{R})$ expresses that if the value of x is used for obtaining the label of a function symbol occurring in r then this must also be true for a function symbol occurring in l, for every rule $l \to r \in \mathcal{R}$ and every variable x occurring in r.

When using matrix interpretations instead of polynomial interpretations we obtain a similar formula $\omega_{\mathrm{FB}}(\mathcal{R})$, only now variables are interpreted as finite vectors of natural numbers. So in addition to x we must also propagate the position in the vector on which the label depends. We omit the straightforward details.

Combining all ingredients gives us now the final formula for executing steps 4 and 5 of our termination procedure simultaneously:

$$\omega_{\mathrm{UR}}(\mathcal{P}, \mathcal{R}) \wedge \omega_{\mathrm{QM}}(\mathcal{R}) \wedge \omega_{\mathrm{FB}}(\mathcal{R}) \wedge \omega_{\mathrm{LAB}}(\mathcal{P}, \mathcal{R}) \wedge \omega_{\mathrm{LPO}}(\mathcal{P}, \mathcal{R})$$

Some clarifying remarks are in order.

The subformula $\omega_{\mathrm{LAB}}(\mathcal{P}, \mathcal{R})$ takes care of computing the labels for all occurrences of all function symbols. (Since the choice of which symbols will be actually labeled is left to the SAT solver, the calculation of labels needs to be encoded for *all* symbols.) This is very similar to the encoding of the algebra computations in $\omega_{\mathrm{QM}}(\mathcal{R})$ and actually we can share most of the code.

The subformula $\omega_{\mathrm{LPO}}(\mathcal{P}, \mathcal{R})$ is the encoding of the specialization of Theorem 8 to LPO. We adopt the encoding given in [3] but since we deal with infinite systems we use as basic building blocks the precedence comparisons sketched on page 419. We compute usable rules with respect to original (unlabeled) system and assume that all labeled versions of a usable unlabeled rule are usable. This gives a correct over-approximation of the usable rules of the labeled TRS.

One thing that seems to be missing in the above formula is the treatment of the rules in $\mathcal{D}ec$. Indeed they are not part of the formula in any way and that is because in the present setting they can be ignored. Regardless of the argument filtering and the precedence (within the constraints of the level/sublevel encoding), the rules in $\mathcal{D}ec$ are all (weakly) oriented, do not contribute to the computation of usable rules, and cannot make the system infinitely branching.

The above formula is given to a SAT solver. Three things can happen as a result:

- the SAT solver returns a satisfying assignment, which is translated back to obtain concrete parameters required to execute steps 4 and 5 of our algorithm, or
- the SAT solver returns "unsatisfiable", in which case we know that our approach is not applicable, or
- the SAT solver runs out of time or other resources, in which case we give up without being able to conclude anything.

5 Experimental Results

We implemented the technique described in the preceding section in the termination prover TPA, using the MiniSat SAT solver [4]. In this section we evaluate our method on a number of examples from the Termination Problem Database (TPDB, see [21]). All experiments involving TPA were performed on a machine equipped with an Intel ® Xeon^{TM} 2.80 GHz processor. Experimental data for other termination tools are taken from the respective publications (due to the difficulty of obtaining those tools in the configuration required for our experiments).

A very natural benchmark for our approach would be the comparison with results from [14]. Unfortunately the substantial difference in the approach to semantic labeling with natural numbers makes any decent comparison difficult. We are convinced however that the direct approach from [14] would be absolutely infeasible for exploring the much larger search space resulting from using arbitrary interpretations with bounded coefficients instead of only a small number of predefined interpretations.

We begin by evaluating two basic ingredients of our implementation, matrix interpretations and LPO with argument filtering (both without semantic or predictive labeling), against reference implementations: [5] for the former and [3] for the latter. Both implementations use more or less the same setup: dependency pairs with usable rules and subterm criterion. The results in Table 1 are based on version 2.0 of the TPDB, more precisely on the 773 TRSs from the termination category of this database. The columns "yes", "time", and "timeout" indicate the number of successful termination proofs, the total time (in seconds) spent on the TRSs in the problem set and the number of timeouts that occurred. We used a 60 seconds time limit.

The experiments for matrix interpretations use 2×2 matrices, 2 bits for the matrix entries, and 3 bits to represent the values of intermediate results. The slightly lower score of TPA compared to Jambox is probably due to a more sophisticated approximation of the dependency graph in the latter. No timing information is given in [5] but the authors write "[...] we took the time limit of 1 minute [...] this time was hardly ever consumed [...] average computation time for all proofs is around 1 second". This suggests that our implementation is far from optimal. Indeed, we did not invest much time in optimizing the encoding.

Table 1. Comparison to other tools

technique	tool	yes	time	timeout
matrix interpretations	Jambox	505	N/A	N/A
	TPA	498	3541	30
LPO	AProVE	380	193	0
	TPA	372	191	0

Table 2. Experiments with TPA on TPDB version 3.2

	technique	60 seconds timeout			10 minutes timeout		
		yes	time	timeout	yes	time	timeout
1×1	SL	440	1178	2	440	1351	0
	PL	456	1193	2	456	1316	0
	PL′	426	752	1	426	893	0
2×2	SL	503	6905	51	506	24577	30
	PL	527	6906	53	532	25582	32
	PL′	522	5211	33	524	11328	8

This seems to be a good starting point for improving the results for predictive labeling presented below.

The slightly higher score of AProVE in the LPO experiments is likely due to a different graph approximation algorithm. The execution speeds are almost the same but one needs to keep in mind that the results were obtained on different machines and hence cannot be compared directly.

Table 2 summarizes the experiments performed with TPA on the 864 TRSs in version 3.2 of the TPDB. All experiments were performed with time limits of 60 seconds and 10 minutes. The first group of results is based on semantic/predictive labeling with matrix interpretations of dimension 1 (equivalent to linear polynomials) used for both interpretations and labels:

- SL means semantic labeling (Theorem 5) where all symbols are labeled and all rules are considered for the quasi-model requirement,
- PL stands for predictive labeling and corresponds to the approach described in this paper,
- PL′ is a variant with a simple heuristic for the choice of labeled symbols; instead of leaving this decision to SAT all dependency pair symbols are labeled and only them.

A first observation is that predictive labeling is more powerful than semantic labeling—it proves termination of an additional 16 TRSs—without incurring any significant increase in execution speed. The heuristic brings a considerable speedup at the expense of termination proving power.

For the second group of results we use the same methods as for the first group but now 2×2 matrices are used for interpretations and labels. Again predictive labeling performs better than semantic labeling. It is interesting to observe that the price in termination proving power of the heuristic is much less than for dimension 1. This can be intuitively explained by the more powerful algebraic structure used for the labeling functions, which makes it possible to put more information in the labels and hence counter the reduced flexibility in the choice of function symbols to label. A similar line of reasoning could lead to the belief that in this case it is also easier to satisfy quasi-model constraints and thereby diminishing the improvement of predictive labeling but the difference of 26 TRSs between SL and PL proves this hypothesis wrong.

It is worth noting that even for the slowest variant (PL with matrices of dimension 2×2) the average time for successful proof is around 3 seconds. Moreover, there are three TRSs which can be proved terminating using this method but not with any tool that participated in the 2006 Termination Competition: Ex26_Luc03b_Z, Ex49_GM04_FR, and ExSec11_1_Luc02a_GM from the TRCSR subcollection.

6   Conclusion and Further Research

In this paper we extended the theory of predictive labeling to a dependency pair setting and we presented the ideas behind the SAT based implementation of this technique in the termination prover TPA. Experimental results confirm the feasibility of our approach. Our technique extends the earlier TPA implementation of semantic labeling with infinite quasi-models described in [14] in several ways:

- the quasi-model restriction is relaxed by using predictive labeling,
- the integration with dependency pairs makes the approach more powerful,
- the SAT encoding enables the use of unrestricted polynomial and matrix interpretations for function symbols, whereas in [14] the interpretations were restricted to a small predefined set in order not to blow up the search space.

There is however one extension in [14] that we fail to cover here and that is the possibility of using min and max as interpretations for binary symbols. This feature really adds power to the whole approach, allowing for instance to easily prove termination of the TRS SUBST [9]. The approach in [14] is to allow at most one binary function symbol to be interpreted as min or max, and to perform a case analysis on all occurrences of that symbol in combination with rule splitting. This approach seems to be difficult to incorporate in our new setting as the whole search procedure is encoded as a SAT problem and we have no way of knowing for which symbols min or max will be chosen and hence cannot do this case analysis and rule splitting in advance. We leave this issue as future work.

An important theoretical question is whether the finite branching condition in Theorem 4 is essential. Disabling the $\omega_{\mathrm{FB}}(\mathcal{R})$ conjunct in our encoding allows to "prove" the termination of two more TRSs from the TPDB. One of these TRSs is presented below.

Example 10. Consider the following TRS (Thiemann/factorial1.trs) computing the factorial function:

$$\text{plus}(0, x) \rightarrow x \qquad\qquad \text{plus}(\text{s}(x), y) \rightarrow \text{s}(\text{plus}(\text{p}(\text{s}(x)), y))$$
$$\text{times}(0, y) \rightarrow 0 \qquad\qquad \text{times}(\text{s}(x), y) \rightarrow \text{plus}(y, \text{times}(\text{p}(\text{s}(x)), y))$$
$$\text{p}(\text{s}(0)) \rightarrow 0 \qquad\qquad \text{p}(\text{s}(\text{s}(x))) \rightarrow \text{s}(\text{p}(\text{s}(x)))$$
$$\text{fac}(0, x) \rightarrow x \qquad\qquad \text{fac}(\text{s}(x), y) \rightarrow \text{fac}(\text{p}(\text{s}(x)), \text{times}(\text{s}(x), y))$$
$$\text{factorial}(x) \rightarrow \text{fac}(x, \text{s}(0))$$

There are ten dependency pairs and the estimated dependency graph contains four single node SCCs. Only one of them, consisting of the dependency pair

$$\text{fac}^{\sharp}(\text{s}(x), y) \rightarrow \text{fac}^{\sharp}(\text{p}(\text{s}(x)), \text{times}(\text{s}(x), y))$$

is problematic. It could be solved using matrices of dimension 2 by labeling s and p, but it is essential that the interpretation of plus depends on its second argument. Then the label of the root symbol of the right-hand side of the rule $\text{plus}(\text{s}(x), y) \rightarrow \text{s}(\text{plus}(\text{p}(\text{s}(x)), y))$ depends on the assignment to y whereas in the left-hand side there is only one labeled s symbol with x as its argument so its label is necessarily independent of the value of y. This makes $\mathcal{R}_{\text{lab}}$ non-finitely branching and hence the termination proof is out of reach with our approach.

At the end of Section 2.1 we already remarked that the proof of Theorem 4 relies on the finite branching condition. The key idea in the proof goes back to a modularity result for termination of Gramlich [8], in which the same finite branching condition is required. By using a much more complicated construction, Ohlebusch [16] showed that the finite branching condition in the modularity result is not essential. It is worthwhile to investigate whether the proof technique in [16] can be used to generalize Theorem 4.

Needless to say, it is not a single technique but rather a careful combination of techniques that makes a successful termination tool. Hence the effect of combining our approach with other techniques should be investigated.

Acknowledgments

We are grateful to Hans Zantema for helpful discussions. The comments of the referees improved the presentation.

References

1. Arts, T., Giesl, J.: Termination of term rewriting using dependency pairs. TCS 236, 133–178 (2000)
2. Baader, F., Nipkow, T.: Term Rewriting and All That. Cambridge University Press, Cambridge (1998)

3. Codish, M., Schneider-Kamp, P., Lagoon, V., Thiemann, R., Giesl, J.: SAT solving for argument filterings. In: Hermann, M., Voronkov, A. (eds.) LPAR 2006. LNCS (LNAI), vol. 4246, pp. 30–44. Springer, Heidelberg (2006)
4. Eén, N., Sörensson, N.: An extensible SAT-solver. In: Giunchiglia, E., Tacchella, A. (eds.) SAT 2003. LNCS, vol. 2919, pp. 502–518. Springer, Heidelberg (2004)
5. Endrullis, J., Waldmann, J., Zantema, H.: Matrix interpretations for proving termination of term rewriting. In: Furbach, U., Shankar, N. (eds.) IJCAR 2006. LNCS (LNAI), vol. 4130, pp. 574–588. Springer, Heidelberg (2006)
6. Giesl, J., Thiemann, R., Schneider-Kamp, P.: The dependency pair framework: Combining techniques for automated termination proofs. In: Baader, F., Voronkov, A. (eds.) LPAR 2004. LNCS (LNAI), vol. 3452, pp. 301–331. Springer, Heidelberg (2005)
7. Giesl, J., Thiemann, R., Schneider-Kamp, P., Falke, S.: Mechanizing and improving dependency pairs. JAR 37(3), 155–203 (2006)
8. Gramlich, B.: Generalized sufficient conditions for modular termination of rewriting. AAECC 5, 131–158 (1994)
9. Hardin, T., Laville, A.: Proof of termination of the rewriting system SUBST on CCL. TCS 46(2-3), 305–312 (1986)
10. Hirokawa, N., Middeldorp, A.: Automating the dependency pair method. Information and Computation 199(1,2), 172–199 (2005)
11. Hirokawa, N., Middeldorp, A.: Predictive labeling. In: Pfenning, F. (ed.) RTA 2006. LNCS, vol. 4098, pp. 313–327. Springer, Heidelberg (2006)
12. Hirokawa, N., Middeldorp, A.: Tyrolean termination tool: Techniques and features. Information and Computation 205(4), 474–511 (2007)
13. Koprowski, A.: TPA: Termination proved automatically. In: Pfenning, F. (ed.) RTA 2006. LNCS, vol. 4098, pp. 257–266. Springer, Heidelberg (2006)
14. Koprowski, A., Zantema, H.: Automation of recursive path ordering for infinite labelled rewrite systems. In: Furbach, U., Shankar, N. (eds.) IJCAR 2006. LNCS (LNAI), vol. 4130, pp. 332–346. Springer, Heidelberg (2006)
15. Lankford, D.: On proving term rewrite systems are noetherian. Technical Report MTP-3, Louisiana Technical University, Ruston, LA, USA (1979)
16. Ohlebusch, E.: On the modularity of termination of term rewriting systems. TCS 136(2), 333–360 (1994)
17. Thiemann, R., Giesl, J.: The size-change principle and dependency pairs for termination of term rewriting. AAECC 16(4), 229–270 (2005)
18. Urbain, X.: Modular & incremental automated termination proofs. JAR 32, 315–355 (2004)
19. Zankl, H., Hirokawa, N., Middeldorp, A.: Constraints for argument filterings. In: van Leeuwen, J., Italiano, G.F., van der Hoek, W., Meinel, C., Sack, H., Plášil, F. (eds.) SOFSEM 2007. LNCS, vol. 4362, pp. 579–590. Springer, Heidelberg (2007)
20. Zantema, H.: Termination of term rewriting by semantic labelling. Fundamenta Informaticae 24, 89–105 (1995)
21. Termination problem data base, version 3.2 (2006) http://www.lri.fr/~marche/tpdb

Dependency Pairs for Rewriting with Non-free Constructors[*]

Stephan Falke and Deepak Kapur

Computer Science Department, University of New Mexico, Albuquerque, NM, USA
{spf,kapur}@cs.unm.edu

Abstract. A method based on dependency pairs for showing termination of functional programs on data structures generated by constructors with relations is proposed. A functional program is specified as an equational rewrite system, where the rewrite system specifies the program and the equations express the relations on the constructors that generate the data structures. Unlike previous approaches, relations on constructors can be collapsing, including idempotency and identity relations. Relations among constructors may be partitioned into two parts: (i) equations that cannot be oriented into terminating rewrite rules, and (ii) equations that can be oriented into terminating rewrite rules, in which case an equivalent convergent system for them is generated. The dependency pair method is extended to normalized rewriting, where constructor-terms in the redex are normalized first. The method has been applied to several examples, including the Calculus of Communicating Systems and the Propositional Sequent Calculus. Various refinements, such as dependency graphs, narrowing, etc., which increase the power of the dependency pair method, are presented for normalized rewriting.

1 Introduction

Algorithms in a functional programming style can be specified elegantly within the framework of term rewrite systems. This is the approach taken by ELAN [14], Maude [3], and theorem provers such as RRL [13], where a function definition is given as a terminating rewrite system on data structures generated using constructors. We will follow that approach in this paper as well, i.e., we assume that a functional program is represented in the form of a term rewrite system. While automated termination methods (a collection of recent papers on termination is [7]) work well for establishing termination of rewrite systems defined on data structures generated using free constructors (such as natural numbers, lists, trees, etc.), they do not extend well to cases where the constructors of the data structures are related. For example, the data structure of finite sets has set union "∪" as a constructor which is not only associative (A) and commutative (C), but also idempotent ($x \cup x \approx x$) and has the other constructor, the empty set "∅", as an identity ($x \cup \emptyset \approx x$). Methods for showing termination of AC-rewrite systems

---

[*] Partially supported by NSF grant CCF-0541315.

F. Pfenning (Ed.): CADE 2007, LNAI 4603, pp. 426–442, 2007.

based on recursive path orderings and dependency pairs have been developed [12,20,16,18]. In [6], the dependency pair method was generalized to equational rewriting with the restriction that equations need to be non-collapsing and have identical unique variables (i.e., each variable occurs exactly once on each side). So termination of rewrite systems defined on a data structure such as finite sets cannot be established using any of these previous approaches.

In this paper, we extend the dependency pair method in order to establish termination of equational rewrite systems in which equations may be collapsing. However, if collapsing relations are included in the equational system, then equational rewriting does not necessarily terminate in cases where this would intuitively be expected. The key idea to handle this problem is to partition the equational system relating the constructors of the data structures into two parts: (i) equations which can be oriented and completed into a convergent subsystem, and (ii) the remaining equations. Rewriting in an equational rewrite system is then done using *normalized rewriting*[1] à la Marché [17]. Before rewriting a term, the constructor-terms in the redex are first *normalized*, and rewriting is thus performed on normalized terms. This approach towards equational rewriting has the major advantage that algorithms can be specified elegantly since, in the specification, the constructor-terms can be assumed to be in normalized form.

Example 1. As an example, we consider the data structure of integers that are built using the constructors 0, s (successor), and p (predecessor). We have the relations $\mathcal{E} = \{p(s(u)) \approx s(p(u)), p(s(u)) \approx u\}$ between these constructors. Defining a simple predicate pos, which checks whether an integer is strictly positive, is highly nontrivial with ordinary equational rewriting. Using the approach of normalized rewriting, we can split $\mathcal{E}$ into $\mathcal{E}_1 = \{p(s(u)) \approx s(p(u))\}$ and $\mathcal{E}_2 = \{p(s(u)) \approx u\}$, where $\mathcal{E}_2$ can be oriented into $\mathcal{S} = \{p(s(u)) \to u\}$, which is convergent modulo $\mathcal{E}_1$. Using normalized rewriting, it is now straightforward to define pos by the rewrite rules $\mathcal{R} = \{pos(0) \to false, pos(s(x)) \to true, pos(p(x)) \to false\}$. The predicate pos indeed correctly determines whether its argument is strictly positive for constructor ground terms since normalizing produces a term of the form 0, $s^i(0)$, or $p^i(0)$ for some $i > 0$. In contrast, evaluation with ordinary equational rewriting using $\mathcal{R}$ and $\mathcal{E}$ does not yield the desired result since, for example, $pos(s(p(p(0))))$ can be rewritten to true, although $s(p(p(0)))$ represents the negative integer -1.   ◊

The results in this paper rely on the property that no equations involving defined symbols (i.e., outermost symbols of left sides of rules in the rewrite system) are allowed. Firstly, this allows us to permit collapsing equations as well, which are not permitted in [6]. Note that orientable equations need not be treated as rewrite rules. Instead, our method provides a uniform framework for termination analysis in both cases. Secondly, even though we allow collapsing equations, the proposed approach is conceptually simpler than the one in [6] since we do not need to consider instantiations of rewrite rules. These instantiations are needed

---

[1] Strictly speaking this should be called *normalized equational rewriting*. We are following Marché's convention of calling it *normalized rewriting*.

for correctness of the method in [6] and can cause problems since they may generate a huge number of rules. Thirdly, using normalized rewriting also enables us to consider equations that do not have identical unique variables, which is another severe restriction of the method in [6]. We allow equations that do not have identical unique variables as long as they can be oriented into rewrite rules. All of these features significantly increase the scope of applicability of the dependency pair approach. The proposed method for showing termination of normalized rewriting has not been implemented yet, but we believe that it can be easily incorporated into a termination tool implementing the dependency pair framework such as AProVE [8].

The paper is organized as follows. In Section 2, we review equational rewriting and, in particular, the distinction between rewriting modulo $\mathcal{E}$ and $\mathcal{E}$-extended rewriting. Normalized rewriting is then discussed in Section 3. It is argued that algorithms can be specified elegantly and in a natural way using $\mathcal{S}$-normalized $\mathcal{E}$-extended rewriting, in which constructor-terms in the redex are first normalized using $\mathcal{S}$ modulo $\mathcal{E}$, where $\mathcal{S}$ is a convergent system capturing (some of the) relations on constructors. In Section 4, the dependency pair method is extended to normalized rewriting. It is shown that if there are no infinite chains of dependency pairs, then $\mathcal{S}$-normalized $\mathcal{E}$-extended rewriting is terminating. A first method for automatically showing that there are no such chains is presented. It uses so-called *reduction pairs*, which are widely used in the dependency pair approach. Reduction pairs have the advantage that they do not need to be monotonic. In Section 5, we extend the recently formulated dependency pair framework to the context of normalized rewriting. This allows flexibility in establishing the termination of complex rewrite systems including the sequent calculus, CCS, etc. In Section 6, dependency pair (DP) processors are discussed. A DP processor transforms a DP problem into a finite set of simpler DP problems in such a way that termination of the simpler DP problems implies termination of the original DP problem. The DP processors presented make use of dependency graphs, reduction pairs, removal of rules, and narrowing.

The method has been applied to interesting and nontrivial examples, many of which cannot be handled otherwise. The Appendix includes an equational rewrite system for the Propositional Sequent Calculus, whose termination can be established using the proposed approach. Due to lack of space, many proofs and detailed discussion of the nontrivial examples are omitted. They may be found in the extended version of this paper [5].

2   Equational Rewriting

We assume familiarity with the concepts of term rewriting [2] and fix some notation in the following. For a finite signature $\mathcal{F}$ and an infinite set $\mathcal{V}$ of variables the set of *terms* over $\mathcal{F}$ and $\mathcal{V}$ is denoted by $\mathcal{T}(\mathcal{F}, \mathcal{V})$. We often write s^* to denote a tuple of terms $s_1, \ldots, s_n$ for some $n \geq 0$. The set of function symbols occurring in the term t is denoted by $\mathcal{F}(t)$. Similarly, $\mathcal{V}(t)$ denotes the variables occurring in t. These operations naturally extends to sets of terms, pairs of terms, and sets of pairs of terms. The outermost function symbol of the term t is denoted by $\text{root}(t)$.

An *equational system* (ES) is a finite set $\mathcal{E} = \{u_1 \approx v_1, \ldots, u_m \approx v_m\}$ of equations, and a *term rewrite system* (TRS) is a finite set of oriented equations (called *rules*) $\mathcal{R} = \{l_1 \to r_1, \ldots, l_n \to r_n\}$, where $l_i \notin \mathcal{V}$ and $\mathcal{V}(r_i) \subseteq \mathcal{V}(l_i)$ for all $1 \leq i \leq n$. The *defined symbols* of a TRS $\mathcal{R}$ are the symbols occurring as $\text{root}(l)$ for some rule $l \to r$ in $\mathcal{R}$. The set of defined symbols of $\mathcal{R}$ is denoted by $\mathcal{D}(\mathcal{R})$. The remaining symbols of $\mathcal{F}(\mathcal{R})$ are *constructors*.

For an ES $\mathcal{E}$ (resp. TRS $\mathcal{R}$), we write $s \to_{\mathcal{E}} t$ (resp. $s \to_{\mathcal{R}} t$) iff there exist an equation $l \approx r$ in $\mathcal{E}$ (resp. rule $l \to r$ in $\mathcal{R}$), a substitution σ, and a position p in s such that $s|_p = l\sigma$ and $t = s[r\sigma]_p$. The symmetric closure of $\to_{\mathcal{E}}$ is denoted by $\vdash_{\mathcal{E}}$, and the reflexive-transitive closure of $\vdash_{\mathcal{E}}$ is denoted by $\sim_{\mathcal{E}}$. For tuples s^*, t^* of the same length n, we write $s^* \sim_{\mathcal{E}} t^*$ iff $s_i \sim_{\mathcal{E}} t_i$ for all $1 \leq i \leq n$.

Definition 2 (Rewriting Modulo $\mathcal{E}$). *Let $\mathcal{R}$ be a TRS and let $\mathcal{E}$ be an ES. The term s rewrites modulo $\mathcal{E}$ to the term t, written $s \to_{\mathcal{R}/\mathcal{E}} t$, iff $s' \to_{\mathcal{R}} t'$ for some terms $s' \sim_{\mathcal{E}} s$ and $t' \sim_{\mathcal{E}} t$.*

Thus, in order to determine whether a term s is reducible w.r.t. $\to_{\mathcal{R}/\mathcal{E}}$, a term that is equivalent to s up to $\sim_{\mathcal{E}}$ and reducible by $\to_{\mathcal{R}}$ has to be found. If the $\mathcal{E}$-equivalence classes are impractically large or even infinite this is not feasible. To avoid this problem, virtually all implementations (e.g., ELAN [14] and Maude [3]) use $\mathcal{E}$-extended rewriting, which builds the equivalence up to $\sim_{\mathcal{E}}$ into the matching process.

Definition 3 ($\mathcal{E}$-Extended Rewriting). *Let $\mathcal{R}$ be a TRS and let $\mathcal{E}$ be an ES. The term s rewrites $\mathcal{E}$-extended to the term t, written $s \to_{\mathcal{E} \backslash \mathcal{R}} t$, iff $s|_p \sim_{\mathcal{E}} l\sigma$ and $t = s[r\sigma]_p$ for some rule $l \to r$ in $\mathcal{R}$, substitution σ, and position p in s.*

An equation $u \approx v$ is *collapsing* iff $u \in \mathcal{V}$ or $v \in \mathcal{V}$, and an ES is said to be collapsing iff it contains a collapsing equation.

Definition 4 (Identical Unique Variables). *Let $\mathcal{E}$ be an ES. Then $\mathcal{E}$ has identical unique variables ($\mathcal{E}$ is i.u.v.) iff u, v are linear and $\mathcal{V}(u) = \mathcal{V}(v)$ for all equations $u \approx v$ in $\mathcal{E}$.*

In this paper we restrict ourselves to i.u.v. ESs. Note, however, that we do allow collapsing equations, in contrast to [6]. Two important cases of i.u.v. ESs are the following, which state that a binary function symbol f is associative and commutative, possibly with a unit 0.

$$\mathsf{AC}_f = \{f(u, f(v, w)) \approx f(f(u, v), w), f(u, v) \approx f(v, u)\}$$
$$\mathsf{ACU}_{f,0} = \mathsf{AC}_f \cup \{f(u, 0) \approx u\}$$

Note that equations like $f(u, u) \approx u$, $f(u, 0) \approx 0$ and $f(u, u) \approx 0$ are not allowed since they are nonlinear and/or not variable-preserving.

The reason for the restriction to i.u.v. ESs is the following lemma, which does not hold true if $\mathcal{E}$ is not i.u.v. Intuitively, it states that subterms t with $\text{root}(t) \notin \mathcal{F}(\mathcal{E})$ persist (modulo $\mathcal{E}$) in terms that are equivalent up to $\sim_{\mathcal{E}}$.

Lemma 5. *Let $\mathcal{E}$ be an i.u.v. ES and let $C[f(s^*)] \sim_{\mathcal{E}} t$ for some context C, some term $f(s^*)$ with $f \notin \mathcal{F}(\mathcal{E})$, and some term t. Then $t = C'[f(s'^*)]$ for some context $C' \sim_{\mathcal{E}} C$ and some term $f(s'^*)$ such that $s^* \sim_{\mathcal{E}} s'^*$.*

3 $\mathcal{S}$-Normalized Rewriting

In this paper we are concerned with proving termination of rewriting with a TRS $\mathcal{R}$ and an i.u.v. ES $\mathcal{E}$, where $\mathcal{F}(\mathcal{E})$ does not contain any defined symbols from $\mathcal{R}$. Thus, $\mathcal{E}$ is an ES of constructors which specifies some properties of the data structures that the functions defined by $\mathcal{R}$ operate on. The first problem that is encountered is that $\mathcal{E}$-extended rewriting does not terminate in many cases where $\mathcal{E}$ is an i.u.v. ES of constructors that is collapsing.

Example 6. Let $\mathcal{E} = \mathsf{ACU}_{+,0}$ and $\mathcal{R} = \{(x + y) \cdot z \to x \cdot z + y \cdot z\}$. Then $\to_{\mathcal{E}\backslash\mathcal{R}}$ is not terminating since

$$0 \cdot z \sim_{\mathcal{E}} (0 + 0) \cdot z \to_{\mathcal{R}} 0 \cdot z + 0 \cdot z \sim_{\mathcal{E}} (0 + 0) \cdot z + 0 \cdot z \to_{\mathcal{R}} \cdots$$

is an infinite $\to_{\mathcal{E}\backslash\mathcal{R}}$ reduction.   ◊

To overcome problems like this, the notion of *normalized rewriting* was introduced by Marché in [17]. In the following we use a slight variation of this notion. The idea is to split an ES $\mathcal{E}$, which does not necessarily need to be i.u.v., into ESs $\mathcal{E}_1$ and $\mathcal{E}_2$ such that $\mathcal{E}_1$ is i.u.v. and $\mathcal{E}_2$ contains the remaining equations. Then, $\mathcal{E}_2$ is completed[2] into a TRS $\mathcal{S}$ that is convergent modulo $\mathcal{E}_1$. Here, *convergence modulo $\mathcal{E}_1$* is defined as follows.

Definition 7 (Confluence and Convergence Modulo $\mathcal{E}$). *Let $\mathcal{S}$ be a TRS and let $\mathcal{E}$ be an ES. Then $\mathcal{S}$ is* confluent modulo $\mathcal{E}$ *iff whenever $t \to_{\mathcal{S}/\mathcal{E}}^{*} t_1$ and $t \to_{\mathcal{S}/\mathcal{E}}^{*} t_2$ for some terms t, t_1, t_2, then there exist terms s_1, s_2 with $s_1 \sim_{\mathcal{E}} s_2$ such that $t_1 \to_{\mathcal{S}/\mathcal{E}}^{*} s_1$ and $t_2 \to_{\mathcal{S}/\mathcal{E}}^{*} s_2$ (thus, $\leftarrow_{\mathcal{S}/\mathcal{E}}^{*} \circ \to_{\mathcal{S}/\mathcal{E}}^{*} \subseteq \to_{\mathcal{S}/\mathcal{E}}^{*} \circ \sim_{\mathcal{E}} \circ \leftarrow_{\mathcal{S}/\mathcal{E}}^{*})$[3]. The TRS $\mathcal{S}$ is* convergent modulo $\mathcal{E}$ *iff $\to_{\mathcal{S}/\mathcal{E}}$ is terminating and $\mathcal{S}$ is confluent modulo $\mathcal{E}$.*

Note that $t \sim_{\mathcal{E}_1} t'$ implies $t{\downarrow}_{\mathcal{S}/\mathcal{E}_1} \sim_{\mathcal{E}_1} t'{\downarrow}_{\mathcal{S}/\mathcal{E}_1}$ if $\mathcal{S}$ is convergent modulo $\mathcal{E}_1$, where $t{\downarrow}_{\mathcal{S}/\mathcal{E}_1}$ denotes the normal form of t w.r.t. $\to_{\mathcal{S}/\mathcal{E}_1}$. We write $t \to_{\mathcal{S}/\mathcal{E}_1}^{!} q$ iff $t \to_{\mathcal{S}/\mathcal{E}_1}^{*} q$ and q is a normal form of t.

In the following table we list how some commonly occurring, not necessarily i.u.v., ESs $\mathcal{E}$ can be split into an i.u.v. ES $\mathcal{E}_1$ and a TRS $\mathcal{S}$ that is convergent modulo $\mathcal{E}_1$.

$\mathcal{E}$	$\mathcal{E}_1$	$\mathcal{S}$
AC_f	AC_f	$\emptyset$
$\mathsf{ACU}_{f,0}$	AC_f	$\{f(u, 0) \to u\}$
$\mathsf{ACI}_f = \mathsf{AC}_f \cup \{f(u, u) \approx u\}$	AC_f	$\{f(u, u) \to u\}$
$\mathsf{ACUI}_{f,0} = \mathsf{ACI}_f \cup \mathsf{ACU}_{f,0}$	AC_f	$\{f(u, 0) \to u, f(u, u) \to u\}$
$\mathsf{AC0}_{f,0} = \mathsf{AC}_f \cup \{f(u, 0) \approx 0\}$	AC_f	$\{f(u, 0) \to 0\}$
$\mathsf{ACN}_{f,0} = \mathsf{AC}_f \cup \{f(u, u) \approx 0\}$	AC_f	$\{f(u, u) \to 0\}$

---

[2] In general, this requires $\mathcal{E}_1$-unification.

[3] Here, $\circ$ denotes composition of relations, i.e., $t \bowtie_1 \circ \bowtie_2 q$ iff $t \bowtie_1 s \bowtie_2 q$ for some s.

As mentioned in Section 2, rewriting with $\rightarrow_{\mathcal{R}/\mathcal{E}}$ tends to be infeasible and rewriting with $\rightarrow_{\mathcal{E}\backslash\mathcal{R}}$ should be used instead. Now $\rightarrow_{\mathcal{E}\backslash\mathcal{R}}$ is clearly contained in $\rightarrow_{\mathcal{R}/\mathcal{E}}$, but the converse is not true in general[4]. For a certain class of TRSs, however, $\rightarrow_{\mathcal{E}\backslash\mathcal{R}}$ and $\rightarrow_{\mathcal{R}/\mathcal{E}}$ are essentially the same.

Definition 8 (Complete TRSs). *Let $\mathcal{R}$ be a TRS and let $\mathcal{E}$ be an i.u.v. ES. Then $\mathcal{R}$ is complete modulo $\mathcal{E}$ iff $\rightarrow_{\mathcal{R}/\mathcal{E}} \subseteq \rightarrow_{\mathcal{E}\backslash\mathcal{R}} \circ \sim_{\mathcal{E}}$, i.e., whenever $s \rightarrow_{\mathcal{R}/\mathcal{E}} t$, then there exists a $t' \sim_{\mathcal{E}} t$ such that $s \rightarrow_{\mathcal{E}\backslash\mathcal{R}} t'$.*

In the following we assume that $\mathcal{S}$ is complete modulo $\mathcal{E}$. For $\mathcal{S}$ to satisfy Definition 8, an extension using $Ext_{\mathcal{E}}(\mathcal{S})$ might be needed, see [19,6]. In case $\mathcal{E} = \bigcup_{f \in \mathcal{G}} \mathsf{AC}_f$ for some set $\mathcal{G}$ of binary functions the extension can be achieved by adding rules $f(l, z) \rightarrow f(r, z)$ for all rules $l \rightarrow r \in \mathcal{S}$ with $root(l) = f \in \mathcal{G}$, where z is a fresh variable. If the rule $l \rightarrow r$ AC-matches the extended rule $f(l, z) \rightarrow f(r, z)$, then the extended rule does not need to be added, see [4, Lemma 6.3]. For example, the extension of $f(u, u) \rightarrow u$ for an AC-symbol f is $f(f(u, u), v) \rightarrow f(u, v)$ for a fresh variable v. Similarly, the extension of $f(u, 0) \rightarrow u$ is $f(f(u, 0), v) \rightarrow f(u, v)$ for a fresh variable v, but this extension does not need to be added since the rule $f(u, 0) \rightarrow u$ AC-matches it.

Since we are only interested in rewriting with non-free constructors, neither $\mathcal{S}$ nor $\mathcal{E}$ contain any defined symbols from $\mathcal{R}$. We thus have the following case.

Definition 9 (Equational Systems). *An equational system $(\mathcal{R}, \mathcal{S}, \mathcal{E})$ consists of two TRSs $\mathcal{R}$ and $\mathcal{S}$ and an i.u.v. ES $\mathcal{E}$ such that $\mathcal{S}$ is complete and convergent modulo $\mathcal{E}$ and $\mathcal{F}(\mathcal{E}) \cap \mathcal{D}(\mathcal{R}) = \mathcal{F}(\mathcal{S}) \cap \mathcal{D}(\mathcal{R}) = \emptyset$.*

Now $\mathcal{S}$-*normalized $\mathcal{E}$-extended rewriting* is done with an equational system $(\mathcal{R}, \mathcal{S}, \mathcal{E})$, and intuitively the arguments to a defined function f need to be normalized with $\rightarrow_{\mathcal{E}\backslash\mathcal{S}}$ before an f-rule from $\mathcal{R}$ may be applied.

Definition 10 ($\mathcal{S}$-Normalized $\mathcal{E}$-Extended Rewriting). *Let $(\mathcal{R}, \mathcal{S}, \mathcal{E})$ be an equational system. The term t rewrites $\mathcal{S}$-normalized $\mathcal{E}$-extended to the term q, written $t \xrightarrow{\mathcal{S}}_{\mathcal{E}\backslash\mathcal{R}} q$, iff $t|_p \downarrow_{\mathcal{E}\backslash\mathcal{S}} \sim_{\mathcal{E}} l\sigma$ and $q = t[r\sigma]_p$ for some rule $l \rightarrow r$ in $\mathcal{R}$, some position p with $root(t|_p) = root(l)$ in t, and some substitution σ.*

Our notion of $\mathcal{S}$-normalized rewriting differs from [17] in that we only normalize the redex w.r.t. $\rightarrow_{\mathcal{E}\backslash\mathcal{S}}$ before the rule from $\mathcal{R}$ is applied, while in [17] the whole term needs to be normalized w.r.t. $\rightarrow_{\mathcal{E}\backslash\mathcal{S}}$.

Example 11. Continuing Example 6, we can split $\mathcal{E}$ into $\mathcal{E}_1 = \mathsf{AC}_+$ and $\mathcal{E}_2 = \{u + 0 \approx u\}$. Then $\mathcal{E}_2$ can be completed into the TRS $\mathcal{S} = \{u + 0 \rightarrow u\}$, which is convergent modulo $\mathcal{E}_1$ and does not need to be extended. Thus, $(\mathcal{R}, \mathcal{S}, \mathcal{E}_1)$ is an equational system and the infinite reduction from Example 6 is not possible anymore if $\xrightarrow{\mathcal{S}}_{\mathcal{E}_1\backslash\mathcal{R}}$ is used since $0 \cdot z$ is in normal form w.r.t. $\rightarrow_{\mathcal{E}_1\backslash\mathcal{S}}$ and no rule of $\mathcal{R}$ applies. Also, the infinite reduction starting with $(0 + 0) \cdot z$ is not possible anymore since $(0 + 0) \cdot z$ would need to be normalized w.r.t. $\rightarrow_{\mathcal{E}_1\backslash\mathcal{S}}$ first, which again gives $0 \cdot z$.   ◊

---

[4] Consider $\mathcal{E} = \{\mathsf{f}(\mathsf{a}) \approx \mathsf{f}(\mathsf{b})\}$ and $\mathcal{R} = \{\mathsf{a} \rightarrow \mathsf{c}\}$. Then $\mathsf{f}(\mathsf{b}) \rightarrow_{\mathcal{R}/\mathcal{E}} \mathsf{f}(\mathsf{c})$, but $\mathsf{f}(\mathsf{b})$ is not reducible by $\rightarrow_{\mathcal{E}\backslash\mathcal{R}}$.

Apart from resulting in a terminating rewrite process in cases where $\to_{\mathcal{E}\backslash\mathcal{R}}$ is not terminating, $\mathcal{S}$-normalized rewriting also has the advantage of giving rise to "natural" function definitions since we can assume that the arguments to a function are in normal form w.r.t. $\to_{\mathcal{E}\backslash\mathcal{S}}$ before the function is evaluated. This would not be true if $\to_{\mathcal{E}\backslash\mathcal{R}\cup\mathcal{S}}$ is used instead.

Example 12. Example 1 already showed an equational system where $\to_{\mathcal{E}\backslash\mathcal{R}\cup\mathcal{S}}$ gives "wrong" results, while $\xrightarrow{\mathcal{S}}_{\mathcal{E}\backslash\mathcal{R}}$ is correct. Even more severely, $\to_{\mathcal{E}\backslash\mathcal{R}\cup\mathcal{S}}$ might not terminate while $\xrightarrow{\mathcal{S}}_{\mathcal{E}\backslash\mathcal{R}}$ does terminate. We define a function for determining whether an integer is non-negative by $\mathcal{R} = \{\mathsf{nonneg}(0) \to \mathsf{true}, \mathsf{nonneg}(\mathsf{s}(x)) \to \mathsf{nonneg}(\mathsf{p}(\mathsf{s}(x))), \mathsf{nonneg}(\mathsf{p}(x)) \to \mathsf{false}\}$, and let $\mathcal{E}_1$ and $\mathcal{S}$ be as in Example 1. Then $\to_{\mathcal{E}_1\backslash\mathcal{R}\cup\mathcal{S}}$ does not terminate since

$$\mathsf{nonneg}(\mathsf{s}(x)) \to_{\mathcal{E}_1\backslash\mathcal{R}\cup\mathcal{S}} \mathsf{nonneg}(\mathsf{p}(\mathsf{s}(x)))$$
$$\to_{\mathcal{E}_1\backslash\mathcal{R}\cup\mathcal{S}} \mathsf{nonneg}(\mathsf{p}(\mathsf{s}(\mathsf{p}(x))))$$
$$\to_{\mathcal{E}_1\backslash\mathcal{R}\cup\mathcal{S}} \cdots$$

In contrast, $\xrightarrow{\mathcal{S}}_{\mathcal{E}_1\backslash\mathcal{R}}$ is terminating since $\mathsf{p}(\mathsf{s}(x))$ in the recursive call of nonneg is normalized to x before the nonneg-rule can be applied again.   ◇

4   Dependency Pairs

In this section we present a termination criterion for normalized rewriting with equational systems that is based on *dependency pairs*. As usual in any approach based on dependency pairs (see, e.g., [1,6]), we extend $\mathcal{F}$ by a fresh *tuple symbol* $f^\sharp$ for each defined symbol $f \in \mathcal{D}(\mathcal{R})$, where $f^\sharp$ has the same arity as f. For any term $t = f(t^*)$, we denote the term $f^\sharp(t^*)$ by $t^\sharp$. The notion of a *dependency pair* is the standard one [1]. Due to the restriction to equations between constructors only we do not need to add instantiations of rules, which is needed in [6].

Definition 13 (Dependency Pairs). *The set of* dependency pairs *for a TRS* $\mathcal{R}$ *is* $\mathsf{DP}(\mathcal{R}) = \{l^\sharp \to t^\sharp \mid l \to r \in \mathcal{R}, t \text{ is a subterm of } r \text{ with } \mathrm{root}(t) \in \mathcal{D}(\mathcal{R})\}$.

In order to verify termination we rely on the notion of *chains*. Intuitively, a dependency pair corresponds to a recursive call, and a chain represents a possible sequence of calls in a reduction. In the following we always assume that different occurrences of (dependency) pairs are variable disjoint, and we consider substitutions whose domain may be infinite.

Definition 14 (($\mathcal{P}, \mathcal{R}, \mathcal{S}, \mathcal{E}$)-Chains). *Let* $\mathcal{P}$ *be a set of pairs and let* $(\mathcal{R}, \mathcal{S}, \mathcal{E})$ *be an equational system. A (possibly infinite) sequence of pairs* $s_1 \to t_1, s_2 \to t_2, \ldots$ *from* $\mathcal{P}$ *is a* $(\mathcal{P}, \mathcal{R}, \mathcal{S}, \mathcal{E})$-*chain iff there exists a substitution* σ *such that* $t_i\sigma \xrightarrow{\mathcal{S}}{}^*_{\mathcal{E}\backslash\mathcal{R}} \circ \to^!_{\mathcal{E}\backslash\mathcal{S}} \circ \sim_{\mathcal{E}} s_{i+1}\sigma$ *and* $s_i\sigma$ *is in normal form w.r.t.* $\to_{\mathcal{E}\backslash\mathcal{S}}$ *for all* $i \geq 1$.

Here, $t_i\sigma \xrightarrow{\mathcal{S}}{}^*_{\mathcal{E}\backslash\mathcal{R}} \circ \to^!_{\mathcal{E}\backslash\mathcal{S}} \circ \sim_{\mathcal{E}} s_{i+1}\sigma$ means that $t_i\sigma$ can be rewritten to a term to which the dependency pair $s_{i+1} \to t_{i+1}$ can be applied.

Example 15. We consider the following equational system $(\mathcal{R}, \mathcal{S}, \mathcal{E})$:

$$\mathcal{R}: \quad \begin{aligned} \mathsf{p}(0) &\to 0 \\ \mathsf{p}(\mathsf{s}(x)) &\to x \\ x - 0 &\to x \\ x - \mathsf{s}(y) &\to \mathsf{p}(x - y) \end{aligned} \qquad \begin{aligned} \mathcal{S}: \qquad & u + 0 \to u \\ & u + \mathsf{s}(v) \to \mathsf{s}(u + v) \\ & (u + \mathsf{s}(v)) + w \to \mathsf{s}(u + v) + w \\ \mathcal{E}: \quad & u + (v + w) \approx (u + v) + w \\ & u + v \approx v + u \end{aligned}$$

Here, $\mathcal{S}$ and $\mathcal{E}$ were obtained from the ES $\{u + 0 \approx u, u + \mathsf{s}(v) \approx \mathsf{s}(u + v)\} \cup \mathsf{AC}_+$, which specifies properties of the natural numbers in Peano representation. The third rule in $\mathcal{S}$ is the extension of the second rule. Then $\mathsf{DP}(\mathcal{R})$ contains the dependency pairs

$$x -^{\sharp} \mathsf{s}(y) \to x -^{\sharp} y, \qquad x -^{\sharp} \mathsf{s}(y) \to \mathsf{p}^{\sharp}(x - y).$$

Using the first dependency pair twice, we can construct the chain

$$x_1 -^{\sharp} \mathsf{s}(y_1) \to x_1 -^{\sharp} y_1, \; x_2 -^{\sharp} \mathsf{s}(y_2) \to x_2 -^{\sharp} y_2$$

by considering the substitution σ with $x_1\sigma = 0, x_2\sigma = 0, y_1\sigma = \mathsf{s}(0), y_2\sigma = 0$. For this substitution, the instantiated right side of the first pair is $0 -^{\sharp} \mathsf{s}(0)$, the same as the instantiated left side of the second pair. Furthermore, both instantiated left sides, $0 -^{\sharp} \mathsf{s}(\mathsf{s}(0))$ and $0 -^{\sharp} \mathsf{s}(0)$, are in normal form w.r.t. $\to_{\mathcal{E} \backslash \mathcal{S}}$. ◊

Using chains, we obtain the following termination criterion, which is the key result of the dependency pair approach.

Theorem 16. *Let $(\mathcal{R}, \mathcal{S}, \mathcal{E})$ be an equational system. If there are no infinite $(\mathsf{DP}(\mathcal{R}), \mathcal{R}, \mathcal{S}, \mathcal{E})$-chains, then $\xrightarrow{\mathcal{S}}_{\mathcal{E} \backslash \mathcal{R}}$ is terminating.*

The proof of this theorem is similar to the proof of the corresponding theorem for regular rewriting ([1, Theorem 6]). In our framework, we need the following important property of normalized rewriting with an equational system: if $s \xrightarrow{\mathcal{S}}_{\mathcal{E} \backslash \mathcal{R}} t$ and $s' \sim_{\mathcal{E}} s$, then $s' \xrightarrow{\mathcal{S}}_{\mathcal{E} \backslash \mathcal{R}} t'$ for some $t' \sim_{\mathcal{E}} t$. For a full proof see [5].

Theorem 16 gives rise to a termination criterion which uses *reduction pairs* [15], which are commonly used in conjunction with dependency pairs.

Definition 17 (Reduction Pairs). *Let $\gtrsim$ be reflexive, transitive, monotonic, and stable[5]. Let $\succ$ be well-founded and stable. Then $(\gtrsim, \succ)$ is a reduction pair iff $\succ$ is compatible with $\gtrsim$, i.e., iff $\gtrsim \circ \succ \subseteq \succ$ or $\succ \circ \gtrsim \subseteq \succ$. We denote the equivalence part $\gtrsim \cap \gtrsim^{-1}$ by $\sim$.*

Note that $\succ$ does not need to be monotonic in a reduction pair. This is the main advantage of the dependency pair approach which enables proving termination of many rewrite systems where simplification orders fail. In order to generate reduction pairs automatically, (monotonic) simplification orders are often used.

---

[5] A relation $\bowtie$ on terms is monotonic iff $s \bowtie t$ implies $C[s] \bowtie C[t]$ for all contexts C. It is stable iff $s \bowtie t$ implies $s\sigma \bowtie t\sigma$ for all substitutions σ.

To benefit from the possibility that $\succ$ does not need to be monotonic, *argument filterings* (which allow the deletion of certain function symbols and arguments) are commonly used in combination with monotonic orders (see [1]).

In the following, let $\mathcal{P}_{\bowtie} = \{(s,t) \in \mathcal{P} \mid s \bowtie t\}$ for any set $\mathcal{P}$ of pairs of terms and any relation $\bowtie$. Thus, for example, $\mathcal{R}_{\succsim} = \mathcal{R}$ means that $l \succsim r$ for all $l \to r \in \mathcal{R}$.

Theorem 18. *Let $(\mathcal{R}, \mathcal{S}, \mathcal{E})$ be an equational system. Then $\xrightarrow{S}_{\mathcal{E}\backslash\mathcal{R}}$ is terminating if there exists a reduction pair $(\succsim, \succ)$ such that*
(i) $\mathsf{DP}(\mathcal{R})_{\succ} = \mathsf{DP}(\mathcal{R})$,   (ii) $\mathcal{R}_{\succsim} = \mathcal{R}$,   (iii) $\mathcal{S}_{\succsim} = \mathcal{S}$, and   (iv) $\mathcal{E}_{\sim} = \mathcal{E}$.

Proof. Assume there exists an infinite $(\mathsf{DP}(\mathcal{R}), \mathcal{R}, \mathcal{S}, \mathcal{E})$-chain $s_1 \to t_1, s_2 \to t_2, \ldots$. Thus, there exists a substitution σ such that $t_i\sigma \xrightarrow{S}{}^*_{\mathcal{E}\backslash\mathcal{R}} \circ \to^!_{\mathcal{E}\backslash\mathcal{S}} \circ \sim_{\mathcal{E}} s_{i+1}\sigma$ for all $i \geq 1$.

Since $l \succsim r$ for all $l \to r \in \mathcal{R} \cup \mathcal{S}$ and $u \sim v$ for all $u \approx v \in \mathcal{E}$, we have $t_i\sigma \succsim s_{i+1}\sigma$. Hence, the infinite chain gives rise to

$$s_1\sigma \succ t_1\sigma \succsim s_2\sigma \succ t_2\sigma \succsim \cdots$$

since $s_i \succ t_i$ for all pairs $s_i \to t_i \in \mathsf{DP}(\mathcal{R})$. Using the compatibility of $\succ$ with $\succsim$, this contradicts the well-foundedness of $\succ$. Thus, there are no infinite chains and $\xrightarrow{S}_{\mathcal{E}\backslash\mathcal{R}}$ is terminating by Theorem 16.   □

Example 19. We now apply Theorem 18 in order to show that $\xrightarrow{S}_{\mathcal{E}\backslash\mathcal{R}}$ is terminating, where $(\mathcal{R}, \mathcal{S}, \mathcal{E})$ is the equational system from Example 15. Thus, we need to find a reduction pair $(\succsim, \succ)$ such that

$$
\begin{array}{ll}
x -^{\sharp} \mathsf{s}(y) \succ x -^{\sharp} y & u + 0 \succsim u \\
x -^{\sharp} \mathsf{s}(y) \succ \mathsf{p}^{\sharp}(x - y) & u + \mathsf{s}(v) \succsim \mathsf{s}(u + v) \\
x - 0 \succsim x & (u + \mathsf{s}(v)) + w \succsim \mathsf{s}(u + v) + w \\
x - \mathsf{s}(y) \succsim \mathsf{p}(x - y) & u + (v + w) \sim (u + v) + w \\
\mathsf{p}(0) \succsim 0 & u + v \sim v + u \\
\mathsf{p}(\mathsf{s}(x)) \succsim x &
\end{array}
$$

Using the reduction pair based on the polynomial order induced by $\mathcal{P}ol(0) = 0, \mathcal{P}ol(\mathsf{s}(x)) = x + 1, \mathcal{P}ol(x + y) = x + y, \mathcal{P}ol(\mathsf{p}(x)) = x, \mathcal{P}ol(\mathsf{p}^{\sharp}(x)) = x, \mathcal{P}ol(x - y) = x + y$, and $\mathcal{P}ol(x -^{\sharp} y) = x + y$, these constraints are satisfied.   ◇

5   Dependency Pair Framework

Theorem 16 provides a first method for proving termination, but this method is inflexible. For regular rewriting, a huge number of techniques has been developed atop the basic dependency pair approach (see, e.g., [9,11,10]). In order to show soundness of these techniques independently, and in order to be able to freely combine them in a flexible manner in implementations like AProVE [8], the notions of DP problems and DP processors were introduced in the context of regular rewriting in [9], giving rise to the DP framework. In [21] the DP framework was extended to equational rewriting under the restrictions of [6]. Here, we extend these notions to normalized rewriting.

Definition 20 (DP Problems). *A* DP problem *is a tuple* $(\mathcal{P}, \mathcal{R}, \mathcal{S}, \mathcal{E})$ *where* $\mathcal{P}$ *is a set of pairs and* $(\mathcal{R}, \mathcal{S}, \mathcal{E})$ *is an equational system.*

DP problems are now classified according to whether they allow the construction of infinite chains.

Definition 21 (Finite DP Problems). *A* DP problem $(\mathcal{P}, \mathcal{R}, \mathcal{S}, \mathcal{E})$ *is* finite *iff there do not exist infinite* $(\mathcal{P}, \mathcal{R}, \mathcal{S}, \mathcal{E})$-*chains. Otherwise, the DP problem is* infinite[6].

According to Theorem 16 we are interested in showing that the DP problem $(\mathsf{DP}(\mathcal{R}), \mathcal{R}, \mathcal{S}, \mathcal{E})$ is finite for an equational system $(\mathcal{R}, \mathcal{S}, \mathcal{E})$. In order to show the finiteness of a DP problem, it is transformed into a set of DP problems whose finiteness has to be shown instead. This transformation is done by *DP processors*.

Definition 22 (DP Processors). *A* DP processor *is a function Proc which takes a DP problem as input and returns a set of DP problems as output. Proc is* sound *iff for all DP problems* $(\mathcal{P}, \mathcal{R}, \mathcal{S}, \mathcal{E})$ *the finiteness of all DP problems in* $Proc(\mathcal{P}, \mathcal{R}, \mathcal{S}, \mathcal{E})$ *implies the finiteness of* $(\mathcal{P}, \mathcal{R}, \mathcal{S}, \mathcal{E})$.

Note that $Proc(\mathcal{P}, \mathcal{R}, \mathcal{S}, \mathcal{E}) = \{(\mathcal{P}, \mathcal{R}, \mathcal{S}, \mathcal{E})\}$ is possible. This can be interpreted as a failure of *Proc* on its input and indicates that a different DP processor should be applied. The following is immediate from Definition 21, Definition 22, and Theorem 16.

Corollary 23. *Let* $(\mathcal{R}, \mathcal{S}, \mathcal{E})$ *be an equational system. Assume there exists a tree whose nodes are labelled with DP problems or "yes" and whose root is labelled with* $(\mathsf{DP}(\mathcal{R}), \mathcal{R}, \mathcal{S}, \mathcal{E})$ *such that for every internal node r labelled with the DP problem d there is a sound DP processor Proc satisfying one of the following conditions:*

- *$Proc(d) = \emptyset$ and r has just one child, labelled with "yes", or*
- *$Proc(d) \neq \emptyset$ and for each DP problem $d' \in Proc(d)$ the node r has a child labelled with d'.*

If all leaves of the tree are labelled with "yes", then $\xrightarrow{\mathcal{S}}_{\mathcal{E} \backslash \mathcal{R}}$ *is terminating.*

6   DP Processors

In this section we introduce a variety of DP processors and prove their soundness. Most DP processors are inspired by similar DP processors in the context of regular rewriting (see [9,10]).

---

[6] Note that this definition of (in)finite DP problems is simpler than the one used in [9]. This simpler notion is sufficient for our purposes.

6.1   A DP Processor Based on Dependency Graphs

The DP processor introduced in this section decomposes a DP problem into several independent DP problems by determining which pairs of $\mathcal{P}$ may follow each other in a $(\mathcal{P}, \mathcal{R}, \mathcal{S}, \mathcal{E})$-chain. The processor relies on the *dependency graph*, which is also used in regular rewriting (see [1]).

Definition 24 (Dependency Graphs). *Let $(\mathcal{P}, \mathcal{R}, \mathcal{S}, \mathcal{E})$ be a DP problem. The nodes of the $(\mathcal{P}, \mathcal{R}, \mathcal{S}, \mathcal{E})$-dependency graph $\mathsf{DG}(\mathcal{P}, \mathcal{R}, \mathcal{S}, \mathcal{E})$ are the pairs in $\mathcal{P}$ and there is an arc from $s_1 \to t_1$ to $s_2 \to t_2$ iff $s_1 \to t_1, s_2 \to t_2$ is a $(\mathcal{P}, \mathcal{R}, \mathcal{S}, \mathcal{E})$-chain.*

A set $\mathcal{P}' \subseteq \mathcal{P}$ of pairs is a *cycle* iff for all pairs $s_1 \to t_1$ and $s_2 \to t_2$ in $\mathcal{P}'$ there exists a path from $s_1 \to t_1$ to $s_2 \to t_2$ that only traverses pairs from $\mathcal{P}'$. A cycle is a *strongly connected component* (SCC) if it is not a proper subset of any other cycle[7]. Now, every infinite $(\mathcal{P}, \mathcal{R}, \mathcal{S}, \mathcal{E})$-chain corresponds to a cycle in $\mathsf{DG}(\mathcal{P}, \mathcal{R}, \mathcal{S}, \mathcal{E})$, and it is thus sufficient to prove the absence of infinite chains for all SCCs.

In general $\mathsf{DG}(\mathcal{P}, \mathcal{R}, \mathcal{S}, \mathcal{E})$ cannot be computed exactly since it is undecidable whether two pairs form a chain. Thus, an estimation has to be used instead. The idea of the estimation is that subterms of t_1 with a defined root symbol are abstracted by a fresh variable. Then, it is checked whether this term and s_2 are $\mathcal{E} \cup \mathcal{S}$-unifiable. This computation of the *estimated dependency graph* $\mathsf{EDG}(\mathcal{P}, \mathcal{R}, \mathcal{S}, \mathcal{E})$ also makes use of the information that certain terms in a chain are in normal form w.r.t. $\to_{\mathcal{E} \backslash \mathcal{S}}$.

Definition 25 (Estimated Dependency Graphs). *Let $(\mathcal{P}, \mathcal{R}, \mathcal{S}, \mathcal{E})$ be a DP problem. The estimated $(\mathcal{P}, \mathcal{R}, \mathcal{S}, \mathcal{E})$-dependency graph $\mathsf{EDG}(\mathcal{P}, \mathcal{R}, \mathcal{S}, \mathcal{E})$ has the pairs in $\mathcal{P}$ as nodes and there is an arc from $s_1 \to t_1$ to $s_2 \to t_2$ iff $\mathrm{CAP}(t_1)$ and s_2 are $\mathcal{E} \cup \mathcal{S}$-unifiable with an unifier μ such that $s_1 \mu$ and $s_2 \mu$ are in normal form w.r.t. $\to_{\mathcal{E} \backslash \mathcal{S}}$. Here, CAP is defined as*

$$\mathrm{CAP}(x) = y \quad \text{for variables } x$$

$$\mathrm{CAP}(f(t_1, \ldots, t_n)) = \begin{cases} y & \text{if } f \in \mathcal{D}(\mathcal{R}) \\ f(\mathrm{CAP}(t_1), \ldots, \mathrm{CAP}(t_n)) & \text{if } f \notin \mathcal{D}(\mathcal{R}) \end{cases}$$

where y is the next variable in an infinite list $y_1, y_2, \ldots$ of fresh variables.

Example 26. With $\mathcal{P} = \{x -^\sharp \mathsf{s}(y) \to x -^\sharp y, x -^\sharp \mathsf{s}(y) \to \mathsf{p}^\sharp(x - y)\}$ and $\mathcal{R}, \mathcal{S}$ and $\mathcal{E}$ as in Example 15 we obtain the following $\mathsf{EDG}(\mathcal{P}, \mathcal{R}, \mathcal{S}, \mathcal{E})$. Since terms headed by $\mathsf{p}^\sharp$ do not $\mathcal{E} \cup \mathcal{S}$-unify with terms headed by $-^\sharp$, there is no arc from the lower dependency pair to itself or to the upper dependency pair.

$\Diamond$

In this example, $\mathsf{EDG}(\mathcal{P}, \mathcal{R}, \mathcal{S}, \mathcal{E})$ and $\mathsf{DG}(\mathcal{P}, \mathcal{R}, \mathcal{S}, \mathcal{E})$ coincide, but in general $\mathsf{EDG}(\mathcal{P}, \mathcal{R}, \mathcal{S}, \mathcal{E})$ is a supergraph of $\mathsf{DG}(\mathcal{P}, \mathcal{R}, \mathcal{S}, \mathcal{E})$. The following DP processor is sound for $\mathsf{DG}(\mathcal{P}, \mathcal{R}, \mathcal{S}, \mathcal{E})$, and hence also for $\mathsf{EDG}(\mathcal{P}, \mathcal{R}, \mathcal{S}, \mathcal{E})$.

Theorem 27 (DP Processor Based on Dependency Graphs). *Let Proc be a DP processor with* $Proc(\mathcal{P}, \mathcal{R}, \mathcal{S}, \mathcal{E}) = \{(\mathcal{P}_1, \mathcal{R}, \mathcal{S}, \mathcal{E}), \dots, (\mathcal{P}_n, \mathcal{R}, \mathcal{S}, \mathcal{E})\}$, *where* $\mathcal{P}_1, \dots, \mathcal{P}_n$ *are the SCCs of* $(\mathsf{E})\mathsf{DG}(\mathcal{P}, \mathcal{R}, \mathcal{S}, \mathcal{E})$[8]. *Then Proc is sound.*

Proof. After a finite number of pairs in the beginning, any infinite $(\mathcal{P}, \mathcal{R}, \mathcal{S}, \mathcal{E})$-chain only contains pairs from some SCC. Hence, every infinite $(\mathcal{P}, \mathcal{R}, \mathcal{S}, \mathcal{E})$-chain gives rise to an infinite $(\mathcal{P}_i, \mathcal{R}, \mathcal{S}, \mathcal{E})$-chain for some $1 \leq i \leq n$. $\square$

Example 28. Continuing Example 26 we have $Proc(\mathcal{P}, \mathcal{R}, \mathcal{S}, \mathcal{E}) = \{(\{x -^\sharp \mathsf{s}(y) \to x -^\sharp y\}, \mathcal{R}, \mathcal{S}, \mathcal{E})\}$. $\Diamond$

6.2 A DP Processor Based on Reduction Pairs

The DP processor presented in this section is closely related to the first termination criterion given in Theorem 18. It now, however, operates on DP problems $(\mathcal{P}, \mathcal{R}, \mathcal{S}, \mathcal{E})$, and we do not require all pairs in $\mathcal{P}$ to be strictly decreasing.

Theorem 29 (DP Processor Based on Reduction Pairs). *Let* $(\gtrsim, \succ)$ *be a reduction pair. The DP processor Proc is sound, where* $Proc(\mathcal{P}, \mathcal{R}, \mathcal{S}, \mathcal{E})$ *returns*

- $\{(\mathcal{P} - \mathcal{P}_\succ, \mathcal{R}, \mathcal{S}, \mathcal{E})\}$, *if*
  (i) $\mathcal{P}_\succ \cup \mathcal{P}_\gtrsim = \mathcal{P}$,   *(ii)* $\mathcal{R}_\gtrsim = \mathcal{R}$,   *(iii)* $\mathcal{S}_\gtrsim = \mathcal{S}$, *and*   *(iv)* $\mathcal{E}_\sim = \mathcal{E}$.
- $\{(\mathcal{P}, \mathcal{R}, \mathcal{S}, \mathcal{E})\}$, *otherwise.*

Proof. The proof for the first case is similar to the proof of Theorem 18. Since $\mathcal{P}$ is finite, any infinite $(\mathcal{P}, \mathcal{R}, \mathcal{S}, \mathcal{E})$-chain has to traverse at least one pair from $\mathcal{P}$ infinitely often. These pairs cannot be in $\mathcal{P}_\succ$ since this would contradict the well-foundedness of $\succ$. In the other case soundness is obvious. $\square$

Example 30. We consider the DP problem $(\mathcal{P}, \mathcal{R}, \mathcal{S}, \mathcal{E})$ with $\mathcal{P} = \{x -^\sharp \mathsf{s}(y) \to x -^\sharp y\}$ from Example 28. Using the reduction pair based on the polynomial order induced by $\mathcal{P}ol(0) = 0, \mathcal{P}ol(\mathsf{s}(x)) = x + 1, \mathcal{P}ol(x + y) = x + y, \mathcal{P}ol(\mathsf{p}(x)) = x, \mathcal{P}ol(x - y) = x + y$, and $\mathcal{P}ol(x -^\sharp y) = x + y$ the constraints for the first case of Theorem 29 are satisfied and the (only) pair $x -^\sharp \mathsf{s}(y) \to x -^\sharp y$ is strictly decreasing. It can thus be removed and we obtain the trivial DP problem $(\emptyset, \mathcal{R}, \mathcal{S}, \mathcal{E})$. $\Diamond$

6.3 A DP Processor Based on Removal of Rules

In this section we present a DP processor for the modular removal of rules. For this, a DP problem $(\mathcal{P}, \mathcal{R}, \mathcal{S}, \mathcal{E})$ may be processed with a monotonic reduction pair $(\gtrsim, \succ)$. Then, rules $l \to r \in \mathcal{R}$ satisfying $l \succ r$ may be removed. For regular rewriting a corresponding DP processor was introduced in [22].

---

[8] Note, in particular, that $Proc(\emptyset, \mathcal{R}, \mathcal{S}, \mathcal{E}) = \emptyset$.

Theorem 31 (DP Processor Based on Removal of Rules). *Let* $(\gtrsim, \succ)$ *be a reduction pair where* $\succ$ *is monotonic. The DP processor Proc is sound, where* $Proc(\mathcal{P}, \mathcal{R}, \mathcal{S}, \mathcal{E})$ *returns*

- $\{(\mathcal{P} - \mathcal{P}_\succ, \mathcal{R} - \mathcal{R}_\succ, \mathcal{S}, \mathcal{E})\}$, *if*
  (i) $\mathcal{P}_\succ \cup \mathcal{P}_\gtrsim = \mathcal{P}$, *(ii)* $\mathcal{R}_\succ \cup \mathcal{R}_\gtrsim = \mathcal{R}$, *(iii)* $\mathcal{S}_\gtrsim = \mathcal{S}$, *and* *(iv)* $\mathcal{E}_\sim = \mathcal{E}$.
- $\{(\mathcal{P}, \mathcal{R}, \mathcal{S}, \mathcal{E})\}$, *otherwise*.

Removing rules has several advantages. Firstly, it might be possible to remove "problematic" rules which prevent finding a reduction pair which yields a strict decrease in at least one pair of $\mathcal{P}$. Secondly, it might happen that $\mathcal{P}$ contains no cycle anymore after some rules are removed from $\mathcal{R}$ since some defined symbols might become constructors.

Example 32. We take the equational system from Example 15, but replace the second "$-$"-rule by

$$x - \mathsf{s}(y) \to \mathsf{p}(x - \mathsf{p}(\mathsf{s}(y)))$$

After computing the estimated dependency graph, we obtain the DP problem $(\mathcal{P}, \mathcal{R}, \mathcal{S}, \mathcal{E})$ with $\mathcal{P} = \{x -^\sharp \mathsf{s}(y) \to x -^\sharp \mathsf{p}(\mathsf{s}(y))\}$. In order to apply the DP processor from Theorem 29 we need to find a reduction pair $(\gtrsim, \succ)$ such that $x -^\sharp \mathsf{s}(y) \succ x -^\sharp \mathsf{p}(\mathsf{s}(y))$ and $\mathsf{p}(\mathsf{s}(x)) \gtrsim x$. It can be shown that there does not exist a reduction pair based on a simplification order with an argument filtering that satisfies these constraints, i.e., an automated proof will most likely fail.

Instead, we may apply the DP processor from Theorem 31 with the monotonic polynomial order induced by $\mathcal{P}ol(0) = 0, \mathcal{P}ol(\mathsf{s}(x)) = x + 1, \mathcal{P}ol(\mathsf{p}(x)) = x, \mathcal{P}ol(x + y) = \mathcal{P}ol(x - y) = \mathcal{P}ol(x -^\sharp y) = x + y$. Then all of $\mathcal{P}, \mathcal{R}$ and $\mathcal{S}$ are at least weakly decreasing, and the rule $\mathsf{p}(\mathsf{s}(x)) \to x$ is strictly decreasing and can thus be removed. Next, we can apply the DP processor from Theorem 29 with the polynomial order based on $\mathcal{P}ol(0) = \mathcal{P}ol(\mathsf{p}(x)) = 0, \mathcal{P}ol(\mathsf{s}(x)) = x + 1, \mathcal{P}ol(x + y) = \mathcal{P}ol(x - y) = \mathcal{P}ol(x -^\sharp y) = x + y$. Then, the pair in $\mathcal{P}$ is strictly decreasing and all rules in $\mathcal{R}$ and $\mathcal{S}$ are at least weakly decreasing, i.e., we obtain the trivial DP problem $(\emptyset, \mathcal{R}, \mathcal{S}, \mathcal{E})$. ◇

As mentioned in [22], the DP processor from Theorem 31 can be automated efficiently by using monotonic polynomial orders induced by linear polynomials.

6.4 A DP Processor Based on Narrowing

In the context of regular rewriting it is often necessary to apply transformations to the dependency pairs in a cycle in order to obtain a successful termination proof (see [1,10]). In this section we introduce one such transformation within our framework.

First, note that $\xrightarrow{\mathcal{S}}_{\mathcal{E} \backslash \mathcal{R}}$ is contained in $\to_{\mathcal{E} \backslash \mathcal{R} \cup \mathcal{S}}$, and we may thus show absence of infinite $(\mathcal{P}, \mathcal{R} \cup \mathcal{S}, \mathcal{E})$-chains instead of absence of infinite $(\mathcal{P}, \mathcal{R}, \mathcal{S}, \mathcal{E})$-chains. Here, a $(\mathcal{P}, \mathcal{R} \cup \mathcal{S}, \mathcal{E})$-chain is defined similarly to a $(\mathcal{P}, \mathcal{R}, \mathcal{S}, \mathcal{E})$-chain by using $\to_{\mathcal{E} \backslash \mathcal{R} \cup \mathcal{S}}$ instead of $\xrightarrow{\mathcal{S}}_{\mathcal{E} \backslash \mathcal{R}}$. The DP processors of Sections 6.1–6.3 can easily be adapted to handle these two kinds of DP problems. For details see [5].

If it now can be ensured that for each $(\mathcal{P}, \mathcal{R} \cup \mathcal{S}, \mathcal{E})$-chain containing a pair $s \to t$, the reduction from the instantiation of t to the instantiation of the left side of the next pair in the chain requires at least one $\to_{\mathcal{E} \backslash \mathcal{R} \cup \mathcal{S}}$-step, then we can perform all possible $\to_{\mathcal{E} \backslash \mathcal{R} \cup \mathcal{S}}$-reductions in order to obtain new pairs that replace the pair $s \to t$. Since we need to determine the instantiations of t, we use *narrowing*. Narrowing of dependency pairs has also been considered in [1,4].

Theorem 33 (DP Processor Based on Narrowing). *The DP processor Proc is sound, where* $Proc(\mathcal{P} \cup \{s \to t\}, \mathcal{R} \cup \mathcal{S}, \mathcal{E})$ *returns*

- $(\mathcal{P} \cup \{s\mu \to t' \mid t \leadsto^{\mu}_{\mathcal{E} \backslash \mathcal{R} \cup \mathcal{S}} t'\}, \mathcal{R} \cup \mathcal{S}, \mathcal{E})^9$, *if*
  - *t is linear, and*
  - *t is not $\mathcal{E}$-unifiable with any (variable-renamed) left side of a pair in $\mathcal{P} \cup \{s \to t\}$.*
- $(\mathcal{P} \cup \{s \to t\}, \mathcal{R} \cup \mathcal{S}, \mathcal{E})$, *otherwise.*

Example 34. We again consider the DP problem $(\mathcal{P}, \mathcal{R}, \mathcal{S}, \mathcal{E})$ from Example 32. As mentioned above, it suffices to show absence of infinite $(\mathcal{P}, \mathcal{R} \cup \mathcal{S}, \mathcal{E})$-chains. For this we first apply the DP processor from Theorem 33 to the only pair $x -^{\sharp} \mathsf{s}(y) \to x -^{\sharp} \mathsf{p}(\mathsf{s}(y))$, which has a linear right side that does not $\mathcal{E}$-unify with the (variable-renamed) left side. We can thus replace that pair by its narrowings. The only narrowing of the pair is the pair $x -^{\sharp} \mathsf{s}(y) \to x -^{\sharp} y$, resulting in a DP problem that can be handled like the one in Example 30. $\Diamond$

7   Conclusions

We have proposed normalized rewriting as an alternative to $\mathcal{E}$-extended rewriting for equational rewrite systems in which equations only relate constructors. The paper extends the dependency pair framework in order to establish termination of normalized rewriting for such equational rewrite systems. It is shown that whereas $\mathcal{E}$-extended rewriting for such systems may not terminate, normalized rewriting often does terminate. Based on our experience in specifying a number of examples on data structures generated by non-free constructors, we are convinced that algorithms can be specified naturally and elegantly as rewrite systems for normalized rewriting (pos is one such example). Unlike previous related work [6], the equations relating constructors may be collapsing and, in some cases, do not need to have identical unique variables. In particular, properties such as idempotency, identity, etc., of constructors on data structures are allowed.

Many functional programming languages use eager evaluation as the evaluation strategy. Then, termination of the functional program corresponds to *innermost* termination of the equational rewrite system. We believe that our method can be extended to show innermost termination, similarly to how this can be done for regular rewriting [1]. This needs to be investigated. An implementation of the proposed approach in AProVE [8] is planned.

---

^{9} Here, $t \leadsto^{\mu}_{\mathcal{E} \backslash \mathcal{R} \cup \mathcal{S}} t'$ denotes that t narrows to t' using the substitution μ. For full details see [5].

References

1. Arts, T., Giesl, J.: Termination of term rewriting using dependency pairs. Theoretical Computer Science 236(1-2), 133–178 (2000)
2. Baader, F., Nipkow, T.: Term Rewriting and All That. Cambridge University Press, Cambridge (1998)
3. Clavel, M., Durán, F., Eker, S., Lincoln, P., Martí-Oliet, N., Meseguer, J., Talcott, C.: The Maude 2.0 system. In: Nieuwenhuis, R. (ed.) RTA 2003. LNCS, vol. 2706, pp. 76–87. Springer, Heidelberg (2003)
4. Falke, S.: Automated termination analysis for equational rewriting. Diplomarbeit, Department of Computer Science, RWTH Aachen University, Germany (2004)
5. Falke, S., Kapur, D.: Dependency pairs for rewriting with non-free constructors. Technical Report TR-CS-2007-07, Department of Computer Science, University of New Mexico (2007) Available at http://www.cs.unm.edu/research/
6. Giesl, J., Kapur, D.: Dependency pairs for equational rewriting. In: Middeldorp, A. (ed.) RTA 2001. LNCS, vol. 2051, pp. 93–108. Springer, Heidelberg (2001)
7. Giesl, J., Kapur, D. (ed.): Journal of Automated Reasoning, 34(2), 34(4) & 37(3), 2005-2006. Special issues on Techniques for Automated Termination Proofs
8. Giesl, J., Schneider-Kamp, P., Thiemann, R.: AProVE 1.2: Automatic termination proofs in the dependency pair framework. In: Furbach, U., Shankar, N. (eds.) IJCAR 2006. LNCS (LNAI), vol. 4130, pp. 281–286. Springer, Heidelberg (2006)
9. Giesl, J., Thiemann, R., Schneider-Kamp, P.: The dependency pair framework. In: Baader, F., Voronkov, A. (eds.) LPAR 2004. LNCS (LNAI), vol. 3452, pp. 301–331. Springer, Heidelberg (2005)
10. Giesl, J., Thiemann, R., Schneider-Kamp, P., Falke, S.: Mechanizing and improving dependency pairs. Journal of Automated Reasoning 37(3), 155–203 (2006)
11. Hirokawa, N., Middeldorp, A.: Tyrolean termination tool: Techniques and features. Information and Computation 205(4), 474–511 (2007)
12. Kapur, D., Sivakumar, G.: Proving associative-commutative termination using RPO-compatible orderings. In: Caferra, R., Salzer, G. (eds.) Automated Deduction in Classical and Non-Classical Logics. LNCS (LNAI), vol. 1761, pp. 40–62. Springer, Heidelberg (2000)
13. Kapur, D., Zhang, H.: An overview of rewrite rule laboratory (RRL). Computers & Mathematics with Applications 29(2), 91–114 (1995)
14. Kirchner, H., Moreau, P.-E.: Promoting rewriting to a programming language. Journal of Functional Programming 11(2), 207–251 (2001)
15. Kusakari, K., Nakamura, M., Toyama, Y.: Argument filtering transformation. In: Nadathur, G. (ed.) PPDP 1999. LNCS, vol. 1702, pp. 47–61. Springer, Heidelberg (1999)
16. Kusakari, K., Toyama, Y.: On proving AC-termination by AC-dependency pairs. IEICE Transactions on Information and Systems E84-D(5), 604–612 (2001)
17. Marché, C.: Normalized rewriting: An alternative to rewriting modulo a set of equations. Journal of Symbolic Computation 21(3), 253–288 (1996)
18. Marché, C., Urbain, X.: Modular and incremental proofs of AC-termination. Journal of Symbolic Computation 38(1), 873–897 (2004)
19. Peterson, G.E., Stickel, M.E.: Complete sets of reductions for some equational theories. Journal of the ACM 28(2), 233–264 (1981)
20. Rubio, A.: A fully syntactic AC-RPO. Information and Computation 178(2), 515–533 (2002)

21. Stein, C.: Das Dependency Pair Framework zur automatischen Terminierungsanalyse von Termersetzung modulo Gleichungen. Diplomarbeit, Department of Computer Science, RWTH Aachen University, Germany (in German) (2006)
22. Thiemann, R., Giesl, J., Schneider-Kamp, P.: Improved modular termination proofs using dependency pairs. In: Basin, D., Rusinowitch, M. (eds.) IJCAR 2004. LNCS (LNAI), vol. 3097, pp. 75–90. Springer, Heidelberg (2004)

A   Propositional Sequent Calculus

We consider the propositional sequent calculus for formulas built from $\wedge$ and $\neg$. Sequents are built from two sets of formulas using $\Longrightarrow$. Sets of formulas are built from the empty set $\emptyset$ using "," to add a formula to a set. Similarly, sets of sequents are built using $\square$ and $\bullet$. Properties of sets are modelled using

$$\mathcal{E}: \quad u, (v, w) \approx v, (u, w) \qquad \mathcal{S}: \quad u, (u, v) \to u, v$$
$$u \bullet (v \bullet w) \approx v \bullet (u \bullet w) \qquad u \bullet (u \bullet v) \to u \bullet v$$

Now the sequent calculus rules for $\wedge$ and $\neg$ are specified by

$$\mathcal{R}: \qquad\qquad \mathsf{eval}(\square) \to \square$$
$$\mathsf{eval}((x, y \Longrightarrow x, z) \bullet s) \to \mathsf{eval}(s)$$
$$\mathsf{eval}((\neg x, y \Longrightarrow z) \bullet s) \to \mathsf{eval}((y \Longrightarrow x, z) \bullet s)$$
$$\mathsf{eval}((x \Longrightarrow \neg y, z) \bullet s) \to \mathsf{eval}((y, x \Longrightarrow z) \bullet s)$$
$$\mathsf{eval}((x \wedge y, z \Longrightarrow z') \bullet s) \to \mathsf{eval}((x, (y, z) \Longrightarrow z') \bullet s)$$
$$\mathsf{eval}((x \Longrightarrow y \wedge z, z') \bullet s) \to \mathsf{eval}((x \Longrightarrow y, z') \bullet ((x \Longrightarrow z, z') \bullet s))$$

For example, the last rewrite rule in $\mathcal{R}$ corresponds to the sequent calculus rule

$$(\Longrightarrow \wedge) \quad \frac{\Gamma \Longrightarrow \Delta, \psi \qquad \Gamma \Longrightarrow \Delta, \phi}{\Gamma \Longrightarrow \Delta, \psi \wedge \phi}$$

Now evaluation w.r.t. $\xrightarrow{\mathcal{S}}_{\mathcal{E} \backslash \mathcal{R}}$ provides a way to prove validity of sequents, provided that $\xrightarrow{\mathcal{S}}_{\mathcal{E} \backslash \mathcal{R}}$ is terminating.

The TRS $\mathcal{R}$ has the following five dependency pairs.

$$\mathsf{eval}^\sharp((x, y \Longrightarrow x, z) \bullet s) \to \mathsf{eval}^\sharp(s)$$
$$\mathsf{eval}^\sharp((\neg x, y \Longrightarrow z) \bullet s) \to \mathsf{eval}^\sharp((y \Longrightarrow x, z) \bullet s)$$
$$\mathsf{eval}^\sharp((x \Longrightarrow \neg y, z) \bullet s) \to \mathsf{eval}^\sharp((y, x \Longrightarrow z) \bullet s)$$
$$\mathsf{eval}^\sharp((x \wedge y, z \Longrightarrow z') \bullet s) \to \mathsf{eval}^\sharp((x, (y, z) \Longrightarrow z') \bullet s)$$
$$\mathsf{eval}^\sharp((x \Longrightarrow y \wedge z, z') \bullet s) \to \mathsf{eval}^\sharp((x \Longrightarrow y, z') \bullet ((x \Longrightarrow z, z') \bullet s))$$

These dependency pairs form an SCC in the (estimated) dependency graph. Termination can now be shown using the DP processor of Theorem 29 three times, with different reduction pairs based on polynomial orders.

We first apply the polynomial order induced by $\mathcal{P}ol(x \wedge y) = xy + x + y + 1$, $\mathcal{P}ol(\neg x) = x$, $\mathcal{P}ol(x \Longrightarrow y) = xy + x + y$, $\mathcal{P}ol(x, y) = xy + x + y$, $\mathcal{P}ol(\square) = 0$, $\mathcal{P}ol(x \bullet y) = x + y$, $\mathcal{P}ol(\mathsf{eval}(x)) = 0$, $\mathcal{P}ol(\mathsf{eval}^\sharp(x)) = x$. In this order, all dependency pairs are at least weakly decreasing. The fourth and fifth dependency pairs are strictly decreasing and may thus be removed.

Next, using the polynomial order induced by $Pol(x \wedge y) = 0$, $Pol(\neg x) = x+1$, $Pol(x \implies y) = x + y$, $Pol(x, y) = x + y$, $Pol(\Box) = 0$, $Pol(x \bullet y) = x + y$, $Pol(\text{eval}(x)) = 0$, $Pol(\text{eval}^\sharp(x)) = x$, the second and third dependency pairs can be removed.

Finally, the polynomial order induced by $Pol(x \wedge y) = 0$, $Pol(\neg x) = 0$, $Pol(x \implies y) = 0$, $Pol(x, y) = 0$, $Pol(\Box) = 0$, $Pol(x \bullet y) = y+1$, $Pol(\text{eval}(x)) = 0$, $Pol(\text{eval}^\sharp(x)) = x$ orients the remaining (first) dependency pair. This concludes the proof of termination of $\xrightarrow{S}_{\mathcal{E} \backslash \mathcal{R}}$.

Proving Termination by Bounded Increase*

Jürgen Giesl, René Thiemann, Stephan Swiderski, and Peter Schneider-Kamp

LuFG Informatik 2, RWTH Aachen, Germany
{giesl,thiemann,swiderski,psk}@informatik.rwth-aachen.de

Abstract. Most methods for termination analysis of term rewrite systems (TRSs) essentially try to find arguments of functions that *decrease* in recursive calls. However, they fail if the reason for termination is that an argument is *increased* in recursive calls repeatedly until it reaches a bound. In this paper, we solve that problem and show how to prove innermost termination of TRSs with bounded increase automatically.

1 Introduction

In programming, one often writes algorithms that terminate because a value is increased until it reaches a bound. Hence, to apply termination techniques of TRSs in practice, they must be able to deal with those algorithms successfully. But unfortunately, all existing methods and tools for automated termination analysis of TRSs fail on such examples. Therefore, proving termination of TRSs with bounded increase was identified as one of the most urgent and challenging problems at the annual *International Competition of Termination Tools* 2006 [16].

Example 1. As an example consider a TRS for subtraction. TRSs of this form often result from the transformation of conditional TRSs or from functional, logic, or imperative programs.

$$\mathsf{minus}(x, y) \to \mathsf{cond}(\mathsf{gt}(x, y), x, y) \quad (1) \qquad\qquad \mathsf{gt}(0, v) \to \mathsf{false} \quad (4)$$
$$\mathsf{cond}(\mathsf{false}, x, y) \to 0 \quad (2) \qquad\qquad \mathsf{gt}(\mathsf{s}(u), 0) \to \mathsf{true} \quad (5)$$
$$\mathsf{cond}(\mathsf{true}, x, y) \to \mathsf{s}(\mathsf{minus}(x, \mathsf{s}(y))) \quad (3) \qquad\qquad \mathsf{gt}(\mathsf{s}(u), \mathsf{s}(v)) \to \mathsf{gt}(u, v) \quad (6)$$

To handle TRSs like Ex. 1, we propose to use polynomial interpretations [14]. But instead of classical polynomial interpretations on natural numbers, we use interpretations on *integers*. Such interpretations can measure the difference between the first and second argument of minus. Indeed, minus is terminating since this difference decreases in each recursive call. However, using integer polynomial interpretations is unsound in the existing termination techniques for TRSs.

This is also true for the *dependency pair (DP) method* [1], which is a powerful method for automated termination analysis of TRSs that is implemented in virtually all current automated termination tools. This method relies on the use of *reduction pairs* $(\succsim, \succ)$ to compare terms. Here, $\succsim$ is a stable quasi-order and $\succ$

---

* Supported by the Deutsche Forschungsgemeinschaft DFG under grant GI 274/5-1 and by the DFG Research Training Group 1298 (*AlgoSyn*).

F. Pfenning (Ed.): CADE 2007, LNAI 4603, pp. 443–459, 2007.

is a stable order, where $\succsim$ and $\succ$ are compatible (i.e., $\succ \circ \succsim \subseteq \succ$ or $\succsim \circ \succ \subseteq \succ$). Moreover, $\succsim$ and $\succ$ have to satisfy the following properties:

(a) $\succsim$ is monotonic   (b) $\succ$ is well founded

After recapitulating the DP method in Sect. 2, in Sect. 3 we extend it to *general* reduction pairs (without requirements (a) and (b)). Then one can also use reduction pairs based on integer polynomial interpretations, which violate the requirements (a) and (b).

In Sect. 4 we extend the DP method further to exploit implicit *conditions*. This is needed to prove that an increase is bounded. For instance, the recursive call of minus in Ex. 1 only takes place under the *condition* $\mathsf{gt}(x, y) = \mathsf{true}$.[1] With our extensions, termination provers based on DPs can handle most algorithms with bounded increase that typically occur in practice. In Sect. 5, we discuss the implementation of our method in our termination tool AProVE [9].

2   Dependency Pairs

We assume familiarity with term rewriting [2] and briefly recapitulate the DP method. See [1,8,10,12,13] for further motivations and extensions.

Definition 2 (Dependency Pairs). *For a TRS $\mathcal{R}$, the* defined symbols $\mathcal{D}$ *are the root symbols of left-hand sides of rules. All other function symbols are called* constructors. *For every defined symbol $f \in \mathcal{D}$, we introduce a fresh* tuple symbol *$f^\sharp$ with the same arity. To ease readability, we often write F instead of $f^\sharp$, etc. If $t = f(t_1, \ldots, t_n)$ with $f \in \mathcal{D}$, we write $t^\sharp$ for $f^\sharp(t_1, \ldots, t_n)$. If $\ell \to r \in \mathcal{R}$ and t is a subterm of r with defined root symbol, then the rule $\ell^\sharp \to t^\sharp$ is a* dependency pair *of $\mathcal{R}$. The set of all dependency pairs of $\mathcal{R}$ is denoted $DP(\mathcal{R})$.*

Ex. 1 has the following DPs, where MINUS is the tuple symbol for minus, etc.

$$\mathsf{MINUS}(x,y) \to \mathsf{COND}(\mathsf{gt}(x,y),x,y) \quad (7) \qquad \mathsf{COND}(\mathsf{true},x,y) \to \mathsf{MINUS}(x,\mathsf{s}(y)) \quad (9)$$
$$\mathsf{MINUS}(x,y) \to \mathsf{GT}(x,y) \quad (8) \qquad\qquad \mathsf{GT}(\mathsf{s}(u),\mathsf{s}(v)) \to \mathsf{GT}(u,v) \quad (10)$$

In this paper, we only focus on *innermost* termination, i.e., we only regard the innermost rewrite relation $\overset{i}{\to}$. The reason is that proving innermost termination is considerably easier than proving full termination and there are large classes of TRSs where innermost termination is already sufficient for termination. In particular, this holds for non-overlapping TRSs like Ex. 1.

---

[1] Proving termination of TRSs like Ex. 1 is far more difficult than proving termination of programs in a language where one uses a *predefined* function gt. (For such languages, there already exist termination techniques that can handle certain forms of bounded increase [5,15].) However, if a function like gt is not predefined but written by the "user", then the termination technique cannot presuppose any knowledge about gt's semantics. In contrast, the termination technique has to deduce any needed informations about gt from the user-defined gt-rules.

The main result of the DP method for innermost termination states that a TRS $\mathcal{R}$ is innermost terminating iff there is no infinite minimal innermost $(DP(\mathcal{R}), \mathcal{R})$-*chain*. For any TRSs $\mathcal{P}$ and $\mathcal{R}$, a minimal innermost $(\mathcal{P}, \mathcal{R})$-*chain* is a sequence of (variable renamed) pairs $s_1 \to t_1, s_2 \to t_2, \ldots$ from $\mathcal{P}$ such that there is a substitution σ (with possibly infinite domain) where $t_i\sigma \xrightarrow{i}{}^*_{\mathcal{R}} s_{i+1}\sigma$, all $s_i\sigma$ are in normal form, and all $t_i\sigma$ are innermost terminating w.r.t. $\mathcal{R}$.

Termination techniques are now called *DP processors* and they operate on sets of dependency pairs (which are called *DP problems*).[2] Formally, a DP processor *Proc* takes a DP problem as input and returns a set of new DP problems which then have to be solved instead. A processor *Proc* is *sound* if for all DP problems $\mathcal{P}$ with infinite minimal innermost $(\mathcal{P}, \mathcal{R})$-chain there is also a $\mathcal{P}' \in Proc(\mathcal{P})$ with infinite minimal innermost $(\mathcal{P}', \mathcal{R})$-chain. Soundness of a DP processor is required to prove innermost termination and in particular, to conclude that there is no infinite minimal innermost $(\mathcal{P}, \mathcal{R})$-chain if $Proc(\mathcal{P}) = \{\varnothing\}$.

So innermost termination proofs in the DP framework start with the initial DP problem $DP(\mathcal{R})$. Then the DP problem is simplified repeatedly by sound DP processors. If all resulting DP problems have been simplified to $\varnothing$, then innermost termination is proved. In Thm. 3, we recapitulate one of the most important processors of the framework, the so-called *reduction pair processor*.

For a DP problem $\mathcal{P}$, the reduction pair processor generates inequality constraints which should be satisfied by a reduction pair $(\succsim, \succ)$. The constraints require that all DPs in $\mathcal{P}$ are strictly or weakly decreasing and all *usable rules* $\mathcal{U}(\mathcal{P})$ are weakly decreasing. Then one can delete all strictly decreasing DPs.

The *usable rules* include all rules that can reduce the terms in right-hand sides of $\mathcal{P}$ when their variables are instantiated with normal forms. More precisely, for a term containing a defined symbol f, all f-rules are usable. Moreover, if the f-rules are usable and g occurs in the right-hand side of an f-rule, then the g-rules are usable as well. In Thm. 3, note that both TRSs and relations can be seen as sets of pairs of terms. Thus, "$\mathcal{P} \setminus \succ$" denotes $\{s \to t \in \mathcal{P} \mid s \not\succ t\}$.

Theorem 3 (Reduction Pair Processor and Usable Rules). *Let* $(\succsim, \succ)$ *be a reduction pair. Then the following DP processor Proc is sound.*

$$Proc(\mathcal{P}) = \begin{cases} \{\mathcal{P} \setminus \succ\} & \text{if } \mathcal{P} \subseteq \succ \cup \succsim \text{ and } \mathcal{U}(\mathcal{P}) \subseteq \succsim \\ \{\mathcal{P}\} & \text{otherwise} \end{cases}$$

For any function symbol f, *let* $Rls(f) = \{\ell \to r \in \mathcal{R} \mid root(\ell) = f\}$. *For any term* t, *the* usable rules $\mathcal{U}(t)$ *are the smallest set such that*

- $\mathcal{U}(x) = \varnothing$ *for every variable* x *and*
- $\mathcal{U}(f(t_1, \ldots, t_n)) = Rls(f) \cup \bigcup_{\ell \to r \in Rls(f)} \mathcal{U}(r) \cup \bigcup_{i=1}^{n} \mathcal{U}(t_i)$

For a set of dependency pairs $\mathcal{P}$, *its* usable rules *are* $\mathcal{U}(\mathcal{P}) = \bigcup_{s \to t \in \mathcal{P}} \mathcal{U}(t)$.

For the TRS of Ex. 1, according to Thm. 3 we search for a reduction pair with $s \underset{(\succsim)}{\succ} t$ for all dependency pairs $s \to t \in DP(\mathcal{R}) = \{(7), \ldots, (10)\}$ and with $\ell \succsim r$ for all usable rules $\ell \to r \in \mathcal{U}(DP(\mathcal{R})) = \{(4), (5), (6)\}$.

---

[2] To ease readability we use a simpler definition of *DP problems* than [8], since this simple definition suffices for the presentation of the new results of this paper.

A popular method to search for suitable relations $\succsim$ and $\succ$ automatically is the use of *polynomial interpretations* [14]. A polynomial interpretation $\mathcal{P}ol$ maps every n-ary function symbol f to a polynomial $f_{\mathcal{P}ol}$ over n variables $x_1, \ldots, x_n$. Traditionally, one uses polynomials with coefficients from $\mathbb{N} = \{0, 1, 2, \ldots\}$. This mapping is then extended to terms by defining $[x]_{\mathcal{P}ol} = x$ for all variables x and by defining $[f(t_1, \ldots, t_n)]_{\mathcal{P}ol} = f_{\mathcal{P}ol}([t_1]_{\mathcal{P}ol}, \ldots, [t_n]_{\mathcal{P}ol})$. If $\mathcal{P}ol$ is clear from the context, we also write $[t]$ instead of $[t]_{\mathcal{P}ol}$. Now one defines $s \succ_{\mathcal{P}ol} t$ (resp. $s \succsim_{\mathcal{P}ol} t$) iff $[s] > [t]$ (resp. $[s] \geq [t]$) holds for all instantiations of the variables with natural numbers. It is easy to see that $(\succsim_{\mathcal{P}ol}, \succ_{\mathcal{P}ol})$ is a reduction pair.

As an example, consider the polynomial interpretation $\mathcal{P}ol_1$ with $\mathsf{GT}_{\mathcal{P}ol_1} = x_1$, $\mathsf{MINUS}_{\mathcal{P}ol_1} = x_1 + 1$, $\mathsf{COND}_{\mathcal{P}ol_1} = x_2 + 1$, $\mathsf{s}_{\mathcal{P}ol_1} = x_1 + 1$, and $f_{\mathcal{P}ol_1} = 0$ for all other function symbols f. Then the DPs (8) and (10) are strictly decreasing. The reason for $\mathsf{GT}(\mathsf{s}(x), \mathsf{s}(y)) \succ_{\mathcal{P}ol_1} \mathsf{GT}(x, y)$ is that $[\mathsf{GT}(\mathsf{s}(x), \mathsf{s}(y))] = x + 1$ is greater than $[\mathsf{GT}(x, y)] = x$ for all natural numbers x. Moreover, all other DPs and the usable rules are weakly decreasing w.r.t. $\succsim_{\mathcal{P}ol_1}$. Thus, the DPs (8) and (10) can be removed and the reduction pair processor transforms the initial DP problem $DP(\mathcal{R})$ into $\{(7), (9)\}$. We refer to [4,7] for efficient algorithms to generate suitable polynomial interpretations automatically. However, it is impossible to transform the problem further into the empty DP problem $\varnothing$. More precisely, there is no reduction pair based on polynomial interpretations (or on any other classical order amenable to automation) where one of the DPs (7) and (9) is strictly decreasing and the other one and the usable rules are weakly decreasing, cf. [11]. Indeed, up to now all implementations of the DP method failed on Ex. 1.

3   General Reduction Pairs

Our aim is to handle *integer* polynomial interpretations. More precisely, we want to use polynomial interpretations where all function symbols except tuple symbols are still mapped to polynomials with natural coefficients, but where tuple symbols may be mapped to polynomials with arbitrary integer coefficients. For such integer polynomial interpretations, we still define $s \succ_{\mathcal{P}ol} t$ (resp. $s \succsim_{\mathcal{P}ol} t$) iff $[s] > [t]$ (resp. $[s] \geq [t]$) holds for all instantiations of the variables with *natural* (not with *integer*) numbers. If $\mathcal{F}$ is the original signature without tuple symbols, then the relations $\succ_{\mathcal{P}ol}$ and $\succsim_{\mathcal{P}ol}$ are $\mathcal{F}$-stable, i.e., $s \underset{(\succsim)}{\succ}_{\mathcal{P}ol} t$ implies $s\sigma \underset{(\succsim)}{\succ}_{\mathcal{P}ol} t\sigma$ for all substitutions σ with terms over $\mathcal{F}$. It is easy to show that $\mathcal{F}$-stability is sufficient for the reduction pairs used in the reduction pair processor.

To solve the remaining DP problem $\{(7), (9)\}$, we want to use the integer polynomial interpretation $\mathcal{P}ol_2$ where $\mathsf{MINUS}_{\mathcal{P}ol_2} = x_1 - x_2$, $\mathsf{COND}_{\mathcal{P}ol_2} = x_2 - x_3$, $\mathsf{s}_{\mathcal{P}ol_2} = x_1 + 1$, and $f_{\mathcal{P}ol_2} = 0$ for all other symbols f. Then DP (9) would be strictly decreasing and could be removed. The resulting DP problem $\{(7)\}$ is easy to solve by $\mathcal{P}ol_3$ with $\mathsf{MINUS}_{\mathcal{P}ol_3} = 1$ and $f_{\mathcal{P}ol_3} = 0$ for all other symbols f.

But such integer interpretations may not be used, since $(\succsim_{\mathcal{P}ol_2}, \succ_{\mathcal{P}ol_2})$ is no reduction pair: $\succsim_{\mathcal{P}ol_2}$ is not monotonic (e.g., $\mathsf{s}(0) \succsim_{\mathcal{P}ol_2} 0$, but $\mathsf{MINUS}(\mathsf{s}(0), \mathsf{s}(0))$ $\not\succsim_{\mathcal{P}ol_2} \mathsf{MINUS}(\mathsf{s}(0), 0)$). Moreover, $\succ_{\mathcal{P}ol_2}$ is not well founded (e.g., $\mathsf{MINUS}(0, 0)$

$\succ_{\mathcal{P}ol_2}$ MINUS$(0, \mathsf{s}(0)) \succ_{\mathcal{P}ol_2}$ MINUS$(0, \mathsf{s}(\mathsf{s}(0))) \succ_{\mathcal{P}ol_2} \ldots$). So integer interpretations violate both requirements (a) and (b) for reduction pairs, cf. Sect. 1.

Indeed, using such polynomial interpretations in Thm. 3 is unsound. As $\succ_{\mathcal{P}ol_2}$ is not well founded (i.e., as it violates requirement (b)), $\mathcal{P}ol_2$ could be used for a wrong innermost termination proof of the TRS $\{\mathsf{minus}(x, y) \to \mathsf{minus}(x, \mathsf{s}(y))\}$. But even if requirement (b) were not violated, a violation of requirement (a) would still render Thm. 3 unsound. We demonstrate this in Ex. 4.

Example 4. Consider the following TRS which is not innermost terminating. Here, round$(x) = x$ if x is even and round$(x) = \mathsf{s}(x)$ if x is odd.

$$\mathsf{minus}(\mathsf{s}(x), x) \to \mathsf{minus}(\mathsf{s}(x), \mathsf{round}(x)) \quad (11) \qquad \mathsf{round}(0) \to 0 \quad (12)$$
$$\mathsf{round}(\mathsf{s}(0)) \to \mathsf{s}(\mathsf{s}(0)) \quad (13)$$
$$\mathsf{round}(\mathsf{s}(\mathsf{s}(x))) \to \mathsf{s}(\mathsf{s}(\mathsf{round}(x))) \quad (14)$$

We use a modification $\mathcal{P}ol_2'$ of $\mathcal{P}ol_2$, where $\mathsf{MINUS}_{\mathcal{P}ol_2'} = (x_1 - x_2)^2$, $\mathsf{round}_{\mathcal{P}ol_2'} = x_1 + 1$, and $\mathsf{ROUND}_{\mathcal{P}ol_2'} = 0$. Now requirement (b) is satisfied. The MINUS-DPs are strictly decreasing (i.e., $\mathsf{MINUS}(\mathsf{s}(x), x) \succ_{\mathcal{P}ol_2'} \mathsf{MINUS}(\mathsf{s}(x), \mathsf{round}(x))$ and $\mathsf{MINUS}(\mathsf{s}(x), x) \succ_{\mathcal{P}ol_2'} \mathsf{ROUND}(x))$ and the ROUND-DP and the usable rules are weakly decreasing. Thus, if we were allowed to use $\mathcal{P}ol_2'$ in Thm. 3, then we could remove the MINUS-DPs. The remaining DP problem is easily solved and thus, we would falsely prove innermost termination of this TRS.

Ex. 4 shows the reason for the unsoundness when dropping requirement (a). Thm. 3 requires $\ell \succsim r$ for all usable rules $\ell \to r$. This is meant to ensure that all reductions with usable rules will weakly decrease the reduced term (w.r.t. $\succsim$). However, this only holds if the quasi-order $\succsim$ is monotonic. In Ex. 4, we have round$(x) \succsim_{\mathcal{P}ol_2'} x$, but $\mathsf{MINUS}(\mathsf{s}(x), \mathsf{round}(x)) \not\succsim_{\mathcal{P}ol_2'} \mathsf{MINUS}(\mathsf{s}(x), x)$.

Therefore, one should take into account on which positions the used quasi-order $\succsim$ is monotonically *increasing* and on which positions it is monotonically *decreasing*. If a defined function symbol f occurs at a monotonically *increasing* position in the right-hand side of a dependency pair, then one should require $\ell \succsim r$ for all f-rules. If f occurs at a monotonically *decreasing* position, then one should require $r \succsim \ell$. Finally, if f occurs at a position which is neither monotonically increasing nor decreasing, one should require $\ell \approx r$. Here, $\approx$ is the equivalence relation associated with $\succsim$, i.e., $\approx \; = \; \succsim \cap \precsim$.

So we modify our definition of usable rules.[3] When computing $\mathcal{U}(f(t_1, ..., t_n))$, for any $i \in \{1, ..., n\}$ we first check how the quasi-order $\succsim$ treats f's i-th argument. We say that f is $\succsim$-*dependent* on i iff there exist terms $t_1, ..., t_n, t_i'$ where $f(t_1, ..., t_i, ..., t_n) \not\approx f(t_1, ..., t_i', ..., t_n)$. Moreover, f is $\succsim$-*monotonically increasing* (resp. *decreasing*) on i iff $t_i \succsim t_i'$ implies $f(t_1, ..., t_i, ..., t_n) \succsim f(t_1, ..., t_i', ..., t_n)$ (resp. $f(t_1, ..., t_i, ..., t_n) \precsim f(t_1, ..., t_i', ..., t_n)$) for all terms $t_1, ..., t_n$ and t_i'.

Now if f is not $\succsim$-dependent on i, then $\mathcal{U}(t_i)$ does not have to be included in $\mathcal{U}(f(t_1, ..., t_n))$ at all. (This idea was already used in recent refined definitions

---

[3] Now $\mathcal{U}(t)$ is no longer a subset of $\mathcal{R}$. We nevertheless refer to $\mathcal{U}(t)$ as "usable" rules in order to keep the similarity to Thm. 3.

of the "usable rules", cf. [10].) Otherwise, we include the usable rules $\mathcal{U}(t_i)$ if f is $\succsim$-monotonically increasing on i. If it is $\succsim$-monotonically decreasing, we include the reversed rules $\mathcal{U}^{-1}(t_i)$ instead. Finally, if f is $\succsim$-dependent on i, but neither $\succsim$-monotonically increasing nor decreasing, then we include the usable rules of t_i in both directions, i.e., we include $\mathcal{U}^2(t_i)$ which is defined to be $\mathcal{U}(t_i) \cup \mathcal{U}^{-1}(t_i)$.

Definition 5 (General Usable Rules). *For any function symbol f and any $i \in \{1, \ldots, \mathrm{arity}(f)\}$, we define*

$$\mathrm{ord}(f,i) = \begin{cases} 0, \text{ if } f \text{ is not } \succsim\text{-dependent on } i \\ 1, \text{ otherwise, if } f \text{ is } \succsim\text{-monotonically increasing on } i \\ -1, \text{ otherwise, if } f \text{ is } \succsim\text{-monotonically decreasing on } i \\ 2, \text{ otherwise} \end{cases}$$

For any TRS U, we define $U^0 = \varnothing$, $U^1 = U$, $U^{-1} = \{r \to \ell \mid \ell \to r \in U\}$, and $U^2 = U \cup U^{-1}$. For any term t, we define $\mathcal{U}(t)$ as the smallest set such that[4]

- $\mathcal{U}(x) = \varnothing$ *for every variable x and*
- $\mathcal{U}(f(t_1, \ldots, t_n)) = Rls(f) \cup \bigcup_{\ell \to r \in Rls(f)} \mathcal{U}(r) \cup \bigcup_{i=1}^n \mathcal{U}^{\mathrm{ord}(f,i)}(t_i)$

For a set of dependency pairs $\mathcal{P}$, we again define $\mathcal{U}(\mathcal{P}) = \bigcup_{s \to t \in \mathcal{P}} \mathcal{U}(t)$.

So in Ex. 4, if $\mathsf{MINUS}_{\mathcal{P}ol_2'} = (x_1 - x_2)^2$ then MINUS is $\succsim_{\mathcal{P}ol_2'}$-dependent on 2, but neither $\succsim_{\mathcal{P}ol_2'}$-monotonically increasing nor decreasing. Hence, the usable rules include $\ell \to r$ and $r \to \ell$ for all round-rules $\ell \to r \in \{(12), (13), (14)\}$. Thus, we cannot falsely prove innermost termination with $\mathcal{P}ol_2'$ anymore. Indeed, with the modified definition of usable rules above, Thm. 3 can also be used for reduction pairs where $\succsim$ is not monotonic, i.e., where requirement (a) is violated.

We now also show how to omit the requirement (b) that the order $\succ$ in a reduction pair has to be well founded. Instead, we replace well-foundedness by the weaker requirement of *non-infinitesimality*.

Definition 6 (Non-Infinitesimal). *A relation $\succ$ is non-infinitesimal if there do not exist any $t, s_0, s_1, \ldots$ with $s_i \succ s_{i+1}$ and $s_i \succ t$ for all $i \in \mathbb{N}$.*

Any well-founded relation is non-infinitesimal. Thm. 7 shows that integer polynomial orders (which are not well founded) are non-infinitesimal as well.[5]

Theorem 7 (Non-Infinitesimality of Integer Polynomial Orders). *Let $\mathcal{P}ol$ be an integer polynomial interpretation. Then $\succ_{\mathcal{P}ol}$ is non-infinitesimal.*

Note that non-infinitesimality of $\succ_{\mathcal{P}ol}$ does not hold for polynomial interpretations on *rational* numbers. To see this, let $\mathsf{a}_{\mathcal{P}ol} = 1$, $\mathsf{b}_{\mathcal{P}ol} = 0$, and $\mathsf{f}_{\mathcal{P}ol} = \frac{x_1}{2}$. For $s_i = \mathsf{f}^i(\mathsf{a})$ and $t = \mathsf{b}$, we get the infinite sequence $\mathsf{a} \succ_{\mathcal{P}ol} \mathsf{f}(\mathsf{a}) \succ_{\mathcal{P}ol} \mathsf{f}(\mathsf{f}(\mathsf{a})) \succ_{\mathcal{P}ol} \ldots$ (i.e., $s_i \succ_{\mathcal{P}ol} s_{i+1}$ for all i) and $\mathsf{f}^i(\mathsf{a}) \succ_{\mathcal{P}ol} \mathsf{b}$ (i.e., $s_i \succ_{\mathcal{P}ol} t$) for all i.

We now extend the reduction pair processor from Thm. 3 to *general* reduction pairs. A *general* reduction pair $(\succsim, \succ)$ consists of an $\mathcal{F}$-stable quasi-order $\succsim$ and

---

[4] To ease readability, for $k \in \{-1, 0, 1, 2\}$ we write "$\mathcal{U}^k(t)$" instead of "$(\mathcal{U}(t))^k$".

[5] All proofs can be found in [11].

a compatible $\mathcal{F}$-stable non-infinitesimal order $\succ$, where $\mathcal{F}$ is the original signature of the TRS, i.e., without tuple symbols. Moreover, the equivalence relation $\approx$ associated with $\succsim$ must be monotonic (i.e., $s \approx t$ implies $u[s]_\pi \approx u[t]_\pi$ for any position π of any term u). But we do not require monotonicity of $\succsim$ or well-foundedness of $\succ$, i.e., both requirements (a) and (b) are dropped. So for any integer polynomial interpretation $\mathcal{P}ol$, $(\succsim_{\mathcal{P}ol}, \succ_{\mathcal{P}ol})$ is a general reduction pair.

In contrast to the reduction pair processor from Thm. 3, the new processor transforms a DP problem into *two* new problems. As before, the first problem results from removing all strictly decreasing dependency pairs. The second DP problem results from removing all DPs $s \to t$ from $\mathcal{P}$ that are *bounded from below*, i.e., DPs which satisfy the inequality $s \succsim c$ for a fresh constant c.

Theorem 8 (General Reduction Pair Processor). *Let $(\succsim, \succ)$ be a general reduction pair. Let c be a fresh constant not occurring in the signature and let $\mathcal{P}_{bound} = \{s \to t \in \mathcal{P} \mid s \succsim c\}$. Then the following DP processor Proc is sound. Here, $\mathcal{U}(\mathcal{P})$ is defined as in Def. 5.*

$$Proc(\mathcal{P}) = \begin{cases} \{\mathcal{P} \setminus \succ, \ \mathcal{P} \setminus \mathcal{P}_{bound}\} & \text{if } \mathcal{P} \subseteq {\succ} \cup {\succsim} \text{ and } \mathcal{U}(\mathcal{P}) \subseteq {\succsim} \\ \{\mathcal{P}\} & \text{otherwise} \end{cases}$$

Example 9. To modify Ex. 4 into an innermost terminating TRS, we replace rule (11) by $\mathsf{minus}(\mathsf{s}(x), x) \to \mathsf{minus}(\mathsf{s}(x), \mathsf{round}(\mathsf{s}(x)))$. *We regard the interpretation* $\mathcal{P}ol_2''$ *with* $\mathsf{MINUS}_{\mathcal{P}ol_2''} = x_1 - x_2$, $\mathsf{s}_{\mathcal{P}ol_2''} = x_1 + 1$, $0_{\mathcal{P}ol_2''} = 0$, $\mathsf{round}_{\mathcal{P}ol_2''} = x_1$, $\mathsf{ROUND}_{\mathcal{P}ol_2''} = 0$, *and* $c_{\mathcal{P}ol_2''} = 0$. *Then the MINUS-DPs are strictly decreasing and the ROUND-DP and the usable rules are weakly decreasing. Here, the usable rules are the reversed round-rules, since* MINUS *is* $\succsim$*-monotonically decreasing on 2. Moreover, all dependency pairs are bounded from below (i.e.,* $\mathsf{MINUS}(\mathsf{s}(x), x) \succsim_{\mathcal{P}ol_2''} c$ *and* $\mathsf{ROUND}(\mathsf{s}(\mathsf{s}(x))) \succsim_{\mathcal{P}ol_2''} c$*). Thus, we can transform the initial DP problem* $\mathcal{P} = DP(\mathcal{R})$ *into* $\mathcal{P} \setminus \mathcal{P}_{bound} = \varnothing$ *and into* $\mathcal{P} \setminus \succ$, *which only contains the ROUND-DP. This remaining DP problem is easily solved and thus, we can prove innermost termination of the TRS.*

Since $\mathcal{U}(\mathcal{P})$ now depends on $\succsim$, the constraints that the reduction pair has to satisfy in Thm. 8 depend on the reduction pair itself. Nevertheless, if one uses reduction pairs based on polynomial interpretations, then the search for suitable reduction pairs can still be mechanized efficiently. More precisely, one can reformulate Thm. 8 in a way where one first generates constraints (that are independent of $\succsim$) and searches for a reduction pair satisfying the constraints afterwards. We showed in [10, Sect. 7.1] how to reformulate "f is $\succsim$-dependent on i" accordingly and "f is $\succsim$-monotonically increasing on i" can be reformulated by requiring that the partial derivative of $f_{\mathcal{P}ol}$ w.r.t. x_i is non-negative, cf. [1, Footnote 11].

There have already been previous approaches to extend the DP method to non-monotonic reduction pairs. Hirokawa and Middeldorp [13] allowed interpretations like $\mathsf{MINUS}_{\mathcal{P}ol} = \max(x_1 - x_2, 0)$.[6] However, instead of detecting $\succsim$-monotonically increasing and decreasing positions, they always require $\ell \approx r$ for

---

[6] While such interpretations always result in well-founded orders, they are difficult to generate automatically. In contrast, the search for integer polynomial interpretations is as for ordinary polynomial interpretations, e.g., by using SAT solving as in [7].

the usable rules. Therefore, their technique fails on Ex. 9, since their constraints cannot be fulfilled by the interpretations considered in their approach, cf. [11].

Another approach was presented in [1, Thm. 33] and further extended in [6]. Essentially, here one permits non-monotonic quasi-orders $\succsim$ provided that f is $\succsim$-monotonically increasing on a position i whenever there is a subterm $f(t_1, ..., t_i, ..., t_n)$ in a right-hand side of a dependency pair or of a usable rule where t_i contains a defined symbol. Then Thm. 3 is still sound (this also follows from Def. 5 and Thm. 8). However, this approach would not allow us to handle arbitrary non-monotonic reduction pairs and therefore, it also fails on Ex. 9.

4 Conditions for Bounded Increase

With Thm. 8 we still cannot use our desired integer polynomial interpretation $\mathcal{P}ol_2$ with $\mathsf{MINUS}_{\mathcal{P}ol_2} = x_1 - x_2$, $\mathsf{COND}_{\mathcal{P}ol_2} = x_2 - x_3$, $\mathsf{s}_{\mathcal{P}ol_2} = x_1 + 1$, and $f_{\mathcal{P}ol_2} = 0$ for all other function symbols f to prove innermost termination of Ex. 1. When trying to solve the remaining DP problem $\{(7), (9)\}$, the DP (9) would be strictly decreasing but none of the two DPs would be bounded. The reason is that we have neither $\mathsf{MINUS}(x, y) \succsim_{\mathcal{P}ol_2} \mathsf{c}$ nor $\mathsf{COND}(\mathsf{true}, x, y) \succsim_{\mathcal{P}ol_2} \mathsf{c}$ for any possible value of $\mathsf{c}_{\mathcal{P}ol_2}$. Thus, the reduction pair processor would return the two DP problems $\{(7)\}$ and $\{(7), (9)\}$, i.e., it would not simplify the DP problem. (Of course since $\{(7)\} \subseteq \{(7), (9)\}$, it suffices to regard just the problem $\{(7), (9)\}$.)

The solution is to consider *conditions* when requiring inequalities like $s \underset{(\succsim)}{\succ} t$ or $s \succsim \mathsf{c}$. For example, to include the DP (7) in $\mathcal{P}_{bound}$, we do not have to demand $\mathsf{MINUS}(x, y) \succsim \mathsf{c}$ for *all* instantiations of x and y. Instead, it suffices to require the inequality only for those instantiations of x and y which can be used in potentially infinite minimal innermost chains. So we require $\mathsf{MINUS}(x, y) \succsim \mathsf{c}$ only for instantiations σ where (7)'s instantiated right-hand side $\mathsf{COND}(\mathsf{gt}(x, y), x, y)\sigma$ reduces to an instantiated left-hand side $u\sigma$ for some DP $u \to v$.[7] Here, $u \to v$ should again be variable renamed. As our DP problem contains two DPs (7) and (9), we get the following two constraints (by considering all possibilities $u \to v \in \{(7), (9)\}$). If both constraints are satisfied, then we can include (7) in $\mathcal{P}_{bound}$.

$$\mathsf{COND}(\mathsf{gt}(x, y), x, y) = \mathsf{MINUS}(x', y') \quad \Rightarrow \quad \mathsf{MINUS}(x, y) \succsim \mathsf{c} \qquad (15)$$
$$\mathsf{COND}(\mathsf{gt}(x, y), x, y) = \mathsf{COND}(\mathsf{true}, x', y') \quad \Rightarrow \quad \mathsf{MINUS}(x, y) \succsim \mathsf{c} \qquad (16)$$

Def. 10 introduces the syntax and semantics of such conditional constraints.

Definition 10 (Conditional Constraint). *For given relations $\succsim$ and $\succ$, the set $\mathcal{C}$ of conditional constraints is the smallest set with*

- $\{TRUE, s \succsim t, s \succ t, s = t\} \subseteq \mathcal{C}$ *for all terms s and t*
- *if $\{\varphi_1, \varphi_2\} \subseteq \mathcal{C}$, then $\varphi_1 \Rightarrow \varphi_2 \in \mathcal{C}$ and $\varphi_1 \wedge \varphi_2 \in \mathcal{C}$*
- *if $\varphi \in \mathcal{C}$ and $y \in \mathcal{V}$, then $\forall y \; \varphi \in \mathcal{C}$*

---

[7] Moreover, $\mathsf{COND}(\mathsf{gt}(x, y), x, y)\sigma$ must be innermost terminating, $\mathsf{COND}(\mathsf{gt}(x, y), x, y)\sigma \xrightarrow{\mathsf{i}}{}^*_{\mathcal{R}} u\sigma$, and $u\sigma$ must be in normal form, since we consider *minimal innermost* chains.

Now we define which normal $\mathcal{F}$-substitutions[8] *σ satisfy a constraint $\varphi \in \mathcal{C}$, denoted "$\sigma \models \varphi$":*

- $\sigma \models TRUE$ for all normal $\mathcal{F}$-substitutions σ
- $\sigma \models s \succsim t$ iff $s\sigma \succsim t\sigma$ and $\sigma \models s \succ t$ iff $s\sigma \succ t\sigma$
- $\sigma \models s = t$ iff $s\sigma$ is innermost terminating, $s\sigma \xrightarrow{i}{}^*_{\mathcal{R}} t\sigma$, $t\sigma$ is a normal form
- $\sigma \models \varphi_1 \Rightarrow \varphi_2$ iff $\sigma \not\models \varphi_1$ or $\sigma \models \varphi_2$
- $\sigma \models \varphi_1 \wedge \varphi_2$ iff $\sigma \models \varphi_1$ and $\sigma \models \varphi_2$
- $\sigma \models \forall y\, \varphi$ iff $\sigma' \models \varphi$ for all normal $\mathcal{F}$-substitutions σ' where $\sigma'(x) = \sigma(x)$ for all $x \neq y$

A constraint φ is valid ("$\models \varphi$") iff $\sigma \models \varphi$ holds for all normal $\mathcal{F}$-substitutions σ.

Now we refine the reduction pair processor by taking conditions into account. To this end, we modify the definition of $\mathcal{P}_{bound}$ and introduce $\mathcal{P}_\succ$ and $\mathcal{P}_\succsim$.

Theorem 11 (Conditional General Reduction Pair Processor). *Let $(\succsim, \succ)$ be a general reduction pair. Let c be a fresh constant and let*

$$\mathcal{P}_\succ = \{\, s \to t \in \mathcal{P} \;\mid\; \models \bigwedge_{u \to v \in \mathcal{P}}(t = u' \Rightarrow s \succ t)\,\}$$
$$\mathcal{P}_\succsim = \{\, s \to t \in \mathcal{P} \;\mid\; \models \bigwedge_{u \to v \in \mathcal{P}}(t = u' \Rightarrow s \succsim t)\,\}$$
$$\mathcal{P}_{bound} = \{\, s \to t \in \mathcal{P} \;\mid\; \models \bigwedge_{u \to v \in \mathcal{P}}(t = u' \Rightarrow s \succsim \mathsf{c})\,\}$$

where u' results from u by renaming its variables into fresh variables. Then the following DP processor Proc is sound. Here, $\mathcal{U}(\mathcal{P})$ is defined as in Def. 5.

$$Proc(\mathcal{P}) = \begin{cases} \{\mathcal{P} \setminus \mathcal{P}_\succ,\ \mathcal{P} \setminus \mathcal{P}_{bound}\} & \text{if } \mathcal{P}_\succ \cup \mathcal{P}_\succsim = \mathcal{P} \text{ and } \mathcal{U}(\mathcal{P}) \subseteq \succsim \\ \{\mathcal{P}\} & otherwise \end{cases}$$

To ease readability, in Thm. 11 we only consider the conditions resulting from *two* DPs $s \to t$ and $u \to v$ which follow each other in minimal innermost chains. To consider also conditions resulting from $n+1$ adjacent DPs, one would have to modify $\mathcal{P}_\succ$ as follows (of course, $\mathcal{P}_\succsim$ and $\mathcal{P}_{bound}$ have to be modified analogously).

$$\mathcal{P}_\succ = \{s \to t \in \mathcal{P} \mid\ \models \bigwedge_{u_1 \to v_1, \ldots, u_n \to v_n \in \mathcal{P}}(t = u'_1 \wedge v'_1 = u'_2 \wedge \ldots \wedge v'_{n-1} = u'_n \Rightarrow s \succ t)\}$$

Here, the variables in u'_i and v'_i must be renamed in order to be disjoint to the variables in u'_j and v'_j for $j \neq i$. Moreover, instead of regarding DPs which *follow* $s \to t$ in chains, one could also regards DPs which *precede* $s \to t$. Then instead of (or in addition to) the premise "$t = u'''$", one would have the premise "$v' = s$".

The question remains how to check whether conditional constraints are valid, since this requires reasoning about reductions resp. reachability. We now introduce a calculus of seven rules to simplify conditional constraints. For example, the constraint (15) is trivially valid, since its condition is unsatisfiable. The reason is that there is no substitution σ with $\sigma \models \mathsf{COND}(\mathsf{gt}(x,y),x,y) = $

---

[8] A *normal $\mathcal{F}$-substitution* σ instantiates all variables by normal forms that do not contain tuple symbols (i.e., for any $x \in \mathcal{V}$, all function symbols in $\sigma(x)$ are from $\mathcal{F}$).

$\mathsf{MINUS}(x', y')$, since COND is no defined function symbol (i.e., it is a *constructor*) and therefore, COND-terms can only be reduced to COND-terms.

This leads to the first inference rule. In a conjunction $\varphi_1 \wedge \ldots \wedge \varphi_n$ of conditional constraints φ_i, these rules can be used to replace a conjunct φ_i by a new formula φ_i'. Of course, $TRUE \wedge \varphi$ can always be simplified to φ. Eventually, the goal is to remove all equalities "$p = q$" from the constraints. The soundness of the rules is shown in Thm. 14: if φ_i is replaced by φ_i', then $\models \varphi_i'$ implies $\models \varphi_i$.

I. Constructor and Different Function Symbol

$$\frac{f(p_1, ..., p_n) = g(q_1, ..., q_m) \wedge \varphi \;\Rightarrow\; \psi}{TRUE} \qquad \text{if } f \text{ is a constructor and } f \neq g$$

Rule (II) handles conditions like $\mathsf{COND}(\mathsf{gt}(x,y), x, y) = \mathsf{COND}(\mathsf{true}, x', y')$ where both terms start with the constructor COND. So (16) is transformed to

$$\mathsf{gt}(x,y) = \mathsf{true} \wedge x = x' \wedge y = y' \quad \Rightarrow \quad \mathsf{MINUS}(x,y) \gtrsim \mathsf{c} \qquad (17)$$

II. Same Constructors on Both Sides

$$\frac{f(p_1, ..., p_n) = f(q_1, ..., q_n) \wedge \varphi \;\Rightarrow\; \psi}{p_1 = q_1 \wedge \ldots \wedge p_n = q_n \wedge \varphi \;\Rightarrow\; \psi} \qquad \text{if } f \text{ is a constructor}$$

Rule (III) removes conditions of the form "$x = q$" or "$q = x$" by applying the substitution $[x/q]$ to the constraint.[9] So (17) is transformed to

$$\mathsf{gt}(x,y) = \mathsf{true} \quad \Rightarrow \quad \mathsf{MINUS}(x,y) \gtrsim \mathsf{c} \qquad (18)$$

III. Variable in Equation

$$\frac{x = q \wedge \varphi \;\Rightarrow\; \psi}{\varphi\sigma \;\Rightarrow\; \psi\sigma} \; \text{if } x \in \mathcal{V} \text{ and } \sigma = [x/q] \qquad \frac{q = x \wedge \varphi \;\Rightarrow\; \psi}{\varphi\sigma \;\Rightarrow\; \psi\sigma} \; \begin{array}{l} \text{if } x \in \mathcal{V}, q \text{ has no} \\ \text{defined symbols,} \\ \sigma = [x/q] \end{array}$$

Of course, one can also omit arbitrary conjuncts from the premise of an implication. To ease notation, we regard a conjunction as a set of formulas. So their order is irrelevant and we write $\varphi' \subseteq \varphi$ iff all conjuncts of φ' are also conjuncts of φ. The empty conjunction is $TRUE$ (i.e., $TRUE \Rightarrow \psi$ can be simplified to ψ).

IV. Delete Conditions

$$\frac{\varphi \;\Rightarrow\; \psi}{\varphi' \;\Rightarrow\; \psi} \qquad \text{if } \varphi' \subseteq \varphi$$

Rule (IV) is especially useful for omitting conditions $q = x$ where x is a variable which does not occur anywhere else. So one could also transform (17) to (18) by Rule (IV). The meaning of (18) is that $\mathsf{MINUS}(x,y)\sigma \gtrsim \mathsf{c}$ must hold

---

[9] To remove the condition $q = x$, we must ensure that for any normal $\mathcal{F}$-substitution δ, the term $q\delta$ is normal, too. Otherwise, Rule (III) would not be sound, cf. [11].

whenever $\mathsf{gt}(x,y)\sigma$ is innermost terminating and $\mathsf{gt}(x,y)\sigma \xrightarrow{\mathsf{i}}_{\mathcal{R}}^* \mathsf{true}$ holds for a normal $\mathcal{F}$-substitution σ. To simplify this constraint further, the next inference rule performs an *induction* on the length of $\mathsf{gt}(x,y)\sigma$'s reduction.[10] Since $\mathsf{gt}(x,y)$ and true do not unify, at least one reduction step is needed, i.e., some rule $\mathsf{gt}(\ell_1,\ell_2) \to r$ must be applied. To detect all possibilities for the first reduction step, we consider all *narrowings* of the term $\mathsf{gt}(x,y)$. We obtain

$$\mathsf{gt}(x,y) \rightsquigarrow_{[x/0,y/v]} \mathsf{false}, \quad \mathsf{gt}(x,y) \rightsquigarrow_{[x/s(u),y/0]} \mathsf{true}, \quad \mathsf{gt}(x,y) \rightsquigarrow_{[x/s(u),y/s(v)]} \mathsf{gt}(u,v)$$

Thus, we could replace (18) by the following three new constraints where we always apply the respective narrowing substitution to the whole constraint:

$$\mathsf{false} = \mathsf{true} \quad \Rightarrow \quad \mathsf{MINUS}(0,v) \succsim \mathsf{c} \tag{19}$$
$$\mathsf{true} = \mathsf{true} \quad \Rightarrow \quad \mathsf{MINUS}(\mathsf{s}(u),0) \succsim \mathsf{c} \tag{20}$$
$$\mathsf{gt}(u,v) = \mathsf{true} \quad \Rightarrow \quad \mathsf{MINUS}(\mathsf{s}(u),\mathsf{s}(v)) \succsim \mathsf{c} \tag{21}$$

So to transform a constraint $f(x_1,\ldots,x_n) = q \wedge \varphi \Rightarrow \psi$, we consider all rules $f(\ell_1,\ldots,\ell_n) \to r$. Then the constraint could be replaced by the new constraints

$$r = q\sigma \wedge \varphi\sigma \Rightarrow \psi\sigma, \qquad \text{where } \sigma = [x_1/\ell_1,\ldots,x_n/\ell_n]. \tag{22}$$

However, we perform a better transformation. Suppose that r contains a recursive call, i.e., a subterm $f(r_1,\ldots,r_n)$, and that the r_i do not contain defined symbols. Obviously, $f(r_1,\ldots,r_n)\sigma$'s reduction is shorter than the reduction of $f(x_1,\ldots,x_n)\sigma$. Thus for $\mu = [x_1/r_1,\ldots,x_n/r_n]$ one can assume

$$\forall y_1,\ldots,y_m \quad f(r_1,\ldots,r_n) = q\mu \wedge \varphi\mu \Rightarrow \psi\mu \tag{23}$$

as *induction hypothesis* when requiring (22).[11] Here, $y_1,\ldots,y_m$ are all occurring variables except those in r. Of course, we may assume that variables in rewrite rules (i.e., in r) are disjoint from variables in constraints (i.e., in q, φ, and ψ). So instead of (22), it suffices to demand (23) $\Rightarrow$ (22), or equivalently

$$r = q\sigma \wedge \varphi\sigma \wedge (23) \Rightarrow \psi\sigma. \tag{24}$$

This leads to Rule (V). Here, $x_1,\ldots,x_n$ denote pairwise different variables.

---

[10] More precisely, we use an induction on $\xrightarrow{\mathsf{i}}_{\mathcal{R}} \circ \trianglerighteq$, where $\trianglerighteq$ is the subterm relation. The idea for this inference rule was inspired by our earlier work on termination of simple first-order functional programs [3]. But [3] only considered a very restricted form of functional programs (left-linear, sufficiently complete, non-overlapping constructor systems without defined symbols in arguments of recursive calls), whereas we regard arbitrary TRSs. Moreover, we integrate this idea of performing induction into the whole framework of termination techniques and tools available for TRSs. Finally, in contrast to [3], we do not need an underlying induction theorem prover. Nevertheless, our approach is significantly stronger (e.g., [3] fails on examples like Ex. 12, cf. [11]).

[11] If there are more recursive calls in r, then one can obtain a corresponding induction hypothesis (23) for each recursive call. But similar to Footnote 9, if the r_i contain defined symbols, then one may not assume (23) as induction hypothesis.

V. Induction (Defined Symbol with Pairwise Different Variables)

$$\frac{f(x_1, ..., x_n) = q \ \wedge \varphi \qquad\qquad\qquad \Rightarrow \psi}{\bigwedge_{f(\ell_1,...,\ell_n)\to r \in \mathcal{R}} (\ r = q\sigma \wedge \varphi\sigma \wedge \varphi' \Rightarrow \psi\sigma\ )} \quad \begin{array}{l}\text{if } f \text{ is a defined symbol and} \\ f(x_1, ..., x_n) \text{ does not unify} \\ \text{with } q \end{array}$$

where $\sigma = [x_1/\ell_1, ..., x_n/\ell_n]$

and $\varphi' = \begin{cases} \forall y_1, ..., y_m \ \ f(r_1, \ldots, r_n) = q\mu \wedge \varphi\mu \Rightarrow \psi\mu, \quad \text{if} \\ \qquad \bullet\ r \text{ contains the subterm } f(r_1, ..., r_n), \\ \qquad \bullet\ \text{there is no defined symbol in any } r_i, \\ \qquad \bullet\ \mu = [x_1/r_1, ..., x_n/r_n], \text{ and} \\ \qquad \bullet\ y_1, ..., y_m \text{ are all occurring variables except } \mathcal{V}(r) \\ TRUE, \quad \text{otherwise} \end{cases}$

In our example, the above rule transforms the original constraint (18) into the three new constraints (19), (20), and (25). Here, (25) is obtained from the narrowing step $\mathsf{gt}(x,y) \rightsquigarrow_{[x/\mathsf{s}(u),y/\mathsf{s}(v)]} \mathsf{gt}(u,v)$, i.e., we have $\sigma = [x/\mathsf{s}(u), y/\mathsf{s}(v)]$, $r_1 = u$, $r_2 = v$, and $\mu = [x/u, y/v]$. There are no variables $y_1, \ldots, y_m$.

$$\begin{array}{c} \mathsf{gt}(u,v) = \mathsf{true} \\ \wedge\,(\mathsf{gt}(u,v) = \mathsf{true} \Rightarrow \mathsf{MINUS}(u,v) \succsim \mathsf{c}) \quad \Rightarrow \quad \mathsf{MINUS}(\mathsf{s}(u),\mathsf{s}(v)) \succsim \mathsf{c} \qquad (25) \end{array}$$

To simplify (25) further, now we can "apply" the induction hypothesis, since its condition $\mathsf{gt}(u,v) = \mathsf{true}$ is guaranteed to hold. So we can transform (25) to

$$\mathsf{gt}(u,v) = \mathsf{true} \wedge \mathsf{MINUS}(u,v) \succsim \mathsf{c} \Rightarrow \mathsf{MINUS}(\mathsf{s}(u),\mathsf{s}(v)) \succsim \mathsf{c}. \qquad (26)$$

In general, to simplify conditions one may of course also instantiate universally quantified variables.[12] This leads to the following rule.

VI. Simplify Condition

$$\frac{\varphi \wedge (\forall y_1, \ldots, y_m \ \varphi' \Rightarrow \psi'\ ) \Rightarrow \psi}{\varphi \wedge \qquad\qquad\qquad \psi'\sigma \Rightarrow \psi} \quad \begin{array}{l} \text{if } DOM(\sigma) \subseteq \{y_1, \ldots, y_m\}, \\ \text{there is no defined symbol and} \\ \text{no tuple symbol in any } \sigma(y_i), \\ \text{and } \varphi'\sigma \subseteq \varphi \end{array}$$

To simplify the remaining constraints (19), (20), and (26), note that (19) can be eliminated by Rule (I) since it has an unsatisfiable condition $\mathsf{false} = \mathsf{true}$. Moreover, Rule (II) can delete the trivial condition $\mathsf{true} = \mathsf{true}$ of the constraint (20). For (26), with Rule (IV) one can of course always omit conditions like $\mathsf{gt}(u,v) = \mathsf{true}$ from conditional constraints. In this way, all conditions with equalities $p = q$ are removed in the end.

So to finish the termination proof of Ex. 1, we can include the DP (7) in $\mathcal{P}_{bound}$ if the constraints $\mathsf{MINUS}(\mathsf{s}(u),0) \succsim \mathsf{c}$ and $\mathsf{MINUS}(u,v) \succsim \mathsf{c} \Rightarrow \mathsf{MINUS}(\mathsf{s}(u),\mathsf{s}(v)) \succsim \mathsf{c}$ are satisfied. Of course, these constraints obviously hold

---

[12] As in Footnote 9, one may only instantiate them by terms without defined symbols.

for $\mathcal{P}ol_2$ if we choose $c_{\mathcal{P}ol_2} = 1$. Then the DP (9) is strictly decreasing and (7) is bounded from below and thus, the reduction pair processor transforms the remaining DP problem $\{(7), (9)\}$ into $\{(7)\}$ and $\{(9)\}$. Now the resulting DP problems are easy to solve and thus, innermost termination of Ex. 1 is proved.

The rules (I) - (VI) are not always sufficient to exploit the conditions of a constraint. We demonstrate this with the following example.

Example 12. We regard a TRS $\mathcal{R}$ containing the gt-rules (4) - (6) together with

$$\mathsf{plus}(n, 0) \to n \qquad\qquad \mathsf{f}(\mathsf{true}, x, y, z) \to \mathsf{f}(\mathsf{gt}(x, \mathsf{plus}(y, z)), x, \mathsf{s}(y), z)$$
$$\mathsf{plus}(n, \mathsf{s}(m)) \to \mathsf{s}(\mathsf{plus}(n, m)) \qquad \mathsf{f}(\mathsf{true}, x, y, z) \to \mathsf{f}(\mathsf{gt}(x, \mathsf{plus}(y, z)), x, y, \mathsf{s}(z))$$

The termination of gt and of plus is easy to show. So the initial DP problem can easily be transformed into $\{(27), (28)\}$ with

$$\mathsf{F}(\mathsf{true}, x, y, z) \to \mathsf{F}(\mathsf{gt}(x, \mathsf{plus}(y, z)), x, \mathsf{s}(y), z) \tag{27}$$
$$\mathsf{F}(\mathsf{true}, x, y, z) \to \mathsf{F}(\mathsf{gt}(x, \mathsf{plus}(y, z)), x, y, \mathsf{s}(z)) \tag{28}$$

To include (27) in $\mathcal{P}_{bound}$, we have to impose the following constraint:

$$\mathsf{F}(\mathsf{gt}(x, \mathsf{plus}(y, z)), x, \mathsf{s}(y), z) = \mathsf{F}(\mathsf{true}, x', y', z') \;\Rightarrow\; \mathsf{F}(\mathsf{true}, x, y, z) \succsim c \tag{29}$$

With the rules (II) and (IV), it can be transformed into

$$\mathsf{gt}(x, \mathsf{plus}(y, z)) = \mathsf{true} \;\Rightarrow\; \mathsf{F}(\mathsf{true}, x, y, z) \succsim c \tag{30}$$

Now we want to use induction. However, Rule (V) is only applicable for conditions $f(x_1, \ldots, x_n) = q$ where $x_1, \ldots, x_n$ are *pairwise different variables*. To obtain such conditions, we use the following rule. Here, x denotes a fresh variable.

VII. Defined Symbol without Pairwise Different Variables

$$\frac{f(p_1, \ldots, p_i, \ldots, p_n) = q \wedge \varphi \Rightarrow \psi}{p_i = x \wedge f(p_1, \ldots, x, \ldots, p_n) = q \wedge \varphi \Rightarrow \psi} \quad \begin{array}{l} \text{if } f \text{ is a defined symbol and} \\ (\, p_i \notin \mathcal{V} \text{ or } p_i = p_j \text{ for a } j \neq i \,) \end{array}$$

So the constraint (30) is transformed into

$$\mathsf{plus}(y, z) = w \wedge \mathsf{gt}(x, w) = \mathsf{true} \;\Rightarrow\; \mathsf{F}(\mathsf{true}, x, y, z) \succsim c$$

Example 13. To continue, we can now perform induction on gt which yields

$$\mathsf{plus}(y, z) = v \wedge \mathsf{false} = \mathsf{true} \Rightarrow \mathsf{F}(\mathsf{true}, 0, y, z) \succsim c \tag{31}$$
$$\mathsf{plus}(y, z) = 0 \wedge \mathsf{true} = \mathsf{true} \Rightarrow \mathsf{F}(\mathsf{true}, \mathsf{s}(u), y, z) \succsim c \tag{32}$$
$$\mathsf{plus}(y, z) = \mathsf{s}(v) \wedge \mathsf{gt}(u, v) = \mathsf{true} \wedge (34) \Rightarrow \mathsf{F}(\mathsf{true}, \mathsf{s}(u), y, z) \succsim c \tag{33}$$

Here, (34) is the induction hypothesis:

$$\forall y, z \;\; \mathsf{plus}(y, z) = v \wedge \mathsf{gt}(u, v) = \mathsf{true} \;\Rightarrow\; \mathsf{F}(\mathsf{true}, u, y, z) \succsim c \tag{34}$$

With Rule (I) we delete constraint (31) and Rule (II) simplifies constraint (32) to "$\mathsf{plus}(y, z) = 0 \;\Rightarrow\; \mathsf{F}(\mathsf{true}, \mathsf{s}(u), y, z) \succsim \mathsf{c}$". Similar to our previous example, by induction via plus and by removing the constraint with the unsatisfiable condition $\mathsf{s}(\mathsf{plus}(n, m)) = 0$, we finally transform it to

$$\mathsf{F}(\mathsf{true}, \mathsf{s}(u), 0, 0) \succsim \mathsf{c} \tag{35}$$

The other constraint (33) is simplified further by induction via plus as well:

$$n = \mathsf{s}(v) \wedge \mathsf{gt}(u, v) = \mathsf{true} \wedge (34) \Rightarrow \mathsf{F}(\mathsf{true}, \mathsf{s}(u), n, 0) \succsim \mathsf{c} \tag{36}$$
$$\mathsf{s}(\mathsf{plus}(n, m)) = \mathsf{s}(v) \wedge \mathsf{gt}(u, v) = \mathsf{true} \wedge (34) \wedge \varphi' \Rightarrow \mathsf{F}(\mathsf{true}, \mathsf{s}(u), n, \mathsf{s}(m)) \succsim \mathsf{c} \tag{37}$$

where φ' is the new induction hypothesis. We apply Rules (III) and (IV) on (36) to obtain "$\mathsf{gt}(u, v) = \mathsf{true} \;\Rightarrow\; \mathsf{F}(\mathsf{true}, \mathsf{s}(u), \mathsf{s}(v), 0) \succsim \mathsf{c}$". By another induction on gt and by applying Rules (I), (II), (IV), and (VI) we get the final constraints

$$\mathsf{F}(\mathsf{true}, \mathsf{s}(\mathsf{s}(i)), \mathsf{s}(0), 0) \succsim \mathsf{c} \tag{38}$$
$$\mathsf{F}(\mathsf{true}, \mathsf{s}(i), \mathsf{s}(j), 0) \succsim \mathsf{c} \Rightarrow \mathsf{F}(\mathsf{true}, \mathsf{s}(\mathsf{s}(i)), \mathsf{s}(\mathsf{s}(j)), 0) \succsim \mathsf{c} \tag{39}$$

In the only remaining constraint (37) we delete φ' with Rule (IV) and by removing the outermost s in the first condition with Rule (II), we get

$$\mathsf{plus}(n, m) = v \wedge \mathsf{gt}(u, v) = \mathsf{true} \wedge (34) \;\Rightarrow\; \mathsf{F}(\mathsf{true}, \mathsf{s}(u), n, \mathsf{s}(m)) \succsim \mathsf{c}$$

Now we can simplify the condition by applying the induction hypothesis (34). In (34), the variables y and z were universally quantified. We instantiate y with n and z with m. With Rule (VI) we replace (34) by the new condition $\mathsf{F}(\mathsf{true}, u, n, m) \succsim \mathsf{c}$. By deleting the first two remaining conditions we finally get

$$\mathsf{F}(\mathsf{true}, u, n, m) \succsim \mathsf{c} \;\Rightarrow\; \mathsf{F}(\mathsf{true}, \mathsf{s}(u), n, \mathsf{s}(m)) \succsim \mathsf{c} \tag{40}$$

So to summarize, the constraint (29) can be transformed into (35), (38), (39), and (40). These constraints are satisfied by the interpretation $\mathcal{P}ol$ where $\mathsf{F}_{\mathcal{P}ol} = x_2 - x_3 - x_4$, $\mathsf{s}_{\mathcal{P}ol} = x_1 + 1$, $0_{\mathcal{P}ol} = 0$, and $\mathsf{c}_{\mathcal{P}ol} = 1$. Therefore, we can include the DP (27) in $\mathcal{P}_{bound}$. For a similar reason, the other DP (28) is also bounded. Moreover, both DPs are strictly decreasing and there are no usable rules since F is not $\succsim_{\mathcal{P}ol}$-dependent on 1. Hence, the reduction pair processor can remove both DPs and innermost termination of Ex. 12 is proved.

We define $\varphi \vdash \varphi'$ iff φ' results from φ by repeatedly applying the above inference rules to the conjuncts of φ. Thm. 14 states that these rules are sound.

Theorem 14 (Soundness). *If $\varphi \vdash \varphi'$, then $\models \varphi'$ implies $\models \varphi$.*

With Thm. 14 we can now refine the reduction pair processor from Thm. 11.

Corollary 15 (Conditional General Reduction Pair Processor with Inference). *Let $(\succsim, \succ)$ be a general reduction pair and let c be a fresh constant. For every $s \to t \in \mathcal{P}$ and every inequality $\psi \in \{s \succ t,\; s \succsim t,\; s \succsim \mathsf{c}\}$, let φ_ψ be a constraint with $\bigwedge_{u \to v \in \mathcal{P}}(t = u' \;\Rightarrow\; \psi) \vdash \varphi_\psi$. Here, u' results from u by renaming its variables into fresh variables. Then the processor Proc from Thm. 11 is still sound if we define $\mathcal{P}_\succ = \{s \to t \in \mathcal{P} \mid \models \varphi_{s \succ t}\}$, $\mathcal{P}_\succsim = \{s \to t \in \mathcal{P} \mid \models \varphi_{s \succsim t}\}$, and $\mathcal{P}_{bound} = \{s \to t \in \mathcal{P} \mid \models \varphi_{s \succsim \mathsf{c}}\}$.*

For automation, one of course needs a strategy for the application of the rules (I) - (VII). Essentially, we propose to apply the rules with the priority (I), (II), (IV)$'$, (VI), (III), (VII), (V), cf. [11]. Here, (IV)$'$ is a restriction of (IV) which only deletes conditions $q = x$ where x is a variable which does not occur anywhere else. Moreover, to ensure termination of the inference rules, one has to impose a limit on the number of inductions with Rule (V). In the end, we use Rule (IV) to remove all remaining conditions containing "=" or "⇒". Moreover, if there are several conditions of the form $s \succsim_{(\sim)} t$, we remove all but one of them.

Thus, the constraints φ_ψ in Cor. 15 are conjunctions where the conjuncts have the form "$t_1 \succsim_{(\sim)} t_2$" or "$s_1 \succsim_{(\sim)} s_2 \Rightarrow t_1 \succsim_{(\sim)} t_2$". However, most existing methods and tools for the generation of orders and of polynomial interpretations can only handle *unconditional* inequalities [4,7]. To transform such conditional constraints into unconditional ones, note that any constraint "$s \succsim c \Rightarrow t \succsim c$" can be replaced by "$t \succsim s$". More generally, if one uses polynomial orders, then any constraint "$s_1 \succsim_{(\sim)} s_2 \Rightarrow t_1 \succsim_{(\sim)} t_2$" can be replaced by "$[t_1] - [t_2] \geq [s_1] - [s_2]$". So in Ex. 13, instead of (39) and (40), we would require $[\mathsf{F}(\mathsf{true}, \mathsf{s}(\mathsf{s}(i)), \mathsf{s}(\mathsf{s}(j)), 0)] \geq [\mathsf{F}(\mathsf{true}, \mathsf{s}(i), \mathsf{s}(j), 0)]$ and $[\mathsf{F}(\mathsf{true}, \mathsf{s}(u), n, \mathsf{s}(m))] \geq [\mathsf{F}(\mathsf{true}, u, n, m)]$.

In practice, it is not recommendable to fix the reduction pair $(\succsim, \succ)$ in advance and to check the validity of the constraints of the reduction pair processor afterwards. Instead, one should leave the reduction pair open and first simplify the constraints of the reduction pair processor using the above inference rules. Afterwards, one uses the existing techniques to generate a reduction pair (e.g., based on integer polynomial interpretations) satisfying the resulting constraints.

More precisely, we start the following procedure REDUCTION_PAIR($\mathcal{P}$) with $\mathcal{P} = DP(\mathcal{R})$. If REDUCTION_PAIR($DP(\mathcal{R})$) returns "*Yes*", then innermost termination is proved. Of course, this procedure can be refined by also applying other DP processors than just the reduction pair processor to $\mathcal{P}$.

Procedure REDUCTION_PAIR($\mathcal{P}$)

1. If $\mathcal{P} = \varnothing$ then stop and return "*Yes*".
2. Choose non-empty subsets $\mathcal{P}_\succ \subseteq \mathcal{P}$ and $\mathcal{P}_{bound} \subseteq \mathcal{P}$. Let $\mathcal{P}_{\succsim} = \mathcal{P} \setminus \mathcal{P}_\succ$.
3. Generate the following constraint φ (where $\succsim$ and $\succ$ are *not yet fixed*):

$$\bigwedge_{s \to t \in \mathcal{P}_\succ,\, u \to v \in \mathcal{P}} (t = u' \Rightarrow s \succ t) \land \bigwedge_{s \to t \in \mathcal{P}_{bound},\, u \to v \in \mathcal{P}} (t = u' \Rightarrow s \succsim \mathsf{c}) \land$$
$$\bigwedge_{s \to t \in \mathcal{P}_{\succsim},\, u \to v \in \mathcal{P}} (t = u' \Rightarrow s \succsim t) \land \bigwedge_{\ell \to r \in \mathcal{U}(\mathcal{P})} (\ell \succsim r)$$

4. Use Rules (I) - (VII) to transform φ to a constraint φ' without "=".
5. Generate an integer polynomial interpretation satisfying φ', cf. e.g. [7].
6. If REDUCTION_PAIR($\mathcal{P}_\succsim$) = "*Yes*" and REDUCTION_PAIR($\mathcal{P} \setminus \mathcal{P}_{bound}$) = "*Yes*", then return "*Yes*". Otherwise, return "*Maybe*".

---

5   Conclusion

We have extended the reduction pair processor of the DP method in order to handle TRSs that terminate because of bounded increase. To be able to measure the *increase* of arguments, we permitted the use of general reduction pairs (e.g., based on integer polynomial interpretations). Moreover, to exploit the *bounds* given by conditions, we developed a calculus based on induction which simplifies the constraints needed for the reduction pair processor.

We implemented the new reduction pair processor of Cor. 15 in our termination prover AProVE [9]. To demonstrate the power of our method, [11] contains a collection of typical TRSs with bounded increase. These include examples with non-boolean (possibly nested) functions in the bound, examples with combinations of bounds, examples containing increasing or decreasing defined symbols, examples with bounds on lists, examples with different increases in different arguments, increasing TRSs that go beyond the shape of functional programs, etc. Although AProVE was the most powerful tool for termination analysis of TRSs in the *International Competition of Termination Tools*, up to now AProVE (as well as all other tools participating in the competition) failed on all TRSs from our collection. In contrast, with the results from this paper, the new version of AProVE can prove innermost termination for all of them. Thus, these results represent a substantial advance in automated termination proving. To experiment with our implementation, the new version of AProVE can be accessed via the web at http://aprove.informatik.rwth-aachen.de/eval/Increasing/.

References

1. Arts, T., Giesl, J.: Termination of term rewriting using dependency pairs. Theoretical Computer Science 236, 133–178 (2000)
2. Baader, F., Nipkow, T.: Term Rewriting and All That. Cambridge (1998)
3. Brauburger, J., Giesl, J.: Termination analysis by inductive evaluation. In: Kirchner, C., Kirchner, H. (eds.) Automated Deduction - CADE-15. LNCS (LNAI), vol. 1421, pp. 254–269. Springer, Heidelberg (1998)
4. Contejean, E., Marché, C., Tomás, A.P., Urbain, X.: Mechanically proving termination using polynomial interpretations. J. Aut. Reason. 34(4), 325–363 (2005)
5. Cook, B., Podelski, A., Rybalchenko, A.: Terminator: Beyond safety. In: Ball, T., Jones, R.B. (eds.) CAV 2006. LNCS, vol. 4144, pp. 415–418. Springer, Heidelberg (2006)
6. Fernández, M.-L.: Relaxing monotonicity for innermost termination. Information Processing Letters 93(3), 117–123 (2005)
7. Fuhs, C., Giesl, J., Middeldorp, A., Schneider-Kamp, P., Thiemann, R., Zankl, H.: SAT solving for termination analysis with polynomial interpretations. In: Marques-Silva, J., Sakallah, K.A. (eds.) SAT 2007. LNCS, vol. 4501, Springer, Heidelberg (2007)
8. Giesl, J., Thiemann, R., Schneider-Kamp, P.: The dependency pair framework: Combining techniques for automated termination proofs. In: Baader, F., Voronkov, A. (eds.) LPAR 2004. LNCS (LNAI), vol. 3452, pp. 301–331. Springer, Heidelberg (2005)
9. Giesl, J., Thiemann, R., Schneider-Kamp, P.: AProVE 1.2: Automatic termination proofs in the DP framework. In: Furbach, U., Shankar, N. (eds.) IJCAR 2006. LNCS (LNAI), vol. 4130, pp. 281–286. Springer, Heidelberg (2006)
10. Giesl, J., Thiemann, R., Schneider-Kamp, P., Falke, S.: Mechanizing and improving dependency pairs. Journal of Automated Reasoning 37(3), 155–203 (2006)

11. Giesl, J., Thiemann, R., Swiderski, S., Schneider-Kamp, P.: Proving termination by bounded increase. Technical Report AIB-2007-03, RWTH Aachen (2007) Available from http://aib.informatik.rwth-aachen.de
12. Hirokawa, N., Middeldorp, A.: Automating the dependency pair method. Information and Computation 199(1,2), 172–199 (2005)
13. Hirokawa, N., Middeldorp, A.: Tyrolean termination tool: Techniques and features. Information and Computation 205(4), 474–511 (2007)
14. Lankford, D.: On proving term rewriting systems are Noetherian. Technical Report MTP-3, Louisiana Technical University, Ruston, LA, USA (1979)
15. Manolios, P., Vroon, D.: Termination analysis with calling context graphs. In: Ball, T., Jones, R.B. (eds.) CAV 2006. LNCS, vol. 4144, pp. 401–414. Springer, Heidelberg (2006)
16. Marché, C., Zantema, H.: The termination competition. In: Proc. RTA '07 (to appear)

Certified Size-Change Termination

Alexander Krauss

Technische Universität München, Institut für Informatik
http://www.in.tum.de/~krauss

Abstract. We develop a formalization of the Size-Change Principle in Isabelle/HOL and use it to construct formally certified termination proofs for recursive functions automatically.

1 Introduction

Program termination plays an important role in verification, and in particular in theorem provers based on logics of total functions, where termination proofs are usually necessary to ensure logical consistency.

Although there has been continuous progress in the field of automated termination proofs, only few of the results have been applied to interactive theorem proving. One possible reason is that many existing methods are relatively complex, often combining several different criteria and heuristics. Another is that they do not usually produce proofs that can be checked by an independent system. This makes their integration difficult, especially when following the LCF approach, where all inferences must be checkable by a minimal logical core.

In this paper, we formalize the size-change principle [14] and prove it correct in Isabelle/HOL [16]. Then we apply it to recursive function definitions in the logic itself, essentially following an approach by Manolios and Vroon [15], but with full proofs. We integrate the results to a fully automated proof procedure to certify size-change termination of Isabelle/HOL functions.

To our knowledge, this is the first formalization of the size-change principle, and also the first mechanically verified implementation. Our results show that it is practically feasible to combine the power of state-of-the-art termination criteria with the high assurance of LCF-style theorem proving. Moreover, we think that the formalization also gives a better insight in the structure of termination proofs, and in particular in the relation between the analysis of Manolios and Vroon and the size-change principle.

As a practical benefit, a significant class of previously hard termination proofs are now automatic.

1.1 Size-Change Termination - Abstractly

"A program is size-change terminating iff every infinite execution of the program would cause an infinite descent in some well-founded data value." Although its first presentation by Lee, Jones and Ben-Amram [14] was in the context of a

F. Pfenning (Ed.): CADE 2007, LNAI 4603, pp. 460–475, 2007.
© Springer-Verlag Berlin Heidelberg 2007

simple functional language, this criterion, called *size-change termination* (SCT), is independent from the actual language or programming paradigm used.

We will emphasize this generality, which leads to a neat abstraction boundary in our formalization, by using slightly more general terminology than the original paper.

SCT abstracts from the actual program by viewing it as a set of *control points* and transitions between them, forming a directed graph (the *control graph*). Each control point has a finite set of abstract *data positions* associated to it, which can be seen as slots, where runtime data is passed around.

Each transition is labeled by a *size-change graph*, which contains information about how the values in the data positions are related. The size-change graph contains an edge $p \xrightarrow{\downarrow} q$, if the value at data position q (after the transition) is always smaller than the value at position p (before the transition), and $p \xrightarrow{\overline{\mp}} q$ if it is smaller or equal. Size-change graphs are usually drawn as bipartite graphs. Fig. 1 shows a simple graph with two control points A and B, with two and three data positions.

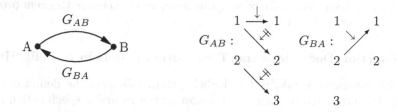

Fig. 1. A simple size-change problem

By connecting the size-change graphs along a control flow path, the data flow becomes visible. Chains of such connected edges are called *threads*. A thread has infinite descent iff it contains infinitely many $\xrightarrow{\downarrow}$-edges.

Definition. *A control graph $\mathcal{A}$ satisfies SCT iff every infinite path has a thread with infinite descent.*

The example in Fig. 1 satisfies SCT, since the only infinite path is $A, B, A, B, \ldots$ and it has a thread going through data positions $1, 2, 1, 2, \ldots$, which has infinite descent.

SCT is decidable:

Theorem. *A control graph $\mathcal{A}$ satisfies SCT iff for every edge in $\mathcal{A}^+$ of the form $n \xrightarrow{G} n$ with $G = G \cdot G$, G has an edge of the form $p \xrightarrow{\downarrow} p$.*

Here, $\mathcal{A}^+$ denotes the transitive closure of $\mathcal{A}$, where the composition of two graphs is defined in the obvious way (for details see §2). This theorem suggests an algorithm which simply computes the transitive closure and checks the above property.

Since SCT is a purely combinatorial graph problem, generating size-change problems from programs is a separate issue.

Here lies the power of the abstraction: Since nothing is said about what the control points and data positions actually are, we can talk about different types of programs. The original paper treated simple functional programs, and used functions as control points. Function calls were the transitions, and the data positions were given by the sizes of the function arguments. For imperative programs, one could take program instructions as control points and program variables as data positions.

Other interpretations are equally valid, as long as (a) infinite executions of the program correspond to infinite paths in the control graph, and (b) the information in the size-change graphs reflects actual size-changes in some well-founded data. Then a non-terminating execution would imply an infinitely decreasing sequence of data values, which is impossible.

Since the $\overset{\top}{\to}$- and $\overset{\downarrow}{\to}$-edges in a size-change graph reflect knowledge about the data flow in the program, a suitable analysis is required to derive this information. The authors of [14] apparently had some syntactic size analysis in mind, but in fact we have the choice of weapons here, and we choose theorem proving, which does very well on this task.

1.2   Function Definitions and Termination Proofs in Isabelle/HOL

Recursive functions are defined in Isabelle/HOL following the definitional approach: An automated package [13] transforms the recursive specification into a non-recursive form, which can be processed by existing means. Then the original specification is proved from this definition. Internally, the package constructs the call relation of the function and a domain predicate characterizing values where the function terminates.

Although the package has some support for partial (i.e. non-terminating) functions (for details, see [13]), reasoning with partial functions is more complicated than with total ones. Specifically, the recursive equations are constrained by the domain predicate.

Now "proving termination" just means showing that the domain predicate is always true or, equivalently, that the call relation is wellfounded.

1.3   No Simple Certificates

Things would be simpler and more elegant, if we could just generate short certificates of some kind, which can be easily checked and which prove that a function is size-change terminating. Then just the checking would have to be proved correct and executed in the theorem prover, while the certificates could be generated by untrusted (but probably more efficient) code.

However, by a complexity argument, such certificates are unlikely to exist, due to the PSPACE-hardness result for SCT [14]:

Corollary 1. *If there were certificates proving* $x \in SCT$ *that could be checked in polynomial time, then* $PSPACE = NP$, *which complexity theorists find unlikely [18].*

Proof. Assume such certificates exist, then SCT $\in$ NP by a simple guess-and-check argument. But SCT is PSPACE-hard, thus PSPACE $\subseteq$ NP.

This result shows that size-change termination is fundamentally different from many other methods in that it does not produce simple and short termination arguments (like simple wellfounded relations). Instead, it is more like an exhaustive search for possible sources of non-termination, ruling them out systematically.

1.4 Related Work

The quest for automated termination proofs is continously receiving a large amount of attention, way too much to be cited here.

But when it comes to full formal certification of termination proofs, the air gets thin: Termination proofs in major proof assistants like Coq [4], PVS [17] and Isabelle are usually based on user-specified measure functions. HOL4 [7], HOL Light [10] and ACL2 [11] support a rudimentary automatic guessing of measures.

Recently, Manolios and Vroon [15] successfully combined the size-change principle with theorem proving to obtain a powerful termination checker for the ACL2 system. They make the following modifications to standard SCT:

- Instead of using the functions as control points, they used the function calls and also take the context of a recursive call into account. This allows to analyze reachability between calls.
- Instead of using a syntactic analysis to generate size-change graphs, they use the ACL2 prover.
- Instead of just looking at the size of concrete data values, they are able to use arbitrary measure functions.
- In an additional processing step, calls can be substituted into one another. This step (called *context merging*) allows for a limited treatment of problems where a temporary increase of data happens.

However, the non-trivial analysis is part of the trusted code base and even if the metatheory is sound, it is not clear if it can be justified within the first-order framework of ACL2. In this paper, we essentially follow their approach (excluding context merging), but we formally verify both the underlying theory and the implementation, which allows us to produce Isabelle proofs.

The CoLoR project [5] aims to provide the formal basis and the tools to certify termination proofs in Coq. Proofs can be imported from various other systems, all from the area of term rewriting. However, since these tools only work on a formalization of term rewriting inside Coq, they cannot easily be applied to Coq function definitions.

1.5 Overview of This Paper

In §2, we describe a formalization of the size-change principle. We formalize Kleene algebras, graphs, paths and threads and define the SCT predicate. Then we present the main theorem, which states the equivalence between the declarative and the algorithmic version of SCT.

In §3, we apply the principle to Isabelle function definitions: We formalize what it means that a control graph approximates a relation. Then we show that for such an approximation, the size-change property implies wellfoundedness of that relation.

It then remains to provide an algorithm for building and inspecting the transitive closure of a graph. In §4 we give a simple implementation and prove it correct. From these three ingredients we obtain a fully automated method to prove termination of recursive functions in Isabelle.

We present some small example applications in §5 and discuss practical implications in §6.

2   Formalizing SCT

2.1   Kleene Algebras

Since the core of SCT checking is the computation of a transitive closure, we will start by defining an axiomatic type class [20] of Kleene algebras, which provide the most general structure for such an operation. With this approach, the formulation of the algorithm is kept seperate from the concrete data structures.

Following the axiomatization by Kozen [12], Kleene algebras are idempotent semirings with an order defined as $(a \leq b) = (a + b = b)$. Additionally, they include a star-operation satisfying the following four laws:

$$1 + a \cdot a^* \leq a^* \qquad\qquad a \cdot x \leq x \implies a^* \cdot x \leq x$$
$$1 + a^* \cdot a \leq a^* \qquad\qquad x \cdot a \leq x \implies x \cdot a^* \leq x$$

These axioms follow from a stronger property, called *-continuity:

$$a \cdot b^* \cdot c = (SUP\ n.\ a \cdot b^n \cdot c)$$

where b^n denotes iterated multiplication. We define transitive closures as $a^+ = a^* \cdot a$.

In §4, we will give the transitive closure algorithm in terms of arbitrary Kleene algebras, which allows us to reason in a very abstract way, using simple algebraic laws. Since our graphs will be special Kleene algebras, the corresponding theorems simply follow as instances.

2.2   Graphs

We represent directed edge-labeled graphs as sets of triples. Graphs may have self-edges, and between two nodes there may be several edges:

datatype. $(\alpha,\ \beta)\ graph = \quad Graph\ ((\alpha \times \beta \times \alpha)\ set)$

Instead of using the set type directly, we wrap graphs into their own type constructor. This will allow us to use axiomatic type classes to overload common notation for graph composition (written as multiplication), exponentiation and transitive closure. We write $x \xrightarrow{\;e\;}_{G} y$ if G has an edge between nodes x and y, which is labeled with e. If we do not care about the label, we just write $x \xrightarrow{}_{G} y$.

If the type of the edges has a multiplication and unit operation, these can be lifted to graphs, preserving monoid structure:

$$p \xrightarrow{\;b\;}_{G \cdot H} q \;\;=\;\; \exists k\, e\, e'.\, p \xrightarrow{\;e\;}_{G} k \xrightarrow{\;e'\;}_{H} q \wedge b = e \cdot e'$$

$$p \xrightarrow{\;b\;}_{1} q \;\;=\;\; p = q \wedge b = 1$$

With addition defined as set union, we get a semiring structure with additive and multiplicative identity. Moreover, by taking the corresponding set operations for supremum and infimum, graphs form a complete lattice and we can define the star operation as $G^* = (SUP\ n.\ G^n)$. It is then not hard to show that graphs form a (*-continuous) Kleene algebra.

2.3   Paths

We represent infinite paths as sequences of node-edge-pairs:

types α *sequence* $=$ *nat* $\Rightarrow \alpha$
    $(\alpha,\, \beta)$ *ipath* $=$ $(\alpha \times \beta)$ *sequence*

The paths of a graph G are characterized by the predicate *has-ipath*:

has-ipath   :: $(\alpha,\, \beta)$ *graph* $\Rightarrow (\alpha,\, \beta)$ *ipath* $\Rightarrow$ *bool*
has-ipath $G\ p = (\forall i.\ fst\ (p\ i) \xrightarrow{\;p_{[i]}\;}_{G} fst\ (p\ (i + 1)))$

Here, $p_{[i]}$ just abbreviates *snd* $(p\ i)$, yielding the value of the i-th edge in p.

For the proofs for size-change termination we also need to talk about finite paths and relate them to infinite paths (by taking sub-paths, constructing infinite paths from finite loops). We omit these details for space reasons, as they are essentially straightforward.

2.4   Size-Change Graphs

Size-change graphs have $\downarrow$ and $\bar{\top}$ as edge labels, and natural numbers as nodes, representing data positions. Control graphs have size-change graphs as their edges.

datatype *sedge* $=$ *LESS* $(\downarrow)$ | *LEQ* $(\bar{\top})$
types
  scg $=$ (*nat*, *sedge*) *graph*
  acg $=$ (*nat*, *scg*) *graph*

Given an infinite path in the control graph, a thread is a sequence of natural numbers denoting argument positions for every node in the path, such that there are corresponding connected edges. A thread is descending, if it contains infinitely many $\downarrow$-edges:

$$is\text{-}desc\text{-}thread \quad :: \quad nat \ sequence \Rightarrow (nat, \ scg) \ ipath \Rightarrow bool$$

$$is\text{-}desc\text{-}thread \ \theta \ p = ((\exists \, n. \ \forall \, i{\geq}n. \ \theta \ i \xrightarrow[p_{[i]}]{} \theta \ (i+1)) \wedge (\exists_{\infty} i. \ \theta \ i \xrightarrow[p_{[i]}]{\downarrow} \theta \ (i+1)))$$

Note that threads may also start at a later point in the path. Now the size-change property is defined as

$$SCT \ \mathcal{A} = (\forall \, p. \ has\text{-}ipath \ \mathcal{A} \ p \longrightarrow (\exists \, \theta. \ is\text{-}desc\text{-}thread \ \theta \ p))$$

The second characterization, which will be proved equivalent, is the basis of the size-change algorithm:

$$SCT_{ex} \ \mathcal{A} = (\forall \, n \ G. \ n \xrightarrow[\mathcal{A}^{+}]{G} n \wedge G{\cdot}G = G \longrightarrow (\exists \, p. \ p \xrightarrow[G]{\downarrow} p))$$

Then the following is our main equivalence result, which corresponds to [14, Thm. 4]:

Theorem 1. *finite-acg* $\mathcal{A} \Longrightarrow SCT \ \mathcal{A} = SCT_{ex} \ \mathcal{A}$

The condition *finite-acg* $\mathcal{A}$ expresses that the control graph and all its size-change graphs are finite. In the original development it is implicit.

The formal proof of Thm. 1[1] consists of about 1200 lines of proof script in the Isar structured proof language, mainly following the informal development in [14], but with many parts spelled out in much more detail. Like in the informal version, the proof uses Ramsey's Theorem, which is already present in Isabelle's Library (the formalization is due to Paulson).

Our proof uses classical logic, including the (infinite, but countable) axiom of choice. It would be interesting to investigate if the proof can be modified to work in a weaker framework.

3 Generating Size-Change Problems

We will now apply the size-change principle to termination problems of a specific form, namely the termination of recursive function definitions in Isabelle itself. For that, we must make the abstract notion of control points and data positions concrete, and give meaning to the size-change graphs and control graphs.

There are multiple possibilities for doing this. In the spirit of the original authors, we could equate control points with functions and transitions with function calls. Instead we take the same route as Manolios and Vroon [15]: We take the

---

[1] The proof can be found in recent versions of the Isabelle library.

calls as control points. A transition is a pair of calls, where one call is reachable from the other. This approach allows to analyze the recursive behaviour at a finer granularity.

As a running example, consider the following function definition[2]:

$$
\begin{aligned}
f\ (n,\ 0) &= n \\
f\ (0,\ Suc\ m) &= f\ (Suc\ m,\ Suc\ m) \\
f\ (Suc\ n,\ Suc\ m) &= f\ (m,\ n)
\end{aligned}
$$

When the definition is made, Isabelle will internally define the recursion relation (or call relation) R_f of the function. In the recursion relation, arguments of recursive calls are "smaller" than the corresponding left hand sides. In this case, R_f is defined as:

$R_f =$
$(\lambda x_1\ x_2.$
   $(\exists m.\ x_1 = (Suc\ m,\ Suc\ m) \wedge x_2 = (0,\ Suc\ m)) \vee$
   $(\exists n\ m.\ x_1 = (m,\ n) \wedge x_2 = (Suc\ n,\ Suc\ m)))$

It is our goal to show that R_f is well-founded.

3.1   Call Descriptors

Recursion relations generated from function definitions are always disjunctions of existential clauses, each corresponding to a recursive call. By providing explicit descriptions for such call relations, we will make this structure accessible to the logic.

A *call descriptor* is a triple $(\Gamma,\ r,\ l)$, which describes a recursive call in a function definition: r is the argument of the recursive call, l is the original argument (from the left hand side of the equation) and Γ is the condition under which the call occurs. All three values depend on variables (the pattern variables), which we replace by a single variable (possibly containing a tuple).

types
   $(\alpha,\ \gamma)\ cdesc \quad = \quad (\gamma \Rightarrow bool) \times (\gamma \Rightarrow \alpha) \times (\gamma \Rightarrow \alpha)$

Here, α is the argument type of the function and γ is the type of the pattern variable.

A list of call descriptors describes a relation in the obvious way:

in-cdesc   :: $(\alpha,\gamma)\ cdesc \Rightarrow \alpha \Rightarrow \alpha \Rightarrow bool$
in-cdesc $(\Gamma,\ r,\ l)\ x\ y = (\exists q.\ x = r\ q \wedge y = l\ q \wedge \Gamma\ q)$

mk-rel :: $(\alpha,\gamma)\ cdesc\ list \Rightarrow \alpha \Rightarrow \alpha \Rightarrow bool$

mk-rel $[\,]\ x\ y \qquad = False$
mk-rel $(c\ \#\ cs)\ x\ y = in\text{-}cdesc\ c\ x\ y \vee mk\text{-}rel\ cs\ x\ y$

---

[2] The function does not compute anything useful.

We can now describe R_f by such a list of call descriptors:

$R_f =$
mk-rel
$[(\lambda(m, n).\ True,\ \lambda(m, n).\ (Suc\ m,\ Suc\ m),\ \lambda(m, n).\ (0,\ Suc\ m)),$
$\ (\lambda(m, n).\ True,\ \lambda(m, n).\ (m, n),\ \lambda(m, n).\ (Suc\ n,\ Suc\ m))]$

Transforming the definition to this form is easily automated by a suitable tactic. The main task here is to determine the type of γ which must be a product large enough to express all the variables in the different clauses. The equivalence to the original version simply follows by unfolding the definitions of mk-rel and in-cdesc.

3.2 Measure Functions

To each call (i.e. each control point in the graph), we will assign a list of measure functions, which correspond to the data positions.

Measure functions capture the notion of size. The whole analysis is independent from the exact form of the measure functions. and any function mapping into a wellfounded domain can be used. For simplicity, our measure functions map into the natural numbers:

types
$\alpha\ measure\quad =\quad \alpha \Rightarrow nat$

Choosing measure functions is a separate problem not addressed here. As a default choice we use just the structural size functions which Isabelle provides for each inductive data type. Product types are split into their components. So for example for an argument type $S \times T$ we use the projections $size_S \circ fst$ and $size_T \circ snd$ as measure functions. Manolios and Vroon [15] describe some other heuristics for choosing measure functions.

3.3 Approximating the Control Graph

We will now show how to construct a size-change problem that corresponds to a relation given by a list of call descriptors.

For two call descriptors C_i and C_j, the predicate no-step is true if a C_i-call can never be followed by a C_j-call:

no-step   :: $(\alpha,\gamma)\ cdesc \Rightarrow (\alpha,\gamma)\ cdesc \Rightarrow bool$

no-step $(\Gamma_1, r_1, l_1)\ (\Gamma_2, r_2, l_2) =$
$(\forall q_1\ q_2.\ \Gamma_1\ q_1 \wedge \Gamma_2\ q_2 \wedge r_1\ q_1 = l_2\ q_2 \longrightarrow False)$

If we can prove no-step $C_i\ C_j$, then we can be sure that these calls can never occur in sequence. Otherwise we must add an edge between i and j to our control graph. This edge will carry a size change graph which approximates the size change behaviour of the call.

The predicates $step_<$ and $step_\leq$ capture strict and non-strict decrease of measures from one call to the next:

$step_<$ :: $(\alpha,\gamma)\ cdesc \Rightarrow (\alpha,\gamma)\ cdesc \Rightarrow \alpha\ measure \Rightarrow \alpha\ measure \Rightarrow bool$
$step_\leq$ :: $(\alpha,\gamma)\ cdesc \Rightarrow (\alpha,\gamma)\ cdesc \Rightarrow \alpha\ measure \Rightarrow \alpha\ measure \Rightarrow bool$

$step_< (\Gamma_1, r_1, l_1) (\Gamma_2, r_2, l_2) \ m_1 \ m_2 =$
$(\forall q_1 \ q_2. \ \Gamma_1 \ q_1 \wedge \Gamma_2 \ q_2 \wedge r_1 \ q_1 = l_2 \ q_2 \longrightarrow m_2 \ (l_2 \ q_2) < m_1 \ (l_1 \ q_1))$

$step_\leq (\Gamma_1, r_1, l_1) (\Gamma_2, r_2, l_2) \ m_1 \ m_2 =$
$(\forall q_1 \ q_2. \ \Gamma_1 \ q_1 \wedge \Gamma_2 \ q_2 \wedge r_1 \ q_1 = l_2 \ q_2 \longrightarrow m_2 \ (l_2 \ q_2) \leq m_1 \ (l_1 \ q_1))$

Now consider a size-change graph G and functions M_1 and M_2 which assign measures to the data positions of C_1 and C_2. We say that G approximates the pair of calls, if the claimed inequalities are actually satisfied by the respective measures. This is expressed by the *approx* predicate:

$approx \ :: \ scg \Rightarrow (\alpha, \gamma) \ cdesc \Rightarrow (\alpha, \gamma) \ cdesc$
$\Rightarrow (nat \Rightarrow \alpha \ measure) \Rightarrow (nat \Rightarrow \alpha \ measure) \Rightarrow bool$

$approx \ G \ C_1 \ C_2 \ M_1 \ M_2 =$
$(\forall i \ j. \ (i \xrightarrow[G]{\downarrow} j \longrightarrow step_< \ C_1 \ C_2 \ (M_1 \ i) \ (M_2 \ j)) \wedge$
$(i \xrightarrow[G]{\bar{\downarrow}} j \longrightarrow step_\leq \ C_1 \ C_2 \ (M_1 \ i) \ (M_2 \ j)))$

Now, a control graph $\mathcal{A}$ is a sound description of a given list of call descriptors and measure functions, if between any two calls, either no step is possible, or $\mathcal{A}$ contains the corresponding edge with a size-change graph approximating the call combination[3]:

$sound\text{-}desc \ :: \ acg \Rightarrow (\alpha, \gamma) \ cdesc \ list \Rightarrow (nat \Rightarrow \alpha \ measure) \ list \Rightarrow bool$

$sound\text{-}desc \ \mathcal{A} \ D \ M =$
$(\forall n < |D|. \ \forall m < |D|. \ no\text{-}step \ D_{[n]} \ D_{[m]} \vee (\exists G. \ n \xrightarrow[\mathcal{A}]{G} m \wedge approx \ G \ D_{[n]} \ D_{[m]} \ M_{[n]}$
$M_{[m]}))$

Now, it is straigtforward to prove the following:

Theorem 2. If *sound-desc* $\mathcal{A} \ D \ M$ and *SCT* $\mathcal{A}$ then *mk-rel* D is wellfounded.

With this theorem, which is basically a formal version of the results in [15], we are able to prove wellfoundedness of a relation, provided we can express it in terms of a list of call descriptors and find an $\mathcal{A}$ which satisfies *SCT* and is a sound estimation of the relation.

3.4   Building Size-Change Problems

It is not hard to build a custom proof tactic to construct $\mathcal{A}$ and prove *sound-desc* $\mathcal{A} \ D \ M$:

– For each pair of calls C_i and C_j, try to prove *no-step* $C_i \ C_j$.
– If this succeeds, no edge needs to be added to $\mathcal{A}$.

---

[3] Here, $xs_{[i]}$ denotes the i-th element of the list xs.

– If it fails, construct a size-change graph G, by proving as many of the $step_<$ and $step_\le$ estimations as possible. For each successful proof, the corresponding edge can be added to the G.

For the *"try to prove ... "* steps in the above algorithm, we simply call Isabelle's `auto` tactic, which combines rewriting, classical reasoning and some arithmetic. Of course, other proof methods could easily be plugged in here.

The result for our example function is given in Fig. 2. The $1 \overset{\downarrow}{\to} 1$ arrow in G_2 is surprising at first: The automated prover discovered that when going from C_2 to C_1, the first argument must get smaller, since for C_1, the first argument must be zero, but before it was nonzero. Also note that there is no arrow from C_1 to itself, which is essential for the termination of the function.

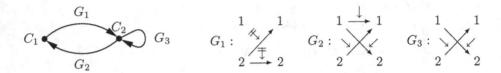

Fig. 2. The control graph and size change graphs for f

4   Implementation Prototype

Finally, an algorithm for checking the predicate SCT_{ex} (cf. §2.4) must be implemented and proved correct. We will present a naive implementation without any optimizations. While this does limit the performance of our system, it is sufficient to explain the ideas and demonstrate the overall approach.

We can use Isabelle's code generator to translate the algorithm into ML. The code generator (originally developed by Berghofer [3]) was recently redesigned by Haftmann [9] to generate code for definitions involving type classes. Type classes are compiled into dictionaries as it is done in Haskell compilers.

The code generation framework also supports the execution of functions involving (finite) sets, which are compiled to lists. By using this functionality, it takes just a few steps to produce a working prototype from our specification.

Recall that our definition of graph composition (cf. §2.2) involves existential quantification, which is of course undecidable in general. However, it is easy to make graph composition executable by proving the following equations and making them available to the code generator:

joinable $((n, e, m), (n', e', m')) = (m = n')$
connect $((n, e, m), (n', e', m')) = (n, e \cdot e', m')$
Graph $G \cdot$ *Graph* $H =$ *Graph* $(connect\ `\ \{x \in G \times H.\ joinable\ x\})$

Note that the bounded comprehension and the image operation (') are executable, as they are compiled to an expression involving *map* and *filter*.

The following function, overloaded on the type class of Kleene algebras, computes transitive closures by a simple iteration:

$mk\text{-}tcl\ A\ X = (if\ X{\cdot}A \leq X\ then\ X\ else\ mk\text{-}tcl\ A\ (X + X{\cdot}A))$

Note that $mk\text{-}tcl$ need not always terminate. However, since the SCT problems we consider are always finite, termination can be proved for these cases.

By straigtforward induction, we can prove that $mk\text{-}tcl$ computes transitive closures of finite graphs:

$finite\text{-}acg\ A \Longrightarrow mk\text{-}tcl\ A\ A = A^{+}$

Then the following function checks SCT_{ex}:

$test\text{-}SCT\ \mathcal{A} =$
$(let\ \mathcal{T} = mk\text{-}tcl\ \mathcal{A}\ \mathcal{A}$
$in\ \forall (n,\ G,\ m){\in}dest\text{-}graph\ \mathcal{T}.$
$\quad n \neq m \lor G{\cdot}G \neq G \lor (\exists (p,\ e,\ q){\in}dest\text{-}graph\ G.\ p = q \land e = \downarrow))$

where $dest\text{-}graph\ (Graph\ G) = G$.

We prove that the function is correct:

Theorem 3. $finite\text{-}acg\ \mathcal{A} \Longrightarrow SCT_{ex}\ \mathcal{A} = test\text{-}SCT\ \mathcal{A}$

Note that the bounded universal and existential quantifiers in the definition of $test\text{-}SCT$ do not prevent code generation: They are translated to the corresponding predicates on lists. Hence, $test\text{-}SCT$ can be translated to ML and executed.

4.1 Putting Everything Together

Connecting the results of the previous sections, we obtain a method to formally certify the termination of functions in Isabelle:

- Define the function as usual, and create a list of call descriptors, representing the call relation.
- Assign suitable measures to each call, and, following the steps outlined in §3.4, construct a size-change problem $\mathcal{A}$.
- Apply Thm. 2. It remains to prove $SCT\ \mathcal{A}$.
- Apply Thm. 1. By construction, $\mathcal{A}$ is finite, so it remains to show $SCT_{ex}\ \mathcal{A}$.
- Apply Thm. 3, obtaining an executable goal.
- Evaluate the goal to $True$, either using the simplifier (which is currently only feasible for small examples), or by translating to ML first.

5 Examples

While our SCT implementation handles all forms of structural recursion and their lexicographic combinations, we are most interested in examples, where simpler analyses fail. The following example is adapted from [14]:

$p\ m\ n\ r = ($if $0 < r$ then $p\ m\ (r - 1)\ n$ else if $0 < n$ then $p\ r\ (n - 1)\ m$ else $m)$

Since the argument is permuted in each recursive call, simple size measures or lexicographic combinations are not sufficient to prove termination. The function from §3 is of a similar nature.

A different example shows the ability of the analysis to detect reachability between calls. The function has a boolean argument which eventually becomes *False*, and then the recursion descends on a different argument:

foo True (Suc n) m = foo True n (Suc m)
foo True 0 m = foo False 0 m
foo False n (Suc m) = foo False (Suc n) m
foo False n 0 = n

A third example is taken from the WST termination competition problem database [2]. The key observation here is that a recursive call can never occur more than once, which is again detected by the reachability analysis between calls, which yields a control graph with no edges.

bar 0 (Suc n) m = bar m m m
bar (Suc v) n m = 0
bar k 0 m = 0

These examples have a certain artificial flavour, as their only reason of existence seems to be to demonstrate termination proofs. So are there also practical examples where size change termination is useful?

The following example comes from a formalization of a descision procedure for equalities in a commutative ring, adapted from similar work in Coq [8] (the Isabelle version was done by Bernhard Häupler). The function adds two polynomials, represented by a datatype with three constructors Pc, Pinj and PX:

add (Pc a) (Pc b) = Pc (a + b)

add (Pc c) (Pinj i P) = Pinj i (add P (Pc c))

add (Pc c) (PX P i Q) = PX P i (add Q (Pc c))

add (Pinj x P) (Pinj y Q) =
(if x = y then mkPinj x (add P Q)
 else if y < x then mkPinj y (add (Pinj (x − y) P) Q)
   else add (Pinj y Q) (Pinj x P))

add (Pinj x P) (PX Q y R) =
(if x = 0 then add P (PX Q y R)
 else if x = 1 then PX Q y (add P R) else PX Q y (add (Pinj (x − 1) P) R))

add (PX P_1 x P_2) (PX Q_1 y Q_2) =
(if x = y then mkPX (add P_1 Q_1) x (add P_2 Q_2)
 else if y < x then mkPX (add (PX P_1 (x − y) (Pc 0)) Q_1) y (add P_2 Q_2)
   else add (PX Q_1 y Q_2) (PX P_1 x P_2))

add (Pinj i P) (Pc c) = add (Pc c) (Pinj i P)

add (PX P i Q) (Pc c) = add (Pc c) (PX P i Q)

add (PX Q y R) (Pinj x P) = add (Pinj x P) (PX Q y R)

In the underlined cases the function just calls itself with permuted arguments. This avoids duplicating the code from other clauses – a sensible programming pattern for commutative functions. However, without an analysis dealing with argument permutation, it is extremely hard to convince Isabelle to accept this definition, which is why the function had to be rewritten in the original version, just for the sake of the termination proof, resulting in significant code duplication.

Note that such duplication does not only concern the function specification, but will turn up again in induction proofs about the function, as the induction rule is generated from the definition. This leads to redundant cases, whose "analogous" proofs have to be copy-and-pasted.

With our prototype, we could automatically prove termination of *add*.

6   Discussion

6.1   Scope of the Method

It is hard to describe the class of problems that can be solved by our tool. While SCT itself is well-understood, the success of the overall method also depends on the quality of the estimations in the size change graphs, which is again determined by the capabilities of Isabelle's `auto` tactic.

While this makes it hard to predict if the method will succeed on a given problem, the advantage is that `auto` can make use of lemmas already present in the current theory. Most static analyses would have a hard time speculating and proving these lemmas, especially when induction is required. In Isabelle, such lemmas can be provided by the user and then used by automated tools.

This shows how interactive theorem proving and automated methods can benefit from each other, when combined: The user can help establishing difficult lemmas and SCT, with its strengths in combinatorics, provides the automated path analysis.

6.2   Practical Applications

Manolios and Vroon tested their system against a large corpus of ACL2 definitions, and observed an impressive gain in automation.

Interestingly, when looking at the function definitions in the current Isabelle distribution and the Archive of Formal Proofs [1], most of the definitions can already be handled by a much simpler search for lexicographic orderings [6]. SCT does solve all these problems, but its real strengths are not used.

A possible explanation could be that users, knowing about Isabelle's limitations in that area, tried to avoid function definitions that would require a difficult manual termination proof, and used other modeling techniques like inductive relations instead. It remains to see whether this changes when SCT becomes generally available in Isabelle. But the *add* function discussed above already shows the potential of SCT.

6.3 Efficiency

Especially in the light of the PSPACE-hardness result, efficiency is a concern. In our setup, there are two critical operations:

First, in order to approximate the size-change problem, many proof goals must be generated and tried by the automated prover, one for each possible edge in each size-change graph. For the *add* function this takes about 2 minutes on a 1GHz laptop. As an improvement, one can implement a more efficient tactic, which is specialized on the kind of inequalities that actually occur, or add a heuristic to filter out subgoals that are likely to be unprovable.

Second, computing the transitive closure can take long. However, our minimalistic implementation represents graphs very inefficiently using sets (implemented by lists). First experiments showed that a better representation (e.g. matrices, implemented by quadtrees) leads to a significant speedup and we plan to integrate such an algorithm soon. Note that the proofs of the metatheory (§2) need not be changed.

7 Conclusion

By formalizing the size-change principle, we made an important termination criterion available for Isabelle. The implemented algorithm is only a proof-of-concept, but it should not be difficult to develop and integrate a more efficient implementation.

Recursive functions are an important application, but they are not the only one: It would be interesting work to apply SCT to other sorts of termination problems. One example is the framework for hoare-logic style verification of imperative programs [19], where termination proofs for loops and recursive procedures currently also need a user-specified well-founded relation. In fact, due to the modularity of SCT, much of the present work should be reusable with little or no change.

Acknowledgements. I want to thank Tobias Nipkow, Christian Sternagel and Lukas Bulwahn for helpful comments on a previous draft of this paper, and Amine Chaieb for pointing me to the *add* example. The anonymous referees provided valuable feedback.

References

1. Archive of Formal Proofs. http://afp.sourceforge.net/
2. Termination Competition.
   http://www.lri.fr/~marche/termination-competition/
3. Berghofer, S., Nipkow, T.: Executing higher order logic. In: Callaghan, P., Luo, Z., McKinna, J., Pollack, R. (eds.) TYPES 2000. LNCS, vol. 2277, pp. 24–40. Springer, Heidelberg (2002)
4. Bertot, Y., Castéran, P.: Interactive theorem proving and program development: Coq'Art: the calculus of inductive constructions. In: Texts in theoretical comp. science, Springer, Heidelberg (2004)

5. Blanqui, F., Coupet-Grimal, S., Delobel, W., Hinderer, S., Koprowski, A.: CoLoR, a Coq library on rewriting and termination. In: Geser, A., Søndergaard, H. (eds.) Eighth International Workshop on Termination, WST'06, Seattle, WA, USA (2006)
6. Bulwahn, L., Krauss, A., Nipkow, T.: Finding Lexicographic Orders for Termination Proofs in Isabelle/HOL. To appear at TPHOLs 2007 (2007)
7. Gordon, M., Melham, T.: Introduction to HOL: A theorem proving environment for higher order logic. Cambridge University Press, Cambridge (1993)
8. Grégoire, B., Mahboubi, A.: Proving equalities in a commutative ring done right in Coq. In: Hurd, J., Melham, T. (eds.) TPHOLs 2005. LNCS, vol. 3603, pp. 98–113. Springer, Heidelberg (2005)
9. Haftmann, F., Nipkow, T.: A design for a generic code generator for the Isabelle/HOL system, Manuscript (2007)
10. Harrison, J.: The HOL Light theorem prover.
    http://www.cl.cam.ac.uk/users/jrh/hol-light
11. Kaufmann, M., Manolios, P., Moore, J S.: Computer-Aided Reasoning: An Approach. Kluwer Academic Publishers, Boston (2000)
12. Kozen, D.: On Kleene algebras and closed semirings. In: Rovan, B. (ed.) Mathematical Foundations of Computer Science 1990. LNCS, vol. 452, pp. 26–47. Springer, Heidelberg (1990)
13. Krauss, A.: Partial recursive functions in higher-order logic. In: Furbach, U., Shankar, N. (eds.) IJCAR 2006. LNCS (LNAI), vol. 4130, pp. 589–603. Springer, Heidelberg (2006)
14. Lee, C.S., Jones, N.D., Ben-Amram, A.M.: The size-change principle for program termination. In: ACM Symposium on Principles of Prog. Languages, pp. 81–92 (2001)
15. Manolios, P., Vroon, D.: Termination analysis with calling context graphs. In: Ball, T., Jones, R.B. (eds.) CAV 2006. LNCS, vol. 4144, pp. 401–414. Springer, Heidelberg (2006)
16. Nipkow, T., Paulson, L.C., Wenzel, M.: Isabelle/HOL. LNCS, vol. 2283. Springer, Heidelberg (2002)
17. Owre, S., Rushby, J.M., Shankar, N.: PVS: A prototype verification system. In: Kapur, D. (ed.) Automated Deduction - CADE-11. LNCS, vol. 607, pp. 748–752. Springer, Heidelberg (1992)
18. Papadimitriou, C.H.: Computational Complexity. Addison-Wesley, New York (1994)
19. Schirmer, N.: A verification environment for sequential imperative programs in Isabelle/HOL. In: Baader, F., Voronkov, A. (eds.) LPAR 2004. LNCS (LNAI), vol. 3452, pp. 398–414. Springer, Heidelberg (2005)
20. Wenzel, M.: Using axiomatic type classes in Isabelle, Isabelle documentation (2000)

Encoding First Order Proofs in SAT

Todd Deshane, Wenjin Hu, Patty Jablonski, Hai Lin, Christopher Lynch,
and Ralph Eric McGregor

Clarkson University

Abstract. We present a method for proving rigid first order theorems
by encoding them as propositional satisfiability problems. We encode the
existence of a first order connection tableau and the satisfiability of unification constraints. Then the first order theorem is rigidly unsatisfiable
if and only if the encoding is propositionally satisfiable. We have implemented this method in our theorem prover CHEWTPTP, and present
experimental results. This method can be useful for general first order
problems, by continually adding more instances of each clause.

1 Introduction

There are two strands of thought in first order theorem proving today. One
line of research is to design general theorem provers which address all of first
order logic. The second line is to design general purpose algorithms for decidable
problems and combine them together. In this paper, we attempt to design an
efficient algorithm for the specialized rigid theorem proving problem, which can
be used as an end in itself, or can be used incrementally to address all of first
order logic.

In standard refutational theorem proving problems we attempt to prove the
unsatisfiability of a set of clauses, and allow an unbounded number of renamed
instances of each clause. In rigid theorem proving, only one instance of each
clause is allowed. Rigid theorem proving has been studied as early as [20,1], and
is used in some tableau style theorem provers[12]. In this case, the rigid theorem
proving problem is used as a means of solving the general theorem proving
problem. But, as we argue in [8] the rigid theorem proving problem is useful in
itself for modeling behavior that only occurs a bounded number of times, such
as cryptographic protocols with a bounded number of sessions.

The most impressive success recently in theorem proving has been the efficiency of SAT solving methods based on the DPLL method[7]. The success of
these methods seems to be based on the fact that the search space is defined in
advance. This means that an exponential number of possibilities can be explored
in polynomial space. It also means that the data structures can be predetermined
in such a way that the algorithm can access everything efficiently. In this paper,
we try to take advantage of such techniques in first order theorem proving. The
obvious idea is to try to incorporate a SAT solver, and also to use it in such
a way that it is not called often, because calling it too many times loses the
advantages mentioned above.

F. Pfenning (Ed.): CADE 2007, LNAI 4603, pp. 476–491, 2007.

In our method, we encode a proof of first order unsatisfiability with propositional clauses. Obviously, we cannot encode full first order unsatisfiability, since that is an undecidable problem. So we chose to encode rigid first order satisfiability. In order to do this, we need to decide what kind of proof should be encoded. One possibility would be to encode a resolution proof, as has been done in [16], although in that paper propositional proofs were encoded and not first order proofs. We chose instead to encode a connection tableau proof. The reason we chose this method is because the number of clauses that are encoded remains fixed for connection tableau whereas resolution proofs introduce clauses not contained in the original set. For that reason, we think a SAT solver will be more directed in the encoding of a connection tableau proof, as opposed to a resolution proof.

Given a propositional encoding of a rigid connection tableau proof (which we describe in this paper), the encoding is sent to a SAT solver (we used MiniSat[9]) which will return RIGIDLY SATISFIABLE if a rigid connection tableau exits, and RIGIDLY UNSATISFIABLE if a closed rigid connection tableau does not exist. If satisfiable, we can recover the tableau from the truth assignment returned by the SAT solver.

The idea of the encoding is the following. We encode the existence of a clause as the root of the connection tableau. We encode the fact that every literal assigned to a non-leaf node is extended with a clause containing a complementary literal. Those things are easy to encode, and do not take up much space. There are three things which are more costly to encode.

First, we must encode the fact that two literals are complementary, in other words that their corresponding atoms are unifiable. For that, we basically have to encode a unification algorithm. In our encoding of unification, we leave out the occurs check, because it is expensive, and because it rarely occurs. We add a check for this after the SAT solver returns the truth assignment. If there really is an occurs check, we add a propositional clause and call MiniSat again.

Second, the above encoding leaves open the possibility that the connection tableau is infinite. Therefore, we must encode the fact that the connection tableau is finite, i.e., that the connection tableau contains no cycle.

Third, we must encode the fact that every literal assigned to a leaf node is closed by a previous literal. Our encoding is simpler for the Horn case, because it is only necessary to close a literal with the previous one on the branch. For the non-Horn case, we must encode the fact that there is a complementary literal higher up in the tree. Since the same clause may occur on two different branches, and a literal on that clause may close with different literals on different branches, we may need to add more than one copy of a clause in the rigid non-Horn case, because of the fact that the literal is closed differently. But we still try to get as much structure sharing in our tree as possible. Note that rigid Horn clause satisfiability is NP-complete, but Rigid non-Horn clause satisfiability is Σ_2^p-complete[11]. So it is not surprising that a SAT solver cannot solve rigid non-Horn clause satisfiability directly.

The original contributions in this paper are to define an encoding of closed rigid connection tableau proofs as a SAT problem; provide rigid-horn, rigid/non-horn, and non-rigid algorithms and proofs of their completeness and soundness; and discuss our implementation along with initial experimental results.

2 Preliminaries

2.1 First Order Logic

We use standard notation to represent classical first order logic formula. Our alphabet consists of variables, constants, functions symbols, predicates, the quantifiers $\forall$ (universal) and $\exists$ (existential), logical connectives $\vee$ (disjunction),$\wedge$ (conjunction), $\neg$ (negation) and parentheses. Terms are defined inductively as follows. Variables and constants are terms. If f is a function with arity n and $t_1..t_n$ are terms then $f(t_1, ..., t_n)$ is a term. Atoms are of the form $P(t_1, ...t_n)$ where P is a predicate of arity n and $t_1, ..., t_n$ are zero or more terms. A literal is defined as a positive or negative atom and a clause is a disjunction of literals. We consider a formula to be constructed from elements in the alphabet according to the standard rules for constructing formula. See [4] for a detailed description of first order logic and a background discussion on the validity of a first order logic formula.

We consider a literal to be ground if it contains no variables. And we define a Horn clause as a clause which contains at most one positive literal. A clause which contains only negative literals is called a negative clause.

A formula is in conjunctive normal form (CNF) if it is a conjunction of literals such that negations are applied only to atoms and all variables are universally quantified.

A substitution σ for F is a map from the set of variables of F to a set of terms. We can view a substitution as a set of equations $x = t$ where x is a variable and t is a term. We call a single equation of a substitution σ an *assignment of σ*. Given a substitution σ, an application of σ on a formula F is denoted $F\sigma$. We say that a substitutions, σ, is a unifier of formulas G and H if $G\sigma = H\sigma$. If σ unifies G and H and for every unifier α of G and H there exists some θ such that $\sigma\theta = \alpha$ then we call σ a most general unifier (mgu) of G and H. A ground instance of G is an instance of G in which all variables are replaced by ground terms.

2.2 Propositional Logic

The alphabet for propositional logic formula consists of propositional variables and the logical connectives $\vee$ (disjunction), $\wedge$ (conjunction), $\neg$ (negation) and parentheses. As with first order logic, we will consider propositional logic formulas to be in CNF and conform to the standard rules for constructing valid propositional logic formulas[4].

2.3 Connection Tableaux

We define rigid clausal tableau as follows.

Definition 1. *Rigid clausal tableaux are trees with nodes labeled with literals, branches labeled either open or closed, and edges labeled with zero or more assignments. Rigid clausal tableaux are inductively defined as follows. Let $S = \{C_1...C_n\}$ be a set of clauses. If T is a tree consisting of a single unlabeled node (the root node) N then T is a rigid clausal tableau for S. The branch consisting of only the root node N is open. If N is a leaf node on an open branch B in the rigid clausal tableaux T for S and one of the following inference rules are applied to T then the resulting tree is a rigid clausal tableaux for S.*

(Expansion rule) Let $C_k = L_{k1} \vee ... \vee L_{ki}$ be a clause in S. Construct a new tableaux T' by adding i nodes to N and labeling them L_{k1} through L_{ki}. Label each of the i branches open.

(Closure rule) Suppose L_{ij} is the literal at N and for some predecessor node M with literal L_{pq} there exists some most general unifier σ such that $L_{ij}\sigma = \neg L_{pq}\sigma$ and the assignments of σ are consistent with the assignments of T. Construct T' from T by labeling the edge from L_{pq} to L_{ij} with the assignments used in the unification and by closing the branch of N.

We call the clause which is added to the root node the start clause and we say that a clause is *in* a tableau if the clause was used in an application of the expansion rule.

Definition 2. *A clausal tableaux is connected if each clause (except the start clause) in the tableaux contains some literal which is unifiable with the negation of its predecessor [13].*

Connection tableaux use an additional macro inference rule called the extension rule.

Definition 3. *(Extension Rule) Let N be a node in the tableau T and let C_k be a clause in S such that there exists a literal L_{ki} in C_k which is unifiable with the negation of N. Apply the expansion rule with C_k and immediately apply the closure rule with L_{ki}.*

The calculus for connection tableaux (or model elimination tableau [13]) therefore consists of the expansion rule (for the start clause only), the closure rule, and the extension rule. We call a tableau closed if each leaf node has been closed by an application of the closure rule.

By [13] we can require that the start clause be a negative clause since there exists a negative clause in any minimally satisfiable set.

2.4   Rigid Unsatisfiability

Unless otherwise stated, we let F be a set of first order logic formulas. The main problem in Automated Theorem Proving is to determine if the set of hypotheses in F implies the conclusion in F. For our purposes we assume that all formula in a problem are in CNF and the conclusion is negated. Therefore we seek to determine if F is (equivalently) unsatisfiable, i.e. there does not exist a model for

F. The problem of rigid unsatisfiability of F seeks to determine whether there exists a ground instance of F which is unsatisfiable.

A result of Tableau Theory is the completeness and soundness of closed (rigid) connection tableaux.

Theorem 1. *There exists a closed (rigid) connection tableau for F iff F is (rigidly) unsatisfiable[12].*

3 Tableau Encoding

Our method to determine the rigid satisfiability of F generates a set of propositional logic clauses for F which encodes a closed rigid connection tableau for F. We provide two encoding, the first for problems which contain only Horn clauses and the second for those containing non-Horn clauses. Given F, we give unique symbols to each of the clauses in F and each of the literals in each clause. We represent clause i by C_i. We represent the jth literal in clause i by L_{ij} (which is used to label the tableaux). Note that as multiple copies of a clause may appear in a rigid connection tableau, multiple nodes may have the same literal label. And whereas the same literal may appear in distinct clauses, they are identified with different labels. We denote A_{ij} to be the atom of L_{ij}. Therefore L_{ij} is either of the form A_{ij} or $\neg A_{ij}$.

3.1 Encoding for Horn Clauses

We define the variables c_m, l_{mn}, e_{mnq}, u_k, p_{mq} as follows: Define $c_m = T$ iff C_m appears in the tableau. Define $l_{mn} = T$ iff L_{mn} is an internal node in the tableau. Define $e_{mnq} = T$ iff C_q is an extension of L_{mn}. Define $u_\tau = T$ iff τ is an assignment implied by the substitutions used in the closure rules. Define $p_{mq} = T$ iff there exists a path from a literal in C_m to C_q.

Below we list the set of clauses that we generate and provide their meaning.

At least one clause containing only negative literals appears in the tableau:

$$\bigvee_{C_m \text{ is a negative clause}} c_m \tag{1}$$

If C_m appears in the tableau and L_{mn} is a negative literal then L_{mn} is an internal node in the tableau:

$$\neg c_m \vee l_{mn} \tag{2}$$

If L_{mn} is an internal node in the tableau then for some q_j, C_{q_j} is an extension of L_{mn}:

$$\neg l_{mn} \vee e_{mnq_1} \vee ... \vee e_{mnq_k} \tag{3}$$

where $\{C_{q_1}...C_{q_k}\}$ represents the set of all clauses whose positive literals are unifiable with L_{mn}

If C_q is an extension of L_{mn} then C_q exists in the tableau:

$$\neg e_{mnq} \vee c_q \tag{4}$$

If C_q is an extension of L_{mn} and τ is an assignment of the mgu used to unify A_{qr} with A_{mn} then τ is implied by the mgu:

$$\neg e_{mnq} \vee u_\tau \text{ where } \tau \in mgu(A_{mn}, A_{qr}) \tag{5}$$

If for two assignments $x = s$ and $x = t$ there does not exist a mgu θ such that $s\theta = t\theta$ then both assignments can not be true:

$$\neg u_{x=s} \vee \neg u_{x=t} \text{ where } s \text{ and } t \text{ are not unifiable} \tag{6}$$

If $x = s$, $x = t$, $\sigma = mgu(s,t)$ and $y = r \in \sigma$ then $y = r$:

$$\neg u_{x=s} \vee \neg u_{x=t} \vee u_{y=r} \text{ where } y = r \in mgu(s,t) \tag{7}$$

If C_q is an extension of L_{mn} then there is a path from C_m to C_q:

$$\neg e_{mnq} \vee p_{mq} \tag{8}$$

Transitivity of the path relation:

$$\neg p_{mq} \vee \neg p_{qs} \vee p_{ms} \tag{9}$$

There are no cycles in the tableau:

$$\neg p_{mm} \tag{10}$$

3.2   Encoding for Non-horn Clauses

For non-Horn problems we use an alternative set of variables and generate a different set of clauses. We say that two literals are *complementary* if they have opposite signs and their atoms are unifiable.

We define the variables s_m, c_{mn}, l_{mn}, e_{mnqj}, u_k, p_{mq}, and q_{mnij} as follows. Define $s_m = T$ iff C_m is the start clause. Define $c_{mn} = T$ iff C_m appears in the tableau and L_{mn} is used to close its parent. Define $l_{mn} = T$ iff L_{mn} is a node in the tableau and is not a leaf node created by an application of the closure rule. Define $e_{mnqj} = T$ iff C_q is an extension of L_{mn} and L_{mn} is used to close L_{qi}. Define $u_\tau = T$ iff τ is an assignment implied by the unifiers used in the applications of the closure rules. Define $o_{ijkl} = T$ iff L_{kl} is used to close L_{ij}. Define $p_{mq} = T$ iff there exists a path from a literal in C_m to C_q. Define $q_{mnij} = T$ iff L_{mn} is a leaf and L_{mn} is closed by a literal between the root node and L_{ij}.

The clauses are as follows.

There exists a start clause in the tableau which only contains negative literals:

$$\bigvee_{s_m \text{ is a negative clause}} s_m \tag{11}$$

If C_m is the start clause in the tableau then each literal L_{mn} of C_m is in the tableau:

$$\neg s_m \vee l_{mn} \tag{12}$$

If C_i appears in the tableau and L_{ij} is the complement of a literal in its parent then all other literals of C_i are in the tableau:

$$\neg c_{ij} \vee l_{ik} \text{ where } j \neq k \tag{13}$$

If L_{ij} exists in the tableau and is not a leaf node created by an application of the closure rule then either L_{ij} is closed by a literal between the root and L_{ij} or there is an extension of L_{ij}:

$$\neg l_{ij} \vee q_{ijij} \bigvee_{k,l} e_{ijkl} \tag{14}$$

If L_{ij} is extended with C_k then C_k is in the tableau and some L_{kl} of C_k is closed by L_{ij}:

$$\neg e_{ijkl} \vee c_{kl} \tag{15}$$

If clause C_m is an extension of L_{ij} and τ is an assignment of the mgu used to unify A_{ml} with A_{ij} then τ is true:

$$\neg e_{ijml} \vee u_\tau \text{ where } \tau \in mgu(A_{ml}, A_{ij}) \tag{16}$$

If for two assignments $x = s$ and $x = t$ there does not exist a mgu θ such that $s\theta = t\theta$ then both assignments can not be true:

$$\neg u_{x=s} \vee \neg u_{x=t} \text{ where } s \text{ and } t \text{ are not unifiable} \tag{17}$$

If $x = s$, $x = t$, $\sigma = mgu(s,t)$ and $y = r \in \sigma$ then $y = r$:

$$\neg u_{x=s} \vee \neg u_{x=t} \vee u_{y=r} \text{ where } y = r \in mgu(s,t) \tag{18}$$

If L_{ij} is used to close L_{kl} then their atoms must be unifiable by some unifier σ, hence each assignment of σ is true:

$$\neg o_{ijkl} \vee u_\tau \text{ where } \tau \in mgu(A_{ij}, A_{kl}) \tag{19}$$

If L_{ij} has the same sign as L_{kl} or their respective atoms are not unifiable then L_{ij} is not used to close L_{kl}:

$$\neg o_{ijkl} \text{ where } L_{ij} \text{ and } L_{kl} \text{ have the same sign or } A_{ij} \text{ and } A_{kl} \text{ are not unifiable} \tag{20}$$

If leaf L_{ij} is closed by a literal between the root and L_{kl} and clause C_k is an extension of L_{mn} then L_{ij} is closed by some literal between the root and L_{mn}:

$$\neg q_{ijkl} \vee \neg e_{mnkl} \vee o_{ijmn} \vee q_{ijmn} \tag{21}$$

If C_k is an extension of L_{ij} then there is a path from clause C_i to clause C_k:

$$\neg e_{ijkl} \vee p_{ik} \tag{22}$$

Transitivity for paths:

$$\neg p_{ij} \vee \neg p_{jk} \vee p_{ik} \tag{23}$$

There are no cycles in the tableau:

$$\neg p_{ii} \tag{24}$$

If C_i is the start clause then there are no extensions into any of the literals in C_i:

$$\neg s_i \vee \neg e_{klij} \tag{25}$$

If C_i is the start clause and L_{mn} is a leaf which is closed by a literal between the root node and L_{ij}, then L_{mn} must be closed with L_{ij}:

$$\neg s_i \vee \neg q_{mnij} \vee o_{mnij} \tag{26}$$

4   Tableau Encoding Algorithm(TE)

We provide three algorithms, each with subtle differences. The first algorithm HTE attempts to find a rigid proof and takes as an argument a problem containing only Horn clauses. The second, $NHTE$, also attempts to find a rigid proof and takes as an argument a non-Horn problem. The last algorithm, $NRTE$, seeks to finds a non-rigid proof and takes either a Horn or non-Horn problem as an argument.

The rigid algorithm for non-Horn problems may require additional copies of the clauses in F in order to generate a proof for F and the non-rigid algorithm may also require additional instances of clauses. In the case of the former, copies of clauses in F are added to the set of problem clauses. The number of copies required can be bounded by k^n where n is the number of clauses in F and k is the maximum number of literals in any clause in F. In the case of the non-rigid algorithm, new instances of clauses in F which are standardized apart are added to the problem clauses.

Each algorithm initially enters a while loop. While in the loop the set of clauses S, which encode the closed rigid connection tableau, is given to an external SAT solver. The SAT solver returns satisfiable or unsatisfiable and if the set of clauses is satisfiable, the SAT solver returns a model M. If the SAT solver returns satisfiable we check if the assignments which are assigned true in M are constent. If not, we add additional clauses to S to resolve these inconsistencies and call the SAT solver again. If the algorithm determines that S is satisfiable and the assignments which are assigned true are consistent, the algorithm returns an indication that F is rigidly unsatisfiable.

The function Unify-Substitutions takes as an argument the model M generated by the SAT solver and generates additional clauses to rectify inconsistencies in the assigments used in the proof. The only inconsistency that can occur among assignments is due to cycles. For example, $\{x_1 = f(x_2), x_2 = f(x_3), x_3 = f(x_1)\}$. If a cycle is found, a clause is created which prevents the conflict. These clauses are added to the original set of clauses generated by the algorithm which are again checked by the SAT solver.

Algorithm 1. Rigid Algorithm For Horn Problems(HTE)

Input: F, a set of FO formula in conjunctive normal form.

Output: RIGIDLY UNSATISFIABLE or RIGIDLY SATISFIABLE

HTE(F)

(1)   Generate S, the set of encodings for F
(2) $S' = \emptyset$
(3)   **while** *true*
(4)   SAT-SOLVER($S \cup S'$)
(5)   **if** SAT-Solver returns SATISFIABLE and and the assignments set true in
             M are consistent
(6)   **return** (RIGIDLY UNSATISFIABLE)
(7)   **else if** SAT-Solver returns SATISFIABLE
(8) $S' =$ UNIFY-SUBSTITUTIONS(M)
(9)   **else**
(10)   **return** (RIGIDLY SATISFIABLE)

Algorithm 2. Rigid Algorithm For Non-Horn Problems(NHTE)

Input: F, a multi-set of FO formula in conjunctive normal form.

Output: RIGIDLY UNSATISFIABLE

NHTE(F)

(1) $F' = F$
(2) $S' = \emptyset$
(3)   **while** *true*
(4)   generate S, the set of encodings for F'
(5) $M =$ SAT-SOLVER($S \cup S'$)
(6)   **if** SAT-Solver returns SATISFIABLE and the assignments set true in M
             are consistent
(7)   **return** (RIGIDLY UNSATISFIABLE)
(8)   **else if** SAT-Solver returns SATISFIABLE
(9) $S' =$ UNIFY-SUBSTITUTIONS(M)
(10)   **else**
(11) $F' = F' \cup F$

5   Completeness and Soundness Theorems for HTE

In the following proofs we refer to the sets of clauses generated by HTE by the enumeration given in Section 3.1.

Theorem 2. *(Completeness) Let F be a set of first order logic Horn clauses. If F is rigidly unsatisfiable, then HTE will return RIGIDLY UNSATISFIABLE.*

Proof. Assume F is rigidly unsatisfiable and let S be the set of clauses for F generated by HTE. As F is rigidly unsatisfiable then by Theorem 1 there exists a closed rigid connection tableaux T. It also follows that the start node of T contains only negative literals. From T we will construct a map from the variables in S to {true, false} so that S is satisfiable.

Algorithm 3. Non-Rigid Algorithm(NRTE)
Input: F, a set of FO formula in conjunctive normal form.
Output: UNSATISFIABLE
NRTE(F)
(1) $F' = F$
(2) $S' = \emptyset$
(3)   **while** 1
(4)   generate S, the set of encodings for F'
(5) $M = $ SAT-SOLVER($S \cup S'$)
(6)   **if** SAT-Solver returns SATISFIABLE and the assignments set true in M
             are consistent
(7)   **return** (UNSATISFIABLE)
(8)   **else if** SAT-Solver returns SATISFIABLE
(9) $S' = $ UNIFY-SUBSTITUTIONS(M)
(10)   **else**
(11)   generate set of new instances, A, of F using variables not occurring in
                 F'
(12) $F' = F' \cup A$

If C_m appears in the tableau set $c_m = true$ otherwise set $c_m = false$. If L_{mn} is an internal node in the tableau set $l_{mn} = true$ otherwise set $l_{mn} = false$. If C_q is an extension of L_{mn} set $e_{mnq} = true$ otherwise set $e_{mnq} = false$. If τ is an assignment implied by the unifiers used applications of the closure rule set $u_\tau = true$ otherwise set $u_\tau = false$ and if there exists a path from C_m to C_q set $p_{mq} = true$ otherwise set $p_{mq} = false$.

As T has a start node containing only negative literals, there exists a variable in Set 1 which is true. Thus Set 1 of S is satisfiable.

As T is a connection tableau and each extension of T closes the branch containing the positive literal of a clause, and since each clause contains at most one positive literal, then each negative literal in T is an interal node. Hence each variable representing a clause in T is true iff its negative literal variables are also true. Thus Set 2 is satisfiable.

Since each negative literal in T must be extended it follows that each variable representing a negative literal in T is true iff the variable representing its extension is true. Therefore Set 3 is satisfiable. Furthermore since each extension of T extends a literal to all the literals in a clause, an extension variable is true iff the clause variable associated with the extension is true. Thus Set 4 is satisfiable.

Since each extension in T unifies complementary literals, it follows that an extension variable is true iff each of the variables representing the assignments in the unifier used in the unification of the complementary literals are true. Hence Set 5 is satisfiable. It also follows by the consistency of T that inconsistent assignments can not both be true, thus for each pair of variables representing inconsistent assignments we have one is true iff the other is false. Hence Set 6 is satisfiable. In addition if two assignments map the same variable to unifiable terms s and t then the assignments used in the unification of s and t must be true. Therefore Set 7 is satisfiable.

Now as there exists paths between literals and clauses via extensions in T, if a variable representing an extension is true then the variable representing the path is true. Thus Set 8 is satisfiable. And since the paths in T have a transitive relation and no cycles exist in T, Sets 9 and 10 are satisfiable respectively.

Therefore since each of the sets of clauses in S are satisfiable, then the SAT solver called in HTE returns a satisfiable model with consistent assignments, hence HTE returns RIGIDLY UNSATISFIABLE. □

Theorem 3. *(Soundness) If HTE on F returns RIGIDLY UNSATISFIABLE then F is rigidly unsatisfiable.*

Our proof of soundness uses the satisfiability map produced by HTE to construct a tableau for F.

Proof. Suppose HTE on F returns RIGIDLY UNSATISFIABLE. Then there exists a set of clauses S generated by HTE and a model M for which S is satisfiable. Furthermore the set of assignment variables that are true in M correspond to a consistent set of assignments. We construct a closed rigid connection tableau T for F using M and S as follows.

Since S is satisfiable the clause $C = c_1 \lor ... \lor c_n$ in Set 1 of S, is satisfiable. Since C is satisfiable at least one of the variables in C are assigned true. Let c_m where $m \in [1..n]$ be a variable of C such that $c_m = true$. We begin constructing T by setting C_m as the start clause of T. [1]

Now as $c_m = true$ and Set 2 is satisfiable, each of the variables corresponding to the literals in C_m are true. Thus for each literal L_{mn} in C_m we create a node directly off the root and label it L_{mn}.

Let L_{mn} be a literal in C_m. Now as l_{mn} is true and Set 3 is satisfiable there exists some variable e_{mnq_i} which is true and as Set 4 is satisfiable $e_{mnq_i} = true$ implies $c_{q_i} = true$. We therefore expand the node labeled L_{mn} in T with clause C_{q_i}. We continue this process until all literal, clause, and extention variables which are assigned true have been addressed. By the satisfiability of Sets $2 - 4$, T is closed.

Now let e_{mnq_i} be a variable in M which is set to true. Since Set 5 is satisfiable, e_{mnq_i} implies that a set of assignments are true. We label the edge from L_{mn} to the positive literal in C_{q_i} with these assignments. Since each extension unifies adjacent complementary literals and the assignments in M are consistent, T is connected and consistent.

The satisfiability of Sets $8 - 10$ ensure that there are no cycles in T, hence T is a tree. It follows then that T is a closed connection tableau. Since each clause in T is in F, T is a closed rigid connection tableau for F. Thus by the soundness theorem for closed rigid connection tableaux, F is rigidly unsatisfiable.   □

---

[1] It may be the case that more than one variable of C is assigned true. This corresponds to the fact that there may be more than one closed rigid connection tableau for F.

6 Completeness and Soundness Theorems for NHTE

Here we provide the completeness theorem of NHTE which takes as input non-Horn problems. In the proofs, we refer to the sets of clauses generated by NHTE by the enumeration given in Section 3.2.

Theorem 4. *(Completeness) Let F be a set of first order clauses. If F is rigidly unsatisfiable, then NHTE will return RIGIDLY UNSATISFIABLE.*

Proof. Assume F is rigidly unsatisfiable and let S be the set of clauses for F generated by NHTE. By Theorem 1, as F is unsatisfiable, there exists a closed rigid connection tableaux T for F. It also follows that the start node of T contains only negative literals. Let S be the set of clauses generated by NHTE. Given T we will construct a map from the variables in S to {true, false} so that S is satisfiable.

Set $s_m = T$ iff C_m is the start clause. Set $c_{mn} = T$ iff C_m appears in the tableau and L_{mn} is closed by an application of the extension rule. Set $l_{mn} = T$ iff L_{mn} is a node in the tableau but is not closed by an application of the extension rule. Set $e_{mnqj} = T$ iff C_q is an extension of L_{mn} and L_{qj} closes L_{mn}. Set $u_\tau = T$ iff τ is a assignment implied by substitutions used in the closure rules. Set $o_{ijkl} = T$ iff L_{kl} is used to close L_{ij} but not during an application of the expansion rule. Set $p_{mq} = T$ iff there exists a path from a literal in C_m to C_q. Set $q_{mnij} = T$ iff L_{mn} is a leaf and is closed by a literal between the root node and L_{ij}.

As T has a start node containing only negative literals, there exists a variable in Set 11 which is true, thus Set 11 of S is satisfiable. Since each of the literals in the start clause are in T and are not closed by an application of the expansion rule then their respective variables are true, therefore Set 12 is satisfiable.

Now as each clause in T (except for the start clause) is the result of an expansion rule, and only one literal in each clause is closed in the process of using the expansion rule, all the other literals are in the tableau but are not closed by an application of the expansion rule. Hence Set 13 of S is satisfiable.

Suppose L_{ij} is in T such that L_{ij} is not closed by an application of the expansion rule. Then either L_{ij} is extended or L_{ij} has been closed by a complementary literal on its path. It follows that Set 14 is satisfiable.

Since each extension in T adds a clause to T, Set 15 is satisfiable. Since each extension in T unifies complementary literals, it follows that an extension variable is true iff each of the variables representing the assignments in the unifier used in the unification of the complementary literals are true. Hence Set 16 is satisfiable. It also follows by the consistency of T that inconsistent assignments cannot both be true, thus for each pair of variables representing inconsistent assignments, one is true iff the other is false. Hence Set 17 is satisfiable. In addition if two assignments map the same variable to unifiable terms s and t then the assignments used in the unification of s and t must be true. Therefore Set 18 is satisfiable.

As each pair of literals which are used in a non-extension closure are complements, if a variable representing the non-extension closure between two literals is true then the variables representing the assignments implied by unification of their atoms are true. Hence Set 19 is satisfiable. Since no two literals with have the same sign or which have atoms that are not unifiable cannot be used in a non-extension closure, Set 20 is satisfiable.

Suppose L_{ij} is a leaf and is closed by a literal between the root and L_{kl}. If the clause containing L_{kl} is an extension of some node L_{mn} then either L_{mn} is a complement of L_{ij} or L_{ij} is closed by a literal between the root node and L_{mn}. It follows that Set 21 is satisfiable.

Now as there exists paths between literals and clauses via extensions in T, if a variable representing an extension is true then the variable representing the path is true. Thus Set 22 is satisfiable. And since the paths in T have a transitive relation and no cycles exist in T, Sets 23 and 24 are satisfiable respectively.

As the start clause has no expansions into it, Set 25 is satisfiable. And since if a leaf, say L_{ij} in T is closed by a non-extension closure by a literal between the root and L_{mn} of the start clause, since there are not literals between the root and the literals of the start clause, then L_{ij} must be closed by L_{mn}. Hence Set 26 is satisfiable.

Therefore as each of the sets of clauses in S are satisfiable, then the SAT solver called in NHTE returns SATISFIABLE. It follows that as T is a tableau the assignments implied by the closure rule are consistent. Hence, NHTE returns RIGIDLY UNSATISFIABLE.

Theorem 5. *(Soundness) If NHTE on F returns RIGIDLY UNSATISFIABLE then F is rigidly unsatisfiable.*

7   CHEWTPTP Implementation

We have implemented our tableau encoding method in a command line program written in C++ called CHEWTPTP. The default options assume the input file is in TPTP CNF format[18]. By default the program assumes the input problem is non-Horn and uses the non-Horn algorithm with one instance of the clauses in the input file. The user may specify alternate settings by including the following flags. The flag -h indicates the problem is Horn, -r specifies the user wishes the program to run one of the rigid algorithms, -i allows the user to input the number of instances of the problem to use, and -p instructs the program to print a proof. Other options are provided to control input and output.

The program initially parses the input file and constructs a data structure to hold the clauses in memory. The program then constructs the sets of clauses defined in section 3. While generating the clauses, a data structure is kept which maps each variable to a unique integer. We use the integers to format the clauses in a MiniSat[9] readable format. CHEWTPTP then forks a process and invokes MiniSat on the set of generated clauses and MiniSat determines the satisfiability of the set. When MiniSat returns, we inspect the file output by MiniSat. If the file contains an indication of satisfiability we check that the substitutions are unifiable and if so, we use the model provided by MiniSat to construct a proof. If MiniSat returns back an indication of unsatisfiable, the program returns

SATISFIABLE in the rigid Horn case, and may add additional clauses and repeat the process in the other cases.

Preliminary results on 1365 Horn and non-Horn CNF problems without equality in the TPTP Library show that 221 of them have rigid proofs requiring a single instance. We have found that CHEWTPTP was able to solve some problems which many theorem provers could not within a 600 second time limit, e.g. the non-Horn problems ANA003-4.p and ANA004-4.p. And although we have not tested the library extensively by adding additional instances, CHEWTPTP was successful solving non-rigid problems that others were unable, e.g. ANA003-2 was proved with 2 instances in less than 5 seconds.

Below are some statistics on the problems mentioned above and a few other problems. The first column identifies the name of the problem in the TPTP library and the second column identifies whether or not the problem is Horn. The third column identifies the number of instances that were required to prove the problem. The fourth column gives the number of seconds CHEWTPTP took to generate the tableau encoding(s) and the fifth column gives the total time (in seconds) that MiniSat ran on the problem. The sixth and last columns give the number of clauses and variables respectively that were input to MiniSat when MiniSat returned SATISFIABLE.

Table 1. Statistics on Selected Problems

Name	Horn	Instances	Clause Gen (sec)	MiniSat (sec)	Clauses	Variables
ALG002-1	N	2	1.2	65.93	411020	13844
ANA003-2	Y	2	.1	4.88	183821	7238
ANA003-4	N	1	1.1	.06	34774	2616
ANA004-4	N	1	1.61	.3	44142	3160
COL121-2	Y	1	1.35	.16	47725	2322
GRP029-2	Y	1	.08	1.41	241272	7943
PUZ031-1	N	1	.24	.71	662145	14672

8   Conclusion

This is not the first paper to suggest an encoding of a proof in propositional logic. [16] has explored the idea of encoding a propositional resolution proof itself in propositional logic. Our emphasis is different from that paper. That paper is interested in using local search methods to find a proof. Since they are only considering propositional proofs, they do not encode unification. In our case, we encode tableau proofs, because we suspect that SAT solver will be able to direct its search better in that case.

We can also compare our recent work with recent papers on instantiation-based theorem proving, which either try to use a SAT solver to create a first order model[6], or else try to use DPLL-like methods directly on first order clauses [3,5,14,19,2]. Those are completely different approaches. They do not try to encode the proof. They try to find a model instead. We argue that the benefit of our approach is that the SAT solver is called rarely. Based on the reasons we understand for the success of SAT solvers, we think this is a big advantage of our method.

In our implementation, we sometimes generate large files for MiniSat to solve. Minisat usually solves them very quickly. Our implementation is still preliminary, but we think it shows promise, given that it can solve some problems quickly that many other theorem provers cannot solve. We do not have a good handle yet on which problems our method does better on. Obviously, it will perform best on problems that do not need many instances of the clauses. From our results, it appears that more than 15% of the problems without equality in the TPTP library are rigidly unsatisfiable, with only one instance of each clause.

For future work, there are several things that need to be done. We need to make our implementation more efficient. There are also several useful extensions. We need to find a good way to represent equality. We need to find a good way to decide exactly which clauses should be copied. We would like a method to decide satisfiability from rigid satisfiability. It would be useful to have an encoding of rigid clauses modulo a non-rigid theory, as discussed in [8]. This way, we could immediately identify some clauses as non-rigid, and work modulo those clauses.

Finally, the most interesting idea to improve the efficiency is to replace the SAT solver by a SAT solver modulo theories. Crude analysis of the input files to the SAT solver shows that for the Horn case less than 1% of the clauses generated are to determine the structure of the tableau whereas nearly 70% are to encode the unification. Instead of encoding the unification problem, we could work modulo a background unification theory. Besides unification, the other things that generate a lot of clauses are the encoding of no cycle in the tree (as much as 30%), and the existence of a complementary literal previously in the tree (as much as 70% in the non-Horn case). They are both somehow concerned with finding cycles. A unification algorithm could also be employed here if it had an efficient occurs check. The existence of a cycle can be succinctly encoded as a unification problem. Unification has a deterministic algorithm. Since this would remove the bulk of our propositional clauses and replace them by a deterministic algorithm, we expect it would improve the efficiency a lot.

References

1. Andrews, P.B.: Theorem Proving via General Matings. Journal of the Association for Computing Machinery 28(2), 193–214 (1981)
2. Baumgartner, P.: FDPLL - A First-Order Davis-Putnam-Logeman-Loveland Procedure. In: McAllester, D. (ed.) Automated Deduction - CADE-17. LNCS, vol. 1831, pp. 200–219. Springer, Heidelberg (2000)
3. Baumgartner, P., Tinelli, C.: The Model Evolution Calculus. In: Baader, F. (ed.) Automated Deduction – CADE-19. LNCS (LNAI), vol. 2741, pp. 350–364. Springer, Heidelberg (2003)
4. Bell, J.L., Slomson, A.B.: Models and Ultraproducts, An Introduction, Dover (1969)

5. Billon, J.: The Disconnection Method: a Confluent Integration of Unifications in the Analytic Framework. In: Miglioli, P., Moscato, U., Ornaghi, M., Mundici, D. (eds.) TABLEAUX 1996. LNCS, vol. 1071, pp. 110–126. Springer, Heidelberg (1996)
6. Chandru, V., Hooker, J., Rago, G., Shrivastava, A.: Partial Instantiation Methods For Inference in First-Order Logic. Journal of Automated Reasoning 28, 371–396 (2002)
7. Davis, M., Logemann, D., Loveland, D.: A Machine Program For Theorem Proving. Communications of the ACM 5(7), 394–397 (1962)
8. Delaune, S., Lin, H., Lynch, C.: Protocol Verification Via Rigid/Flexible Resolution, submitted (2007)
9. Eén, N., Sörensson, N.: An Extensible SAT. Solver. In: Giunchiglia, E., Tacchella, A. (eds.) SAT 2003. LNCS, vol. 2919, pp. 502–518. Springer, Heidelberg (2004)
10. Ganzinger, H., Hagen, G., Nieuwenhuis, R., Oliveras, A., Tinelli, C.: DPLL(T): Fast Decision Procedures. In: 16th International Conference on Computer Aided Verification (CAV), Boston (USA) (2004)
11. Goubault, J.: The Complexity of Resource-Bounded First-Order Classical Logic. In: Enjalbert, P., Mayr, E.W., Wagner, K.W. (eds.) STACS 94. LNCS, vol. 775, pp. 59–70. Springer, Heidelberg (1994)
12. Hähnle, R.: Tableaux and Related Methods. In: Robinson, A., Voronkov, A. (eds.) Handbook of Automated Reasoning (ch. 3), vol. 1, pp. 101–177. Elsevier, North-Holland (2001)
13. Letz, R., Stenz, G.: Model Elimination and Connection Tableau Procedures. In: Robinson, A., Voronkov, A. (eds.) Handbook of Automated Reasoning, ch. 28, 28th edn., vol. 2, pp. 2015–2113. Elsevier, North-Holland (2001)
14. Letz, R., Gernot, S.: Proof and Model Generation With Disconnection Tableaux. In: Baader, F., Voronkov, A. (eds.) LPAR 2004. LNCS (LNAI), vol. 3452, pp. 289–306. Springer, Heidelberg (2005)
15. McCune, W.: A Davis-Putnam Program and its Application to Finite First-Order Model Search: Quasigroup Existence Problems, Technical Report ANL/MCS-TM-194, Argonne National Laboratory (1994)
16. Prestwich, S., Lynce, I.: Local Search for Unsatisfiability. In: Biere, A., Gomes, C.P. (eds.) SAT 2006. LNCS, vol. 4121, pp. 283–296. Springer, Heidelberg (2006)
17. Riazanov, A., Voronkov, A.: The design and implementation of VAMPIRE. AI Communications, CASC 15(2-3), 91–110 (2002)
18. Sutcliffe, G., Suttner, C.B.: The TPTP Problem Library: CNF Release v1.2.1. Journal of Automated Reasoning 21(2), 177–203 (1998)
19. Stenz, G.: The Disconnection Tableaux, PhD thesis, TU München (2002)
20. Chang, C., Lee, C.R.: Symbolic Logic and Mechanical Theorem Proving. Academic Press, New York and London (1973)

Hyper Tableaux with Equality

Peter Baumgartner[1], Ulrich Furbach[2], and Björn Pelzer[2]

[1] NICTA, Canberra, Australia
Peter.Baumgartner@nicta.com.au
[2] Universität Koblenz-Landau, Koblenz, Germany
{uli,bpelzer}@uni-koblenz.de

Abstract. In most theorem proving applications, a proper treatment of equational theories or equality is mandatory. In this paper we show how to integrate a modern treatment of equality in the hyper tableau calculus. It is based on splitting of positive clauses and an adapted version of the superposition inference rule, where equations used for paramodulation are drawn (only) from a set of positive unit clauses, the candidate model. The calculus also features a generic, semantically justified simplification rule which covers many redundancy elimination techniques known from superposition theorem proving. Our main results are soundness and completeness, but we briefly describe the implementation, too.

1 Introduction

Tableau calculi play an important role in theorem proving, knowledge representation and in logic programming. Yet, for automated first-order theorem proving the influence of tableau calculi decreased in the last decade. The CASC competition [SS06] is dominated by saturation-based provers, and a tableau system like SETHEO, which was several times among CASC winners, is not even entering the competition any more. Among the reasons are the problems tableau calculi have with efficient handling of equality. Of course there are numerous papers on equality handling in tableau calculi. Various approaches have been discussed, for instance, in [Bec97]. It is not clear, however, whether they can be a basis for high performance theorem proving. This has to do with the usage of free variables in most semantic tableau calculi. The nature of these free variables, their rigidness, seems to be a major source for difficulties to define efficient proof procedures, even without equality. For instance, proof procedures often suffer from excessive backtracking and enumerate whole tableaux in an iterative-deepening fashion, typically based on the number of γ-rule applications in a tableau.

To avoid the problems of rigid variables for equality reasoning, in [DV96] the authors combine a superposition based equality reasoning system with a top down semantic tableau reasoner. Yet, certain substitutions still have to be applied globally to all variables in the tableau, which thus are still treated rigidly. As with most free-variable tableau calculi, the important property of *proof confluence* does not hold or is not known to hold.

Other free-variable tableau methods are based on solving (simultaneous) rigid E-unifiability problems [DV98] but still face the same problem of not exploiting proof confluence.

F. Pfenning (Ed.): CADE 2007, LNAI 4603, pp. 492–507, 2007.
© Springer-Verlag Berlin Heidelberg 2007

A more recent stream of equality handling in free-variable tableaux has been initiated by Martin Giese. It is (also) motivated by addressing the excessive backtracking of the methods mentioned above. In [Gie02] the author gives a calculus for free variable tableaux with superposition-type inference and proves completeness by adapting the model generation technique for superposition [BG98,NR01]. One improvement, compared with [DV96] and other free-variable methods is that unification constraints leading to a closed tableau are now held locally together with tableau literals. This allows one to avoid backtracking over the tableaux generated in a derivation, but instead amounts to combining local substitutions in a compatible way for the purpose to witness a closed tableau (see [Gie01] for details). A drawback of this approach is its potentially high memory consumption, as, in essence, it does not admit a one-branch-at-a-time proof procedure.

In [Gie03], simplification rules and reasoning with universal variables[1] are added to the framework of [Gie02], *but without equality*. Equality aside, the most relevant contribution in [Gie03] from the viewpoint of this paper is the instantiation of the calculus there to a variant of the hyper tableau calculus [BFN96].[2] An important difference to [BFN96] is that [Gie03] uses rigid variables for variables that are shared between positive literals in clauses. For instance, a clause like $\forall x, y \ (p(x,y) \lor q(x))$ then is treated by β-expansion with the formulas $\forall y \ p(X,y)$ and $q(X)$, where X is a rigid variable shared between branches. In contrast, the hyper tableaux of [BFN96] would branch out on the formulas $\forall y \ p(t,y)$ and $q(t)$, where t is some "guessed" ground term of the input signature.[3]

In this paper we stick with the hyper tableau calculus and its "obviously inefficient" approach of guessing ground terms for shared variables, as opposed to using free variables. More precisely, we show how to incorporate efficient ordering-based equality inference rules and redundancy elimination techniques from the superposition calculus [BG98, NR01] into a tableau calculus. We believe the hyper tableau calculus [BFN96] is a good basis for doing that, for the following reasons.

- All variables in a hyper tableau are universally quantified in the branch literal they occur. This facilitates the adaption of the superposition framework and enables powerful redundancy criteria.
- As far as we know, none of the free-variable calculi mentioned above can be used as a non-trivial decision procedure for function-free clause logic. The same holds true for any known resolution refinement.

  On the other hand, our calculus is a non-trivial decision procedure for this fragment (with equality), which captures the complexity class NEXPTIME.

---

[1] Variables that are local to a clause or literal and that are universally quantified.

[2] Hyper tableaux is a tableau model generation method, which is applied to clauses and needs only one inference rule, which can be seen as a tableaux β-rule. It is applied in a "hyper-way", such that all negative literals are "resolved away" by positive literals in the branch. The remaining literals are positive and are split after that. This basic idea stems from SATCHMO [MB88], which is extended in hyper tableaux by making better use of universally quantified variables.

[3] Notice that Resolution- or Superposition calculi, also those with Splitting [Wei01], do not split $\forall x, y \ (p(x,y) \lor q(x))$.

Many practically relevant problems are NEXPTIME-complete, e.g. first-order model expansion (relevant for constraint solving).
- Advanced techniques are available to restrict the domain of the guessed ground terms (like t above). For instance, the preprocessing technique in [BS06] can readily be used in conjunction with our calculus without any change.[4]
- Specific to the theory of equality and in presence of simplification inference rules, that domain can even be further reduced. This occasionally shows unexpected (positive) effects, leading to termination of our system, where e.g. superposition based systems do not terminate. See Section 5 for details.
- The hyper tableau calculus is the basis of the KRHyper prover, which is used in various applications [FO06, ?, BFGHS04, e.g.] from which we learned that an efficient handling of equality would increase its usability even more.

The closest approximation of the superposition calculus to E-hyper tableaux is obtained by using a selection function that selects all negative literals and using a prover that supports splitting, like SPASS [Wei01]. Even then, there remain differences. We discuss these issues in Section 5.

In [BT05], the model evolution calculus is extended by equality. Model evolution is a lifting of propositional DPLL to the first order case. The model construction method behind admits semantically justified redundancy elimination criteria. This calculus, as well as other instance-based methods (with equality, like [LS02]) are conceptually rather different to resolution- or tableau calculi as considered here.

This paper is organised as follows: we start with preliminaries in the following section. In Section 3 we present superposition inference rules for clauses together with a static completeness result. In Section 4 we introduce E-hyper tableaux and soundness and completeness properties. In Section 5 we consider improvements for splitting and discuss the relation with splitting in the SPASS prover. Section 6 describes the implementation of the E-KRHyper system. Detailed proofs of all results can be found in the long version of this paper.

2   Preliminaries

Most of the notions and notation we use in this paper are the standard ones in the field. We report here only notable differences and additions.

We will use an infinite set of variables X, and x and y denote elements of X. We fix a signature Σ throughout the paper. Unless otherwise specified, when we say term we will mean Σ-term. If t is a term we denote by $\mathcal{V}ar(t)$ the set of t's variables. A term t is *ground* iff $\mathcal{V}ar(t) = \emptyset$.

The notation $s[t]_p$ denotes the replacement of a subterm of s at position p with a term t, as usual. We leave away the subscript p if clear from the context. All of the above is extended from terms to literals in the obvious way.

---

[4] For example, the calculus described here does not admit a finite (fair) derivation from the clause set $\{\forall x \, p(x) \lor q(x), r(f(c))\}$, but in conjunction with the techniques in [BS06] it does.

In this paper we restrict ourselves to equational clause logic. Therefore, and essentially without loss of generality, we assume that the only predicate symbol in Σ is $\simeq$. Any atom A that is originally not an equation can be represented as the equation $A \simeq \mathbf{t}$, where $\mathbf{t}$ is some distinguished constant not appearing elsewhere. (But we continue to write, say, $P(a)$ instead of the official $P(a) \simeq \mathbf{t}$.) This move is harmless, in particular from an operational point of view.[5] An atom then is always an equation, and a literal then is always an equation or the negation of an equation. Literals of the latter kind, i.e., literals of the form $(s \simeq t)$ are also called *negative equations* and generally written $s \not\simeq t$ instead. We call a literal *trivial* if it is of the form $t \simeq t$ or $t \not\simeq t$.

We denote atoms by the letters A and B, literals by the letters K and L and by $\overline{L}$ the complement of a literal L.

A clause is a finite multiset of literals, written as a disjunction $A_1 \vee \cdots \vee A_m \vee \neg B_1 \vee \cdots \vee \neg B_n$ or an implication $A_1, \ldots, A_m \leftarrow B_1, \ldots, B_n$, where $m, n \geq 0$. Each atom A_i, for $i = 1, \ldots, m$, is called a *head atom*, and each atom B_j, for $j = 1, \ldots, n$, is called a *body atom*. We write $A, \mathcal{A} \leftarrow B, \mathcal{B}$ to denote a clause with head atoms $\{A\} \cup \mathcal{A}$ and body atoms $\{B\} \cup \mathcal{B}$, where $\mathcal{A}$ and $\mathcal{B}$ are multisets of atoms. As usual, clauses are implicitly universally quantified.

We suppose as given a reduction ordering $\succ$ that is total on ground Σ-terms.[6] The non-strict ordering induced by $\succ$ is denoted by $\succeq$, and $\prec$ and $\preceq$ denote the converse of $\succ$ and $\succeq$. The reduction ordering $\succ$ has to be extended to rewrite rules, equations and clauses. Following usual techniques [BG98, NR01, e.g.], to a given ground clause $\mathcal{A} \leftarrow \mathcal{B}$ we associate to each head atom $s \simeq t$ in $\mathcal{A}$ the multiset $\{s, t\}$ and to each body atom $u \simeq v$ in $\mathcal{B}$ the multiset $\{u, u, v, v\}$. Two atoms then (head or body) are compared by using the multiset extension of $\succ$, which is also denoted by $\succ$. This will have the effect of a lexicographic ordering, where, first, the bigger terms of two equations are compared, then the sign (body atoms are bigger) and at last the smaller sides of the equations. To compare clauses the two-fold multiset extension of $\succ$ is used, likewise denoted by $\succ$. When comparing ground rewrite rules they are treated as unit clauses.

A central notion for hyper tableaux is that of a *pure* clause [BFN96]: a clause $A_1, \ldots, A_m \leftarrow B_1, \ldots, B_n$ is called *pure* iff $\mathcal{V}ar(A_i) \cap \mathcal{V}ar(A_j) = \emptyset$, for all $1 \leq i, j \leq m$ with $i \neq j$. That is, in a pure clause variables are not shared among head literals. (In the rest of this paper we will need this concept for positive clauses only.) Any substitution that turns a clause C into a pure instance $C\pi$ is called a *purifying substitution (for C)*.

A *(Herbrand) interpretation* I is a set of ground Σ-equations—those that are true in the interpretation. Satisfiability/validity of ground Σ-literals, Σ-clauses,

---

[5] Strictly speaking, one has to move to a two-sorted signature with different signatures for function symbols and predicate symbols, and all variables are of the sort of terms. We ignore this aspect throughout the paper because it does not cause any complications.

[6] A *reduction ordering* is a strict partial ordering that is well-founded and is closed unter context i.e., $s \succ s'$ implies $t[s] \succ t[s']$ for all terms t, and liftable, i.e., $s \succ t$ implies $s\delta \succ t\delta$ for every term s and t and substitution δ.

and clause sets in a Herbrand interpretation is defined as usual. We write $I \models F$ to denote that I satisfies F, where F is a ground Σ-literal or a Σ-clause (set).

Since every interpretation defines in effect a binary relation on ground Σ-terms, and every binary relation on such terms defines an interpretation, we will identify the two notions in the sequel.

An *E-interpretation* is an interpretation that is also a congruence relation on the Σ-terms. If I is an interpretation, we denote by I^E the smallest congruence relation on the Σ-terms that includes I. We say that I *E-satisfies* F iff $I^E \models F$. Instead of $I^E \models F$ we generally write $I \models_E F$. We say that F *E-entails* F', written $F \models_E F'$, iff every E-interpretation that satisfies F also satisfies F'. We say that F and F' are *E-equivalent* iff $F \models_E F'$ and $F' \models_E F$.

Redundant Clauses. Intuitively, a clause is redundant iff it follows from a set of smaller clauses. We will formalize this now, following [BG98]. There is a related notion of "redundant inference" which will be introduced in Section 3.1 below.

If D is a ground clause and $\mathcal{C}$ is a set of ground clauses then let $\mathcal{C}_D = \{C \in \mathcal{C} \mid D \succ C\}$. When $\mathcal{C}$ is a set of non-ground clauses and when writing $\mathcal{C}_D$ we identify $\mathcal{C}$ with the set of all ground instances of all its clauses.

Now, a ground clause D is *redundant wrt. a set of clauses* $\mathcal{C}$ iff $\mathcal{C}_D \models_E D$. That is, D is redundant wrt. $\mathcal{C}$ iff D follows from smaller clauses taken from $\mathcal{C}$.[7] When D is a non-ground clause we say that D is redundant wrt. $\mathcal{C}$ iff every ground instance of D is redundant wrt. $\mathcal{C}$. For instance, using any simplification ordering, $P(f(a)) \leftarrow$ is redundant wrt. $\{P(a) \leftarrow , f(x) \simeq x \leftarrow \}$, because $\{P(a) \leftarrow , f(a) \simeq a \leftarrow \} \models_E P(f(a)) \leftarrow$ and each clause in the premise is smaller than $P(f(a)) \leftarrow$.

3   Inference Rules on Clauses

The following three inference rules are taken from the superposition calculus [BG98] and adapted to our needs. We need in addition a splitting rule that will be defined afterwards. All rules will later be embedded into the hyper tableau derivation rules.

An equation $l \simeq r$ always also denotes its symmetric version $r \simeq l$.

The sup-left rule (*superposition left*[8]) applies a superposition step to a body literal:

$$\text{sup-left}(\sigma) \quad \frac{\mathcal{A} \leftarrow s[l'] \simeq t, \mathcal{B} \qquad l \simeq r \leftarrow}{(\mathcal{A} \leftarrow s[r] \simeq t, \mathcal{B})\sigma} \quad \text{if} \begin{cases} l' \text{ is not a variable,} \\ \sigma \text{ is a mgu of } l \text{ and } l', \\ l\sigma \not\preceq r\sigma, \text{ and} \\ s\sigma \not\preceq t\sigma \end{cases}$$

---

[7] By compactness, even from a *finite* set of clauses.

[8] With our notation for clauses, the name superposition *left* is actually counterintuitive, but we keep it for compatibility with corresponding rules in the superposition calculus.

The last condition can be dropped, and the resulting inference rule is then called *ordered paramodulation left*.

The unit-sup-right rule (*unit superposition right*) applies a superposition step to a positive *unit* clause:

$$\text{unit-sup-right}(\sigma) \quad \frac{s[l'] \simeq t \leftarrow \qquad l \simeq r \leftarrow}{(s[r] \simeq t \leftarrow)\sigma} \quad \text{if} \begin{cases} l' \text{ is not a variable,} \\ \sigma \text{ is a mgu of } l \text{ and } l', \\ (s \simeq t)\sigma \not\preceq (l \simeq r)\sigma, \\ l\sigma \not\preceq r\sigma, \text{ and} \\ s\sigma \not\preceq t\sigma \end{cases}$$

The last condition can be dropped, and the resulting inference rule is then called *ordered unit paramodulation right*.

The general superposition right inference rule of [BG98] between non-unit clauses is not needed, essentially due to the presence of the splitting rule below.

The ref rule (*reflexivity*) eliminates a body literal on the grounds of being trivially true (after applying a substitution).

$$\text{ref}(\sigma) \quad \frac{\mathcal{A} \leftarrow s \simeq t, \mathcal{B}}{(\mathcal{A} \leftarrow \mathcal{B})\sigma} \quad \text{if } \sigma \text{ is a mgu of } s \text{ and } t$$

Finally, the announced splitting rule. It takes a disjunctive fact, applies a purifying substitution π to it and returns the instantiated head atoms, one conclusion per head atom.

$$\text{split}(\pi) \quad \frac{A_1, \ldots, A_m \leftarrow}{A_1\pi \leftarrow \quad \cdots \quad A_m\pi \leftarrow} \quad \text{if} \begin{cases} m \geq 2, \text{ and} \\ \pi \text{ is a purifying substitution for } A_1, \ldots, A_m \leftarrow \end{cases}$$

3.1   Redundant Inferences and Saturation

We write $C, D \Rightarrow_{\text{sup-left}(\sigma)} E$ to denote a sup-left inference, i.e., an instance of the sup-left inference rule with left premise C, right premise D, conclusion E and substitution σ that satisfies the rule's side condition. We use analogous notation for an application of the sup-right inference rule, and for an application of ref we write, similarly, $C \Rightarrow_{\text{ref}(\sigma)} E$. Likewise, $C \Rightarrow_{\text{split}(\pi)} A_1 \leftarrow, \ldots, A_m \leftarrow$ denotes a split inference with premise C, purifying substitution π and conclusions $A_1 \leftarrow, \ldots, A_m \leftarrow$.

An R-inference, with $R \in \{\text{sup-left}, \text{unit-sup-right}, \text{ref}\}$ is *ground* iff its constituent clauses C, D and E are ground. The substitution σ in a ground inference is irrelevant and may be assumed, without loss of generality, to be the empty substitution ϵ.

If $C, D \Rightarrow_{R(\sigma)} E$ is an R-inference (with D absent in the case of ref) and γ is a substitution such that $C\sigma\gamma, D\sigma\gamma \Rightarrow_{R(\epsilon)} E\gamma$ is a ground inference, then the latter inference is called a *ground instance* of the inference $C, D \Rightarrow_{R(\sigma)} E$.

For instance, by taking $\gamma = \{x \mapsto a\}$ one sees that the ground inference

$$(P(f(a)) \leftarrow), (f(a) \simeq a \leftarrow) \Rightarrow_{\text{sup-right}(\epsilon)} P(a) \leftarrow$$

is a ground instance of the inference

$$(P(f(x)) \leftarrow \,), (f(y) \simeq y \leftarrow \,) \Rightarrow_{\text{sup-right}(\{y \mapsto x\})} P(x) \leftarrow \quad.$$

In contrast,

$$(P(f(f(a))) \leftarrow \,), (f(a) \simeq a \leftarrow \,) \Rightarrow_{\text{sup-right}(\epsilon)} P(f(a)) \leftarrow$$

is not a ground instance of the inference above, for any substitution γ. Intuitively, only such ground inferences can be ground instances of inferences where paramodulation takes place at positions that exist also at the non-ground level. This excludes ground inferences that are not liftable because they would require paramodulation into or below variables. We can define these notions for the split rule analogously: a split inference is *ground* if the premise is ground (and hence all its conclusions are ground). Similarly as above for the other rules, the purifying substitution π can always be assumed to be the empty substitution then.

If $C \Rightarrow_{\text{split}(\pi)} A_1 \leftarrow \,, \ldots, A_m \leftarrow$ is a split inference and γ is a substitution such that $C\pi\gamma \Rightarrow_{\text{split}(\epsilon)} A_1\gamma \leftarrow \,, \ldots, A_m\gamma \leftarrow$ is a ground split inference, then the latter inference is called a *ground instance* of the former inference.

Let $\mathcal{D}$ be a set of (possibly non-ground) clauses. A ground inference $C, D \Rightarrow_{\text{sup-left}(\epsilon)} E$ or $C, D \Rightarrow_{\text{sup-right}(\epsilon)} E$ is *redundant wrt.* $\mathcal{D}$ iff E is redundant wrt. $\mathcal{D}_C \cup \{D\}$. A ground inference $C \Rightarrow_{\text{ref}(\epsilon)} E$ is *redundant wrt.* $\mathcal{D}$ iff E is redundant wrt. $\mathcal{D}_C$. And a ground inference $C \Rightarrow_{\text{split}(\epsilon)} A_1 \leftarrow \,, \ldots, A_m \leftarrow$ is *redundant wrt.* $\mathcal{D}$ iff there is an i with $1 \leq i \leq m$ such that $A_i \leftarrow$ is redundant wrt. $\mathcal{D}_C$.

For all inference rules sup-left, unit-sup-right, ref and split, a (possibly non-ground) inference is *redundant wrt.* $\mathcal{D}$ iff each of its ground instances is redundant wrt. $\mathcal{D}$.

Intuitively a ground inference is redundant wrt. $\mathcal{D}$ iff its conclusion follows from a set of smaller clauses than the left premise, while fixing the right premise. Because all (ground) inferences work in a strictly order-decreasing way, adding the conclusion of an inference to the clause set the premises are taken from renders the inference redundant wrt. that set.[9] For instance, adding $P(a) \leftarrow$ to the set $\{(P(f(a)) \leftarrow \,), (f(a) \simeq a \leftarrow \,)\}$ renders the obvious sup-right inference redundant wrt. the resulting set.

It is not only redundant inferences that can be neglected. Also inferences where one or both parent clauses are redundant can be neglected. This is captured by the following definition.

Definition 3.1 (Saturation up to redundancy). *A clause set* $\mathcal{C}$ *is saturated up to redundancy iff for all clauses $C \in \mathcal{C}$ such that C is not redundant wrt.* $\mathcal{C}$ *all of the following hold:*

1. *Every inference $C \Rightarrow_{\text{split}(\pi)} A_1 \leftarrow \,, \ldots, A_m \leftarrow$ such that $C\pi$ is not redundant wrt.* $\mathcal{C}$*, is redundant wrt.* $\mathcal{C}$*.*
2. *Every inference $C, D \Rightarrow_{R(\sigma)} E$, where $R \in \{\text{sup-left}, \text{unit-sup-right}\}$ and D is a fresh variant of a positive unit clause from $\mathcal{C}$, such that neither $C\sigma$ nor $D\sigma$ is redundant wrt.* $\mathcal{C}$*, is redundant wrt.* $\mathcal{C}$*.*

---

[9] This property makes it obvious that fair derivations, as defined later, exist.

3. *Every inference $C \Rightarrow_{\mathsf{ref}(\sigma)} E$ such that $C\sigma$ is not redundant wrt. C, is redundant wrt. C.*

For instance, the (satisfiable) propositional clause set $C = \{(A, B \leftarrow), (\leftarrow A)\}$ is *not* saturated up to redundancy. By an application of the split rule to $A, B \leftarrow$ one can infer $A \leftarrow$ and $B \leftarrow$, and adding, say, $B \leftarrow$ to C renders the clause $A, B \leftarrow$ redundant.

As an example for a non-ground split inference consider a clause $P(x), Q(x) \leftarrow$ from some clause set. One may want to avoid applying all purifying substitutions to it. Fortunately, Definition 3.1-1 does not prescribe that at all. For instance, when the clause set includes an equation $a \simeq b \leftarrow$ (where $a \succ b$), then purifying $P(x), Q(x) \leftarrow$ by $\pi = \{x/b\}$, yielding $P(b), Q(b) \leftarrow$, and adding $P(b) \leftarrow$ to the clause set is sufficient to render the split inference with purifying substitution $\{x/a\}$ redundant, as the clause $P(a) \leftarrow$ follows from $P(b) \leftarrow$ and $a \simeq b \leftarrow$, both of which are smaller than $P(a), Q(a) \leftarrow$.

Theorem 3.2 (Static Completeness). *Let C be a clause set saturated up to redundancy. If $\Box \notin C$ then C is E-satisfiable.*

The proof employs the model-construction technique originally developed for the superposition calculus, but adapted to our needs. The difference come from the facts that in our case all side premises are unit clauses, and so there is no equality factoring (or merging paramodulation) inference rule, and that we need a splitting rule.

Notice that Theorem 3.2 applies to a *statically* given clause set C. The connection to the *dynamic* derivation process of the E-hyper tableau calculus will be given later, and Theorem 3.2 will be essential in proving the completeness of the E-hyper tableau calculus.

4   E-Hyper Tableaux

In [BFN96], based on [LMG94], hyper tableau have been introduced as labeled trees over *literals* (which are universally quantified, and hence can be seen as unit clauses). For our purposes, however, a generalization towards trees over *clauses* is better suited. This is, because *new* clauses can now be derived as the derivation proceeds, and these clauses are context dependant (branch local), and tableaux are an obvious data structure to deal with this context dependency.

A *labeled tree over a set M* is a pair $(\mathcal{T}, \lambda)$ consisting of a finite, ordered tree $\mathcal{T}$ and a labeling function λ that maps each node of $\mathcal{T}$ to some element from M. A *(clausal) tableau over a signature Σ* is a labeled tree over the set of Σ-clauses. We use the letter $\mathbf{T}$ to denote tableaux.

Let $\mathbf{B}$ be a branch of a tableau $\mathbf{T}$ of length n, i.e., a sequence of nodes $(\mathbf{N}_1, \ldots, \mathbf{N}_n)$, for some $n \geq 0$, where $\mathbf{N}_1$ is the root and $\mathbf{N}_n$ is the leaf of $\mathbf{B}$. Each of the clauses $\lambda(\mathbf{N}_i)$, for $i = 1, \ldots, n$, is called a *(tableau) clause of $\mathbf{B}$*.

Occasionally it is convenient to read a branch $\mathbf{B}$ as the multiset of its tableau clauses $\lambda(\mathbf{B}) := \{D \mid D \text{ is a tableau clause of } \mathbf{B}\}$. This allows us to write, for instance, $C \in \mathbf{B}$ instead of $C \in \lambda(\mathbf{B})$. Furthermore, if $\mathbf{B}$ is a branch of a tableau $\mathbf{T}$ we write $\mathbf{B} \cdot C$ and mean the tableau obtained from $\mathbf{T}$ by adding an edge from the leaf of $\mathbf{B}$ to a fresh node labeled with C. Furthermore, we write $\mathbf{B} \cdot \mathbf{B}'$ to denote the branch obtained by concatenating the branch $\mathbf{B}$ and the node sequence $\mathbf{B}'$.

4.1   Extension Rules

We define two derivation rules for extending branches in a given tableau.

The Split rule branches out on an instance of a positive clause; its conclusions are labeled as "decision clauses", as indicated by the annotation ^{d}. The role of this labeling will become clear below in Section 4.2.

$$\text{Split} \quad \frac{\mathbf{B}}{\mathbf{B} \cdot A_1 \leftarrow^{\mathrm{d}} \quad \cdots \quad \mathbf{B} \cdot A_m \leftarrow^{\mathrm{d}}} \quad \text{if} \begin{cases} \text{there is a clause } C \in \mathbf{B} \text{ and} \\ \text{a substitution } \pi \text{ such that} \\ C \Rightarrow_{\mathsf{split}(\pi)} A_1 \leftarrow, \ldots, A_m \leftarrow \text{ and} \\ \mathbf{B} \text{ contains no variant of } A_i \leftarrow, \\ \text{for each } i = 1, \ldots, m \end{cases}$$

The clause C is called the *selected clause (of a Split inference)*.

The Equality rule applies an inference rule for equality reasoning from Section 3 to a body literal.

$$\text{Equality} \quad \frac{\mathbf{B}}{\mathbf{B} \cdot E} \quad \text{if} \begin{cases} \text{there is a clause } C \in \mathbf{B}, \\ \text{a fresh variant } D \text{ of a positive unit clause in } \mathbf{B}, \text{ and} \\ \text{a substitution } \sigma \text{ such that} \\ C, D \Rightarrow_{R(\sigma)} E \text{ with } R \in \{\mathsf{sup\text{-}left}, \mathsf{unit\text{-}sup\text{-}right}\} \text{ or} \\ C \Rightarrow_{\mathsf{ref}(\sigma)} E, \text{ and} \\ \mathbf{B} \text{ contains no variant of } E \end{cases}$$

In both rules, the test for the conclusion(s) being not contained in $\mathbf{B}$ is needed in interplay with deletion of clauses based on non-proper subsumption (see the Del below).

For later use, we say that an application of a Split, Sup-left, Unit-sup-right or Ref derivation rule to a branch $\mathbf{B}$ is *redundant* iff its conclusion (at least one of its conclusions, in the case of Split) is redundant wrt. $\mathbf{B}$.

4.2   Deletion and Simplification Rules

From a practical point of view, deletion of redundant clauses and simplification operations on clauses are crucial. We will introduce these now. Adding such rules is a major addition to the hyper tableau calculus and involves a more sophisticted technical treatment than that in [BFN96]. This is, because hyper tableau as defined in [BFN96] are *non-destructive*, in the sense that extending a branch goes along with increasing the set of its corresponding labels (unit clauses). This is no longer the case in presence of, for instance, the Del rule (*deletion*) below, which removes a clause that is redundant in a branch or subsumed by another clause in the branch.

Also, to preserve the calculus' soundness, arbitrary deletion of redundant clauses is not possible. A clause can be deleted only on the condition that none of the clauses which make the clause redundant is a clause which has been introduced at a later "decision level" (i.e. one that occurs further down in the tree below a more leafwards decision clause). This is formalized next.

$$\text{Del} \;\; \frac{\mathbf{B} \cdot C^{(\mathrm{d})} \cdot \mathbf{B}_1 \cdot \mathbf{B}_2}{\mathbf{B} \cdot t \simeq t \leftarrow^{(\mathrm{d})} \cdot \mathbf{B}_1 \cdot \mathbf{B}_2} \;\; \text{if} \; \begin{cases} (1) \; C \text{ is redundant wrt. } \mathbf{B} \cdot \mathbf{B}_1, \text{ or some} \\ \quad \text{clause in } \mathbf{B} \cdot \mathbf{B}_1 \text{ non-properly subsumes } C, \text{ and} \\ (2) \; \mathbf{B}_1 \text{ does not contain a decision clause} \end{cases}$$

The notation $^{(\mathrm{d})}$ is meant to say that if there is a label ^{d}, it is preserved when replacing C by $t \simeq t \leftarrow$.

Observe that our redundancy notion does not cover non-proper subsumption.[10] For instance, the clause $P(a) \leftarrow$ is *not* redundant wrt. $\{P(x) \leftarrow \}$ (and neither is the clause $P(y) \leftarrow$). Therefore, deletion of non-properly subsumed clauses has been taken care of explicitly.

The next rule, Simp (simplification), replaces a clause by another one that is smaller in the ordering:

$$\text{Simp} \;\; \frac{\mathbf{B} \cdot C^{(\mathrm{d})} \cdot \mathbf{B}_1 \cdot \mathbf{B}_2}{\mathbf{B} \cdot D^{(\mathrm{d})} \cdot \mathbf{B}_1 \cdot \mathbf{B}_2} \;\; \text{if} \; \begin{cases} (1) \; \mathbf{B} \cdot C \cdot \mathbf{B}_1 \models_{\mathrm{E}} D, \\ (2) \; C \text{ is redundant wrt. } \mathbf{B} \cdot D \cdot \mathbf{B}_1, \text{ and} \\ (3) \; \mathbf{B}_1 \text{ does not contain a decision clause} \end{cases}$$

The Simp rule covers, for instance, standard rewriting by unit clauses.

The condition (2) in Del is needed for completeness reasons, and the condition (3) in Simp is needed for both completeness and soundness reasons. They make sure that no deletion or simplification step is justified by a clause from a decision level further down in the tableau. Such a step would in general be justified only in the branch containing the used clauses, but not in the other branches. For illustration consider the following clause set.

$$P(a) \leftarrow \quad (1) \qquad \leftarrow P(b) \quad (2) \qquad a \simeq b, \, Q \leftarrow \quad (3)$$

After a Split with clause (3) a branch containing the decision clause $a \simeq b \leftarrow$ comes up. If condition (3) in Simp were dropped (and $a \succ b$), then clause (1) could be simplified to $P(b) \leftarrow$, leading to a refutation. This would be unsound because the simplification is not justified in the branch containing $Q \leftarrow$ although it would contain the simplified literal. But with the restrictions in place we arrive at the following lemma.

Lemma 4.1. *For each of the derivation rules* Split, Equality, Del *and* Simp, *if the premise of the rule is* E-*satisfiable, then one of its conclusions is* E-*satisfiable as well.*

---

[10] A clause C non-properly subsumes a clause D iff $C\sigma = D$ for some substitution σ.

For similar reasons as for Simp, the Del rule cannot just delete the clause C^{d} mentioned in the premise, as the deletion would remove the separation of $\mathbf{B}$ and $\mathbf{B}_1$ by a decision clause (while the replacement by $\mathbf{t} \simeq \mathbf{t} \leftarrow^{\mathrm{d}}$ preserves the separation).

A different approach to deletion and simplification is implemented in the SPASS prover [Wei01]. The corresponding rules in SPASS are even more general than ours as they allow to ignore the decision levels. But then, in general, a deleted or simplified clause must be reinserted on backtracking to an earlier decision level. This is never necessary in our case, essentially because of disallowing "backward" deletion and simplification steps across decision levels, as just discussed in the previous example.

4.3   Derivations

We say that a branch of a tableau is *closed* iff it contains the empty clause $\square$.[11] A branch that is not closed is also called *open*. A tableau is *closed* iff each of its branches is closed, and it is *open* iff it is not closed (i.e., if it has an open branch).

An *(E-hyper tableau) derivation* from a set $\{C_1, \ldots, C_n\}$ of Σ-clauses is a possibly infinite sequence of tableaux $\mathbf{D} = (\mathbf{T}_i)_{0 \le i < \kappa}$ such that

1. $\mathbf{T}_0$ is the clausal tableau over Σ that consists of a single branch of length n with tableau clauses $C_1, \ldots, C_n$.[12], and
2. for all $i > 0$, $\mathbf{T}_i$ is obtained from $\mathbf{T}_{i-1}$ by a single application of one of the derivation rules in Sections 4.1 and 4.2 to some open branch of $\mathbf{T}_{i-1}$, called the *selected branch*.

Recall that a tableau $\mathbf{T}$ is of the form $(\mathcal{T}, \lambda)$, where $\mathcal{T}$ is a tree, i.e., a pair $(\mathcal{N}, \mathcal{E})$ where $\mathcal{N}$ is the set of the nodes of $\mathcal{T}$ and $\mathcal{E}$ is the set of the edges of $\mathcal{T}$.

A derivation $\mathbf{D} = ((\mathcal{N}_i, \mathcal{E}_i), \lambda_i)_{i < \kappa}$ determines a *limit tree* $((\bigcup_{i < \kappa} \mathcal{N}_i, \bigcup_{i < \kappa} \mathcal{E}_i)$. It is easy to show that a limit tree of a derivation $\mathbf{D}$ is indeed a (possibly infinite) tree.

Now let $\mathbf{T}$ be the limit tree of some derivation, let $\mathbf{B} = (\mathbf{N}_i)_{i < \kappa}$ be a (possibly infinite) branch in $\mathbf{T}$ with κ nodes, and let $\mathbf{B}_i = (\mathbf{N}_1, \ldots, \mathbf{N}_i)$ be the initial segment of $\mathbf{B}$ with i nodes, for all $i < \kappa$. Define $\mathbf{B}_\infty = \bigcup_{i < \kappa} \bigcap_{i \le j < \kappa} \lambda_j(\mathbf{B}_j)$, the set of *persistent clauses (of $\mathbf{B}$)*.

Definition 4.2 (Exhausted Branch). *Let $\mathbf{T}$ be a limit tree, and let $\mathbf{B} = (\mathbf{N}_i)_{i < \kappa}$ be a branch in $\mathbf{T}$ with κ nodes. The branch $\mathbf{B}$ is* exhausted *iff it does not contain the empty clause, and for every clause $C \in \mathbf{B}_\infty$ and every fresh variant D of every positive unit clause in $\mathbf{B}_\infty$ such that neither C nor D is redundant wrt. $\mathbf{B}_\infty$ all of the following hold, for all $i < \kappa$ such that $C \in \mathbf{B}_i$ and D is a variant of a clause in $\mathbf{B}_i$:*

---

[11] We write $\square$ instead of " $\leftarrow$ ".

[12] The order does not matter, as the collection of tableau clauses of a branch will be seen as sets. For technical reasons we assume that no clause C_i is a variant of a clause C_j, for all $1 \le i < j \le n$, but this is obviously not an essential restriction.

1. *if* Split *is applicable to* $\mathbf{B}_i$ *with underlying inference*
   $C \Rightarrow_{\mathsf{split}(\pi)} A_1 \leftarrow , \ldots, A_m \leftarrow$ *and* $C\pi$ *is not redundant wrt.* $\mathbf{B}_i$, *then there is a* $j < \kappa$ *such that the inference* $C \Rightarrow_{\mathsf{split}(\pi)} A_1 \leftarrow , \ldots, A_m \leftarrow$ *is redundant wrt.* $\mathbf{B}_j$.

2. *if* Equality *is applicable to* $\mathbf{B}_i$ *with underlying inference* $C, D \Rightarrow_{R(\sigma)} E$, *for some* $R \in \{\mathsf{sup\text{-}left}, \mathsf{unit\text{-}sup\text{-}right}\}$, *and neither* $C\sigma$ *nor* $D\sigma$ *is redundant wrt.* $\mathbf{B}_i$, *then there is a* $j < \kappa$ *such that the inference* $C, D \Rightarrow_{R(\sigma)} E$ *is redundant wrt.* $\mathbf{B}_j$.

3. *if* Equality *is applicable to* $\mathbf{B}_i$ *with underlying inference* $C \Rightarrow_{\mathsf{ref}(\sigma)} E$ *and* $C\sigma$ *is not redundant wrt.* $\mathbf{B}_i$, *then there is a* $j < \kappa$ *such that the inference* $C \Rightarrow_{\mathsf{ref}(\sigma)} E$ *is redundant wrt.* $\mathbf{B}_j$.

A *refutation of a clause set* C is a finite derivation of C that ends in a closed tableau.

A derivation is *fair* iff it is a refutation or its limit tree has an exhausted branch.

In the preceeding definition, actually carrying out a Split inference with a clause C and (irreducible) purifying substitution π, when applicable, will achieve the conclusion, i.e. make $C\pi$ redundant wrt. $\mathbf{B}_j$. The analogous holds for the Equality inferences in items 2 and 3. This observation indicates that proof procedures implementing fair derivations indeed can be given.

Theorem 4.3 (Soundness of E-Hyper Tableaux). *Let* C *be a clause set that has a refutation. Then* C *is* E-*unsatisfiable.*

For the completeness direction we need the following result:

Proposition 4.4 (Exhausted branches are saturated up to redundancy). *If* $\mathbf{B}$ *is an exhausted branch of a limit tree of some fair derivation then* $\mathbf{B}_\infty$ *is saturated up to redundancy.*

Proposition 4.4 and Theorem 3.2 entails our main result:

Theorem 4.5 (Completeness of E-Hyper Tableaux). *Let* C *be a clause set and* $\mathbf{T}$ *be the limit tree of a fair derivation* $\mathbf{D}$ *of* C. *If* $\mathbf{D}$ *is not a refutation then* C *is satisfiable.*

Because the proof of this theorem refers to the proof of Theorem 3.2, the model constructed in the proof of Theorem 3.2 provides a strengthening of Theorem 4.5 by being more specific.

Corollary 4.6 (Bernays-Schönfinkel Class with Equality). *The* E-*hyper tableau calculus can be used as a decision procedure for the Bernays-Schönfinkel class with equality, i.e., for function free formulae with the quantifier prefix* $\exists^*\forall^*$.

The proof of Corollary 4.6 follows from the soundness and completeness results, and the facts that the calculus cannot derive clauses that grow in length, or that grow in term depth (using the assumption that no non-nullary function symbols are present) or that are variants of clauses already contained in the branch. Therefore any (exhausted) branch derivable must be finite.[13] Because of the finite branching of hyper tableaux and by Koenig's Lemma it follows that any (limit) derivation must be finite.

5   Restricting Split and the Relation to Splitting in SPASS

For performance reasons it is mandatory to restrict the search space induced by having to apply purifying substitutions in Split rule applications. The fairness criteria in Definition 4.2 already support that. For instance, one can take advantage of avoiding purifying substitutions that are *reducible*, as they lead to redundant inferences.

Definition 5.1 (Reducible substitution). *Let C be a clause set and σ a substitution. We say that σ is reducible wrt. C iff there is a term $t \in \mathcal{R}an(\sigma)$[14], a unit clause $l \simeq r \leftarrow \ \in C$ and a (matching) substitution μ such that $l\mu$ occurs in t and $l\mu \succ r\mu$.*

We say that σ is *irreducible wrt.* C if σ is not reducible wrt. C.

Obviously, for each (positive) clause $C = A_1, \ldots, A_m \leftarrow$ in a branch $\mathbf{B}$ and each purifying substitution π_0 for C there is a maximal chain $C\pi_0 \succ C\pi_1 \succ \cdots \succ C\pi_n$, for some $n \geq 0$, where π_i is obtained from π_{i-1} by one-step rewriting a term of its range with a positive unit clause from $\mathbf{B}$ and such that π_n is irreducible wrt. $\mathbf{B}$. It is not difficult to see that, by equality, applying Split with $C\pi_n$ renders the Split inferences with $C\pi_0, \ldots, C\pi_{n-1}$ redundant (wrt. all branches obtained by splitting $C\pi_n$). No reducible purifying substitution need therefore ever be considered in Split inferences to obtain an exhausted branch.

An example of such a situation is $C = P(x), Q(x) \leftarrow$, $a \simeq b \leftarrow \ \in \mathbf{B}$, $a \succ b$, $\pi_0 = \{x/a\}$ and $\pi_1 = \{x/b\}$. Split with $P(b), Q(b) \leftarrow$ alone to extend $\mathbf{B}$ is sufficient.

A significantly different split rule is implemented in the SPASS prover [Wei01]. It does not apply a purifying substitution to force partitioning a clause into variable disjoint parts. Instead, it can split on clauses only that are already partitioned.

We do not claim that our approach is always preferrable in practice. Yet, there are situations where indeed it is. By way of example, consider the following clauses

$$f(a) \simeq a \leftarrow \quad (1) \qquad\qquad f(g(x)) \simeq g(f(x)) \leftarrow \quad (3)$$
$$g(a) \simeq a \leftarrow \quad (2) \qquad\qquad p(f(x)), p(g(x)) \leftarrow \quad (4)$$

Suppose a precedence $f \succ g \succ a$ (or $g \succ f \succ a$, as the problem is symmetric in f and g), lifted to any simplification ordering. All superposition inferences among the clauses 1-3 are redundant, and a prover like SPASS will detect that.

---

[13] The situation is slightly more complicated due to the Simp and Del rules.
[14] As usual, the *range* of a substitution σ is $\mathcal{R}an(\sigma) = \{x\sigma \mid x\sigma \neq x\}$.

Among others, there is a superposition inference between clause 4 and 3, which yields the clause

$$p(g(f(x))), p(g(g(x))) \leftarrow \quad . \tag{5}$$

In fact this inference is redundant, too. To see this, consider any ground substitution γ. It must map x to some term comprised of a combination of fs, gs and (one) a, e.g. $\gamma = \{x/f(f(g(f(a))))\}$. Now, any ground instance obtained from clause 5 in this way can be reduced by the unit clauses 1-3 in one or more steps to the clause $p(f(a)), p(g(a)) \leftarrow$ (they can be reduced even further), which is a ground instance of clause 4 and which is smaller in the ordering than the ground instance of clause 5 we started with. By this argument the superposition inference leading to clause 5 is redundant (and need not be carried out).

Notice that this argumentation takes the clause set's signature into account. However, the commonly implemented redundancy criteria do not do that. In particular, for instance, SPASS does not find a finite saturation of the clause set above. In contrast, E-hyper tableaux are aware of the input signature and the redundancy criteria based on irreducible purifying substitutions, as mentioned above, are strong enough to achieve termination.[15] To see this, it is enough to observe that every purifying substitution, like $\pi = \{x/f(f(g(f(a))))\}$, is reducible (to $\pi = \{x/a\}$) wrt. every branch containing clauses 1 and 2. Thus, the *only* instance of clause 4 to be considered for splitting (in presence of 1-3) is $p(f(a)), p(g(a)) \leftarrow$ (which can be simplified further). Moreover, this can easily be achieved by adding the following "logic program"

$$ran(a) \leftarrow \quad (6) \qquad ran(f(x)) \leftarrow ran(x) \quad (7) \qquad ran(g(x)) \leftarrow ran(x) \quad (8)$$

which, in combination with rewriting by unit clauses will enumerate in its *ran* predicate the ground terms of the input signature that are irreducible wrt. the orientable current positive unit clauses. In presence of clauses 1 and 2 this is the singleton $\{a\}$. The general form of the "logic program" has, of course, already been used within SATCHMO [MB88] and some descendants. To our knowledge, though, it was never observed before that equational reasoning can help to confine the *ran*-predicate.

6   Implementation

We have implemented the E-hyper tableau calculus by extending our existing KRHyper system. KRHyper is a hyper tableaux theorem prover, and as such it lacked equality handling in the original version. The modified system, called E-KRHyper, adapts the methods of its precursor to accommodate the new inferences, while at the same time retaining the original functionality.

The derivation proceeds in a bottom-up manner. Internally, clauses are divided into three sets, one containing the positive non-equational units (*facts*),

---

[15] More precisely, there is a finite derivation in the E-hyper tableau calculus, and any reasonable implementation, like our E-KRHyper system, will find it.

the other consisting of the positive non-unit clauses (*disjunctions*), and the third including both the unit equations and the clauses with negative literals (*rules*). The hyper extension inference of KRHyper is equivalent to a series of Sup-left, Ref and Split applications, and therefore it is kept in place in E-KRHyper as a shortcut inference for the resolution of non-equational atoms. The E-hyper tableau is generated depth first, with the current state of the three clause sets always representing a single branch. The Split on a disjunction is only executed when the other inference possibilities have been exhausted. An iterative deepening strategy with a limit on the maximum term weight of generated clauses is employed. This ensures the refutational completeness and a fair search control, as it prevents splitting from being delayed indefinitely by other inferences.

Clauses are derived by a loop iterating over the rules, with each rule in turn accessing indexes in the search for inference partners. The inferred clauses are added to their respective sets after having passed the weight and subsumption tests. The dynamic nature of the rule set represents a major change compared to the previous system version. As the hyper tableaux calculus has no inferences that generate new rule clauses, this set remained fixed throughout the derivation of KRHyper, and many optimizations on the input could be delegated to preprocessing. Operations like the clause subsumption test are necessary for the new calculus, and they are now employed to optimize the input clauses as well.

The superposition inferences utilize a discrimination-tree based index [McC92] over the subterms of clauses, and terms are ordered according to the recursive path ordering (RPO). As an option, the backtracking mechanism allows the removal of redundant clauses from the entire current branch, beyond the limits set in Section 4.2. More details about the system can be found in [PW07]; it is available under the GNU Public License from the E-KRHyper website at http://www.uni-koblenz.de/~bpelzer/ekrhyper.

7   Conclusion

We have presented a tableau calculus with equality, by integrating superposition based inference rules into the hyper tableau calculus rules. Our main result is its soundness and completeness, the latter in combination with redundancy criteria. The calculus is implemented in the E-KRHyper system, an extension of our existing KRHyper prover.

Acknowledgements. We thank the anonymous reviewers for their useful comments on improving the paper's presentation.

References

[Bec97]   Beckert, B.: Semantic Tableaux With Equality. Journal of Logic and Computation 7(1), 39–58 (1997)

[BFGHS04] Baumgartner, P., Furbach, U., Gross-Hardt, M., Sinner, A.: Living Book – Deduction, Slicing, and Interaction. J. of Aut. Reasoning 32(3) (2004)

[BFN96]   Baumgartner, P., Furbach, U., Niemelä, I.: Hyper Tableaux. In: Orłowska,
            E., Alferes, J.J., Moniz Pereira, L. (eds.) JELIA 1996. LNCS, vol. 1126,
            Springer, Heidelberg (1996)
[BG98]   Bachmair, L., Ganzinger, H.: Chapter 11: Equational Reasoning in
            Saturation-Based Theorem Proving. In: Bibel, W., Schmitt, P.H. (eds.)
            Automated Deduction. A Basis for Applications, vol. 1, Kluwer, Dor-
            drecht (1998)
[BS06]   Baumgartner, P., Schmidt, R.: Blocking and Other Enhancements for
            Bottom-up Model Generation Methods. In: Furbach, U., Shankar, N.
            (eds.) IJCAR 2006. LNCS (LNAI), vol. 4130, Springer, Heidelberg (2006)
[BT05]   Baumgartner, P., Tinelli, C.: The Model Evolution Calculus with Equal-
            ity. In: Nieuwenhuis, R. (ed.) Automated Deduction – CADE-20. LNCS
            (LNAI), vol. 3632, Springer, Heidelberg (2005)
[DV96]   Degtyarev, A., Voronkov, A.: Equality Elimination for the Tableau
            Method. In: Limongelli, C., Calmet, J. (eds.) DISCO 1996. LNCS,
            vol. 1128, Springer, Heidelberg (1996)
[DV98]   Degtyarev, A., Voronkov, A.: What you Always Wanted to Know About
            Rigid E-Unification. Journal of Automated Reasoning 20(1), 47–80 (1998)
[FO06]   Furbach, U., Obermaier, C.: Applications of Automated Reasoning. In:
            Freksa, C., Kohlhase, M., Schill, K. (eds.) KI 2006. LNCS (LNAI),
            vol. 4314, Springer, Heidelberg (2007)
[Gie01]   Giese, M.: Incremental Closure of Free Variable Tableaux. In: Goré, R.P.,
            Leitsch, A., Nipkow, T. (eds.) IJCAR 2001. LNCS (LNAI), vol. 2083,
            Springer, Heidelberg (2001)
[Gie02]   Giese, M.: A Model Generation Style Completeness Proof For Con-
            straint Tableaux With Superposition. In: Egly, U., Fermüller, C. (eds.)
            TABLEAUX 2002. LNCS (LNAI), vol. 2381, Springer, Heidelberg (2002)
[Gie03]   Giese, M.: Simplification Rules for Constrained Formula Tableaux. In:
            Mayer, M.C., Pirri, F. (eds.) TABLEAUX 2003. LNCS, vol. 2796,
            Springer, Heidelberg (2003)
[LMG94]   Letz, R., Mayr, K., Goller, C.: Controlled Integrations of the Cut Rule
            into Connection Tableau Calculi. J. of Aut. Reasoning 13 (1994)
[LS02]   Letz, R., Stenz, G.: Integration of Equality Reasoning into the Discon-
            nection Calculus. In: Egly, U., Fermüller, C. (eds.) TABLEAUX 2002.
            LNCS (LNAI), vol. 2381, Springer, Heidelberg (2002)
[MB88]   Manthey, R., Bry, F.: SATCHMO: a Theorem Prover Implemented in
            Prolog. In: Lusk, E.R., Overbeek, R. (eds.) 9th International Conference
            on Automated Deduction. LNCS, vol. 310, Springer, Heidelberg (1988)
[McC92]   McCune, W.: Experiments with Discrimination-Tree Indexing and Path
            Indexing for Term Retrieval. J. of Aut. Reasoning 9(2), 147–167 (1992)
[NR01]   Nieuwenhuis, R., Rubio, A.: Paramodulation-based Theorem Proving. In:
            Robinson, J.A., Voronkov, A. (eds.) Handbook of Automated Reasoning,
            Elsevier and MIT Press (2001)
[PW07]   Pelzer, B., Wernhard, C.: System Description: E-KRHyper. In: Pfenning,
            F. (ed.) CADE-21. LNCS, Springer, Heidelberg (2007)
[SS06]   Sutcliffe, G., Suttner, C.: The State of CASC. AI Communications 19(1),
            35–48 (2006)
[Wei01]   Weidenbach, C.: Combining Superposition, Sorts and Splitting. In:
            Robinson, A., Voronkov, A. (eds.) Handbook of Automated Reasoning.
            North Holland (2001)

System Description: E-KRHyper

Björn Pelzer and Christoph Wernhard

Universität Koblenz-Landau, Koblenz, Germany
{bpelzer,wernhard}@uni-koblenz.de

Abstract. The E-KRHyper system is a model generator and theorem prover for first-order logic with equality. It implements the new E-hyper tableau calculus, which integrates a superposition-based handling of equality into the hyper tableau calculus. E-KRHyper extends our previous KRHyper system, which has been used in a number of applications in the field of knowledge representation. In contrast to most first order theorem provers, it supports features important for such applications, for example queries with predicate extensions as answers, handling of large sets of uniformly structured input facts, arithmetic evaluation and stratified negation as failure. It is our goal to extend the range of application possibilities of KRHyper by adding equality reasoning.

1 Introduction

E-*KRHyper* is a theorem proving and model generation system for first-order logic with equality. It is an implementation of the E-*hyper tableau calculus* [1], which integrates a superposition-based handling of equality [2] into the hyper tableau calculus [3]. If E-KRHyper terminates without finding a refutation, it leaves a finite set of positive unit clauses representing a model of the input. Continued operation effects that alternative models are enumerated, allowing the use of E-KRHyper as a model generator for answer set computation.

E-KRHyper is an extended version of our KRHyper system [4], which is based on the original hyper tableau calculus and therefore lacks a dedicated mechanism for equality reasoning. So far KRHyper has been used as an embedded knowledge processing engine in several applications including content composition for e-learning [5,6], document management [7], database schema processing [8], semantic information retrieval [9], ontology reasoning [10], and planning [11]. An excerpt of KRHyper has been ported to Mobile Java and is employed for user profile matching on mobile devices [12]. We intend to further this usage with the enhanced reasoning capabilities of our upgraded system. This includes reasoning in modal and description logics, which is only possible in a restricted way with the original KRHyper [13], and which will allow a more accurate modelling of application domains.

2 Language, Usage and Availability

E-KRHyper accepts formulas of first order logic in clausal form. The system supports several language extensions, including stratified negation as failure and

F. Pfenning (Ed.): CADE 2007, LNAI 4603, pp. 508–513, 2007.
© Springer-Verlag Berlin Heidelberg 2007

a stratified set abstraction construct. The arithmetic constant types, evaluable arithmetic functors and arithmetic built-ins specified in the ISO standard for Prolog are provided. The input syntax is the *Protein* format, which is supported by the *TPTP* tools. The syntax of in- and output complies with ISO standard Prolog. Proofs of refutations and derivations of facts in models can be output as terms which can be visualized with the *Graphviz* tool. The system is implemented in the functional/imperative language *OCaml* with additional pre-processing scripts in *SWI-Prolog*. E-KRHyper runs on Unix and MS-Windows platforms and is available under the GNU Public License from the E-KRHyper website at `http://www.uni-koblenz.de/~bpelzer/ekrhyper`.

3   E-Hyper Tableaux

An E-hyper tableau [1] is a tree whose nodes are labeled with clauses and which is built up by the application of the inference rules of the E-hyper tableau calculus. The calculus rules are designed such that most of the reasoning is performed using positive unit clauses. A branch can be extended with new clauses that have been derived from the clauses of that branch.

A positive disjunction can be used to split a branch, creating a new branch for each disjunct. No variables may be shared between branches, and if a case-split creates branches with shared variables, then these are immediately substituted by ground terms. The grounding substitution is arbitrary as long as the terms in its range are *irreducible*: the branch being split may not contain a positive equational unit which can simplify a substituting term, i.e. rewrite it with one that is smaller according to a reduction ordering [2,15]. When multiple irreducible substitutions are possible, each of them must be applied in consecutive splittings in order to preserve completeness.

Redundancy rules allow the detection and removal of clauses that are redundant with respect to a branch.

4   Model Generation and Theorem Proving Method

The E-hyper tableau is generated depth-first, with E-KRHyper always working on a single branch. Refutational completeness and a fair search control are ensured by an iterative deepening strategy with a limit on the maximum term weight of generated clauses.

E-KRHyper maintains the clauses on the working branch grouped into two sets, the first containing positive non-equational units and the second containing equational units and clauses that include negative literals. A third set is used to maintain positive non-unit clauses. If all other inference possibilities have been exhausted, the spliting rule picks a clause from this set and extends the working branch by attaching a child for each disjunct to its leaf node. One of the resulting branches is then selected as the new working branch.

If the computation of a branch reaches a fixed point, then a model has been found. If on the other hand a contradiction within a branch is detected, then that branch is abandoned, and the computation backtracks to the next branch. If there is no next branch, computation halts with the result that there is no [more] model.

A model is represented by a set of positive unit clauses. These correspond to a convergent rewrite system that is complete with respect to the equational theory represented by the set of input clauses [1]. For example, consider the input clauses displayed in Fig. 1. At the first fixed point of E-KRHyper's derivation, the branch contains the positive unit clauses $\{C_1, C_2, C_3, p(x)\}$, which corresponds to the model $M_1 = \{a \simeq b, q(a), r(d), p(x)\}$. The second and final fixed point corresponds to the model $M_2 = \{q(a), r(c), c \simeq d\}$ – note that C_3 has been simplified into the atom $r(c)$.

$$\begin{aligned} C_1 &= a \simeq b. \\ C_2 &= q(a). \\ C_3 &= r(d). \\ C_4 &= p(x) \vee c \simeq d \leftarrow q(b). \end{aligned}$$

Fig. 1. Example Input

Optionally two refinements of theorem proving methods based on model generation are employed: *level cut* [3], a form of dependency directed backtracking, and *complement splitting* [17], which also can be used for the computation of minimal models. The *hyper extension* inference from the original hyper tableau calculus is equivalent to a series of E-hyper tableau calculus inference applications. Therefore the implementation of the hyper extension in KRHyper by a variant of semi-naive evaluation [16] is retained in E-KRHyper, where it serves as a shortcut inference for the resolution of non-equational literals.

5   Comparison to KRHyper

Both KRHyper and E-KRHyper are written in OCaml. The integration of the new calculus in E-KRHyper has required approximately 10,500 lines of additional code compared to KRHyper, representing a size increase of 79 percent. Apart from implementing the new inference rules, it was also necessary to modify a number of original operations. KRHyper only ever adds positive unit clauses to its hyper tableaux, and the indexing is similarly confined to positive units. Also, there is no support for destructive tableau modifications, as the original calculus does not include any such operations. In E-KRHyper the clause indexing has been extended to cover the full range of clauses, and both the derivation loop and the indexing take into account the dynamically growing and shrinking clause sets of the new calculus. On problems without equality, the changes result in E-KRHyper being 24 percent slower than KRHyper.

6   Related Systems and Performance Evaluation

The SPASS system is a superposition-based theorem prover for first-order logic, that however cannot straightforwardly be used for model computation. Like E-KRHyper, SPASS splits on disjunctions. SPASS can only split when the resulting parts are variable disjoint, though. This inability to split on all disjunctions is responsible for failing to decide certain classes of formulas that are decided by E-KRHyper [1].

The basic concept of theorem proving by model generation, as employed in E-KRHyper, stems from *Satchmo* [17]. *Satchmo Compiler* [19] and *MGTP* [20] have been earlier efforts to implement such a system efficiently. GEO [21] is a recent system for theorem proving and computation of finite models in first order logic, which, like E-KRHyper, works by integrating equality processing into model based search. The approach in GEO is not based on superposition and has no redundancy treatment, and while the splitting method is similar to the one in E-KRHyper, the number of eligible grounding substitutions is not limited to those that are irreducible. *Smodels* [22] and *DLV* [23] are systems which efficiently compute stable models but can handle first-order features such as nested terms and nonground terms only in very restricted ways.

We have tested E-KRHyper on several problem groups eligible for the CASC 2006 [24]. The tests were carried out on a 1.5 GHz Pentium M computer with 1.5 GB RAM and a timeout limit of 400 seconds. Table 1 shows the results for those

Table 1. Results on CASC J3 problems

Problem class	NNE	HEQ	NEQ	UEQ
Number of problems	20	20	70	100
Solved by E-KRHyper	6	9	18	2
Solved by Otter 3.3	10	12	20	28

problems finally selected for the competition. As a comparison the official competition results of the Otter 3.3 system [25] are listed as well.[1] In comparision with the competition entrants, E-KRHyper ranks in the middle for Horn and Non-Horn problems with equality (HEQ and NEQ) and in the lower ranges for Non-Horn problems without equality (NNE). For unit equation problems (UEQ) the system is uncompetitive. E-KRHyper retains the general characteristics of KRHyper and thus performs well on certain problem classes without equality [4]. So far the development of the KRHyper line has focused more on the application possibilities than on competition performance, but we hope to optimize the operation in the future. More detailed information and test results are provided on the E-KRHyper website.

7 Conclusion

KRHyper has successfully been deployed in real-world applications for knowledge representation. However, its lack of dedicated equality handling has been a limitation in certain areas like reasoning with description logics. The implementation of the new calculus with equality in E-KRHyper has cleared this obstacle and opened the way for new integration opportunities. Given that the field of automated theorem proving has come to be dominated by saturation based systems in recent years, we also hope that E-KRHyper will be a first step towards an efficient and competitive tableau based theorem prover with equality.

---

[1] The Otter system represents the state of the art in first-order theorem proving around 1996 and regularly participates in the CASC to provide a stable benchmark.

Acknowledgements. The authors wish to thank Peter Baumgartner and Ulrich Furbach for opening to them the world of model based deduction with hyper tableaux and for their help in implementing the new calculus, as well as the anonymous reviewers for their constructive suggestions on improving this paper.

References

1. Baumgartner, P., Furbach, U., Pelzer, B.: Hyper Tableau with Equality. In: Fachberichte Informatik 12–2007, Universität Koblenz-Landau (2007)
2. Bachmair, L., Ganzinger, H.: Chapter 11: Reasoning in Saturation-Based Theorem Proving. In: Bibel, W., Schmitt, P.H. (eds.) Automated Deduction – A Basis for Applications, vol. I, pp. 352–397. Kluwer, Dordrecht (1998)
3. Baumgartner, P., Furbach, U., Niemelä, I.: Hyper Tableaux. In: Orłowska, E., Alferes, J.J., Moniz Pereira, L. (eds.) JELIA 1996. LNCS, vol. 1126, Springer, Heidelberg (1996)
4. Wernhard, C.: System Description: KRHyper. In: Fachberichte Informatik 14-2003, Universität Koblenz Landau (2003)
5. Baumgartner, P., Furbach, U.: Living Books, Automated Deduction and other Strange Things. In: Hutter, D., Stephan, W. (eds.) Mechanizing Mathematical Reasoning. LNCS (LNAI), vol. 2605, pp. 255–274. Springer, Heidelberg (2005)
6. Baumgartner, P., Furbach, U., Gross-Hardt, M., Sinner, A.: Living Book: deduction, slicing, and interaction. J. of Autom. Reasoning 32(3), 259–286 (2004)
7. Baumgartner, P., Furbach, U., Gross-Hardt, M., Kleemann, T., Wernhard, C.: KRHyper Inside - Model Based Deduction in Applications. In: Baader, F. (ed.) Automated Deduction – CADE-19. LNCS (LNAI), vol. 2741, Springer, Heidelberg (2003)
8. Baumgartner, P., Furbach, U., Gross-Hardtand, M., Kleemann, T.: Model Based Deduction for Database Schema Reasoning. In: Biundo, S., Frühwirth, T., Palm, G. (eds.) KI 2004. LNCS (LNAI), vol. 3238, pp. 168–182. Springer, Heidelberg (2004)
9. Baumgartner, P., Burchardt, A.: Logic Programming Infrastructure for Inferences on FrameNet. In: Alferes, J.J., Leite, J.A. (eds.) JELIA 2004. LNCS (LNAI), vol. 3229, pp. 591–603. Springer, Heidelberg (2004)
10. Baumgartner, P., Suchanek, F.M.: Automated Reasoning Support for First-Order Ontologies. In: Alferes, J.J., Bailey, J., May, W., Schwertel, U. (eds.) PPSWR 2006. LNCS, vol. 4187, pp. 18–32. Springer, Heidelberg (2006)
11. Baumgartner, P., Mediratta, A.: Improving Stable Models Based Planning by Bidirectional Search. In: International Conference on Knowledge Based Computer Systems (KBCS), Hyderabad, India (2004)
12. Kleemann, T., Sinner, A.: KRHyper - In Your Pocket, System Description. In: Nieuwenhuis, R. (ed.) Automated Deduction – CADE-20. LNCS (LNAI), vol. 3632, Springer, Heidelberg (2005)
13. Baumgartner, P., Schmidt, R.: Blocking and Other Enhancements of Bottom-Up Model Generation Methods. In: Furbach, U., Shankar, N. (eds.) IJCAR 2006. LNCS (LNAI), vol. 4130, Springer, Heidelberg (2006)
14. Deransart, P., et al.: Prolog: The standard: reference manual. Berlin (1996)
15. Nieuwenhuis, R., Rubio, A.: Paramodulation-based theorem proving. In: Robinson, J.A., Voronkov, A. (eds.) Handbook of Automated Reasoning, pp. 371–443. Elsevier and MIT Press (2001)

16. Ullman, J.D.: Principles of Database and Knowledge-Base Bystems, Rockville, Maryland (1989)
17. Manthey, R., Bry, F.: SATCHMO: A theorem prover implemented in Prolog. In: Lusk, E.R., Overbeek, R. (eds.) 9th International Conference on Automated Deduction. LNCS, vol. 310, pp. 415–434. Springer, Heidelberg (1988)
18. Weidenbach, C.: Combining Superposition, Sorts and Splitting. In: Robinson, A., Voronkov, A. (eds.) Handbook of Automated Reasoning, North Holland (2001)
19. Schütz, H., Geisler, T.: Efficient model generation through compilation. In: McRobbie, M.A., Slaney, J.K. (eds.) Automated Deduction - Cade-13. LNCS, vol. 1104, pp. 433–447. Springer, Heidelberg (1996)
20. Hasegawa, R., Fujita, H., Koshimura, M.: MGTP: A Model Generation Theorem Prover — its advanced features and applications. In: Galmiche, D. (ed.) TABLEAUX 1997. LNCS, vol. 1227, pp. 1–15. Springer, Heidelberg (1997)
21. de Nivelle, H., Meng, J.: Geometric Resolution: A Proof Procedure Based on Finite Model Search. In: Furbach, U., Shankar, N. (eds.) IJCAR 2006. LNCS (LNAI), vol. 4130, pp. 303–317. Springer, Heidelberg (2006)
22. Niemelä, I., Simons, P.: Smodels – An implementation of the stable model and well-founded semantics for normal logic programs. In: Dix, J., Furbach, U., Nerode, A. (eds.) Proc. of the 4th Int. Conf. on Logic Programming and Non-Monotonic Reasoning, pp. 420–429 (1997)
23. Leone, N., Pfeifer, G., Faber, W., Eiter, T., Gottlob, G., Koch, C., Mateis, C., Perri, S., Scarcello, F.: The DLV System for Knowledge Representation and Reasoning. INFSYS RR-1843-02-14, Technische Universität Wien (2002)
24. Sutcliffe, G., Suttner, C.: The State of CASC. AI Communications 19(1), 35–48 (2006)
25. McCune, W.: OTTER 3.3 Reference Manual. Argonne National Laboratory, Argonne, Illinois, ANL/MCS-TM-263 (2003)

System Description: SPASS Version 3.0

Christoph Weidenbach[1], Renate A. Schmidt[2], Thomas Hillenbrand[1],
Rostislav Rusev[1], and Dalibor Topic[1]

[1] Max-Planck-Institut für Informatik, Germany
spass@mpi-sb.mpg.de
[2] University of Manchester, UK
spass@mpi-sb.mpg.de

Abstract. SPASS is an automated theorem prover for full first-order logic with equality and a number of non-classical logics. This system description provides an overview of our recent developments in SPASS 3.0, including support for dynamic modal logics, relational logics and expressive description logics, additional renaming and selection strategies, and significant interface enhancements for human and machine users.

1 Introduction

New in SPASS 3.0 are facilities for supporting automated reasoning in a large class of related logics which we refer to as *EML* logics (extended modal logics). These include (traditional) propositional modal logics such as $K_{(m)}$, $KD_{(m)}$, $KT4_{(m)}$ etc., which are widely used for studying and formalizing e.g. multi-agent systems, but have many applications in other areas of computer science as well as mathematics, linguistics and philosophy. *EML* logics also include dynamic modal logics which are PDL-like modal logics in which the modal operators are parameterized by relational formulas [6]. These can be used to formalize dynamic notions such as actions or programs and are useful in linguistic and AI applications. Examples of dynamic modal logics are Boolean modal logic, tense logic, information logics, logics expressing inaccessibility and sufficiency as well as a large class of description logics. The *EML* class further includes relational logics, i.e. logical versions of Tarski's relation algebras. SPASS handles these logics by translation to first-order logic, see Sect. 2.

For most decidable *EML* logics, SPASS is actually a decision procedure on the first-order formulas resulting from the translation. For some logics, e.g., description logics including negation of roles, it is currently the only available decision procedure. SPASS is competitive even with special-purpose systems.

Further enhancements in SPASS 3.0 are additional renaming and selection strategies, see Sect. 3, and an improved user/machine interface including an extended formula-clause relationship handling, input and output of saturated clause sets and documentation, see Sect. 4 and 5.

F. Pfenning (Ed.): CADE 2007, LNAI 4603, pp. 514–520, 2007.

2   Modal Logics, Relational Logics and Description Logics

The facilities in SPASS 3.0 for supporting automated reasoning in *EML* logics were first implemented from 1998 onwards in the MSPASS theorem prover [2,4] as an extension of SPASS 1.0. This code has been upgraded and integrated into SPASS 3.0 (and FLOTTER 3.0) so that support for modal, relational and description logic reasoning is now immediately available to SPASS users and the latest SPASS technology is immediately available to MSPASS users.

The dfg input language of SPASS was extended to support the input of *EML* problems without changing the syntax for formulas in first-order logic or clause form. There are three types of *EML* formulas which can be used simultaneously in one file: first-order formulas, Boolean type formulas and relational type formulas. Boolean and relational type formulas can be constructed using common modal, relational and description logic operators. The predefined logical operators are:

- the standard Boolean operators (for all three types of formulas): true, false, not, and, or, implies (subsumed by), implied (subsumes), equiv,
- multi-modal operators with atomic or complex relational arguments: dia and box (synonyms are some and all), as well as domain and range,
- additional relational operators: comp (composition), sum (relative sum), conv (converse), id (the identity relation), div (the diversity relation), and
- test (test), domrestr (domain restriction) and ranrestr (range restriction).

We give three examples of *EML* formulas, two Boolean type formulas and one relational type formula.

$$\text{prop\_formula(implies(box(bel1,p), box(know1,box(bel1,p)))).} \quad (1)$$

$$\text{concept\_formula(implies(expert\_AR,} \quad (2)$$
$$\text{not(some(not(has\_studied),proof\_methods)))).}$$

$$\text{rel\_formula(implies(comp(r,r), r)).} \quad (3)$$

(1) is an example from modal logic and says that if agent 1 believes p then it knows that it believes p, i.e. it is aware that it believes p. The example (2) is a description logic example; it says that an expert in automated reasoning is someone who has studied every proof method. This kind of example cannot be handled by current tableau-based description logic provers because it requires negation of roles. (3) expresses transitivity of a relation in relational logic (or in description logics).

Table 1 summarizes the implemented translation methods. The different translation methods are based on first-order encodings of the different ways of defining the semantics of the logics. The basis for the *relational translation* method, or *standard translation* method, is the standard set-theoretic semantics of *EML* logics. It is implemented for all Boolean and relational *EML* formulas.

The basis for the different *functional translations* is the functional semantics of traditional modal logics. The *optimized functional translations* are obtained from the functional translations by a non-standard quantifier exchange operation,

Table 1. Available translation methods

Translation method	Options
relational translation	`-EMLTranslation=0` (default)
(monadic) functional translation	`-EMLTranslation=1`
polyadic functional translation	`-EMLTranslation=1 -EMLFuncNary=1`
(monadic) optimized functional translation	`-EMLTranslation=2`
polyadic optimized functional translation	`-EMLTranslation=2 -EMLFuncNary=1`
semi-functional translation	`-EMLTranslation=3`
relational-functional translation	`-EMLTranslation=0 -EMLFuncNary=1`
relational-relational translation	`-EML2Rel=1 [-EMLTranslation=0]`

which is implemented by replacing non-constant Skolem terms by Skolem constants. The *polyadic functional translation* methods are variations of functional translation methods and differ in the way they encode world paths (transition sequences). The polyadic translations avoid the use of an extra function symbol by using n-ary predicates of different arities. The *semi-functional translation* approach is a mixture of the relational and functional translation approaches. It translates box modalities in the standard relational way, while diamond modalities are translated functionally. The (monadic) functional translations and the semi-functional translation are implemented for the basic multi-modal logic $K_{(m)}$ possibly with serial (total) modalities, plus frames or models, and non-logical axioms. The corresponding description logics are $\mathcal{ALC}$ with concept ABox and TBox statements, possibly with total roles. The polyadic functional translations are implemented for the basic multi-modal logic $K_{(m)}$ possibly with D (serial) modalities. The corresponding description logic is $\mathcal{ALC}$ possibly with total roles.

The *relational-functional translation* method, or *tree-layered relational translation*, is a variation of the relational translation specialized for the basic modal logic $K_{(m)}$. The *relational-relational translation* converts Boolean *EML* formulas into the relational formulas via a cylindrification operation. This translation is implemented for $K_{(m)}$.

All translation methods are sound and complete for the logics they are implemented for and have linear time complexity.

There are various additional *EML* options. For example, the `-EMLTheory` option can be used to add standard relational properties to the background theory. There are also options for varying the translation methods and the preprocessing done on *EML* formulas. The functional translations can be varied slightly with the two options `-EMLFuncNdeQ` and `-EMLFFSorts`. With the option `-EMLElimComp=1` top-level occurrences of relational composition in modal parameters can be eliminated as part of preprocessing. When enabled, the option `-QuantExch=1` causes non-constant Skolem terms in the clausal form to be replaced by constants. The option is automatically set for the optimized functional translation methods. The option can also be used for classical formulas and clauses, but it is not sound in general and therefore switched off by default.

With the new *EML* facilities SPASS supports reasoning for *EML* logics with the following additional additional features.

1. For dynamic modal logics and relational logics: non-logical axioms, modal operators characterized by any first-order frame correspondence properties and accessibility relations satisfying any first-order properties, specification of concrete worlds as constants, (first-order) relationships between concrete worlds, specifications of frames and models.
2. For description logics: the corresponding features, including in particular terminological axioms, TBox and RBox statements, and ABox statements for concept and role expressions.

Because SPASS is a first-order superposition based prover its capabilities as a modal, relational or description logic prover are very different and more varied than those of other provers for these logics. It is possible to use SPASS as a decision procedure for a large class of *EML* logics. For instance, it decides extensions of Boolean modal logic with converse, domain/range restriction, and positive occurrences of composition, and the corresponding description logics, i.e. extensions of $\mathcal{ALB}$ with positive occurrences of composition. No other (special-purpose) prover currently decides these logics. SPASS can be used as a decision procedure for many solvable first-order fragments including the guarded fragment, Maslov's class K, first-order logic in two variables, the clausal class DL*, and many decidable quantifier prefix classes. Using the new features it is possible to approximate the behavior of modal and description logic tableau provers with SPASS. Additionally, it can be used as a model finder.

For definitions of the different translation methods and further details, the various applications and references to original work, the reader is invited to consult the survey paper [6]. The paper [3] surveys decidable first-order fragments relevant to description logics. References to resolution decision procedures of *EML* logics and first-order fragments can be found in both [6] and [3].

3 Renaming and Selection Enhancements

Renaming transformations, or structural transformations, are not standard in current first-order theorem provers but have various advantages. They are essential for linear conversion of first-order formulas into clausal form. They are useful to control the way the search is performed in order to enhance the performance of a prover or to define decision procedures. They preserve the structure of the input formulas and make it easier to read resolution derivations and translate them back into first-order logic or the original *EML* logic. Renaming transformations introduce new predicate symbols for subformulas in the input problem. The renaming strategy available in SPASS 2.2 [7] is aimed at minimizing the number of eventually generated clauses [5]. A subformula is renamed if the replacement of the subformula by an atom headed with a new Skolem predicate plus the definition of the Skolem atom eventually results in fewer clauses. We added two more renaming strategies to SPASS 3.0: *complex formula renaming* and *quantified formula renaming*. Complex formula renaming introduces a new Skolem predicate for any subformula that is not an atom and does not start with a negation symbol. Quantified formula renaming introduces a new Skolem predicate for any subformula that starts with an existential or universal quantifier. The definition formulas for the Skolem predicates are generated in a polarity dependent way for all three versions. The renaming strategy is controlled via the -CNFRenaming=n flag where $n = 1$ selects minimizing renaming, $n = 2$ selects complex renaming, and $n = 3$ selects quantified renaming.

For the finite saturation of many first-order theories it is indispensable to select certain literals in order to protect variables in different literals of the same clause. An example is the (simplified) formalization of LAN router functionality that contains clauses of the form below. The clause states that if a packet is to be routed to the destination xdst and there is a route entry saying that all destination addresses "anded" with the mask xmsk produce the network xnet can be forwarded to xhop, then the packet is actually forwarded to xhop.

$$[\text{RouteIP}(\text{packet}(\text{xsrc}, \text{xdst}, \text{xpld})), \text{RouteEntry}(\text{xmsk}, \text{xnet}, \text{xhop}),$$
$$\text{ipand}(\text{xdst}, \text{xmsk}) \approx \text{xnet}] \rightarrow \text{Send}(\text{xhop}, \text{packet}(\text{xsrc}, \text{xdst}, \text{xpld}))$$

As all symbols starting with 'x' are variables, superposition left inferences can produce many clauses with the clause above and the theory for logical "and" on bit vectors (the function ipand). If the literals RouteIP and RouteEntry are selected then these inferences can be avoided.

Such situations are supported by enhanced selection mechanisms in SPASS 3.0. First, via the command set_selection a list of predicates can be defined in the input file to be candidates for selection. Second, this list can be combined with the following selection strategies that are set via the -Select=n option. For $n = 1$ in any clause with more than one maximal literal one negative literal is selected. Either a negative literal with a predicate from the selection list is chosen or if no such negative literal is available, a negative literal with maximal weight is chosen. For $n = 2$ in any clause containing at least one negative literal, a negative literal is selected. Again, either a negative literal with a predicate from the selection list is chosen or if no such negative literal is available, a negative literal with maximal weight is chosen. For $n = 3$ in any clause containing negative literals with predicates specified by the selection list, one negative literal out of these is selected.

In SPASS 3.0 we changed the heuristic for selecting splitting clauses. SPASS now selects the clause with the highest unit reduction potential after splitting.

4   Interface Enhancements

Starting with SPASS 3.0, FLOTTER writes the formula-clause relation into the setting part of the clause normal form output file. When processing such a .cnf file SPASS is now also able to tell which input formulas were used in an eventually found proof.

When SPASS finitely saturates a set of clauses, the result can be output to a file via the -FPModel option. So far the generated file did not contain any information about the selection of literals. Hence, it could happen that running

SPASS again on such a file would produce further clauses by inferences. With SPASS 3.0 we have defined an additional clause input format that is similar to the clause output given by SPASS at run time and includes the possibility to mark negative literals in clauses to be selected. In SPASS 3.0 this format is used when -FPModel is set and inferences on saturated sets produce no additional clauses when such sets are resubmitted to SPASS.

At run time, SPASS now selects literals before it prints the Given clause. This improves manual inspection of the SPASS output.

5   Conclusion and Future Work

Finally, we want to point the reader to the new handbook [8] distributed with SPASS. It contains detailed descriptions of the most important features and facilities implemented in the prover, covering the sophisticated reasoning technology, the superposition calculus implemented in SPASS, the theory and implementation details for the translation methods for *EML* logics, and the theory behind the clause set transformations of dfg2dfg. A detailed, formal specification of the extended input language can be found in the SPASS documentation [9]. It also includes examples of input files for the different *EML* logics supported by SPASS.

A start has been made at implementing the techniques introduced and studied in [1] for the bottom-up model generation paradigm in SPASS. Moreover, we are developing efficient superposition based reasoning techniques for finite domains, further improving the performance of the prover for several *EML* logics.

SPASS 3.0 is available from http://spass.mpi-sb.mpg.de.

Acknowledgements. We thank the SPASS user community for delivering enhancement requests as well as bug reports, and the reviewers for their comments.

References

1. Baumgartner, P., Schmidt, R.A.: Blocking and other enhancements for bottom-up model generation methods. In: Furbach, U., Shankar, N. (eds.) IJCAR 2006. LNCS (LNAI), vol. 4130, pp. 125–139. Springer, Heidelberg (2006)
2. Hustadt, U., Schmidt, R.A.: MSPASS: Modal reasoning by translation and first-order resolution. In: Dyckhoff, R. (ed.) TABLEAUX 2000. LNCS, vol. 1847, pp. 67–71. Springer, Heidelberg (2000)
3. Hustadt, U., Schmidt, R.A., Georgieva, L.: A survey of decidable first-order fragments and description logics. J. Relational Meth. in Computer Sci. 1, 251–276 (2004)
4. Hustadt, U., Schmidt, R.A., Weidenbach, C., MSPASS,: Subsumption testing with SPASS. In: Proc. DL'99, pp. 136–137. Linköping University (1999)
5. Nonnengart, A., Weidenbach, C.: Computing small clause normal forms. In: Handbook of Automated Reasoning, pp. 335–367. Elsevier, Amsterdam (2001)

6. Schmidt, R.A., Hustadt, U.: First-order resolution methods for modal logics. In: Volume in memoriam of Harald Ganzinger, Springer. LNCS, Springer, Heidelberg (2006) (to appear),
   http://www.cs.man.ac.uk/~schmidt/publications/SchmidtHustadt06a.html
7. Weidenbach, C., Brahm, U., Hillenbrand, T., Keen, E., Theobald, C., Topic, D.: SPASS version 2.0. In: Voronkov, A. (ed.) Automated Deduction - CADE-18. LNCS (LNAI), vol. 2392, pp. 275–279. Springer, Heidelberg (2002)
8. Weidenbach, C., Schmidt, R.A., Keen, E.: SPASS handbook version 3.0. Contained in the distribution of SPASS Version 3.0 (2007)
9. Weidenbach, C., Schmidt, R.A., Topic, D.: SPASS input syntax version 3.0. Contained in the distribution of SPASS Version 3.0 (2007)

Author Index

Lecture Notes in Artificial Intelligence (LNAI)

Vol. 4335: S.A. Brueckner, S. Hassas, M. Jelasity, D. Yamins (Eds.), Engineering Self-Organising Systems. XII, 212 pages. 2007.

Vol. 4334: B. Beckert, R. Hähnle, P.H. Schmitt (Eds.), Verification of Object-Oriented Software. XXIX, 658 pages. 2007.

Vol. 4333: U. Reimer, D. Karagiannis (Eds.), Practical Aspects of Knowledge Management. XII, 338 pages. 2006.

Vol. 4327: M. Baldoni, U. Endriss (Eds.), Declarative Agent Languages and Technologies IV. VIII, 257 pages. 2006.

Vol. 4314: C. Freksa, M. Kohlhase, K. Schill (Eds.), KI 2006: Advances in Artificial Intelligence. XII, 458 pages. 2007.

Vol. 4304: A. Sattar, B.-h. Kang (Eds.), AI 2006: Advances in Artificial Intelligence. XXVII, 1303 pages. 2006.

Vol. 4303: A. Hoffmann, B.-h. Kang, D. Richards, S. Tsumoto (Eds.), Advances in Knowledge Acquisition and Management. XI, 259 pages. 2006.

Vol. 4293: A. Gelbukh, C.A. Reyes-Garcia (Eds.), MICAI 2006: Advances in Artificial Intelligence. XXVIII, 1232 pages. 2006.

Vol. 4289: M. Ackermann, B. Berendt, M. Grobelnik, A. Hotho, D. Mladenič, G. Semeraro, M. Spiliopoulou, G. Stumme, V. Svátek, M. van Someren (Eds.), Semantics, Web and Mining. X, 197 pages. 2006.

Vol. 4285: Y. Matsumoto, R.W. Sproat, K.-F. Wong, M. Zhang (Eds.), Computer Processing of Oriental Languages. XVII, 544 pages. 2006.

Vol. 4274: Q. Huo, B. Ma, E.-S. Chng, H. Li (Eds.), Chinese Spoken Language Processing. XXIV, 805 pages. 2006.

Vol. 4265: L. Todorovski, N. Lavrač, K.P. Jantke (Eds.), Discovery Science. XIV, 384 pages. 2006.

Vol. 4264: J.L. Balcázar, P.M. Long, F. Stephan (Eds.), Algorithmic Learning Theory. XIII, 393 pages. 2006.

Vol. 4259: S. Greco, Y. Hata, S. Hirano, M. Inuiguchi, S. Miyamoto, H.S. Nguyen, R. Słowiński (Eds.), Rough Sets and Current Trends in Computing. XXII, 951 pages. 2006.

Vol. 4253: B. Gabrys, R.J. Howlett, L.C. Jain (Eds.), Knowledge-Based Intelligent Information and Engineering Systems, Part III. XXXII, 1301 pages. 2006.

Vol. 4252: B. Gabrys, R.J. Howlett, L.C. Jain (Eds.), Knowledge-Based Intelligent Information and Engineering Systems, Part II. XXXIII, 1335 pages. 2006.

Vol. 4251: B. Gabrys, R.J. Howlett, L.C. Jain (Eds.), Knowledge-Based Intelligent Information and Engineering Systems, Part I. LXVI, 1297 pages. 2006.

Vol. 4248: S. Staab, V. Svátek (Eds.), Managing Knowledge in a World of Networks. XIV, 400 pages. 2006.

Vol. 4246: M. Hermann, A. Voronkov (Eds.), Logic for Programming, Artificial Intelligence, and Reasoning. XIII, 588 pages. 2006.

Vol. 4223: L. Wang, L. Jiao, G. Shi, X. Li, J. Liu (Eds.), Fuzzy Systems and Knowledge Discovery. XXVIII, 1335 pages. 2006.

Vol. 4213: J. Fürnkranz, T. Scheffer, M. Spiliopoulou (Eds.), Knowledge Discovery in Databases: PKDD 2006. XXII, 660 pages. 2006.

Vol. 4212: J. Fürnkranz, T. Scheffer, M. Spiliopoulou (Eds.), Machine Learning: ECML 2006. XXIII, 851 pages. 2006.

Vol. 4211: P. Vogt, Y. Sugita, E. Tuci, C.L. Nehaniv (Eds.), Symbol Grounding and Beyond. VIII, 237 pages. 2006.

Vol. 4203: F. Esposito, Z.W. Raś, D. Malerba, G. Semeraro (Eds.), Foundations of Intelligent Systems. XVIII, 767 pages. 2006.

Vol. 4201: Y. Sakakibara, S. Kobayashi, K. Sato, T. Nishino, E. Tomita (Eds.), Grammatical Inference: Algorithms and Applications. XII, 359 pages. 2006.

Vol. 4200: I.F.C. Smith (Ed.), Intelligent Computing in Engineering and Architecture. XIII, 692 pages. 2006.

Vol. 4198: O. Nasraoui, O. Zaïane, M. Spiliopoulou, B. Mobasher, B. Masand, P.S. Yu (Eds.), Advances in Web Mining and Web Usage Analysis. IX, 177 pages. 2006.

Vol. 4196: K. Fischer, I.J. Timm, E. André, N. Zhong (Eds.), Multiagent System Technologies. X, 185 pages. 2006.

Vol. 4188: P. Sojka, I. Kopeček, K. Pala (Eds.), Text, Speech and Dialogue. XV, 721 pages. 2006.

Vol. 4183: J. Euzenat, J. Domingue (Eds.), Artificial Intelligence: Methodology, Systems, and Applications. XIII, 291 pages. 2006.

Vol. 4180: M. Kohlhase, OMDoc – An Open Markup Format for Mathematical Documents [version 1.2]. XIX, 428 pages. 2006.

Vol. 4177: R. Marín, E. Onaindía, A. Bugarín, J. Santos (Eds.), Current Topics in Artificial Intelligence. XV, 482 pages. 2006.

Vol. 4160: M. Fisher, W. van der Hoek, B. Konev, A. Lisitsa (Eds.), Logics in Artificial Intelligence. XII, 516 pages. 2006.

Vol. 4155: O. Stock, M. Schaerf (Eds.), Reasoning, Action and Interaction in AI Theories and Systems. XVIII, 343 pages. 2006.

Vol. 4149: M. Klusch, M. Rovatsos, T.R. Payne (Eds.), Cooperative Information Agents X. XII, 477 pages. 2006.

Vol. 4140: J.S. Sichman, H. Coelho, S.O. Rezende (Eds.), Advances in Artificial Intelligence - IBERAMIA-SBIA 2006. XXIII, 635 pages. 2006.

Vol. 4139: T. Salakoski, F. Ginter, S. Pyysalo, T. Pahikkala (Eds.), Advances in Natural Language Processing. XVI, 771 pages. 2006.

Vol. 4133: J. Gratch, M. Young, R. Aylett, D. Ballin, P. Olivier (Eds.), Intelligent Virtual Agents. XIV, 472 pages. 2006.

Vol. 4130: U. Furbach, N. Shankar (Eds.), Automated Reasoning. XV, 680 pages. 2006.

Vol. 4120: J. Calmet, T. Ida, D. Wang (Eds.), Artificial Intelligence and Symbolic Computation. XIII, 269 pages. 2006.